The Story of Christianity

Century by Century

TONY PINNINGTON

THE CHOIR PRESS

First published in the United Kingdom in 2023 by
The Choir Press

ISBN 978-1-78963-421-1

Back cover photograph kindly supplied by Sebastian Gibbs

for Buff, Phil, Danielle, Tom and
our loving memory of David

Contents

Foreword

This is a story of the formation and reformation of Christianity during the first two thousand years, ending with a glimpse of a possible path to transformation.

People have always mostly recognised that a greater power or God must exist which created the universe and life, even if they may not understand it. Spontaneous creation is unsatisfactory so human nature led them to seek, learn and know something about such a power so that they may pay due homage to it. This drive evolved and there are now myriad beliefs.

Few would dispute there are distinct differences between people and all other animal species. I believe the distinction lies in a soul. I have long held that mathematics should be as closely related to classics and art as to science. There are relationships between maths and music as well as poetry, appreciation of which speaks of our soul – a spiritual side that goes beyond reationality in a quest for another dimension.

Today a large proportion of the people in the world follow one of the so-called Abrahamic religions – Judaism (14 million), Christinity (2.2 billion), or Islam (1.5 billion). This book is about the story of Christianity and its relation to these and other faiths. Claiming no intellectual, theological or doctrinal superiority, it is intended to track Christianity's background, origins, thinking and influence over two millennia, also referring to other relevant lines of belief. It is not intended as a proselytising work but just as a readable story of a quest for a moral way of life interwoven with the reality and pitfalls of human, organisational, technical and social development in its first two thousand years.

Some major religions have become centralised human institutions at some expense to their closeness to God. Christianity is no exception, having arguably strayed from the Church that Christ, its founder told apostle Peter to take forward. Thanks partly to the proximity to the very life of Christ on earth, it weathered its early formation and rapid growth in the face of persecution. Since the fourth century AD it has lived under autocratic or monarchial governments with human ambition and greed, which often influenced its practice. As other cultures and parts of the world have been discovered and developed since the Middle Ages, it has failed to adapt as Christ himself would have done. It retained a predominantly 'Western' religion but there are signs of change. It became human, institutional and divided. Schisms arose and ultimately reformation, resulting in devastating divisions. Is it now time for transformation and reunification, coming closer to Jesus Christ's original stated intentions? Any religious institution claims a pathway to God but ultimately the relationship of any one of us with our maker is direct through ourselves.

The appeal and acceptance of Christianity continues to grow in the developing world while rather declining from favour in the developed Western world where it enjoyed such historic success. There have been few if any times when atheism has been so widespread and 'evangelistic' as at present. The Christian religion is not, in Karl Marx's words 'the opium of the people'. It was always intended for ordinary people – "a Church of the poor for the poor" – but also for great minds, which through the centuries have examined, validated and adopted it as well as helping develop its worship, philosophy and social teaching.

Before I came to the end of a busy industrial career, I had plans to fill my retirement with various new interests and voluntary work, but I had not envisaged the kind of work involved in this book. It just evolved from events as a while after retiring I was asked to help a proposed monthly magazine for my parish by contributing a regular 'view from the pew' type of article. After a few dozen issues and feeling I was beginning to run short of ideas, I thought I would try tracing the development of Christianity from the time of Christ to the present day, something I had long thought of doing for myself. Thus the series continued setting me on an intriguing journey of discovery within a faith that I thought I knew. There was neither enough space in the articles to convey more than a brief summary of what my early research revealed nor sufficient time between them for more than superficial research. I have spent a further ten years' reading, so there will be far more in these pages, but never enough, as I try to strike a balance between readability and satisfying interest that may stimulate the reader to pursue further any particular subjects that capture their further interest. This research and writing has been helpful to my own faith while giving me a more balanced view of it as well as greater respect for other traditions. I hope it may foster mutual understanding in the reader, who may find similar reward.

Details of Christ's life and work have not been covered, as the gospels and New Testament are well known or easily accessible for this. Also, I feel obliged to share with the reader St Ignatius' counsel against falling in love with religion. If you believe in God, it is God you must love. The point he makes is that religion is the worldly organisation of a channel to knowledge and worship of God. As an organisation of humans, it is subject to pride and error. Please realise this book is an attempt by a totally fallible, lay individual, not even a theologian, philosopher or historian but a mere retired engineer and industrial manager, to relate the growth of the Christian Church from its scriptural and Jewish origins, concentrating on the first twenty centuries since Jesus Christ. The twenty first is only beginning to unfold, so is not included.

I felt fairly relaxed in this approach when it came to religion and history, but with God it is more challenging. Indeed the words of the prophet Isaiah (55:8-9) warn us all of that – "for my thoughts are not your thoughts and your ways are not my ways," says the Lord, "for the heavens are as high above the earth as my ways are different from your ways, my thoughts are above your thoughts." But I can humbly try.

So this is not a scholarly work so much as the result of a journey of my deeper research into origins and development of the Christian faith I was born into. Accepting my own limitations and to keep the book readable, I have sought to avoid becoming too involved in details of philosophy and theology, though some is inevitable, so superficial description is given of such issues when they are relevant to understanding Church development and history. I am conscious any such overviews will beg questions and argument from people far better informed than me on individual issues, but even some appreciation of these offers insight into the reasons for historical dialogue, conflict and division around the Church.

When researching distance degree courses, I was confronted by a variety of courses and providers, but could not find a suitable one specific to my objective and I did not wish to be tied in to the personal views of any individual academic in seeking relevant qualification. Nor did I need a degree. So I determined to do my own research and found direction and guidance from some trusted and respected people.

If theology is defined as 'faith seeking understanding', then most thinking people are theologians to some extent, so I have allowed myself the occasional commentary, hopefully objective and not judgmental. The question of the Trinity and the origins and nature of Jesus Christ and his relationship with the Holy Spirit and God the Father have been such subjects for intricate debate and causes of angst and schism from the early days of the Church, that they have to feature. As no more of a 'theologian' than the above definition, I have tried to convey the bones of theories without diving too deep into the matter, taking Jesus at his word when he said God would not test us beyond our abilities. Plenty of experts have done more over time and readers can easily dig deeper if they are so inclined, for I can claim no such expertise.

The first five hundred years is a fascinating period when one considers what Christ asked of his followers. Before his believed incarnation – his arrival on earth as a human – God had interacted with the Hebrews through inspiration, recorded in the Torah, the original law-based covenant with plenty of rules on how to please a perceived rather fearsome God. Inspiration took various forms. Very occasionally, he was believed to intervene directly in a dream or as an apparition or a voice from heaven to a chosen prophet. God is not human, needs no gender, but in those days men were regarded as of the dominant gender, so God was referred to as 'He'. Then about two thousand years ago he apparently came to earth, incarnate as Jesus Christ, a man born into the Middle East, neither white nor black. In his brief recorded life, Jesus brought to all people the opportunity of a closer relationship with God, based more on principles than hard and fast rules. The old Law of the Torah is superseded by this new covenant. Jesus claimed to be God, the Messiah promised by prophets in the Torah, regarded as the only route to salvation. He certainly existed, so the stark choice facing us is to believe this claim or consider him deluded; there is no satisfactory middle way.

Christianity, the Church Jesus founded then appointed apostle Peter as his first successor as leader, has shown remarkable resilience in the face of adversity over time – Roman persecutions, Saracens, Mongolian 'Storm from the East', Ottomans, Tudors, USSR under Communism and more recent persecution around Christ's homeland and elsewhere.

In the very early days following Christ's death, church 'centres' developed in some cities where Christianity had found a large enough following, such as Rome, Antioch, Caesarea (in Asia Minor), Alexandria. Each centre had a separate leadership, though all kept in touch through correspondence and synods to check matters of faith. Naturally enough, some regional differences of view and organisation developed, but with the spirit of Christ still fresh, they were good at reaching measures of agreement based on what they deemed was Jesus Christ's intention for them. The senior bishops in these centres thus acted individually in leading their flocks, without there being an overall leader, reminiscent of the Orthodox Churches today. Various schisms then reformation in Western Christianity over centuries have led to diversity in practice and worship such that it is now hard to envisage a full return to unity. However, it is conceivable that there is something to be learned from the original order described above and at least an effective 'conference' of Christian Churches could be sought in which mutual respect and understanding could grow and the aspects that unite the various denominations be better mutually recognised, developed and respected. It seems spiritual, social and financial folly to have several church buildings in the same community competing in worship of the same God, each with hard stretched ministers. So bearing in mind Jesus' expressed wish for unity, some compromise and sharing is surely worthy of serious prayer and action.

I found the research and writing process full of interest, though cross-referencing was never easy or tidy. It always troubled me that in spite of the Holy Spirit's guidance and Christ's promise that "the gates of hell would not prevail against" his Church, which should therefore ensure its goodness and a sufficient degree of infallibility, without any need for human declarations to that effect, it has suffered schisms, conflict and been undermined by all manner of human weakness. But I have drawn consolation from learning how Hellenic philosophical thought processes adapted in the post-apostolic period and from the prayerful dedication and learning of some of the Fathers of the Church. They set standards for fellow members and helped guide those who wished to dedicate their lives to God by asceticism and laying foundations for monasticism for both men and women. If there was a prize for a person best supporting Christ in defining the concept of a human true Christian for all time, there are a number of candidates described in this book. On the evidence, I might vote for Clement of Alexandria, who is probably better known in the Eastern Orthodox Church, or Augustine of Hippo in 'City of God', though neither could be described as perfect.

As an engineer, I seek to understand how things work and I also like certainty. No religion offers the latter. If it did there would be no argument and no need for faith and hope. So the over-simplified perception of Old Testament versus New Testament as tensions between the God of wrath and retribution versus the God of love and mercy, which leads to the field of theodicy – a study of the justice and love of a God who created a world in which evil and suffering exist – is difficult for us all to grasp. However, if we are looking at human level arguments for the divinity and goodness of God, Jesus provides cogent material, even if no incontrovertible truth. So let's get used to it – Christianity, as any faith, holds no certainty. But there are powerful arguments and evidence in its favour which give comfort yet still require faith.

Even the Gospels can be questioned – from their authors and timing to their consistency with each other in terms of content and related events to which they refer. The same applies to the Old Testament of the Bible. Such is the nature of events recounted down the ages by word of mouth when most people could not read or write. So in the absence of certainty Christians are asked to have faith and hope in the message.

In a public discussion on religion between a celebrity Catholic lay person, the comedian and occasional Times columnist, Frank Skinner and the then Archbishop of Canterbury, Dr Rowan Williams, Frank said he was a man of both faith and doubt and he worried about people who have no doubt, be they people of faith or committed atheists. Even Jesus showed doubt – "My God, My God, why have you forsaken me?" demonstrating his real humanity. Archbishop Rowan concurred and said that doubt always exists and Faith gave you "the confidence to take the next step". The Archbishop also told of his trip to Taizé in France with a party of youngsters the previous year. His abiding memory was the wonder of the sound of the silence of 5000 teenagers. "Yes, I've had gigs like that", mused the comedian, wistfully.

So the story in this book may appear challenging and even negative at times but it does seem quite miraculous that the Christian Church has survived in spite of, as much as because of, its human leaders. The Church Christ founded would not be the only one to grow doctrines and practices going beyond his teaching, even if with the best intentions to remain true to his message. I believe that when unsure of a Church's tenet being right, we should always refer back to Christ its founder. He specified his desire for it to be one united Church, but over centuries it would divide, almost entirely over 'man-made' rules. It is never long before a human organisation and its officers tend lose focus on its true raison d'être and regard it as an end in itself, the focus of its own care and protection. Power politics and competitive tribal instincts emerge which do not reflect its mission. At my Christian Brothers' school in Crosby, I was taught what to think. University, then the workplace and broader life experience have taught me how to think. I am a Christian first, a questioning but committed Roman Catholic second. I have huge respect for the Orthodox Churches and sympathetic understanding for the Reformation, so strong ecumenical tendencies, for I see the differences within Christianity as less important than what is held in common. As will be flagged up frequently in the course of this book, once faith falls into the hands of a human organisation, as it does in 'religion' or 'the Church', trouble ensues.

I have endeavoured to convey reasoning behind the schisms yet still find them unfathomable as given good will on both sides they all seem to have been so avoidable – and repairable, though it is far more difficult to mend a broken pot than it is to break it in the first place as witnessed by so many failed attempts to repair the Eastern Schism for example. Humans are frail and imperfect, whatever their earthly power. We take stands on points of detail, losing sight of God's broader vision as conveyed quite simply through Jesus. We should always be asking whether Christ would approve of what we are doing, especially those who have answered his call to set example and evangelise as his pastors, for surely that is the reference point for personal conscience. Although I write as a straight white English man with a Roman Catholic background, I hope to have given a fair and reasonably balanced account of what has taken place over time, for I yearn for that unity and inclusivity that Christ was clear in desiring yet I observe two millennia of less than full-hearted attempts to achieve it.

Jesus Christ never sought power, just to influence others by example. He was here as a divine yet wholly human manifestation and as ambassador of God the Father to show the way to salvation. The often turbulent story of Christianity embraces many good people of real faith who understand what Christ is about and seek to share this by humble example, word and charity. Most will never make the news or be recognised as 'saints' in that imperfect honours system. I say that because just a few years ago I was asked who I considered an inspirational heroic person of the age and I replied "Jean Vanier founder of L'Arche organisation". The organisation is a true force for good, but he let himself down and with it the institution. At the end of this 'story', the human frailty of the institutions that are now 'the Church' and the contrast with their founder's message are highlighted. It is high time for unification and some radical action to reappraise and correct their approach and role to align with Christ's message.

I have so far referred to only two of the three great monotheistic Abrahamic faiths. There is of course also Islam in which Jesus is accepted as an important prophet, but not as the Son of God. With 1.5 billion followers, Islam is second only to Christianity in terms of world following and plays a significant part in this story. If all these three religions are right in believing there is only one God, then would it be too outrageous to suggest it is the same God, however differently each faith visualises and worships him? Let us not be misled by the extremists, the fanatics.

Please understand that where language may not be inclusive, it is a reflection of the society of the place at the time being referred to; an attempt to be true to the narrative with no intent to give offence of any kind. I have tried to be consistent in the use of capital letters and have avoided their use when using pronouns for God or Jesus Christ. This is not irreverence, but an effort to avoid distracting people new to the subject. When using titles, such as bishop, emperor or pope, I only use capitals when relating them to specific names or places, e.g. Pope John or Bishop of Milan. Capital C is used in Church as a specific organisation, while lower case applies to the church as a building or generality.

Not wishing to over-punctuate this story, I agonised over the inclusion of dates, but decided that they do help readers relate to the greater map of history. Some people find this distracting, but dates can help understand the sequence and can be ignored by the reader who so chooses. Without any provocative intention, I have used the terms BC (Before Christ) and AD (*Anno Domini*, Year of Our Lord) as appropriate to an essentially Christian work, in preference to the new non-theistic terms BCE and CE (Common Era). The story is related in historical sequence, though in order to cover some subjects fully in one place, reference is occasionally made to past or future events that put them into context or fully explain them without further repetition or the need for the reader to jump back and forth too much. Sub-headings have been added to ease reference by people who like to refer back or just dip in.

Since this is a long story though not a full reference book, and again seeking readability, I have not included detailed references for research of which I soon lost track, they became so copious in the early chapters. I simply mentioned just a few of the countless sources and references from which I have drawn information over the years of study in the text, for all of which I am truly grateful. The many on-line encyclopedias are also helpful in checking, though sometimes reflecting personal or prejudiced views of contributors. I have stitched together this patchwork quilt of a story in a way that hopefully includes a lot of the relevant detail without being too dull. But the core information relies on work and research already done by many others, so although the results of my lengthy research, I do not claim that as my own original work, only that I have collected and merged it in my own words to form a cohesive record. That has sometimes involved making my best judgement between conflicting accounts, though I have tried to be fully objective in the story.

The thread of history is truly fascinating. Continuing echoes of the biblical era in spots around the Mediterranean coast illustrate this. I shall share just one peripheral anecdote I unearthed. It concerns byssos. Today in the 21st century, a woman called Chiara Vigo on a remote island off Sardinia goes diving every Spring to harvest the solidified saliva of a large clam Pinna Nobilis. She learned unique skills handed down the generations through which she can identify and harvest the material, then spin it and infuse it with a handed down recipe of lemon juice and spices to give it a golden lustre. She then uses her technique of weaving this very rare and lightweight thread to make 'sea silk' or byssos. She says the skill was taught by Princess Berenice, great-granddaughter of Herod the Great in the late first century AD. It was priceless, far and away the finest fabric known to ancient Egypt. Some believe it to have been the cloth God asked Moses to lay on the first altar. Chiara remains a Jew although most others in the area converted to Christianity. She does not sell the fabric and may be the last full practitioner of this skill, including the recipe and realisation of its unique golden lustre in sunlight. She learned this from her grandmother and is passing it on to her daughter.

CHAPTER 1

Israel Leading up to Christ

Modern science has gone some way towards understanding the beginnings of the universe, but the more we learn, the more we realise that we do not know and science continues to run into error. It is of course unlikely that human kind began literally as described in Genesis, the first chapter of the Bible, but that is not to discredit it, as will be explained. Humans have always believed or wanted to believe in the existence of a higher creative power – a god or gods – exercising ongoing control and order over the world and the vast universe; there is an irresistible drive for us thinking, rational, creative beings to seek out how we came to be here and to give some meaning to our lives as well as to acknowledge and even offer worship or sacrifices to that creative power. Prayer is often used as a means of asking god to tip the order in our favour.

Christianity is the most widespread religion with the greatest following on this earth, some 2.2 billion people. To understand the birth and growth of Christianity it is worth first looking at the background from which it emerged. There is no doubt Jesus did live, but was he the Christ, the Messiah the Jews were expecting and was he really the Son of God? He was born a Jew and always lived among Jews. Their land had fairly recently become part of the Roman Empire. It was in a region with strong Greek cultural influence, affected by the Greek philosophers and originally brought there by Alexander the Great.

Jews and the Bible

The founding fathers of the Jews, known as the patriarchs, were Abraham, Isaac and Jacob (c.1900 BC). Judaism as a religion began with an event during the escape journey of the enslaved descendants of Jacob and his twelve children from Egypt (c.1400 BC). There were over half a million of them and the event had been the 'great revelation' when God gave the Ten Commandments to Moses on Mount Sinai in the Sinai desert.

The ancient Jews handed down the story of creation and their thread of history, verbally from generation to generation. They believed they were then the chosen people of the world, as do many Jews today. The most important part to them of their Hebrew Bible is the Torah, the 'Law', which consists of the first five books – Genesis, Exodus, Leviticus, Numbers and Deuteronomy. It is known by Christians as the Pentateuch and is the beginning of the Old Testament in the Christian Bible. Since these older books and many of those that follow in the Old Testament, were passed on by word of mouth over centuries, questions naturally arise over their reliability. But believers regard this verbal sharing as having been sourced by wise men or prophets guided by God, the Holy Spirit over time.

The three great monotheistic Abrahamic religions of the world – Judaism, Christianity and Islam, broadly follow the Bible accounts, though with variations. Islam's Qur'an contains much of the Old and some of the New Testament, the differences arising from corrections by Mohammed, their most recent prophet.

The Old Testament

Although it is not the purpose of this book to examine the Hebrew Bible (*Tanakh*), broadly known to Christians as the Old Testament, it is a key element in the background to Christian faith and most of it is accepted by the various Christian churches as canonical (approved after due study). It is seen as a fundamental document and often referred to in the New Testament of the Christian Bible and by notable Christian scholars throughout history.

It is a gathering of selected writings that record word-of-mouth recollections passed down the ages from about two thousand years before Jesus Christ was born. Some parts are much older and few archaeological clues have been found to prove their history. But the great majority of the Bible stories were written down in hundreds rather than thousands of years before Christ, being edited works weaving together the sources. All five books of the Pentateuch are of similar length and at the time they were written each was more or less sufficient to fill a scroll. Although traditionally attributed to Moses, most students now agree that while he may have originated at least some of the accounts, there are at least four different styles of authorship and these books are a mix of work dating from the sixth century BC.

The series of books that follow the Pentateuch – Joshua, Judges, Samuel and Kings through to the Maccabees, are known as the Historical Books and cover some five hundred years of the history of Israel with its cycle of sin, punishment (usually by invasion), repentance and rescue (from the occupier), which may be argued to show history serving theology.

The third set comprise the Wisdom Books from Job to Wisdom, including Psalms (another mix of works, some poetry, or songs, from many ages and places) and the final set, the Prophets – Isaiah, Jeremiah,

Ezekiel, and the briefer twelve, Daniel, Hosea, Joel, Amos, Jonah, Micah, Nahum, Habakkuk, Zephaniah, Hagar, Zechariah and Malachi. Isaiah was quoted by Jesus, but there were actually two Isaiahs. One author is Isaiah of Jerusalem, of the 8th century BC. The second part from about chapter 40 is about a later Isaiah of the 6th century BC and speaks of the Persian king Cyrus II the Great (c.580-530 BC). There were even later contributors, one being Daniel and it was all drawn together probably as late as the 4th century BC.

Just to take one brief example for mention – Jonah; his book gives a clear warning against taking the Bible too literally or as an accurate historical account. He refers to the King of Nineveh and his people being converted but no trace of a historical record has been found of any conversion of the king of Nineveh or its people. The brief prophecy of Jonah could be read as a tongue-in-cheek instruction to read the Bible as allegorical. Their purpose was to record the spiritual wishes of God within the context of the times in which they were first recorded. Advances of learning, society and technology in the physical world reveal many factual changes since then, so contextual errors will be apparent to us. They should not be interpreted too rigidly. Even the darkest threat of God contains his mercy as he pardons the repentant. Jonah condemns racism, pointing out that God is the God of all his creation, gentiles as well as Jews and the nature of all living things, animal and vegetable and the productive world around us. We are to safeguard it.

So there is no certitude in the Bible stories and yet the Hebrew Bible, the Old Testament, became part of the Scriptures and an essential guide to salvation. It adapts for application to different life situations and to changing ages and cultures. As a collection of accounts spanning such a large timescale itself, several of its 'books' carry interpretation of others e.g. Chronicles partly reinterprets Kings, Zechariah does the same with Ezekiel and so on, so it builds on itself. We have no evidence to be sure of the Jewish system for selecting which writings they accepted as canonical. Consistency with received history would have been a factor in some, as would acceptance and relevance of moral messages whether comfortable or not, in others. However a wide spread of students from all backgrounds believed it was guided by God, that it gave powerful moral guidance and was helpful in living a good life. They also accepted it as difficult, allegorical, in need of interpretation and some parts are plain ambiguous, readable in several ways.

A Greek translation of the Pentateuch by Hellenist Jews in Alexandria, a great seat of learning, was available by the end of the third century BC and the whole of the Hebrew Bible by 132 BC. This work was commissioned by Ptolemy II Philadelphus, who employed 72 Jewish scholars, from which it derived the name 'Septuagint', often referred to simply as LXX. Being the earliest Greek direct translation of the Hebrew Old Testament it is invaluable for translation research. The Jews used it from well before the Christian era and in Christ's time it was the accepted legitimate text from which the Apostles and Evangelists drew. Being in Greek, it embedded theological terms which helped the Evangelists to be understood when spreading their message throughout the Greek speaking world.

A reasonable amount of archaeological evidence related to the Bible stories has been unearthed in the Holy Land. Remains of a 10th or 11th century BC fortified city about 20 miles north of Jerusalem date from King David's time and include a palace where he is believed to have stayed. A stone slab known as the Tel Dan Stele from about the 9th century BC was unearthed in 1993, bearing an inscription in Aramaic that seems to refer to the killing of Jehoram, son of Ahab mentioned in 2 Kings. An 8th century BC seal inscribed 'Nathan Melech. Servant of the King' tallies with a recorded servant of King Josiah in 2 Kings. There is also evidence of the Israeli-Edomite rivalry in Southern Israel, descendants of brothers Jacob and Esau respectively. In I Kings, Israeli King Solomon fights Edomite King Hadad, who was raised by the Egyptian pharaohs. There is little archaeological evidence so far of the theologically important exodus from Egypt, though the main landmarks are well known. But of course, nomads are unlikely to leave permanent traces in their wake. The fall of Jerusalem to Nebuchadnezzar's Babylonian army in the 6th century BC is witnessed by the discovery of arrowheads of the type known to have been used by the Babylonians.

Predictions of the Messiah's Coming

The Old Testament of the Bible included over forty instances of prophecies by prophets and in the Psalms, first by Isaiah around 750 BC. These foresaw not only the arrival of the expected Messiah but the manner of it as well as a number of other happenings in Christ's life. These included preparation for the Messiah's arrival, then his birth to a virgin woman in Bethlehem; that he would come from the line of Abraham, Isaac and Jacob, the tribe of Judah and King David; he would be called Emmanuel; he would spend time in Egypt; and there would be a massacre of children where he was born.

As for the life of Jesus Christ, it was prophesied that he would be a prophet; called a Nazarene; rejected by his own people; hailed as the Son of God; would bring light to Galilee, such a troubled region in Isaiah's time; speak in parables; heal the sick and broken-hearted; be praised by children; he would pray for his enemies; be betrayed 'for the price of a potter's field'; keep silence while being falsely accused, mocked and ridiculed; be spat upon and struck; be crucified with criminals, given vinegar to drink and his hands and feet would be pierced but none of his bones would be broken; his side would also be pierced; soldiers would draw lots for his garments; he would feel forsaken by God, his Father; be buried with the wealthy; rise from the dead; and finally be seated at God's side.

Greek Philosophers

Most people still pursued a religion to help them find a reason and meaning for life. Only the Jews followed the monotheistic scriptures and most others still followed their traditional polytheistic religions although philosophies then gaining the attention of intellectuals undermined these. Plato argued quite cogently in favour of there being room for only one God – monotheism.

The philosophers are worthy of mention because some of them laid foundations on which Christian theologians and philosophers would build. Greek civilisation had long surpassed that of its neighbours in the last millennium before Christ and had produced a wave of philosophers who brought radical new thinking to life, government and morals. The Greeks worshipped dozens of gods, with Apollo, Atlas, Aphrodite, right through the alphabet to the top God Zeus. Philosophy was a revered subject and some philosophers addressed issues that would have an influence on future Christian thought, so there follows a cursory summary of some better-known ones.

Socrates (470-399BC) is regarded as the first moral philosopher of Western ethics. He developed the Socratic Method of seeking ultimate truth, which involved dialectics, a form of debate without subjective input, using solely objective arguments to distil 'Good' or 'Justice'. Socrates believed in divine gods and in people having a soul, but also that he had been sent as a messenger from the gods. He thought that too many people were more concerned for their temporal interests and careers than for the welfare of their souls. He was an influential figure in Athens, preaching strongly that people should pursue virtue rather than security and wealth. Virtue should lead to living a simple life, though he did not appear to promote asceticism, which came later with the Stoics (about 281 BC) and would be adopted by hermits and monks in the course of their quest for virtue.

Plato (420s-c.344 BC) was a student of Socrates and effectively became his mouthpiece. He is better known than Socrates because his copious writings survived and have been widely translated and read. His frequent references to Socrates, make it difficult to distinguish between much of their thought although Plato also followed others, including Pythagoras, who was born about 200 years earlier. He advanced the written dialogue and dialectic forms of philosophy and used this approach to consider both 'myth' (*mythos*) and 'word' (*logos*). Myths are non-verifiable accounts yet can be tested by human reason; words are verifiable. Those of interest to him which most relate to the subject of this book are a) the origins of our universe and b) the origin and destiny of human beings, morals and the soul. His teachings provided new ways of looking at and interpreting the world which gained popularity and would be adopted by Christians through to Thomas Aquinas and beyond, gaining the reference 'Platonism'.

Aristotle (384-322BC) was a pupil of Plato and inherited much of Plato's work but later concentrated his efforts on the empirical study of natural then physical sciences rather than on metaphysical or spiritual matters and the origins or destiny of creation. His view of soul was perhaps more pragmatic than spiritual, believing that vegetable, animal and human souls existed in ascending order. The human soul incorporated the assets of both the others but with the added dimension of rationality, having the unique ability to compare forms of other things using intellect (*nous*) and reason.

Aristotle left Athens in 343 BC for King Philip II of Macedonia, who wanted him to tutor his son, destined to become Alexander the Great (356-323 BC). It was a relationship of mutual benefit, enabling Aristotle to install a library in the Lyceum, the great temple to Apollo and produce hundreds of papyrus scrolls, the books of the time. His work on physical science endured into the Renaissance era and beyond. It was also influential in early Christian theology with Neoplatonism and also highly respected by Islamic scholars in the Middle Ages. He believed that philanthropy enhanced the moral character of the donor when offered in the right spirit and relationship to genuinely needy recipients. His ethics followed Socrates and have recently been revisited by the rise of 'virtue ethics' in the latter half of the 20th century. Aristotle was also a pioneer in the study of logic.

Epicurus (341-270) set up his own school in Athens and had the novel policy of including women. His philosophy was directed at achieving in life a happy, calm peaceful state with freedom from worry, fear and pain. He believed in Gods but they were unconcerned with people and would not judge or punish them as he saw death as the end of body and soul, so it should not be feared. Just make the most of life, friends, happiness and pleasure. However, people had free will and should lead a moral life to avoid the complications of feeling guilt.

The Stoics originated from a Cypriot, Zeno (335-263 BC), who had set up a school in Athens, *Stoa Pockile* (Painted Portico), after which they were named. Stoicism has held an enduring appeal and following and many of its beliefs are perceived as reflecting quite a sensible view and way of life. To them, reason is at the core of everything and virtue is the basis for happiness. There is no point in struggling against powerful forces and since we are such an insignificant part of nature, the wise choice is for us to work in harmony with creation and nature, accept what life throws at us and make the most of it. This leads to happiness, which arises from a healthy state of mind in which one's judgment is likely to be sound. Behaviour that contravenes nature arises from poor judgments and results in unhappiness and a disturbed mind. Stoics therefore assess people more by their actions than words. Things such as health, wealth and pleasure are not seen as good or bad but their intrinsic value lies in them being matters which virtue can influence.

Early Stoics dismissed the mythical concept of the multiple gods of most 'religions' as irreconcilable with their view of natural law dictating events. Nor could they accept that rites and sacrifices could find favour with a creator spirit. Their 'spirit' was not perceived as particularly caring; if it cared at all, they suggested that the right way of living would be to be virtuous, involving respect for fellow men and the rest of creation. Their ideal virtuous person was one who exercised self-control, consideration, unselfishness, awareness of duty and displayed courage and accepted their life was of little significance in the grand scheme of things. They warned against vanity of possessions as it restricted one's freedom unnecessarily. Wise people should be impassive and at ease within themselves and their environment.

Stoics did not recognise a personal god and thus had no related spirituality. They promoted heroism, thought little of love, saw no point in remorse or seeking forgiveness and paid little heed to the needy. Attaching little value to human life beyond self-interest, they supported suicide to avoid pain or indignity in death. They were basically fatalists, 'stoically' accepting whatever life threw at them, not believing in miracles or oracles as these did not fall under the law of nature, which they believed were the sole determinant of events. Stoics share common ground with Christians – one God, creator and ruler of the universe, our duty to behave well with personal beneficence, though they favoured the elite over the disadvantaged.

Legacy of Alexander the Great (356-323 BC) and the Romans

Alexander the Great then later the Romans should be credited with laying the cultural and connective foundations that would eventually enable Christianity to spread as far and fast as it did. In a brief life of similar length to Jesus, Alexander established an empire that stretched east from his homeland Greece as far as the Indian sub-continent and south to Egypt. The lands in his empire adopted the Greek language and Hellenic philosophy and thinking, which had a unifying effect. When the Romans later overcame the western end of these territories, they built impressive port and road infrastructure to support their military logistics which provided excellent international communications and travel facilities within their empire.

Alexander had the strategy and strength to conquer Palestine, something that many, apart from the Babylonians in the 6th century BC, had failed to do, but the defeated Jews upheld unyieldingly the commandments and law of their religion which absolutely forbade the worship of any images of a god. Alexander sensed it would be unwise to take a stand on this. But when the Greeks appointed Antiochus IV Epiphanes, a member of the neighbouring Seleucid (Syrian) dynasty to rule Palestine, he took a hard line. He applied the letter of the Hellenist policy, banning circumcision, observance of the Sabbath and scripture-reading as well as opening up the Jews' sacred Temple to the whole population who were free to bring images. He aimed thus to deny the Jews their distinctive identity, but had underestimated their passion and commitment to their faith. They formed an armed guerrilla resistance movement known as the 'Maccabees' which defeated Antiochus's army, forcing him to soften his line. It was an early example of the Jews' ongoing incorrigibility. They derived strength from the fact they still regarded themselves as God's chosen people and expected the Messiah.

In the second century BC, Rome conquered the Greeks and western Asia Minor having already acquired much of the north coast of Africa including Egypt, but not Palestine, which became the 'missing link'. The Jews had a long history of success in defending it from attacks, which were frequent as it lay on vital trade routes between ambitious regions. King Mithradates of Pontus (in the region of present-day Anatolia, south of the Black Sea), and his son-in-law Tigranes of Armenia ventured south to take Cappadocia and Cilicia, then threatened Syria and settled into Antioch.

The Romans always defended their hard-won territory, so they sent General Pompey in 64 BC to win Syria from these invaders and the remains of the Seleucids, the previous rulers. They then tried once more to complete the Mediterranean loop by gaining Palestine. They had also become more aware of the need to secure their eastern border which had been safe while King Alexander Jannaeus (105-78 BC), a descendant of the Maccabees ruled Judaea. But when his sons fell out over the crown, each sought help from the Romans, so it fell into Roman hands through General Pompey in 63 BC despite stiff resistance. Jewish independence was lost as Palestine was absorbed into the Roman administration of Syria and one of Jannaeus' sons, Hyrcanus II was appointed High Priest and titular leader. Hyrcanus appointed Antipater I (100-43 BC), as one of his ministers.

General Pompey took a hard line, but Antipater found favour with Julius Caesar and the senate and he negotiated freedom from taxes and military service for the Jews. Caesar saw sense in this – why give the best military training to such resourceful people? Antipater was founder of the Herodian dynasty and became a strong leader; however the Jews, suspicious of his Roman sympathies, assassinated him. His two sons, Phasael in Jerusalem and Herod in Galilee, held on to their governorships of two of the five states of Israel. Phasael committed suicide when Jerusalem was over-run by Antigonus. Herod followed the victorious Mark Antony through Egypt to Rome where the senate made him Jewish king in 40 BC. Antigonus held Jerusalem but in 37 BC, Herod the Great besieged the city and married princess Mariamne of the deposed Maccabees, thus legitimising his claim to the throne and reunifying Judaea.

Octavian was the great nephew and adopted son and heir to Caesar in 31 BC. Mark Antony was a successful general who commanded the support of many of the military, but he lost the battle of Actium to Octavian's General Agrippa. Antony's mistress, Pharaoh Cleopatra (69-30 BC), the last active Pharaoh of Egypt also lost at Actium, ending a dynasty spanning five millennia. The Roman ring was thus completed around the Mediterranean Sea. Octavian's acceptance by the senate was sealed by his appointment as Augustus and he soon adopted that name in the hope of marking a new more peaceful era.

The wily Herod once more found favour with the victor and his area of influence was enlarged, although he was always regarded by the Jews as a foreigner, being a Roman protégé and coming from Idumea/ Edom, a state bordering Judea south of the Dead Sea. Nonetheless he ruled for nearly 40 years, securing the bridge between Egypt and Syria for the Romans. He was vigorous in building infrastructure and temples, notably rebuilding the great temple of Jerusalem. But his architecture reflected that of the Greeks and the temples were dedicated to pagan gods and emperor worship which fuelled the people's hatred.

Herod the Great is believed to have died in 4 BC, probably the actual year of Jesus' birth. He had a number of sons by ten wives and had been ruthless in culling them by assassination, so only three younger sons remained to inherit his specified parts of his kingdom. Herod Philip took on the remote region of Batanea to the north and east of the Sea of Galilee; Herod Antipas was given Galilee and Perea, probably being the person referred to in the New Testament as playing a role in the death of John the Baptist and the trial of Jesus; Herod Archelaus was given charge of the main part of the kingdom – Judea proper, Edom and Samaria.

Thanks to his friendship with Emperor Caligula, Herod's grandson Agrippa I became ruler of most of these territories as his father and uncles left them, thus reuniting them once more as king until his death in 44 AD. Another uprising took place when the Romans ousted his son in favour of a Roman governor, leading to a full scale revolution in 66 AD. The Romans, led by Titus, spared nothing and overcame this and virtually destroyed Jerusalem in the process. This was a major event involving the famous sacking of the magnificent Temple of Jerusalem.

Religious Factions in Israel

In the New Testament there are references to some different religious groups among the Israelis, so for clarity, it is worth summarising the main ones as follows.

Saducees were quite a small but influential group comprising senior priests and aristocrats including many members of the **Sanhedrin**, the ruling Jewish Council. They adhered to the strict interpretation of the Law of Moses, whom they regarded as the only true prophet from Divine Revelation.

Pharisees were found among people with a reliable occupation and income or full-time study. Being more numerous, they had local 'chapters', each with its own management committee and rules. They were generally respected by the Jews and interpreted the Law less strictly than the Saducees. This eased their relationships with the Romans, few of whom had any concept of the scriptures. The Pharisees believed in life after death and accepted the Hebrew Scriptures. Their rules were generally easier for the middle classes to follow than for ordinary workers and the poor. Jesus, who may well have had Pharisee relatives, did not hold them in high regard, since he was more concerned at the situation of poorer people, who tended to be marginalised in Jewish society.

Zealots came mainly from among the Pharisees and believed that God was their only master. So they wanted absolute freedom from Roman rule and formed a resistance movement.

Essenes were devout and held themselves largely apart from Jewry and society, which they rejected as corrupt. They believed that God would reassert control. Much smaller in number than the Sadducees or Pharisees, the Essenes were mostly to be found in various cities. They are today connected with the Dead Sea scrolls, which were found in the 1940s in caves in the Qumran area at the north end of the Dead Sea. This was a fairly barren and isolated part in which some Essenes had separated themselves from society. They tended to live in communal groups dedicated to asceticism – some groups practiced celibacy, daily bathing in cold water and poverty, similar to future monastics. Hebrew Scriptures often suggest a causal relationship between adherence to religious teaching and worldly fortune, i.e. the good would be rewarded and the evil punished. There was constant expectation of improvement among the faithful. This could have related to the life to come, although many Jews do not believe in an afterlife.

Birth of Christ

For any Christian, keen interest centres on the birth of Jesus Christ. Some puzzling inconsistencies arise in dating that and some of the surrounding events referred to in the gospels.

Quirinius, the Roman governor of Syria who oversaw Israel, held his famous census for the emperor, Augustus Octavian, grandnephew of Julius Caesar, in 6 AD. Mary, daughter of Joachim and Anne, and her betrothed, Joseph travelled to Bethlehem, to register for that census according to Luke (2:1-4). Mary was expecting Jesus' birth imminently. There is clearly some confusion of dates here as the Gregorian calendar regards Christ's birth as being either at the end of 1 BC or the beginning of 1 AD (there was no year zero, so it is even possible that the year of Christ's birth was left out). The confusion is augmented in Matthew's gospel (2: 7-8) where he describes how Herod asked the 'visitors from the East' to report back to him on the whereabouts of the 'baby born to be King of the Jews' and also (Matt 2:13-15), the Holy Family's consequent escape to Egypt. He also confirms that the King in question was Herod the Great, not one of his sons. But Herod the Great is believed to have died sometime after an eclipse of the moon. There were such eclipses in 4 BC and 1 BC.

Discussion continues, although it is fair to say that the Gregorian calendar we currently use was established as far back as 1582, there was possibly more than one census and there were a number of lunar eclipses, so the uncertainty may persist for some time. The BC/AD (or BCE/CE) system may be flawed in that it possibly misrepresents the birth of Jesus by up to 7 years. This could mean that Jesus' active ministry did not begin around the year 30, but possibly from as early as 23 AD. Likewise, Pentecost, usually regarded as the origin of the Christian Church, may not be dated to 33 but possibly 26 AD. This may help reduce the confusion over Christ's birth date, but it would still require some date verification regarding Herod's death and Quirinius' census.

Regardless of the date issue, the conception and birth of Jesus, his nature and relationship with God as well as the nature of God and the Holy Trinity have been challenging subjects of keen study and debate both within Christianity and among non-Christians. These will be covered as this story unfolds, but two key matters should be flagged up at this stage.

Firstly, the Gospels of Matthew (1:18) and Luke (1:35), both refer to Christ's conception being 'of the Holy Spirit'. The Holy Spirit is one of the three members of the Holy Trinity, the other two being God the Father and his son Jesus Christ. Debate on the Trinity surrounds its nature and whether any one part preceded the others. Many believe the debate is futile as it is a concept that surpasses human understanding, serving to enhance the human intellectual challenge.

Secondly, there are also several angles of debate as to the nature of Jesus, all related to his humanity and his divinity – to what extent he was truly human and truly God.

Jesus' birth and some references to part of his childhood are made in the gospels, but his active mission did not really begin until his Baptism at about the age of thirty, so it only lasted for around three years.

His teaching and example in life revealed qualities of God that were not so clearly communicated in the Old Testament. Christ insisted that a reluctant relative John the Baptist baptise him, which involved forgiveness of sins. That was followed by his suffering of temptation in the desert. After living nearly thirty years of a humble working class life he preached for three years then suffered ghastly torture and execution. Through all this, he demonstrated the importance of serving and accepting hardship and suffering in this life. In the end, he offered us hope through his death, resurrection and ascension. Yet still many Christians ask how a God of love and mercy could allow the hardships and suffering that we all experience and witness.

Instead of the Ten Commandments given through Moses, Jesus taught that one can live a good life by following just two as will be described in the next chapter.

There are several references to the coming of a Messiah in the Hebrew Bible, and all Jews were expecting his arrival, but when Jesus came, he did not at all match the image of the Messiah expected by the Jews. They imagined a grand arrival of a glorious God; certainly not one of humble birth and life followed by execution. So, while some Jews were convinced that Jesus was the Messiah and followed him, many do not to this day.

CHAPTER 2

Acts, Jesus Christ's Message and the First Missions

This chapter differs from the rest in that it is a précis of eye witness accounts of the first decades of Christianity from Christ's teaching period until his death and the beginnings of the Church as reported in the Acts of the Apostles, written by Luke and regarded by Christian bodies as a canonical part of the New Testament. It lays the ground for the story of Christianity to be taken forward in the hands of people. Being taken from a part of scripture, its style is different from the rest of this book, with more detail of events as well as references to apparitions, miracles and angels. There are differences of opinion today as to what extent angels are called upon as explanations of apparently supernatural events – are they dreams or flashes of imagination? These are all reasonable questions, but if there is a personal God such things could also be valid communication channels between God and humans; if the creator God exists and Jesus was the Son of God, then such things as angels and what seem like miracles to us cannot be discounted. Events such as the Ascension – Jesus' rise to heaven – for example could not be described by any other word than miracle in human terms.

The scriptures derive from people's memory, mostly through word of mouth, then words written mostly well after the event. They have been translated one or more times, so there is adequate room for some misinterpretation. There is also much mention of the Holy Spirit. Again, if one accepts the Holy Trinity, of which an explanation will be attempted later, there is nothing remarkable in this – it could help explain the incredibly rapid spread of Christian faith in and beyond the century following Christ's death, which is a well-recorded fact. Subsequent chapters will be more earthly based, and recounted in more conversational style. However sceptical one may be about celestial interventions, the letters that St Paul wrote to people in so many of the places he had visited confirm those earlier journeys described in Acts of the Apostles.

God's Message Updated and Simplified

Christianity is based on the teaching and example of Jesus Christ, who conveyed this renewed impression of God from that of the Old Testament. Christians believe that Jesus came as God both to fulfil these scriptures and to reinterpret them through his teaching. Jesus' life has been covered by the gospels, so needs no repetition here, though the actual writing of the gospels will be touched on later. For readers who may not be familiar with the gospels, Mark (12:30-31) records that Jesus Christ left a simple and clear message to clarify earlier scripture and the Ten Commandments. The principal two commandments to be obeyed by his followers are:

1. To love the Lord your God with all your heart, with all your soul, with all your mind, and with all your strength.
2. To love your neighbour as yourself

These are positive commandments rather than the negative 'do not...' Whilst they do not negate or replace the Ten Commandments, they distil them and support their relevance in accommodating developments in society and technology.

Just a reminder of the generally recognised Ten Commandments as delivered by God to Moses:

1. Do not have any other gods before me nor make any graven images and worship them.
2. Do not take the name of the Lord your God in vain.
3. Remember to keep the Sabbath Day holy
4. Honour your mother and father
5. Do not kill.
6. Do not commit adultery.
7. Do not steal
8. Do not bear false witness against your neighbour.
9. Do not covet your neighbour's spouse.
10. Do not covet your neighbour's possessions.

So with his two commandments came Christ's message of evolution of a religion from one of apparent condemnation and retribution to one of love and forgiveness. Its entreaty is for people to love their creator and all his creation, not forgetting themselves, perhaps reversing the natural order of priority, which means doing no harm to others and the brotherhood and sisterhood of people. Luke's gospel, chapter 10 follows this with the parable of the Good Samaritan for illustration. Matthew (7:12) underscores this in quoting Jesus' 'Golden Rule', which is normally expressed in English as "Do unto others as you would have them do unto you." It is expanded in John (6). The Jews say that this effectively expresses the whole Torah; the rest is just commentary. Nearly every faith from Buddhism to Hinduism to Taoism, Baha'i to Islam to Zoroastrianism has the same or equivalent injunction.

So this statement encapsulates all Christian teaching and that of nearly every serious faith or religion regarding our behaviour. The world would be an orderly and peaceful place if everybody followed it. Complications arise in the natural human search for explanations and origins of 'truth' and the meaning of life, which lead perversely to differences and dispute.

The Old Testament related the transmission of God's message through prophets to the Israelis then from the time of Moses, to the Jews. But now the Son was sent to bring direct, clearer guidance to the world in which the New Testament records his activities and messages as the basis for the Christian era. Christ did not come to change God's word but to complete it.

Founding the Church, Succession Planning

The Gospel of John (1:41-42) relates that Jesus changed Simon's name to Cephas (Aramaic for 'Rock', or Peter). In the bible a male name change indicates a leader. Then in Matthew 16:18-19: "And I say to you, that **you are Peter, and upon this rock I will build my church**, and the gates of Hell shall not prevail against it. And I will give you the keys of the kingdom of heaven. And whatever you shall bind on earth shall be bound, even in heaven. And whatever you shall loose on earth shall be loosed, even in heaven." This was after the Transfiguration and before Jesus told the apostles of his forthcoming death. He was preparing his succession, appointing Peter to head his Church. This was a moment of immense importance to all Christians, as Peter had proven human weaknesses and was destined soon to emphasise these when Jesus was taken into custody by the Jews from the Garden of Gethsemane and Peter denied his connection with Jesus three times. This first leader from whom the papacy of the Roman Catholic Church claims descent was far from infallible. It may be argued that he was not then under the full guidance of the Holy Spirit, but that would in turn raise the issue of the behaviour of some of the forthcoming leaders of the Church.

Towards the end of Luke's gospel, after Jesus's crucifixion and the discovery of his Resurrection, the eleven remaining apostles were in a state of shock and disarray, knowing they could be pursued and possibly killed. They closeted themselves in a room for fear of hostility without the protection of their leader. The next day, they were visited by the two followers who had just met Jesus on the road to Emmaus and as they were describing the encounter, Jesus himself appeared in the room, showing them his wounded hands and feet. He stressed the importance of the old scriptures having been fulfilled by his death and resurrection and asked them to stay together in Jerusalem because in a few days he would send them the Holy Spirit as promised by God the Father. Luke says that he then took them for a short walk out of the city to the Mount of Olives in Bethany and they watched him for the last time as he ascended into heaven.

They returned to Jerusalem as Jesus had asked, knowing they had a mission to perform in spreading the word of Christ. There were twelve Apostles – Peter, brothers John and James, Andrew, Philip, Thomas, Bartholomew, Matthew, James the son of Alphaeus, Simon the Zealot, and Thaddaeus. The twelfth, Judas Iscariot, who had betrayed Jesus to the Romans and then committed suicide, had since been replaced by Matthias. The twelve remained together for days to await the promised Holy Spirit.

Pentecost and the Christian Church after Jesus

Jesus Christ had been crucified just before the Jewish Passover feast. God sent the Holy Spirit to fill the twelve apostles, those first Jewish believers in Jesus with the Holy Spirit to guide and strengthen them 50 days later, Pentecost, which tied in with the Jewish Festival of Shavuot. Jewish people 'from every nation' of the known world were staying in Jerusalem to celebrate this festival. Shavuot is held 50 days after the Passover and is celebrated for two reasons. First it is a thanksgiving for the beginning of the wheat harvest (Lev 23:17). The second reason was that Moses received the Law, the Torah – teaching from God – at Shavuot. 'Pentecost' derives from a Greek word meaning 'fifty' and it is the Greek word used to describe the Jewish feast of Shavuot.

A key element in Shavuot is God's revelation of himself and his Torah, his teaching, to his people, as told in Exodus chapters 19 and 20. In that revelation God taught Moses and delivered his commandments to him on Mount Sinai, accompanied by thunder, lightning and a trumpet blast. The voice of the Lord called to Moses (Exodus 19: 16-19) – an event that was witnessed not only by Israelites, but also by "many other people", (Exodus 12:38) – literally a mixed multitude – accompanying the Israelites on their journey. There are several things in common between this event and the 'new' Pentecost:

- When God revealed his teaching to Moses there was thunder and a loud trumpet blast. When the Holy Spirit of God came upon those first Jewish believers in Jesus "a sound like the blowing of a violent wind came from heaven and filled the whole house".
- On Mount Sinai when God revealed his teaching to Moses he descended upon the mountain in fire. When the Holy Spirit came on the day of Pentecost the believers "saw what seemed to be tongues of fire that separated and came to rest on each of them" as they felt the presence of God.
- The mountainside was surrounded not only by Israelites but also a mixed multitude. On the day of Pentecost there were in town 'God-fearing Jews from every known nation' for Shavuot.
- On the mountain God delivered his Torah – his teaching. On the day of Pentecost God was giving believers his Holy Spirit, and one of the functions of the Holy Spirit is to be the teacher.

The evident parallels between Shavuot and Pentecost speak of a God of perfect timing and the clear new message of God through Jesus. The New Testament had begun as God came on earth through the incarnation and gave his message directly to the world rather than through prophets. His timing of the arrival of Jesus coincided with improved recording of the written word and communications.

On the night he was betrayed Jesus had spoken to his disciples and whilst teaching them he said: "All this I have spoken while still with you. But the Counsellor, the Holy Spirit, whom the Father will send in my name, will teach you all things and will remind you of everything I have said to you" (John 14:25-26).

Summary of the 'Acts of the Apostles'

The Acts of the Apostles is a continued account by Luke, summarising the events in his gospel and going on to describe the Pentecost, when the Holy Spirit came upon them 'in tongues of fire', imparting the full knowledge of Christ's message as well as the gift of tongues, so they could begin their mission by preaching to the international crowds gathered in Jerusalem for Shavuot and be understood by all. Acts goes on to recount how the very early believers, guided now by the Holy Spirit, began to spread the faith among the Jews and Samaritans then 'Gentiles' further afield in the known world. There was also a political dimension in that Luke sought to assure the Romans that Christians posed no threat to their Empire, a prescient move that would be severely tested over the first few centuries prior to Christianity being adopted some three centuries later as the official Roman faith.

Peter publicly addressed the Jews, relating the events of Christ's life, some of them miraculous, then his crucifixion and his crowning resurrection and ascension. He said there was no doubt this was the Messiah whom the Jews awaited. He urged them to be baptised and receive the Holy Spirit and faith in Jesus Christ. On one occasion, Peter and John called on God to cure a beggar who had been lame throughout his life. When he was cured, the local people flocked to them but they were called before the High Priest Annas and the elders, who arrested them. Some 5,000 people had been converted so the Council, aware of their support, set Peter and John free but warned them never again to speak publicly in the name of Jesus, a warning they could not accept.

The disciples of Christ multiplied rapidly in spite of the considerable commitment asked of them. Not only was there the lurking danger of persecution, but they were asked to sell all their assets and give all the money to the group, who distributed money daily according to the needs of the members. As their numbers grew, so did friction between the native Jewish (Hebrews) and the Greek-speaking Jewish disciples (Hellenists from the Greek diaspora), the latter claiming that their widows were being relatively less well supported. So the twelve Apostles held a meeting with all available followers and it was agreed to appoint seven overseers to administer the funds fairly, thus freeing the others to concentrate on their mission of evangelisation.

Stephen was an early deacon and influential preacher but he was opposed by many members of the synagogue in Jerusalem and they arrested him for blasphemy. When he appeared before them he rather undiplomatically berated the members of the council for having killed the Messiah foretold by Moses, so they took him out and stoned him to death with the approval of Saul of Tarsus, who held their cloaks. Stephen thus became the first Christian martyr after Jesus. Saul was a Pharisee and also a Roman citizen who then vowed to destroy the Christian Church, and from that day, the followers of Christ were persecuted and scattered throughout Judea and Samaria. Saul searched for believers from house to house, throwing those he found into jail. Philip travelled to Samaria, converting and baptising many people. When the Apostles heard of this Peter and John went there to pray that they may receive the Holy Spirit. Today, the Christian Confirmation is a formal replay of that process and is regarded as sacramental by most. An angel then sent Philip to Gaza and on the way he met and baptised an Ethiopian official who was returning from Jerusalem to his country, where Christianity subsequently grew.

Meanwhile, Saul's passionate persecution of the followers of Christ continued and he set out with a squad to ride to Damascus in the cause. As he approached his destination, a powerful light flashed from the sky around him and he fell from his horse. He and his followers heard the voice of Jesus saying, "Saul, Saul, why do you persecute me?"

He replied "Who are you, Lord?"

"I am Jesus, whom you persecute. But get up and go into the city, where you will be told what to do."

Saul got up but was blind, so his men led him into Damascus. For three days he could not see and did not eat or drink.

A Damascan believer called Ananias had a vision in which the Lord told him to go to the house of Judas in Straight Street and ask for Saul from Tarsus. He went and placed his hands on Saul's head saying that Jesus had sent him. Saul's sight was restored and when he had eaten, his strength returned also. He appears to have received great learning and understanding of Christ's teaching from the Holy Spirit, for he was converted and started to preach so powerfully in the synagogues that the Hellenist Jews plotted to kill him. He hid from them before being helped to escape through a hole in the city wall by being lowered in a basket before returning to Jerusalem, where the Apostles fearfully avoided him until Barnabas pleaded his cause. Barnabas was a Cypriot Jew, who had become one of the earliest active disciples in Jerusalem. They then helped Saul return to Tarsus, his homeland and a peaceful period ensued, during which the Holy Spirit strengthened them all to help grow the Church. Mark the Evangelist was not an apostle but a helper, son of a cousin of Barnabas called Mary. Mark would accompany Paul on his first missionary journey and was with Paul and Peter later in Rome. The Copts believe he then went to Egypt and founded the Church there.

A number of miracles were worked through Peter in his travels and a couple are worth recounting here. Peter was in Lydda where a man called Aeneas had been paralysed and bed-ridden for eight years. Peter said "Jesus Christ makes you well. Get up and make your bed." Aeneas did so and all the people in the town converted. Peter was then called to Jaffa, where Tabitha, a great benefactor and helper of the poor had fallen ill and died. Peter came and prayed over her body, then told her to get up. She opened her eyes and seeing Peter, she sat up. He showed Tabitha fully alive to the people who had called for him.

Cornelius, a Roman soldier captain in Caesarea was told by an angel to seek Peter in Jaffa. When his messengers approached, Peter was told by the Holy Spirit to do as his visitors asked and they took him to Cornelius who had gathered a lot of people to hear what Peter had to say. Peter was taken aback by their numbers and diversity but being a Jew, he said "You know well that a Jew is not allowed by his religion to visit or associate with Gentiles. But God has just shown me that I must not consider anybody ritually unclean or defiled. I came without objection but why did you call me?" Cornelius asked to be baptised. This was an important moment when Peter realised that God had called him also to baptise Gentiles and other non-Jews, who had not been circumcised. The other apostles, also Jews were critical of him until he told them of his vision of the Holy Spirit. Then Barnabas went to Antioch (now Antakya in Turkey) where he was well received. He asked Paul to join him and they spent a year there, preaching. It was here that believers were first called Christians.

King Herod Agrippa (ruled 41-44 AD), began to persecute some members of the Church and had James the brother of John assassinated. Then he had Peter put in jail, heavily shackled and guarded. An angel freed Peter and he walked out to the home of Mary, mother of John Mark, where his friends had gathered to pray. They hid him from Herod's searchers and word continued to spread; Barnabas and Saul returned from Antioch and took John Mark with them. Saul had Roman citizenship through his Roman father and was finding it better for his missions overseas to use the Roman version of his name, Paul, which he adopted. They travelled to Salonica and Cyprus, where the governor Sergius Paulus asked to see them. His Jewish magician tried to deny them entry and Paul told him in front of the governor he would be blinded for a while, whereupon a dark mist enveloped him and he could not see. As a result, the governor believed.

They sailed on to Perga, where John Mark left them, then to Antalya and the other Antioch nearby. Here Paul taught the Jews in a lengthy sermon in the synagogue how God had brought the Israelites from their exile in Egypt, their forty years in the desert, through King David, John the Baptist, then the life and death of Jesus, his resurrection and how it all fitted with their scriptural prophecies. He was invited back for more the following Sabbath and almost the whole town turned up, including many Gentiles. The Jews were resentful and angrily disputed what Paul was saying. Paul and Barnabas pointed out that they had been given the honour of hearing the message first, but they would go on to attend to the Gentiles as in Christ's command "I have made you a light to the Gentiles so that the whole world may be saved." Many Gentiles embraced the faith.

Influential Jews made it impossible for Paul and Barnabas to stay, so they moved east to Iconium, where much the same thing happened and they went on to the city of Lystra. There, after they cured a man who had been lame from birth, the crowds hailed them as Gods, calling Barnabas Zeus and Paul Hermes and wanting to offer sacrifices to them. They persuaded the people that they were not gods but men charged by God the creator with his message and the people should give up offering sacrifice to worthless things. Some Jews came on from nearby Antioch and rallied a group against them, stoning Paul and leaving him outside the city for dead.

But when the believers gathered round him, he got up and went back into the town. The next day they travelled further east to Derbe to preach there and in surrounding villages. After preaching to as many people as possible in these places, they retraced their steps, stopping briefly at each of these towns to encourage and strengthen the believers and appoint elders to lead them and then they sailed back directly from Perga to the other Antioch in Syria, having won many disciples.

There they gathered the people of the church together and told them how, with God's help they had opened the way for Gentiles to believe. Some men came from Judea and began to teach the believers that they could not be saved unless they were circumcised as the Law of Moses required. Paul and Barnabas strongly contested this, so they went to Jerusalem to settle the matter with the Apostles and elders. As they travelled through Phoenicia and Samaria, they shared the news of how many Gentiles had turned to God, which the people greeted with delight.

Back in Jerusalem, they were welcomed by the Apostles and the elders, to whom they recounted what God had done through them. Some of them who had been brought up as Pharisees supported the argument that Gentiles must be circumcised and follow the Law of Moses. So a meeting was held to discuss the matter but the debate was cut short as, following his experience with Cornelius, Peter pronounced that God had guided him to preach the Good News to the Gentiles, so they could hear and believe. He pointed out that God, who knows the thoughts of everyone showed his approval of the Gentiles by giving the Holy Spirit to them, "…just as he has done to us. He forgave their sins because they believed." He ended emphatically "We believe and are saved by the grace of the Lord Jesus, just as they are." James supported this, quoting an adaptation of Amos 9:11-12 – 'And so all the rest of the human race will come to me, all the Gentiles who I have called my own.' James also felt they should not trouble the Gentiles who were turning to God, but write asking them not to eat any food that has been offered to idols; to keep themselves from sexual immorality; and not to eat any animal that has been strangled, nor any blood. This meeting is sometimes referred to as the Council of Jerusalem, the very first council of the Church.

The apostles and elders sent Paul and Barnabas back with two respected believers – Judas, known as Barrabas, and Silas – with a letter asking the Gentiles to do what James said. The messengers and the message were greeted with great joy and Judas and Silas spoke at length, giving the people courage and strength. Paul and Barnabas wanted to revisit places where they had been successful. Barnabas wanted to include John Mark but Paul did not believe he had the staying power, so they agreed to go separate ways, Barnabas and John Mark to Cyprus and Paul with Silas to

Syria and Cilicia, all to strengthen the churches. Paul travelled on to Derbe and Lystra, where a Christian named Timothy lived. His mother was a Christian Jew, his father Greek. They travelled on together through Phrygia and Galatia. According to Acts (16:7), the Holy Spirit would not let them take their message to the province of Asia (Turkey, east of the Dardanelles), so they went to Mysia and Troas, where Paul had another vision calling him to Macedonia. They went by ship from Troas to Neapolis (Kavalla today) via the island of Samothrace, then inland to Philippi, which was a Roman colony in Macedonia. There they stayed with Lydia, a Jewess whom they converted at a place where the Jews gathered to pray and which the evangelists visited daily. They were followed constantly by a servant girl possessed by evil spirits which gave her amazing power to predict the future. This was annoying and one day, Paul's patience snapped and he called on Jesus to banish the spirit from her. She lost her predictive powers and thereby her value to her owners. They held Paul and Silas to account in public and the authorities had them whipped and jailed. They prayed and sang to God in the presence of other prisoners and there was an earthquake that loosened all their chains. The jailer was converted and when the authorities learned that Paul and Silas were Roman citizens, they came to apologise but asked them to leave the city.

So they moved via Amphipolis and Apollonia to Thessalonica where there was a synagogue in which, over three Sabbaths they persuaded many Jews and Greeks that Jesus was indeed the expected Messiah. Those Jews they had not converted stirred unrest and incited mobs to seek them, but the believers moved them by night to Berea where they converted many more before the mob from Thessalonica came. Paul was spirited away to the coast, while Silas and Timothy stayed discreetly a while longer in Berea until the men who had helped Paul as far as Athens told them to join them. Meanwhile Paul held discussions with Jews and Gentiles in the synagogue. Athens regarded itself as a centre for contemporary thought and practice, so Paul was taken to share his preaching with the city leaders. He had seen temples to unknown gods and commented on the religious nature of the people but said that he could tell them about the real God who had sent his son to earth to reveal his message and had raised him from death. Some, led by Dionysius believed him.

Paul then went on to Corinth where he met a Jew called Aquila who had come from Pontius in Italy with his wife Priscila when Emperor Claudius had expelled all Jews from Rome. Paul stayed with them and worked with them for a while. He was a tentmaker and this was their business too. Every Sabbath he held discussions in the synagogue, then when Silas and Timothy joined him, they all evangelised full time. When some Jews turned against him, Paul preached to the Gentiles. He stayed there for 18 months before sailing with Aquila and Priscila towards Syria. On their arrival in Ephesus, Paul went to the synagogue for discussions and they asked him to stay longer but he needed to move on, saying that God willing, he would return. Aquila and Priscila chose to remain there. Paul briefly greeted the church in Jerusalem then moved to Antioch to preach before going again through Galatia and Phrygia to strengthen believers there.

At that time a Jew called Apollos came to Ephesus and preached the Way of the Lord. Aquila and Priscila found his enthusiasm was not matched by his knowledge so they took him home and gave him more instruction. He then went to Achaia and helped the believers there, proving very strong in his arguments with the Jews in public debates. While Apollos was later in Corinth Paul travelled through the interior of the province and in Ephesus he took his teaching forward from John's baptism to baptism in the name of Jesus, bringing the Holy Spirit to believers. After about three months using the synagogue, some Jews became truculent, so for the next two years Paul taught in the lecture hall of Tyrannus. This helped bring the Good News to most of the people of the province of Asia. God performed unusual miracles through Paul and even his belongings were curing people and driving out evil spirits.

Paul moved tirelessly on to Macedonia and Achaia then back to Jerusalem before resolving to see Rome. He sent Timothy and Erastus to Macedonia while he spent time in Asia. Some serious trouble arose in Ephesus as a silversmith called Demetrius and friends were making a great deal of money from making statues of the Goddess Artemis to whom there was a large temple and following in the city. Uproar against Christian Jews was quelled by the Town Clerk as Paul had been restrained from addressing a crowded stadium. Paul travelled to Macedonia then Achaia and back to Macedonia to calm unrest among the Jews, then to a large gathering and community meal in Troas where he spoke to the people.

After this, Paul went to Assos, then with his friends to Miletus, a three day journey via Samos. When in Miletus, Paul sent a message to the elders in Ephesus, asking them to meet him as he wanted to leave Asia and return to Jerusalem for Pentecost. In Ephesus he announced that this would be his last visit but he left them the responsibility of keeping and spreading the faith. He had given them three years of his time recounting all that Jesus stood for. He told them he had faced violence and threats and they should be prepared for the same. There was an emotional farewell as they escorted him to the ship, on which he sailed with his friends via Cos, Rhodes and Patara eventually to disembark at Tyre.

They stayed with believers who were guided by the Holy Spirit to tell Paul not to go to Jerusalem. So they sailed on to Ptolemais and stayed one day with Christians and on to Caesarea and stayed with Philip the evangelist. Paul received another warning from a prophet, Agabus who came from Judea to deliver it, but Paul insisted he was prepared to die for the Lord Jesus and they went and were welcomed in Jerusalem. Next day, Paul went with all the church elders to see James. They went to the temple where Paul was captured by the crowd, who accused him of teaching the Gentiles contrary to Moses' Law. The Romans intervened and let him address the crowd in Hebrew. He talked of his history persecuting Christians, what happened on the road to Damascus, how Ananius restored his sight, washed his sins and baptised him. He had held the cloaks of Stephen's murderers. But the crowd called for his death. The Romans shaved and beat him but released him when on learning he was a Roman citizen. They took him before the council.

Paul had been a Pharisee who believed in life after death, angels and spirits. He noticed there were both Pharisees and Sadducees in the group and the latter do not believe in life after death. He announced that he was a Pharisee, son of Pharisees and it seemed odd that he was on trial because of his belief that the dead could rise to a new life. At this there was division among his accusers and as violence arose, the Roman commander sent his troops to take Paul to the fort. That night Jesus appeared to him telling him not to be afraid. He had given good witness to him in Jerusalem and would yet do the same in Rome. A group of Jews plotted to assassinate Paul but his sister's son found out and reported the plot to Paul and the commander, so Paul was sent with a strong guard to Caesarea with a letter to Governor Felix.

The High Priest Ananias and lawyer Tertullus put their case that Paul was a dangerous nuisance, who started riots among Jews and was a leader of the Nazarenes. No verdict was given but Felix held Paul for two years before being succeeded by Porcius Festus, who held a retrial. Since no proof could be found, Paul appealed to the Emperor. A while later, Agrippa (Emperor from 41-44AD) and Bernice made a formal visit to Caesarea to greet the new Governor Festus. Paul was given a hearing and told of his full history – persecution, conversion and preaching according to the Law of Moses, and that Jesus was the expected Messiah. It was agreed Paul had done nothing to deserve death or even imprisonment. This meant that he was free to sail to Rome under the care of Julius, an officer in the Emperor's Regiment. But the ship encountered a storm and was driven by strong North Easterly winds, eventually foundering in a bay in Malta. It was a frightening journey but an angel reassured Paul they would be saved; and they were. Paul cured some Maltese natives and when winter was over they sailed again for Rome and he got to work with the Jews with some success.

There the Acts of the Apostles ends. There was no mention of Emperor

Nero's persecution of Christians or the Jewish wars and fall of the Temple in Jerusalem in the 60s AD, but the same applied to other political events of the period, so this was perhaps regarded as being within the scope of politics rather than evangelism. Nor are the deaths of Peter and Paul mentioned, but these might have occurred after publication of the Acts. Luke lived until about 84 AD and died in Greece.

Regarding how Paul, a natural leader and orator, acquired such detailed knowledge of the scriptures and firm views on the teaching of the Church, which he taught so lucidly, Christians believe he was given such insights directly by God through the Holy Spirit during or soon after his experience on the road to Damascus. This is what prophets are – people blessed and inspired by God's revelation. Paul set up Christian groups, or 'Churches' in the main centres he visited, so these became known for example as the 'Church of Rome' or the 'Church of the Corinthians' and so on. He still had personal struggles with apparent conflicts as a born Jew, between God's teaching through Christ and that in the Torah, especially the fact that although the Israelites regarded themselves as God's chosen people in the Old Testament, this status did not survive Jesus Christ's teaching. This is well illustrated in Paul's epistle to the Romans, Chapter 9, which includes (Good News Version): "How great is my sorrow, how endless the pain in my heart for my own people, my own flesh and blood…. They are God's people, he made them his children and revealed his glory to them, made his covenants with them and gave them the Law; they have the true worship; they have received God's promises."

The Christian faith had been established and grown in the East Mediterranean to face over two millennia of further growth and development in the face of multiple difficulties, both internal and external.

CHAPTER 3

First Century AD

Early Roman Leaders

100-44 BC   Julius Caesar
83-30 BC   Marc Antony with Lepidus & Octavian

Emperors

27 BC–14 AD	Augustus (Octavian), first emperor	69-79 AD	Vespasian
14–37 AD	Tiberius	79-81 AD	Titus
37-41 AD	Caligula	81-96 AD	Domitian
41-54 AD	Claudius	96-98 AD	Nerva
54-68 AD	Nero	98-117 AD	Trajan
68-69 AD	Galba then Otho and Vitelius,		

This century naturally overlaps with the last chapter, Acts of the Apostles, as well as superficially scanning the life of Jesus. The nascent Christian religion, with its Jewish origins, emerges as a more open new faith and approach based on the teaching of Jesus Christ which also appeals to non-Jews. It begins to form an organisational structure as well as services of worship, weekly practice, seasons in the year, all quite close to classical Judaism as a natural starting point. At the same time, its beliefs open new avenues of scrutiny and study from students and teachers. To ensure consistency and correctness of belief, clergy leaders write the first catechism, the 'Didache'. Even at this early stage, some Roman emperors perceive Christianity's influence and spread as a threat and launch persecution against it.

Influential Writers

Philo of Alexandria's (20BC to 40AD) life spanned that of Jesus. He lived in that ancient Egyptian city of culture and learning and was the only Hellenist Jewish Rabbi and philosopher to publish parts of his sermons and lectures. Although totally committed to his religion, he believed that literal interpretations of the Old Testament would stifle humanity's view and perception of God, who is beyond description in human terms, so suggested it is allegorical, that is to say an abstract or figurative account of people and events that requires interpretation to reveal its true moral meaning. This word 'allegorical' will crop up during the course of this story and Philo applied himself to the difficult task of interpreting the real meaning of some of the scripture and wrote commentaries that would probably have been palatable to the Greek philosophers. The post-evangelist Barnabas agreed, suggesting the texts' relevance to Christianity lay in their spiritual message, a view that was shared and developed by others who followed.

Josephus (37-100AD) was a Jerusalem-born former army general who was defeated and captured by the Romans and became a historian and friend of Emperor Vespasian's son, Titus. He wrote a history of the Jews covering the period from just before Christ to early Christianity. He too wrote with appeal to Greek philosophy and ethics to attract contemporary readers and his account is fairly consistent with the Gospels in describing John's message as seeking complete righteousness in life by following the divine ethical commands. The Gospels represented baptism in water as the repentance and forgiveness of sins, but Josephus also regarded baptism as sanctifying the body once the sin had been cleansed. He refers to Jesus as a wise teacher crucified on the orders of Pontius Pilate.

Birth and Life of Jesus

Augustus (BC 63-AD 14) succeeded his great uncle, Julius Caesar the dictator of the Roman Republic in 43 BC after a number of military successes (including the landing in Britain). He dropped the post of dictator and became the first emperor of the Roman Empire and was held in almost god-like admiration by Romans throughout the empire. The Roman military presence in Israel, added stability to the region and while they raised taxes, the Jews themselves were left mostly to administer their religion, law and government.

Jesus grew up as a Jew in the Galilean village of Nazareth. Since only Mary is mentioned, his father Joseph may have died quite young, though possibly not before he fathered four 'brothers' (James, Joseph, Jude and Simon) and several sisters of Jesus. The term brother in this period and region can refer to cousin or half-brother. But he probably lived at least some fifteen years as it is known that Jesus worked with him, learning the carpenter's trade and may have applied these skills to boat building and repair as they lived close to Lake Galilee. Jesus met fishermen there, including his first four disciples, Simon (Peter), Andrew, James and John, all fishermen. Little is known of Jesus' life between late teens and most of his twenties, but he downed tools in his late twenties for pilgrimage to the River Jordan to be baptised by John the Baptist. Only then did he go into the desert for the famous 'forty days' before beginning his missionary work as the Son of God.

John the Baptist

John, son of Mary's cousin Elizabeth, was the precursor of Jesus Christ, as prophesied some 700 years earlier by Micah and Isaiah – "God said I will send my messenger ahead of you to clear the way for you...". He was an ascetic living in the wilderness on locusts and wild honey and began his public mission during the reign of Herod Antipas in the Galilee region. John preached the imminent coming of 'the stronger one', and the need for urgent repentance for which he offered baptism in the waters of the river Jordan. He was in the Scriptural tradition, a 'fire and brimstone' preacher of repentance and divine judgment. The Jews' expectation of the Messiah included judgment, but they believed that as descendants of Abraham and marked with circumcision, they were God's chosen people, meriting salvation. John sought to disabuse them of this comfort. It was almost always adults who John blessed in baptism, as candidates had to declare repentance and resolve to avoid sin in future in order to find forgiveness.

John was seen as a prophet and the sheer size of his following disturbed Herod Antipas. Shortly after he baptised Jesus, John was seized and held in the castle prison at Machaerus near the east coast of the Dead Sea (Mark 6:17-19).

Jesus in the Wilderness, the Apostles

Following his baptism by John, Jesus went into the wilderness where, being human, he struggled to connect in prayer with God the Father and fend off temptations of the devil. Some considered him deranged while he was in the desert as he made seemingly outrageous declarations, such as that no man could be his disciple who "does not hate his own father and mother and wife and children... and his own life also" (Luke 14:26), which sits uneasily with the fourth Commandment, "Honour your father and your mother". This was a time when Jesus seemed to display his true humanity, affected like us all by the stressful conditions. Another time was later on when he lost patience with the traders and money lenders in the Temple, which was probably a major factor in leading to their call for his crucifixion. Again, as he was crucified he called out to his heavenly Father "...Why have you forsaken me?"

After John the Baptist was arrested, Jesus returned home from the wilderness and resumed John's teaching, but in a softer way than either John's or his own recent pronouncements. He stressed that suffering and tears would cease in God's kingdom. He used parables, many of which need some explanation or guidance though even then there seem to be some difficult ambiguity in message, such as the value of family, referred to above, or wealth – the parable of the 'talents' versus that of the 'rich man, camel and needle' – which relate to every-day matters for us all. In such apparent contradictions, there were similarities with the Old Testament, though Jesus' message was more one of God's love and mercy than that of retribution and punishment heavily portrayed in the Old Testament.

He drew a large following with most of those who had followed John the Baptist and he selected a dozen close disciples including the initial four. They became known as the twelve apostles, some of whom left their home and livelihood to work with him:

- **Simon,** renamed **Peter** (Jesus' name for him, 'Cephas' in Aramaic, meaning rock), who was married
- **Andrew,** Peter's brother
- **James,** son of Zebedee, a prosperous fisherman
- **John,** brother of James, referred to in John's gospel as 'the one Jesus loved'.
- **Philip**
- **Bartholomew** (also referred to in John's gospel as Nathaniel)
- **Thomas,** (also known as Didimus)
- **Matthew,** tax collector, son of Alphaeus, brother of James the Lesser.
- **James,** sometimes called James the Lesser
- **Thaddeus,** referred to in Luke as Jude, son of James and in John as Jude, not Iscariot
- **Simon,** the Cananean; referred to in Luke as Simon the zealot
- **Judas Iscariot,** referred to in John as Jude, son of Simon Iscariot.

After the crucifixion, Judas Iscariot was replaced by another follower **Matthias,** selected by drawing lots.

All these apostles were Jews, as was Jesus himself and those who came later such as Barnabas, Paul, Mark and James, 'brother' of Jesus and a future leader. They saw themselves as true Jews, from the chosen race of the Jewish scripture, for whom the Messiah had come. They followed the Scriptures and their respect for the Old Testament was undiminished by knowing Jesus – it was after all the handed-down basis of their faith and knowledge of God and had included foresight of the Messiah's birth, life, death and resurrection.

As well as preaching, Jesus publicly performed prolific miracles, healing the lame, blind, deaf, dumb, leprous and the possessed and he even raised some who had died. Given the copious sources and records, there can be little doubt that he was endowed with supernatural powers and used them. His main ministry activities are recorded in the Gospels, which were written over some decades beginning in the 60s AD.

The Gospels Record Jesus' Active Life

The Gospels tell the life story of Jesus as far as his major works are concerned, then Luke's Acts of the Apostles describe the aftermath – starting with Pentecost, then the rapid spread of the Christian Church around the Mediterranean by the missionary work of apostles and disciples, especially Paul and Barnabus. These events are widely known and easily accessible as records and communications were improving beyond word-of-mouth transmission which is always susceptible to exaggeration or error.

The principal Gospels, now accepted as canonical, were written by the four evangelists **Matthew, Mark, Luke and John,** of whom only Matthew may have been one of the apostles. The evangelists saw no need to write down the gospels until some considerable time later. There were three reasons for this. First, on the basis of some Old Testament passages from Isaiah to Malachi, they expected the 'second coming' would be quite soon, so thoughts of posterity were remote. Secondly there was no time to be wasted in spreading the news as Jesus had asked just before his ascension to heaven, so they had not looked beyond transmitting the story of Jesus verbally. The third reason was that with their humble backgrounds, not all the apostles were literate, so some needed friends to write down their recollections once the importance of doing so was realised. When some did get writing, their accounts emerged as a series of anecdotes. Some people wrote falsehoods then and later, so all contributions eventually had to be sifted by Church experts, which led to a delay in sorting, selecting and agreeing which important texts should be accepted and published as the New Testament. There were delays, for example, before the Christian East came round to accepting Revelation and the West to accepting Hebrews. It was also agreed following lengthy debate that the Book of Wisdom should be left in the Old Testament. So it would not be until as late as AD 400 that the bulk of the New Testament was released in a form that was agreed to be canonically correct.

The first three gospels – Matthew, Mark and Luke – are called the Synoptic Gospels, because they have much in common with each other, albeit with a few apparent conflicts. Students have deduced that many of the commonalities in Matthew and Luke come clearly from Mark, but believe others may come from another unidentified source, often referred to as Q (from German '*quelle*' meaning source).

Mark (c.3-68 AD) is now widely accepted to have written the first gospel – in Rome in the 60s AD. He is believed to be 'John Mark', three years younger than Jesus, who although not one of the twelve, was one of the 'seventy' disciples sent throughout Judea to spread the word (Luke 10:1-3). He is mentioned in Acts, accompanied Paul and Barnabas on at least two of their missions and knew Peter, whom he met again on his way to Rome in 42 AD, becoming his interpreter. According to the later historian Eusebius of Caesarea, in his famous Ecclesiastical History (3.39.15), Papias, a contemporary Church leader said Mark's gospel was a collection of summaries of Peter's sermons. Both Irenaeus ("Against Heretics" 1.1.1) and Clement of Alexandria (Eusebius' Ecclesiastical History 6.14.6) linked Mark's gospel to Peter and these views have more recently been confirmed by expert analysis of its contents.

Many believe Mark travelled to Alexandria about 49AD, established the Church there and became bishop of that important early centre of Christianity and gateway to Africa. Today the Greek Orthodox Church of Alexandria and the Coptic Orthodox Church claim direct succession from this community and believe Mark was martyred there in AD 68.

Matthew is thought by some to be one of the twelve, son of Alphaeus and brother of James the Lesser. This is possible, because, as a tax collector, he was probably literate in Aramaic and Greek. Tax collectors were regarded as generally corrupt, but he followed Jesus as a penitent. However, it is now regarded as quite likely that another Matthew wrote this gospel because the text seems to rely heavily on Mark, who was not there with Jesus. It was probably written between AD 80 and 100, a time when many Christians regarded themselves as Messianic Jews – a sect of Judaism rather than a separate religion, who believed that Jesus was the Messiah.

Luke (c 1-84 AD) was born a Gentile in Antioch in Syria. He accompanied Paul on some of his travels, thus gaining the basis of his record of Christian 'history' in Acts of the Apostles. He wrote his gospel and the Acts of the Apostles in Antioch, before his death in the 80s originally as one work following the fall of Jerusalem (70 AD). It was aimed at Gentiles. He was a physician and is also known to have spent some time in Rome. There were many attributions to Luke, including from Paul (Collossians), Irenaeus, Clement of Alexandria, Tertullian and Origen. Many historians regard him as having been a highly competent historian of his time, though some feel he dwells too much on accounts of the supernatural. Luke died about 84 AD in Greece.

John (15- c100AD), wrote the fourth gospel, probably much later than the others, which covered some quite different events from the other three. He was clearly well educated, as was the author of the Epistle to the Hebrews.

Given the expectation of imminent apocalypse and the simple artisan backgrounds of most of Jesus' disciples and evangelists, their tendency was to share the news of Jesus as far and wide as possible by word of mouth. Nonetheless, the gospels began to be published during the lifetimes of many of them.

John, 'Logos', Revelation

John's Gospel, quite different in style and content, begins with his dramatic insight into the nature of God:

"In the beginning was the word and the word was with God and the word was God. All things were made by Him and without Him was not anything made that has been made. And the Lord became flesh and dwelt among us and we behold His glory, as the only-begotten of the Father, full of grace and truth."

The Greek for 'word' (as in the first sentence of this quotation) is 'Logos', but it can also be translated as 'reason' or 'plan'. The theory of the Logos appeared for the first time in Heraclitus (535-475 BC), first among the Greek philosophers. He was regarded by St Justin (First Apology I; 46) as a 'Christian before Christ'. For him the Logos is the universal principle or energy which animates and rules the world. According to the Encyclopaedia Britannica, 'it became particularly significant in Christian writings and doctrines to describe or define the role of Jesus Christ as the principle of God active in the creation and the continuous structuring of the cosmos and in revealing the divine plan of salvation to man'. It therefore underlies the basic Christian doctrine of the pre-existence of the Son. So Christ is the earthly manifestation of the divine logos as a human. He had been part of God since before time began and now he had returned to the Father where he abides in glory. (John 8:38, 58; 3:13; 6:62; 12:16)

In his writings, John reveals God. These writings are consistent with being post-Paul, when Judaism had become so much less relevant to the converts. John speaks to the Jews as "you" and in his prologue he says "God gave the Law to Moses but grace and truth came from Jesus Christ". So for Christians, most of whom were either Jewish converts or their descendants and thus held an inherited reverence for the Old Testament, it was seen by many as having lasting significance only as a book of prophesy leading towards the coming of Christ and the Law had been superseded by Jesus' teaching. It was in Matthew (22:36-40) and Mark (12:28-34) that Jesus paraphrased the message of the Pentateuch with the 'two commandments' – Love the Lord your God with all your heart, with all your soul and with all your mind; Love your neighbour as yourself. So over time, some of Christ's followers questioned the validity of the Jewish Scriptures, which largely represent the Old Testament. There was not yet a 'New Testament', but there was sufficient reluctance within the new religion to dropping the good book for it to be adopted for all its enigmatic and apparently self-contradictory content and they continued to sing the Psalms. Some claim that the Old Testament was about the God of Justice (an eye for an eye and a tooth for a tooth, Exodus 21:24), and the New Testament was of the God of love (turn the other cheek, Matt 5:39), two quite opposed approaches.

John's gospel continues with the witness and affirmation of John the Baptist, accounts of the life of Jesus and concludes with Jesus' death, resurrection and his further appearances. But who is John? In Chapter 21 of the Gospel, reference is made to the Gospel being the work of the "disciple whom Jesus loved". Early Church tradition held this to be John, one of the twelve Apostles. This is supported by its style and content being so similar to that of the three surviving epistles of John. Scholars regarded these four books together with the Book of Revelation as the 'Johannine literature' until fairly recently. Revelation is the only one that identifies its author as a John and today most scholars doubt that John the Apostle was the author of any of them. The similarity in style of the Gospel and epistles has led to the belief that they have a common author, whereas Revelation is almost certainly from a different author.

Given that John's Gospel was written after AD 70 and possibly even into the second century, even if John the Apostle was 15 when he joined Christ, he would have been very old when he wrote or recounted the Johannine works. As the son of a fisherman, swept up to follow Jesus at that age, he would only have spoken Aramaic and it is doubtful he had the learning or even the literacy for such a work. For John's gospel is a learned work that examines the contemporary Church-Synagogue. It could have been written by an experienced writer, based on John the Apostle's spoken account. He certainly had more revealed to him of heaven than the other apostles.

So the 'John' in what follows, refers to whoever is the author of the works attributed to him.

John's Gospel is distinct from the 'synoptic gospels' in that it aims to expose the significance of Jesus' words and actions. It lays greater emphasis than the synoptics on worship and the sacraments and uses contrasting couplets (light-darkness, truth-lies), similar to later Gnostic thinking. It also exhibits some Jewish ideas current at the time such as those recently revealed in the Essene documents known as the Dead Sea Scrolls which were found in caves near Qumran in the 1940s. (The Essenes were a sect of Judaism that flourished from the 2nd century BC to the 1st century AD – see end of Chapter 1.)

The famous beginning of John's Gospel prologue, "In the beginning was the Word... etc." is particularly significant in Christian doctrine as it defines the role of Jesus Christ as having been God prior to and taking part in creation of the Universe long before briefly becoming man to reveal directly and participate in the divine plan of salvation through love. Thus Jesus is the earthly manifestation of the divine Logos as a human. He had been mystically integral with God since before time began and now he had rejoined the Father in whom he always abided. (John 8:38,58; 3:13; 6:62; 12:16)

There are some inconsistencies between the gospels and other writings on the life and works of Jesus Christ as well as doubt as to the exact chronology especially of his birth, but the key events are difficult to deny. The baptism and crucifixion of Jesus are almost universally agreed upon by scholars as historically authentic, while there are varying degrees of certainty as to the accuracy of dates and detail of other events. Christ always stressed the importance of faith and left room for the degree of faith demanded by God. The resurrection is crucial in this and Hans Lietzmann in 'The History of the Early Church' expressed it thus: "...but the verdict on the true nature of the event described as the resurrection of Jesus, an event of immeasurable significance for the history of the world, does not come within the province of historical enquiry into the nature of the past; it belongs to the place where the human soul touches the eternal."

The Jews always expected the arrival of a Messiah due to prophesies of the Old Testament, but many refused to accept that Jesus was that Messiah. So although Christianity was born among the Jews, it spread rapidly both within and beyond their faith and community. Jesus gave his 'brother' James a leadership role in the Church in Jerusalem, according to the non-canonical gospel of St Thomas. Clement of Alexandria called him the first Bishop of Jerusalem a century later. James was closely attached to the Jewish tradition, but early on the Christian Church diverged from Jewish practice. There is disagreement as to whether Jesus' brothers and sisters briefly referred to in the synoptic gospels were actually the issue of Mary and Joseph. Roman Catholic, Orthodox and some Protestants hold to belief in the perpetual virginity of Mary and the term 'brother' has a wider embrace than 'sibling' in the Middle East.

The Jewish Law had been given to the Israelites through the prophets in the Torah and the Ten Commandments given to Moses by God on Mount Sinai. They had developed the Law to include circumcision of male children, prohibition of eating pork or any meat not slaughtered in the correct way, the Saturday Sabbath and forms of dress to display a visible distinction between them and the pagans.

Crucifixion, Resurrection

The Crucifixion included the torture and inquisition of Jesus by the Romans led by their governor Pontius Pilate at the insistence of the people of Jerusalem, many of whom had hailed his return to Jerusalem some days earlier, followed by his sentence immediately to die on the cross. Pontius Pilate scourged Jesus and applied the 'crown of thorns', then paraded him thus humiliated in front of the crowd, hoping this would satisfy them and they would instead choose another criminal to die, but they insisted Christ be crucified. After that, Jesus was compelled to carry and drag the heavy cross through the town to a hill outside called Calvary. He was held by his captors to this cross as nails were driven through his hands and feet, before it was raised and dropped into a post-hole in the ground. He suffered extreme pain and a lingering death between two thieves who were also crucified. The cross would become the symbol of Christianity, representing Jesus Christ's life in the service, education and healing of people according to God's wishes, then his sacrificial death. The crucifixion is remembered by Christians on Good Friday.

As the prophets foretold, none of Christ's bones were broken and he rose again on the third day after the crucifixion. This resurrection is the key element on which Christian faith is based. It confirms that Jesus Christ was indeed the Messiah the Jews were expecting and conveys the eternity of human life, where the death of earthly bodies is just a transition point in the eternal life of their souls in what became known as 'The Communion of Saints' in the fourth century. The resurrection is celebrated on Easter Sunday.

Other feasts based on events around the culmination of Christ's time on earth are Pentecost, representing Christ's appearance to the closeted apostles and the starting point of the Church on earth mentioned in the previous chapter; the Transfiguration of Christ on the mountain; and his Ascension into heaven.

Other Accounts of Christ's Life

There were several other writings describing Christ's life and works, but the four gospels were eventually decided to be canonical and sufficient.

The same selection process was applied to various epistles found, some without attribution to a particular author. They have provided researchers with plenty of scope for analysis, so it is worth dwelling on a few of these.

The so-called Pastoral Epistles written possibly by Paul to Timothy and Titus offer advice of the time on organisation of local churches, conduct required of their officers, forms of worship and prayer, the importance of conveying the true message of Christ untainted by outside errant messages and encouraging ethical moral behaviour of their followers.

'Hebrews' was written after Paul, but in his style and expanding on his thinking. It stressed the significance of the incarnation of the Son of God. It expanded Paul's description of Christ obedient unto death, venturing into his agony in the Garden of Gethsemane, where "having been made perfect, He ... became the author of salvation." Yet whoever wrote Hebrews, still quite unknown, took an even harder line than Paul on sin, distinguishing between the forgivable (10:14-19) and the unforgivable (10:26), venial and mortal sin respectively, for ultimate salvation. This is supported in Matthew 12:30-37 and Mark 3:30.

Peter wrote in similar vein. In this world, suffering for Christ's sake was an actual stark reality in the face of prevailing widespread persecution of Christians with deprivation, torture and grisly executions.

Barnabas wrote that the Son had existed already with the Father at the creation of the world. The Son came to earth "to preach to Israelis' deaf ears". He pointed out that Christianity had been forecast by prophets of the Old Testament. His epistle is included in one of the oldest extant codices, the Codex Sainaiticus, which shows his view of the Old Testament to be close to that of Philo of Alexandria, believing its real importance lies in its spiritual message rather than the narrative to which this is attached.

Jesus acted above the old Law. When he spoke with the Samaritan woman at Jacob's well of how people would pray to the Father, he was saying that the old religion and its places of worship would be replaced by Christianity and its Churches. But Judaism did live on and even became a persecutor of Christianity in the early days, as were other parties then and in the longer term. The world outside Christianity had not recognised Christ, the logos.

Christian Symbols

Tertullian, a Roman writer and contemporary of Barnabus, called Christians '*crucis religiosi*', or 'devotees of the cross'. His 204 AD book *De Corona* mentions their tradition of repetitively tracing the sign of the cross on their foreheads. The crucifix may not have appeared in Europe as a symbol until the 5th century, though it may well have been predated by the

'St Thomas cross' in southern India, with clover leaf ends to its head and arms. Thomas the Apostle is reputed to have introduced Christianity to the sub-continent. Nearly all Malabar churches in Kerala display a characteristic granite cross outside still featuring the clover leaves, with its post let into a socket in the base, which is usually carved in the form of a lotus flower.

Other symbols developed and used in the early days are summarised in the box below.

Early 'Branding', Symbols of Christianity

The '*Icthus*' or fish was probably first and most important, being quite a clever construct from the initial letters of the Greek words for the phrase 'Jesus Christ, Son of God, Saviour', IΧΘΥΣ. Augustine of Hippo explains this in '*Civitate Dei*', noting that the sentence contains 27 letters (33), conveying 'power'.

AΩ Another popular one was the first and last letters of the Greek alphabet, alpha and omega **AΩ**, symbolising Christ's words in Revelation (22:13) 'I am the first and the last, the beginning and the end'.

Known as the Chi Rho or Chrismon, this monogram symbol is a superimposition of the first two letters of the word Christ in Greek. Although of early origin, it had become widespread by the time of Constantine in the 4th century and he had it inscribed on his army's shields when he attacked Rome in 312 AD.

A similar monogram is the iota eta, **IH**, likewise using the first two Greek letters in their word for Jesus. They are often superimposed. Well known quite early, it was mentioned by Barnabus and Clement of Alexandria.

IHS This is another, from the first three Greek capital letters of the name Jesus – iota, eta, sigma. For Latin speakers, it gained traction from another interpretation – *Jesus Hominum Salvator* meaning Jesus, saviour of men, so the I is often seen as a J. Perhaps due to the Latin, it has become the most widely used Christogram on vestments, crucifixes and altar vessels etc. It often has a crucifix mounted on the H cross-bar.

Written Records, Scrolls, Materials

Jesus seems to have timed his earthly arrival just before wide adoption of durable written records. He stressed the need for faith and one wonders if this timing was intended to ensure debate about details of his life on earth. The gospels would have been written originally on fairly long lengths of papyrus, known as scrolls, each rolled up on two wooden rods with handles to avoid touching them by hand. This was quite an inexpensive and available form of rough paper, made from woven, glued and pressed pith of the water-borne, reed-like papyrus plant. This material was introduced about the second century BC and it had limited life expectancy. Also, its porosity varied and most affordable inks were of poor quality, so the unrolling and rerolling of the scrolls for reading and storage respectively tended to flake the ink off in places. With minimal or no punctuation or gaps between words, a typical scroll would contain up to 10,000 or maximum 20,000 words, which usually determined the length of say, a gospel. This limited length restricted the narrative to events so the gospels were short on descriptive elements such as environmental, political, economic or family detail and many other surrounding facts which would be of interest to scholars today, though their absence may also reflect the style of the time.

When a written work was in demand, as the gospels were, their idea of mass-reproduction was a '*scriptorium*', a room in which many scribes would hand-write copies of the manuscript on scrolls as a reader dictated from the original text. The same applied when translations were made for distribution.

If a work was highly valued, expensive parchment (treated, stretched and dried animal skin such as sheep or goat) could be used, or the even more expensive vellum (from calf skin). These had been used in Egypt for many centuries before the arrival of papyrus and the scroll lengths could be up to 36 metres, with the rectangular cut skins being sewn together with strong twine or animal tendons and having a longer life expectancy than parchment. The 'codex' was an early form of book as we know it, with the sheets or pages of parchment or more usually vellum bound together at one end, rather than in a continuous scroll. These codices began to appear during the first century AD.

Thus the timing of Jesus ensured that none but the select few could have certainty from direct knowledge of his life, so most needed the gift of faith backed by the Holy Spirit to do his bidding.

Martyrs and the Travelling Evangelists

About a year after Christ's death, in 34 AD, Christianity's first recorded martyr, St Stephen was stoned to death after delivering an uncompromising sermon which upset the Sanhedrin (the Jewish synagogue court). This hardened the resolve of his fellow apostles, who consisted almost entirely of converts from Judaism and were naturally more at ease preaching to Jews, but they now began to embrace Gentiles. Their inclusion began in Antioch in Northern Syria, the remains of which lie near Antakya, now in Turkey. Barnabas, an energetic and articulate converted Jew descended from the tribe of Levi, was sent from his native Cyprus to consolidate and spread the message that had found considerable support in Antioch. His success was such that after a year he called for further help from Paul of Tarsus. Paul was surely the mission's most successful and ubiquitous recruit, in spite of his unpromising start.

Paul's family was probably of Palestinian origin and fairly well off, having moved to Tarsus before his birth. His given name was the Hebrew Saul. They moved on to Jerusalem, where he had a good rabbinical education, becoming a committed Pharisee, faithful to Jewish traditional Law who detested the upcoming Christian movement. He may have planned to become a Rabbi, for which path he needed a supplementary salary, so he trained as an apprentice tentmaker while still obeying the Sanhedrin.

He had played a supportive role in the stoning of Stephen and followed up with more active and widespread persecution of Christians. At one point, a Sanhedrin had ordered him to travel to Damascus to counter the success of Christian missionary work there. This was when the well-known 'Damascus moment' (see previous Chapter), took place – God's apparent direct intervention and conversion of Saul. He shed his Hebrew name and adopted the Roman version, Paul, as more appropriate to his new mission.

Paul appears to have then been imbued with detailed knowledge of the life of Christ. Converted within days as his eyesight returned, he believed strongly that in becoming a Christian, one received the Spirit and the flesh should no longer prevail; a true Christian lives in the hope of eventual full redemption – liberation from the body and transfiguration through death to the heavenly experience. Paul regarded baptism as a transformatory sacrament where in immersion in water, the 'old self' figuratively dies and one resurfaces as a purer being through the Spirit.

He held the view that Christ provided humans with the opportunity of a holy path and it pained him whenever he encountered evidence to the contrary; such as the strife between his followers and those of Apollos in Corinth (1Cor 3:2-4).

Paul was keenly aware of Christ's intention that Christians should be one united body, as Jesus prayed to his Father "as you and I are one" (John 17:11,23). Paul's letters are peppered with confirmation of this sentiment (Romans, Ephesians etc.) He believed that prior to Christ, sin and judgement were the lot of humans, whereas after him, they had been left all the guidance needed to avoid sin. He came to realise that not all people were as strong as Christ, however human he was and that Christians were also subject to sin. Their free will gave them choice which did not always follow the direction of their consciences and the Spirit. His ideas developed on this theme from initial hard-line conviction of 'sinlessness' and salvation of Christians versus rejection and damnation of non-Christians. As they matured, his ideas swung towards degrees of God's acceptance ranging from the highest one of immediate salvation, through eventual salvation after atonement by punishment for unforgiven sins (Purgatory), to rejection (Hell). The judgment depends on success or otherwise of one's use of free will in the face of worldly temptation. In taking Christ back, God left the less visible, audible and tangible Holy Spirit to guide and support people in their faith.

How Could the Church Continue Among Humans?

The apostles were mostly contemporaries of Jesus, so should survive him by another thirty plus years if they were to meet a natural end, which not all of them did. Christ himself appointed Peter to be the first leader of the Church and promised that no evil would prevail against it. But how would the Church carry on after Peter? What structure was in place to ensure continuity? Of course if a creator god exists, he has the power to achieve this and the case of Paul was an example of this. After his miraculous conversion and enlightenment, he proved an effective and tireless advocate and evangelist of Christianity in the face of powerful Jewish opposition. Barnabas and others followed him and elsewhere a number of others studied Christianity and began to develop theology as a subject for study.

The term 'Apostolic Fathers' or 'Fathers of the Early Church' generally refers to some writers who were seen as immediate or early successors to the Apostles. Many of these also became regional bishops or presbyters, these terms being almost synonymous at the time. Bishops had absolute leadership of their flocks and their instruction was the rule in their diocese during the first couple of centuries after Christ.

As a result, the Father-Son relationship of God and the humanity and divinity of Jesus became subjected to intellectual scrutiny already in this first century. The Holy Spirit and thoughts on the Trinity would take just a little longer. Theologians would take stances on mere intellectual surmise, seek followers and confront those with different views. Thus no doubt well-meaning thinkers fomented argument, schism and even war between sincere Christians, all of whom believed they were defending their faith against heresy but over time would feed divisions within Christianity, contrary to the expressed wish of Christ.

After Jesus' death and into the first half of the second century there was an upsurge of people claiming to be prophets. A few were genuine but many were false prophets, not only among the Gnostics, and they could write convincingly and attribute false words to Jesus. They were spiritual preachers and writers ('pneumatics') and the Church had to work hard to discern which were genuine prophets in the style of the Old Testament and eventually to decide which writings should be included in canon on a level such as Paul's epistles. This was further complicated by some who wrote under the name of Paul and others.

Judaism, Diaspora and Spreading Christianity

Meanwhile, Judaism itself remained a closely united religion and at the same time drew a clear line between itself and the world about it, as it still does today. Yet in the diaspora, where migrants had spread it abroad, it proselytised energetically and successfully to gain converts from among the pagans, drawing the bitter comment from Seneca in Nero's time, "The conquered have given their laws to the conquerors." For although the converts took enthusiastically to the Jewish Law, they could never be 'blood' Jews; they had to pray to the 'God of the fathers of Israel' instead of the 'God of our fathers'. The blood Jews held themselves aloof and cool towards proselytes, never fully embracing them, so they grouped together in their own enclaves. The Romans were reluctant to free converts from duties to their Roman gods in the way they did the born Jews. Converts from the nobility were treated especially harshly.

In Emperor Caligula's time (12-41 AD), when Jews in Alexandria agitated for full recognition, the Prefect Flaccus turned their gregariousness against them and ordered them to be confined to living in their own designated 'quarter', which was actually less than a fifth of the city. Jews were cleared from other parts of the city, but many could find no room in the Jewish quarter and those returning to the cleared areas were treated brutally and many killed. The next emperor, Claudius (41-54 AD) demanded tolerance and punished Flaccus with death for over-zealousness. Strong anti-Semitic feelings persisted. In 66 AD during Nero's reign (54-68 AD), the Jews rebelled in Palestine. Hostility erupted in Alexandria once more and there were 50,000 deaths in the city and yet more through the rest of Egypt. The 'Jewish quarter' then became commonplace in cities throughout Europe and North Africa. Hadrian (Emperor 117-138 AD) forbade conversion to Judaism as well as the practice of circumcision. While their skills and acumen were recognised, Jews were subject to suspicion and hostility.

As Jesus Christ had begun his mission, his initial following came almost entirely from those among the Jews who recognised him as the expected Messiah. They began to form, in Paul's words, an "elect race... a holy nation", all confident that they were at the beginning of something new and of great significance. They believed they were part of something far beyond any national or geographical boundary, united by the Son of God, the Messiah and guided by the Holy Spirit. As a body, they were the Church, inextricably linked to Christ and his angels and saints.

Judaism had evolved somewhat during its spread in the diaspora before the time of Christ, the principal new influence coming from Greek philosophy, primarily that of Plato, from which it picked up forgiveness of sins and life after death and thus the concept of the immortal soul. There are still differing views within Judaism on this. But hitherto it had been strictly based on their Holy Scripture, worshipping God, the almighty King of Heaven, Lord of creation, who punishes the wicked and offers special protection to the people of Israel and the city of Jerusalem. Immortality was restricted to God and heavenly beings; they believed humans were denied this following their exile from the Garden of Eden. Their prayers are well represented in the Psalms. So Christianity began among these people, but brought with it resentment and scorn from among those who did not accept Jesus as the promised Messiah.

Christian practice first spread among some temple Jews and the Hellenists in Israel. After Christ many of the apostles followed his 'great commission' and embarked on missions to spread the Christian faith 'to all nations' (Matt 28:19-20). These forays proved highly effective thanks to their first-hand knowledge of Christ as, supported by his grace and the Holy Spirit, they spoke with convincing authority and contagious enthusiasm so that ever-increasing numbers of various peoples were converted to Christianity and most would hold to it under the intense suppression and persecution which came later.

Travelling around the periphery of the Mediterranean, which borders upon three continents, was not difficult as it was a thriving trading region. The Romans had established good road systems, originally for military purposes, but they also became well-used for trade. Many boats plied trade around the main population centres. Some larger vessels ventured further round the Iberian Peninsula into Britain and Northern Europe, while travel overland took messages eastwards to Mesopotamia and well beyond. Philip was possibly the first 'foreign missionary', spreading the faith to

Samaria, north of Judea, overseen to some extent by Peter. Then more people took the message further afield, including east beyond Mesopotamia, which is less well documented. Many believe that St Thomas travelled to India and died there in Chennai, also that Mark expanded the faith into Egypt.

The extent and speed of spread of Christianity were remarkable for that era. Less than twenty years after Jesus was crucified, people were journeying from all over Asia Minor, Mesopotamia, Pontus and greater Asia and all-round the eastern Mediterranean rim from Libya to Italy to hear Peter's early orations. Jesus' followers may have been mostly humble working people, but their message was well received by cultured sophisticated audiences. Most conversions were within the Roman Empire but the ground for this had almost certainly been prepared by Alexander the Great (356-323 BC), who in his all-too-brief active life had created an Empire stretching from Greece to the Indian sub-continent. The unifying force so astutely used by Alexander was the adoption of 'Hellenism' – the Greek language and way of thinking, fertilised by some helpful elements of Platonism. The empire had endured for a while after Alexander's death, but no adequate successor appeared to continue his work and hold the empire together. The Romans prevailed in its more Western reaches and brought their good roads, so travel inland became easier and safer while the common Greek language also fostered international interchange, speeding the Christian message.

The busy era of the great Greek philosophers had passed and general intellectual standards languished. There were still the **Stoics**, encountered by Paul in Athens (Acts 17:18), who advocated making the most of life while you had it as there was nothing beyond. Most pagans hedged their bets and followed their gods, conscious but regardless of Plato's support of monotheism.

Many found Christianity an attractive alternative, its way having been paved by earlier waves of Eastern influence and ideas, with their fascination for the universe and astrology as potential windows on a higher existence. Philosophers had argued that with so much evil and restlessness in our known world, there must be another, better world. Could this be a way to seek it? **Gnosticism** (from Greek *gnosis*, meaning knowledge), grew in the first couple of centuries AD from extension of similar lines of thought, claiming there were two worlds, the spiritual and the material. They believed the material world was corrupt and evil, while the spiritual world was good and worthy, with a supreme deity, holy and pure. That deity would not involve itself in the unworthy material world. People consisted of a material body and a spiritual soul. Our only hope of escape from the material world was death, by which we leave the body behind while our soul seeks to enter the spiritual world. In order to do this, a divine spark in the person would be essential; if that spark was absent, the soul would be united with another body to endure a further material life. To gain that spark, some Gnostics tried to negate their material life by self-denial, abstinence and asceticism, while others tried the opposite extreme of aiming to sicken it with excess. The latter were associated with a 'devil' figure, known as the 'demiurge', who with his minions ('*archons*'), tried barring the gates to the spiritual world and could only be overcome if the spark had knowledge, or '*gnosis*' of its nature and the nature of salvation.

Judaism was relatively new to the Hellenic experience as the Jewish diaspora moved into lands beyond Israel and introduced another reasonably accessible monotheistic understanding of existence. The Greeks and Romans held in respect the Jewish standards of individual morality and social responsibility compared with the prevailing permissiveness within their own cultures. Some actually converted and there were two levels of conversion; a few embraced full conversion as proselytes, accepting fully the Old Testament, while most took on the moral teaching and standards, becoming accepted as 'God fearers'.

When Christianity came along, it struck a chord with these non-Jewish converts and showed a far more open welcome, offering access to total integration with their faith through eventual baptism. Paul had approached such people and communities before others, exhibiting a clear understanding of their moral and spiritual hunger.

The world seemed ready for Christianity. Philosophical thought had reached the point where such a breakthrough was needed. The appetite was there for better personal understanding of the meaning and clear sense of purpose in life from the ideas, faiths and ideologies available. Christianity offered much to feed this. The Old Testament had already been translated into Greek so it was fairly familiar and available; Christianity held to the highest morals of Judaism and accepted the Old Testament, but also offered more tangible knowledge of God through Christ and a clear route to salvation. Those who Jesus sent forth to spread the gospel "to the ends of the earth" had visited all the accessible major cities and centres of population, establishing communities of Christian believers who lived and demonstrated that sense of meaning and purpose for which so many yearned.

This was the strength of Christianity. It was a positive step beyond such world-negating philosophies as Gnosticism in that it taught a meaningful yet human way of life whereby a true relationship can be built with God. No more the need to separate from daily life or dream of another existence; here was the way, the truth and the life. It was and remains a religion that can be followed individually and communally, filling a spiritual emptiness, feeding that human hunger.

Sabbath, Prayer and Liturgy

The Sabbath was the rest day, such as God took in Genesis after six 'days' of creation. So one day per week was put aside to worship the creator God. Whilst the Jews observed the Saturday Sabbath, Christians chose the 'Sun's day' as their Sabbath because it is supposed to be the first day on which God put darkness and chaos to flight and made the world and perhaps more significantly because Sunday was the day of Christ's resurrection, ultimate proof of Christ's divinity. They called it the 'Lord's Day', in recognition of the resurrection and David's prophecy a thousand years earlier in Psalm 16 that Christ's body would not be left to decay. Their service of worship included celebration of the Lord's Last Supper as he had asked.

The Jews used fasting two days a week on Mondays and Thursdays as regular means of self-denial. Fasting was adopted by those who converted to Christianity and since Friday was the day on which Christ was crucified, it was deemed an appropriate day for fasting and abstinence, while Wednesday was chosen as their second fast day, perhaps because it was the day Jesus was arrested.

Christians in the first century AD said personal prayers to God, their most commonly used prayer being The Lord's Prayer, from Matthew (6:9-13). Those who could would read from the Bible, most likely Psalms.

There is no recorded order of service from liturgy of that time but writings suggest that worship assemblies more or less followed the Jewish form. This involved readings from the bible, an informative address, often interpreting the day's readings, prophetic declarations, possibly with glossolalia, sung psalms, confession and expression of sorrow for sins, praising and thanking God and praying for his help for the sick, bereaved and suffering. Rhetoric and philosophy were revered subjects at the time, so there was emphasis on preaching, which was often quite lengthy and the address would usually be delivered by a trained preacher. But in addition to all this was the new dimension of the *Eucharist* (thanksgiving), based on Jesus Christ's own personal request during the Last Supper that they 'do this in memory of me' i.e. eat bread and drink wine as his body and blood respectively in commemoration of his death on the cross for the salvation of all sinners. The Eucharist and Sunday Sabbath, were the key differences in Christian worship from that of Jews. Since for many this new Sabbath remained a working day, the service was often held either early morning before work, or in the evening, like the Last Supper.

The format seems to have been left quite free, which encouraged a tradition of poetry and music. The latter was simple, often using early psalms or canticles. Probably the best known three canticles are in Luke's gospel – the Song of Mary or Magnificat (Luke1:46-55), Zechariah's Prophecy (1:68-79) and Simeon's Nunc Dimittis (2:29-32). These carry through to todays' Vespers and Anglican Evensong.

Paul preached to both Gentiles and Jews, often in synagogues, by arrangement since they were not usually active on a Sunday. He was called to give some direction to the Corinthians and followed up with his famous epistles to them. They had embraced the Spirit over-enthusiastically, overplaying the speaking in tongues, glossolalia, often with several persons simultaneously jabbering unintelligibly. Paul (I Cor 14) stressed that love should be their aim and those who speak in tongues speak only to God, not to their companions. He therefore insisted that no more than one or two 'prophets' could so address the congregation in the same meeting speaking one at a time and always with an interpreter present to convey the meaning of what they were saying for the benefit of the whole congregation. Any meeting for worship should have as its objective to inform and improve the participants rather than to stir up a spiritual frenzy.

It was quite common for gatherings for Christian teaching or worship to take place in synagogues by arrangement with the Jews, this being facilitated by the different Sabbaths. Gradually over this first century, Christian worship gravitated towards the Hellenic Jewish form, which was the initial basis from which the services today evolved with the addition of the celebration of the Lord's Supper, which was then reserved solely to full members of the Church. Paul taught that this service should be held in the evening and it took the form of a communal feast or 'fellowship meal', preceded by the blessing, then breaking of a loaf, pieces of which were distributed as the body of Christ, uniting all present to each other in his body. At the end of the meal, the president or principal celebrant blessed a glass of wine and it was shared around as the blood of Christ. This was the main worship for the love of God and an occasion on which members were expected to make a monetary contribution according to their individual means.

Loosening Links to Judaism, Council of Jerusalem

As the age of the Apostles approached its end, Christianity was already heading towards being a 'world' religion and the ties to its Jewish origins were being strained, only to be tested further when the Herodian dynasty reappeared. Agrippa I, a grandson of Herod the Great was made king of most of Israel by the Romans in 37 AD. He had been sent to Rome as a young man after the murder of his father and became a close friend of Emperor Tiberius' son Drusus at school, but grew into something of a playboy and spent extravagantly. His friend Caligula succeeded Tiberius and he let Agrippa return to Israel and made him king of some of the Jewish lands. Two years later he engineered the removal of his uncle Herod Antipas and was awarded Galilee and Perea, creating a partial Jewish kingdom which was duly completed by the addition of Judea and Samaria in 41 AD. Agrippa was a passionate Jew and persecuted Christians but he died in 44 AD, whereupon the Roman Procurator took over the rule of the whole nation once more.

In the meantime, inherited Jewish traditions in that early Christianity called for review when they began to affect missionary work among Gentiles. The first major Council was held in Jerusalem in the early 50s AD (see previous Chapter and Acts 15:1-21). Its main purpose was to resolve the Christian view of circumcision. Peter led and those present included Paul, Barnabas and James among others. Since the early Christians considered themselves a branch of Judaism, they still maintained many of the basic traditions and practices of the Jewish faith, but with the added belief that Christ was the expected Messiah. Circumcision was important to them as originating from Abraham's time and being embodied in Mosaic Law to the extent that a Jew could not sit at the same table as an uncircumcised Gentile without being regarded as unclean. They grew up with the view that circumcision was necessary for salvation, as were Jewish rules on the treatment of meat. The converted Pharisees in particular wanted to take a hard line on this.

Paul carried the credibility of having been very successful in converting Gentiles in Antioch to Christianity and he clearly saw any insistence on circumcision especially, as a potential barrier to further success. He argued that Jesus Christ had made no mention of these things, so confirmation of such rules could constitute human interference with the word of God. After lively discussion, the Council concluded that Gentile converts should be left free to choose on the matter of circumcision, but were forbidden to eat the meat of improperly slain animals or ingest blood. For good measure, they must also obey the commandments regarding fornication and idolatry. It was a compromise that Paul was prepared to accept.

Although the Council of Jerusalem was seen as a forerunner of Ecumenical Councils to come, it only addressed life practices and not real theological issues based on Christ's teaching, so would not be recognised today as a full council. Those involved were finding their way starting with established Jewish culture; only now the Messiah had come and given guidance as to which of those ethics he had ordained should now be shared with people of all other cultures and traditions, though the Gospels were only then being written. This council held that the path to salvation should be open to all people as God's children.

Even when the evangelists embraced other pagan races as converts and dropped the requirement of circumcision, kosher food and the Old Testament, the story of the God of the Jews still held its prominence in Christianity. Jewish feasts were retained, such as the Passover which had transformed into Easter, a celebration of the resurrection; Pentecost (the Greek for the Jewish festival of Shavuot, marking the spring harvest festival and the day of delivery of the ten commandments on Mount Sinai;'50 days' after Passover), now the 'new birthday' of the Church celebrating the emergence of the apostles from hiding, fired with the inspiration of the Holy Spirit 50 days after Easter.

Persecution of Christians was already occurring but sporadic. James, the 'brother' of Christ and local leader of the Church, was taken to the High Court in 62 AD under the Roman Procurator, Florius and sentenced to death by stoning, suggesting it was on the grounds of religious malpractice. The Christians were coming under increasing pressure and in 66 AD, during the Jewish rebellion, many left Jerusalem for the Gentile city of Pella in Transjordan, east of Samaria, where they were welcomed and sheltered. Elsewhere the universal or Catholic Church was expanding vigorously.

Early Church Organisation

In terms of leadership at the beginning of Christianity, Peter was nearly always the first Apostle mentioned in Gospel anecdotes. Jesus changed his name, choosing him as the 'rock' on which his Church on earth would be built (Matt 16:18. Christ also gave his 'brother' James a special leadership role in the Church in Jerusalem, assisted by 'presbyters' – an Old Testament minister's office. As individual Churches, were established in other lands, they tended to be led by groups of presbyters.

God had effectively made an honorary Apostle of Paul in whose time, as Churches were becoming established, Christian hierarchical roles tended to be based on how active they were in spreading God's word:

1. Apostles, sometimes known as the new evangelists, who travelled to preach Christianity,
2. Prophets, who worked from a fixed base, and preached as messengers of divine revelation,
3. Teachers, who acted as heralds of the Lord.

In at least the first and early second centuries, Paul and Barnabas chose local Church leaders from among the learned faithful at each centre in which they found success. For example in Galatia, "And when they had appointed elders for them in every church, with prayer and fasting they committed them to the Lord in whom they had believed." (Acts 14-23); then again in Titus 1:5, "This is why I [*Paul*] left you [*Titus*] in Crete, so that you might put what remained into order, and appoint elders in every town as I directed you". A generation later, Clement I says that apostles and then later "other men of repute"… were… "appointed elders"… "with the consent of the whole church." (1 Clement 44:3)

The decades that followed the Apostles and publication of Acts, saw a waning of the occurrence of signs, dreams, wonders and miracles and this 'normalisation' was matched by increasingly firm rules and guidelines from Church leaders to the faithful. One attempt at tis lay in the 'Didache' as follows.

Didache – the First Catechism

The Didache was probably written in Syria around the third quarter of the first century and is often regarded as the first catechism, though it was never accepted as canonical or as part of the New Testament. It seems more like the writing of an administrator recording received wisdom rather than divine inspiration, but this is perhaps the role of a 'catechism' – a guide for instruction. First references to the Didache were found in a manuscript dated 1056 in a Constantinople library in 1875, then a Greek version of the original was discovered in Constantinople in 1883 just before original copies of it were found around 1900.

The Didache addresses Christian behaviour and salvation. It outlines the higher moral standards expected of a Christian and offers a guide to living as such. It points to the duty of every living Christian as being to use all their power to know and follow Jesus' teaching with a view to achieving eternal salvation, which means living in God's company, seeking and following the guidance of the Holy Spirit. This may not always chime too well with a modern-day lifestyle but as well as a conscience, people are endowed with the freedom to choose. A selection of key passages from the Didache shown in the box should convey its gist.

Excerpts from the Didache

1 There Are Two Ways

1:1 There are two ways, one of life and one of death and there is a great difference between the two ways.

1:2 The way of life is this: First, you shall love God who made you. And second, love your neighbour as yourself, and do not do to others what you would not want done to you.

1:3 The meaning of these sayings is this: Bless those who curse you, and pray for your enemies, and fast for those who persecute you. For what reward is there for loving those who love you? Do not the heathens do the same? But you should love those who hate you, and then you shall have no enemies.

1:4 Abstain from fleshly and bodily lusts: If someone strikes your right cheek, turn the other also, and be perfect. If someone forces you to go one mile, go two. If someone takes your cloak, give also your coat. If someone takes from you what is yours, don't ask for it back.

1:5 Give to everyone who asks you, and don't ask for it back. The Father wants his blessings shared ...

2:2 Do not commit murder; do not commit adultery; do not corrupt children; do not have illicit sex; do not steal; do not practice magic; do not practice witchcraft; you shall not murder a child, whether it be born or unborn. Do not covet the things of your neighbour.

2:3 Do not swear or bear false witness. Do not speak evil of others; do not bear grudges ...

2:6 Do not be covetous, or greedy, or hypocritical, or malicious, or arrogant.

3:1 Flee evil of all kinds.

3:2 Do not be prone to anger, for anger leads to murder. Do not be jealous or quarrelsome or hot-tempered, for all these things lead to murder.

3:3 Do not be lustful, for lust leads to illicit sex. Do not be a filthy talker or allow your eyes a free reign, for these lead to adultery.

3:4 Do not observe omens, since it leads to idolatry. Do not be an enchanter, or an astrologer, or a purifier, or be willing to see or hear about these things, for these all lead to idolatry.

3:5 Do not be a liar, since a lie leads to theft. Do not love money or seek glory, for these things lead to thievery.

3:6 Do not grumble, since it leads to blasphemy, and Do not be self-willed or evil-minded, for all these things lead to blasphemy.

3:7 On the contrary, be gentle, since the gentle will inherit the earth.

3:8 Be long-suffering and pitiful and guileless and gentle and good.

3:9 Do not be on intimate terms with mighty people, but with just and lowly ones.

3:10 Accept whatever happens to you as a blessing ...

4:7 Do not hesitate to give, and do not complain about it.

4:8 Do not turn away from one who is in want; rather, share all things with your brother, and do not say that they are your own.

4:9 Do not remove your hand from your son or daughter; teach them the fear of God from their youth....

4:14 In your gatherings, confess your transgressions, and do not come for prayer with a guilty conscience.

5 The Way of Death

5:1 The way of death, is this: It is evil and accursed—murders, adulteries, lust, illicit sex, thefts, idolatries, magical arts, sorceries, robberies, false testimonies, hypocrisy, double- dealing, deceit, haughtiness, depravity, self-will, greediness, filthy talking, jealousy, over-confidence, loftiness, boastfulness—those who do not fear God.

5:2 The way of death is the way of those who persecute the good, hate the truth, love lies, and do not understand the reward for righteousness. They do not cleave to good or righteous judgment; they do not watch for what is good, but for what is evil. They are strangers to meekness and patience, loving vanities, pursuing revenge, without pity for the needy and oppressed. They do not know their Creator; they are murderers of children, destroyers of God's image. They turn away from those who are in need, making matters worse for those who are distressed. They are advocates for the rich, unjust judges of the poor. In a word, the way of death is full of those who are steeped in sin. Be delivered, children, from all of this! ...

6:1 See that no one leads you astray from the way of this teaching, since all other teachings train you without God ...

Concerning Baptism

7:1 You should baptize this way: After first explaining all things, baptize in the name of the Father, and of the Son, and of the Holy Spirit, in flowing water....

8 Your Fasts and prayers

8:1 Your fasts should not be with the hypocrites, for they fast on Mondays and Thursdays. You should fast on Wednesdays and Fridays.

8:2 Do not pray like the hypocrites, but rather as the Lord commanded in the gospel: Our Father in heaven, holy be your name. Your kingdom come. Your will be done, on earth as it is in heaven. Give us enough bread day-by-day. And forgive us our debts, as we also have forgiven our debtors. And do not bring us to the time of trial, but rescue us from the evil one.

8:3 Say this prayer three times each day ...

9 Concerning the Eucharist ...

10 After the Eucharist ...

11 Welcome the Teacher ...

12 Welcome Anyone Coming in the Name of the Lord ...

13 Every Genuine prophet
13:1 Every genuine prophet who wants to live among you is worthy of support.
13:2 So also, every true teacher is, like a workman, entitled to his support....
14 On the Lord's Day
14:1 On the Lord's day, gather yourselves together and break bread, give thanks, but first confess your sins so that your sacrifice may be pure....
15 Appoint Bishops for Yourselves
15:1 Appoint bishops for yourselves, as well as deacons, worthy of the Lord, of meek disposition, unattached to money, truthful and proven; for they also render to you the service of prophets and teachers....
16 Watch Over Your Life
16:1 Watch over your life, that your lamps are never quenched, and that your loins are never unloosed. Be ready, for you do not know on what day your Lord is coming....
16:8 Finally, "Then the sign of the Son of Man will appear in heaven, and then all the tribes of the earth will mourn, and they will see the Son of Man coming on the clouds of heaven' with power and great glory."

In the pastoral epistles attributed to Paul, it became clear that realisation was dawning on leading Christians that the 'second coming' may not arrive as soon as had been assumed. Therefore the Church should organise for the long term in supporting members in testing the value of their lives. The Lord would come, but in his own time. The Christian way would not be easy. Peter wrote in similar vein and indeed in the world, suffering for Christ's sake was an actual stark reality in the face of prevailing widespread persecution of Christians with deprivation, torture and executions. If the Church of Christ were to spread further it called for clearer norms for organisation, structure and worship.

Church Appointments and Clerical Attire

The Didache states that Christians should "appoint for themselves bishops and deacons worthy of the Lord" (15.1). Ignatius, Bishop of Antioch was clear in his view towards the end of the first century. He saw three ranks in the Church – 1. Bishops; 2. Presbyters; 3. Deacons.

The bishop was to be received as the Lord Himself, with all in his designated region subject to him, including presbyters. At the very end of the first century Clement of Rome posited the doctrine of divine appointment of bishops, but Ignatius completed the spiritual monarchical episcopate, that is to say he was the ultimate spiritual leader within his diocese. This was accepted in Syria and Asia Minor and became the classical authority for the Roman Catholic concept of bishops.

As regional Church communities were established abroad, the office of bishop signified the head of the Church in his designated territory. He was regarded as a direct successor to the original Apostles. A college of presbyters formed a supporting council for advice, but the bishop was undisputed sole leader.

Any sense of urgency in organising the Church with a wider structure was undermined by many who still thought that the second coming of God, the Apocalypse and the end of the world would come quite soon.

By the middle of the second century in Rome, bishops and deacons took on special responsibility for widows, orphans and the poor, while also carrying out normal 'priestly' functions and worship, becoming true pastors, shepherds of their 'flocks'. Of course, human instincts surfaced and there was competition for status within the hierarchy of the Church and defensiveness on the part of the college of presbyters, but by the end of the second century, the bishop of Rome would come to hold a clear sole leadership role in the sphere of the Roman Church.

These ministers of the faith followed no special pattern of dress even in the worship assemblies, just as Jesus had not done as he had led the call for humility. If anything, they tended to wear the plain white normal style dress of the time. This also helped them not to stand out, as white was common and helped avoid drawing attention to their roles in the prevailing waves of persecution.

Sanctity of Life, Celibacy and Marriage

In imitation of Jesus, the early Christians believed to the letter the sixth commandment "Thou shalt not kill", in contrast to the Jews, who had always linked Israel so closely with God and felt quite justified in killing attackers who threatened them. Any killing was forbidden for true Christians. Quite apart from the commandment, life was God's creation so it was not theirs to destroy be it for war, punishment or for any other reason.

Ignatius (c 50-108 AD), second bishop of Antioch, who is recognised as a 'Father of the Early Church' went even further than Paul (Phil 1:23) in his Christian zeal for perfection and to be a martyr. He saw the Eucharist as uniting the recipient's body, which Paul described as the 'Temple of the Holy Spirit' (1 Cor 6:19-20), with that of Christ, so long as he then kept it free from any kind of immorality. Ignatius practised total sexual abstinence, believing his body would then be resurrected as was that of Jesus and he directed his life to that end with total resolve and confidence.

His essential elements of Christian life were:

1. Fellowship with Christ
2. Faith and love – faith the beginning and love the end of perfection, both becoming united.

He broke new ground in his efforts to express his own theology and to influence the developing creed of the Church, preaching that people must seek to live a life of honesty and purity which will be found all the easier if they really learn to love God and all fellow human beings as well as the rest of his creation. For love is the purest expression of the Holy Spirit.

Paul never married. He was sceptical and saw no benefit in intercourse, the satisfaction of animal instinct and he regarded marriage as a means of regularising it. While he did not say marriage was wrong, he felt that it was often the cause of hardship and worries, best avoided given his early belief that the world was about to end. However Jesus gave his blessing to marriage with his first miracle at Cana (John 2) and again in Mark 10:9 and Matthew 19:6 "So they are no longer two, but one flesh; therefore what God has joined together let no man put asunder." The latter suggests the indissolubility of marriage in his eyes.

Role of Women in the Early Church

Paul is often represented as a misogynist, a conclusion easily drawn from some of his epistles. Such writings are seized upon by those opposed to any move towards equality of women in the Church. The principal text of Paul cited in favour of the exclusion of women from ordination was in 1 Cor (14:33-35) "As in all Churches of God's people, women are to remain quiet in the assemblies since they have no permission to speak. Theirs is a subordinate part, as the Law itself says if there is anything they want to know they should ask their husbands at home; it is shameful for a woman to speak in the assembly."

But this needs putting into context first of the contemporary social attitudes to and of women and secondly of the reason behind the writing of this letter in the first place. It followed his receipt of reports of general misbehaviour during fellowship meals, participants getting drunk, women with heads uncovered, some poor going hungry and many speaking in tongues at once. Some students argue that this passage was a later addition to the epistle, which may seem plausible if one compares it with an earlier passage in the same epistle (1Cor 11:5) "For any woman to pray or prophecy with her head uncovered shows disrespect..." the implicit suggestion being that it is quite in order for a woman with her head covered to take part in the assembly by praying or prophesying aloud.

However, in his letter to Timothy in Ephesus, Paul says "I give no permission for a woman to teach or have authority over a man. A woman ought to be quiet because Adam was formed first and Eve afterwards and it was not Adam who was led astray, but the woman..." (1Tim 2:12-14). That sounds outrageous now, but was not altogether out of place in its time and location. There are questions over the authorship of the 'pastoral epistles' although they were accepted as part of the canonical New Testament.

Looking to the gospels for guidance, they record several women disciples, including Mary Magdalene, Joanna and Susanna, who at times accompanied Christ during his ministry and gave some financial or material support (Luke 8:13). Women were also the first witnesses to the Resurrection. Women are mentioned in the New Testament as supporting the Church or opening their houses for assemblies, to wit Lydia (Acts 16:11-15); even Paul pays tribute to Phoebe, Chloe, Priscilla, Rufus' mother, Tryphena and Tryphosa who "labour for the Lord's work" and Junua, a "prominent apostle". There were certainly women deaconesses, who administered baptism, which involved total immersion and was therefore appropriate for the propriety of women. There is even some evidence that Priscilla was appointed as a local leader of the Church. Dr. Guy Macy in his book 'The Hidden History of Women's Ordination' (OUP 2007), states that some women were ordained between 100 and 1100AD.

In Paul's defence and in support of the argument against even today's level of discrimination against women in the Church, one can look at another epistle (Gal 3:26-28) in which Paul says "... for all of you are the children of God, through faith, in Christ Jesus, since every one of you that has been baptised has been clothed in Christ. There can be neither Jew nor Greek, there can be neither slave nor freeman, there can be **neither male nor female** – you are all one in Christ Jesus."

The Corinthians also agonised over the issue of divorce with particular concern for mixed marriages. Divorce was frequent and legally simple in their society. Christians were aware of Christ's words that marriage was indissoluble. Mark (10:6-12) says "a man leaves his father and mother and the two become one flesh ... what God has united, human beings must not divide." Matthew (19:9) also held that a man who divorces his wife and marries another commits adultery against his wife and vice-versa. Paul believed that a man and wife should not divorce but if they did, there should be no remarriage even if one party was pagan.

Jewish War, Destruction of the Temple

A Jewish war took place in AD 60, following sporadic uprisings throughout Palestine. The Jews had tried to buy the support of Florius in fighting the Greeks at Caesarea, but he demanded double the price offered by the Temple treasury. The result was an uprising and King Agrippa II, who ruled only the remote Eastern and Northern parts of Palestine, was powerless to mediate. Undermanned Roman garrisons were overrun by the Jews, while in Gentile centres, especially Caesarea, Jews were massacred. The Roman legate of Syria marched his limited army south into Judea, but it was insufficient and on its retreat was defeated near the coast by the Jews. Israel proclaimed and rejoiced in its freedom and minted its own currency once more and its own aristocracy finally lent support.

Emperor Nero gave Vespasian the task of recovering Judea. Vespasian raised an army of 60,000 that travelled east and in 67 AD began to overwhelm stubborn resistance, conquering Perea and southern Israel in a 12 month campaign. Nero died in 68 AD and as successors rapidly came and went, Vespasian stayed his hand but at the end of 69 AD, he handed over leadership of the army to his son Titus, a senior general, while he returned to Italy to bid for the throne. In the spring of 70 AD, Titus marched his forces on Jerusalem. After a fierce 5-month battle, he prevailed and the Temple of Jerusalem was burned and destroyed on 8th August. A number of fortified cities in the hands of the Jews remained defiant, but were gradually besieged and overcome, the last being the southern outpost of Masada in which the Jews' famous last act was mass suicide as their food ran out. The Romans faced the horrific reality of this victory in early 73 as they entered without resistance to see the bodies and blood running from the cut throats. Judea became a Roman province and the full tenth legion was camped there. Between 132-135 AD, there was a brief fanatical rebellion under Bar Kochba, which was soon snuffed out and the Emperor Hadrian responded by building a Roman colony over Jerusalem's remains and establishing the death penalty for any Jews trying to enter. Judea would not see statehood again for nearly two thousand years and even then prove a controversial and destabilising presence in the region.

Fire of Rome and Nero's Persecution

In 64 AD, about two thirds of Rome was destroyed by a fire. Nero was criticised for the tragedy and in his quest for scapegoats, he pointed the finger of blame at the Christians, who at that point were a new movement in Rome arising from amidst the Jews, mainly among the poor of the population. He mistrusted them because they believed a new king was about to come, which he regarded as a potential threat, so he had them rounded up and put to death in the most barbaric ways as public entertainment. The Roman historian Tacitus, who was a young boy at the time, later wrote in 'Annals' :

"...to stifle the rumour [that Nero had set Rome on fire], he falsely charged with guilt and punished with the most fearful tortures, the persons commonly called Christians, who were hated for their enormities. Christus, their founder, was put to death as a criminal by Pontius Pilate, procurator of Judea, in the reign of Tiberius ... In their very deaths they were made the subjects of sport: for they were covered with the hides of wild beasts, and worried to death by dogs, or nailed to crosses... and when the day waned, burned to serve for the evening lights. Nero even offered his own garden players for the spectacle, so a feeling of compassion arose towards the martyrs. Even if they were guilty and deserving of exemplary capital punishment ... they were not being slain for the public good, but to satisfy the extreme anger of one man."

Three months later, on 13th October, Peter was crucified, probably head downwards (at his request since according to Origen he wished not to be honoured with the same end as Jesus), as part of celebrations for the 10th anniversary of Nero's reign as Emperor. The public crucifixion of the first head of the Church appointed by Jesus, took place outside the city wall on the site where the basilica of St Peters now stands. Paul was reported to have been beheaded in the same year, probably also as part of Nero's retribution. The deaths of these two figures there ensured that Rome was destined to be a major centre of the Christian Church.

That autumn, according to Tacitus "The Gods also marked by storms and diseases a year made shameful by so many crimes. Campania was devastated by a hurricane ... the fury of which extended to the vicinity of the City in which a violent pestilence was carrying away every class of human beings... houses were filled with dead bodies, the streets with funerals..." But apart from suppression of the Jews and Christians, the war in Jerusalem and a few other local matters, the Roman Empire enjoyed relative peace in the first century. One notable event in the period was their landing and eventual conquest of Britain which began under Claudius in 43 AD.

Fathers of the Church

Managing growth is a challenge for all organisations and the rapid and widespread growth of the Christian Church from its inception made it an extreme case. Until the second half of the first century, this was mostly by word-of-mouth, in a sceptical and quite unruly and troubled world. Paul's letters to Timothy and Titus made it clear that realisation had dawned that the 'second coming' may not be as imminent as was widely assumed, so the Church must organise for the long term in order to support members in testing the value of their lives – the Lord would come, but in his own time.

This led to a wave of writers, philosophers, theologians and historians studying the life of Jesus and the growth of early Christianity and to record what they learned from these studies for the benefit of future generations, who would be increasingly separated by time from the actual events. First-hand accounts of Jesus were becoming less easy to find as time passed. A handful of learned authors succeeding the apostles from the first into the fifth century, all of varying backgrounds, character and ways of thinking, set about recording Church teachings, devotion and practice in order to defend it from distortion by time and non-believers to secure a correct Christian creed for the future. Those who have come to prominence are generally known as the 'Fathers of the Church'. They also translated Christ's message into modes of contemporary thinking outside the Hellenic Jewish areas, since these men differed widely in character, personality, background and lifestyle, presaging the very nature of the future Universal or Catholic Church.

Apart from a few core members, it seems that every listing of the Church Fathers is different. The list in the box includes those common to most lists, though not exhaustive. Those recognised by the Western (Roman Catholic) Church are shown in **bold**; those accepted by the East (most Orthodox Churches) are in *italics;* some are both. The conditions of qualification for the Roman Catholic Church are antiquity (pre-eighth century), doctrinal orthodoxy, personal sanctity and approval by the Church, whereas the Orthodox Churches have similar conditions but apply no time limit.

The following are some more commonly recognised 'Church Fathers' but others are often included:

Clement of Rome (c.35-99 AD) Bishop of Rome. first recognised Apostolic Father

Ignatius of Antioch (c35-c110) Bishop, Apostolic Father, student of John

Papias of Hierapolis (c.60-120s AD), bishop of Hierapolis, author, Apostolic Father

Polycarp of Smyrna (69-155) Bishop, Apostolic Father, disciple of John

Justin Martyr (100-165 AD) Christian apologist, logos interpreter

Irenaeus of Lyons (130-202) Christian apologist, early theologian

The author of an **Epistle to Diagnetus** (late 2nd Century), name uncertain

Clement of Alexandria (150-215) convert, theologian, taught at famous catechetical school, Alexandria
Origen of Alexandria(185-254) theologian, ascetic
Tertullian **(160-220),** early Christian author in Latin
Cyprian of Carthage(200-258) Berber, convert, bishop
Athanasius of Alexandria(296-373) bishop, theologian trinitarian
Basil the Great 330-379 Archbishop of Caesarea, Cappodocian
Cyril of Jerusalem (313-386) theologian
Gregory of Nazianzus **(329-390)** Archbishop of Constantinople, theologian
Gregory of Nyssa **(335-394)** bishop
Ambrose of Milan (337-397) Roman governor then Archbishop of Milan
Augustine of Hippo **(345-430)** theologian and philosopher
John Chrysostom **(347-407)** preacher**,** ascetic and Archbishop of Constantinople
Jerome **(347-420)** Translator of the Vulgate Bible
Cyril of Alexandria **(c.375-444)** Christologist, Patriarch of Alexandria
Cyril of Alexandria (400-461) Roman aristocrat, Pope
Gregory the Great **(540-604)** Pope who sent first large mission to Britain,

Both Western and Eastern Churches recognised four 'Great Fathers', but different for each Church. The Western four were Ambrose, Jerome, Augustine and Gregory the Great; the Eastern four were Basil the Great, Athanasius, Gregory of Nazianzus and John Chrysostom. The others who overlapped and probably met one or more of the original Apostles (Clement of Rome, Ignatius and Polycarp) are referred to as **Apostolic Fathers** and all later ones are designated Greek, Latin or Syriac Fathers. There were also a few Desert Fathers, who appear a couple of centuries later.

There is no official list, so more are often included; the Orthodox Church does not consider the age of Church Fathers to be over and it includes later influential writers in its list.

Rome, Clement I and Christian Behaviour

Back in Rome the Church had been subdued for a while following Nero's purge and records became sparse for some years, but reappeared again as trouble broke out in Corinth between the old and young members of the new Church towards the end of the first century. The dispute led to the removal from office of several deacons. Since none of the deacons were charged with moral offences, a Bishop Clement in Rome declared their sacking as high-handed and unjustified. The Church authorities in Rome, keen to maintain peace and unity in this volatile part of the Empire, commissioned Clement to broker peace.

Clement is credited with an anonymous letter in Paul's written style to the turbulent Corinthians, accusing the young faction of envy and seeking their humility and obeisance while urging prayer and reconciliation. It is reasonable to suppose the author of the letter was a bishop and the official list of Popes or Bishops of Rome shows St Clement I (88-97 AD). These dates tally with the contents of the letter, which suggest mid-nineties. Tertullian suggests Clement was appointed by Peter as his successor, but the official list shows Peter was followed by Linus then Cletus before Clement. It is possible that two bishops in Rome laid claim to the papacy, one (Cletus) Pauline, the other (Clement) Petrine. However, the identity of the author is less important than the content of the letter, which provides useful insight to the Church in Rome just six or seven decades after Jesus Christ's death. The picture is a settled, grounded one in which there are no ecstasies, demons or miracles, nor the expectation of an imminent second coming. The letter addresses organisation, liturgy and ministry of the local Church, demonstrating a moral influence confident in its knowledge of a living God, the message of love and mercy, redemption and eternal life from Jesus Christ. Christians offered a peaceful example in a disordered Rome and sought the same for Corinth.

Bishops and deacons at the time were often regarded as functionary officials rather than inspirational leaders compared to the charismatics, who were regarded as more possessed of God's spirit. But gradually, as the numbers of gifted charismatics waned, the bishops and deacons became more practised at matching their spiritual skills to those of administration. This point was made in the letter attributed to Clement, which claimed Old Testament support, laying out clear instructions for all spiritual functions. To behave contrary to these instructions would be to sin against God. Divine revelation had come from God, who sent Jesus, then his apostles, who appointed bishops to succeed them for life, as well as deacons. He thus formalised the divinity of clerical ordination and apostolic succession. Bishops are appointed by bishops and the members of the Church have only the 'right of assent'. Clement's letter also laid down clear claim to the Old Testament as the word of God, if oftentimes allegorical. It had become as important to Christians as it had been to the Jews, in the absence then of a New Testament to which one could turn.

Divine Law requires above all else adherence to the commandments. Christians were blessed with confirmation of the availability of forgiveness of sin, hence of salvation through the death and resurrection of God's son Jesus Christ, who also taught all that they needed to achieve it. Against these advantages, there was no mention of 'chosen people'; one would be chosen at the final judgement on the basis of one's performance in this life on earth.

Early Fathers

Ignatius of Antioch (c 35- c108AD) converted to Christianity as a young man and became the second Bishop of Antioch in 67 AD, succeeding Euodius and was reported as having been chosen by St Peter for this. Antioch was the cradle of Gentile Christianity, beginning with Paul's stay there, which had a strong influence on Ignatius, as did the writings of John. Ignatius was important pioneering 'Christology', the study of Christ and his approach influenced future development of it and the concept of a forgiving merciful God, leading much later to the introduction of confession and absolution of sins. He drew from both Paul and John, taking particular inspiration from John's words "God is love and he who abides in love abides in God and God in him" (1 John 4:16). Ignatius was arrested by Emperor Trajan during a visit to Asia Minor and was condemned to death, probably for refusing to accept the Roman Gods. Unusually, he was sent from Antioch to Rome for execution. On his way there, he wrote at least seven letters in the style of Paul to his Churches and those of Asia Minor most of which were collected by his friend, Polycarp. They said much including that "Jesus, the son of Mary and of God reveals the Father, bestows immortality through his resurrection. The Spirit is the charisma of Christ and Christianity is the Christ in us." The letters repeatedly include the theme of "unity and submission to ecclesiastical authority represented primarily by the bishop. Unity is the very condition of Christianity..." Ignatius was killed by wild animals in the Coliseum.

Papias of Hierapolis (c.60-120s AD), bishop of Hierapolis (now Pamukkale in Turkey), was the author of Expositions of the Sayings of the Lord, an important contemporary record of much of the origins of the canonical gospels. He was most likely a student of John the Apostle.

Polycarp of Smyrna (69-155) was said to have been appointed as Bishop of Smyrna by St John the Apostle, whom he followed. He wrote about the Church, but his only surviving letter is that to the Phillipians. He was martyred for his faith by being burned at the stake, but witnesses told that when the flames did not touch him, he was stabbed to death.

Christians and Pagan, Sun and Light

When the post-evangelists, led by Paul and Barnabas, brought Christianity to non-Jews and pagans, they realised over time that these new members brought in return valuable new perceptions and practices to Christianity, some of which were absorbed to the enrichment of the faith. It had been common since the beginning of time for humans to believe in or seek a Supreme Being, or god. The great societies of Greeks, Romans, Persians, Hindus and Egyptians worshipped numerous gods. They prayed to these gods and many of their rites of worship included communal meals, so the Christian Eucharistic celebration came easily to converts. There were other points in common, such as a view on light versus darkness. Christianity sees light as representing good or knowledge and darkness as evil or ignorance. This was supported by Old Testament references, such as Psalm 119:105 "Your word is a lamp to my feet and a light to my path"; the prophet Malachi wrote (4:2) "... shall the sun of righteousness arise with healing in its wings"; Psalm 27:1 "The Lord is my light and my salvation..." and numerous mentions in John's and Matthew's gospels. After all, darkness never overcomes light, while light always dispels darkness.

The most visible heavenly objects are the sun and the moon. Seen as sources of light, so potential goodness, both were subjects of worship by some and little wonder that the sun attracted worship from many widespread races, including Indo-Europeans various, Egyptian Ra, Norse Sol, African Liza, Roman Sol Invictus, Greek Helios and Aztec Huitzilopotchli. It also made sense as the sun is our source of warmth and light, without which no crops would grow and life would be unthinkable.

Christians adopted from other religions the practice of facing the east, towards the rise of the sun, with prayer and Churches traditionally oriented that way. The first known hymn not derived from a Psalm of David is *Phos Hilaron*, from the 3rd century praising the Son of God reflecting the rays of his Father's glory. It is now a Greek Orthodox hymn, 'The Gladdening Light' which is to this day sung in every Orthodox evening service. Its opening words are:

"Jesus Christ,
The gladdening light
Of the deathless Father's holy glory,
The Heavenly
Holy blessed one."

The Sabbath is named after the sun in northern European languages, while in the south it was named after the Latin for the Lord's Day, *dies dominica–* Domenica, Dominica, Dimanche etc.

Significant Christian Dates and Seasons

As already explained, some Jewish feasts were adapted for Christian worshippers, such as the Passover which had been transformed into **Easter**, celebrating the resurrection, and Shavuot, now **Pentecost**, fifty days later.

From earliest times, Christians observed a forty day period of fasting and almsgiving leading up to Easter.

The term 'Forty days' is significantly used several times in the bible, perhaps colloquially signifying 'a long time'. Preparing to receive the Ten Commandments, Moses stayed with the Lord on Mount Sinai for forty days and forty nights without eating or drinking (Ex 34:28); Elijah walked forty days and forty nights to the mountain of the Lord, Mount Horeb in Sinai (1 Kings 19:8); Jesus fasted and prayed for forty days and forty nights in the desert before beginning his public ministry (Matt 4:2).

Christmas and Epiphany – the Winter solstice, when the sun is at its lowest point and starts rising again, was a guide in fixing the birth date of Christ, which nobody knew exactly, even to the year. Early Christians alighted on either 25th December or 6th January, an existing Egyptian festival. Later, in the fifth century, the Church settled for the date nearer the solstice, while keeping 6th January as the Epiphany, celebrating the visit of the wise men in the Western Church and the baptism of Jesus in other parts. The wise men were said to have borne three gifts, gold, frankincense and myrrh, from which it was assumed there were three of them. Psalm 72:10 mentions three kings bearing gifts, so the wise men are often referred to as three kings. There is no astronomical evidence of any special star or conjunction that can explain the guiding star for the visitors. There are also some questions as to the exact dates of the census which required Joseph and the pregnant Mary to travel to Bethlehem and the dates of the rule of Herod the Great, which cloud the exact year of Jesus' birth, the basis of the Gregorian calendar.

The Christmas tree is a recent addition borrowed from German folklore, with no Christian connection. Father Christmas derives from a 4th century bishop St Nicholas who was renowned for his kindness to children and often referred to in English as Santa Claus (from Dutch Sinterklaas).

Demons and Exorcism

In the early years of the Church there was also the issue of exorcism, the casting out of evil spirits and demons. This was fairly common and established practice in the pagan religions. One of the commonest calls on it was the general misconception of epilepsy as the possession of the sufferer by demons, a concept held by some until quite recently, although Hippocrates had correctly identified it as an illness. But there were other perceived manifestations of demons and Christians continued the practice of exorcism for both health and religious reasons. They came to adopt a quieter and more peaceful method which enjoyed some success, involving the laying on of hands, in line with Jesus' use of his hands for healing. A modest version of this was even incorporated in the baptism service during the third century. Today, when child baptism is the norm, it remains simply as a verbal renunciation of the devil and all his works by the Godparents on behalf of the person being baptised.

Demons persisted as an issue in the Western Church and would later become the basis for the witch-hunts of the sixteenth century. However, the Eastern Church was more relaxed on the matter, regarding Christ as having overcome the forces of darkness.

Emerging Centres of Early Christianity

Jerusalem is where much of Christianity began as recorded in Acts of the Apostles. The growth of the Church and the sources of opposition to it here are recorded already as is the fluctuating relationship with Rome, which led to an exodus of many Christians to Pella about 66 AD and eventually to a transfer of administrative centre to Caesarea in the second century.

Caesarea, (which had a namesake in Asia Minor) lies northwest of Jerusalem on the coast and was built by Herod the Great about 25–13 BC, becoming the capital of Judaea Province. It was initially called Caesarea Maritima, then from 133 AD (when Hadrian lay siege to Jerusalem) Caesarea Palaestina and later Palaestina Prima. It was there that Peter baptized the centurion Cornelius, who is considered the first Gentile convert. Paul sought refuge there, once staying at the house of Philip the Evangelist, and later being imprisoned in the town for two years (probably 57–59 AD). At the end of the second century a council was held there to regulate the date of Easter. According to the Catholic Encyclopedia, after Hadrian's siege of Jerusalem, Caesarea became the metropolitan see (like an archdiocese in the West these days) with the bishop of Jerusalem as one of its suffragens (subordinates). There was a theological school there and a famous library which was later destroyed, either by the Persians in 614 or the Saracens around 637.

Antioch – was a major Hellenistic centre, the third-most important city of the Roman Empire, part of the province of Syria, but today it is a ruin near Antakya, Turkey. It was where Christians were first so called and also where the early disagreement between Peter and Paul regarding the conversion of Gentiles took place, which led to the Council of Jerusalem. Paul's view was that Mosaic Law in its fullness of practice (including diet, dress and especially circumcision) should be relaxed while the Jewish Christian view stood firm and suggested that Gentile converts should be considered at a lower level, based on Noahid law, a selection of seven Mosaic laws. Antioch was the site of an early church, traditionally said to be founded by Peter who is considered by some to have been its first bishop.

Alexandria, in the Nile Delta, was established by Alexander the Great of Macedonia (356-323 BC). It was a major port and its famous libraries were a significant centre of Hellenist learning. The Septuagint translation of the Old Testament began there. It had a sizeable Jewish population, of whom Philo of Alexandria is probably their best known author.

About 49 AD, Mark is reputed to have travelled to Alexandria, established the Church there and became bishop of that important early centre of Christianity and gateway to Africa. Today the Greek Orthodox Church of Alexandria and the Coptic Orthodox Church claim direct succession to this community and believe he was martyred there in 68 AD.

Its famous theological college produced superior scripture and notable Church Fathers, such as Clement, Origen, and Athanasius, as well as later Desert Fathers to the south west. By the end of the century, Alexandria, Rome, and Antioch were accorded authority over other metropolitans. The Council of Nicaea in Canon VI would affirm Alexandria's traditional authority over Egypt, Libya, and Pentapolis (North Africa) and probably granted Alexandria the right to declare a universal date for the observance of Easter.

Asia Minor, now Anatolia was the birthplace or residence of a number of notables in the early years of Christianity. It was the near-eastern part of modern Turkey, called by the Romans the western part the Province of Asia. The tradition of John the Apostle was strong there. The Johannine Works were plausibly written in Ephesus, *c.* 90-110 AD. The Book of Revelation, the last book of the New Testament in which Seven Churches of Asia are mentioned, is believed by some to be authored by another John, John of Patmos, a Greek island about 30 miles off the coast, which was used by the Romans as a penal colony. Paul came from Tarsus in south-central Anatolia and carried out many of his missions in the region. The First Epistle of St Peter (1:1-2) is addressed to Anatolian regions. Inhabitants of Pontus, a Greek colony on the southeast shore of the Black Sea were some of the very early converts to Christianity. Of the seven surviving authentic letters of Ignatius of Antioch, five are to Anatolian cities, and the sixth is to Polycarp, the bishop who reportedly knew the Apostle John personally and lived in Smyrna (now Izmir), as did his student Irenaeus (130-202).

CHAPTER 4

2nd Century

Bishops of Rome	Roman Emperors
Alexander (105-115) Sixtus (115-125)	Trajan 98-117
Telesphorous (125-136)	Hadrian 117-138
Hyginus (136-140)	Antoninus Pius 138-161
Pius I (140-155)	Lucius Verus 161-169
Anicetus (155-166)	Marcus Aurelius 161-180
Soterius (166-174)	Commodus 180-192.
Eleutherius (174-189) Martyr	Pertinax Jan-March 193.
Victor (189-199)	Didius Julianus March-June 193
Theodotus of Byzantium;	Severus Septimus 193-211
Zephyrinus (199-217)	

Christianity approached its second century having spread fast, thanks to the good Roman-built roads and trade routes around the Mediterranean, easing missionary travel westward and to some extent northward from the Holy Land. Converts grew fast in number in spite of ongoing persecution and many martyrs. Christians were held in awe for their endurance, even by their strongest critics. Tertullian (160-220 AD), a prolific early Christian author and perhaps the first to address directly the Trinity as "three persons, one substance", mentioned meeting a pagan who expressed amazement at how Christians show love for one another, setting up organisations to teach and care for the sick and the poor, widows and orphans. They were also impressed by the cures of the sick that took place, many seeming miraculous to them, which all attracted converts. Cures were the only recourse of the poor, who could not afford physicians. This century saw the sheer numbers, faith and respectability of Christians meaning they could no longer be ignored.

The Church as a whole was already suffering some leadership challenges. Humans have been blessed with intelligence, free will and a conscience, which usually lead them to a range of firmly-held convictions and Church leaders were not yet ready with the confidence or skill to handle these well.

From the beginning, even when it was outlawed, Christianity preached peace and respect for the law. Its followers were encouraged to pray for the State and rejoice in its strength. So even though the Romans continued to worship in their pagan tradition, in general they now tended to regard Christians as non-threatening and good citizens. This did not prevent some emperors initiating sporadic new persecutions, which forced practice of the religion literally underground into the catacombs outside the city walls of Rome, which were originally used as places to bury their dead.

As Christianity gained respectability, middle and upper classes began to convert and attend services. As a consequence of this and rising levels of education among the faithful, philosophy, which was still a favoured subject of study, entered the Christian arena. The ideas of Plato from the 4th century BC, were highly popular. An offshoot from his line of thinking, the Stoics were quite helpful to Christianity, even though some of their beliefs and practices were unacceptable.

Records

Records of Christian thinkers and writers became more widespread and durable from about this century as literacy, materials and formats improved. The Codex was invented, which consisted of written sheets collated in rudimentary book form with protective cover panels, although the familiar and cheaper scrolls would remain popular until around the 4th century as the compactness, easy access and durability benefits of the book form became fully realised. So from this time onwards, our first-hand information gains reliability.

Worship and the Sabbath

The service of public worship lay as it still lies at the centre of Christian life. It was a way for Christians to connect with God, his angels, each other and all those beyond death, remaining a celebration of the Last Supper, just as it did in Paul's time. Early guides as to the early form of the assembly, show the president blessed the bread and wine, welcomed those who were holy and asked those who were not to repent, before saying "*Marana tha*" (Come, O Lord). Those who were free of grievous sin then attended the communion service. All moved to a table for a communal meal. As the meal ended, the leader prayed in thanks for their spiritual food and for the eternal life which Christ had won for them. Prayers were said for the whole Church on earth and for the world to come.

During the first half of this century, Paul's guidance prevailed leading to a change in the order, format and timing. The sacramental service was preserved and proceedings were transferred to the morning to dissociate it from the habitual evening meal. It was still evolving and would do so further over the next couple of centuries. There was a collection at every meeting where each gave according to what he or she could afford as their offering.

Evening gatherings still took place, but were less formal and tended towards social events, usually with a meal followed by often quite lengthy readings from the gospels, then the Old Testament, singing psalms and perhaps some discussion before a sermon exhorting people to greater effort and involvement in the faith. Poorer members of the Church would sometimes be invited to join the gathering. If possible a cleric would preside and start proceedings by blessing and breaking bread – the *Eulogia* or Eulogy as opposed to the sacramental Eucharist. There was also a simpler, briefer form of service without the full liturgy, in which the congregation were given parcels of food to take away for home consumption.

The main divine service in the morning evolved during the century so that the first part began with the call to repent and the clerics would give absolution, then readings and the sermon were open to all comers – practising Christians, catechumens, potential converts, strangers and the merely curious. The second, sacramental Eucharistic part, was reserved to those who had been baptised. After the departure of those excluded, there were prayers followed by shared embraces of peace. Then bread and a vessel of wine mixed with water were presented to the celebrant, who blessed them with the Eucharistic prayer, which was considered the key part of the service during which the consecration of the bread and wine took place. Presented then with the "Body of Christ" and the "Blood of Christ" by the celebrant, the congregation responded 'Amen' ('so be it') before receiving communion from the deacons. Later on, an *Anaphora*, Greek equivalent of Eucharistic prayer often attributed to Hippolytus dated about 215 AD, was an introductory dialogue and text of the Eucharistic prayer that is astonishingly similar to those in use to this day. It has the current structure, begins with thanks to the Lord for sending his Son to earth to point the way to salvation and institute this sacred meal. Matthew (26:26-28), Mark (14:23,24), Luke (22:19,20) and Paul (1 Cor 11:24-5) all relate his key words in the institution of the Eucharist at the Last Supper on the eve of his passion:

Over the bread: *Take this, all of you, and eat of it: for* **this is my body** *which will be given up for you.*

Then the wine: *Take this, all of you, and drink from it: for* **this is** *the chalice of* **my blood***, the blood of the new and eternal covenant which will be poured out for you and for many for the forgiveness of sins.* (Wine)

Do this in memory of me.

These come during the Eucharistic prayer in today's Mass or Communion service, the precursors for which are mentioned below.

Fast Days and Feast Days

With Sunday established as the Sabbath, day of worship, the next days to be marked were Wednesdays and Fridays as fasting became common practice. According to Tertullian, people habitually fasted until 3pm on one or both of these days, the more devout extending the fast to include the evening meal. The Church specified only Good Friday and Holy Saturday as obligatory fast days. Easter became a centre of controversy arising from disagreement on establishing its date, which is examined below. Pentecost was always marked as 50 days after Easter. Then the feast celebrating Jesus' baptism began in Egypt in the second century, later becoming more widespread as the Epiphany.

Places of Worship, Vestments, Language

The first Christians were sometimes allowed by the local Jews to use synagogues for preaching and prayers, as the respective Sabbaths were on different days. They often tended to meet in houses. As they grew in number in larger towns, a funded house church would be specially built for the purpose, with a large room for meetings. It would be put in the hands of a trustee or *episcopus*, who would usually be the accepted local Christian leader. Churches as 'public' buildings began to be built about AD 200, but due to ongoing persecution, they were usually incognito as to their purpose and there was no set pattern for their design. They were plain, usually rectangular and in Jewish tradition featured no images or pictures, especially not of God. As it was a place with God's presence, congregations dressed smartly but normally as did the celebrants – again avoiding identification during persecutions. Leaders still tended to wear plain white, which was in common use anyway. The early language for services and prayers was Greek, as that of the New Testament, even in Rome until Latin began to be used early in the third century.

Alexander, the bishop of Rome from 105-115, introduced a new practice of blessing the houses of the faithful with 'holy water' (i.e. formally blessed water), as potential places of worship.

Church Fathers of the Second Century

The Early Church Fathers, or Patristics are mentioned in the previous chapter. During this century, many of them were digging deep for understanding of the true nature of God and his message – this God, whose promised Messiah had been incarnate as a man and who in turn promised that the Holy Spirit would guide and protect the Church into the future. Questions arose as to how God would wish to organise the Church on earth to guide individual behaviour, the individual and collective worship of God, as well as the human soul and its destiny. Christ had provided guidance but not such detail, so there was a thirst for deeper understanding, which led to theories, some conflicting, so not all of them could be right. The Church had to organise to examine these and decide which would be accepted as canon belief and which could not. There were and remain some variations of emphasis and acceptance of the Church Fathers as well as some of the writings of the time between different regional branches of the Church Universal. Also, the Orthodox churches still regard the Patristic Period as ongoing.

These men focused on the following issues among others – the relationship of Christianity to Judaism; which writings were canonically acceptable for the New Testament; apologetics (arguments for the existence of a god, extended in their case to the Christian concept of God); the nature of that God; doctrines important in helping achieve a consistency of faith; developing ecumenical creeds; the Trinity and Christology (the study of the divine/human nature of Jesus Christ); and the doctrine of divine grace.

Between them, the Church Fathers established a triad of disciplines for the Christian life – prayer, almsgiving and fasting. This basic template would develop in future centuries with the monastic rules.

Diognetus is only known through an epistle addressed to him by an unknown Christian author, referred to as Mathetes, generally accepted as written in the mid-to late 2nd century. This was an apologist work, its main aim being to demonstrate a peaceful and loving God, the attractiveness of the Christian way of life and how it enhanced rather than opposed the authority of the State. The following excerpts convey the flavour of the letter:

"God sent a messenger ... not to rule as a tyrant ... in gentleness and mildness; as a king sending his royal son; He sent Him as God ... to men, saving them, persuading, not exercising force (for force is no attribute of God) ... summoning men, not prosecuting them; as loving, not judging ... Do you not see that as more of them are punished [by others on earth], so others abound the more? These things do not seem to be the works of men but the power of God. .... proofs of his presence. ... What men had any knowledge at all of the character of God before Christ came? ... God revealed himself through faith, by which alone it is granted to see God."

The final phrase is essential to believers because they have a mass of evidence regarding the true nature of Christ, but none of it conclusive, whereas non-believers dismiss faith as a tame excuse.

The original manuscript existed until 1870, when it was destroyed by a fire in Strasbourg during the Franco-Prussian war, but numerous copies of that original survive.

Justin Martyr (c100-165) was a Christian apologist, arguing and explaining Christian faith and practice, but he was not a theologian. Born in Flavia Neapolis (now Nablus), about 50 miles north of Jerusalem, he was keen on philosophy in early life, became a Christian in Ephesus, went to Rome, taught philosophy, wrote prolifically and with commitment to the faith. He made the earliest known reference to people's use of the sign of the cross and promoted its use. He also deals with baptism – regeneration through water and describes the regular worship of the Eucharist (thanksgiving) service, as all assemble on the Sun's day. He confirms the form of worship much as described above and adds that it is followed by the deacons taking communion to those who are absent through age, illness or disability. The collection is passed to the president, who distributes it as aid to orphans, widows and all those who are in want through sickness and it supports those in prison, foreigners and the needy.

Justin mentioned the concept of the Trinity which was by then taking shape, although he regarded it as a hierarchy with God the Creator at the top, the Son, Jesus Christ in second place and the 'prophetic spirit' in third. This was at odds with his own declared acceptance of the Son as the logos, identical with the Spirit which revealed itself to the prophets. He refuted the pagan condemnation of monotheism as atheism by confirming his belief in angels and he equates Christianity to 'incorruptibility'.

Although Justin says that Christianity is not rational he argued that as Jesus was the incarnate divine reason, everything reasonable supports Christianity. Athenagoras of Athens (133-190) raised his writing's level of respectability by placing it on an equal footing with philosophy. Justin wrote his 'Apologia' about 150 AD to Antoninus Pius and his philosopher son Marcus Aurelius, then followed with the fuller 'Dialogue'. He condemned polytheism and included a summary of God the creator and the logos, quoting Proverbs (8:22) and Isaiah's prophesy (7:14) of Christ incarnate.

His pupil, **Tatian** was a vegetarian and ascetic celibate, regarded by Eusebius of Caesarea as not being helpful to the Church. Tatian was noted for writing 'Diatesseron' in which he merged extracts from the four gospels as a single continuous story, which was used by the Syrian Church in its worship for about two hundred years before they reverted to the canonical four gospels.

Irenaeus (130-202) was taught by Polycarp of Smyrna (69-155), who was close to John and witness to his original gospel writing. Polycarp travelled to Gaul where he became bishop of Lyons. He is often linked with **Tertullian**, who came a little later, both of them being referred to sometimes as the first Catholic Fathers having been clear defenders of the main faith tradition of the Church against Gnostic heresy.

Irenaeus helped to forge strong links between Asia Minor in the east and Lyons and Vienne in the Rhone valley. The Asia Minor region was converted early to Hellenic Christianity. Irenaeus had been strongly influenced by Polycarp and is regarded as one of the most influential of the Church Fathers.

He displayed impatience with middle-class intellectuals who made more of scriptures than he felt was there, in the manner of the Gnostics. He wrote that it was far better to be simple and lack learning yet to come close to God in love. In this he spoke for many of the Church Fathers – keep it simple and humble, as Jesus did, surrounding himself by artisans and fishermen.

Irenaeus may have been the first to refer to the New Testament as Scripture, but it was his view that the four Gospels were sufficient and that no more needed to be added to Church canon. He saw the New Testament canon as comprising the four gospels and Paul's epistles, the Revelation of John, I Peter plus the prophetic writing of the Shepherd of Hermas. The knowledge contained in these condensed into the 'Rule of Faith' which was adopted by the Church as the basis of 'The Apostles' Creed'. (See below – Doctrine, Creeds and the Trinity)

He was a strong Trinitarian and probably the first to suggest the eternal existence of the Holy Trinity. He combined Jewish traditions of the Spirit with New Testament theology in becoming the first post-New Testament author to address the theology of the Holy Spirit.

Irenaeus bridged East and West and presented his faith in simple understandable terms. He believed that one could be a Christian without a Bible and that the original source of Christian teaching was really that of the Apostles which was passed down through their appointed successors, the bishops, its truth guaranteed by Christ's promise and the Holy Spirit. He cites the Roman Church, founded by the Apostles, Peter and Paul as the oldest and most eminent example of such apostolic succession and he believed it should be held as the predominant conservator of the true faith. He based his argument on faith, not on law. He also envisaged Christ and Mary as symbolising God's reincarnation of Adam and Eve in perfect form, i.e. without the fall, thus restoring the divine plan for mankind – salvation.

He preached that people sin with body and soul. Sacraments offer revival and give the grace of new life, uniting recipients with God. Baptism unites our bodies with God, making them incorruptible and our souls with the Holy Spirit, conveying the potential of eternal life. Irenaeus believed this immortality was not restricted to the soul alone, but the body and soul together. It is reception of the Eucharist as the body and blood of Christ that renders the participant a member of the eternal body of Christ.

Irenaeus' theories were more grounded and Christ-based and less highbrow than those of the apologists. Most of the Western Church regarded his ideas as being of enormous importance at such an early stage. God became man in order to teach us directly how God wishes us to live – in full obedience to his will in order to gain ultimate immortality in his presence. He endowed all people with free will and his Son showed the way in which they should use it to join his eternal company. Intellectual leaders of the Church then and since sought more on an advanced philosophical level than the grounded, prayerful and pragmatic Irenaeus offered. Their assured pride often contributed to dispute and schism.

Irenaeus wrote a pentalogy 'The Refutation of False Gnosis', exposing Gnostic fantasies, expounding Christian teaching and in the final book, covering Christ's Resurrection and part of the brief history of Christianity since. He was a biblical theologian and regarded the Old Testament as an inspired record of God's progressive revelation of himself to people, which culminated naturally in the incarnation of Christ among them. He believed Christ was the heralded Logos, fulfilling the revelation of God's love. He confronted the Gnostic view in agreeing the eternal co-existence of the Logos with the Father, as in the prologue to John's Gospel, 'In the beginning was the Word (*Logos*)...' Irenaeus also concurs with Paul that Christ was like a second Adam, enabling people to fulfil their potential. Though not born perfect and immortal, they have the potential for self-improvement and through Christ for learning and earning these. He is believed to have been the first to refer to original sin and he preached that to reach their full potential, each person has to learn more of good and evil for guidance in the exercise of their own free will. The presence of evil is essential to moral and spiritual growth. These views make for interesting comparison with Augustine of Hippo, in the fourth century.

Hippolytus (170-235) was a theologian and writer and although not normally included as a Church Father, he is believed to have been a disciple of Irenaeus. He was an important theologian and perhaps the most prolific Christian writer and exegetist of his time relating to Old and New Testaments, liturgy and especially studies of heresies. He wrote 'On Christ and Antichrist' around 202AD.

Hippolytus was active well into the 3rd century and referred to by

Jerome and Eusebius, a later historian, as a bishop. He denounced the Bishop of Rome Zephyrinus for not condemning Callixtus as a Modalist and when Callixtus succeeded Zephyrinus as Bishop of Rome about 218, Hippolytus was so exasperated that he declared himself antipope. He held to this claim through Callixtus' successors Urban (223-230) and Pontius (230-35) and was erased from the list of bishops. Hence there remains no record of his see. He was exiled to Sardinia under Emperor Maximinus Thrax, probably to work in the mines there, until about 235. While he was there, he became reconciled with the local bishop and the Catholic Church. We can assume he was accepted back as he was referred to as a martyr by the year 255 and canonised a saint in Eastern and Western Churches. The manuscript 'Philosophumena' discovered in the 19th century on Mount Athos, in refutation of heresies, is believed to be genuinely his work.

Christian Apologists

Some learned people wrote powerful detractions of Christianity. By the early 2nd century, its rapid spread began to fuel opposition and repression more widely than just among the Jews as had been the case in the past. The apologists sought to rebut such negativity by laying out the arguments for the existence of God, explaining Christianity and defending it against paganism, at the same time as helping win converts and providing guidance for new Christian communities. Another early Christian apologist after Justin was **Aristedes of Athens**, who wrote what is generally regarded as a fairly superficial and tedious argument in about 140 AD fell short of matching the quality of debate of the mainstream Greek philosophers.

Melito of Sardis (c108-180 AD), was recognised for his spirituality and had an important influence on early Christianity, with some work on the Old Testament. He became Bishop of Sardis, near Smyrna and had keen interest in the controversy over the date of Easter. He is perhaps best known for his 'Apology for Christianity', which he wrote to Marcus Aurelius.

Theophilus, bishop of Antioch, wrote soon after AD 180 that the Christian is rewarded with immortality, becoming one with God. He claimed that Greek wisdom based on the philosophers would not stand comparison with the more ancient teachings of the Old Testament.

Practices Now Known as Sacraments

Original sin and Baptism

Irenaeus was the first to refer to the concept of original sin. He believed all human beings participate in Adam's sin and share his guilt. This may seem to run contrary to Jesus' merciful and forgiving approach, being more like an extension of Old Testament thinking, in which the 'sins of the father' could be carried down several generations of offspring. It met the Gnostics tenet – 'material bad, spiritual good'.

Augustine of Hippo (354-430) would later develop the concept of original sin into a doctrine based on Paul's epistles to the Romans (5:12-21) and 1Corinthians (15:22) plus Psalm 51:5 from the Old Testament. The idea impacted on the practice of Baptism. In the early days after Christ, Baptism had been administered later on in life for salvation, often towards the end of life, to qualifying adults unless a life-threatening illness or accident happened to a child. Infant baptism consequently became more common from about this era of the 2nd century. Its emphasis now swung towards the 'exorcism' of original sin, rather than forgiveness of actual sins committed, as well as being a source of sacramental grace for the recipient. Because forgiveness required remorse and resolve, God-parents were introduced to speak on behalf of the child and oversee its spiritual upbringing, since baptism preceded the power of both faith and remorse for the infant ('paedobaptism' versus 'credobaptism'). It was also regarded and accepted by converted Jews as a Christian equivalent to their circumcision.

Confession, Penance and Confirmation

The practice of **Confession** had already been recognised in the Old Testament (Numbers 5:7, Nehemiah 9:2-3). Matthew and Mark both refer to the confession of sins being a prerequisite to baptism by John the Baptist. In 1 John 1:9, "If we confess our sins, [God] is faithful and just and will forgive us our sins and purify us from all unrighteousness." But the key New Testament basis comes from John 20:23, where Jesus breathed the Holy Spirit into the Apostles, saying, "Whose sins you shall forgive, they are forgiven them; and whose sins you shall retain, they are retained," and to James in 5:16: "Confess therefore your sins one to another ..."

Early Bishops and clergy were sometimes approached by people with troubled consciences and soon had to deal with those who broke the Commandments by sins such as theft, murder and fornication. This raised the issue of **'penance'**, a means by which the subject could make retribution to God for their sins. There was little consistency and the lack of guidelines for this led to precedent often being set locally, usually in the form of an act of penitence, such as prayer, good deeds, fasting or almsgiving.

The issue of apostasy, renouncing their religion, arose especially during persecution, when Christians sometimes yielded to the pressure to make sacrifice to pagan Gods. This was seen as a serious matter, punishable by a ban from practice of their Christian faith – known as excommunication, as they were cut off from the Eucharistic sacrament. The early form of this sanction was to prevent them from sharing in the Eucharistic part of the mass, so that they had to sit near the rear and at a certain point in the service, a curtain further forward of them was drawn to hide the rest of the service from those at the back of the church, who also included catechumens (people preparing to join the Church). Those people tended to leave the premises then. It was viewed as an eventually retrievable situation, depending on the gravity of the sin and the level of remorse and repentance of the sinner.

The Church believes the Holy Spirit guides receptive members and clergy to follow God's will in the practice and understanding of the faith. **Confirmation** is generally accepted as a celebration of the Spirit within and it affirms the recipients' early Baptism, so they must have reached the 'age of reason' before it.

In the early Church the three sacraments of initiation as we know them today — Baptism, Confirmation, and first Eucharist—were effectively celebrated in the same ceremony for adult catechumens at the Easter Vigil. The catechumens, each of whom had a Christian sponsor, plunged into a pool where they were baptized "in the name of the Father, the Son, and the Holy Spirit". On emerging, they donned a white robe, and the bishop laid hands on them and anointed them with oil as confirmation. They could then receive the sacrament of the Eucharist for the first time, so the three sacraments were included in one ceremony as is still the practice in the Eastern Orthodox Church.

In the Western Church, Confirmation became separated, partly because of the increase in child baptism and also for practical reasons as the Church grew it was difficult for bishops, who were now also involved in governing the Church, to preside at every Baptism. The bishops of the East handled this logistical challenge pragmatically by blessing the oil to be used and sending it to presbyters, to whom they delegated the performance of the sacraments of initiation. In the West, Baptism and First Communion could be carried out by priests, but the bishops retained the rite of Confirmation, which was therefore administered in parishes once every few years and some years after Baptism. In the Middle-Ages, it became regarded as the sacrament of maturity and as such was administered near adolescence, when recipients were old enough to be regarded as valid witnesses for Christ in Confirmation and fortified by grace and the Spirit's gifts to be messengers of Christ charged with spreading the faith by word and example.

Death and Burial

While generally fitting in with the customs of their country of residence, one thing Christians insisted on was burial, as applied to Jesus, rather than cremation of their dead. They were buried in underground catacombs and Christian art had its origin in the decoration of tombs of martyrs, whom they always held in highest esteem. The style of Christian art developed as the tombs were decorated with increasingly elaborate paintings and carvings with scenes from the Old, then the New Testament, probably initially in invocation of faith teachings but then growing into a teaching medium itself.

Theodotian – Old Testament Translation

Theodotian was a 2nd century scholar, believed to have translated the original Hebrew Bible into Greek about 150 AD for Greek-speaking Christians. There was no New Testament at the time. Such translations, known as the Septuagint or LXX had already been done in the 3rd and 2nd centuries BC for Jews in Egypt.

The New Testament

There was a belated drive to write down Jesus' message for posterity. The Jews had relied on remembered words of the great teachers of history, memorised, repeated and thus handed down the generations before being written down as the Old Testament. Literacy and writing materials being more available and improving fast, helped the apostles' memories of the active life and teaching of Jesus to be recorded while still fresh and first-hand.

Early Christians had three sources of divine revelation –the Old Testament, the teaching of Jesus Christ and third, the Holy Spirit communicating through the prophets. The prophets were losing credibility by the second century due to the rise of gnostics and other false prophets. The oral tradition was still strong and continued, which may help explain some apparent 'add-ons' to the gospels beyond the most original copies discovered. Mark's is the earliest available.

There are clear dangers of imagination, exaggeration and

reconstruction as with the gnostics. Similar amendments may have occurred in other gospels than Matthew, Mark, Luke and John, such as those of the Hebrews, Egyptians, Thomas, Matthias, Peter and James in varying degrees. There are also some difficulties regarding Jesus' early years from his birth to age 12 in the temple. The early Christians were naturally curious about his birth and childhood and were obliged in this by Matthew and Luke. There are historical inconsistencies in parts of the overlap in their commentaries.

Luke addressed his gospel to Theophilus, a respected elder. Luke's writings are more learned than the other gospels and his Acts is now regarded, following centuries of close scrutiny, as a faithful account of later events. The lengthy sermons, although of his composition, do represent broad Christian beliefs at the time. Chapter 20 onwards is written in the first person plural and was probably written by or with a travelling companion of the apostle, perhaps another Luke, the physician. Some scholars think the epistle to the Ephesians attributed to Paul was written by Luke because the church structures mentioned seem more developed than in Paul's time and the writing style resembles that of Acts.

Acts of Peter and Acts of Paul are regarded as romances with dubious miraculous stories, including those of Thecla the virgin and of lionesses killing in defence of Paul in the amphitheatre. Acts of Thomas and John contained even more questionable miracles including anthropomorphist animal tales such as preaching donkeys. They were written around the end of the second century, generations beyond the life spans of those to whom they were attributed so they were treated as 'faction' and never canonically approved.

There were a worrying number of apocryphal writings attributed to or written by well-respected names around the first half of the second century. The Church eventually deemed canonical just the four gospels written by or for the evangelists, these being the only ones with sufficient supporting evidence to be instruments of divine revelation. The Greeks always revered Paul's letters and the Church recognised him as an authority inspired by the Holy Spirit, so some of his epistles were also included in what was to become the New Testament, which is more a selection of writings than it is exhaustive.

The Church in Alexandria kept close to Rome and used the Western canon. Clement of Alexandria quoted 1 Peter, 1 and 2 John and Jude. Alexandria also recognised the epistles of Barnabus and Clement 1 of Rome as apostolic and also added the Didache to Holy Scripture. Even Origen, who amongst his other qualities was respected as a literary critic, accepted these texts. Codex Sinaiticus from about 350 AD, written in Greek and discovered in 1859, includes Barnabas as well as Hermas'

Shepherd in an appendix. Codex Alexandrinus, written between 400 and 440 AD, has an appendix with both epistles of Clement of Rome. But the authors of these appendices both failed the test of apostolic principle for canonical acceptance.

So, apart from Paul, combining the canonical epistles of the West with those of Antioch, there are seven epistles – James, 1 and 2 Peter, 1,2and 3 John and Jude as recorded by the historian Eusebius of Caesarea about 320 AD, which eventually found canonical acceptance in Egypt. The Book of Acts, continuing Luke's gospel was also elevated to the canon, although it was not prominent in much of Christendom, while the Syrian Church held it as of equal significance with Paul's epistles.

Conversely the Apocalypses, regardless of claiming the authority of the Holy Spirit, were only accepted with difficulty. John's prophetic Revelation defies any attempt to alter a single word. Nevertheless, its acceptance spread in the West, Egypt and Africa during the 2nd Century.

Doctrine, Creeds and the Trinity

Doctrine is remarkably well covered in Paul's epistles, always emphasising the genuine humanity of Jesus. Ignatius of Antioch did the same, describing Jesus' true birth, persecution and crucifixion, suffering pain, hunger, thirst and exhaustion. Jesus ate and drank and wept as at the death of his friend Lazarus. Ignatius contested the docetic belief that Christ, being God, did not experience life and death as a true human.

Justin Martyr, then Irenaeus, Tertullian and Hippolytus left records of the development of Trinitarian thought. There was a brief early Roman nine-point **creed**, which soon spread to Egypt:

> "I believe in God, the Father, the Almighty; And in Jesus Christ, His only begotten Son, Our Lord; And in the Holy Ghost, the Holy Church, the resurrection of the flesh."

This was developed further with several additions, principally of Christology. There were varying extensions in the East, revealing some of the differences in emphasis between the early Church Fathers. However the Creed was accepted as emanating from Jesus Christ himself with the guidance and teaching of the Holy Spirit. The Church accepted it as being on a par with the apostolic succession of bishops and the canonical New Testament in importance as to its teaching value since it summarised important beliefs that Christians would then have learned as children or catechumens. The first full and clear summary of Christian doctrine appeared in the **Apostle's Creed** in the second century:

"I believe in God, the Father almighty, Creator of heaven and earth and in Jesus Christ, His only Son, Our Lord,

who was conceived by the Holy Spirit, born of the Virgin Mary, suffered under Pontius Pilate, was crucified, died and was buried;

He descended into hell; on the third day He rose again from the dead; He ascended into heaven and is seated at the right hand of God the Father almighty;

from there He will come to judge the living and the dead.

I believe in the Holy Spirit, the Holy Catholic Church, the communion of saints, the forgiveness of sins, the resurrection of the body, and life everlasting. Amen."

The Apostles Creed is believed to have evolved from Matthew 28:19 and been first written down about 180 AD. Another theory is that it emanated from the joint product of the apostles inspired by the Holy Spirit, each providing one of the articles. An early revised version may have been compiled by Ambrose, Bishop of Milan for Pope Sirius at the Council of Milan in 390 AD.

It is worth thinking about the three key articles of the creed – the Father, the Son and the Holy Spirit. It can be taken as read that the Father, the creator of all is omnipotent, almighty. Long before Christ the word 'father' was attributed to gods, for example in Homer and in Hellenist Judaism, but it also conveys monotheism, i.e. "Father of all".

For his time on earth, the Son was the only begotten of God, through the Holy Spirit and Mary (Matt 1:18). Apart from his conception and birth, the other absolutely key events in his life on earth were his passion, death and resurrection, as witnessed by their inclusion in the extended creeds, both East and West versions. Although not included in the Creed, his Baptism, fasting in the desert, teaching and miracles were also foundations of faith.

The only mention of the **Holy Trinity** in all the Gospels is in Matt 28:19 'Go therefore, make disciples of all nations; baptise them in the name of the Father and of the Son and of the Holy Spirit'. There have been various theories regarding the origin and nature of the Trinity causing controversy, vehement argument and even serious schism in the Church over the centuries. To mention just a few, much simplified:

- One is that of the *logos;* that the Son was one with the Father and the Holy Spirit from the very beginning. This lies close to the 'pneumatic theory', i.e. that Jesus existed with God from the beginning, appearing on earth at a pre-determined time then ascended to resume his place with the Father.
- Another is the 'adoptionist' theory, postulating that Jesus was

adopted by the Father at his baptism on account of his perfection. Support for this is drawn from the Western text of Luke 3:22, in which a voice came from heaven: "You are my Son; today I have fathered you".

- A similar theory was penned by Hermas in Rome about 150 AD, suggesting Jesus was elevated to God's throne in recognition of his work on earth and joined the Holy Spirit and the angels as God's counsellor.

All three together with the short prayer below would appear to undermine the Roman Church's wish to include '*filioque*' (Latin for 'and the Son') in the Nicene Creed passage 'I believe in the Holy Spirit, the Lord, the giver of life, who proceeds from the Father **and the Son...**', which the Eastern Churches logically rejected as implying a lesser role for the Holy Spirit. Human attempts to explain the inexplicable in the Holy Trinity would result in divisions in Christianity later on.

A widely used prayer today perhaps says enough:

"Glory be to the Father, the Son and the Holy Spirit, as it was in the beginning, is now and ever shall be, world without end. Amen". This surely is incompatible with '*filioque*'.

Church Organisation

The organisation of the growing Church played its part in that relatively trivial but destructive East-West misalignment regarding Easter which has continued to the present day. All parts of Christendom had evolved from its foundation by Christ, all accepting similar scriptures and beliefs, but with autocephalous leaderships – Rome, Alexandria, Antioch, Africa, Gaul (Lyons), Armenia, Crete etc. Their leaders were senior bishops and in a few of the greater centres, were sometimes referred to as Pope or Metropolitan. As this universal Church grew, more bishops were appointed. These normally accepted one of the 'mother' cities as the centre of their loyalty and were autonomous rather than autocephalous. The difference is that autocephalous bishops were totally independent leaders who made their own rules with due reference to ecumenical councils and praying for guidance from the Holy Spirit, while the autonomous bishops ruled their local domain in Church matters but sought agreement and approval from their 'mother' Church for the more serious or wide-ranging decisions.

As for communication between regional Churches, in the first and second centuries they held occasional synods where the bishops gathered together to discuss and consult on doctrine and organisation. Less frequently, gatherings of the whole universal or Catholic Church at 'Ecumenical Councils' were convoked. There were times when they failed to obtain full consensus on all issues, in which case dissenters usually refused to recognise the conclusions, as was the case with the question of Easter. These synods were not necessarily binding, although unanimous conclusions were usually accepted as binding. However, there was no over-arching authority and each senior bishop had complete apostolic authority in matters of doctrine and discipline relating to his own Church domain. Their combined authority conveyed power to broad synods and councils and given their acceptance that the Holy Spirit guided the Church through the bishops as successors to the apostles, the Church was seen as united in Christ and the Holy Spirit.

Rome in the 2nd century

Although the empire remained relatively peaceful, Trajan (Emperor 98-117) was aware of threats to its borders, especially from the Dacians from the region of today's Rumania and from the Persians seeking coastal access via the eastern border of Syria. So he invaded those areas but stretched his resources and in eventual victory, integration and control of these peoples into the empire would remain an ongoing challenge.

On Trajan's death in 115, his successor Hadrian decided that the resulting overstretch of resources endangered the empire, so he drew back from Mesopotamia, Assyria and Armenia, but held on to Dacia. He then embarked on a campaign to build fortified defences to help secure land borders, including the one across the width of Northern Britain which still carries his name.

Meanwhile, especially under Hadrian, Rome looked more to Greek culture and religion, a spiritual change covered in the Roman historian Tacitus' book 'Agricola'. Philosophy made a come-back as a favoured subject. Greek author, Plutarch (46-120 AD, became a pagan priest in Delphi, reviving the use of oracles and adopting Apollo as monotheistic god of the universe. He agreed with Plato on the immortality of the soul. A ban on circumcision led to a series of insurrections by Jews, then massacres in response.

Many Christian missionaries came to Rome, and disparate Christian groups in this large city gradually joined up and grew from localised collegiate structures to the intended community model under a bishop leader. Christianity grew apace to become a dominant force, largely thanks to the missionary work of converted Jews. Detailed records are lacking, but the apostolic tradition seems to have been followed. Marcion arrived there in 140 AD, but was excluded from the Church, as were other accused heretics such as Valentine the Gnostic. The Christian apologist Justin became the Christians' accepted theologian.

By the middle of the second century, Roman bishops and deacons had special responsibility for widows, orphans and the poor as well as normal priestly functions and leading worship. There is no doubt there was competition for status within the hierarchy of the Church and defensiveness on the part of the college of presbyters, but by the end of the second century, the Bishop of Rome held a clear sole monarchical role in the Western Church, assured of an honoured place in the eventual list of successors to Peter.

Persecutions

An underlying reason for Roman persecutions of Christians was the refusal of Christians to accept emperor worship, which some Roman leaders saw as the glue uniting all the nations and cultures in their Empire. There was no legal ban on being a Christian, but many who came to public notice were martyred for their refusal when required to offer sacrifices or give worship to the emperor. This arose mainly away from Rome in occupied lands. In the second century, there were two major persecutions of Christians:

> 156 AD – persecution in Asia Minor resulting in the immolation of Polycarp aged 80, among others.
> 177 AD – persecutions in Lyons and Vienne in Gaul.
> Far worse and more widespread persecutions would follow in the next century.

Non-Christians were impressed by the courageous willingness of Christians to stand by their faith in the face of death and by their emulation of Christ in their lives, obeying the Lord's commandments and practising fraternal love regardless of social strata. Their evident power to transform life and marginalise death attracted many converts. The conversion process was simple and welcoming, in contrast with Judaism which shared monotheistic belief, but Christianity was far more active in seeking converts. So their numbers grew fast in spite of many losses to martyrdom and even their severest critics respected that.

Christians did not seek heroism except in God's cause, but showed more heart and hope, believing in the power of love, the sanctity of all human life and its equality of value in God's eyes. **Tertullian**, an early Christian author, mentioned a pagan who expressed amazement at the love

Christians showed for each other, setting up organisations to care for the sick and the poor, widows and orphans. Eventually the sheer numbers and respectability of Christians could no longer be ignored though the faith would have to wait until 313 AD to be fully legalised as middle and upper classes began to be converted and attend services.

Justin 'Martyr' (100-165) using his intellect and reading, settled on Christianity as the most reasonable philosophy. He eventually set up a school in Rome, which was legally acceptable, whereas preaching and church meetings were not.

Sanctity of Life and Forbidden Activities

The Jews linked God closely with Israel. Believing they had scriptural support, they felt quite justified in killing anybody who threatened them or their land. For the early Christians killing was a red line. Imitating Jesus, they observed to the letter the commandment "Thou shalt not kill". Quite apart from the commandment, life was God's creation so it was not theirs to destroy be it for war, punishment for a crime or for any other reason. The memory of Christ's admonishment to Peter in the garden of Gethsemane was still fresh in the memory "those who take up the sword shall perish by the sword." Military service was forbidden as it potentially involved killing and this was a firmly held view right through persecutions until about AD 200. Towards that time, as recruits were badly needed for securing the lengthening borders of the Roman Empire, numbers of Christians were drawn into the Roman army in spite of this view and regardless of the practice of their faith being proscribed in Rome.

Some were even invited to be magistrates, which posed a dilemma because of the potential need to pass judgement on capital cases. This would later be cleared at the synod of Elvira in Spain, held early in the fourth century, from which Canon 56 stated "Magistrates are not to enter the church during the year in which they serve as '*duumvir*', the government official who presides at public occasions and national feasts." This did not refer directly to the capital punishment issue, but seemed to relate more to the necessity of eating with pagans and Jews, forbidden by other canons of the same synod. This dilemma was complicated by Paul's rather imprecise suggestion (Romans 13:1-2) that the state has God-given authority, which would include the right to punish wrongdoing. Regardless of the ongoing debate, there have since been many examples of Popes as state leaders who have delivered judgment or decisions that have led directly to death. Augustine and later Martin Luther would argue that the Church and State are separate realms. The first seeks peace and abjures force; the second is responsible for a stable and safe society and needs laws to punish miscreants to this end. The Church has to work within its local environment while maintaining its ethic. Subsequent changes in society and technical developments have raised even more complex issues to which such argument may be relevant.

The Church held views on members' occupations and even on leisure activities, some of which even had to be renounced if people were to be accepted into the faith. In terms of occupations, prostitution was irreconcilable, as being directly contrary to a commandment. Christians were forbidden to join the military or to hold government office which intrinsically involved military activity (the willingness to kill) and pagan ceremony. But the Church also deemed as unworthy or trivial the occupations of actors, astrologers, soothsayers, gladiators, chariot racers and related or supporting activities. Playing dice and even visiting the barber shops and bazaars were discouraged. Sculptors and painters had to avoid depicting pagan gods and teachers had to avoid teaching pagan mythology. Traders were warned to avoid making exaggerated claims about their wares or to behave in any way fraudulently.

The delicate balance between the ideal and the practical was exemplified by the conscientious objection of Christians to paying temple dues. This brought them into direct conflict with local laws, so was never strictly observed or applied. There were some exceptions granted and a degree of pragmatic tolerance applied, but pressure for their observance was always present. The rules affected the behaviour and leisure activities of Christians, but in reality many of them would find the attraction of attending drama, racing or the coliseum too great to resist sampling from time to time. The Church also frowned upon the widespread practice of public bathing, which actually provided recreational and social benefits as well as its primary purpose, so it contented itself with prohibiting mixed bathing, though enforcement even of that was difficult in the prevailing Roman culture. So even this early, ordinary Christians had to learn to balance the differences between the culture of their society and the demands of their faith.

The Easter Controversy

Jews celebrated the feast of Passover rejoicing in the memory of their ancestors' escape from bondage in Egypt. Since it coincided with Christ's passion, death and resurrection, Jewish Christians adapted it to commemorate these events, naturally picking the same date, initially on the day of the first full moon after the beginning of Spring, then under Bishop of Rome Soterius (reign c 166-174 AD) on the first Sunday after that full moon. The feast soon became known as Easter or the Paschal

Feast. In the East, there were more variations in the calendar and this led to Easter often being celebrated around different new moons.

Bishop Polycarp of Smyrna visited Rome in the late 150s AD and conferred with Bishop Anicetus on Church matters, including the question of Passover celebration. Rome would not accept Asia Minor's practice of celebrating on the day of the Passover – it was felt to be too closely associated with Judaism. It was known as the 'quartodecima', by which on biblical tradition, the Passover was celebrated on the 14th day of 'Nisan', the first month of the Jewish ecclesiastical year. Nonetheless the celebration of Easter was spreading as a practice in the Catholic Church and Bishop Soterius, successor to Anicetus, introduced the practice to Rome as a Sunday festival of the Resurrection rather than as in Asia Minor, where it was linked to the full moon on whichever night of the week it fell. However, Soter did not wish to fall out over this and visitors would be allowed to celebrate according to their tradition and were still welcome as members of the Roman communion, just as Polycarp was invited to celebrate the Eucharist.

Bishop of Rome Victor (reign 189-199 AD), called a synod there on the matter in 196 AD and asked all the main Christian centres to do the same. Of African origin and with a confrontational rather than persuasive style, he tended to impose Rome's views on the other centres. This alienated Polycrates (130-196), Bishop of Ephesus, who was reported by Eusebius as replying "It is more important to obey God than men." All apart from Asia Minor sided with Rome. Polycrates held a local synod as requested but they would not accept the proposal so Victor controversially cut them off from the Church family. Some bishops were concerned at his unyielding, high-handed way and wrote to Irenaeus, Bishop of Lyons, who beseeched Victor to maintain peace and unity with Asia (where Irenaeus had grown up).

Philosophy and Christianity, Stoics, Gnostics

Stoics feature in the first chapter of this book, but the following broadly compares some their ideas with those of Christianity. They had plenty in common with Christians – one God, the creator and ruler of the universe; the duty to behave well with personal targets to do good, though they differed in this by favouring the elite over the disadvantaged; the belief that virtue and reason are the basis for happiness; moral corruption is disruptive; suppress anger; there is a natural law dictating events, which negates the concept of multiple gods; we should accept that we are but a tiny part of nature and the universe so we should make the most of those if we are to achieve happiness; everything is rooted in nature, which must be cared for as we need to live in harmony with it; the totality of creation is so vast that sense can only be made of it if a single spirit created and sustains it. This all encouraged behaviour that helped support a stable society much as was the case with the Ten Commandments, with which there was some overlap.

Stoics differed from Christians in lacking a personal god and thus basic spirituality and they missed a few links that Christians see as vital. They promoted heroism, thought little of love, saw no point in remorse or seeking forgiveness and paid little heed to the needy. Attaching little intrinsic value to human life, they supported suicide to avoid pain or indignity in death, which was utterly rejected by Christians as contrary to the fifth commandment. Stoics were basically fatalists, 'stoically' accepting whatever life threw at them, never believing in miracles or oracles as these did not fall under the law of nature, by which alone they believed events were determined.

Epictetus (c. AD 55-135) was a leading stoic philosopher, born a slave with a crippled leg but encouraged in education by his wealthy owner as he showed such an interest in philosophy. He claimed all external events are determined by fate and therefore beyond our control, so we should accept whatever happens calmly and dispassionately. However, he also recognised that we are individually responsible for our own actions, which we can consider and control through rigorous self-discipline. Another notable stoic was Seneca (c. BC 4 – AD 65), a Roman philosopher and prolific writer, reputed to have later become a Christian. He was an advisor to Nero, who was friendly with Epictetus' owner. Both men's writings have been studied by Christians, Epictetus for his early study of prayer and Seneca's book 'On Mercy' from which Jean Calvin took extracts for Christian use.

Gnosticism grew from a fusion of early pagan Roman, Greek and Oriental religious myths plus astrology, with a few contemporary philosophical ideas. Begun before Christ, it spread with increasing momentum as Christianity was beginning. It is thought to be one of the main subjects of Paul's warnings in his letter to the Colossians (2:13-18) who were at the time in the Lycus Valley, a cradle for 'new age' thinking. Paul expresses concern about some of them accepting without question spiritual authorities, worshipping and holding rituals around celestial bodies such as the sun, moon and stars.

In mankind's eternal search for a widely acceptable explanation of creation, syncretism – in this case the co-mingling of various mythical deities, such as Egyptian, Greek, Persian, Babylonian – became fashionable from the beginning of the second century to the fourth century. It was perhaps a quest for a common thread in the various mythical religions and the Gnostics found a following, their basic belief being that only spiritual things had the potential to be good while material things, including people, were not good.

At the beginning of the 2nd century Dion of Brussa linked the Greek and Roman gods – Zeus to Jupiter and so on. Plutarch introduced Isis and Osiris from Egyptian mythology into the mix, which some had already found attractive, so the step to embracing Persian and Babylonian influences was not difficult. The Jews were always great salesmen. Their powerful projections of the Torah no doubt played a part in the adoption of excerpts of the scriptures into gnostic tracts.

Even though many Christians already allegorised the scriptures, most Gnostics exceeded tolerable limits. Christianity would be seriously challenged if Gnostic-style 'god-prophets' were to be used in overcoming doubts about the Old Testament as described by the theological writer Hippolytus. His idea of Jesus as just one of a number of God's messengers condemned it for Christians. There were a couple of additional Gnostic heresies in the mid-second century, the doctrines of Basilides followed by Isidor and that of Valentine and his disciple Ptolemy. They included reference to the Old Testament and to Jesus Christ the redeemer and convincingly argued elaborate perceptions of the godhead which bore more resemblance to pagan myths already well known to people east of Greece and Alexandria than any Christian view. The Church saw danger in their Christian character, Old Testament style interpretation, cogent descriptions of the nature and number of divine gods and demons, but above all in their total denial of the Old Testament. The significance of the Holy Trinity came to prominence in Christianity in this century.

Gnosticism's basic "Spiritual good; material evil", offered a basis for at least one of the following heresies.

Heresies and the Old Testament

The Christian Church began in a period following the famous philosophers. Humans as naturally curious beings, continued to explore thoughts on the new religion, many of which the Church had to consider and judge. Theories deemed contrary to its true teaching were decried as heresies. A few notable heresies arose in the second century. To Gnosticism could be added Docetism, Marcionism, Monarchianism, Montanism and Sabellianism, all of which arose either from difficulties in accepting the Old Testament literally or developing concepts of the nature of Jesus and the Holy Trinity, while otherwise accepting the teaching of Jesus Christ.

The theologian Hippolytus, did some major work on heresies up to his time.

Docetism held that Christ's body was not human but either a phenomenon or of real but celestial substance, and that therefore his sufferings were only apparent. Gnostics embraced this, but it was clearly heretical Christology in the Church's eyes, denying its view of Christ's divinity and humanity.

Marcionism – Marcion of Sinope (85-160 AD), son of the Bishop of Sinope was excommunicated by his father, Polycarp on theological grounds as a young adult. He moved to Smyrna seeking followers. Marcion applied his own logic in contrasting the nature and teaching of God as revealed in the Old Testament with that of Jesus Christ as represented in the four gospels.

This touched a raw nerve for the Church as it could reconcile the clear contradictions only by accepting that the Old Testament should not be taken too literally. Marcion rejected this argument as specious and inadequate, maintaining that its authors had always intended it to be read literally. Known to be sceptical of philosophy, Marcion envisaged two distinct deities – the Old Testament God of retribution (dark and evil) and the New Testament God of love (light and good). Thus, Marcion perceived an offensive nature in God of the Old Testament, who created humans and the world with gross imperfections. When people sinned in keeping with the nature he had given them, he seemed to show forgiveness to the favoured ones while visiting dreadful punishment on others. Why, he asked, did God create snakes, scorpions, crocodiles and other dangerous beasts and insects of no clear benefit? Why must procreation and birth involve such revolting processes? It was with strongly held views like these, perhaps arising from his privileged upbringing, that Marcion antagonised the Church and incurred its anger and ultimate excommunication.

He accepted as truth the picture of God the creator as painted in the Old Testament. But this was not a perfect God if the world he created failed to match up to his aims. His law, the commandments, although indeed holy and righteous, even spiritual, had to be enforced by a retaliatory system of punishment – an eye for an eye for example, and the sins of a father could be carried down as many as four generations of successors. The Jews accepted this 'righteousness' in spite of its inherent cruelty and inconsistency.

Marcion regarded Jesus Christ as clearly rejecting the Old Testament righteousness, preaching in its place patience, forgiveness and love. He practised gentleness, humility and compassion, believing the Sermon on the Mount in Matthew's gospel covers it well and the Beatitudes offer a fresh set of ideals focused on these qualities and Jesus' teachings on spirituality and compassion rather than demand and sanction.

But in reading the Sermon on the Mount as denying the old Law, Marcion deduced that Christ could not be one with 'the Creator'. Marcion believed in both; he accepted the righteous creator God of the Old Testament and Genesis as proclaimed by Moses; he also believed in Jesus Christ, who revealed the God of love, compassion and mercy who was supreme, and accepted his teachings, many of which seemed to him to run counter to the Old Testament. This different and more recent God delivered mankind from the earlier and lesser one, clearly not a monotheistic proposition. Nevertheless, he is by no means alone in noting contradictions between the Old and New Testaments and we now know that the Genesis story of creation was more graphically simplified than real.

Marcion might have been influenced by Persian belief that civilisation truly began when a transition from devil-worship to god-worship took place. Zoroaster, who lived in the late seventh to mid-sixth century BC was the great prophet of their faith in Mazda, 'the omniscient one'. He founded Persian dualism, which in crude terms involves two gods, one evil and one perfect. Its echoes in Marcionism are clear.

The Church could not accept Marcion's hypothesis, which was gaining popularity. It was declared heretical. But Marcion was not easily put down as he also firmly believed that St Paul had grasped the teachings of Jesus better than the apostles. He held that fearing the apostles misreading his message, Christ had to call on Paul to deliver it correctly. Marcion went further, saying that the Church wrongly claimed apostolic origin of the four gospels even though none of the apostles wrote them. He did, however, recognise Luke as a disciple of Paul and therefore took Luke's gospel more seriously.

While Marcion was persuasive, his sect survived his death only for a short while in the West, but for a couple more centuries in the East and Asia Minor, partly thanks to an effective disciple called Apelles. Also, Origen was to preserve some of the thoughts from one of his works, 'Syllogisms', which stresses the inferior nature of the Old Testament.

Marcion once protested "In truth I do not know how there could be an uncreated God, but I believe it." It is a thought appropriate even today, as faith transcends human logical analysis.

A later development which certainly emanated from Persia and spread widely was '**Manichaeism**' which introduced the struggle between the evil god of darkness and the physical world versus the good god of light and the spirit, linked to Mesopotamian Gnostic beliefs. It was introduced by the

Persian prophet Mani (Latin Manichaeus) who lived about 216-275 AD, a dualist belief with some resemblance to Zoroastrianism which was also closely involved with astrology, spreading rapidly as far east as China where it endured until the fourteenth century. Nonetheless, its philosophy held attraction for some further west such as Augustine of Hippo in Numidia (Algeria) in his late youth a few centuries later.

Asia Minor Herecies, Monarchianism and Montanists

Stimulated by the recent time of Jesus Christ, self-proclaimed prophets found eager audiences. The Gnostics did not dampen the ardour of people seeking further divine guidance. But Church leaders in Rome were learning to take a more considered approach in examining further apparent revelations of the Spirit. So even at this early juncture, mechanisms were burgeoning to protect 'absolute truth' as far as it can fully be recognised, as faithfully as possible in a genuine attempt to ensure valid trustworthiness of its dogma.

The missions had begun in Asia Minor with Paul's visit to Ephesus. From there, Christianity found fertile ground first in the Western, Greek-speaking areas, then spread north along the coasts including Byzantium, Nicomedia and Sinope (now respectively Istanbul, ruins near Izmir and Sinop, all in Turkey), before moving inland and into Phrygia. Smyrna (now Izmir) soon became a second centre of growth. The Church in Asia Minor had some of its own particular Orthodox characteristics, which would spread west through Irenaeus.

Monarchianism – Theodotus, an early Christian writer from Byzantium, with Praxeas, a priest from Asia Minor who went to Rome, were both concerned that the concept of the Holy Trinity challenged and was logically irreconcilable with that of monotheism. They consequently promoted a new theory of Christology – 'Monarchianism'. Sabellius, a priest and theologian from North Africa who taught in Rome, was another proponent. All three were excommunicated for heretical preaching.

Their belief was along the lines that the one and only God had become flesh and walked on earth as Jesus Christ. They won a sizeable following locally. Their theses were not entirely consistent and ran counter to the Christian logos theory as well as the idea of the Holy Trinity, which was then growing. Two contradictory models emerged, with Theodotus propounding 'Dynamic', also referred to as 'Adoptionist' Monarchianism, while Praxeus and Sabellius favoured 'Modalism' or 'Sabellianism'. Dynamism holds that God is one being, wholly indivisible, and of one nature and that the Son was not eternal like the Father, but was essentially adopted and imbued with divine wisdom and powers. Modalism basically considers God to be one entity appearing and operating in the different modes of the Father, the Son, and the Holy Spirit, thus contrary to the trinitarian belief in three entities in one substance.

There was much theological and philosophical argument about Monarchianism, but it was to maintain a core following into the fifth century in spite of strong opposition from the Logos theologians such as Hippolytus, Clement of Alexandria and Origen.

Montanism – In the more isolated regions of Asia Minor, as Christianity took hold a new 'prophesy' emerged by the end of the second century, which would become known as Montanism. The numerous heresies of this period whose names begin with M are confusing. Following his baptism in adulthood about 150 AD, a known ascetic called Montanus, had gone into frantic ecstasy and spoke in tongues before reverting to intelligible speech. Some around him believed he was a prophet of the Spirit. Montanus' disciples recorded his sermons as sacred writings on a par with the gospels and epistles. His success ran contrary to the recent perception that there remained few, if any true new prophets, but many false ones. Jesus had left his message over a century and a half earlier and was followed immediately by his trusted apostles. Hippolytus claimed that manifestations of the Spirit mostly ended following John's Revelation around 100 AD.

Montanus argued that the reduction in such manifestations resulted from the Church's moral decline in matters such as divorce and less fasting. He claimed direct apparitions of the Spirit. Tertullian was a follower, describing a "sister among us who has been granted gifts of revelations". At least two of Montanus' disciples, women called Prisca and Maximillia, also occasionally exhibited glossolalia. The Church authorities were wary and nervous of Montanism and tended either to deride or condemn it.

Maximillia claimed to be the last true prophet before the second coming and Montanus professed to be as the Son of God, one of the Trinity with the Lord and the Paraclete, come again to teach. Over time, he established a Montanist canon of the New Testament – a list of books from which readings could be used in church services. This reappears in the following chapter with further heresies.

Africa

The Romans had absorbed much of North Africa into their Empire, including Numidia which is now broadly Libya, Tunisia and Algeria, its capital city being Carthage, today a suburb of Tunis. It proved fertile ground for Christianity, which grew with strong roots, although including a number of heretical sects. This area was subjected to as much persecution as any province within the Roman Empire. Many Christians avoided the ultimate punishment by agreeing to Roman demands to offer sacrifice. A synod was called in Carthage in 198 by the local Bishop Agrippus and attended by 70 bishops, at which it was decided that heretics and schismatics and those who had simply weakened, who wished to return to the mainstream must apply to be re-baptised to ensure they display repentance and re-commit before being accepted back as Christians.

Egypt

Most of the first two centuries of Christianity in Egypt seem to have involved a pervading Gnostic influence. Many locals believe that Mark founded the Church there during Nero's reign in the middle of the first century and also established the famous catechetical school in Alexandria that is still there, the oldest in the world. But in preference to the four usually accepted gospels, they used the Greek Gospel of the Egyptians (as opposed to the slightly later Coptic one) and that of the Hebrews, until the official canonical coding of the gospels towards the end of the 4th century. The Western (Roman) Church considered both those gospels Gnostic to the point of being heretical.

Basilides in Hadrian's time and Valentine were celebrated early Gnostic teachers. Apelles also appeared in Egypt and with much of their work translated into Coptic, its circulation and influence lasted for some time.

The earliest records of the Catholic Church in Egypt date back further than Demetrius, who was Bishop of Alexandria 189-231 AD to Clement of Alexandria (150-215), a Greek-born pagan who converted to Christianity and was supported by the Roman Church. In 189 AD Clement joined another great teacher, Pantaenus in Egypt. According to the historian Eusebius who described him as the head of the Alexandrian catechumen school, Pantaenus had been a stoic and had led a mission to India. Origen (185-254) was a subsequent leader of St Mark's school which by then was an already renowned centre of Christian learning attended by people of all religions and philosophies. Alexandria was a seriously important centre of culture, providing ripe ground for Christianity. Clement and Origen will be considered in further detail in the following chapter as that is when most of their work had effect.

East of Jerusalem

According to tradition, the gospel message had been carried further eastward by Thomas the Apostle. He took it to the Parthian Empire, much of which is now Iran, where the prevailing religions were the cults of Mithra, and Zoroastrianism. He then travelled further, reaching India, probably by sea as his main work was in the south of the sub-continent. Not much is recorded about these areas, but there were substantial eastern pockets of Christianity in the early centuries, mainly around Persia, southern India, Mongolia and parts of China, the last two no doubt the work of other missionaries.

CHAPTER 5

3rd Century

Bishops of Rome

Zephyrinus 190–217
Callixtus I 217-222
Urban I 222-230
Pontian 230-235
Anterus 235-236
Fabian 236-250
Cornelius 251-253
(Novation antipope 251-258)
Stephen I 254-257
Sixtus II 257-258
Dionysius 259-268
Felix I 269-274
Eutychian 275-283
Caius 283-296
Marcellinus 296-304

Roman Emperors:

Severus Septimus 193-211
Caracella 211-217.*
Geta (son of Septimus) co-emperor w
Septimus 209-211, with Caracella
Feb-December 211.*
Macrinus & Diadumenam co-emperors
217-218.
Elagabulus 218-222.*
Severus Alexander 222-235.*
Maximus Thrax 235-238.*
Gordian I & Gordion II (son),
co-emprors March-April 238. GI
committed suicide on news of GII's death
in battle.
Pupienus* & Balbinus* April-July 238,
co-emperors.

Gordian III 238-244.*
Philip I, the Arab 244-249. Made son
Philip II co-emperor in 247. Philip I
killed in battle; P!!*
Decius 249-251. Defeated Philip I in
battle, made Herrenius Etruscus
co-emperor 251, both died in battle.
Hostilian June –November 251, died of
plague
Trebonius Gallus & Velusianus father and
son co-emperors 251-253. **
Aemilian Aug-Oct 253.*
Valerian 253-260. Died in captivity by
Persians.
Galienus 253-268. Co-emperor with
Valerian, and briefly with his son
(Salonenus).*.
Salonenus July 260.*
Claudius Gothicus 268-270, died of
plague
Quintillus Jan-Sept 270
Aurelian 270-275.*
Tacitus 275-276
Florianus June-Sept 276.*
Probus 276-282
Carus 282-283
Carenus 283-285, died in battle &
Numerian co-emperor 283-284.*
Diocletian 284-286, then Emperor East
286-305 Abdicated.
Maximium 286-305, Emperor West.

*Believed assassinated.

Following a century of growth, organisation and consolidation, albeit with some persecution and heretical thought growth, the third century began in a period of relative peace for Christianity. Imperial policy broadly allowed the largely law-abiding Christians to be tolerated and practice of their faith was not seen as disloyal to the empire. Leadership of the Church seems to have been held by devout Christians more driven by the desire to follow in the footsteps of the apostles than tainted by the sense of power until nearly half-way through this century, when a dispute over the leadership would spoil this record. At the other extreme, this century saw some Christian individuals seeking a solitary contemplative life, which would eventually lead to the monastic movement. But the Roman Empire would run into more problems as witnessed by the numerous emperors and their precarious longevity with over fifty percent chance of assassination, execution or captivity. Persecution of Christians would also recur during this century.

Roman citizenship was held for the most part only by Italian inhabitants, expatriates or selected loyal nobility in other countries within the empire. But in 212, Emperor Caracella established the 'Antonine Constitution', an edict declaring universal citizenship within the Roman Empire, meaning that all freeborn men and women in the Roman Empire were to be given Roman citizenship.

The Roman Empire in Crisis

From the prosperous period of Trajan (reign 98-117 AD) to Decius (249-251), a huge population decline took place in Rome due to reducing birth rate, two serious bouts of plague, significantly reduced net immigration from the provinces as well as the departure of existing immigrants. The Antonine Constitution was a step to reverse this flow. The stark population figures tell the story: AD150 – 1.25 million, 200 – 1 m, 300 – 0.5 m.

So productivity and the economy suffered, while the military sought ever more funding for defence, around the Empire's lengthy borders, presenting challenges for government and society. Conversely, Christianity prospered and grew during this period as it gained in influence.

In the first half of the third century in particular, the denarius devalued from a pure silver coin to an impure copper, plunging to less than one thirtieth of the currency value it had held under Trajan. The army, essential for stability, was financially insatiable and successive governments bled the landed classes dry to support their spending. The state was toppling as its perceived lack of fairness led to widespread robbery and piracy while the army, now heavily staffed by foreign soldiers, became weaker. The throne became threatened and the borders of the empire suffered breaches by enemies, always scenting any weakness.

So the third century was a testing time for the Empire, which nearly collapsed under the pressures of plague, invasion, civil disturbance and economic decline. The 'Imperial Crisis of the Third Century' from 235-284, began with the assassination of Emperor Severus Alexander by his own troops. There followed over the ensuing 50 years, twenty six claimants to be Emperor, most of them senior military officers.

By 271, the empire had broadly three parts – the Gallic (Gaul and Britain); the Palmyrene (Syria, Palestine and Egypt); and the Roman, which covered southern Europe, Asia Minor and North Africa. Aurelian (Emperor 270-275) reunited the empire and the crisis ended when Diocletian introduced his tetrarchic reforms in 284. Diocletian made Nicomedia in Greece (near today's Izmir in Turkey) the capital of the Eastern Roman Empire in 286.

The Church in North Africa

The Church in Roman-occupied North Africa grew in strength both among the earlier invading Phoenicians and the fair-skinned Berbers, descendants of immigrants from Persia around 7000 BC. Carthage became the second city to Rome. Latin and the Phoenicians' Punic, were the main spoken languages there and their solid Christian growth and commitment surpassed that of Europe in the late second and early third centuries. In fact, Latin was used as the Church language here even before it replaced Greek in Rome.

So Africa was an important centre of the Church and had nearly 200 bishops. Its numbers were swelled both by people converting and by those switching from various schismatic or heretical groups, these latter having been ruled to require re-baptism.

Bishop Agrippenus of Carthage may have been succeeded by an early Donatus, not to be confused with the better known bishop of the same name in the fourth century. The first Donatus of Carthage probably presided at the synod of Lambaesis c. 240 AD. This small town had grown around a Roman military camp and was the designated capital of the new Roman province Southern Numidia. Its synod was called to remove a heretical bishop. Cyprian succeeded Donatus and through his strong personality became one of the most powerful Christian voices of the time. Born a pagan, he had led a loose youth but grew to deplore the public and private immorality around him as well as the greed, corruption and cruelty prevalent in wealthy society. After instruction and baptism into

Christianity he felt cleansed and liberated from his despair and empowered to live a moral life. Against opposition from some elderly presbyters, he was consecrated 'pope', a title then reserved for the bishops of Rome, Carthage and Alexandria only.

In 249 AD, Emperor Decius ordered that throughout the Empire, all people should come before special officers and formally declare their allegiance to the Roman gods then prove it by offering a sacrifice. His aim was to destroy Christians inwardly, rather than disturb the wider population with mass executions. His officials went for top clerical figures first, to undermine Church leadership and many were subject to threats of selective execution. Some of the leaders escaped before they were challenged and provided guidance to their congregations from their places of sanctuary.

Many Christians, softened by a lengthy period of comfortable living and relatively peaceful existence, recanted their faith. Others were tortured, including the respected teacher Origen, who survived the ordeal. Cyprian, aware he would not offer sacrifices and could be executed as an example before completing his work, went into hiding and led the Church from there. Bishop of Rome, Fabian was martyred there in 250, the position remaining vacant for a year during which Roman authorities realised the persecution was ineffective, so it was lifted. Decius, killed in battle in 251, was succeeded by Valerian.

Cyprian came out of hiding and was restored to his see in Carthage. The African Church, unlike some in Rome, took quite a lenient view of the defectors and opened its arms to receive many back as remorseful penitents. This raised strong feelings of grievance among those who had endured extreme hardships or lost family members for their loyalty, but under Cyprian's strong guidance things soon returned to normal.

Novation and Marcian

Cornelius was elected by the bishops to the vacant position of Bishop of Rome in 251. An opposing priest, Novatian, with the support of a few dissident Italian bishops and some presbyters in Africa who opposed Cyprian, also claimed the seat. Novation's opposition to Cornelius was based on the hard line taken by Cornelius and the Roman Church regarding excommunication of those who had lapsed or yielded to pressure to offer pagan sacrifice during the Decian persecution. Novation had supporters for a more moderate approach to penitent defectors and found Cyprian sympathetic, though not to the extent of supporting his claim to be bishop of Rome. Cornelius knew he was no match for the intellect of Novatian and excommunicated him in his first year. Emperor

Decius banished Cornelius from Rome and he was killed in exile in 253. Cornelius had little time to achieve, but he supported exorcism in the Church and since his time, each diocese in Christendom has been canonically required to appoint an exorcist.

Two issues within the Church then centred on heresies, most of them relating to theories around the Trinity, and how to deal with people returning either from heresy or having agreed to offer sacrifices under considerable duress. The organisation of the Church was then neither sufficiently unified nor supported by qualified theologians or lawyers to make informed judgements, so declarations were made according to the strength of conviction of the leaders at the time and place.

Stephen I, succeeded Cornelius as Bishop of Rome. Faustinus, Bishop of Lyons asked him to decry Bishop Marcian of Arles for denying penance and communion to returnees, especially Novatianists. Church argument over this issue centred on the balance between the mercy and justice of Christ. Excommunication then involved denial of forgiveness and the sacraments, even on the death bed, so it was a devastating sentence with which many conscientious followers of Christ were deeply uncomfortable.

Valerian Persecution and Capture, Border Breaches

Valerian was quite a tolerant emperor, but in AD 257, his Treasurer, Macrianus persuaded him to clamp down on Christians again and history was repeated. First they were ordered to make sacrifices to the Roman gods or face banishment, then after a year, an order was issued to execute their leaders. In 260 Valerian was defeated and captured, the first Roman Emperor to be so, by the Persians in the battle of Essene. His son Gallienus, now Emperor, reversed his father's order against the Christians and the persecutions duly subsided, though too late for some bishops. Gallienus declared the first public and official edict of tolerance of Christianity, ruling that Christians were not to be interfered with in their practices, meaning they emerged stronger than hitherto. This 'little peace of the Church' heralded forty years in which the faith flourished while the Roman Empire faced new challenges.

The Persians' capture of Valerian caused shock-waves around the Roman Empire and emboldened their enemies, leading to sensed vulnerability of the empire's borders. Breaches included:

- The Franks crossed the Rhine from Northern Germany into Gaul and beyond.
- Further south, the Alemanni moved west into the Black Forest then across the Rhine and down to the Rhone as far as the Mediterranean

while also crossing the Alps and taking parts of northern Italy where Gallienus held the line just north of Milan.

- To the east, the Goths in alliance with other Germanic tribes and the Sarmatians took the northern Balkans and crossed the Black Sea and took major cities on the Bosphorus, also invading northern Greece and advancing almost as far as Athens.
- The Persians breached the empire's eastern borders and advanced through Mesopotamia and Syria as far as the city of Antioch.

These aggressors were mainly non-Christian people. As the Roman Empire officially tolerated Christians under Gallienus, the Church now regarded it as something of a haven and prayed in support of it.

Gallienus, intelligent and valiant as he was, had insufficient resources to cover all the breaches, so the threatened regions of the Empire had to organise their own defence, assuming new levels of autonomy, sometimes even withdrawing allegiance to the empire. For example, Western parts of Gaul, joined with Britain and Spain in adopting Postumus, a seasoned general as emperor to protect and maintain the benefits of civilisation introduced by the Romans. He did that successfully between 258 and 268 AD from his established base in Tréves. His successors, Victorinus and Tetricus were to prove less successful.

Claudius II, Aurelian, Empire Recovers

In 268, Emperor Claudius II in Rome began a major recovery of the empire as his army, led by General Aurelian vanquished the Alemanni then the following year engaged the Goths and expelled them from Greece and the northern Balkans. Then Aurelian, while defending the borders in Europe, was made Emperor. He secured territory south of the Danube and established the river as a border before going on to re-take Syria, Asia Minor and Egypt in 273. Aurelian then marched on the autonomous western Empire in 274, which Tetricus ceded. All this took a further heavy toll on the stretched Roman economy.

As Aurelian was lauded for restoring the Empire, he asked all patriotic Romans to follow him in paying tribute to the Sun God, the "one and only God of the Empire". He built Rome's city walls which still stand as testimony to his successes, but his next objective of restoring economic activity and strength, while reducing the burden of local bureaucracy was halted by his assassination. A succession of seven Emperors over the next nine years saw the Empire facing another decline. The last of those seven emperors was assassinated and the surprising candidate deemed to have the strength and dedication to be a worthy successor in the mould of

Aurelian was the head of the elite imperial bodyguard. Diocletian, a man of humble origin but a distinguished military career took the crown in 284 AD

With work still to be done in Gaul and Britain, Diocletian adopted a trusted young colleague, Maximian as his brother and appointed him Caesar, charging him with the military tasks first to hold the Rhine as an eastern border then quell a peasant disturbance in part of Gaul. Distant Britain remained a challenge. A Celtic fleet commander, Carausius had set up as leader of Britain and parts of the North Sea coast from Boulogne to the Rhine delta won by the late Postumous. Carausius was brought on-side by apparent peaceful acceptance as Maximian was busy enough elsewhere. Mainly pagan Britain had become less disciplined after Postumus. The venerable Bede wrote of 'cruel persecution' of Christians and the execution of St Alban, the first known English Martyr was recorded.

By the year 293 Diocletian and Maximian were legally recognised joint Emperors. While appearing in harmony as Maximian ruled the west and Diocletian the east of the empire, each of them was privately setting up an eventual successor as sole emperor. Maximian chose Constantius to whom he set the test of conquering Carausius. Diocletian suppressed a similar uprising in Egypt while Maximian fought further west in North Africa. More territory was won in Valeria (now in Hungary) as well as against the Persians around Armenia. So nearly forty years after the borders had begun to crumble, the boundaries of the Empire had been secured anew and even extended. But this recovery had been costly as the army had been expanded.

Needing to increase taxes Diocletian revised the Empire's administration and divided it into many provinces with each having similar productive value. He had devised a scheme of taking tax partly in money and partly in a share of goods produced in the province, the latter having the greater value. With a well-designed and tight administrative structure, he achieved almost universal collection and a sense of fairness, enabling him to balance his books. But, inflation grew and people became restless as they sensed they were becoming poorer. Diocletian issued a draconian edict controlling market prices of essential goods and services. Anybody either demanding or paying more than the declared prices or who refused to sell at them faced the death penalty. It did little to improve the atmosphere or the economy for some time but the tax revenue enabled the army to be maintained to ensure reasonable security and stability.

One casualty of the ailing economy in the latter stages of the third century was the arts, accompanied by declines in literature, poetry, sculpture and oratory because the usual patrons and purchasers were now so much less well-off. But things gradually improved and Diocletian commissioned an infrastructure revival in grand building works, some of the larger ones involving elaborate relief carvings which encouraged a revival of those skills and provided much-needed employment. The improved tax revenue and relative stability of the Empire supported such public works and helped improve the economy. The Romans continued to worship and offer sacrifices to their traditional gods.

Diocletian moved the capital from Rome to Milan in 286 but chose to reside in Nicomedia in the East, leaving Maximian in charge in Milan. Although further north, Diocletian felt that Milan was more defensible than Rome against potential attack from the barbarian Vandals from Eastern Germany who were growing in military power and territorial ambition. Diocletian saw their main threat to Rome as being seaborne from their enclave in the Balkans and via the west coast.

Coptic Desert Fathers, Seeds of Monasticism

The Jewish sect of the Essenes had lived like monks from the second century BC, wearing white robes, dining in silence and practising celibacy, living in male-only communities. In earlier times it had been a practice of various ascetics, who together with some Jews rejected carnal pleasure, and regarded celibacy as a holy and noble state. There is no mention in the gospels of celibacy being necessary for holiness, nor is the celibacy of Jesus lauded. Indeed, Peter, appointed by Jesus to lead the Church on earth, was a married man. The first Christian celibate groups were in fact women, partly for demographic reasons – they outnumbered men in the known world. However, women always held a secondary, supportive role in societies of that time and little has changed within the Church since, regardless of progression outside. There would be a sea-change in their roles and standing towards equality in the 20th century, and they are now well on course to achieving it in Western developed society and most Christian Churches.

The monastic movement began with a number of Egyptian Coptic Christian ascetics venturing into the nearby desert seeking solitude to pray, study or work, living as individual hermits in rudimentary huts or caves. What drew them to this life may have been a search for inner knowledge, holiness and peace, perhaps aggravated by risk of persecution, or just an escape from the distractions of daily struggle, heavy taxation and austerity prevalent in the Roman Empire. There were hundreds of them, finding caves or building huts within reach of oases distant from Cairo and other towns. The solitary life carried risks as they were easy pickings for bandits, which led to a tendency for them to form groups while still living alone at some distance from each other. Some would weave mats and baskets to earn enough to buy occasional basic food. The earliest known groupings were at Nitria and Cellia. Thus began the 'Desert Fathers'. One of the first recorded was Paul of Thebes (c.227-341), but perhaps the best known is Antony the Great (c.251-356 AD), thanks to Athanasius later writing Antony's biography.

With time and age some of them fell ill, requiring the help of others, leading to better organised communities forming. This move was strengthened by other factors. Many missed regular worship services; others had learned that lengthy periods of absolute solitude and inactivity could not simply be filled with prayer and far from generating peace of mind, they could suffer melancholy, boredom and even insanity and struggles with demons. Solitude did not guarantee freedom from carnal temptations, which added to their worries. The solitary life clearly did not suit everybody, so the advent of the safe walled monastery with individual cells for solitude was a natural development. Some zealots continued in the open desert and either attended services at a nearby monastery or met together in groups on Sundays, a practice that continues today mainly in the East, but also among the Carthusian order in the West.

The first such monastery is believed to have been set up by Pachomius (292-348) the following century at Tabenissi on the east side of the Nile in Upper Egypt, where single men lived in a collection of buildings as a community of individuals who prayed together at set times and lived according to written rules under an elected abbot or 'father'. They undertook organised work according to their skills and sold the resulting goods such as produce, handicrafts, furniture locally and services like education, health and building, to help finance the community. It was also a self-help community supporting each other's needs.

This type of arrangement was particularly suited to women seeking such a life and soon such communities were separately established by them. Some had already adopted the solitary life, but the monastic model offered a safe way for them to follow in their own holy and prayerful communities of nuns, and in the interests of safety, nunneries were usually located on the outskirts of a town, or not too far from a monastery in rural or remote areas. Few monks and nuns seem to have been ordained by the Church.

Antony also helped set up a monastic community. He introduced Macarius (300-391), a Coptic man of wisdom, to the monastic life. Macarius became known as the 'Lamp of the Desert' and he was ordained after ten years there, becoming president of the monastery. Thus, over time two modes of contemplative living had developed – solitary (eremitic) and communal (coenobitic), with practitioners sometimes interchanging between the two. The communal model attracted most followers while the solitary model was regarded in Egypt as the higher form. In either case, the ascetic existence appeared to work wonders for their longevity. Antony and Paul of Thebes lived to over 100 and were by no means alone in this.

The ideals of the celibate and prayerful contemplative life of the Egyptian hermits spread slowly west along the North African coast. Later, it also grew along the coasts of Gaul and Spain, where it followed the writings of John Cassian, an exile in Marseilles who analysed its psychology in about 432. His book 'Conferences' served as a useful guide to future monastic rules.

That trinity of disciplines already promoted by the Church Fathers – **Prayer** (strengthens relationship with God), **Almsgiving** (reinforces relationship with other people) and **Fasting** (helps our relationship with ourselves) was the basis of their lifestyle. Jesus himself had actually shown the way when he went into the desert, fasted and was subjected to heavy temptation to follow worldly values –prestige, power, pride – rather than Messianic values, but he resisted. The message was that this was his example which Christians should all try to follow and Church leaders especially so, perhaps a subject for discussion elsewhere.

Prayer Practice of Christians

As to personal religious practice for the more mainstream Christians, a number of people proposed prescriptions for individual prayer patterns around the beginning of the third century. Established Jewish custom was to repeat their '*Shemoneh Esrei*' three times daily – early morning, afternoon and evening. This translated early on to Christians as recitation of the Lord's Prayer three times a day as mentioned in the Didache (8:3). In 200 AD, Tertullian suggested extending this to five times a day, adding 9.00 am (mid-morning) and noon. Others introduced the idea of prayers during the night and Hippolytus of Rome proposed adding midnight and cock-crow, taking the suggestion of Daniel (6:10) "Seven times a day I have given praise to thee". The seven canonical hours were adopted by ascetics and monastic orders and were to form part of the Benedictine Rule. But most early Christians said prayer three times a day, while churches developed morning and evening services (lauds and vespers) to support the practice, these being in addition to the Eucharistic service, which was then mainly held on Sundays.

Repetitive prayer has been used by several great religions. Hindus used prayer beads (*Rudrashka*) over two centuries before Christ to help with repetitive prayer they call *Japa*; Bhuddist monks have used repetition of the Bhudda's name and increased their usage following the Bhakti movement in the 15th century with the Hare Krishna mantra. In

Christianity the knotted prayer rope was adopted by the Desert Fathers and this has endured as the Orthodox equivalent of the Western rosary beads, which were probably introduced as late as the 13th century. Repetitive prayer, *hesychasm* in Greek, is regarded as a useful vehicle for meditation and prayer for various intentions.

Church Fathers of the 3rd Century

This century with the previous and next saw many learned written works on Christianity by prominent thinking churchmen and theologians, some of whom would be honoured as Fathers of the Church.

Tertullian (155-240 AD) Quintus Septimus Florens Tertullianus was born in Carthage, the son of a pagan officer in the Roman army, Tertullian studied law in Rome. A positive and assertive character with a strong work ethic, he married a Christian. He converted in 193, having been impressed like many others by the courageous bearing of Christians in the face of torture and execution. Tertullian was an austere rigorist as were many of the African fathers in the early Church. Around AD 200, Tertullian attacked heresy in a much admired work, applicable for all time "*Liber de Praescriptione Haereticorum*" (Book of Heretical Beliefs). He referred to lax discipline in the Church of Rome. In 203, he effectively embraced Montanism with its ascetic leaning and belief in the continuation of prophets, which the Church would later declare heretical. His writings on public amusements, the veiling of virgins and the conduct of women for example, give expression to his particular moral views. He was a misogynist, claiming that all women share Eve's guilt in causing the fall of Adam, who was created in God's likeness. Tertullian left the Church about 211, when Carthage followed Rome in declaring Montanism heretical and excommunicated many of its followers.

Contrary to Irenaeus, who preached the faith in a manner that appealed to Hellenist thought, Tertullian was wary of philosophy as having nourished Gnosticism. But he agreed with Irenaeus in insisting that Church teaching is based on Scripture as delivered by the Apostles and preserved by their successors the bishops. He dismissed the Gnostics for denying the vital humanity of Jesus and the reality of his sufferings.

Over thirty of Tertullian's writings remain, covering all aspects of life and faith, including apologetics, heresies, and morals. These reflect his legal training, such as his argument that since the Church was self-supporting and was the source of the most peaceful citizens, government should not persecute its members but protect and encourage them. He also observed that persecution seemed to strengthen the Church rather than weaken it, just as pruning can improve shrubs. But regarding religious practice, sin and especially penance and women, his views are regarded as overly severe. Augustine would later refer to him as moody, changeable and self-centred.

Clement of Alexandria (150-215 AD) was born of pagan parents in 150 AD in Athens, studied philosophy and travelled widely. He found comfort in Christianity in Alexandria, a busy multi-cultural port and wealthy trading centre which was a centre for intellectuality. He succeeded Pantanaeus as head of the Catechetical school there. His was a more kindly Christianity than that which developed in the West in later times.

Clement saw the Logos as being there in the beginning, creating the world, sending us Christ the Saviour, to teach us a way of living leading to immortality. His writing style softened the black and white style of the apologists and the clinical incisiveness of Tertullian while conveying a refreshingly upbeat Christian sense of vitality and optimism leading to eternal life with God. He wrote an elegant and readable trilogy of books – Exhortation *Protrepticus* (195 AD), Tutor *Paedogogus* (198), and Miscellany *Stromateis* (198-203).

'Exhortation' illustrates his wide knowledge of pagan mythology and theology. He tracks the history of Greek pagan beliefs from the worship of sun, moon and stars, through that of agricultural products then random stone and wood objects to sculpted or carved images made from them as idols. The latter plus the Commandment led the early Church to resist the presence of 'graven images', even paintings in churches.

The second book, 'Tutor', develops his thinking on Christian ethics, based on belief in the Logos incarnate.

The third had been intended as a didactic work, *Didaskalos* covering Christian knowledge and revelation, but the requirements of academic stringency for such a work simply did not sit comfortably with his intuitive style. He was at his best communicating on a more relaxed and 'human' level, so the world was treated to a far more digestible book in 'Miscellany'.

He denied the Gnostics' belief that faith and knowledge are far apart – they believed the *psychics* on one side had blind faith in and literal understanding of the Old Testament while the *pneumatics,* on the other, were helped by the Spirit who revealed to them deeper meanings in the scriptural words. Clement's Christianity was one of forgiving moderation – no extreme asceticism, no greed but still a light footprint on the earth; measured control of our human weaknesses; nothing wrong with honestly acquired wealth used well and in moderation; life should give enjoyment but not at emotional or temporal cost to others.

Clement believed that the Holy Scriptures held back from revealing ultimate divine truths, thus requiring earnest effort in personal search to get closer to a real understanding. He did not condemn philosophy, which had worried many theologians, who could always quote the Gnostics in their polemics. Clement felt it was a God-given gift to Greek culture which helped sort some order and truth from a patchwork of gleaned knowledge. If philosophy helped some in the discovery process, it gave him no problem, but truth is truth no matter how one approaches it. The truth comprised in faith is the food necessary for spiritual life. He wrote persuasively and is another who believed that the Old Testament must be read allegorically to make sense, but when done so he believed the fruits could match those of the philosophers.

Clement believed that all baptised Christians possess the Holy Spirit, facilitating salvation. The differences between individuals are down to the effort they make towards achieving higher perfection and moral strength. A pagan convert gains faith in the sense of what is necessary. A seasoned believer needs to go further in seeking what faith contains based on Christ's teaching, leading to a trusting belief rather than mere acceptance. This is the route to a genuine love of God which can lead to realising his promised vision and rendering believers like angels. It lifts the relationship with God far beyond the fear of punishment and desire for salvation to a real love and thirst for a closer knowledge and presence of him. In seeking this, celibacy and asceticism is not essential but it may help some. Living close to God in prayer kindles a warm relationship, kindness to strangers as well as friends, visible empathy which brings one closer to God than faith alone offers. This is why so many people have dedicated their lives to its pursuit.

Clement needed no examination of the relationship between the Logos, the Father and the Holy Spirit. The ideas of Irenaeus meant little to him; his was a religion based on a direct relationship, seeking personal closeness with God bordering on intimacy. This may be why this remarkably pure thinker and writer is rather side-lined by Western and some Orthodox Christianity. Or was it because he did not go out and about to teach as Christ had asked or that he was overshadowed by Origen who was to follow as a great teacher of the Eastern Greek Church. The Church that so loved Clement's writing in his time would come to regard him as suspect to the point of erroneous centuries later. The Roman Church side-lined Clement in the 17th century, but Anglicanism still regards him highly. It may be that Clement suffers for recounting it as he saw it, without academic rigour, but he was a great communicator. Eusebius fortunately preserved an account of Clement's life in his sixth book of the History of the Church.

Photios I, Ecumenical Patriarch of Constantinople in the late 9th century excommunicated Clement *post mortem,* for heretical thoughts or beliefs. In this, Photios drew from Clement's writings suggestion that the universe pre-dated creation, inconsistency with the Church's view of the Logos and the Holy Trinity, ambivalence towards Docetism and erroneous treatment of the creation of Eve and sexuality of angels. But he is now regarded as a saint in most of Orthodoxy as well as Anglicanism.

Origen (185-254 AD), was born in Alexandria, the first of the Church Fathers known to have Christian parents. His father, Leonidas was a prosperous Roman citizen and played a large part in his child prodigy's early education, but was imprisoned and martyred in 203. Origen was saved from a similar fate by his astute mother. Their home had been confiscated and ensuing poverty led to the family being split up. Origen benefitted from the patronage of a wealthy devout Christian lady who adopted him and ensured his education. He became passionately opposed to Gnosticism after rejecting the views of a co-adoptee called Paul. When he left that home he found a teaching job, supporting his birth mother and siblings with his earnings

Origen's academic education enabled him to make a living as a tutor. Since the persecution had closed Alexandria's catechetical school, his knowledge of Christianity was also much in demand, so he taught theology for no pay with such success that he came to the notice of the bishop. Bishop Demetrius. called on Origen at 18, to give up his paid work in teaching secular subjects in 203 to revive the school. Clement had succeeded its founder Pantaenus as the Principal in 190 and it had closed during Severus' persecution. The persecution seemed to be aimed more at converts to Christianity which may have left Origen at less risk. He sold his beloved library in return for a modest annuity and ran the religious school by day. He also learned Hebrew to aid his study of the original Old Testament and started work on *Hexapla,* his ambitious and complex comparison of previous translations of the Bible. For good measure, he studied pagan philosophy and attended lectures by Ammonius Sakkas on Neoplatonism. He met Heraclas (who later taught Plotinus referred to later) there. He was working all hours and living on a pittance as a committed ascetic and according to Eusebius the historian, he went to the extreme of castrating himself.

Origen visited Rome when Zephyranus was Bishop there and Caracella was Emperor. Some while after that, about 215, there was an uprising by some residents of Alexandria, which Caracella had forcibly subdued at the cost of considerable destruction, including closure of the school again and expelled all foreigners. Ambrose, a wealthy friend of Origen and a non-Christian foreigner moved to Caesarea in Palestine and Origen followed him at the invitation of Bishop Theocstistos of Caesarea, leaving his early pupil Heraclas in temporary charge of what was left of the school.

In Caesarea Origen lectured on the Bible. The bishops also invited him to preach on the scriptures, but his home Bishop Demetrius was uncomfortable with this and recalled him to Alexandria, as peace had been restored. One important lasting consequence of this was the conversion of his benefactor Ambrose, who went on to help Origen become probably the most prolific writer of his age. Ambrose set up a publishing workshop with seven shorthand writers, seven copyists and some expert calligraphers, from which came a commentary on John's Gospel and the book '*de Principis*', On First Principles. The mass of written record did no harm to Origen's lifetime and future standing. Origen's enhanced reputation saw him becoming the unofficial representative, arbiter and peacemaker of the Eastern Church even as a layman.

His view of Christ as the same substance as God was orthodox, but it is not clear whether he extended that to the Holy Trinity. Origen is reported as believing the Holy Spirit proceeded from the Son as the third phase of the unfolding Godhead, at odds with Orthodox wisdom and some gospel passages such as in Luke 1:35 and Matt 1:30, which clearly state that the Son of God was conceived by the power of the Holy Spirit. Possibly a misunderstanding, this was partly why some in the Church held a jaundiced view of Origen.

About 230 AD, Origen fell foul of Bishop Demetrius by accepting ordination as a presbyter by his friends the bishops of Caesarea and Jerusalem while visiting Greece, which was not canonically correct as bishops were not supposed to ordain anybody from another jurisdiction. Demetrius had been annoyed by the first incident when Origen preached in Caesarea, another diocese under another bishop, and by the story that Origen had in his youth castrated himself. Demetrius, incensed by this latest transgression, called a synod which banished Origen from Egypt with Rome's agreement about 232. Heraclas succeeded Origen as head of the catechetical school, and later succeeded Demetrius as Bishop of Alexandria.

Origen moved back to Caesarea in 230 and stayed there issuing frequent sermons and also writing scriptural commentaries on both New and Old Testaments until his death at 69 in 254, which was hastened by torture three years earlier under Emperor Decius' persecution. He left the memory of a very open teacher, who shared excellent rapport and trust with his students. One called Gregory Thaumaturgus spoke of this "divinely-inspired man" who "kindled in our hearts love of the divine Logos..."

Probably Origen's most famous work was his '*Hexapla*' (sixfold) – a huge exegetic comparative edition of the Old Testament in six columns comparing the early Hebrew text with:

- Secunda, a transliteration into the Greek alphabet,
- Aquila of Sinope's literal version,
- Symmachus' Greek translation, a revised edition of the Septuagint, LXX, marked up with variations from the original Hebrew version and
- Theodotion's revision of the LXX in 150 AD.
- Two other translations of the Psalms by unknown authors

This massive work began as a quest for the earliest divine revelation and his own theology from the Bible in which God spoke through his prophets. The sheer effort in this is impressive and he always encouraged his students to seek ultimate truth in the scriptures but to realise that God, the ultimate creator of all things is beyond the full comprehension of humans. Origen taught that God is omnipotent, of spiritual, not material nature, though he created all material things. His world is not constrained by the dimension of time as it is eternal. His begotten Son had always been a part of him and would for ever be so, but because Christians' knowledge of God has mainly come from indirect records of the Son's limited time on earth, they cannot be expected to have a full understanding of him and less still of the Holy Trinity. Hence genuine faith is a gift of God's grace and helps consolidate the truth and to understand better the Holy Spirit's messages in the Bible. Few people have put so much work and commitment into forming their view on these things.

Clement began with learning from the Bible and Origen took that to another level. Origen described the Old Testament as being "like a man – it has body, soul and spirit. The body is in its literal meaning, which anybody could understand; the soul is the moral message, clear to believers when explained; the spirit is in the allegorical reading". His real interest was to discern the underlying spiritual meaning, wherein lay difficulty, inconsistency and even incomprehensibility, demanding the support of faith.

Visions and ecstasy never featured large in Origen's personal religion. He still held reservations regarding Paul and the Gospels, especially John. He lived in the bible to a level beyond most other notable Christians and was generally accepted as one of the greatest Christian thinkers. At the fifth Ecumenical Council in Constantinople in the sixth century, various anathemas were tabled, perhaps the most serious being his apparent questioning of the Resurrection, though the Church may have been misled by the translation of his original statement on this. Nonetheless, he was rated by some as a heretic.

The Roman Catholic Church has been lukewarm on Origen and regards him more as an Ecclesiastical Writer than a Church Father or a saint. Pope Benedict XVI, an accomplished theologian, recently referred to him more warmly, but Origen's views on the pre-existence of souls, the final reconciliation of all creatures, possibly including Satan and his suggested subordination of God the Son to the Father were simply not in line with Christian orthodox teaching. To be fair, these matters all fall under Origen's own expressed umbrella 'beyond the full comprehension of humans'.

Cyprian (200-258 AD) was born in Carthage, studied law and was only converted in 246, living only twelve more years in which to make his name in Christianity. But this natural leader's studies and practice in law had prepared him to be an ecclesiastical statesman and he already enjoyed a good social standing and solid reputation. So he was soon on a steep upward trajectory in the Church and was appointed bishop within two years of his baptism, arousing resentment among some faithful long-serving fellow clerics. After a further two years, he was driven into hiding as Emperor Decius began his persecution in 250.

Following that relatively brief but intensely cruel Decian persecution, a controversial spiritual 'trade' in forgiveness developed, which was misused in similar fashion to indulgences in the future. During the persecution, many brave Christians who refused to offer sacrifice to the Emperor and therefore suffered torture and execution, signed certificates of 'credit' to members who had in effect apostatised or left the faith by offering sacrifice to save their lives. A form of logic had emerged that through their suffering, the strong had won credit beyond their debt, so the balance could be offered to weaker brethren by means of such certificates. The Church authorities were thus challenged in effectively assessing the credit value of honoured martyrs. It was a convenient tactic given the high numbers that had weakened and the Church could ill afford to lose, but it was open to obvious abuse. The manoeuvring involved would open the way to future schism with the rise of 'Donatism' which will be examined in the fourth century.

This was just the first of a few serious tests of Cyprian's statesmanship, in the face of resentment at his rapid rise in the hierarchy and compounded by the fact that by going into hiding he himself had dodged having to make that choice between offering sacrifice and possible martyrdom. There was a body of opinion in favour of leniency to the lapsers, which found a champion in a presbyter called Novatus, who travelled to Rome to present his case to a sympathetic, if confusingly named, Novatian, a bishop with a following. It suited Novatian to defy Bishop Cornelius, so a twin conflict arose – Novatus, Presbyter versus his bishop Cyprian in Carthage and Novatian, claimant versus Cornelius, incumbent Bishop of Rome.

Cyprian decided to start by excluding all voluntary lapsers from the faith, then allowing them to appeal. He would then consider each lapser's case on its merits, imposing commensurate penance, or if the lapser was a member of clergy, limiting their readmission to ministry. Cornelius took a similar line in Rome. But when a new persecution under Gallus threatened in 252, a Council of Bishops in 253 realised that the recanters needed to be kept on side to limit the chances of them repeating or passing on their weakness. All penitents showing remorse were offered amnesty. Former clerics could also return, but only as laymen.

The second test came when Stephen I was Bishop of Rome. Cyprian refused admission to the Church of people who had been baptised by heretics, insisting on their re-baptism. He argued that heretical ministers were by definition outside the Church and "No man can have God as his Father unless he has the Church as his mother." Stephen took a hard line against re-baptism and excommunicated those who offered it. Cyprian wrote directly to Faustius of Lyons whom he knew had sought that Marcianus of Arles be deposed for still refusing reconciliation of voluntary lapsers.

A further test confronted Cyprian as renewed persecution began under Emperor Valerian in 256. He was close to the proconsul but refused to pay homage or give sacrifice to pagan gods and loudly professed his loyalty to Christ. So he was initially banished to an outlying town for a year, but when he became terminally ill, a new proconsul put him under house arrest in his villa. Meanwhile, Valerian had issued orders for more severe penalties for uncooperative clerics. Cyprian was called before the proconsul, refused once more to bow to the Roman gods and was sentenced to death by the sword for crimes and leading a disloyal organisation. Cyprian responded simply,"Thanks be to God" and he was led outside where the sentence was carried out immediately.

Other Notable Names of the Time

While some of this does not relate immediately to Christianity, it is worth recording as background to the role that the Roman Empire played in both challenging and helping the faith. But along with the arts, spirituality in the Empire had subsided in the third century.

Plotinus (204-270 AD), was an exception. He revered Plato, so his works were categorised **Neoplatonism.** Not a very assertive man, he did rail against the Gnostics. He could not accept the world as basically evil; it was good, glorious; the beauty in nature and the majesty of the skies, especially at night and the harmony of creation are witness to this. Sincere reflection on these glories demands acceptance of a supreme creator. Who could imagine a new world beyond this or speak of the sinful fall of the cosmos or of repentance and punishments in hell? The ultimate source of the world was the One, the highest Good, the *Nous*, the 'supreme creator of the world'. The world was formed from random matter by *Logos* which sprang from *Nous* (addressing the old question "What was there before God's creation?"). So the world was the second stage of existence and the third was its soul, born of ideas. This scant coverage of what was a far deeper philosophy does him little justice, but to go deeper would diverge from the aim of this book.

Emperor Gallienus, who succeeded his father Valerian in 260, reversed his orders against the Christians and showed favour to Plotinus who had no wealth and mostly depended on living in friends' houses. The closest Plotinus came to his dream of setting up a community of philosophers was in gathering an international group of like-minded people in Rome to meet together frequently. Significant among them was Porphyry, who left some notes on this community, describing Plotinus as a philosophy teacher totally dedicated to the ideals of Plato. Deeply spiritual, he was neither an orator nor a gifted writer, but he was gifted teacher, exhibited self-effacing humility and little concern for his appearance or health and he came over as utterly sincere. He had no enemies but won many friends. Plotinus became seriously ill and died at the home of a friend outside the city in 270 AD.

Porphyry (c 234-305 AD), a fairly 'high-born' but grounded Phoenician Jew from Tyre, was affected by the various religions around Rome and was familiar enough with Christianity to attend Origen's lectures there. In his early days he was fascinated by magic, the occult, astrology and dabbled in exorcism which he linked with religion before encountering Plotinus. His own writing and oratory were better than those of Plotinus, he respected him as a superior philosopher and accepted all his teaching. He processed it so that he could communicate it better to others. His communication was excellent and pitched at a level that reasonably intelligent people could assimilate. He deduced the existence of individual souls which had characteristics and potential closer to God, the creator and ultimate good, than to the world. He accepted that the aim of one's life was to bring the soul to a state acceptable to God.

Porphyry's supreme God of the universe was the Greek God Zeus, with other gods related to different aspects of nature. He believed that the redemption of the soul required the attainment of the godly state through asceticism, vegetarianism and rejection of worldly pleasures, including marriage. The four principles of his own philosophical religion were faith, truth, love and hope, not far from those of Christianity. Yet Porphyry was obstinately hostile to Christianity – he found the idea of a son of God on earth, the crucifixion and resurrection irrational and inconceivable. As a proud rationalist and in spite of similarities in their philosophical thought processes and lifestyle he argued against Origen and fast-growing Christianity with the pen as his weapon. Christianity still continued to grow, although given the multiplicity of beliefs at the time, some followers retained parts of various faiths, mythologies or philosophies, known as syncretism. Many of these involved astrology or 'purification' practices such as celibacy, never proposed by Jesus but possibly influencing some Desert Fathers and early monastics.

Peace Helps Christianity Grow

There followed a period of relative peace for Christians into the beginning of the fourth century. By 284, as Diocletian became Emperor, the Christian faith was growing in acceptance and confidence and many who had lapsed in the face of the Decian persecution were again Christians. Meanwhile, the brave martyrs, many of whom had come from the influential upper classes, gained widespread recognition and celebration. That a top scholar such as Origen was amongst them impressed the Romans. That and the rising class status of Christians helped foster their greater participation in public life, all showing general acceptance, if not always agreement. By 300 AD, Christians had reached high offices in the administration and the army and were by now quite free to profess their faith. A sign of the changing atmosphere was the conversion of Emperor Diocletians' consort Prisca and daughter Valeria to Christianity, following which there was an eruption of church-building to accommodate the growing numbers of the faithful.

Defensiveness Against Heresies

Heresy is a word used quite selectively today as it is seen as drastic condemnation. In those early times, the Church readily reverted to its use to supress even quite mild questioning or variation of doctrines. The sufferings of the victims of persecution had reduced tolerance levels of any dubious theories which were seen as a threat to hard-won stability. This also led to over-use of the sanction of excommunication, an extreme measure of enormous consequence feared by any of the devout. It would continue for centuries to come. It held dangers to the Church being both a disincentive to theological exploration and a cause of resentment among genuine followers. The Church hierarchy already seemed one of fierce domination as distinct from one of service such as Christ, its founder who had preached love, mercy and forgiveness. This perhaps grew from its leaders' inexperience, inadequate training and hence defensiveness.

In mitigation, the background was different in those early days. The Church took its mission seriously and faced enormous difficulties in carrying it out, given the strength and potential violence of opposition. Also as has been seen, there were many persuasive false prophets and people interpreting the scriptures in ways which the Church could not accept. The most direct way in which to provide clear guidance was for the Church to agree its positions on various matters through the use of prayer, synods and Councils, invoking the guidance of the Holy Spirit then to use its network and influence to ensure their promulgation and protection. As the Church grew, reaching agreement in the first place became increasingly difficult, requiring humility and generosity from regional leaders to reach consensus. The Holy Spirit sometimes took second place to personal pride, regional and personal ambition or unyielding dogmatism. John Henry Newman in the 19th century admired the Alexandrian teaching based on "mystical principle" and he believed the need for pronouncement of dogma and doctrine was sadly forced upon the Church in the face of heresies. Some of the better known heresies are worth recalling and are shown in the box.

Summary of Some Early Heresies

Adoptionism (See Theodotus of Byzantium's Dynamism, Modalism and Sabellianism below)

Arianism (next century)

Docetism – held that Christ's body was not human but either a phenomenon or of real but celestial substance, and that therefore his sufferings were only apparent.

Dynamism – Theodotus; that God is one being, wholly indivisible, and of one nature and that the Son was not co-eternal with the Father, but essentially adopted (either at baptism or ascension) for the plans of God and for his own perfect life and works (variation of the adoptionist theory)

Gnosticism – there are two worlds, spiritual, good and physical, bad with a single deity, pure and holy. People consist of physical body and spiritual soul. One could try to improve the physical body by self-denial, but the only sure route to purity is death which releases the soul into the spiritual world.

Marcionism – there are two distinct deities – the Old Testament God of retribution (dark and evil) and the New Testament God of love (light and good).

Modalism (Sabellianism) – considers God to be one entity appearing and operating in the different modes of the Father, the Son, and the Holy Spirit (variation of the adoptionist theory).

Monarchianism (Noëtos of Smyrna supported by Praxeas Asia Minor) – the one and only God had become flesh and walked on earth as Jesus Christ.

Montanism (Montanus etc.) Montanus accepted the Old Testament verbatim and claimed to be the last prophet before the second coming. He also said he was part of the Holy Trinity of the Father, Son and 'Paraclete'(advocate or helper), or Holy Spirit. See more below.

Novationism – Anti-Cyprian dogma of Novation that lapsers should never be readmitted to Holy Communion.

Sabellianism (Modalism) - considers God to be one entity appearing and operating in the different modes of the Father, the Son, and the Holy Spirit (variation of the adoptionist theory).

Montanism

During the Decian persecutions (249-251), the Montanists took a far harder line with the 'lapsers' than the Roman Church, thereby increasing mutual antagonism. Montanus' growing movement, described in the previous chapter, openly encouraged female preachers, which raised eyebrows though there was no formal prohibition of this in the wider Church. Sometimes compared to the charismatic churches of today, its followers believed the apocalypse was imminent and the promised New Jerusalem would descend in or near a small town called Pepuzza in Phrygia, where its headquarters had duly been located. Montanists had ascetic tendencies, believing that celibacy was a mark of genuine Christianity and fasting was valuable spiritual preparation for the approaching second coming. Some of them went to extremes by selling homes and belongings and Montanists attracted ridicule for always living for the apocalypse and seeming to desire martyrdom. It had still successfully spread to Rome, Gaul and Africa. Some of their preaching and practise bore similarities to the Church, but not Montanus' claims to his involvement in the Holy Trinity. Their prophets made dubious claims. Tertullian showed sympathy for them but Montanism was ultimately condemned and declared a heretical sect by synods in Asia Minor, invalidating its baptism.

Asia Minor-born Bishop Irenaeus, Bishop of Lyons and Vienne wrote to Eleutheros, bishop of Rome, pleading for him to over-rule the Asia Minor synods. Nothing came of it although Rome and Carthage, where there was wide acceptance of the Asia Minor view, were in dispute. The sect's influence gradually waned back to the region around Phrygia during the fourth century and died out altogether in the fifth.

Sabellianism

One of the first North African mini-schisms based on Christology arose in in the late 250s. It related to the nature of Jesus Christ, denying the Holy Trinity. A controversial 'Sabellian' theology emerged in the city of Ptolemais in Libya, which claimed that the one and only God was unitary and had visited earth physically in the person of Jesus Christ to redeem people by his death and resurrection. This conflicted with the Logos theory accepted by most Christians, whereby the second member of the Holy Trinity was the Logos, present in God and who played an important part in the creation and arrangement of the universe with the Father and the Holy Spirit.

Bishop Dionysius of Alexandria, a past pupil of Origen, was drawn in to arbitrate and eventually stated that the Son of God was not identical with the Father; he was a separate being who sprang from the creative act of the Father. A complaint on the matter was then referred to another Bishop Dionysius, of Rome, who held a synod which found firmly against the Sabellians and informed Dionysius of Alexandria of the verdict. The latter wrote an apology (260), admitting that he could have expressed his views better. He held firmly to the view that the Son and Holy Spirit were individual entities (*hypostases*), both of whom are eternal and one in essence (*homoousios*) with God, in accord with the teachings of Origen. His candour and humble acceptance of dissent and his own error were quite exceptional in the history of learned people in the Church hierarchy and served to underline the growing closeness of Alexandria with Rome.

Alexandria and Antioch were both proud and ancient cities as well as long-term strong rivals. In AD 260, Paul of Samosota (200-275) was consecrated Bishop of Antioch. He was thought to be a believer in Monarchianism. His teachings reflected Adoptionism and he made no secret of his antipathy and rejection of Origen's teachings. Dionysius was ageing by now but many other Eastern bishops, most of whom owing their learning to Origen, found common cause against Paul and gathered in Antioch. They came to meet with Paul several times over the next few years. After the final synod in 268, they deposed Paul as a heretic appointing Domnus, son of Paul's predecessor Demetrian in his place. Domnus' appointment was initially deemed invalid as Antioch was ruled by Zenobia, Queen of Palmyra and only on her defeat by Aurelius in 272 was Paul deposed.

Most of this was recorded by the principal recorder of early Church history, Eusebius of Caesarea, who will be mentioned later. His work was helped by the wealthy patron, Pamphilus, who had taught in Caesarea and then collected Origen's writings and copied nearly all of them out personally towards the end of the 3rd century. He preserved these in an impressive library centred on the remains of Origen's collection, much of which had been damaged or ruined during Decius' persecution.

CHAPTER 6

4th Century

Pontiffs

Marcellinus 296-304
Eusebius 309-310
Miltiades 311-314
Sylvester I 314-335
Mark Jan-Oct 336

Julius I 337-352
Liberius 352-366
Damasus I 366-384
Siricius 384-399
Anastasius 399-401

Roman Emperors

Diocletian 286-305, Emperor East
Maximium 286-305, Emperor West.
Galerius 305-311, Emperor East
Constantus Chlorus, Emperor West 305-306.
Valerius Severus, Emperor West 306-307.
Constantine the Great, 306-324, Emperor West, then 324-337, sole Emperor
Maxentius claimed Caesar 306, supported by his father Maximian 307.
Licinius 308-324 Emperor East.
Licinius made Valerian Valens in 313 and Martinian in 317 Emperors West.
Maximinus II 311-313 claimed Emperor East.
Constantine II 337-340, Emperor West.
Constantius II 337-340 Emperor East, then 356-361 Emperor East and West.
Constans I 337-350 Emperor Central, then 340-350 West.
Vetrianus March-December 350.
Julian 360-361 Emperor West, 361-363 East and West.
Jovian 363-364 Emperor East & West
Valentinian I 364-375 Emperor West
Valens Emperor East 364-378; Gratian (Valentinian's son) 367-375 junior Augustus
Gratian 375-383 co-emperor West. Assassinated
Valentinian II co-emperor West 375-392.
Magnus Maximus and son Victor 383-388 co-emperors Britannia and Gaul.
Theodosius I 392-395
Honorius 395-423

This century begins as something of a roller-coaster in relations between the Roman Empire and the Catholic Church, so this chapter will include a condensed coverage of the politics of both. The apparently favourable outcome brought with it wider power and responsibilities for the Christian Church but would introduce conflicts between its spiritual and temporal duties into the future. North Africa remained a powerhouse of philosophy and theology and considerable controversy was taking place there, related to diverse views on Christology and the Holy Trinity with sub-plots of ambition, leading to some polarisation between eastern and western bishops. Two particular developments were the Arian Controversy and the supportive rise of Emperor Constantine with his Catholic mother.

A milestone for Christianity was reached early in the fourth century as Armenia, a mountainous Kingdom surrounding Mount Arafat, became the first sovereign nation formally to adopt Christianity as its official religion in 301 AD.

Diocletian Persecution, Mini-Schisms

The 40 year lull in persecution since Valerian, seemed to set the stage for further entrenchment of Christianity within the structures of the Roman Empire, but history has a habit of springing surprises. In 303 AD, Galerius, an avowed anti-Christian of Bulgarian origin urged Eastern leader Diocletian to destroy a church in Nicomedia, near Byzantium, in retaliation for an alleged arson attack on the Imperial Palace.

Diocletian was more of an intellectual than a warrior, but unlike his Christian wife and daughter, he held no love for Christians, as he leaned towards sustaining the Roman state religion. So he issued the edict and responded to ensuing widespread protests with the most intense persecution of Christians to date. There was widespread slaughter especially in the Eastern Empire and in some regions in Anatolia entire Christian populations were wiped out. Four years later, this bloodshed subsided but harsh new penalties were introduced for Christians refusing to offer sacrifice to the Roman Gods, which consisted of crippling one leg and blinding one eye, followed in the case of continued refusal by forfeit of all property and a life sentence to work in quarries in Palestine or Silesia. The Romans re-established priesthood in their own religion and began rebuilding temples in order to strengthen their position. Diocletian abdicated following the failure of his economic policy and was succeeded in 305 by Galerius.

Christianity in North Africa suffered a series of mini-schisms during the fourth century. A new Bishop of Alexandria, Peter, consecrated in 300 AD, was imprisoned early on during Diocletian's persecution but continued to run his diocese from captivity. Another Egyptian bishop, **Meletius** from Lykopolis (now Asyut) in the south, seized the opportunity and travelled widely to cover Peter's flock and those of other imprisoned northern bishops as well as his own diocese. He also consecrated in those dioceses new presbyters and deacons in churches that had no clergy. This was well outside his jurisdiction and four other bishops complained to him. Meletius ignored their protests and went to Alexandria where he persuaded many deacons and presbyters to support him. Alexandria was the accepted lead diocese in Egypt, so he was effectively promoting himself in place of the imprisoned Peter. Two presbyters, Isidoros and Arius helped him before he was imprisoned himself in 305 AD. Peter wrote warning his followers to have no more to do with Meletius.

Before the end of the Diocletian persecution, Peter issued instructions to his presbyters and deacons regarding the penance to be served by Christians who had weakened in the face of it. As after past persecutions, there were different levels of penance – those who had agreed immediately to offer sacrifice to the Roman gods were to spend a year outside Communion with the Church before returning and being given penance. Clerics who had denied the faith but later given themselves up were to be granted absolution and a return to the Church after penance but were not allowed back into office. His orders were entirely in line with the established practice of the Church, but were regarded as lenient by those who had suffered severely from the persecution, many of whom had even welcomed it as a chance to display their absolute commitment. Peter pointed to the example of the Apostles, demonstrating that even they had shown flight from persecution and that Christians should be reminded of just one example of this every time they heard a cock crow.

As always when people feel they have not been given due recognition, factions develop of extreme fundamentalists versus main-stream moderates and even while in the quarries, there was a divide between the fundamentalist 'Church of the Martyrs' and the orthodox followers of Bishop Peter. So, in 311 AD, when the quarries and prisons released Christians, the debilitating punishments they had endured meant that there were many extremists among them who were ready to side with Bishop Meletius, who opposed Peter's decision, set up independent Christian churches and began ordaining new clerics. The mainstream Church objected and before his own execution in 311, Bishop Peter pronounced their baptisms invalid, meaning excommunication of the recipients. Meletius still had 28 bishops by 325 AD. The strain of the persecutions had led to this Meletian mini-schism and another one, Donatism, further west.

By 310 AD, cripples of the persecution in some of the quarries had set up makeshift churches there, but in that year, they again began to be killed or tortured. Their impressive forbearance and the Holy Spirit had kept the Church alive during this worst period of persecution and Eusebius of Caesarea, the historian recorded in his History of Christianity that in April 311, soon before he died, Emperor Galerius issued an edict of partial tolerance of Christians, admitting that this act of clemency was in recognition of their sheer bravery in refusing to accept Roman practice. He licenced Christianity and church worship so long as they included in their prayers to their God the well-being of the Emperor and the Empire. In fact it is believed that Constantine (Emperor 306-337), then Emperor in the West, had pushed for cessation of the persecution on account of its failure being not only an issue of division, but an embarrassment to the empire. Maximinus II was now the leading Augustus in the East (310-312) and issued the orders, whereupon partially blind Christians limped out of prisons and quarries all over the Eastern Mediterranean.

In AD 311 another schism grew among the indigenous Berber Christians in Numidia, followers of Bishop Donatus Magnus. This was another result of Diocletian's persecution, during which the local Governor had been fairly lenient and only required Christians to hand over holy books to escape punishment. Those who refused, mainly the poor, became known as 'rigorists' and were persecuted. They resented those who yielded, scorning them as '*traditores*'.

When a moderate archdeacon, Caecilian was consecrated as the new Bishop of Carthage by an alleged *traditor*, the rigorists, who believed the Church should be one of saints and intolerant of sinners, consecrated their own bishop, Donatus, starting the **Donatist Schism.** Emperor Constantine asked the bishop of Rome, Miltiades to set up a Council to consider the Donatists' case, for which he loaned the Lateran family's Palace in Rome in 313. Donatus appeared in person as defendant and the Council found against him and his followers. Two more appeals were heard, one heard in Arles a year later, then another in Milan. The dispute rumbled on for a decade with some serious conflict in Numidia. These zealots had suffered severe persecution for their faith and felt aggrieved that many had 'bought' themselves relief. The Donatists never spread but continued in separate practice, claiming to be 'the only true Church' until overwhelmed by the forces of Islam a few centuries later. Their view was understandable, but they too had set a higher standard than even the apostles, overlooking Christ's teaching of love, mercy and forgiveness.

Arian Controversy

Meanwhile, a serious new schismatic controversy was brewing along the North African coast. Arius (c250-336), a Libyan theologian of Berber descent studied at the Antioch school and became well connected in the East. He teamed up with Lucius and Meletius in the Egyptian schism against Bishop Peter I of Alexandria. Following reconciliation, Peter ordained Arius as a deacon in 306. But it soon became clear Arius' teachings on Christology were not in line with Christian belief. He regarded Jesus Christ as neither fully God nor fully man. He referenced John's Gospel (14:28), quoting Christ "You heard me say I am going away and I shall return. If you loved me, you would be glad that I am going to the Father, for the Father is greater than I." From this he was not the first to conclude that the Son of God had not always existed, but was created by God the Father. Arius also considered the Holy Spirit to be a created being or a high-ranking angel. So in addition to an unacceptable Christology, he denied the concept of the Holy Trinity.

Peter I's successor in Alexandria, Alexander (bishop 313-326) could not accept this Arianism, though he would have preferred to handle his disagreement discreetly. But his hand was forced by the Meletians who supported Arius' view and felt that Alexander's orthodoxy was questionable as his theology was close to that of Origen. Alexander also carelessly modified Origen's logic in asserting that the arrival on earth of the Son and his death for the salvation of mankind made for a closer relationship that amounted to a 'deification' of mankind. This helped Arius to marshal support in defence of his cause.

In 318 AD, a synod of most of the bishops in Egypt rejected Arius and his followers. But Arius' scattered friends rallied behind him after he wrote to them and even journeyed to Palestine to argue against some flaws in the logic of Alexander's theology. Over the next five or six years, the split within the Egyptian Church deepened and spread to affect the broader Eastern Church, not helped by Emperor (of the East) Licinius and his anti-Christian sentiments and action. When Constantine overthrew Licinius, the new Emperor lost no time in addressing these issues as he linked the unity of the Christian Church closely to that of the Empire. He regarded the differences between the Christian factions as theological detail rather than key matters of faith. This approach was resented in the Church where his adversaries believed the conflict was not one of detail, but went to the very heart of the faith and saw Constantine as trying to impose political convenience on their religion. Alexander also resented the fact that Arius was seemingly being considered as of equivalent status. Constantine was falling foul of Eastern culture – by no means the last Western leader to do so.

A synod was held in Ancyra (now Ankara) in 314 with the aim of agreeing the penalties and penance for the lapsers during the Diocletian/Lycinian persecution, so as to prevent a repeat of the aggravation and inconsistencies arising from previous ones. Although not well attended, the synod came up with a list of canons mainly concerning errant clerics, giving guidance that usually involved spending specified times as a hearer then a prostrator before receiving the Eucharist again. Not all could expect to regain their posts.

Constantine

The leadership of the Roman Empire had been shared early in this century between four main characters involved – Licinius, Maximinus, Maxentius and Constantine, an untenable situation. Constantine, co-emperor of the West with Maxentius, was the son of Constantius I and Helena, a Christian now regarded as a saint and credited with discovering the true cross. Constantine strongly supported his mother's Christianity. His sister Constantia was married to Licinius who shared rule of the East with Maximinus. Maxentius in Rome sided with Maximinus sensing danger from the Constantine dynasty.

Constantine marched an experienced army south over the Alps to Rome, having prayed to the Godhead and Jesus Christ for victory and decorated his soldiers' shields with the Christian chi-ro monogram, ☧. Maxentius died in losing the battle, so Constantine became sole ruler of the Western Empire and was greeted as the supreme Augustus by the Senate. Maximinus eventually attacked Licinius but lost that battle and his life, leaving Licinius as sole ruler of the Eastern Empire beyond the mouth of the Danube. In 324 AD, Constantine became sole Emperor of the whole Roman Empire after defeating and imprisoning Licinius. As well as any true conviction he had, Constantine recognised the appeal of a single religion with a single God. Christianity also had the practical advantage to him that it could encourage unity in his Empire. So from 313 AD onwards, Christian worship was officially tolerated within the Roman Empire. Constantine's faith is not so certain but his astute application of support proved a godsend to the Church.

However such apparent benefits usually come at a price. This would not be fully realised until about the 8th century. Whilst imperial protection helped the Christian faith grow, it fundamentally changed its operation and governance as well as its perception from outside the Roman Empire with a hint of colonialism. This was perhaps the origin of Roman Catholicism later being perceived as a Western rather than a universal Church, 'Catholic' meaning 'universal'. Christianity had penetrated most of the known world, though only to a limited and fragile extent to the east and south, which included Arabia. Another potential change in governance in the Church would be that its leaders would have an eye over their shoulders to the emperor when making decisions, even some regarding faith and morals or when selecting a pope. This raised the danger of the focus of motivation and mission of the Church becoming wider than that of Jesus Christ.

Constantine was pragmatic and innovative. Realising that the centre of gravity of the empire now lay to the East of Rome, he therefore considered building a new capital on the plain of Troy in Turkey. Construction had just begun when he apparently had a dream that he interpreted as an instruction from God to build his new capital at Byzantium, a far more suitable location strategically, guarding the entrance to the Bosphorus. The building process lasted some years before its eventual ceremonial opening in 330 AD. He also built himself a palace near the new city, now renamed Constantinople. His empire became known as the Byzantine Empire, which would last until 1453.

That the centre of gravity of Christianity had indeed moved eastwards was borne out by the fact that the first seven full Ecumenical Councils of the Church would be held either in Constantinople or Anatolia.

Following his triumph over Licinius, Constantine anticipated a fairly clear period of consolidation ahead, helped by his manifest sympathy towards Christians. But he had reckoned without the simmering Arian controversy which would grow into a serious and widespread rift within the Eastern Church. Rival bishops and learned theologians would line up with authority on opposing sides.

Meanwhile, Alexandria went through its own evolution of leadership in the Church in Egypt. The presbyters traditionally elected the lead bishop from among their number, but Bishop Alexander had opened the post beyond the 'inner circle' and would nominate one such, Athanasius to succeed him (AD 328) as head of the Egyptian Church. The popular Arius was defrocked in 321. In his protests he quoted from Origen, among others as well as the scriptures in his defence. Arius attracted widespread following within the Church.

First Council of Nicaea

By 325, Constantine was tiring of the numerous schisms in the Eastern Church, some of which had resulted directly from Licinius' persecution. He engaged the help of Bishop Ossius of Cordoba, who visited rivals Antioch and Alexandria to explore common ground for possible reconciliation but was faced with Middle-Eastern intractability. So Constantine called the first Ecumenical General Council to agree broadly acceptable definitions of Christian beliefs and practice including a clear majority Church view and action on Arianism. It was held at Nicaea, where his Imperial Palace could accommodate a large gathering. A similar approach had largely succeeded against the Donatists (in Rome, 313) and this time he decided to participate personally, underlining his wish for both political and religious unity in the Empire. This novel combination also opened the potential for centralising authority within the Church, otherwise unlikely at this stage of its growth. This council in 325 was to prove a masterstroke, a milestone in the Church's definition of its beliefs and organisation, also an important precedent for universal decrees of the Church.

About three hundred Eastern bishops by far outnumbered a disappointing ten or so from the West (though many from the West had sent delegates), perhaps because the Western bishops did not feel as directly involved in the Arian controversy. For impartiality, joint presidents of the council were Bishops Ossius and Alexander I of Alexandria. Constantine took pains to demonstrate his respect for the bishops as "priests of God and servants of Our Lord and Saviour", clearly conveying the new era which raised the Church to a higher level of dignity and influence. He took his place of honour on a golden throne at the end of the grand hall and parallel rows of Church representatives lined the length, facing each other. Eusebius, the local Bishop of Nicomedia opened proceedings with a welcome and thanks to the Emperor. Constantine replied expressing hope that this council may match military defeats of the persecutors by victory over dissension within the Church leading to unity, peace and concord for the whole world. He spoke in Latin to emphasise that this was as an important state occasion as well as a religious one, although ensuing discussions were mainly in Greek, with which more of the Africans were familiar.

Business began with the crucial debate on the divinity of Christ and the issue of the Holy Trinity. Bishop Ossius proposed the Greek term *homoousios* (of the same substance) to describe the essential nature of Father and Son, his logic being "If there is one God and Christ is God, he must be God in the same sense that the Father is God." The Cappadocians developed this into "There is but one substance in the Trinity, one essential stuff of Godhead." One cannot, in other words separate the creator of all things from the source of salvation, thus Christ must be divine. This was accepted by all except the Arians, who did not believe that Jesus, *logos,* was an integral part of an eternal Trinity. Athanasius was secretary and advisor to Bishop Alexander at the council and his dogged opposition to Arius was a major contributor to the content of the first part of the Nicene Creed which was one of the enduring results of this council.

There was then discussion on Church organisation and discipline with special reference to coping with the separatist Meletians. A compromise decision was taken that Meletius could retain his title of bishop but should stay within his city of Lycopolis, though any clergy who had been ordained by him or his followers had to be re-ordained and confirm their acceptance of the authority of Bishop Alexander. This resulted in partial reconciliation of affected clergy but also in the removal of some powers from Meletian bishops. Though Alexander was not overly content with the compromise, he was partly mollified by a clear canon from the Council confirming that the patriarchate of Alexandria extended to cover all of Egypt, Libya and its eastern coastal region, the Pentapolis. This carried the mark of Constantine's negotiating skill and elevated Alexandria to a level approaching that of the Roman patriarchate. However, Meletians and Arians continued to agitate which would lead Constantine to reconvene the General Council in Nicaea late in 327.

The Easter Controversy

Another contentious subject at Nicaea was to resolve the determination of a date for Easter. The argument had been between continued reliance on the Jewish calendar and the simpler Roman approach. It was apparently resolved by endorsing the latter which had been in common use in Rome and Alexandria. Easter was henceforward to be a Sunday in a lunar month chosen according to Christian criteria rather than as defined by Jews. This and a demand for universal conformity were the only rules for Easter laid down by the council. But no actual method for calculation of the date was defined, leaving most regions carrying on as before, resulting in different dates of celebrating Easter, leaving the matter unsettled.

Different bishops had been celebrating Easter on different dates. Some chose the fourteenth day or the day of the full moon in the month of Nisan in the Jewish lunar calendar, believing this was the day on which Christ was crucified. Nisan is the 7th month of the Jewish calendar year, the first month of their ecclesiastical year and falls in the March-April period of the Gregorian calendar. Some opted for the following Sunday, while others sought to sever the link with the Jewish calendar altogether. Since Nicaea, the Western Church has celebrated Easter on the Sunday immediately after the first full moon following the Spring equinox, fixed as 21st March. So it can vary from 22nd March to 25th April. The Eastern Orthodox Churches accepted the formula, but now they continue to use the Julian calendar whereas the West adopted the Gregorian, so the Orthodox celebration takes place later, between 4th April and 8th May.

Another canon arising from the council was the affirmation of Rome's primacy in cases of regional or doctrinal dispute; another was confirmation of the close link between Alexandria and Rome and their agreement regarding the date of Easter. Some Eastern bishops published a separate set of findings, one of which disputed the validity of the unprecedented Western predominance especially over some issues that only concerned the East. For example they condemned a number of prominent bishops and showed no change of heart towards Athanasius and Marcellus. They also condemned some beliefs regarding the Trinity as heretical and issued their own dating of Easter based on the Jewish Passover.

Church Feast Days and Other Canons of Nicaea

Easter had initially been the only Holy Day, although Holy Week began as now with Palm Sunday, celebrating Jesus' final entry to Jerusalem when he was greeted by the welcoming crowd, many of whom would some days later be calling for his execution. The forty day Lenten fast was observed in the West, while only Good Friday or sometimes up to forty hours from Maundy Thursday was the extent of the fast in the East until Athanasius brought Lent to Egypt in AD 337 from his exile in Tréves.

Pentecost (Whitsunday) was added as a Holy Day, falling about 50 days after Easter. Christmas was added in the West in the 330s as a fixed feast, its date being chosen by when the sun started rising again. In the East, later in the century, the Epiphany was added on the twelfth day after Christmas as the celebration of Christ's baptism and became a major feast in the West to mark the Magi, the Three Kings. Over time, other dates were selected to celebrate major events and figures in the Church such as Saints Peter and Paul, All Saints and All Souls which still vary from region to region.

The delegates also discussed the matter of the celibacy of the clergy that had been recommended at a Council of Elvira in 306 (perhaps the first written reference to this subject). The idea was strongly opposed by Bishop Paphnutius of Egypt, who had chosen not to marry, but argued passionately that apart from being too rigorous it would be unwise in that such a rule would serve no better purpose than to create many sinners among the clergy and thus damage to the Church (which in hindsight seems like prophetic wisdom). The proposal was thus shelved.

Among other new church laws (canons) agreed at the 325 Council were the following:

- prohibition of self-castration.
- establishment of a minimum term for preparation of catechumens (persons studying for baptism).

- prohibition of the presence of a younger woman in the house of a cleric to avoid suspicion.
- confirmation of long-established jurisdiction over large regions to bishops of Alexandria, Rome and Antioch and recognition of honorary rights of the see of Jerusalem.
- prohibition of usury among the clergy.
- abolition of kneeling on Sundays and during the Pentecost (the fifty days commencing at Easter). Standing was the normative posture for prayer at this time and remains so among the Eastern and Orthodox Christians. Kneeling was considered appropriate only for penitential prayer, as distinct from the festive nature of Eastertide and its remembrance every Sunday. This canon was intended to ensure uniformity of practice.

Many of the outcomes of this high profile and historic Council were ambiguous or unsatisfactory, which may be a reflection on the limited effectiveness of a non-Church chairman without a grip of the subtleties, even though there was no doubting Constantine's power and influence at the actual meetings. Yet Nicaea I remains highly influential in today's Christian prayers, practices and beliefs. The new creed is believed to have been produced here, though it has undergone some important changes through the ages.

The second gathering, in 327, was again led by Constantine and culminated in the settlement of disputes with Arians and the Meletians, all of whom accepted the Nicene Creed, given that its ambiguity offered sufficient flexibility to suit several theological variations. So Constantine was satisfied with the outcome. It was however to prove a missed opportunity of unimaginable importance to the Church as the resulting creed neither clearly negated Arius' views, nor acknowledged that the whole concept of the Holy Trinity was beyond full human understanding. The theologians present appear not to have given matters profound consideration, which may be understandable – they mainly represented the Eastern Church, which still bore the consequences of persecution and now found themselves faced with this majestic occasion and the prospect of peace and unity with the Emperor's authority behind them. Nevertheless, the results would not only lead to further short term disputes but also more durable arguments and schisms far into the future. In nearly all cases these conflicts arose either from individual attempts at explaining the unexplainable or from human pride or lack of Christian understanding or any combination.

Athanasius, Church Father

Athanasius is attributed with the 'Athanasian Creed', the *'Quicumque vult'* (Whosoever wishes). Its main statement is "we worship one God in Trinity, and Trinity in Unity; neither confounding the Persons, nor dividing the Essence." and "in this Trinity none is before, or after another; none is greater, or less than another. But the whole three Persons are coeternal, and coequal. So in all things, the Unity in Trinity, and the Trinity in Unity, is to be worshipped."

Following Bishop Alexander's death in 328, Athanasius, born in 296 and avid reader of the scriptures, was elected to succeed him as **Bishop of Alexandria** (328-373). Alexander had noticed him as a young man and employed him as secretary before ordaining him deacon in 321. Regarded by some as the last of the Church Fathers, and a prominent Church figure in this century, his episcopate would be turbulent, spanning 45 years punctuated by five periods of exile and several escapes from assassination attempts. Initially he visited widely, including hermits and monks in the desert, one of which was Pachomius, who would be helpful later. The Meletians spread dissension and false claims against Athanasius, which annoyed Constantine since he had worked hard at the Council for peace between the factions. He called a Synod in 334 to look into the list of accusations assembled by Arians against Athanasius. Their allegations included bribery of the Emperor's messenger; sacrilege when he sent a presbyter to apprehend another which resulted in a scuffle that caused damage to a Church and a communion chalice; and more. The synod was held at a royal villa near Nicomedia in the New Year 332. Athanasius was judged innocent and returned to Egypt the following March with a document declaring the allegations untrue and extolling him as innocent and as a godly person which was intended to moderate anticipated local hostility towards him.

Constantine warned the Meletians (now led by Meletius' successor, John Archaphos), against a repeat of such behaviour. Arius had a tense relationship with the emperor but he confidently suggested to him that if Athanasius continued to refuse to admit him, he should be free to set up a church of his own. This was anathema to Constantine in his earnest quest for unity, so he threatened heavy tax penalties on any such organisation, ordered the destruction of Arius' writings and the death penalty for anyone found with copies. Strangely, Constantine about the same time invited Arius to visit the court and prove personally to the emperor the validity of his faith.

Emboldened by this, Meletius' successor John Archaphos, raised an accusation that Athanasius had murdered a bishop called Arsenius. A favoured deacon was sent by Athanasius and found Arsenius alive and well in a monastery, but apparently sympathetic to Archaphos. Bishop Arsenius was brought to Tyre, where the local Bishop Paul confirmed his identity. When Constantine heard of this, he threatened the Meletians with state proceedings in the event of any similar deceptions in future.

The see of Antioch, a persistent rival of Alexandria began to lose its high level of influence towards 330 AD as its Bishop Eustathios was deposed and deported to Thrace at Constantine's command. He had a strong following in Antioch and his dismissal led to a regional division of loyalties. A synod of Antioch was called and Eusebius of Caesarea, who had recently declined to move there to fill the vacancy left by Eustathios, was the lead delegate.

Bishop Eusebius of Nicomedia (not to be confused with Eusebius of Caesarea), who had led the Arians at Nicaea, later demanded that Arius be reinstated and he won Constantine's support. Athanasius remained an implacable opponent to this, but also faced further accusations of violence towards some bishops.

Meanwhile, Constantine had ordered Bishop Makarius of Jerusalem to destroy a temple to Aphrodite and build the basilica of the Holy Sepulchre in its place next to the rock of Golgotha where Christ was laid to rest and Constantine planned for its consecration on the 30th anniversary of his appointment. He also planned to celebrate it with another Grand Council on the lines of that held ten years previously in Nicea.

But he wanted to ensure order within the Church before such an event and to that end arranged a synod at Tyre at which Eusebius of Nicomedia would preside as head of the Eastern Church and test the case against Athanasius. Constantine's Consul Dionysius was sent with a guard to ensure order and with instructions to imprison any of the accused who resisted. This synod began in July 335 and the Meletian bishops were ranged against those loyal to Athanasius. Uproar ensued during which Athanasius slipped away from Tyre and made his way to Constantinople to seek imperial justice. In his absence he had been found guilty and it was recommended that Athanasius be brought before the Imperial Court of Justice.

In September 335, the new Holy Sepulchre church at Golgotha was consecrated amidst celebrations. Constantine ordered the reinstatement of Arius in Alexandria before returning to his capital for further anniversary celebrations. Athanasius obtained an audience with him as his caravan travelled and won him over with his charm, leading Constantine to call yet another synod in Constantinople. The very next day, the anti-Athanasius Eusebians had an urgent audience with the Emperor and told him a concocted story that Athanasius planned to block the shipping of corn from Alexandria to Constantinople, great quantities of which were needed daily. Such a move would soon cause famine and in a fit of rage, Constantine immediately banished Athanasius to Tréves without further hearing.

He ignored passionate appeals from Alexandria including those from the reclusive but well-known ascetic and saintly Antony, who argued that Constantine had no right to support such emotional and partisan judgements in the name of the Church. John Archaphos tried to take Athanasius' place but this was strongly opposed, so the Emperor exiled him in the interests of peace, leaving Alexandria leaderless.

Arius died about that time, while Constantine was distracted by greater affairs of state, having to oversee his two young sons' battles to defend the Empire's frontiers – Constantine II to the North from the Alemanni and then the Goths; Constantius to the East against the Persians over the River Euphrates. In 337, Constantine became terminally ill and was baptised a Christian just before his death aged 65. He was buried among the images of the apostles in the rotunda of the Church of the Apostles in Constantinople, built at his command for that purpose. The site is now occupied by the Fatih Mosque.

Constantine's legacy

The differences in views between the relatively sparse intellectual thinkers of the first three centuries regarding the nature of the Christian God and their conclusions on Christ's message demonstrate the likely inadequacies and pitfalls to befall human institutional religion. But the apostles' task had been passed down the generations. The first inklings of significant geographical differences in thinking regarding the Church on earth were arising from theologians in the two main areas of Christianity in Constantine's time, West and East. Each felt pride of place and their eventual divergence related more to culture and humanity than to spirituality, although each remained Christ-based.

Despite the confusions and disputes already mentioned, the importance of Constantine to the spread and respectability of Christianity within his empire was enormous and he had applied imperial funds generously for building or rebuilding countless churches. Lacking similar support, the established pagan religions soon fell away. Constantine was influenced from childhood by his mother in support of Christianity and he always believed he was destined for greatness. He felt empowered by God, believing that Christ brought peace to earth, which made him feel competent to chair Councils and intervene in Church disputes. He was broad-minded in accepting other religions, holding always integrity and unity of the empire foremost in his mind. His unconventional interplay of Church and state served both parties' temporal interests albeit sometimes raising alarm regarding the spiritual.

With the benefit of hindsight we may see that this laid the ground for future political power play and self-interest among Church leaders, though that may well have happened anyway. The Nicene Creed certainly left a disputable legacy which would give rise to future difficulties for the Church. When the rivalry and manoeuvrings of many Church leaders over the ages are examined, it could reasonably be argued that they would have had less success without Constantine's intervention. In keeping with his intrinsic creativity and attraction to the East and some of its customs, he had a tendency to make rapid intuitive decisions rather than consult broadly and follow the letter of Roman law. As a natural leader and decisive manager, his decisions seemed more often to be right than wrong. He never fully embraced the faith, but was known to pray regularly and had confidence that God was guiding him in leadership, though he was fallible as displayed in many of his impromptu decisions and changes of mind. It was only at the very end of his life that he was baptised and he received absolution.

Constantine provided a legal basis for Church possessions through a law in 321 AD qualifying the Church to hold and transfer property. He then started a trend for significant donations to the Church in gifting it with the Lateran Palace. This was followed over the years by wealthy families of Roman nobility whose names were eternalised on properties and lands given to the Church, which became known as the 'Patrimonial Possessions of St Peter'.

He restored and protected the unity of the Roman Empire and although he had reached the pinnacle of power by military competence and success, Constantine eventually initiated the process of separating the civil administration from the military which had been a wish of his predecessor Diocletian. This included a flatter command structure in the military, reducing the risk of a military coup but carried with it increased defence costs, adding further strain on the fragile economy. He introduced the gold standard to stabilise the currency but high taxes suppressed individual creativity and enterprise, though encouraging corruption and a black economy as a route to individual financial and social progress. This endured through generations, long enough to become embedded long-term in the Latin culture.

Constantine displayed a skill in balancing affairs of state with religion that would never be matched by his successors. Prior to his reign, not only did Christians have to accept ethics and discipline that meant foregoing some earthly advantages and pleasures, but they also ran the risk of cruel persecution for the privilege of membership of a group that was often not tolerated by government. So that faith held less appeal to the poor or common people struggling to make a living and support a family, a group with whom Jesus had been at pains to identify, than for those better off who were perhaps seeking an ethical and spiritual dimension towards the 'meaning of life'. Thus it was a major event for the Roman Empire to recognise and formally accept the Church and encourage a firmer structure for it. Subsequent emperors varied in the extent of their support, but Christianity had become a valid source of guidance to behaviour – especially so later that century, when Theodosius (the last Emperor of both East and West 379-395) declared Orthodox Nicene Christianity the official and sole religion of the Empire. This completed a reversal as the common person would now need more courage not to practice Christianity than to do so.

Church Turbulence Post-Constantine

Realising that none of his sons matched his leadership skills, Constantine proposed to split the Empire between five relatives. But the military judged that this stretched dynastic succession too far, and pressed him to reduce it to three sons. So the Senate appointed the three to Augustus status – Constantine II to the West, 12-year-old Constans to Italy, Africa and Greece and Constantius to the East and territory south of the Danube. Constantius thus became heavily involved in defending the threatened borders to the north and particularly the east where the Persians still sought coastal access to the Mediterranean. But it was also in his region that underlying Church divisions and their tendency to erupt were most prominent. They arose from a mixture of theology and personal ambition among the clergy. Theological debate still raged around the origin and divinity of Christ, overshadowed by Sabellians, Meletians and Arians, who had all by then lost their founders but retained passionate adherents.

The sub-division of the Empire after Constantine's death provided opportunities for the Church and its internal dissidents which if exercised unchecked, risked its own further division, potentially affecting the unity of both the Empire and the Church. Constantius' Semi-Arian sympathies did not help. Semi-Arian and the orthodox views on Christ were that Arians believed he was of 'similar substance' (*homoiousios)* to God the Father, versus the orthodox 'same substance' (*homoousios)*.

The Athanasius saga continued. Confined by exile in Tréves in the territory of Constantine II, but seeking return to Alexandria which was under the rule of Constantius, he was released by Constantine with a letter of authority to Constantius. Athanasius took time and detours in his journey to make representations in many patriarchates on the way, diverting though central Asia Minor. He had two meetings with Constantius, who was keen to minimise any trouble. Athanasius met Bishop Marcellus, a fellow deportee who had returned to his old base at Ancyra, to ensure his support.

Athanasius arrived back in Alexandria in November 337, five months after leaving Tréves. Eusebius of Nicomedia, whose see had waned in influence, was kept abreast of developments. Determined to maintain leadership, Eusebius secured the dismissal and deportation of Paul of Constantinople and took his seat. Three other influential bishops, including Marcellus were also banished, with Constantius' support. Athanasius took back his vacant post in Alexandria, but not for long as the Eusebians refused to recognise his authority, which he had resumed without consultation or synod.

There followed a series of synods on either side as a tug-of-war took place between Julius and the orthodox Western bishops versus Eusebius and the Arian-leaning bishops of the East backed by the Eastern Emperor. Many of the orthodox anti-Arian bishops in the East had fled or been exiled to the West. So effectively the leadership division of the empire had exacerbated that in the Church.

Meanwhile, the young Constans expected to be on an equal footing to his older brothers. This irritated Constantine II who invaded parts of Northern Italy in an attempt to stamp his own seniority. Constans could not stand for this and in the ensuing war, Constantine II was killed early 340 AD in an ambush, so his fast-maturing young half-brother took charge of two thirds of the Empire, in defence of which his military prowess yielded many successes. However, his arrogant manner and his open and vaunted homosexuality plus the unsavoury company he kept, undermined his popularity with his troops and the people.

Julius as Bishop of Rome sought to arrange a full-Church synod in Rome to reconsider some excommunications, the subjects of which included Novation, Marcellus and Athanasius. Eusebius at first did not reply, then early in 341 responded objecting to the tone of Julius' demand for a synod and for the short notice, pointing out that while respecting the apostolic origin of the Roman Church, the Apostles themselves had come from the East. Also, the importance of any particular church did not depend on the size of a city or the number of followers, as all bishops are equal, so why had Julius had seen fit to overrule the synods that had deposed Athanasius and Marcellus by accepting them back into the Church, in contrast with the East's earlier silent acceptance when Julius excommunicated Novatian with whom they had found no fault.

Fortified by a synod of mostly Italian bishops in Rome, who endorsed

Julius's approach in support of re-instating Athanasius and Marcellus and aware that Constans was by now no longer over-committed on military issues, Julius decided to take a hard line with Eusebius' response to his mild invitation, which was compliant with Church canon law that required involvement of the Western Church. He noted the growing number of Eastern bishops fleeing to Rome to escape the attentions of activists in the East who seemed determined on a path to Arian schism. He accepted the point about Novatian but drew the similarity of this to Eusebius' excommunication of Paul of Samosata. In neither of these cases had there been disagreement with the verdict expressed by the other party, whereas in the cases of Athanasius and Marcellus there most certainly had.

Following the death of Eusebius of Constantinople and further dispute regarding leadership of the Eastern Churches, the general synod that Rome had called for was eventually held at the end of 342 in Serdica (now Sofia). Ossius of Cordoba, now elderly, co-chaired the synod with a local bishop. Julius' view prevailed, in support of Athanasius, who was present and he was reinstated. As a result, the Eastern contingent of a mere 76 bishops left the nearly 300 from the West and returned home to hold their own synod in Philoppopolis in Thrace. One result of the Serdica synod was a letter addressed to Constantius asking him to instruct his governors to restrict their activities to political, military and public order matters rather than getting involved with the realm of the Church either in judgement or action. As to the canons arising from this Serdica synod, one was the unsurprising affirmation of Rome's primacy in cases of regional or doctrinal dispute; others were reaffirmation of the close link between Alexandria and Rome and their agreement regarding the date of Easter.

Meanwhile the breakaway Eastern synod in Thrace denounced Athanasius and the stance of the Roman Church and prevailed on Constantius to take drastic measures, contrary to his letter from Serdica. He issued an edict that should Athanasius return to Alexandria or be captured elsewhere, he was to be killed.

The two synods had abjectly failed to find common ground and further exposed the growing rift between Western and Eastern Churches. Surprisingly, they were to maintain quite close links for a further 700 years. Constantius underwent an unexpected change of approach in his support of the Eastern Church over the next couple of years, with his view of Athanasius softening and he invited him to Antioch for a meeting. Athanasius was understandably cautious and sent emissaries. The Eastern bishops sensed this softening of approach during 344 and sent a delegation to a synod in Milan seeking to repair relationships, to no avail.

When Gregory of Alexandria died in 345, Constans warned his brother Constantius that he would resist any interference with the return of

Athanasius. In view of the strength of this warning and his own preoccupation with ongoing incursions along the Persian border, Constantius agreed. Athanasius was naturally dubious but he was persuaded to return to Alexandria, travelling via Rome and onward by the northern land route, meeting in Ancyra with Constantius, who welcomed him graciously and sent him back to a triumphant return to his seat in 346.

At the beginning of AD 350, Constans had lost the faith of people in the Western Empire and the respect of the military. Magnentius, a Germanic general put forward his claim as emperor, a move that found rapid and widespread support. Constans fled only to be apprehended and murdered near the Spanish border.

Although Magnentius was not a Christian, he expressed his support for Athanasius in order to keep Egypt on side. He consolidated his leadership over the following year, but lost Illyria in the Western Balkans (roughly from Albania up to Slovenia including parts of Serbia, Bosnia and Croatia today) to Constantius in the East. The scene was set for a battle of succession as Constantius saw the threat to the dynasty. East was pitched against West in the political as well as the religious arena. Both faced ongoing external threats to their borders which led to each appointing a senior military leader early AD 351 – Decentius, brother of Magnentius in the West to secure the Rhine border against the persistent Alemanni; and Gallus, nephew of Constantius in the East, who married Constantius' sister, Constantia and was posted to Antioch to oversee defence against the equally persistent Persians.

Religion and philosophy were both undergoing change around this time. Magnentius once more allowed temple worship and sacrifices in Rome. Throughout the Empire and especially in the East and Egypt, Christian philosophers such as the blind but intelligent and influential Didymos wrote copiously on the Trinity and views of Arius and Origen. Photinus, Bishop of Sermium promoted the extreme belief that Christ was neither divine nor one with God. The Trinity was still a key area of genuine debate as people struggled to translate the essentially spiritual and mystical concept into the physical. It transcended any scriptural writings and even the New Testament held insufficient detail of the genesis and relationships of the Son and Holy Spirit to the Father to allow a firm resolution to be determined. About 350 AD, Cyril of Jerusalem published a series of sermons which amounted to a catechism of the day, giving valuable insight into the ordinary practice of the faith at that time.

Constantius had only recently gone to Rome and was impressed by the city and its grand buildings. He and Magnentius met but could not agree co-leadership in negotiations. Their political antagonism became military and later in 351, Constantius advanced. After initial skirmishes in which his troops were unconvincing, the two sides met in full force at Mursa near the confluence of the Drava and the Danube (in today's Croatia), where the bloodiest battle in Roman history took place with more than 50,000 casualties, well over half the total combatants. This resulted in victory for Constantius. In contrast to his brother, who had been a leader from the front in battle, he had left his troops in order to pray at a nearby church housing the tomb of a Christian martyr. Due to his celebrity status, he was recognised and it was there that Valens, the Bishop of Mursa gave him the news of his army's great victory over the pagan force. This encounter spawned an alliance between Emperor and bishop that would endure with broad consequences.

In 351, a council was held in Sirmium (in what is now Serbia) where Constantius had a residence. Basil of Ancyra who led the Semi-Arians, secured a deposition from Photinus, Bishop of Sermium, rejecting that the Son existed before the human birth of Jesus, which was taken in effect as a denial that Christ was God. This encouraged Arian Illyria to become a durable irritant to the Church of nearby Rome.

Meanwhile, the fleets had regained Africa and won Spain and Sicily from Magnentius, who retreated back to Gaul, yielding Illyria and also Italy. Constantius set up a new, more strategic base in Milan in 352. In the summer of 353, he moved on Gaul and was again victorious in a battle near Arles in the south of France and as Gallic support collapsed, Magnentius killed himself, as did his brother Decentius just after trouncing the Alemanni. Constantius, the son misjudged by his father as least likely to succeed him, was now sole Emperor and set up court for the time being in Arles.

Bishop Julius of Rome had died in the spring of 352, having failed to repair the rift between Eastern and Western Churches and was succeeded by Liberius, who was aware of the difficulties around Athanasius. Emperor Constantius called a Council in Arles in 353, in support of Arianism, but Liberius did not attend and refused to sign it off on account of the stacked electorate and suppression of opposition, leaving Constantius to do his own work. Athanasius was consequently deposed and arrested for the fourth time. The Eastern bishops had sensed the change of atmosphere and had written to Liberius suggesting another wider synod now be held to reconsider Athanasius' case. Liberius was keen to take this up, so he asked the Emperor to call a general council. After some hesitation as his hands were full with absorbing the Western Empire, Constantius agreed to a new Council in Milan to be held mid-355. Unlike his father he did not preside, but listened in to several sessions and made his wishes known. Liberius invited Bishop Eusebius of Vercelli (unrelated to his two namesakes, both of whom had died around 340), who accompanied Lucifer of Cagliari to plead with Constantius on behalf of Athanasius that serious consideration be given to ratifying the Nicene Creed. However, support for Athanasius at the synod was insufficient and he was again condemned to exile, as were other bishops, including Eusebius and Lucifer.

Athanasius went into exile in the southern desert where he lived with monks and wrote copious arguments against Arianism. Liberius resisted Constantius' efforts to make him accept at least Semi-Arianism so he was banished to Thrace in 356 and replaced as Bishop of Rome by Felix, an Arian sympathiser. Attempts by Constantius' appointees to enter churches in Egypt were resisted by Athanasius' strong following. Eventually the Roman army was sent in to Alexandria, whereupon Athanasius went into hiding in February 356 while his followers occupied the churches for some months before being forced out by the army. Later that year, a new bishop, George of Cappadocia was installed in Alexandria but was highly unpopular and an uprising resulted in his hasty departure in October 358.

During this time, Constantius was distracted from Church matters by renewed border threats. The borders of the Eastern Empire to the west of the Upper Euphrates were being attacked by the Isaurians who came from around the Taurus mountain range in what is now Southern Turkey. His deputy Gallus was deposed. Then in the northern Rhine area, the Franks and Alemanni advanced westwards and over the Rhine. Julian, the studious half-brother of Gallus and the only remaining member of Constantine's dynasty, was called from Athens to be made deputy leader and married to Constantius' sister Helena in November 355. This academic confounded all by proving a highly successful general, beating the Alemanni back over the Rhine after a victory at Strasbourg and clearing the Franks from Gaul.

When Constantius II asked Julian to release more of his troops to help in renewed fighting against Persia, the Gallic soldiers resisted and proclaimed Julian as emperor. Once Constantius could leave the Persian front, he headed west to confront his cousin but suffered fever on his way.

Auxentius in Milan

Another outcome of the 355 Milan synod was that Arian bishop Auxentius was installed in Milan. In 359 Auxentius was prominent in the Council of Rimini, which confirmed the Semi-Arian doctrines that had been adopted by the second Council of Sirmium (351). The new Emperor Julian was busy with military matters and social reform as well as regenerating the Roman religion, so Auxentius suffered little interference from that quarter.

The puppet bishop of Rome, Felix, was never accepted by the people. Liberius, who was never comfortable outside Rome, was highly distressed in exile. To achieve a return to Rome, he was either coerced or deceived into signing a document acceding to Constantius and the declarations of the 357 synod at Sirmium that had condemned Athanasius and others. In 358, after nearly three years in exile Liberius was authorised by the Romans to return as bishop of Rome but Felix was also to remain in office, which was not a satisfactory situation, because neither was an effective leader. Liberius carried no political influence and made little impact on Church matters. Basil of Ancyra was by now lead bishop in the East.

Having been severely affected by his exile in Thrace Liberius was never going to cause problems on his return, although he did reconcile Athanasius and also made some effort to restore relations with the East by accepting back some of the more moderate Arians. He stayed in office until he died in 366, a year after Felix. Both had their following and on Liberius' death, his followers appointed a deacon Ursinus as Bishop of Rome, based in the basilica Juli (now Santa Maria in Trastevere), while those loyal to Felix appointed a well-connected and ambitious deacon Damasus, to the throne in what is now San Lorenzo in Lucina. An unprecedented battle ensued in the city, with Damasus protected in the Lateran Palace while over 130 of his followers were killed in an attack on a church where Santa Maria Maggiore now stands. It was a brief, localised but astonishingly violent spat, quickly resolved as Damasus prevailed.

However helpful Constantine had been to the Church, its leadership had been rendered less effective since he had introduced the involvement of the Emperor in its decision-making. Not all emperors were knowledgeable or devout in their own faith. So the Bishop of Rome as Church leader had to set the spiritual and ecclesiastical standards with one eye on any political implications they may carry.

After Emperor Julian died in 363 and Christian emperors ruled once more, the orthodox Western Church with Hilary of Poitiers to the fore, followed by Eusebius of Vercelli and Athanasius himself rallied to bolster the Nicean view and counter Arianism in any form. One of their first objectives was to secure the removal of Auxentius, but he managed obstinately to remain in his seat until his death in 374.

East-West Church Debate Continues

Heated debate continued in the Church over the Trinity and the Nicene Creed, accompanied by sporadic allegations of Arianism, which was locally revived in well-argued papers by Aetios, assistant to Eudoxios the new bishop of Antioch in 357.

An imperial synod was called to be held in 358 in Nicomedia, but due to the ravages of an earthquake there it was finally held in early 359. Emperor

Constantius II ordered it be held in two concurrent parts, with the Western bishops meeting in Rimini and the Eastern ones in Seleucia in Isauria, (now Silifke in Turkey). Before it started, Constantius drew up the agenda and also a desired confession of faith regarding the Son that was the work of his advisers, bishops Valens (his friend from Musa) and Ursacius of Singidunum (now Belgrade). He intended that each meeting would seek agreement on the matters listed then a delegation of ten bishops from each would meet with the Emperor to discuss items with each other to seek resolution. It was bigger than Nicea, with 400 delegates at Rimini alone. The Western meeting started in May, reporting in July with a consensus disagreeing with the proposed confession of faith, declaring it heretical, and supporting the Nicene Creed. But all delegates were held until they recanted and accepted, which they eventually did when Constantius told them to stay and await his return from another campaign against the Persian Sassanid Empire.

The Eastern meeting of 140 delegates began at the end of September and there too, were divisions of opinion but in the end the ten delegates went early December 359 to Constantius, now back in Constantinople. In common with the Western delegates, they could not agree with the proposed formula but were forced to sign it at the very end of the year. The entire exercise had clearly been a farce and a fix by the Emperor and his church confidantes. The ten delegates on each side had submitted to extreme persuasion and the conviction of the rest had to be seen as dubious. It was difficult to do much about this in the West but in the East there was yet another round of banishments including Basil of Ancyra and Makedonios of Constantinople. Eudoxios moved from Antioch to replace the latter with superb timing as he could celebrate by consecrating the Hagia Sophia, which still stands impressively today, one of the largest unsupported dome spans in the world.

The unfortunately named Lucifer, exiled bishop of Cagliari plagued Constantius with criticism and direct insults. He was becoming regarded by others in the Church as a demented loose cannon so Constantius, wishing to avoid creating martyrs, felt able to ignore his rants.

The Persians attacked the borders once more in 359, so Constantius was obliged yet again to travel East in 360 with a force and to over-winter there. During his return he fell ill and he died in November 361 soon after being baptised by Euzoios, Arian Bishop of Antioch, though he had been the cause of much division within the Christian family. Before dying he confirmed Julian as his successor, being the only remaining male descendant of Constantine. Though a pagan he had proven himself a capable leader.

The Persian wars had been a recurring thorn in the side of the Roman

Empire, but they had been an even more unfortunate block to spreading Christianity further east, where for example Zoroastrianism (founded in the 6th century BC) and more recently Manichaeism had spread east from their Persian origins, making significant inroads further into Asia as far as China. The main channel of Christian mission into Asia in these early days had to be by sea following St Thomas' voyage in AD 52 to Southern India where he is believed to have spread the faith from just north of Kochi where he landed in the West, over to Chennai in the East.

Emperor Julian Revives Roman Paganism and Philosophy

It was a blow to Christianity as Julian became Emperor, having rejected the Christian religion in which he had been raised in favour of paganism. He attempted to reorganize the highly decentralized pagan cults on similar lines to the Christian Church, but his reign was short-lived (361-363).

Around this time nearly all the recorded philosophy and dialectic of the day came from the East and the African coastline. But coming to the fore in Rome was a philosopher of African origin called Marius Victorinus (c. 300-370), who had already been recognised by the Senate as a prominent teacher by the mid-350s and was baptised as a Christian soon after. He was a Neoplatonist and had come to recognise the close parallels of Plato's philosophy with much of the theology of Christianity, leading him to become a Christian by conviction. He wrote heavy condemnations of Arian theory about 360 AD and came down in emphatic support of the Nicene concept of *homoousios,* 'same substance' regarding the Trinity. Seeking to rid the schools of Christian teachers and influence, Julian issued a declaration mandating that all state appointed professors must receive official approval. Victorinus was obliged to retire in June 362 from his teaching work, due to Julian's anti-Christian edict but he continued to write copiously, including Latin translations and commentaries on the Epistles of Paul. Another talented writer, Bishop Hilary of Poitiers, spread these thoughts on the genesis of the Son and the Trinity further westwards.

Julian travelled to Constantinople to receive the body of Constantius and ensure that it was buried with full honours next to his father in the Church of the Apostles. He then set about purging his perceived enemies at court and praised his gods for his good fortune. As a teenager he had covertly followed the classical Greek teachings of Libanius, which introduced him to this world of pagan gods. Now he was free to reintroduce openly traditional worship and practice in Roman and Greek territories, ordering the restoration and reopening of temples. This led to some localised sporadic retribution and mob violence against Christians but no serious persecution except in turbulent Alexandria where Bishop

George was killed. At the same time Julian enhanced the status and pride of the Hellenic lands including the capital Constantinople. He referred to Christians as 'Galileans' and in trying to appear reasonably even-handed, did not actively suppress Christianity. He quite reasonably took the view that their self-evident propensity for dispute with each other was at least as great a danger to them as that of any outside forces. He even felt confident enough to allow repatriation of the many exiled bishops and the return of their confiscated possessions, though not always their positions in the Church.

Athanasius, one of those exiles, returned yet again to Alexandria in 362 and was able to resume his office as Bishop George had still not been replaced. This led the Arians in Alexandria pointedly to install Lucius as their own bishop. Ever the activist, Athanasius consulted Eusebius of Vercelli who was travelling home with Lucifer of Calabria from their own exile in Upper Egypt. Athanasius called the Synod of Alexandria in 362, once more aiming to unite the faithful behind the Nicene concepts. In his book 'Speeches against the Arians', Athanasius argues logically in favour of Christ's divinity and 'oneness' with God the Father. He had held doggedly to his beliefs and proved to be an astute survivor against heavy opposition.

Lucifer, meanwhile left in haste for Antioch, where the Church was in dire need of guidance following inadequate successors to Eudoxios after his move to Constantinople. Lucifer delegated two Presbyters to attend the Alexandria synod on his behalf.

The synod was not heavily attended but the delegates raised a proposal that may lead to peace. This stated that the Holy Spirit was not a created being but was of the same substance as the Father and Son. Hitherto the philosophical arguments had mainly covered the Father–Son relationship, sidestepping the Spirit. It included definitions of the terms 'being' and 'substance' in line with the Greek '*hypostasis*' and '*ousia*', simple and clear, reflecting the Nicene Creed description of the Trinity as it then existed. The synod openly invited back those Arian clerics who could accept this Nicene formula rejecting the idea of the Holy Spirit as a separate being from Christ. The synod condemned to excommunication those who persisted in Arianism. Since the lead parties in the synod were Athanasius and Eusebius, it offered a path to unity between East and West even if it seemed there were many who determinedly sought another path.

Meanwhile in that troubled centre Antioch, the mercurial radical Lucifer had achieved the very opposite of unity and his precipitate appointment of Paulinus as bishop allowed the establishment of four distinct groups, divided almost entirely by their interpretations of the origin and nature of the Son, which meant the findings of the synod of Alexandria stood little chance of making impact. Nobody could then have imagined the later consequences of those findings. Julian once more banished Athanasius 'for incompetence'.

Christianity was so widespread and embedded throughout the Empire that Julian could see the folly of any persecution, so he took a long-term view and issued an edict in 362 requiring local authorities everywhere to test all applicants for advanced teaching posts as to their 'character' as a basis for deciding which ones would qualify for teaching in further education establishments. Lists of those approved were then to be submitted to the Emperor for his confirmation. He made it clear that 'character' meant sincerity, so their teaching had to be in full accordance with Roman beliefs. This was clearly read as an astute way of weeding out Christians as they could hardly hold to their faith and yet teach reverence for the works of the Roman classical writers Homer, Herodotus and so on, which were based on the traditional Roman gods. Julian believed he was on track to throttle Christianity within a generation. Fortunately for Christianity there was much resistance and through his advisors, always aware of an Emperor's wish for a good epitaph, he was persuaded instead to turn his attention to pushing the Persians back and establishing himself as a legendary leader on the lines of Alexander the Great. In his travels eastwards, he was disappointed to find only lukewarm adherence to the pagan feast days.

Julian established himself as the Chief Priest of the Empire and sent High Priests to each province to recruit local priests, whose entire families were required to worship regularly with them and the faithful. Julian had noted the success of the Jewish and Christian faiths in preaching and showing love and care to their neighbours, travellers, the poor, sick, dead and bereaved. He never won the respect of the people of Antioch and he departed for war in the spring of 363, swearing never to return there. He was killed in battle with the Persians and was succeeded by a Christian, General Jovian. Jovian was obliged to submit to the Persians on their terms then he was allowed to return to Syria to bury Julian in Tarsus fulfilling his last wish. Julian was the last of the Constantine dynasty and the last pagan Emperor in Rome.

Jovian wasted little time in restoring the Church's legal status, income and privileges. He issued an order prohibiting the offering of sacrifices and insisting that only Almighty God and Christ be worshipped with Christian teaching fully resumed. Despite strong pleas from opposing factions, Athanasius was confirmed yet again in his office in Alexandria early 364. Wasting no time, he gathered a synod of Egyptian bishops which affirmed the 362 view that the Nicene Creed is the only basis for the true faith.

Jovian died at the young age of 23 from carbon monoxide poisoning from a charcoal fire. He was succeeded by Valentinian (reign 364-375), an officer of the imperial guard. The army insisted on having a second emperor, so he chose his younger brother Valens, giving him responsibility for the eastern provinces. Valentinian adopted an 'arms-length' approach to the fractious bishops, especially after the fatal riots in Rome following the Ursinus-Damasus conflict in 366. He took the view that the Church was strong enough to settle its own affairs and refused to be drawn into theological or clerical judgements; in other words, he was putting the authority of Church affairs firmly in the hands of the Church rather than the State, so separating Church and State leadership for the first time since Constantine. Converting that desire into practice proved elusive, however, not least because the Church leadership was out of practice, so unprepared. In State matters Valentinian was proving a poor strategist and Emperor, alienating people by imposing high taxes while allowing inevitable corruption and nepotism to take hold once more.

Perhaps emboldened by Valentinian's support for the Church, Bishop of Rome Damasus I called a synod there in 372. In the course of this he found support in condemning Auxentius as a heretic. Auxentius still managed to hold on to his seat in Milan until he died two years later, although orthodox Christians there meantime tended to look to a priest called Philastrus, who would later be consecrated Bishop of Brescia.

Basil of Caesarea (330-379)

The Western Church generally accepted the Nicene Creed while bickering continued in the East. When Eusebius of Caesarea died, he was succeeded by Basil who had been born in Cappadocia, a deeply religious and ascetic man who proposed practices and lifestyle for monastic life as described in the previous chapter. His grandmother, a stalwart of the Church and follower of Origen was a strong influence in Basil's love of theology. He emerged as an impressive leader, personality and diplomat able to win Valens' ear. He had to firefight more local disputes over interpretational nuances of the Nicene Creed, arising from its sad lack of clarity. He saw the need to transcend local rivalries, pride and argument over minutiae. In short, he had a natural skill in balancing theology and politics and sought a broad Catholic approach. He requested that a fully authorised delegation from the West travel and meet a full Eastern contingent for open discussion with a view to reaching joint agreement on a creed for the whole Church.

Given the special relationship between Rome and Alexandria, Basil picked Athanasius as the ideal delegate to persuade Rome to arrange this, offering him the tempting opportunity to leave a lasting legacy by achieving East-West reconciliation. But it would have meant Athanasius accepting Meletius, the incumbent as the rightful bishop of Antioch (not to be confused with Meletius of Lycopolis, who had been Athanasius' opponent in Alexandria). Meletius and Athanasius nurtured a deep and unchristian dislike of each other paralleling the historic antipathy between the two sees and aggravated by suspicion linking Meletius with Semi-Arianism. Basil continued in his attempts but Athanasius died in 373, having consecrated a close presbyter, Peter as his successor as Bishop of Alexandria. Peter rebuffed a further attempt by Basil and was then removed by Valens' agents who travelled from Antioch to Alexandria to depose him.

Basil had exercised statesmanship and restraint in efforts to persuade the inward-looking Roman Church to denounce the bishops he regarded as heretical. These included Arian sympathisers and other possible heretics, sympathisers with recently deceased Marcellus of Ancyra. By 377, he was exasperated enough to challenge Rome directly to hold a synod to expose the heretical leaders in the East. A synod was held but with Rome's closeness to Peter of Alexandria, it limited its response to a message broadly condemning the heresies that Basil had mentioned and insinuating criticism of Meletius without naming him. Basil, a saintly man of towering potential died in 379, his wishes for unity even within the Eastern Church unfulfilled. He is regarded in Orthodoxy as one of the Cappadocian Fathers, together with Gregory of Nazianzus and Gregory of Nyssa. The Eastern Orthodox Church regards these as two of three Holy Hierarchs, similar to the Doctors of the Western Church the third being John Chrysostom, below.

There were hundreds of monasteries and nunneries and literally thousands of cells and caves throughout the Egyptian desert by the end of the 4th century. Basil the Great as Archbishop of Caesarea and Cappadocia in Asia Minor and founder of the monastic movement there visited Egypt about 357 AD. The rule he developed as a result is followed by the Eastern Orthodox Churches who have a great tradition of building amazing monasteries in some of the most unlikely and inaccessible places. It would yet be a while before the monastic movement spread in the Western Church.

Bishop of Rome Damasus

Damasus was another bishop of Rome who, although a holy man, was not blessed with leadership qualities and showed myopic reluctance to interfere too much in matters beyond Rome where troubles persisted. His position was strengthened by a synod of Italian bishops held in Rome in late AD 378 which led to a law backed by Emperor Gratian (reign 367-383) declaring that the state would support the bishop of Rome in ensuring the expulsion from office of any bishop he deposed. Bishops in outlying sees, who could discipline their own clerics, were in turn subject to the jurisdiction of Rome. Damasus felt empowered by the relative non-interference of Valentinian and was regarded as the senior man of Christianity.

Basil and Peter, the Eastern prelates showed deference to Damasus and felt the need of support from the Western Church in solving their intransigent local differences. But Damasus missed an opportunity to put his strong position to good use, partly because he bore an irrational distrust of Basil of Caesarea, who desperately desired his support in countering the growing and spreading confidence of the Arians in the East and the comfort Meletius was giving them in Antioch. Peter II of Alexandria escaped from an Arian persecution and Damasus gave him sanctuary in Rome but would not travel.

In over 18 years as bishop, probably the main thing for which Damasus would be remembered was asking his secretary Jerome to collate and revise old Latin versions of the Bible New Testament and the Septuagint translated from Greek. This resulted in the 'Vulgate' (meaning commonly used), which would eventually become the recognised Latin Bible.

Ambrose of Milan

While Auxentius was Bishop of Milan (355-374), Arians felt free to lobby and spread dissension. Damasus excommunicated many of them, but Emperor Valentinian I supported him in leaving Auxentius in Milan against Athanasius' wishes. On Auxentius death in 374, the Roman governor of Liguria-Emilia, Ambrose filled the vacancy. Ambrose was a catechumen and was swiftly baptised. He was a close associate of future Emperor Gratian and his political experience and leadership qualities helped him become influential and popular, arguably having a more important role in many respects than Damasus.

Ambrose was confessor to Valentinian I and advisor to Gratian on religious and Church matters, but his job was not an easy one as by the time he took over from Auxentius, many people, clergy and especially the military were either deeply Arian or sympathetic to Arianism. Valentia, the mother of Valentinian was very keen to have Ambrose replaced by another Auxentius – the Younger, Bishop of Durostorum.

Ambrose took under his wing the young Augustine of Hippo who held him in high regard as shall be seen. Ambrose would become one of the four original Doctors of the Roman Church. He popularised antiphonal chant and is believed to have composed the hymn *Veni redemptor gentium.*

Church and State

Valentinian I died in 375 and was succeeded as ruler of the Western empire by his young sons. Gratian was promoted from Junior to Senior Augustus of the West and the child Valentinian II became Junior Augustus of the East. Valens was meanwhile preoccupied in defending the borders of the Empire in the North Eastern part of Asia Minor, Thrace (now Eastern Bulgaria) against the Goths, and tribes such as the Alans and Huns – fierce horsemen of Mongolian descent from the Caucasus. Valens was killed in the Battle of Adrianople in 378 and Gratian moved with reinforcements to Sirmium in Serbia. He meanwhile promoted Theodosius, a young Spanish commander who had distinguished himself in the field, and told him to take command of the Illyrian army south of the Danube to quell another threat, which he did to good effect. Theodosius became Augustus at the beginning of 379, with full authority to defend the part of the Balkan peninsular that belonged to the Western Empire. To help secure the Danube border, he managed the controlled immigration of Goths, who actually proved useful mercenary reinforcements in the army.

Gratian was a committed Christian and aware of the activities of his late uncle Valens. He issued an edict from Sirmium late 378 that all exiled bishops were to be repatriated again. There was to be freedom of Christian worship with the exceptions of Manicheans, Sabellians and Arians, whom he banned. Contrary to his intention, the practical effect of this was encouragement rather than suppression of divisions in the Eastern Church. Meletius of Antioch and Peter of Alexandria renewed hostilities. Meletius' views had moved closer to the Nicene Creed and he called a synod in Antioch which attracted 153 bishops, ratifying the Nicene Creed and Damasus' view of the faith, including *homoousios.*

Meanwhile the Western Church, earlier disturbed by the violence of Arian-leaning Constantius, had settled down under Jovian and Valentinian. The radical Lucifer of Cagliari, having stirred up matters in the east during his exile had returned to his base in Sardinia and had built a significant following of 'Luciferians' as far spread as Gaul, Rome, Egypt and Palestine, which dwindled to nought after his death in 370.

Gratian returned to Milan where he had commissioned Bishop Ambrose to draw up a summary of the Christian faith. One of the resulting contentions was that the incursions of the Goths south of the Danube had been a divine retribution to the Arian heresy prevalent there. Gratian reversed his earlier edict of tolerance from Sirmium. Emperor Theodosius backed this in 380 declaring that all the faithful in his part of the Empire should follow Christianity as preached by the Apostle Peter and accept the Holy Trinity in line with Damasus and Peter of Alexandria, i.e. "We believe in one Godhead and in the equal majesty of the Father, the Son and the Holy Spirit." Any variation from this was heretical and would be punishable. This freed Ambrose to address the widespread Arianism in Northern Italy and Illyria. His subsequent attempt to include the East by calling a full general synod failed and he was astute enough to decide to live with this.

Damasus was still bishop of Rome and while Ambrose was Gratian's advisor on Church and religious policy, Ausonius was his spiritual mentor. Emperor Gratian was a studious and devout man as well as being physically strong and a good sportsman. He trusted Ausonius and in line with Roman culture, ensured his whole family benefitted from his patronage. Such 'grace and favour' beneficence would also become part of the practice of Church leadership in Rome for centuries. Gratian and Theodosius worked well together as emperors and took a common line on religious matters, ending any public displays of paganism. Both emperors decreed jointly in 383 that renunciation of the Christian faith would be illegal, intrinsically signalling to the bishops the emperors' seniority over them in what they regarded as the state Church.

Britain

The arrival of Christianity in Britain tends to be associated with the mission of Augustine of Canterbury in 597 AD. But in reality Christianity arrived long before that. As early as the 1st Century AD, there had been an organised attempt to convert the British. This began when Roman artisans and traders who followed the military arrival in Britain were accompanied by evangelists. These spread the story of Jesus while the Roman military also introduced their Pagan deities.

Christianity was just one cult among many, but unlike those of Rome, monotheistic Christianity demanded exclusive allegiance from its followers. This powerful commitment to Jesus and intolerance of other gods had rattled the Roman authorities, another factor behind the persecutions. During the 4th Century, British Christianity became more visible but it had only managed to win over a minority of the population in which pagan beliefs still abounded.

Gratian had rather taken his eyes off his Western Empire due to other preoccupations around the Eastern Mediterranean. The Roman military In Britain, were feeling isolated and side-lined by Rome, so they rebelled and installed their own general Maximus as emperor. This rebellion spread to Gaul, which triggered a response from Gratian, who led his troops into Gaul, but they deserted him near Paris and he was killed in AD 383 aged only 24. His younger brother Valentinian II, at 12 years of age, was appointed emperor in Milan and defences were established in the Alpine passes to deter invasion south by Maximus. Agreement was then negotiated on a new three-way division of the empire as Theodosius recognised Maximus, a fellow Spaniard and possible relative of his.

Theodosius I and Gratian

Over the previous century and this one, the Vandals in central and southern Poland and Eastern Germany spread in various directions and one of their branches, the Thervingi in the Danube plains became known as the Visigoths, had established a foothold in Pannonia (Hungary with parts of Austria, Croatia and Serbia). Valens had recruited Theodosius to help with defence in Illyria, but then he moved on to engagement with the Vandals and Visigoths. When Valens died in battle, Theodosius became co-emperor. In 382, the Vandals and Visigoths advanced southward and defeated an attack by the Romans. Following negotiation, Theodosius signed a treaty with them granting their occupation of part of Northern Dacia and Thrace, but specifying that the land remained sovereign Roman territory. Part of the deal was that they would do Roman military service but other than such agreed provisos, they were autonomous. The Emperor realised that if the Visigoths became adventurous, Rome was vulnerable from the sea in the west, which was behind his moving the capital in 386 once more to Milan as a large enough city, further inland and more defensible than Rome.

Following Valens' death, Gratian's intended peace-making move in the Eastern Church and Theodosius' promotion, Theodosius made an offer to the incumbent Arian Bishop Demophilus of Constantinople, of retaining his position if he accepted the Nicene Creed, but Demophilus rejected this. He was deposed within two days of Theodosius' arrival in Constantinople. Theodosius accepted the advice of Meletius, whom he had appointed patriarch of Antioch and replaced Demophilus with Gregory of Nazianzus (329-390) and tasked him to convert Constantinople to Nicene orthodoxy. Gregory had already built up a strong following before his arrival in Constantinople in 380 and was known for his stylish rhetoric and passionate support for the Nicene concept of the Trinity. This is well illustrated in an excerpt from his recorded addresses – *"Look at these facts: Christ is born; the Holy Spirit is His Forerunner. Christ is baptised, the Spirit bears witness to this. Christ works miracles and the Spirit accompanies them. Christ ascends, the Spirit takes His place. What great things are there in the concept of God which are beyond His power?"*

First Council of Constantinople

The following Spring 381, Meletius arrived in Constantinople to chair the First Council of Constantinople, called by Theodosius I, which was attended by 150 Eastern bishops, but excluded those from Egypt. Meletius hoped to repair relationships between East and West, but died before any progress could be made. Gregory took the chair and Theodosius, in a further bid to unite East and West, then insisted that the Egyptians and Macedonians be invited to join the synod. They arrived but refused to recognise Gregory as Bishop of Constantinople, claiming his transfer to have been illegal. Gregory resigned to enable the Council to proceed as harmoniously as possible, delivering a stirring speech that persuaded Theodosius to let him leave and return to his original diocese of Nazianzus in Cappadocia. His surprise successor, chosen by Theodosius, was an unknown catechumen called Nectarius, who was rapidly baptised, consecrated and chaired the council to its conclusion and continued in post until his death in 397, to be followed by John Chrysostom.

This Ecumenical Council of Constantinople gave the Bishop of Constantinople precedence over all the Eastern Church, second only to the Bishop of Rome. This disappointed Alexandria even though it was given special standing and extended authority, together with Antioch. Other canons emphasised prohibition of bishops interfering with other dioceses and the ecclesiastical administrative autonomy of each of the five eastern provinces of the empire – Egypt, Orient, Asia, Pontus and Thrace. The creed that emerged from the council became known as the Nicene-Constantinopolitan Symbol, which is the one used today in the West, (plus the later disputed addition of the word '*filioque*' – 'and the Son'). Another canon condemned all types of Arianism, which was dealt a serious blow. The Holy Spirit had been accepted as an equal member of the Holy Trinity and therefore a valid subject of worship by the faithful. The Eastern Church now accepted the impossibility of worldly interpretation explaining the mystery of the Trinity as in Paul 1 Cor 2:10 "It was to us that God made known his secret by means of his Spirit. The Spirit searches everything, even the hidden depths of God's purposes", a conclusion also reached separately by Augustine of Hippo (354-430) in Numidia and accepted in the West. The new canons of the Church were sent to Emperor Theodosius requesting his approval as only then would they be legally valid, a move that demonstrated acceptance of the principle of a State Church with the Emperor at its head.

Having succeeded Valens in the East, when Gratian died in 383, Theodosius took charge of the West, so became sole emperor of the Roman Empire. He was passionate in his support of the Nicene Creed. He subsequently directed that the Nicene Trinitarian Creed be universally accepted as had been decided at the Council of Constantinople in 381. He derided any variations on this and also ended any state support for traditional polytheist religions and practices.

John Chrysostom (347-407)

Born in Antioch in 347AD, John became a student of theology while practising extreme asceticism. He led a hermit life from about 375 then returned to Antioch due to poor health a couple of years later. Regarded as a Holy Hierarch in the Orthodox Churches and as a Doctor of the Church by Roman Catholics, he became known for his eloquent rhetoric and asceticism and denunciation of abuse of authority in the Church and the Empire. He was ordained deacon in 381 by Meletius of Antioch, and as presbyter five years later, gaining wide respect for his perceptive clarification of Bible passages and moral teaching.

In 397, John was consecrated Bishop of Constantinople despite his reluctance which was based on the elaborate privileges that would come with the appointment. During his time as bishop he avoided hosting lavish entertainments, which although winning the popularity of common people, did not go down well with the wealthy or the clergy, which left him uneasy. Theophilus, the Bishop of Alexandria opposed John's appointment to Constantinople, as he wanted to bring that see under his own influence. Theophilus was uncomfortable with the teachings of Origen, to which he accused John of being too partial.

John was fearless in denouncing offences in high places, which gained him influential enemies. A synod held in 403 accused John, of following Origen's beliefs so he was deposed and banished. But the people of the city knew a good man when they saw one and were deeply angered by this. Their restlessness ensured his early reinstatement. He died after being exiled once more, following which he was named Chrysostom from Greek, 'golden mouth'. His remains were brought back to Constantinople about 30 years after his death. They were stolen from there by crusaders in 1204 and brought to Rome, but Pope John Paul II ordered their return in 2004.

Spain and Priscillian

The Church in Spain had kept its distance from the arguments within the Church east of the Pyrenees, but faced a growing challenge of its own in this fourth century. Priscillian, a Spanish nobleman, had given up all his wealth to become an ascetic and preacher and built a serious following. To put his view simply, he saw the world as intrinsically sinful and man as a combination of "works of the flesh" and "works of the spirit". The latter made each of us into a temple of God which is achieved involving three processes.

- Modesty should tame the worldly passions of the flesh.
- The soul regains its divine character only if it resists the sins which tempt and infect it.
- God dwells within us, seeing and judging all our behaviour

Priscillian said "For salvation, we should follow the commandments of the bible, forsake parents and children, gifts and goods, even our own soul and love God more than anything else. All must fight the realm of the flesh, animal instinct and darkness... The perfect sons of God neither marry nor are given in marriage; they neither beget nor are begotten, but are like the angels of God." He allows for God's mercy being available to those who cannot match up fully to these standards so long as they submit to "God's supervision and command".

Sexism (neither a word in the language nor a recognised concept at that time) and an over-riding preoccupation with 'sins of the flesh' have echoed down the centuries in the Church. The world would not be populated for long if all were Priscillian's 'perfect sons of God' – note 'sons' not 'children'. His followers included a handful of bishops and perhaps surprisingly a majority of women, because he was a gifted orator, who used biblical language and references and practised what he preached. But Priscillianism was regarded by some as a heresy. Although a layman, his followers consecrated him bishop of Avila in 380. This created uproar and when appeals to Damasus and Bishop Ambrose of Milan, proved fruitless, a final appeal to Maximus, the Spanish self-styled Emperor of Britain and Gaul, resulted in a synod in Bordeaux to examine the matter. A civil trial was eventually held in Trier, where Maximus was based, which led to the execution of Priscillian and most of his senior followers for 'sorcery and immorality' in 385. It was a harsh sanction for a zealot, but it did avoid a repeat of a Western Arian-style division.

Valentinian II and Ambrose of Milan

Nonetheless, this challenge provided fuel for a highly respected aristocrat in Rome, Symmachus. He took this incident as a cue to raise with Valentinian II the issue of state grants for resumption of traditional state worship and re-installing the altar of Victory in the Senate building. The persuasive style, argument and presentation of his supplication were brilliantly composed and still impress researchers. It took a strong letter of admonition from Ambrose, Valentinian's confessor, even going so far as to raise the spectre of excommunication, to close the matter and confirm the Emperor as 'a soldier of God' with the divine duty to protect the Church as a legally constituted part of the state. This underlined how the power of an emperor in Church matters as assumed by Valentinian, and later more directly by Theodosius I, carried with it serious fundamental responsibilities.

Intervention from another source came soon after this. Valentinian II's mother, Juliana, who espoused the Illyrian (Western Balkan) Arians, supported one of their bishops called Auxentius as a replacement for Ambrose. Valentinian II had been offended by another stand-off by Ambrose the previous year and sided with his mother. In an attempted statesman-like resolution, he proposed that Ambrose and Auxentius argue their cases before a consistory, a formal meeting of cardinals. Auxentius agreed but Ambrose did not and he reminded young Valentinian that in matters of faith it is not for emperors to pronounce judgement on bishops but the opposite. He pointed out that Valentinian was not baptised. He crowned this by delivering a famous sermon on Palm Sunday 386, including "Give to Caesar what belongs to Caesar and to God what belongs to God. Caesar is the son of the Church and part of the Church, not superior to it." The sermon was reproduced in a widely distributed pamphlet and it soon became the basis of Western interpretation of the constitution of the church-state.

Valentinian had lost respect in these exchanges and his support for the Arians had shaken the Western empire, so Maximus seized his chance and after declaring his fealty to the bishop of Rome, then Siricius, successor to Damasus in late 384, he marched into Italy late in 387. Valentinian fled to Salonika and the reluctant protection of Theodosius who was by now his brother-in-law. In the East, Maximus was regarded as a usurper and Theodosius took an army westward in the summer of 388, defeating and killing Maximus. Theodosius entered Milan that October, effectively becoming sole emperor.

Bishop Ambrose in Milan remained as Theodosius' confessor and moral guide. There were a number of incidents after which Ambrose demanded Theodosius' penitence before resuming communion for him, thus asserting the full authority of the Church over the Christian emperor. In 391, encouraged by Ambrose, Theodosius introduced a law in Rome that forbade all pagan worship, sacrifices and even prayer in temples. This was quickly replicated in Egypt after a spell of brutal combat between Christians and pagans which included the demolition of many temples, including the biggest – the Serapium in Alexandria. Theodosius enacted similar laws for the Eastern Church, plus others that aligned Rome with Constantinople.

Final Defeat of Greco-Roman Paganism

The turbulence of this century continued into its last decade, as new threats to the empire emerged from the West. The Frankish King Arbogast broke the news that Valentinian II had died by suicide in May 392, though it was suspected that Arbogast had a hand in it. Arbogast promoted his friend Flavius Eugenius to Augustus of the West and both men wrote to Bishop Ambrose, who did not answer either. So Eugenius wrote to Theodosius in Constantinople and in frustration at still receiving no response, he began to threaten Italy, prompting Ambrose to break his silence only to show his solidarity with those threatened. He was clearly opposed to Eugenius in spite of the latter having announced his Christian sympathies, but he was known to have promoted the ancient cults while he was teaching in Rome some years earlier.

When approached by the senate for a grant to enable them to resume temple worship, Eugenius drew from the experience of predecessors and avoided antagonising Ambrose. But he did send a personal donation to cover the senate's request, which Ambrose took as an act of war. As Eugenius advanced towards Milan early 393, Ambrose decamped to Florence and wrote to Eugenius accusing him of disobeying God and betraying Christ by his support of the senate, behaviour to be expected of him and which was the reason Ambrose had not responded to the earlier letters.

This signalled to the whole Church and Eugenius, that it should oppose him. Eugenius countered by promoting Flavian, who had been prefect under Theodosius, to pretender chancellor of Italy. Flavian allowed the resurgence of the old religions and sacrifices, risking possible religious war. Arbogast, Eugenius and Flavian fought Theodosius in September 394 carrying standards of Hercules and Jupiter. Theodosius' envoys had consulted a reclusive Egyptian monk in Lycopolis, who prophesied a costly but decisive victory. Theodosius prayed earnestly before this battle of the Vipana River in what is now Western Slovenia. He emerged victorious but ascribed this success to the miracle of a chance Alpine hurricane handicapping the enemy. The rebel leaders died during or just after the battle, which was the last such challenge to the Christianisation of the Empire and secured the final defeat of Greco-Roman polytheism.

Ambrose returned to Milan in the August following Eugenius' death. Having heard of the victory by letter from Theodosius he held a thanksgiving Mass. He responded to the Emperor that he had returned to

Milan knowing that victory was assured, sent his congratulations and begged mercy for any repentant prisoners, or those who had sought the Church's protection. He then travelled to meet Theodosius in Aquilea, where Theodosius showed humble respect and gratitude for Ambrose's prayers and support, thus confirming the inter-dependence between Emperor and Church. Theodosius died from diabetes a mere four months after the victory. Ambrose addressed the funeral gathering, which was attended by Theodosius' ten-year-old son Honorius with his guardian Stilicho, and advised them to follow up Theodosius' later edicts. Ambrose left the political scene at that point, having had an important influence on the continuation of Christianity at the highest level during the latter half of this momentous century. He returned to Milan to concentrate on his episcopal duties and died in 397.

Popes and the Papacy

The title 'Pope' had been used by the senior bishops of the major centres Rome, Constantinople, Alexandria and Carthage but late in this century it became generally accepted as referring just to the Bishop of Rome. The Greek term 'Pappas' (Daddy) was applied to abbots and bishops early on in the east and priests are still referred to as 'father'. In the west the first recorded usage of 'pope' was an inscription on the tomb of Liberius who died in 366, but its first general use was in the fifth century. Bishops of Rome saw themselves as direct successors to Saint Peter, regarded as the first Bishop of Rome, so they assumed overall authority over the whole Christian Church. The title of Pope came to signify this, but was affected by the two main seats of Christianity, Rome which was looked to by the west and Constantinople by the east. Rome's claim to absolute ascendency was enhanced by the council of Constantinople and the recent tendency for Emperors to take up permanent residence in Rome instead of Milan.

Pope Siricius, a Roman, had joined the priesthood at an early age and succeeded Damasus. He focused on discipline in religious practice and is best known for being the first pope to write an instruction ordering celibacy for priests in correspondence with the bishop of Tarragona in 386. It was also during his reign that the 27 books of the New Testament were accepted as canonical and brought together in 398.

Practice and Worship

Worship by the faithful had continued with little change through all the political upheavals and philosophical disputes of the senior clergy. Cyril of Jerusalem recorded the Sunday Eucharistic Service in his catechism which was adopted and broadcast from Constantinople around the middle of the century. At the time, the Service was quite lengthy, mainly used in the larger churches and celebrated by a bishop or senior presbyter as described in the box. Men and women would use separate entrances and sit in separate groups and there was usually a further sub-division of young and old.

Service of Worship

The service proper usually began with two readings from the Old Testament followed by a psalm, normally sung, with responses or 'Hallelujah' after each verse. There followed a reading from the epistles of St Paul before the congregation rose for a deacon or presbyter to read a Gospel passage from the lectern.

Then the sermons were delivered by those officiating clergy who wished to speak in ascending order of rank – deacon, presbyter then bishop. Prayers and benediction were said over the unbaptised and Catechumens (those being instructed for baptism) present, each clause of the benediction having the response "Kyrie Eleison" (Lord have mercy). They then left the service, followed by the penitents, who gathered just inside the doors, followed in turn by the sick after they were blessed. During all this time the altar was concealed behind curtains and it continued thus until the Eucharistic prayers and Communion. The rest of the service was reserved to the baptised believers, so the doors were now closed. A deacon then said aloud Church prayers and intercessions, to each of which the congregation responded "Kyrie Eleison". Then the deacon said "Let us greet one another with a holy kiss" at which those on the altar would exchange kisses, as would the men in their group and the women in theirs, confirming the love between fellow Christians present. Then the deacon announced there were now no catechumens, unbaptised or unbelievers, heretics, hypocrites nor hate between people present and called all to stand upright before the Lord in fear and trembling. A bowl of water was handed to the bishop or senior presbyter, who symbolically washed his hands before deacons passed him the bread and wine. He prayed silently over these gifts while deacons placed a decorative robe over his shoulders recognising the solemnity of the occasion. Returning to the centre of the altar, he recited the 'Grace' – "May the Grace of God, the love of Christ and the fellowship of the Holy Spirit be with us all ever more". The traditional responses followed:

R And with your Spirit
P Lift up your hearts
R We raise them with the Lord
P Let us thank the Lord
R That is worthy and fitting

Only now did the Eucharistic prayer begin with "It is worthy and fitting to sing praise to You before all, You who are truly God". There followed an intoned lengthy prayer of thanks and praise for creation, Jesus and biblical events, then raising his voice, giving honour to the almighty Lord and joining all the angels at some length in His praise, to which the congregation respond, "Holy, Holy, Holy is the Lord of hosts; Heaven and earth are full of His glory; blessed be He for ever. Amen"

There was an air of devotion as the celebrant thanked and praised God for all he had done for humankind's redemption, reciting most of the Creed's description of him before saying of Jesus "Mindful of all He suffered for us, we thank you almighty God, not as we should but as well as we are able, and we fulfil His will, for on the night He was betrayed He took the bread..." over the host, "and cup..." over the chalice, and consecrated them, to which the faithful said "Amen". This was the sacrificial part of the service after which the Spirit miraculously transformed the bread and wine into the tortured body and blood of Christ who died in reparation for our sins. The curtains were now drawn back to reveal the altar and the celebrant took communion then distributed it to the clergy before descending to distribute to the congregation at the foot of the altar, saying "Body of Christ" with the bread and "Blood of Christ" with the wine, to each of which the recipient would say "Amen". During the distribution, the choir and congregation would usually sing Psalm 34. After quiet time for contemplation, there would be a thanksgiving, followed by a blessing which marked the end of the service.

Towards the end of the fourth century, two processional events were introduced to the service – one preceding the Gospel and the other bringing the bread and wine offerings to the altar.

It is interesting that apart from lasting a good two hours, the order of service would still be recognisable today in Catholic Mass and Anglican Communion Service and others. Although the present day Mass is referred to as a sacrifice, the re-enactment of the Last Supper is hard to read as a sacrifice, but the communion most certainly is. Apart from some regional variations of the service the core format was fairly consistent and although there is a lack of records dating back so far in the West, it is reasonable to assume their services followed similar lines, given the frequent interchange of bishops either by appointment or exile. It is recorded that by the first half of the third century, a Eucharistic service was held daily in the West and in the fourth century at least three days per week in some Churches in the East.

Pilgrimage, Vestments

Another development in the fourth century was the idea of pilgrimage as a commitment of self-denial and homage to God. An obvious destination was the Holy Land and New Testament sites. Helena, Constantine's Greek mother played an early part in this and promoted the building of churches in Bethlehem and on the Mount of Olives, the places of Christ's birth and Ascension. Her son followed, building the Church of the Holy Sepulchre over the cave where Christ's body was laid. Helena also reportedly identified the rock of Golgotha and the remaining wood of the bases of the three crosses in the ground.

Since gaining the blessing of Constantine as the accepted religion of the Empire, the Christian Church had gained considerable wealth. It applied some of this to the greater glory of God in grand buildings, elaborate decoration of Churches and altars and magnificent vestments for presbyters and bishops, the senior clergy being emboldened to imitate the senators of Rome in wearing magenta. Grand clerical vestments were a departure from the early days, when those officiating at services wore their best, yet still modest garments as they would have done whenever in public focus. In this, they differed notably from Christ, who never wore fine clothes. It is fair to question whether such self-aggrandisement would have gained Christ's approval regardless of the claimed reasoning, which related to human expectation, though they suggested clerical vanity and pride. Hermits, monks and nuns maintained humility and practicality in their attire.

Baptism, Penance, Absolution, Pursuit of Perfection

Many of those who flocked to churches were not baptised. They had to take instruction for baptism as catechumens. Until baptised, they were ineligible to stay for the communion part of Mass and the altar was hidden from their view by a thick curtain, beyond which only the baptised could venture, similar to the Holy of Holies in the synagogue. Baptism was then regarded in the Church as the only sacrament that could annul sin. The sacrament of penance would not be introduced until the 11th century. But as Christ said to the Apostles when he appeared to them after the resurrection, "As the Father sent me, so I send you. Receive the Holy Spirit. If you forgive people's sins they are forgiven; if you retain them they are retained." (John 20:22, 23). In recognition of this, grave sins could be forgiven by a bishop after a period of due remorse, prayer, almsgiving or good deeds involving exceptional efforts. Lenten penance was common practice but regarded as a source of grace rather than absolution. This led people to leave Baptism until as late as possible in life, even to just before death as in the case of Constantine and at least two of his sons, to help ensure forgiveness and salvation carried forward. This was seen by clergy as a dangerous ploy and they pushed for infant baptism, but the norm continued and children were generally only baptised if very ill. Thus most adults did not qualify to attend the full Eucharistic service, probably not Christ's intention.

Preparation for baptism was taken seriously and generally consisted of catechetical lectures based on the catechism. Cyril of Jerusalem started these about 350 AD in the Church of the Holy Sepulchre. At each session the catechumens (candidates), were first exorcised to expel evil and bring in the Holy Spirit.

The contents of the Didache, the first catechism encouraged fortifying the will of a person to resist temptation and behave morally. In this regard, Lent was an important period of penance by self-denial. Baptism was the sole source of forgiveness and route to salvation and that led later to the concept of Limbo. Baptism was regarded as 'rebirth' – born again. Absolution also involved part of the exorcism, with anointment by holy oil, myrrh and chrism, which was used to bring the Holy Spirit into the new-born Christian as today it is used in Confirmation. These oils are outward signs of sacramental grace. Although with origins in pagan traditional practices, they were adapted to their current spiritual purpose.

Nicetas (335-414), bishop of Remesiana in present-day Serbia, wrote a six-volume 'Instructions for Candidates for Baptism'. Significant parts of this have survived, in which he made the first recorded reference to 'The Communion of Saints'. This concept is a vitally important part of Christian belief referring to a mystical eternal family of all good people, living and dead. It renders life on earth and death as merely a natural part of the eternal sequence of an individual's full life.

It had become the practice of a few zealot faithful to adopt asceticism, which, though in the name of Christianity, was not unrelated to earlier pagan practice. Even today there remain signs of the old and the new in most faith traditions. Asceticism echoed early belief that the body was the enemy of the soul (as in Gnosticism). Thus self-denial included fasting, often wearing uncomfortable clothing, avoidance of eating meat and of sexual intercourse, this latter arguably suppressing of the status of women. Jesus told the rich young man who wanted to follow him to sell all his possessions, according to Mark (10:21), although Matthew (19:21) softened the same message by adding "..If you want to be perfect".

This was indeed a counsel for perfection rather than a commandment. In just the same way, Jesus supported marriage as a good thing, though he never married and there was the suggestion from Paul that it was even better to eschew marriage and possessions and lead a pure life. Christianity embraced asceticism as a good and valid practice even if only as an aspiration, as intimated in the Didache 6:2 – "If you are able to carry the entire yoke of the Lord, you will attain perfection; but if you are unable, do as much as you can." Then again from Barnabas 19:8 "Let your neighbour share in all that you possess and refuse to call anything your own. As far as you can you must live continently for the sake of your soul."

Ascetics and Monastics, Pachomius, Basil, Eustathius, John Chrysostom

Ascetics still had to be warned against spiritual pride as many regarded themselves superior to clergy, so humility was added to their aims. A few parts of the early Christian Church such as Mesopotamia preached celibacy, but the broad Catholic Church (meaning 'Universal Church', East and West) regarded these views as extreme and impracticable, although it held the ascetic life in high regard.

Some ascetics aimed to cut themselves off from the temptations of the world, while others sought solitude to bring them closer to God. The latter were the seeds of hermitage and the monasteries, for which Egypt was renowned. Monasteries emerged as a custom grew of several ascetics, each living entirely alone but within reasonable walking distance of each other both for security and to be able to gather together once a week for communal worship. As many of the early ascetics aged or fell ill, the arrangement of each living separately in his own cell but within a large single complex or building offered some practical assurance of support. In fact, women probably adopted this movement earlier as they were more vulnerable on their own and needed the protection. Also, women outnumbered men in the world at the time.

Pachomius, born 292, introduced a more structured idea of monastic life in Egypt in which ascetics came together but lived and worked in their own individual cells or gardens within buildings enclosed from the outside world by a wall. He established rules and an organisational structure involving defined cycles of work, prayer, worship and two communal meals a day. These were initially formed in Egypt close to fertile land along the Nile during the 4th century and became extremely popular. For example the town of Oxyrynchus became over-run by monasteries to the extent that a new monastic town had to be built outside its walls in order to house 10,000 monks and 20,000 nuns. These were huge numbers given the population at the time. Monasteries spread north within Egypt, across the Sinai Peninsula then into Palestine, Syria and Asia Minor. Their growth was driven for some by founders persuading the faithful that the world was full of 'demons' – today we would probably use the word temptations or distractions – which could draw them away from God and the ideal Christian life.

For the very poor there would have been the added attraction of regular food and a roof over their heads. Life outside was hard, so the privations within were not alien. The organisation was such as to gain maximum spiritual benefit for the individual whilst the work regime supported a cohesive whole that ensured economic security for the group as well as self-sufficiency in food, clothing and furniture. The produce and products surplus to their requirements were sold and became an important element in the local economy outside in the case of the larger establishments.

One criticism of the ascetic or monastic life then was that being a dawn-to-dusk regime of prayer, hard work, barely essential sustenance and very little sleep, all with no conversation, it was a life of devotion and penance alright, but it provided little by way of evangelism and theological development. The prayer and worship included psalms, biblical reading and learning. But there was little examination of philosophy or the finer points of, say, the Trinity (both of which would have involved distraction, or discussion and therefore association with others) that were causing such dissension and strife in the 'real' world outside the monastery walls. In truth, the life was somewhat one-dimensional in so far as while perhaps bringing practitioners closer to God than to the world, it did little to increase one's knowledge and understanding of God or his message. With a preponderance of women in the outside population, the movement was also depriving the world of potentially productive men. They were doing little to help fellow men, although they would argue that they helped the world by their prayers. Regardless, Antony, Pachomius and other leading ascetics were honoured as saints, so the Church clearly approved.

The weekly Eucharistic celebration including the sacrament of Communion was an important feature. This had to be administered by a presbyter, but the ascetics were rarely qualified or ordained and had to rely on either a resident or visiting priest. Towards the end of the fourth century and beyond, some ascetics sought ordination but there was a tension, as given their responsibilities to others and their less arduous prayer routines, they were no longer regarded by the purists as fully ascetic and Pachomius for one would not have approved of their new ministry.

The Church had concerns about the proliferation of extreme forms of asceticism, especially around Syria, whereby exponents went to further extremes and for example confined themselves in tiny cages, exposed themselves to extremes of weather or became stylites ('pillar saints'), dendrites (tree-dwellers) or Adamites, who went naked. The Church would like to have condemned them, but their intentions were clearly good and they were so numerous that they were tolerated, although always regarded as odd extremists and there are obvious comparisons for example with Hindu sadhus and some Buddhists. Public opinion supported them and when Simeon Stylites, the renowned pillar saint died in 459, he was honoured by the construction of a great church complex with a magnificent cloister around his pillar in Syria, the cloister being fully intact until the Syrian civil war in the twenty-teens.

In fact, ascetics became so numerous that even they sometimes formed groups 'like choirs of angels' which held themselves superior to the secularised institution of the Church, tending to regard people who were married or had possessions as beyond salvation. Eustathius of Sebaste, a charismatic ascetic from Armenia, was a powerful influence and supported Basil of Ancyra, an accomplished scholar. They adopted a degree of monasticism which led to joint activities such as bible study and developing improved liturgies. Basil founded a monastery of the Egyptian model in the second half of the 4th century and became a celebrated teacher and writer on the role of monasticism in the Church. Basil and Eustathius held differing views on the subject of consubstantiality and *homoousios* but they always respected each other.

Following his baptism and dedication to the spiritual life, in 357 Basil travelled to Egypt to observe at first hand the ascetics and monastics there and spend some time as a hermit in the desert before returning via Palestine and Syria to his native Caesarea. In 358, he gathered his brother and a few like-minded friends together to establish a community on the family estate. He wrote about monastic life and set out guidelines on rules for it, thus becoming the pioneer of Eastern monasticism, which flourished. John Cassian and St Benedict would be similar pioneers later in the West.

The clergy enjoyed high prestige and privileges in Constantinople which resisted the establishment of monasteries in the city, but they arrived in the early 380s, supported by John Chrysostom. Asceticism was slower to develop in the West, but an early proponent was St Martin. Born in Hungary, he served a while in Julian's army then left to become a hermit and moved around before settling near Poitiers. He became Bishop of Tours in 372 but never abandoned his ascetic way of life. His cell some way out of town soon became surrounded by cells of followers and effectively became a monastic community from which eventually grew the renowned monastery of Marmoutier.

In 380, Euagrios, Bishop of Antioch translated Athanasius' 'Life of Antony' and this spread the word about asceticism more widely. A monastery outside Tréves used a copy to enthuse many, including Augustine of Hippo who came to study in Europe, having been born and brought up in a part of Numidia that is now Algeria. Monasteries and nunneries sprang up all over France and it became popular to site them on islands in wide rivers or just off coasts. They spread into Spain in spite of resistance from some bishops who were fond of their palaces and worldly comforts; also into Africa with Augustine's encouragement. He will feature in the fifth century when most of his work was carried out.

Not all Church leaders saw the point of the monastic life when so many workers were needed to support and spread the faith. One such was Vigilantius (c365-407), a priest from South-west France who had no time for asceticism, celibacy or the reverence of relics. Another was Jovinian (340-405), a monk who upset the establishment by abandoning the closeted life, but who kept his habit and many practices, similar to the friars who came later. He wrote a powerful critique of monastic life. He did not believe celibacy represented holiness even though he maintained it himself, nor could he see the point of asceticism or anything wrong with marriage. After all, as Helvidius, who was the first to suggest that Mary's virginity did not last as she had other children (an assertion strenuously denied by Jerome), had pointed out around 383 that Abraham, Isaac, Jacob and others all had wives. He quoted many married Biblical characters, also noting praise of sexual love in the Old Testament Song of Songs. Even Jesus' appointed head of his Church on earth, Peter was married. Jovinian similarly doubted the value of fasting and abstinence as prejudicing bodily strength and stamina for useful worldly work. God promised equal reward for all who reach his kingdom as illustrated by the parable of the vineyard workers (Matt20:1-16). Jovinian's view upset some and a synod of bishops led by Pope Siricius and Ambrose had him whipped and deported. He died soon after. The Church denounced him as a heretic, and Jerome called him a second Epicurus, while much later, John Henry Newman saw him as a forerunner of Protestantism, drawing a parallel with Jean Calvin.

Celibacy and Male-only Clerics

The question of clerical celibacy also faced differing views as to its wisdom, just as the role of women in the early Church was a challenging subject. Jesus never gave guidance on either. True, he never married and had all-male disciples, but that was entirely normal in his region in that era.

Paul is often quoted on both sides of both arguments. He himself appointed women leaders in some areas that he had evangelised. His messages on the subject were ambiguous in his epistles, e.g. 1 Corinthians 7 could be read selectively either way. More specifically, there were apparent contradictions. For example, compare the text that gave him the label of misogynist with others, seemingly contrary:

- 1Timothy 2:11-14 – "During instruction, a woman should be quiet and respectful. I give no permission for a woman to teach or have authority over a man. A woman ought to be quiet because Adam was formed first and Eve afterwards, and it was not Adam who was led astray but the woman who was led astray and fell into sin."
- Galatians 3:27, 28 – "...every one of you that has been baptised has been clothed in Christ. There can be neither Jew nor Greek, there can be neither slave nor free man, there can be neither male nor female – you are all one in Christ Jesus."

On the matter of women leaders in the Church, he says in the epistle to the Romans (16) – "I commend to you our sister Phoebe, a deaconess of the church at Cenchreae; give her, in the Lord, a welcome worthy of God's holy people and help her with whatever she needs from you – she herself has come to the help of many people, including myself." Here, Paul goes on to greet over two dozen more people, men and women in Rome for whom he has strong feelings of respect for their work in and for the Church.

The Bible on balance encourages but does not demand celibacy of Church leaders and it was not an issue in the early centuries of Christianity. Bishops were commonly married, including some who are regarded as saints. Many of these, including a number of popes, had children.

Christianity and Heresies

This century showed how much passion, energy, argument and even bloodshed was spent on debate as to the nature of Christ – Christology. It embraced all levels in the Church which had been charged by Christ himself with spreading the news of him and maintaining its unity. Of course his true nature is important to the faith, as illustrated by the alternative beliefs of Judaism and Islam; but from the Christian point of view alone it may have helped if the Church had paused to consider how Jesus Christ would have viewed and handled such debate. It is hard to envisage Jesus banishing people for genuinely reasoned opinions, or ever excommunicating them and certainly not killing them. Yet in seeking to give clear guidance on the basis agreed at councils, this is what people of the Church encouraged or took part in. The Church needed now as ever to use prayer and spiritual guidance.

The dissension was aggravated rather than eased by the interplay between Church and empire that developed during the Constantine dynasty. Power and politics became interdependent with Church and faith, yielding some beneficial effects but others not so good.

Some of the Debates on the Nature of Christ and the Holy Trinity

Logos theology – The concept derives from John 1:1 "In the beginning was the Word, and the Word was with God, and the Word was God." 'Word' is the translation we have of the Greek *logos*, but *logos* has a wider significance, including a 'spiritual entity', which might seem more accessible in this context.

Origen – was the first to use the word '*homoousios'* in the sense of the Son being 'of the same substance' as the Father. A highly respected philosopher in his own time, Origen was first to perceive that our concept of time did not apply to God. Thus the Son was eternally begotten by the Father. The Son was therefore of the same nature as the Father, being created out of him and thus subordinate to him. This idea of logos who was also the Son corresponded with the Platonic view. Origen was reported to have believed the Holy Spirit proceeded from the Son as the third phase of the unfolding Godhead and all three made up the single spiritual Godhead. (Somewhat at odds with Luke 1:35 and Matt 1:18)

Clement – First Century bishop in Alexandria, he was mainly preoccupied with the Old Testament and regarded the Holy Spirit as significant in its revelation. He refers to the Trinity in the confessional formula "We have one God and one Christ and one Spirit of grace poured upon us and one calling through Christ."

Justin – God the Creator; the Son, Jesus Christ in second place; the *logos* identical with the 'prophetic spirit' in third place. He believed in angels. His Trinity was difficult to reconcile with the *logos* theory.

Tertullian – the Trinity is of one essence and one power, but the Son is the second and the Spirit the third person of the Trinity. For Tertullian, Christ was god and man, one person in two substances.

Monarchianism – Belief in a unitary as against trinitarian God, deemed heretical.

Sabellians (Modalists) – Based on Sabellius, a third century cleric and theologian probably from Libya who taught in Rome and rejected the logos theology and the concept of the Holy Trinity. It was much in line with the earlier Monarchianism, believing that God is unitary and he appeared on earth in the form of Jesus Christ and redeemed mankind by his death on the Cross.

Paul of Samosata – followed Luke 1:35, that Jesus was begotten of the Holy Spirit and the Virgin Mary. The divine *logos* lived and worked within this Son of God just as if in a temple, but was a separate entity from Jesus, having worked previously within foregoing prophets. In other words, the *logos* was one in essence with God, but not with the Son who, by such inference, could not be one with the Father. This was why his view was deemed heretical, as it logically denied the Trinity.

Meletians – followers of Bishop Meletius from Lycopolis, including Isidoros and Arius, whom he recruited while trespassing in the diocese of Peter of Alexandria while the latter was in prison, thus initiating schism in the Egyptian Church. Meletius claimed the divine logos was coeternal with God and became incarnate in Jesus, thus rendering it impossible for the Son to be subordinate to the Father, while yet being human.

Arius – one of Meletius' early recruits who promoted his 'Arian' theology, which was condemned as heretical. This postulated that the Father was superior to the Son. There had been a time when God was alone as the Father and at some point he begot or created the Son from nothing, at which point time began and the Universe was created. Arius did not accept that the Son was eternal, nor that he had equal status with the Father. Nor, in his view could the Father and Son be 'consubstantial', so he clearly rejected the concept of homoousios. He saw the Trinity as three individuals (hypostases), only one of which could be the true Godhead, this being the Father.

Nestorianism – Nestorius (386-450) denied the union of divinity and humanity in the one person (hypostasis) of Christ.

Apollinarinism – Apollinaris of Laodicea said Jesus had a human body but a divine mind instead of a human soul.

Pneumatomachoi – (trans. 'opponents of the spirit'), founded by Macedonius in the 4th century. They believed that Jesus was divine but the same could not be said of the Spirit. Their belief was rejected by the Church and repudiated at the Council of Constantinople, which confirmed the full divinity of the Holy Spirit.

CHAPTER 7

5th Century

Popes

401-417 Innocent I
417-418 Zosimus
418-419 Eulalius
418-422 Boniface I
422-432 Celestine I
432-440 Sixtus III
440-461 Leo I (The Great)

461-468 Hilary
468-483 Simplicius
483-492 Felix III
492-496 Gelasius I
496-498 Anastasius II
498-514 Symmachus (Sardinia)
498-506 Laurentin (Rome)

Roman Emperors

Constantine III 409-411, self-declared in West in 407, accepted as co-emperor West by Honorius 409. Executed.
Constantius III Feb-Sept 421
Joannes 423-425 (not recognised in the East}
Valentinian III 424-455 Emperor West
Petronius Maximus March-May 455. Assassinated.
Avitus 455-456

Majorian 457-461
Libius Severus 461-465 Not recognised in East. Assassinated.
Anthemius 465-472. Assassinated.
Olibrius July-Sept 472
Glycerius 473-474. Deposed, became bishop.
Julius Nepos 474-475 Assassinated.
Romulus Augustulus 475-476, parts of Italy only, deposed.

This century saw more advancement in thinking around the Church, creation and human behaviour concerning religion and various moral dilemmas, including Just War theory. The Oriental Church went its own way, choosing to follow 'Nestorian Christianity', which was considered heretical by the mainstream. This schism would have enormous consequences over time for the Universal Church. The Roman Empire fell and Christianity overtook druidic practices and belief in Ireland.

The 'Filioque' Debate

"[I believe] in the Holy Spirit, the Lord, the giver of life, who proceeds from the Father **and the Son**..."
Latin: *"[Credo] in Spiritus Sanctus Dominum et vivificantem qui ex Patre **et filioque** procedit..."*

Debate frequently recurred during the 5th century as to whether to add to the Nicene Creed the phrase 'and the Son', or '*et filioque*' as above. Recent research suggests that it was first proposed at a local Council of Seleucia-Ctesiphon, (capital of the Sassanid Empire in Persia, south-east of today's Baghdad on the River Tigris), called by Bishop Mar Isaac, as early as 410 AD. This council was a remarkable turn-round in that region, as Christianity had been a proscribed religion in parts of this Zoroastrian enclave until one year previously when the Zoroastrian King Yazdegerd I had given permission for Christianity to exist and hold open worship. He had then allowed sacked churches to be rebuilt, but strictly forbade proselytisation.

The King asked the Bishop to call this council to establish a homogeneous organisation for the minority Christian Church in his empire. Based on the lines of the First Council of Nicaea, it would be headed by an Archbishop or, using the Orthodox term, a Metropolitan, resident in the capital Seleucia-Ctesiphon, with bishops in each designated province reporting to the Metropolitan. It was named the Church of the East and in the course of agreeing a Creed, debate arose between two Syriac versions which differed in their reference to the Holy Spirit. The East Syriac version simply expressed belief "…in the Holy Spirit", while the West Syriac version, used by the Syrian Orthodox Church had "…in the Holy Spirit… who is from the Father and the Son", which some scholars believe is the earliest known example of the 'filioque' clause.

This may sound like a minor semantic issue, but the Eastern Orthodox Church saw the addition of this phrase as relegating the Holy Spirit's place in the Holy Trinity. The Western addition had been intended as a positive challenge to the Arian heresy. But it is incompatible with the Trinitarian *homoousios* concept. It seems to run contrary to the common prayer the 'Glory Be': '*Glory be to the Father, the Son and the Holy Spirit, as it was in the beginning, is now and ever shall be. Amen*', with no suggestion of the Holy Spirit arriving later or being inferior to the Son in the Holy Trinity. The debate raised such intense passion that a few centuries later Pope Leo III (795-816) rejected and forbade the '*et filioque*' version and had the Nicene Creed engraved in Latin on the wall of St Peter's without the words, so satisfying both Roman Catholicism and Eastern Orthodoxy. But the matter would certainly not end there.

Augustine of Hippo (354- 430)

Augustine was born of a Christian mother and pagan father in Numidia in what is now the Annaba region of Algeria. His eventual view on original sin grew from a childhood incident when he stole fruit from a neighbouring garden "not because I was hungry, but because it was not allowed". He deduced from this that the human is naturally inclined to sin and in need of the grace of God. In his late teens, he studied rhetoric in Carthage but he was quite a playboy in his youth, a stage that produced that prayer "Grant me chastity and continence, Lord, but not just yet". As he grew up, he left the Church, influenced by Manichaeism (see 2nd Century), but he later became sceptical of this and was drawn to study the ideas of Plato, the Stoics, Plotinus, Porphyry and Neoplatonism, leading to a passion for philosophy.

Aged 19 in 373 he took a lover for over ten years. They had a son they named Adeodatus ('gift of God'). He later left his lover and much of his past behind and took Adeodatus to Rome and set up a school there. They moved to Milan in 384 where he admired and was noticed by Bishop Ambrose, who took him under his wing, brought him back to Christianity and baptised him in 387 aged 32 together with Adeodatus, who excelled academically. When his mother died, Augustine and his son returned home but soon after, he was even more grief-stricken when Adeodatus died aged just 16. He offloaded possessions and turned his family home into a monastery. He was ordained to the priesthood in 391 then consecrated Bishop of Hippo Regius in 396. Augustine gave his property to the church in Thagaste and began the life's work for which he became famous, now recognised as one of the great philosophers and a saint by all Christian Churches.

After his conversion and baptism, he demonstrated deep thinking as he began to develop and expound his own philosophy and theology. Believing that divine grace was indispensable to human development, he helped formulate the doctrine of original sin and contributed greatly to unfolding 'Just War' theory. The books for which he is best known are 'City of God', the autobiographical 'Confessions' and 'On the Trinity', which confirmed the concept of the Trinity as defined by the Councils of Nicaea and Constantinople. As the Roman Empire in the West began to collapse, Augustine developed the concept of the Church as a 'City of God', a spiritual rather than a physical entity and wrote the book of that title to console fellow Christians after the sacking of Rome in 410. In it he describes the Church as a heavenly kingdom ruled by love and transcending all earthly empires because the latter are essentially ruled by pride and self-indulgence. He believed that Bishops and priests have God-given authority as successors of the Apostles.

Augustine recognised that intellectuals had more difficulty with faith than the average person, who did not need to question what they were told, especially true in those days of limited education, books or literacy.

Regarding Augustine's theology, there are a number of headline points.

The Bible, Creation

Regarding the Old Testament, Augustine began by admitting similar difficulty to many others in accepting the literal interpretation of the book of Genesis. He was dismissive of the idea of 6-day creation and saw creation as more likely a single event. In fact he saw no wrong in factually rejecting any content of the Old Testament that conflicted with scientific knowledge or God-given reason. Nor did the New Testament escape such analysis. For example, Revelation 20:1-10 says that Jesus will reign on earth for 1000 years, which Augustine took as symbolic rather than a truth. He was far from being the first to suggest the Bible should not be read literally, going further by describing any insistence on doing so as a pointless obstruction to the ability of intelligent people to accept Christianity. However, he did recognise the Bible as a record of serious prophecy, teaching and guidance on God's will for humankind.

Human Christianity

Augustine regarded the human being as a perfect unity of soul and body, both of them sacred as a creation of God, the soul being the superior partner. He was therefore opposed to abortion once the foetus had been infused with a soul, the timing of which he was unsure. He also believed that procreation was an important part of marriage and therefore he also opposed any other means of preventing the birth of a child such as sterilisation or contraception. All of these were known and occasionally practised in this era though abortion was a highly dangerous procedure for the mother.

Original Sin, Free Will, Sexuality, Predestination

Whatever he did or did not believe about the Garden of Eden, Augustine was willing to take on the message conveyed in the story of Adam and Eve and the fragility and fall of the human race. The real original sin was their disobedience in tasting the one and only forbidden fruit, following which came realisation and possibly the beginning of human sexuality – embarrassment, fig leaves and so on.

Augustine's arguments eventually led the Church to accept the concept of the inheritance of original sin and this set off a trend towards widespread infant baptism. Original sin was in line with some passages in the Old Testament suggesting that the sons inherit the sins of the father, though there it is limited to three or four generations (Exodus, Numbers, Deuteronomy). However, there are also explicitly contradictory passages (Ezekiel and strangely, Deuteronomy – 24:16 versus 5:9).

He viewed Adam and Eve's original sin as disobedience to God, with their human desires overcoming the expressed will of their creator. God created humans with the moral capacity of doing good or evil. From the beginning, he gifted them free will in making the choice, then later the Ten Commandments for clear guidance in that choice. Divine grace was essential to human ability to obey the Commandments and it is there for the asking. God created humans and angels as rational beings with free will. This gives them the capacity to sin but free will is not prepared equally for good and evil. Sin limits its freedom, creating dissatisfaction and guilt, while grace restores this freedom.

Pelagius, a British ascetic theologian and orator (of whom more below) contested Augustine's view of original sin. For him, the original sin did not affect future generations, nor could human will and mind have been wounded by it. The human person still maintained the capacity for good and evil and the free will to choose either. Pelagius upset theologians by saying humans could achieve salvation by their own efforts, implying that those who are strong enough may not even need divine grace to help them.

Augustine clearly disagreed, citing the ever-present overbearing desires of the flesh, disobedient both to the Spirit and what the human knows to be right. He saw this as springing directly from the original sin, the ongoing punishment of humans for the sin of Adam and Eve and thus strongly affirmed the existence of original sin, the need for infant baptism and the impossibility of a sinless life without Christ and his grace.

Self-examination and self-justification may have influenced Augustine's conclusion, including the childhood theft incident, his youth and passion for his lover. The last was accepted by some in the Church as having been a loyal and genuine love, even if outside of marriage. Nevertheless, Augustine followed Plato and many others before or since in eschewing further carnal contacts after his reconversion. In 'Confessions' he accepts his own natural sensuality. He saw the sacrament of marriage as permission for conjugal acts, going some way towards healing the effects on human sexuality of the original sin. Full healing would be achieved in the resurrection of the body. Augustine and Pelagius' views here were poles apart.

Augustine deduced that all human beings inherited the original sin because they are conceived by concupiscence, so suffer a weakened free will, more disposed to choose wrong than right. His belief in original sin was endorsed by councils in Carthage (417), Ephesus (431), Orange (529) and much later, Florence (1442) and Trent (1546), some of which supported baptism for infants as early as possible. Many theologians and saints went along with original sin, without accepting Augustine's link with concupiscence.

Pondering the apparent conflicts between free will, omniscience of God and predestination, Augustine concluded that "God wills all men to be saved... every kind of man is among them..." God orders all things while preserving human freedom. People ask how there can be no predestination if God is omniscient. Humans are constrained in their thoughts by the time dimension in life, while God is not. Thus he can give us free will, the exercise of which will determine our destiny, while it is quite reasonable that God can see this end without interfering in our choices. Scholars have differing views in this respect.

The strength of Augustine's view and writing may have been influenced by his disagreement with Pelagius, perhaps feeling that he had to take an equivalent but opposite extreme position. This led him to appear to suggest some sort of predestination and punishment whereby humans are completely powerless in their ultimate destiny, be it salvation or damnation. They live out their lives according to a predetermined divine plan. This concept was too extreme for many, who consequently sided with Pelagius.

Just War Theory

Augustine probably originated the term Just War in 'City of God', although the subject had been previously addressed in the Indian epic, the Mahabharata, the longest known piece of poetry probably dating back to at least 700 years before Christ.

In the first three centuries after Christ, Christians were totally opposed to the use of lethal force even in self-defence then some flexibility on this had crept in latterly as a matter of pragmatism as mentioned earlier. Augustine found war repulsive and believed that Christians should be pacifists in the model of Christ. But in line with Ambrose of Milan's thinking, he realised war can be an inevitable way of resolving unsurmountable difficulties between states. He believed God had given government the sword and Christians called by their government to declare or join war to fight evil or gain peace should feel no guilt, even if it involves killing, so long as that is done with a heavy heart. He stresses the importance of adopting a suitable "...inward disposition. The sacred seat of virtue is the heart." He said that remaining passive in the face of unyielding serious evil would be sinful, while self-defence or the defence of weaker others is also justified. So carrying out such obligations in a just cause is justified against the Commandment 'Do not kill'. All war should be lamented and unjust war condemned. Opponents of Just War theory argue that while war always brings loss to both sides, it never brings tangible benefit to any participant.

Christianity holds that all legitimate authority is God-given. Augustine says that individual Christians called up to war by their government in an immoral war "by divine edict have no choice but to subject themselves to their political masters and seek to execute their duty in combat as justly as possible."

Debate on this issue would develop over later centuries and Thomas Aquinas would take it further, offering guiding moral principles for national governments to weigh when contemplating military action.

Pelagius (c357-418)

Born in the late 350s of British or Irish origin and very well educated, perhaps by monks, Pelagius was evidently clever and a fluent speaker and writer in Latin and Greek. He had a striking appearance, tall and well built in spite of following an austerely ascetic life. He was also endowed with a powerful and persuasive rhetoric, which together with his asceticism gained him rapid notoriety when he moved to Rome in 380. He was still there when Alaric sacked the city in 410. After Rome's fall, Pelagius and his close follower Caelestius went to Carthage and it was probably there that he and Augustine first locked horns. Pelagius moved on to the Holy Land five years later.

In accepting the idea of free will, Pelagius believed strongly that this put peoples' destinies firmly into their own hands, so he opposed any suggestion of predestination. He derided Augustine's idea of people inheriting original sin, referring to Deuteronomy 24:16 "Parents must not be put to death for their children, nor children for their parents, but each must be put to death for his own crime". He worried about the moral laxity of Christians at the time blaming the teaching on divine grace espoused by Augustine and others. He believed people are quite able to keep to the Law without divine aid, perhaps a view one could expect from a determined ascetic and celibate, who would tend to regard this as a personal objective.

Pelagius saw "grace" as comprising the gift of free will, the Law of Moses, and the teachings of Jesus. Armed with these, a person would always be able to determine the moral course of action and follow it. Prayer, fasting, and asceticism supported the will to do good. Augustine accused him of thinking of God's grace as consisting only of external support.

The personal animosity between Pelagius and Augustine was more than just intellectual rivalry. They were two good, articulate and intelligent thinkers seeking Christian perfection, yet they were so different and competitive in their theology. Augustine referred to his rival's beliefs as Pelagianism and successfully pushed for a synod in Carthage. It took place in 418, led by Bishop Aurelius of Carthage and supported Augustine, denouncing Pelagius' views on original sin and human perfectibility. The synod alleged that Pelagianism denied nine Church beliefs:

1. Death came from sin, not from man's physical nature
2. Infants must be baptized to be cleansed from original sin.
3. Justifying grace covers past sins and helps avoid future sins.
4. The grace of Christ imparts strength and will to act out God's Commandments.
5. No good works can come without God's grace.
6. We confess we are sinners not from humility, but because it is true.
7. The saints ask for forgiveness for their own sins.
8. The saints also confess to be sinners because they are.
9. Children dying unbaptised are excluded from both the kingdom of heaven and eternal life.

The last item raises the matter of Limbo, a place for the souls of the unbaptised – see box on the next page.

The wider Church was not certain about the nine beliefs. Pelagius wrote a letter from Jerusalem to Pope Innocent, clarifying his beliefs. It included the claim that good works can only be done with the help of God's grace, that infants must be baptized for salvation (today no longer deemed essential by all Christian Churches), and that the saints were not always sinless, but that some at least have been able to stop sinning. Pelagius stated, "This free will is in all good works always assisted by divine help," and in an accompanying confession of faith, he said that he believed God would never ask the impossible of anyone and obedience of the Commandments is not beyond anyone. By the time the letter reached Rome in 417, Innocent had died and it was received by Pope Zosimus.

Augustine's famous riposte to this was "I cannot not sin." (*Non possum non peccare*). The African bishops and Emperor Honorius brought such pressure to bear on the pope that Pelagius and his key followers were excommunicated in 418. He was expelled from Jerusalem and given sanctuary by Cyril of Alexandria in Egypt and left the public eye.

LIMBO

Given the concepts of heaven for the saved and hell for the damned, applied to those who followed Jesus, who died on the cross to enable baptised believers to be saved, theological debate arose about the prospects for a) all those who had died before Christ and b) infants who died before baptism. This ignored a significant third group – unbaptised people of other faiths or none – which will be covered under Thomas Aquinas in 13th century. There is no scriptural reference to any of this and it is entirely supposition arising from learned debate, none of it being embodied in the Christian faith. The word 'Limbo' is not used in the latest Catholic catechism, though it does refer to 'the realm of the dead'.

It was believed that when Christ died he descended to hell, which had a compartment for the serious sinner with positive punishment and one for the just, which included Abraham and did not involve such punishment. This became known as the Patriarchs' Limbo and there was a belief that Christ would bring the latter group with him to join him in heaven together with all those saved in the AD period after him. Clement of Alexandria remarked on how unjust it would be if those God created who preceded Christ's presence on earth were excluded from the benefits of those who followed it. Would the same apply to those who had never become Christians?

As to children, there was a further compartment known as Infant's' Limbo, which involves no positive punishment, but the denial of the actual presence and company of God in heaven, surely punishment in itself. Tertullian believed there was no need for infant baptism as infants are innocent. Ambrose taught that original sin, if it exists, is an inherited capacity and inclination to sin, but did not in itself carry guilt deserving of any punishment. Punishment is reserved for sins actually committed by an individual.

This was the scene into which Augustine pitched his less severe views. Anselm agreed with him that unbaptised infants share in at least some of the punishment of the damned. Later thoughts, including views from Peter Abelard and Thomas Aquinas are covered in the 13th century and present days.

The Church took the matter seriously as Bishop Germanus of Auxerre was sent to Britain to combat Pelagianism there around 429. The Palagianists seem to have been drawn from the wealthy and known for their fine attire, with a large proletariat following. In their public meeting, they proved no match for Germanus in debate and rhetoric and he made a convincing case for the Augustinian view of divine grace. There is no record of what wider impact he had, but he became known for some apparent miracles and for tactically helping the British Christians win a battle in North Wales against Picts and Saxons. There are dubious legends around him including that St Patrick was his pupil. There were also connections with the erstwhile St Alban, of whom he is supposed to have had a visionary dream.

Wales was quite a Christian stronghold around this time. In the following century Welsh Bishop Paul Aurelius called a synod at Llandewi Brefi with condemnation of Palagianism on its agenda. Paul persuaded Dubricius, the senior bishop there to allow a bright young monk David, who opposed Pelagius' views to address the assembly. David's eloquence encouraged Dubricius to retire and leave the see in David's capable hands. David followed this later with another synod about 569 at Caerleon, which condemned Pelagianism. This became known as the Synod of Victory. David is now the patron saint of Wales.

It is difficult to make a fair judgement today on Pelagius because our knowledge of him and his beliefs comes only from the writings of his opponents, which may well include distortions. He was confirmed a heretic at the First Council of Ephesus in 431 and thus never honoured by the Church. Recent scholars supported by extant letters of his that have since been discovered tend to take a kinder view of him.

Jerome (347-420)

Jerome was born into a wealthy Christian family near present day Ljubljana, Slovenia, which was in North East Italy in 347. He went to Rome for his education leading to studies in rhetoric and philosophy. He was baptised in his teens and in common with many of his peers, decided to travel to broaden his experience. He went to a monastery near Trier, now in Germany, joined a group of ascetics then moved on to a similar group in Aquilea in Italy, meeting Rufinius, the translator of much of Origen's work. This dispersed in 373 and Jerome went to the Holy Land and became a nomadic hermit until he arrived in Antioch where he resumed Greek studies. One of his teachers was Apollinaris of Laodicia who was later to be declared a heretic for believing that Jesus was only human in body, but not in mind or will.

In 375, during Lent, Jerome had a dream or vision of his final judgement in which he was accused of following pagan literature in preference to Christ. So he dropped secular study and devoted his life to God, mainly through the Bible. He went once more into the desert of Syria to live the ascetic life with "none but scorpions and wild beasts for companions" and found loneliness brought with it temptations of "the ardent heat of my nature" which fasting failed to dispel. As his physical frailty and exhaustion became intolerable, he craved company and learned Hebrew from a Jewish convert. This helped him on the track for which he would become best known, offering him access to the original Hebrew Bible as it had been before its translation into Greek.

He returned to Antioch around 379 where Bishop Paulinus, recognising him as a monk, hastened to ordain him as a priest, which he accepted on the condition he did not have to carry out normal priestly functions. He went to Constantinople and sank himself in studying Scripture, some of the time under Gregory Nazianzus, then was summoned to Rome to be secretary to Pope Damasus, who asked him to review and revise the New Testament of the Latin Bible based on Greek manuscripts. Several existed already, but these were rather loose translations from the Greek. He began this work, translating from the Greek while also applying his acquired knowledge of Hebrew to keep as close to the original as possible.

Jerome's status and lifestyle led to a following of aristocratic women who yearned for a monastic life. This together with his frequent criticism of the relatively indulgent lives of secular clergy drew their retaliatory criticism. He mocked their lack of charity, their accumulation of wealth, their vanity regarding clothes and perfume, their pride in their beards and their lack of knowledge of Scripture. Some of his followers blamed him for the death of one of the women following a strict fast. When Damasus died in 384, leaving Jerome vulnerable without his patronage, the clergy struck back, alleging his misconduct with one of his female followers, Paula. He stepped down and went to the Holy Land, but the women kept in touch through correspondence. They tried to maintain his influence in Rome, circulated his letters to make clear they were intended for the wider audience. Meanwhile, a wealthy follower of Jerome, probably Paula, established a monastery in Bethlehem for him to lead, including cloisters for women and a visitors' hostel.

Jerome moved in to the monastery and still spent most of his time following Damasus' instructions to translate the Bible from the original Greek Old Testament, the Septuagint, since Damasus felt the past Latin versions were so varied, having been produced by inaccurate translators, and the blundering alterations of confident but ignorant critics, and "…inserted or changed by copyists more asleep than awake." Jerome still further improved the reliability of his translation by checking it against the original Hebrew, diligently consulting Jewish rabbis and converts where he was unsure, setting a high standard for subsequent translators. His New Testament translation was also from the Greek. Jerome's Bible in Latin became known as the Vulgate (common language of the people), a work which took him 23 years and became the accepted Bible of the Roman Church for over 1000 years, although a number of copyist errors crept in that were corrected when the Council of Trent in the sixteenth century promoted it as the only authentic Latin text. This was a significant factor in the continuing use of Latin in all Roman Church services for a further five hundred years regardless of the fact that a majority of lay people would not understand the content of their liturgy anyway. The hierarchy rested satisfied that its biblical content was reliable.

Jerome was never regarded as a great theologian or philosopher. He did write a number of 'Contra' works against certain well known people's beliefs, for example Herodius, who believed firstly that Mary bore children to Joseph after Jesus and secondly that from a religious viewpoint, the state of marriage is not inferior to celibacy. Another was Vigilantius, who he thought undervalued the monastic life and the veneration of saints and relics; then Jovinian for his criticism of asceticism. These were hardly core issues of doctrine, so it is little wonder that Jerome was never regarded as a theologian. He interpreted ecclesiastical doctrine but his breadth and originality was no match for that of Augustine, so his fame only really stems from his grand work on the Vulgate.

Another subject of Jerome's criticism was Bishop John of Jerusalem. Firstly, Jerome was emboldened by a visit to Jerusalem by Epiphanius bishop of Salamis in Cyprus, who backed him in accusing John of 'Origenism', the allegedly erroneous beliefs of Origen attributed to John, these being:

- the Son was subordinate to God the Father
- souls are imprisoned in earthly bodies
- the devil could find salvation
- God clothed Adam and Eve in human bodies
- our bodies at their resurrection will be without gender
- Scriptural descriptions of Paradise are allegorical: trees meaning angels, rivers the heavenly virtues, the waters above and below the firmament being angels and devils
- man in the image of God was altogether lost at the Fall

John defended himself against these criticisms, writing that he always followed the genius of Origen but not his creed in entirety and surely some of these views were reasonable food for debate without censure?

Epiphanius tended to agree with Jerome and advised him and his friends to distance themselves from John, their bishop. He offended further against fellow-bishop John when he ordained Paulinian, Jerome's brother. This was entirely irregular, being outside Epiphanius' sphere of authority and John of Jerusalem appealed to Bishop Theophilus of Alexandria, winning his support which led to a lengthy dispute. The altercation broke out afresh when Jerome criticized John for receiving some of the 300 Origenist monks of Nitria when they were expelled from the Egyptian deserts. About fifty of these monks with John Cassian were welcomed to Constantinople by the bishop, John Chrysostom in 401.

Orosius, a pupil of Augustine who shared his contrary views on Pelagius, visited Jerome in Bethlehem in 414. They jointly condemned Pelagius, in particular for his dismissal of original sin. Bishop John, of Jerusalem, a personal friend of Pelagius, called a council in 415. Orosius, not being fluent in Greek, made a weak case while John's Eastern background helped him to agree that humans were not inherently sinful. No verdict was reached and because Pelagius, Jerome and Orosius were all followers of Rome the issue was passed to Pope Innocent in Rome. It came to nothing, attracting a mild rebuke warning John as to his diplomacy, which may not even have reached John before both he and Innocent died in 417.

The title 'Saint' has been largely avoided in this book but the foregoing scan of some saints – Augustine of Hippo, John of Jerusalem, Jerome and some others conveniently cues into the issue of sainthood.

Sainthood

Any belief system needs role models and in Christianity, Jesus is the ultimate role model and the only one worthy of worship, but perhaps human beings also need the comfort of less divine examples that they may seek to emulate or with whom they can identify where human weakness has been apparently overcome. The first people given the honour of sainthood were the known martyrs, who had given their lives for their Christian faith. There were of course many more unknown or unsung yet qualifying martyrs who will never be recognised. A day was set aside for remembrance of martyrs which is mentioned in a hymn by a Syrian writer in 359 and became referred to as All Saints Day by the 600s.

The Eastern Orthodox Church held reservations about the reverence the Roman Church showed the saints seeing it as potentially diluting the focus of worship on Christ. Sainthood was based on human judgment alone and it rankled with them that every Bishop of Rome up to the fifth Century had been canonised.

Over the centuries, the world of saints grew into an ecclesiastical honours list, which invites questions both over its own authenticity and about the unrecognised deserving ones, risking devaluation of this human honour. An omniscient God who is aware of all people's thoughts and actions knows countless more saints and worthy people than are recognised by the Church. The Gospels show Peter had his frailties, and Paul could hardly be described as 'good' in his early days, however conscientious. Yet Christ chose Peter as first Church leader and Paul as lead evangelist, effectively giving them such honours. Pelagius made the wry comment that "the saints were not always sinless, but some at least have been able to stop sinning."

The Greek word '*hagios*' translates either as saint or holy. Initially all Christians were regarded as '*hagios*' and members of the 'Communion of Saints'. A higher order of 'hagios' was found in Mary, mother of Jesus and in Stephen, the first martyr in 35 AD, since whom all known martyrs have been made saints. When Polycarp was burned to death, his bones were preserved and valued, perhaps the first such honoured relics. They were placed in a decorated tomb which served as a focus for annual celebrations on the anniversary of his martyrdom. Many saints have their feast day on the believed date of their death.

The title 'Saint' was not used before someone's name until the 6th century. It was then 'Sanctus' and confirmed by the bishop of the subject's diocese and was often a reflection of the numbers of people visiting the tomb or celebrating the anniversary. This meant they were nearly all local saints. Not until the 13th century did the Pope use his office to appoint saints according to Western Church law. People in the West continued to regard various holy people, heroes, monarchs and popes as saints, while in the East, most saints were Metropolitans, monks or nuns, including many of those from the West.

As mentioned, Mary, the mother of Jesus soon became regarded as a special saint and a helpful mother figure through whom petitions could be requested in the hope that those which caught her sympathy would be passed on to God through a voice he respected, just as children sometimes use their mother as a kind intermediary when confessing bad news that their father probably needs to know. People were always warned that they should not worship anyone but God, but it was quite in order to pray to God through the intermediary of saints, some of whom are regarded as patrons of particular causes or places.

Nestorian Controversy, Councils of Ephesus

When Nestorius was appointed Bishop of Constantinople by Theodosius II in 428, he was immediately active in opposing Arians and 'Quartodecimans' – those who based their date of Easter on the Jewish formula of 14 days (*quartodecima*) after Nisan. Nestorius came from Antioch, where he had studied, a major reason he was not well received by the Constantinople clergy among whom there had been strong claimants to the post. He was unfortunate to fall between a weak emperor in Theodosius II and a strong prelate of Alexandria in Cyril. Pope Celestine I had succeeded Boniface II in 422 and expelled a number of Pelagian clerics. Nestorius did not help his relations with Celestine by offering the expelled clerics good hospitality in Constantinople. Moreover, Nestorius had been influenced in his Christology by Theodore of Mopsuestia in the School of Antioch who promoted the view that the human and divine natures of Jesus were separate. This may sound like Arianism, to which they were passionately opposed, but small differences took on huge importance in Christology. The following is a brief simplistic distinction between Arianism, Apollinarianism and Nestorianism:

- Arius taught that in the course of the incarnation the Logos took a human body while his divine nature became its soul. Thus his divinity and humanity are not of the same substance (denying *homoousios*).
- Apollinaris taught that Christ had human body and soul, but that the divine Logos replaced his rational mind – similar objection as to Arianism.
- The School of Antioch, hence Nestorius, held to the completeness of human body and soul in Jesus but taught that at the incarnation the *Logos* took over or assumed this person, which effectively separated Christ's humanity from God's divinity.

Theologians would regard this summary as over-simplification, but the point is that the whole issue was too technical for the average person and rather beyond Christ's mission and teachings; which raises the question of how religion equates faith with moral direction. Jesus Christ gave clear guidance on faith and morals but little on theological issues. Human nature seeks knowledge and understanding, but academics who dedicate their lives to this, naturally find simplification of their speciality insufficient and unpalatable.

All this may have passed without challenge had there not already been ill-will regarding Nestorius' appointment and, more importantly, had he not taken his beliefs further. He accepted calling Mary the Mother of Christ but challenged the validity of the claim that Mary was the Mother of God (Greek *Theotokos*, God-bearer) on the basis of questionable theology, clearly not in line with the Nicean definition of the Trinity – God being three persons in one substance. That 'Nestorianism' was a serious mistake on his part that led to condemnation, his theory now carrying a pejorative element. Pope Celestine engaged the willing support of Cyril of Alexandria in this condemnation and events led via a synod in Rome in 430, to the First Council of Ephesus in 431.

The Western Church regards the First Council of Ephesus as the Third Ecumenical Council. About 250 bishops attended and the debate was heated. Nestorius was convinced that Cyril was an Apollinarian and would lose the case for that reason. He was therefore surprised when the council sided with Cyril in the ratification of Athanasius' beliefs that the Nicaean Council had correctly defined the Holy Trinity and that Mary was the mother of God. Nestorius was accused of heresy and unseated, withdrawing from the public view to a monastery in Antioch. Schism resulted as the Assyrian Church (today centering on Northern Iraq and adjacent territories in Syria and Turkey) went its own way.

A Second Council of Ephesus was called in 449, presided over by Dioscorus I of Alexandria, mainly covering Christology. It was never recognised as a full Ecumenical Council and its findings and canons were never taken too seriously by bishops from east or west. It upheld the 'hypostatic union' – that Jesus is fully God and fully man but found that Jesus had just one incarnate nature (monophysite) as generally accepted by the Eastern Church. This led to clarification in the full Ecumenical Council of Chalcedon.

Council of Chalcedon, Oriental Schism

The Council of Chalcedon took place in 451 in an attempt to heal divisions and to correct some of the unsatisfactory aspects of the second Council of Ephesus. In calling the council, Emperor Marcian had been trying to bring peace to the table, though Bishop Diosconus of Alexandria said the emperor should not interfere with church affairs. This was regarded as the 4th Ecumenical Council with over 500 bishops present. Many Protestants accept only the four and none of those that followed.

The Oriental Orthodox Churches aligned with the Ephesus definition that defined the single nature in Christ, composed of both Godhead and manhood, whereas the accepted wisdom in East and West was that he had two natures – divine and human – in one substance. Each is complete and there is no partial synthesis of the two. Although a seemingly fine point of Christological detail, it was regarded as important and the second Council of Ephesus declared in its favour. The Council of Chalcedon emphasised its determination by anathematising the already deposed Nestorius and all his writings were to be burned.

Almost inevitably this triggered the 'Chalcedonian Schism' which began later that same year, as one-by-one the Oriental Churches separated away. The term Oriental rather than Eastern can be confusing, especially when there was also the Nestorian-leaning 'Church of the East' in Persia. But in this case it served to distinguish the six autocephalous Orthodox Churches – Coptic Orthodox Church of Alexandria, Ethiopian Orthodox Tewahedo Church, Eritrean Orthodox Tewahedo Church,

Syriac Orthodox Church, Armenian Apostolic Church and the Indian Malankara Orthodox Church from the 'Eastern' ones – Constantinople and the three Greek Orthodox patriarchates of Alexandria, Antioch and Jerusalem. As each one left, they took no part in future Councils, in spite of all still proclaiming to be Catholic and universal with true apostolic succession. Autocephalous is beyond autonomous in that it means fully independent and self-determining by its senior bishop or Patriarch, who does not report to any higher-ranking authority.

The Chalcedonian Churches, i.e. Roman and Eastern Orthodox, took the view that the Oriental Churches' stance denies Christ's true humanity, a view nowadays also accepted by most Protestant Churches. It seems a moot point but in fairness, the Church was building what was still quite a new missionary Church and had to carry the message to people of far longer established faiths as they took it further afield, so their evangelists deserved the confidence of certainty in the accuracy of their knowledge. However, the point cannot be escaped that through poor handling and the obduracy of the participants, which ignored Nestorius' large loyal following in the Church of the East, Chalcedon nourished the early stages of the Oriental schism, sometimes called the Nestorian Schism, as the Oriental Church went its own way. This would have long-lasting and serious effect on all future missionary efforts further east as it became more than just a matter of argument about the human and divine nature of Christ.

This breach was particularly damaging for Christianity as the Sassanid dynasty, which had ruled Persia since 224 and would endure until 651, had built up the Sassanid Empire. This had huge influence further east and rivalled the Roman-Byzantine Empire. It stretched North-East from Egypt to Central Asia as far as Tajikistan and from Eastern Turkey to Pakistan, including Eastern Arabia and the Yemen. Nestorian missionaries would go on to convert Mongols from about the 7th century and Chinese during the Tang dynasty (7th to 10th centuries), so without doubt the Oriental Church was a major player, eventually covering a vast geographical area.

This latest council also issued 27 disciplinary canons determining church administration, clerical behaviour and authority and in its 28th decree, confirmed that the See of Constantinople, referred to as New Rome, ranked second only to Rome and as 'first among equals' of the heads of the several autocephalous churches that make up the Eastern Orthodox Church. Appointment of metropolitans of any of the autocephalous branches was to be consecrated by the patriarch of Constantinople but, once so ordained the provincial metropolitan would be in total charge of his province. Constantinople is still widely regarded as the spiritual centre of the 300 million Orthodox Christians worldwide.

Persian Church, Nestorianism, Gateway to the Orient

Christianity had existed in Persia since the early days especially in Parthia, but had ranked as minor compared to the national religion of Zoroastrianism. Christian Persians were represented at the Council of Nicaea in 325 by John of Persis. The Persians were in constant confrontation and frequently at war with the Romans. So long as the Romans were persecuting Christians, the Persians were reasonably tolerant of Christianity, adopting the principle 'my enemy's enemy is my friend'. But when Constantine showed favour to Christians and wrote to Persian King Shapur II in 315, asking him to protect and care for Christians, suspicion arose as to the where the loyalty of Christians in Persia might lie. Most Christians in Persia were converted Jews and Syrians, but at that time there was also a growth in conversion of ethnic Persians.

Following Constantine's death in 337, Persia began to take measures against Christians, doubling their taxes and requiring their bishops to collect these. One bishop who refused, saying he was the Lord's shepherd not a tax collector, was executed on Good Friday, along with some other members of the clergy. The majority Zoroastrians disliked Christians for some of their practices including the fact that their clergy regarded celibacy as holiness. Persecution gathered pace with the sacking of churches and execution of clergy refusing sun worship as well as prominent converted Persians, intended as a deterrent to others. But Persian Christians proved as resilient in their faith as those in the Roman Empire had done.

Roman Emperor Jovian reached agreement with King Shapur in 363 AD by which the Romans handed over control of Mesopotamia and Armenia to Persia, leading to a period of peace between the empires. The persecution eased as a result and in 409, Persian King Yazdegerd issued an edict of toleration.

In 364, the Metropolitan of Seleucia-Ctesiphon, Mar Isaac presided over the Synod of Seleucia and opened it with a prayer for King Yazdegerd. The main decision was that the Bishop of Seleucia-Ctesiphon would henceforth be the nominated primate (Catholicos) of the Persian Church. Thus the royal capital became the centre of Christianity in the Seleucid Empire with Yazdegerd's official approval. There would be just one bishop for each see, approved by the Catholicos. Importantly, the Nicene Creed was also accepted, though the first suggestion of adding the contentious *filioque* may have arisen here.

Yazdegerd's acceptance of the organisation of the Church in Persia as included in the Synod of Seleucia was conditional upon the appointment of future primates being approved also by the king and the Church being answerable to the state through the primate, which meant tight state control over the Church.

In 420 some persecution returned and the following year one of its victims who had been imprisoned, Mar Dadyeshu was elected Catholicos. He called a synod in 424 which proclaimed that no ecclesiastical authority is above the Catholicos, who is the sole head of the Persian Church, which is totally independent of the Byzantine and Roman Churches. This denial of allegiance to any foreign authority pleased the king.

This all provided fertile ground for the developing Nestorian Schism which was confirmed at Chalcedon some years later. In 486, Bishop Barsauma of Nisibis in Persia recognised Theodore of Mopsuestia who had been Nestorius' main mentor in Antioch, as a spiritual authority. Pope Celestine had pronounced Theodore a heretic. Three years later, the Byzantine Emperor Zeno closed the School of Edessa in Mesopotamia, so the school moved to Nisibis, where it was welcomed and followed by other migrations of Nestorian-leaning institutions. This all added strength to the Oriental Church in which Persia became a leading missionary force eastwards and also in the adjacent Arabian Peninsula, a short boat journey over the Gulf. Nestorian missionaries spread into the 'Stans' of central Asia, the Indian sub-continent and became well entrenched in China by the 7th century. Even after the Muslim conquest of Persia in 644 the Persian Christian Church at home and abroad continued to expand until the 10th century, when a rapid decline of Nestorianism began.

Incense

Incense is known to have been used in religious rituals in China about 2000BC. Its use spread west and is often mentioned in the Bible and used in Jewish worship, so it would have been known to Christians converted from Judaism. Its earliest recorded use in Christian liturgy was in the Eastern Church for liturgies of Saint James and Saint Mark in the 5th century before appearing in Good Friday processions in the West in the 7th century. Its use for blessing the gospel book during Mass was first mentioned in the 11th century, since when it has regularly featured at 'High Mass'.

Fall of the Roman Empire

In the 430s, Emperor Theodosius II realised that Roman Law had become chaotically labyrinthine as each Emperor had added new laws, many of which were conflicting or ambiguous with established laws and the overlay of post-pagan principles by Christian ones added further complexity. It had become difficult to learn, manage and apply law consistently. So he set up a committee of senior lawyers to define the Theodosian Code in 439. It covered State law embodying Christian principles, though it fell short of adequate simplification as it still required huge libraries of commentaries and many contradictions remained. Justinian I eventually approved a new Code in 534, known as the Digest or Pandect. Again based on Christian principles, it included standards for behaviour for the clergy, including a ban on gambling; separation of monasteries from nunneries; duty of care for prisoners and abandoned foundlings; bishops to oversee marriage of clerics and honesty of financial accounts.

Theodosius II, the last Emperor of both East and West, moved to Constantinople. Since Milan had meanwhile almost been captured in the course of wars, in 402 the Western capital was moved to Ravenna, which was felt even better equipped than Milan for defence, with a good port on the Adriatic and being surrounded inland by swamps.

Rome was finally humiliated and sacked as Alaric's Visigoths broke in during August 410 and spent three days pillaging the city. They were restrained in so far as there was no widespread slaughter and most buildings and monuments survived as did the two great basilicas of St Peter and St Paul as respected sanctuaries. Valuables that disappeared were mostly portable and Rome crucially retained its sovereignty.

Rome, as the seat of Peter, was confirmed as the base of the Roman Church after some debate when the capital of the Western Roman Empire had moved from there to Milan in 286. The Visigoth attack on the city and continuing pagan pressure encouraged Augustine of Hippo to write 'The City of God' in its defence. Rome continued to be the centre of the Western Church through the eviction of the Visigoths and the subsequent rule of the Ostrogoths, who established the Italian Kingdom in 493, including some territories adjacent to the Italy we now know. Led by Theoderic the Great, they overthrew the interregnum in Northern Italy, which had earlier deposed the emperor of the Western Roman Empire, Romulus Augustus. Theoderic agreed with the then Eastern Roman Emperor Anastasius in 497 that he would rule Italy as Anastasius' deputy, which kept Italy within the empire and suited both men as Anastasius reduced a potential threat to his empire while Theoderic found wider acceptance by the Italian population. The Italian Kingdom at its height ran from today's French border in the west into Serbia in the East. Theoderic liked to be known as the King of the Goths and the Romans.

Iberian Peninsula, Northern Europe, Celts

Following the sacking of Rome, the Visigoths expanded into southern Gaul and founded their Kingdom of Toulouse in 412. They then aimed westwards and crossed the Pyrenees into Spain in 415 AD and conquered most of the Iberian Peninsula. The Vandals and Alans who had earlier occupied some of this area mostly went on to North Africa. Meanwhile, the Visigoths' own monarchy had embraced Roman Catholicism and would rule most of the peninsula until the 8th century.

Members of Germanic tribes from central and northern Europe had started settling in the Roman Empire from the third century as parcels of land were offered to immigrant mercenaries willing to settle and commit to the Roman army.

But pressure mounted on the Roman Empire into the early 5th century with frontiers crumbling at the hands of German chiefs crossing the Rhine, especially when it froze over in the hard winter of 406. Franks poured into Gaul, Visigoths across southern Gaul and into most of Spain, Ostrogoths and Lombards to Italy, Vandals to Africa, while Angles and Saxons took the sea route to Britain.

Society in the West was thus in flux, but the Church remained a strong point of reference and a valued link with the old order. Law and order was in disarray and monasteries raised their walls. Many of the insurgents were Christians albeit still retaining some traditional folk practices.

Germanic tribes of central northern Europe had overcome and occupied most of Scandinavia and further west and south to the natural borders of the Rhine and Danube rivers. The Franks, Angles, Jutes, Saxons and other tribes were heathens who mostly followed a polytheistic religion, though it was not a matter of great importance in their lives.

The Franks were Germanic people, mostly from the Salian area of Gaul that now includes Belgium, north eastern France and south Netherlands, but would conquer Gaul and eventually spread back into Germany and further south. Their Gods were more worldly than spiritual, the main one being the water God Quinotar. Frankish influence grew and expanded in Gaul and eventually the nation adopted a version of their name, as also happened in England with the Angles.

Jutes, Angles and Saxons were other Germanic tribes from the Jutland peninsular, Saxony and Denmark. A fourth century Anglo-Saxon invasion of Britain's east coast had been repelled. They moved successfully on the British Isles again after the Romans left them defenceless in 407. These pagans swept westward, leaving Christian enclaves only on the Western fringes of Britain.

The Celts were an ancient people, originating from near the source of the Danube and populating a region known as Hallstatt around Switzerland, Austria and southern Bavaria. Their wealth was built on the Bavarian salt mines and their empire expanded from about 800 BC eventually stretching from Portugal to Turkey, including Gaul over following centuries. Good craftsmen and fierce in combat, they tended more to individual enterprise than teamwork, falling short on political, military and organisational skills. They lived in conically thatched round houses, but never seemed to build towns or defences. They invaded Britain around 480 BC, and spread so that Britons were mainly Celts while the Picts, an amalgam of peoples, occupied Scotland north of the Firth of Forth. The Celts were no match for the Romans when they invaded, so in France they were pushed west to Brittany and in Britain likewise to Cornwall, Wales and Ireland – the Celtic fringes – as well as north to south-west Scotland.

The Romans had introduced Christianity to Britain but did not go far out of their way to convert the natives, though some took to the faith. After the Roman legions withdrew, starting from the west and north about 383, the Celts tried gradually moving east. The Picts tended to collect in the east of Scotland and far north east of England They were limited by better organised pagan tribes – mainly Angles and Saxons, but also some Jutes and Franks – who settled eastern and southern parts of Britain after the final Roman departure in 407, leading to a waning of the Christian faith although the Celtic-controlled western parts retained some Christianity. The faith did not die completely in the Anglo-Saxon kingdoms, as witnessed by Saxon churches, some of which are still standing, mainly in pockets around St Albans, Lichfield and Glastonbury.

The Celts had not taken to Roman Christianity, but in Ireland and western Wales, they were widely introduced and converted to the faith through direct contact with some maritime travelling Desert Fathers, who also brought to them the solitary hermit lifestyle as well as the monastic communal life. This was soon reflected in further missionary efforts from Ireland into Scotland and Northern England. Since there were no large towns in the Celtic kingdoms, monasteries were attractive to nearby settlements due to safety in numbers. Celtic Christians were thus heavily influenced by the Eastern traditions of the Desert Fathers.

But somebody else would end up being credited with the conversion of Ireland. Patrick was born about 387AD to Calpurnius, a Roman and Conchessa, a relative of St. Martin of Tours. He arrived there the first time in his mid-teens and quite unwillingly, for he was kidnapped by a Celtic raiding party and sold into slavery in Ireland. He escaped from Ireland some six years later and visited monasteries in Europe then studied to be a priest, eventually being ordained by Germanus, Bishop of Auxerre.

One of the most productive decisions of Pope Celestine I was perhaps his last before dying, as he sent Patrick in 431 to take the faith to Ireland, a country that would for centuries produce numerous scholars and send out a diaspora to all corners of the world. So Patrick was able to fulfil his dream to convert Ireland from its Druidic traditions to Christianity, having long believed that if he could go to "the very ends of the earth" and convert them, this would be an ultimate achievement before the end of the world. Patrick supplemented considerably the work of the resident monks, who spent most of their days within monastery walls, preoccupied with praying and working for their subsistence while doing some trading with the locals.

The tale of Patrick's bonfire on Slain Hill on the Easter Vigil in 432 AD being lit just before the local King's fire to a pagan God on nearby Tora Hill and proving inextinguishable is perhaps a mythical story by a 7th century cleric, supposedly drawn from the Book of Daniel to an Irish setting. There is a lot of myth and symbolism surrounding Patrick, such as driving snakes out of Ireland – it is true there are no snakes there, but his 'snake' was thought probably to have been paganism. There is also the shamrock symbolism of the Trinity and so on. He died satisfied, saying "I have given Ireland the gift of God".

This now native Church would become centred on monasteries rather than bishoprics, developed largely in isolation from Rome. Other distinguishing characteristics grew such as its calculation of the date of Easter and the style of the tonsure haircut wore by their clerics. Following Patrick, the Celtic Christians passed on the practice of 'pilgrimage', which involved a learned member travelling into unknown territory seeking quiet, peace and prayer while those leaning more to the sociable sought to pass on the faith – as Christ had ordered "to the ends of the earth" (Acts 1:8). Thus Columba (521-597) would sail north in 563 with twelve fellow monks across to Kintyre and then settle on the island of Iona off Scotland's west coast, part of the Irish kingdom of Dál Riata. It was here they founded a new abbey as a base for spreading Christianity among the pagan Pictish kingdoms east across the Grampian Mountains and into north east England. The Celtic Church would encounter the Roman Church again in the 7th Century as their missionary work took them further.

CHAPTER 8

6th Century

Popes

498-514 Symmachus

514-523 Hormisdas

523-526 John I

526-530 Felix IV

530-532 Boniface II

533-535 John II

535-536 Agapetus

536-537 Sylverius

537-555 Vigilius

556-561 Pelagius I

561-574 John III

575-579 Benedict I

579-590 Pelagius II

590-604 Gregory I

Emperors

Anastasius I	491-518	Tiberius II	578-582
Justin I	518-527	Maurice	582-602
Justinian I	527-565	Theodosius	590-602
Justine II	585-578		

During the first five hundred years of Christianity the faith had learned something about the buffeting it could receive, not only from political forces but even from sincere and well-intentioned human passions and intellectual enquiry within, thus far with Rome and Constantinople still holding together.

The 5th and 6th centuries are closely interlinked, spanning decline of the Roman Empire, The sacking of Rome, shifts in Northern Europe and Britain, the Nestorian schism and evolution in Christian thinking and practice as well as in church architecture, decoration and music. The Western Church suffered from weak papal leadership for nearly a century after Pope Gelasius I died in 496. Rome's leadership had been missing the close attention and support of emperors since their move to Constantinople. Eventually, Pope Gregory I, 'The Great', restored some authority which offered encouragement for the future.

Monasticism Comes to Europe, John Cassian, Benedict

John Cassian (c.360-435) may have been the first to bring monastic practice and rules from Egypt to mainland Europe. Born in Scythia Minor, west of the Black Sea and fluent in Latin and Greek, as a young man he joined a friend, Germanus in entering a hermitage in the Holy Land for about three years. Seeking a higher level of sanctity, they then joined a monastery in the Egyptian desert. John developed a practice of private confession, which was adopted by the Irish monks soon after. About 15 years later, John and Germanus went with a delegation to Alexandria protesting to Bishop Theophilus about a paschal letter which suggested an unacceptable Christology. Theophilus was profoundly anti-Origen and this led to him executing numerous monks for their believed Origenist views, which led to John Cassian leaving Egypt accompanied by about 300 fellow monks. Bishop John Chrysostom welcomed them and in time ordained John Cassian as a deacon, employing him in his cathedral. When Chrysostom, in dispute with the Emperor and Theophilus, was exiled a second time, Cassian was sent to Rome to plead with Pope Innocent I on Chrysostom's behalf. He was probably raised to the priesthood during his ten-year stay there. He moved on close to Marseilles, where he set up two monasteries, one for men and one for women, with rules he adapted from the desert monasteries, staying in that area until his death. His best known writings were 'Institutes, and 'Conferences', drawing heavily on what he had learned in Egypt.

Born in Nursia, some 70 miles from Rome, **Benedict** (480-547) studied liberal arts. He was aghast at the immorality and corruption of fellow students. This so concerned him that he left Rome for a life of solitude, first in the hills east of Rome, then in a cave near Subiaco in Lazio province, central Italy. There he discovered his own 'demons' as had the Desert Fathers, so he prayed fervently for God's grace to strengthen him. His reputation as a holy man spread and he soon attracted disciples, gradually establishing up to thirteen communities, limiting each to twelve disciples, following the model of Jesus. At least one of these was for women, which endures to this day, the Abbey of St Scholastica, dedicated to his twin sister.

Benedict moved on again and set up his famous hilltop monastery at Monte Cassino and this is where he wrote his 'Rule of Benedict', which has been used widely as a basis for the spiritual and administrative operation of the Western monasteries. It was probably influenced both by his reading of John Cassian and the anonymous 'Rule of the Master', written some decades earlier, but Benedict struck an engaging balance of the spiritual and the practical without extreme asceticism. According to his Rule, each monastery had an abbot, who would be chosen by and from the resident monks for the role of patriarch in directing the community, teaching and caring for each member within it. The Rule constantly reminds the abbot to pray and primarily to follow the will of God and be fair, wise and humble in this role. It impresses on all monks that life is a journey of change and growth, initially requiring obedience to the abbot, stability and conversion of each one's own heart and passive acceptance of discomforts.

The Rule holds the central task and focus of the community as the Divine Office (Opus Dei), with its structure of prayer (about 4 hours per day), work (6) and study (4). All personal wealth and assets had to be renounced. Life, the gift of God, is rooted in work, supported by prayer and contemplation; it is deeds rather than words that witness to Christian life. Seeking God is a lifelong process of advancing towards him through our complete dependence on his grace, contrary to Pelagian self-sufficiency. Followers must examine themselves honestly, recognising their faults and weak areas to understand their need of God's mercy and grace to grow in him. Prayer provides important encounters with God and one's daily life should be offered to God as a means of staying in his presence. Periods of silence allow one to listen to God and establish a relationship with him. It could be alluring to those seeking truth and spirituality as integral with life itself if they find faith in Christ, so long as they can accept the rigours that go with it. The Rule involves an austere timetable, with eight set prayer times spread through the day and night:

Matins	(2.30-3 am)
Lauds	(5-6am Dawn)
Prime	(Approx. 7am)
Terce	(Approx. 9am)
Sext	(Noon)
Nones	(Sunset or early evening)
Compline	(Before sleep – usually about 8pm)

The only time a monk receives special treatment or dispensation is when he is sick. Any non-clerical visitors are subject to the abbot during their stay.

Benedict thus set up the first durable monastic order in the West. In deference to the heroic privations of the Desert Fathers he claimed his rule as 'one for beginners'. It is a pacific life which shows love and respect for creation, nature, the universe and people around, but is not subject to the normal worldly pressures of earning a living or supporting a family. The perceived value of celibacy in such context may be more understandable than in the pastoral role of a secular priest dealing with families and worldly issues. Benedict's rule became the benchmark for subsequent orders and monasteries with fairly minor variations.

Benedictines developed a tradition of praying for the dead during this century, relating this to 2 Maccabees 12:46, "It is a holy and wholesome thought to pray for the dead that they may be loosed from their sins."

Different terms became applied to the various forms of seeking spiritual seclusion from secular life:

Syllabite – in a monastery,
Anchorite – hermit or loner,
Sarabites – small groups who set their own rules,
Gyrovagues – drifters, itinerant holy people.
Stylites were no more.

Constantinople, Nika Riots, Hagia Sophia

In 532 probably the most serious riots ever in the history of Europe, took place – the Nika riots, initiated by hooliganism surrounding the chariot racing. This sport commanded widespread fanaticism and intense 'tribal' factionalism similar to football today, but on this occasion on a totally different scale. The venue was the Hippodrome, next door to the Emperor's palace and Constantine's 'Holy Wisdom' church. Underlying social unrest and resentment at high taxes and inequality surfaced at the races, fuelled by the fact that Emperor Justinian I was watching on from the overlooking palace balcony. Tens of thousands of people died in the fighting and as the mob went out on the rampage, many buildings were burned down, including the church. The army was severely stretched in protecting the palace and quelling the unrest.

Justinian had a magnificent basilica built on the site of Hagia Sophia Church in 537, which still stands today, a major feature of the city. It was a triumph of contemporary architecture with the largest indoor area unsupported by pillars in the world, having a dome 33metres diameter and a height of 56m. It remained the biggest Church in Christendom until Seville Cathedral in 1520. The dome has collapsed three times during its long life – in 558, 984 and 1346 AD – each time being rebuilt by benefactors with improved design and materials. It was also sacked and looted by the fourth crusade in 1204. The Turks turned it into a mosque when they overtook the city in 1453. The remnants of the wonderful mosaics left from the crusaders looting were anathema to the Muslims since they included images of creatures and saints, but rather than destroy them, they colour washed over them.

It was also during Justinian's reign that the monastery of St Catherine was built on Mount Sinai, still active and a place of pilgrimage and tourism today. In the absence of iconoclasts there (of which more later), one of the oldest known paintings of the Transfiguration, when Moses and Elijah appeared to Jesus watched by Peter, James and John, still adorns the ceiling of the half dome behind the apse in its chapel.

Church Buildings, Art, Bells

Christian worship was originally carried out in homes of supportive benefactors, in synagogues and in times of repression and persecution, below ground in catacombs. When numbers of worshippers in a community outgrew homes, to accommodate them, communities would build new or convert existing buildings into churches usually discreetly to avoid antagonising authority and other established religions of the area. Once the main danger of persecution passed in the Constantine era and churches could be openly identifiable, a pattern for their design began to emerge. This evolved differently between East and West as the participation of congregations in services followed different patterns.

In the West, they evolved as rectangular in plan, oriented with the congregation in the nave or main area facing east towards the celebrant who was in the apse, usually under a semi-dome at one end of the building. The celebrant faced the congregation, from behind a wooden table known as the *altare* ('place of sacrifice' in Latin), often on a raised platform, for the Eucharistic bread and wine.

Hagia Sophia was built when mosaics, frescos and icons were becoming more widely adopted as a uniquely Christian expression of devotion in art. The first depictions of Christ had not been broadly agreed until about the 6th century but have remained common since then with his long hair and beard, just as in the 'Turin Shroud'. This image of him was used in the earliest icons, painted on wood.

Icons spread as an art form in Byzantine Eastern Christian churches, also extending to pictures of saints. They became more than just pictures, but rather channels of prayer, petitions and thanksgiving addressed to the saint. They focused prayer, often being touched or kissed, nearly equivalent to the relic in the West.

In the East, the building tended to be round or square, still with an apse for the celebrant at the east end and a bell tower at the west. The apse containing the sacraments was separated from the nave by a low barrier or tempion, behind which the altar could be hidden by curtains which would be drawn across this divide for parts of the service. Curtains later evolved into fixed screens, which soon began to be used for displaying icons which had become a tradition in the Eastern Church from the 3rd century, so the screens became known as iconostases. As the demand grew to hang more icons, the screens were raised to the extent of hiding the altar and the celebrants so doors were incorporated. The priest emerges from the central 'royal' doors for the main parts of the Eucharist but is out of sight for much of the service, adding to its mystery but also introducing a further distinction between the Eastern and Western rites. Two side doors were installed for use by deacons and servers. There were few seats, just enough for the elderly and frail as the tradition of kneeling was reserved in the east for confession and penance in front of a priest. The congregation mostly stood throughout the service.

From about the time of Justinian in the sixth century, side apses were built, so Orthodox Churches feature a 'triapse' with three part-circular walls topped with partial domes. In the north one, the sacred vessels for communion were stored, with a shelf on which the bread and wine for the Eucharist were prepared. The south side is similar to the vestry in the West. This contains the celebrants' vestments, altar cloths and decoration as well as a wash basin for the priest to wash his hands before the preparation and equipment to boil water for cleaning the chalice. The whole area behind the iconostasis is regarded as a holy place, only accessible to those with a specific liturgical role.

The first five hundred years saw little by way of **art or images** enter churches, in contrast with pagan places of worship. Those Christians who had converted from Judaism inherited their predecessors' disdain for pictures in church, which were banned from synagogues as being too close to the graven images forbidden by the second commandment. Jews being the majority of the very early Christians, their view prevailed initially. Most citizens of the Roman Empire were less restrained and familiar with images of their pagan gods in temples, so found portraits and biblical scenes helpful. So Roman and even Hellenic Jewish converts used paintings and carvings and some still survive, almost all of it from the catacombs, dating back to the second and third centuries. Their imagery tended towards ambiguity; for example, an image of a shepherd carrying a sheep carved on a sarcophagus, or painted on a catacomb wall could then have been either pagan or Christian, although today the true meaning is probably clear. But at that time caution had to be exercised to avoid its destruction by Roman officials during the frequent periods of persecution. The Chi-Rho symbol, ☧, which only Christians would recognise, was commonly painted.

At the synod of Elvira in 305 AD, canon 36 stated "Pictures are not to be placed in churches, so that they do not become objects of worship and adoration." There was much agonising about this over the early centuries but as the sixth century neared its end, Pope Gregory, acknowledging that most Christians could neither read nor write and many spoke no Latin, felt paintings on the walls of churches would help them to recall lessons about the Bible, Christ and his religion. The bishops began to realise that paintings, mosaics and frescos may enhance the beauty and grandeur of a church and also inspire prayer.

Pictures of God were initially avoided, but church's patron saints started appearing which drew prayers of intercession and veneration from congregants, which ran the unacceptable risk of developing into worship. To focus adoration and worship, images of God the *Pantocrater,* creator of all, had been allowed on the apse ceiling, normally a semi-dome above the altar, from about the late fourth century.

In the Eastern Church, icons began to appear in St Catherine's monastery in Sinai about the sixth century, but it would be a couple of centuries before they became much more widespread and they would have to survive the violent opposition of iconoclasm before that.

Both Eusebius of Caesarea and Irenaeus wrote about a cloth that Pilot held to the face of Jesus which resulted in an imprinted portrait of his face. Referred to as the Image of Edessa, this became a broadly discussed relic. It relates to a story about King Abgar V of Edessa, who sent a message to Jesus begging a cure to his illness. Jesus could not come, but promised that one of his disciples would visit him in the future. After Jesus' death, one of the seventy disciples, Thaddeus brought the words of Jesus and the cloth bearing Jesus' image to King Abgar and he was cured. Parallels have naturally been drawn with the Turin shroud, discovered in the 14th century, but the two are believed unlikely to be directly linked.

The **bell** came from China well before Christ and hand-bells were used in pagan rites, rung vigorously to induce ecstasy, for which they were frowned upon by early Christians. Buddhists used them in meditation. However, once Constantine had raised Christianity to the religion of the empire, it could openly announce its presence. Larger, louder bells could now be made and they began to be used by desert monasteries to signal imminent worship or times of prayer to the hermits scattered around the area. This idea gradually spread north and westward, thanks partly to the Celtic missionaries. The Benedictines established foundries to manufacture larger bells, which also had an effect on church design, with the addition of either a free-standing campanile or an integral bell tower, usually at the church's west end.

Language

The Greeks, with their cultural and philosophical heritage, had been among the first converts and were the first to translate the Old Testament into their own language, while much of the New Testament was originally written in Greek anyway. This was naturally a source of pride to them and enhanced their sense of direct linkage to the apostles. They regarded Western Christianity as an offshoot from them and regarded Latin as a crude language. Against this, they had to admit that both Peter, Jesus' chosen leader for the Church and Paul, the great evangelist settled and died as martyrs in Rome, which made a strong case for it as the Church's base. So Latin was used throughout the West for worship services in church and would remain so for Catholics until half-way through the 20th century which meant that for most of this time, although they could recite the common prayers and responses, most of the congregation did not understand the language and those who could were becoming fewer as time passed. Greek was the main language used in the Eastern Church, with scope there for use of the vernacular where Greek would not be understood. This was just one of a number of points of difference between East and West.

Franks

Originating in the region around today's Holland, Belgium and North West France, the Merovingian dynasty was founded by Childeric (440-481), son of Merovech the leader of the Salian Franks after the Romans had withdrawn. They overran Gaul, establishing the most powerful empire in Europe of the post-Roman era. Francia, as it then became known by the Romans was a collection of states, each run by a royal chieftain who served on the ruling council. The national kingdom was established by Clovis I (466-511), son of Childeric about 496, when he united all the Frankish tribes under his single rule. In 493, King Clovis married Clotilde, a Burgundian who urged him to become a Christian, which he did in 496. He was baptised as a Catholic in 508, rather than the Arianism which many Germanic Christians had adopted. Three thousand of his knights were converted with him and many senior Franks followed his example, so that nation which then covered France, Holland, Belgium and Northern Germany became Roman Catholic.

Late in his life, Clovis called for a synod of bishops, the first Council of Orléans, to agree some reforms to the Church and strengthen links between the Royal family and the bishops. It conferred on Church property and places of worship the right to provide sanctuary; defined a number of duties and rights for individuals and disciplines for clergy; required bishops to ensure the welfare of the poor and the sick. In seeking Clovis' approval the Church suggested it was a formal treaty between the Church and Francia.

Following the established Frankish tradition of dividing patrimonies as evenly as possible among sons, when Clovis died his kingdom was divided between his four sons. The result was that Francia was ruled nominally as one state, but was divided into autonomous sub-kingdoms – Rheims, Orléans, Paris and Soissons. Each subsequent generation involved further sub-division and any dispute or loss of good will between parties inevitably bred disunity. However, the family tended to unite against any outside threat or hostility that arose against any one of them, enabling the Merovingian dynasty to last until half-way through the 8th century.

Rise of the Byzantine Empire, Byzantine Papacy

Having its origins in Constantine's move early in the 4th century, the Eastern Roman Empire enjoyed especially healthy growth between about 470 and 550 AD, when it was more frequently referred to as the Byzantine Empire.

Emperor Justin I (reign 518-527) was from peasant stock, poorly educated and spoke only Latin. He became the Byzantine (previously Eastern Roman) emperor and was quite ruthless in disposing of opponents, relying heavily on his nephew Justinian as an advisor. He was a devout Orthodox Christian and together with the patriarch of Constantinople, John of Cappadocia, he took steps to repair relations with Rome.

His successor, Justinian I (reign 527-565), set out to regain much of the Western Roman Empire that had been overcome more than a century earlier by barbarian tribes. He unleashed the Gothic War in 535 between the Eastern Roman Empire and the Ostrogothic Italian Kingdom.

Ravenna in north-eastern Italy was soon overcome and Witiges, the Ostrogoth's ruler was captured there. This would affect the papacy in that from 537 the elected popes had to be approved by the Byzantine emperor before being consecrated, beginning a period known as the Byzantine Papacy, which would last until the mid-8th century. This power was exercised through the Exarchate of Ravenna, whose incumbent was appointed by Constantinople.

The Ostrogoths eventually fell in 553, after two invasions, long sieges and reinvasion. Justinian's ambition was to restore the full Roman Empire. In addition to the Ostrogothic Kingdom, his army and Navy also won back North Africa from the Vandals as well as the southern fringes of Spania. Justinian I personally confirmed the appointment of the three popes that followed his defeat of the Ostrogoths and the tradition of the emperor confirming the pope's appointment continued under his successors.

Pope Gregory I (The Great) (590-604)

Gregory was born in Rome in 540, as Justinian I's Eastern Roman Empire was winning control of the city from the Ostrogoths. He was a descendant of Pope Felix III and his father Gordianus was a senator in Rome and for a while Prefect, the highest civil office in the city. They had a family villa on the Caelian Hill, one of Rome's Seven Hills. They also owned large estates in Sicily, where he probably spent part of his early childhood when Rome was sacked by the Ostrogoths. Rome was also ravaged and its population decimated by a plague that swept round the Mediterranean during the 540s. Peace returned to the city in 552 and an invasion by the Franks was repulsed two years later.

Gregory had a good education and excelled in most subjects including rhetoric, dialectic and law. He was more a practical, caring and pious man than a philosopher and followed his father into public service, showing precocious management talent and rising to Prefect of Rome by the age of thirty three. But he felt unfulfilled and after much prayer he opted for a monastic life about 574. After inheriting the family estates following the death of his father, he had the family's Caelian villa converted into a monastery dedicated to St Andrew. He withdrew from public life to live as a monk and followed the strictest regime at some expense to his future health. He fully accepted the rule of poverty and donated the family estates on Sicily to the Church as "property of the poor" and established six monasteries there in the Benedictine tradition. The meat, food and grain from the farms were to be distributed by the Church to the poor.

After what he called the three happiest years of his life, as the Vandals advanced through Italy from the north in 558, he was plucked from the monastery by Pope Pelagius II. Pelagius ordained him one of the seven deacons of Rome then in early 559 dispatched him with an emissary to seek the help of Emperor Tiberius in Constantinople in protecting Rome from the Vandal army. Gregory became Permanent Papal Ambassador to the court of Byzantium which he found to be an extravagant contrast to the monastic life to which he had become so attached. Fortunately, some of his fellow monks had accompanied him and together they made time to pray and study scripture together. He never learned to speak Greek. He challenged Patriarch Eutychius of Constantinople over the latter's published view of the nature of the resurrection, which Emperor Tiberius settled in Gregory's favour shortly before the emperor's and Eutichius' death.

Having failed to gain Tiberius' help for Rome Gregory soon learned that the Byzantine Emperors' distance from it put Rome low in their priority list. In about 585 Pope Pelagius recalled Gregory to Rome and he was thrilled to be able to return to the full monastic life at St Andrew's, soon becoming abbot. His life there was not fully reclusive as he gave a number of public lectures and many internal talks about parts of the Old Testament, also completing a literary work on his studies of the Book of Job which had begun in Constantinople and he published as '*Magna Moralia*'.

A chance meeting with some young English slaves in the Forum, left him determined to take a missionary group to convert the Anglo-Saxons. Three days into the venture, the Roman military were horrified to hear of this and brought the party back to Rome. He was by then a famous and valued figure in Rome and had a role as virtual advisor and secretary to Pope Pelagius II, although still working from the monastery. In 589, prolonged torrential rains led to overflowing rivers and serious widespread floods in many parts of Italy, including Rome. Homes were swept away as were grain and food stores. The unsanitary living conditions and ensuing famine nurtured a reappearance of the plague with heavy population loss. Business came to a standstill as all efforts were directed to burying the dead, cleaning up and restoring homes.

In 590, Pope Pelagius II died and Gregory was quickly elected by the clergy and people of Rome to the papacy. He dreaded leaving the contemplative life behind and hoped Emperor Maurice would not confirm the appointment. But Maurice knew of his work and its importance after the disaster in Italy. When his confirmation was received, the reluctant monk almost had to be dragged to the Chair of St Peter to be consecrated, still yearning for the cloistered life.

As the first monk to become pope he showed great energy and organisation in spite of by then suffering persistent ill health. He supported clerical celibacy and he published a short guide, 'Book of the Office of Bishop', which was used by bishops for centuries to come. He re-established papal authority in Spain, which had seen almost no papal contact in a century and in France, where the Church had become self-sufficient with influential families providing bishops.

Gregory also realised his missionary ambition by sending a party led by Augustine, a colleague from St Andrew's, with Paulinus and other Benedictine monks to convert the Anglo-Saxons in England. A re-alignment of Barbarians, the Franks, Lombards and Visigoths from their Arian leanings to allegiance to Rome enabled well-organised Gregory to turn his focus onto the Donatist heresy in North Africa and paganism in Gaul as well as threatened schism in Istria and part of Northern Italy.

As the depleted city of Rome recovered, immigrants flocked there from countryside flood devastation. The military were mostly elsewhere, so in addition to his civil and spiritual duties, Gregory also effectively became military leader in the city. No Pope had been so effective since Gelasius I had died in 496. Drawing from his natural deep compassion and in order to forestall further pestilence or discontented uprisings, Gregory organised for food to be brought from the Church estates, mainly in Sicily plus supplements from the 'office of alms' in each surrounding ecclesiastical district to feed the growing needy masses gathering in Rome.

He was still a monk at heart and identified with the poor. So thorough was his grasp of accounts that the tenants and agents of the Church estates soon began to find it more difficult to deceive or cheat him than former masters by siphoning off income or giving short measures. Gregory regarded his Church as that of the poor and his use of reserves accordingly raised some criticism.

He was uncompromising in asserting his leadership as the successor of St Peter, of the entire universal Church, which included the Western and all the Orthodox Eastern Churches. He was a strong supporter of papal supremacy in jurisdiction over his clergy, so he opposed clerics being subjected to trial by civil authorities. He regarded the Emperor as the secular leader and himself on a more-or-less equal footing in ecclesiastical matters, the two being distinct and independent of each other. Gregory believed that the emperor as secular leader had a duty to protect the Church.

His passion for justice extended to the Jews as he defended their right to freedom of worship and action within the law. He also refused to approve their compulsory baptism, while continuing the prohibition on their ownership of Christian slaves.

Gregory was canonised a saint – 'Saint Gregory the Great' – soon after his death and is also recognised as a Father of the Church and Doctor of the Church by Catholics.

Britain, Augustine of Canterbury

There is no evidence that the native Christians in the south eastern parts of England had tried to convert the Anglo-Saxons. Invasions from the east had destroyed most remnants of Roman civilisation including economic and religious structures in areas now held by Saxons and related tribes. King Ethelbert of Kent (560-616) had married Merovingian princess Bertha, accepting her father King Charibert I's condition that she would be allowed to continue practicing her Catholic faith. Bertha was Clovis' great-granddaughter. Francia was now the most powerful state in Western Europe and as an influential Catholic she may well have conveyed her disappointment to Pope Gregory at the lack of faith in that part of England.

Pope Gregory selected his trusted colleague from his old monastery in Sicily to take a group of about three dozen colleagues as missionaries to south-east England. This Benedictine expedition under Augustine left Rome in 596 and arrived in England in 597 AD. There was a pause in the party's progress as they heard of the crude and belligerent nature of the English on their journey. So they waited in Provence as Augustine returned to Rome where the pope encouraged him with improved supporting documents and authority.

King Ethelbert was sufficiently impressed by these monks to take instruction from Augustine and he converted to Christianity, which boosted their missionary spirits and effort. The king donated land in Canterbury for the building of a church, which would become Canterbury Cathedral. Ethelbert was baptised in 597 and many of his subjects followed, including thousands baptised on Christmas Day that same year. Pope Gregory was thus encouraged to send more missionaries to England to support and build on this initial success. As they spread the gospel, Augustine's deputy Paulinus became Bishop of York.

Such was the success of this Gregorian mission that English missionaries were soon being sent to Holland and Germany. It set the future course of Christianity in England, with a strong alliance between Christianity and the monarch and the Venerable Bede (672-735) would later report on it this way.

As already noted, monastic Christianity came to Ireland around 400 AD. In his 'Ecclesiastical History of the English People', Bede would describe the tension between the Celtic Christianity epitomised by Saint Columba (521-597) and the international Roman brand of Christianity which had been brought to southern England by Augustine. Bede, a man of order and discipline, ends his Ecclesiastical History bemoaning the lazy Anglo-Saxons whom he regarded as half-hearted Christians still observing some pagan practices. An organised and disciplined parish life, which would regulate the beliefs and behaviour of the British people, was yet to mature. Bede saw a Christian England as part of God's master-plan and that the destiny of the Anglo-Saxons was to become Christians, united in a single Christian nation.

Meanwhile, in the far west and north of Britain, the Celts were busy spreading their own Christian message as Columba sailed to Iona and mainland Scotland in 563 and others set up a few pockets in Wales. With faith and practice heavily influenced by the Desert Fathers from the Egyptian Coptic tradition, and in view of events since the Council of Chalcedon, it would be interesting to see the results when they eventually came face-to-face with the Roman Augustinian Christians from the south and east of England as both groups spread their faith towards a meeting point in the British Isles during the forthcoming century.

Third Council of Toledo (589)

Bishop Leander of Seville called a council in Toledo primarily aimed at bringing the Visigoths round from Arianism. They had been taught this by an early 4th century bishop Wulfila, who had initially converted them to Christianity from paganism. Bishop Leander had tried to convert the Visigoth kings to orthodox Christian beliefs and had eventually found success with King Reccared, who sponsored this meeting and sent an opening address carrying such detail as to suggest that it must have been prompted by Leander.

Only eight Arian bishops attended. These were heavily outnumbered by the Catholic bishops present. Leander took a conciliatory approach, stressing they had been led by others into Arianism, so no blame attached to them. One of the Catholic bishops asked that they declare themselves likewise opposed to the Arian heresy, and would thenceforth preach accordingly. All eight agreed.

Another canon of note of that council was to require the addition of the *filioque* to the Nicene Creed, though Eastern opposition prevented its formal adoption.

Lombards

The Gothic War had depleted Italy's resources and the Byzantine Empire was short of funds and forces following its expansion into Italy and western Mediterranean fringes as well as continuing defensive wars against Persia in the east. Italy was susceptible to invasion. Following Justinian's death, in 568 AD the Lombards' new young king Alboin decided they should take their opportunity. They over-ran north and central Italy by the early 570s then spread further south. The Lombards were descendants of the small Winnili tribe originally from southern Scandinavia, who had moved to live among the Suebi on the Baltic coast of Germany by the first century AD. Their community grew and moved south, settling in territory north of the Danube, roughly Austria and Slovakia today, then westwards and south of the Alps to the northern part of Italy. The Romans called them '*longobardi*' (long-beards), which corrupted to Lombards.

King Alboin was murdered in 572 and his successor Cleph was assassinated after a brief but brutal reign, following which there was about a five year period without an overall king. Italy had been divided into dozens of duchies and during the interregnum the dukes had free rein to rule their duchies, a period of turbulence which attracted the attention of Francia, who were allied to the Byzantine Empire.

Cleph's son Authari was crowned king in 579. He married the Duke of Bavaria's daughter, Theolinda, a Catholic and friend of Pope Gregory I. Authari recognised the need to reconcile the kingdom and reform its administration. The duchies agreed to contribute part of their estates and income to maintain the royal court. Authari also deployed delicate diplomacy to ease the threat of Franco-Byzantine interference.

Before their invasion of Italy, the Lombards were split in their religious beliefs between inherited paganism and a Germanic Arian flavour of Christianity similar to the Goths, which did not endear them to the Roman Church. As this was the result of received wisdom rather than theological conviction, over time they drew closer to the Roman model as their rule continued well into the following century. Theolinda was destined to be queen from 616-628. By then more Lombards had become Catholic, but some of these still Arian.

One stream of income for the Church since Constantine's day had been gifts and property bequests from wealthy noble Roman families, some of which were large estates with epitaphic intention to perpetuate the memory of the donor. That practice tailed off during this century as many such families had struggled to maintain their wealth during the wars with the Lombards, while the Byzantine Emperors more or less ended the Roman tradition of Emperors giving gifts and lands to the papal estates through the pope in Rome, preferring instead to support the Church in Constantinople.

Islam

Away from the theological and cultural struggles within Christianity, an unexpected external challenge was brewing as Mohammad ibn Abdullah was born in Mecca about 570AD. He would grow up to be acclaimed by his Arabian followers as the 'last Prophet'. He founded Islam, a new Abrahamic and monotheistic faith at the turn of the century. This would sweep the Arabian Peninsula, which due to its inaccessibility, had never been widely converted to Christianity. Islam would expand further mainly by conquest, north and eastwards into important strongly Christian territory that had produced many influential figures and thinkers for Christianity.

CHAPTER 9

7th Century

Popes

590-604 Gregory I	654-657 Eugene I
604-606 Sabinian	657-672 Vitalian
607 Feb-Nov Boniface III	672-676 Adeodatus II
608-615 Boniface IV	676-678 Donus
615-618 Adeodatus I	678-681 Agatho
619-625 Boniface V	682-683 Leo II
625-638 Honorius I	684-685 Benedict II
640 May-Aug Severinus	685-686 John V
640-642 John IV	686-687 Conon
642-649 Theodore I	687-701 Sergius I
649-654 Martin I	

Roman Emperors

Phocas	602-610	Justinian II	685-695
Heraclius	610-641	Leontios	695-698
Constans II	641-668	Tiberios III	698-705
ConstantineIV	668-685		

The centuries since Jesus Christ had seen much advance and change in human, social, cultural and spiritual matters. The Church that Jesus left in the hands of his followers had grown regardless of unimaginable levels of persecution by its opponents and serious internal disputes. Jesus had promised the Holy Spirit would be there to support its followers as needed, but from early on strains began to show. All human institutions can risk their founding objectives being clouded by a human tendency to see them as ends in themselves, thus suffering self-weakening even destructive internal differences. Christianity proved no exception although the Church survived and would continue to do so, even if frequently in spite of rather than because of its own human leaders and clerics.

As the Christian Church developed among diverse nations and groups, differences of interpretation and opinion arose, influenced by cultural variations, intellectual rivalry and personal pride or ambition. Parts of the Oriental, mostly Middle-Eastern Church had gone their separate way in the Chalcedonian or Nestorian Schism then tensions grew between Rome and Constantinople. Roman and Sassanid Empires had fought each other to the point of both being existentially weakened. Schism and tensions within the Eastern Church, together with the faltering power base and reach of the Roman Empire would all prove handicaps in the face of the arrival of a nascent fervent religious movement in the Arabian Peninsula, an area which had only recently been recognised as ripe for conversion to Christianity.

Islam and the Middle East

Arabia was separated from its neighbours by a huge expanse of desert, which had hindered missionary access by land. Society and politics were undeveloped there. Arabs are descended from Ishmael, son of Abraham, but had split into tribes, many of them nomadic, in order to survive in their harsh landscape and climate. The only organisation of society was tribal law, largely dependent on the whim of individual tribal leaders. It was a hard life, lacking in spirituality but indulging in idolatry and star-worship and a local quarrel could ignite war in which they relished the application of their skills, honed as sport in leisure time, mostly in horse-riding and fighting as well as subsistence survival in the most hostile terrain.

Yet the hospitality, generosity and protection they afforded to guests were legendary in spite of scarcity of provisions. Many of life's necessities were fetched or brought by traders from the north by camel train or the west from Egypt over the narrow Red Sea. Arabia's main city Mecca gained wealth as the centre of such trade but also from pilgrim visitors as it had been regarded as a holy place since before Christianity. There were pockets of Jews there and many of the Arabs shared the Jews' belief that a new prophet would come and teach them to worship the God of Abraham, who they believed built the sacred Ka'ba in Mecca, an eight meter high rectangular stone construction which drew pilgrims to the city.

Mohammed was born in 570 AD near Mecca into a wealthy family. He became known for his wisdom and honesty and he struggled with the tribal strife, corruption, abuse of authority, social injustice and discrimination, especially against women in his country. He yearned for peace and holiness and took the occasional retreat alone in a cave on Mount Jabaal an Noor (Light) about five kilometres north of Mecca. One night in 610 he was visited in his sleep by the archangel Gabriel in a cave. The apparition gave him a verse of the Qur'an (Koran) saying it was a message from God and he was to remember and recite it. The words eventually became the opening verses of Chapter 96 of the Qur'an. "Read.

In the name of the Lord. Who created man from a clot. Read. And your Lord is the most generous."

Over many subsequent visits to the cave, usually lasting several days, he received the fullness of the Holy Qu'ran, which became the key 'Bible' of a new faith, Islam. Three years later, he had another vision telling him to spread the word of God. He began to build a following by preaching from a hill in Mecca calling on people to abandon evil and follow the straight path of God. The Arabs were not alone in tending to follow strong leaders and some wanted to regard him as a God himself, but he denied and discouraged that.

Mohammed spread the Muslim faith in just ten years throughout the Arabian Peninsula beginning in 622 and in so doing, more or less united its volatile people. There was negligible competition due to the inaccessibility of the region, consolidated by Muslim control of the trade routes that could have been used by Christian evangelists. The new faith punished apostasy or conversion by death, so once a Muslim, always a Muslim.

Mohammed's death in Medina in 632 was announced by his caliph Abu Bakr, who ruled out any idea of his divinity, saying "Whosoever worshipped Mohammed, let him know that Mohammed is dead, but whosoever worships God, let him know that God lives and never dies." Mohammed is therefore regarded by Muslims as the messenger of God, Allah.

Key Islamic beliefs were not altogether alien to Christianity, though as a religion it differed considerably in theology and practice. Both religions believe in one God, omniscient, just, loving and merciful; that God has revealed messages and commandments to prophets; and they accept the first five books of the Old Testament (the 'Pentateuch' as revealed to Moses), the psalms (to David) and the Gospel (through Jesus). Islam accepts these books as part of their scriptures, which are completed by the Qu'ran and the 'scrolls of Abraham' (Suhuf Ibrahim), which they believe are currently lost. They contend there are some errors and distortions in the Scriptures due to the way they were handed down, but not in the Qu'ran as this was divinely revealed to and faithfully recorded by Mohammed. Jesus is recognised by Muslims as an important prophet, but not as divine, not as the Son of God. This is not a mere point of Christological argument, but an unbridgeable difference between Islam and Christianity in spite of how much they have in common.

Once the people of the Arabian Peninsula accepted this faith, they helped spread it further afield eastward across the Persian Gulf to Iran, where they soon mostly supplanted Zoroastrianism. Lacking political skills and diplomatic persuasion, they achieved this in the way they knew best, by violent conquest. This was not the way Mohammed had taught, but these insular, tribal and war-like people attached little value to foreign and especially non-believers' lives.

Following Mohammed's death, the Rashidun caliphate (succession) began. It only lasted until 661 but in that time Islam moved north and east and conquered the Middle East, including the Holy Land and Syria as well as Afghanistan and Persia. Once their ferocity had achieved submission and control of a region, the Muslims settled to live side-by-side with the indigenous Jews and Christians, who often still constituted the majority in many of these countries. Religion, politics and the law were closely linked in Islam. God's divine law, which they call sharia law derived from the Qur'an, was the backbone of Islamic administration. There was always pressure exerted on non-Muslims in the population in the form of discrimination and high taxes, which led to further conversions. Christian evangelisation was no longer allowed and the trade routes were tightly controlled, so there could be little, if any Christian growth in the occupied countries.

This period also saw the beginning of similar expansion westward into Egypt and Libya, which had been strong Christian territory with close relationships to Rome. Some of the hermits and monastics in the Egyptian desert were disturbed enough to begin considering alternative locations. After the conquest of Alexandria, the Eastern Orthodox Church of Egypt became a minority group, even among the Christians.

Turkey

Christianity was well established in Turkey and its missions were launching eastwards along the Silk Road and other major trade routes beyond the Caspian Sea towards North West China with remarkable success on the way. Christianity found little difficulty in showing itself to be a deeper faith than the polytheistic local religions and these regions were probably less aware of Islam at the time as its proselytisation tended to be accompanied by conquest.

Roman and Persian Empires

The situation in the West was fluid as regular changes in territory and leadership occurred. During the previous century the Roman Empire and Sassanid Persian Empire had waged decades of war leaving the power of both empires depleted and in decline. Rome had fallen but the Western Church kept its base there, further straining ties with Constantinople. But Persia was in a direct path of the Islamic tide.

Europe

With the loss of central imperial authority from Rome, some states had become restless and more localised leaders emerged. The Western Church still looked to Rome for its leadership but the brevity of successive papal reigns rendered it a less stable beacon for the faith which still missed an emperor's backing for theological norming. Thus its development and teaching became more distributed and local, with many people looking towards monasteries for teaching and guidance as they were well supported by wealthy aristocratic families and encouraged deep thinking on theology and practice of faith.

A tradition arose of wealthy nobles donating parts of their estates to monks for adaption or building monasteries and development of horticulture or farming, often on the understanding that prayers and masses would be said for their family and their forebears who had died. These arrangements generally worked well and the farms were highly productive. All farming faced a cooling climate in that era and the monastery farms were better invested and organised than the self-sufficiency peasant farming of the age. They also allowed the employment of outside workers, freeing the monks to spend more time studying. It also made the monastic life more attractive to quality recruits, so enhancing the status and influence of monasteries as their knowledge bank grew.

As a consequence of looking to local monasteries rather than central guidance from Rome for teaching, some variations arose between for example, Italian, Frankish, and British theologies and practices, comparable to those which had already occurred in the Eastern Church. Britain was one example of this, magnified by the separate proselytisation processes at different times of Celtic monastics from the west and Roman missions from the south together with a mix of self-learning among secular clergy. This example of Britain, where desert monasticism via the north approached Benedictine Western European monasticism from the south, is examined more closely below. Each region had its own challenges.

Celtic Christianity Reaches Northumbria – Edwin, Oswald, Aiden, Hilda, Cuthbert

The 7th century saw much activity in the North of England, involving several learned and holy men, some from aristocracy and even royal families of the time. The story of Christianity in Britain would not be complete without mention of some of these people – Kings Edwin and Oswald, Saints Aiden, Cuthbert, Biscop, Wilfrid, Hilda and others. But as ever, the fortunes of religion were intricately tied to royal power struggles, so at least a superficial view of the political background helps in understanding the development of Christianity in this century which was an important one for the Church in Britain.

In the early part of this century, three kingdoms existed in the North East of England – Bernicia (roughly north of the Tees to the Scottish border), Deira (between rivers Humber and Tees) and Elmet (West Yorkshire plus). Edwin (586-633), was king of Deira and Bernicia, which together constituted Northumbria, from 616 to his death.

When the powerful Ethelbert of Kent died, both King Raedwald of East Anglia and Edwin of Northumbria were well placed to dominate England, which Raedwald did until his death in the mid-620s. At that point the less decisive and assertive Edwin took over rule of the minor kingdom of Elmet and then the larger Lindsey (Lincolnshire).

Edwin and Eadbald of Kent (son of Ethelbert and Bertha) were allies and Edwin sought to marry Eadbald's sister Ethelburgh. According to Bede, Eadbald would agree to the marriage only if Edwin accepted her continuing Christianity, which he promised to do. She was accompanied north by her chaplain, Paulinus of York, who had come to England with Augustine in 601. In 627 Edwin was baptised a Christian in York as was his whole court, which included a 13-year-old Hilda, daughter of his nephew.

It was commonplace in those times for a king to wage more or less annual wars with neighbours to obtain submission, tribute, and slaves. It was probably in this way that Edwin's expansion west was achieved, extending his kingdom from the Humber to the Mersey and eventually as far west as the Isle of Man and north to southern Scotland. All this expansion served also as a vehicle for Christian mission.

Edwin died in battle in 633, losing Northumbria to the Briton King of Gwynedd, Cadwallon ap Cadfan with King Penda of Mercia, a pagan. The Britons were in what are now Wales, Cumbria, south western Scotland and the far south-west of England, having been driven westward by the Anglo-Saxon invaders.

Oswald (604-642), son of Ethelfrith, previous king of Bernicia, had escaped west with Acha, a Deiran princess, as a youngster when his father fell in defeat to Edwin. He had spent part of his long exile in Iona and converted to Christianity there.

About a year after Edwin's defeat, Oswald gathered an army and erected a wooden cross above Heavenfield near Hexham. The night before battle against Cadwallon and his British army, Oswald told his warriors to pray for bravery and victory before the cross. The following day, they engaged with the British army which well out-numbered them, but they won and Cadwallon was killed. Oswald became a benign king, reunited

Northumbria, and re-established the historical supremacy of Bernicia. He was eventually killed in battle against the Mercians and succeeded by his brother Oswiu, who ruled from 642 – 670.

Following a request from Oswald to the Irish bishop for a missionary, a senior monk, **Aiden** (590-651) travelled from Iona to Northumberland in 634. Oswald was based at Bamburgh Castle and offered Aiden any site of his choice to build a monastery. He chose Lindisfarne, off the east coast, where he remained as bishop, still mixing frequent missionary travels with his monastic life. He died on 31st August 651, the very night on which a 17-year-old Cuthbert in Melrose had a vision of Aiden's soul being carried to heaven by angels. Aiden was succeeded on Lindisfarne by Finian, who built the thatched oak chapel. The community continued in the monastic life and Lindisfarne remained the main springboard for Christian evangelisation in Northern England, also sending a successful mission further south to pagan Mercia.

Hilda (614-680) was born into Deira royalty, as daughter of Hereric, nephew of King Edwin. Her father died when she was an infant, so when Edwin created Northumbria and became its king Hilda grew up, was educated and allotted tasks as a court member. She became a capable administrator and also learned to teach younger members of court. She inherited some land from her father and therefore employed people as shepherds, cattle and arable farmers and woodcutters. Hilda became well known for her wisdom and judgement to the extent that other royal figures sought her advice. She was also a devout Christian and in 647, bishop Aiden called her to Lindisfarne where she became a nun. She was soon appointed abbess of Hartlepool Abbey then in 647 became abbess of the recently built double (monks and nuns) monastery Whitby Abbey, where she lived out the rest of her life.

Cuthbert (634-687) grew up near Melrose Abbey, which was an offshoot of Lindisfarne Abbey. He had decided to become a monk after his vision of St Aiden's death, following brief service as a soldier. Once a monk, Cuthbert became guest-master at the new monastery at Ripon soon after 655, but returned to Melrose when Wilfrid was put in charge at Ripon. Around 662 Cuthbert became prior at Melrose, then three years later, prior of Lindisfarne. In 684 he was made bishop of Lindisfarne but by late 686 resigned and took up a solitary life on Inner Farne Island, a couple of miles off the coast from Bamburgh Castle, the king's seat. He died there of a painful illness in 687 AD. He was buried at Lindisfarne the same day, but to escape looting by the Danes his coffin was subsequently moved about before being reburied at Durham, leading to the founding of Durham City and Cathedral. The coffin was re-opened eleven years after his death, and according to biographies, including one by Bede from about 720, his remains had suffered no decay. The historically important St Cuthbert's Gospel is among the objects recovered from his coffin.

Roman and Celtic Christianity Meet; Synod of Whitby

As Roman Christianity had moved north and the Celtic tradition moved south in a missionary pincer-like movement in Britain, they intermingled and realised some differences in practice, 'Roman' tradition being more geared to secular practice and 'Ionian' to the monastic. Other differences existed, for example in Rule, routines and dress as well as the tonsure haircut of the monks, There were also some important liturgical issues to resolve such as the way of calculating the date of Easter, the key feast day of the Christian year. A joint synod was held at Whitby in 664 to explore ways of reconciling and unifying practice in Britain. King Oswiu presided over proceedings although he did not take part in the ecclesiastical debates. Broad agreement was reached mainly favouring Roman ways, but many Celts retained their traditional observance of Easter for a couple more generations and some continued their hair shaving.

Biscop (aka Benedict, 628-690)

Biscop was an Anglo Saxon who served King Oswald as a soldier in Northumbria until 653, when he went with the young Wilfrid on a pilgrimage to Rome. He travelled to Rome again with Alhfrith, son of Oswiu (612-670) and eventual successor as King of Northumbria. Biscop was tonsured in France where he adopted the monastic name Benedict. He returned from a third visit to Rome in 669 with Theodore of Tarsus, archbishop of Canterbury, who made him abbot of St Augustine's monastery in Canterbury.

Benedict moved back north to oversee the construction of Tyneside monasteries. In 674, he founded the first monastery building of St Peter's, Monkwearmouth on donated land overlooking the river. He wanted to build an inspirational model monastery for England, sharing his knowledge of the Roman traditions in this area that had been brought up in Celtic tradition of Christianity. To do this he brought in specialist skilled Franks to build these churches, as they were the first ecclesiastical structures in Britain to be built of stone and with glass windows. There are references to stained glass, which was then unknown in England, in some of the windows; even plain glass in windows was unusual at that time in spite of the fact the Romans had introduced glass, having learned the skill from Egyptians in the second century. There are supporting records of Frankish glassmakers having set up a workshop at Monkwearmouth. Benedict donated pictures, service books and an impressive library he had collected on his travels.

A papal letter in 678 awarded the monastery autonomy, and in 682 king Oswiu, so delighted at the success of St Peter's, gave Benedict more land in Jarrow, seven miles away along the river, for a sister foundation, which became St Paul's monastery. Benedict visited Rome again and brought back with him considerable additions to St Paul's fine library. He appointed Ceolfrith as superior at Jarrow, who took with him twenty monks, including his protégé the young Bede. The two monasteries at Monkwearmouth and Jarrow were so closely connected in their early history that they are often referred to as one. Benedict stipulated that the two sites should function as 'one monastery in two places'. Jarrow became the centre of Anglo-Saxon learning in the north of England and one of the most influential such centres in all of Europe in the 7th and 8th centuries. It produced the greatest Anglo-Saxon scholar in Bede, who wrote most of his works in Jarrow.

Wilfrid (c633-c709) and Bishop Theodore (602-690)

Wilfrid was born of Northumbrian nobility and although always a flamboyant character, he entered religious life as a teenager, studying at Lindisfarne, then briefly in Canterbury before travelling to Rome with Biscop. There he learned new practices including the Roman calculation of the date of Easter. On their way back, he decided to stay in Lyons while Biscop continued on his way home. Wilfrid learned Frankish practices from his hosts, Benedictine monks. He returned to Northumbria in about 658 and soon became the abbot of the recently built monastery at Ripon, where he used Frankish masons to dig a crypt so he could introduce Roman style burials.

In 664 Wilfrid spoke up for the Roman ways at the Synod of Whitby, He gained plaudits for his speech advocating that the Roman calculation of the date of Easter should be adopted, which prompted the king's son, Ahlfrith, to appoint him Bishop of Northumbria based at York. A dispute between Ahlfrith and King Oswiu delayed this appointment but in 668, Theodore of Tarsus became Archbishop of Canterbury and set about appointing more bishops to vacant sees around Britain, finally negotiating Wilfrid's installation at York. He also suggested dividing larger dioceses, including Northumbria, which Wilfrid resisted, building tension between himself and Theodore. Wilfrid subsequently founded Hexham Abbey and had it built in the Roman basilica style, following Benedict's (Biscop's) example of employing Franks as masons, who took much of their stone pre-dressed from Hadrian's Wall, which ran conveniently close by.

Following a synod at Hertford in 672, Bishop Theodore called the first general synod of the English Church. Decisions were taken to impose the Roman date of Easter, normalise practice, require obedience of clerics and monks to the Church, forbid bishops from interfering outside their own dioceses as well as reaffirm teachings on marriage, consanguinity and divorce. The controversial issue of dividing larger dioceses was postponed, but Theodore and Wilfrid fell out again. In 678 Wilfrid was deposed and travelled once more to Rome seeking the Pope's support. He then returned to England accepting Theodore's position in the argument. While Wilfrid set up a new diocese in the Kingdom of Sussex, Theodore had divided the Northumbrian diocese, leading to Wilfrid's reinstatement at Ripon. However Aldfrith, who had succeeded Egfrith in 685, expelled him again in 691, so Wilfrid went to help missionaries in Mercia. The Pope intervened, ruling in his favour and he was restored to Ripon and Hexham abbeys.

Bede (672-735)

Bede's family sent him to the abbey of St Peter at Monkwearmouth at the age of seven to be educated under Benedict, in line with common practice among noble families. When Benedict sent Ceolfrith to run the sister abbey at Jarrow in 682, Bede went with Ceolfrith and may have been involved in some of the building work, as young trainees were expected to do their share of menial work.

A plague hit Jarrow in 686 and only two of the surviving monks continued to be able to sing the full daily office – Ceolfrith and 14-year-old Bede. Bede was appointed deacon by John, Bishop of Hexham in 692, at about five years younger than the normal age for such office; he was ordained priest ten years later. As well as writing, he taught mostly scripture and history but mainly spent his life as an enclosed monastic absorbed in reading, writing and prayer. He also entertained fellow monks by singing and reciting poetry.

The only Englishman recognised as a Doctor of the Church by Roman Catholicism, Bede is still famous as an author and scholar and like Eusebius before him as the greatest Church historian of his time. His most famous work was 'Ecclesiastical History of the English People'. He was also an accomplished linguist and translator, so had no difficulty in reading the Greek and Latin writings of the early Church Fathers and making them accessible to English people.

Integration of Celtic Christianity, Penance

The Celts' legendary hunger for knowledge attracted strong support from many, including Bede. Following the synod of Whitby, in which they willingly participated, they mostly adopted Roman ways or compromises. Dissidents were mainly elderly monks, more comfortable in their traditional ways. Their colleagues showed them sympathy and tolerance, so the changes took place more or less trouble-free.

Always independent, the Welsh carried on as before, in a show of respect for their specially venerated Saint David (500-589), an early hermit, who had become Bishop of Mynyw. St David's cathedral there became a popular place of pilgrimage and worship. Wales continued to use the old Latin Bible long after other countries had adopted St Jerome's improved translation, the vulgate, originally published in 382.

As well as a thirst for knowledge and endeavour, the Celts had art and craft skills which they applied to some beautiful samples of illuminated gospels. The Book of Durrow was produced in Ireland around 700 AD, the Lindisfarne Gospel by Bishop Eadfrith a couple of decades later, then the book of Kells in Ireland around 800. In St Gall around 880, Abbott Hartmut organised the Lundau Gospels, which were subsequently bound together with a cover of metal plate and inset gemstones and now reside in the JP Morgan collection in New York. These were all serious Celtic works of art inspired by the important history and messages of their contents. The Abbey of St Gall, just mentioned, was founded in the 7th century by a Celtic monk from Ireland, Gallus, who had travelled through Gaul to Northeast Switzerland near the original home of the Celts, with a group who carried out missionary work around Austria and Bavaria.

In this century, Christianity in Britain had come a long way from being divided between Roman and Celtic Churches and seriously threatened by endemic and resurgent paganism to being a strongly growing Church in unity with the Church Universal. Paganism ceased to be a force in England with the death of its last pagan monarch, Jutish King Arwald of the Isle of Wight around 686 AD.

Penance had developed differently in Celtic Christian Britain from the Roman practice. Until the 7th century, in its isolation it had no knowledge or guidance regarding public confessions. Celtic penance had been influenced by John Cassian and involved personal confession to a priest and acceptance of a sanction, an act of penance determined by the priest, the fulfilment of which earned forgiveness and reconciliation. The priest would draw on suggested 'tariff penances' from published penitential books, which had evolved in the British Isles. For example, for a man confessing adultery, the recommended tariff was one year on bread and water and no sleeping with his wife. The use of such tariff penances was introduced to continental Europe by the monks from Britain, who had no knowledge of the practice that prevailed in Europe, which featured a public penance in the community of the church involving sanctions backed by canon law. In many areas it was a once only forgiveness which could not be given for a repeat offence.

Northern Europe, Franks and Germanic Areas, Italy

Apart from numerous forays westward, Saxony and what is now Denmark and Scandinavia was little changed, remaining pagan territory, but missionary activity there increased from the late 7th century, including some from England who are quite well documented.

Such missionaries included Willibrord (658-739) and Boniface (675-754). Willibrord, a Northumbrian missionary, brought Christianity to Northern Netherlands and Friesland, later settling as Bishop of Utrecht.

Boniface was a Devonian monk who worked mainly in the 8th century on the conversion of Northern Germany, where he installed many Catholic institutions and later became Bishop of Mainz.

Christianity had reached the northern extremities of the old Roman Empire and would extend further.

Merovingian King Clotaire II was a strong enough leader to unite his family and the dynasty lasted out the 7th century with stable borders to their realm. Their aristocracy had adopted Christianity in the wake of Childeric's conversion and this gradually percolated through to impress the Alemanni east of the Rhine, north of the Alps. Columban (543-615), another Celtic monk from Ireland was a celebrated missionary who led a group on to continental Europe and managed to establish monasteries in the Alemanni region and over the border in Lombardy, the northern part of Italy.

The Lombard rule with passive Byzantine support, as well as the Byzantine papacy, continued through this century although the Byzantine Empire faced growing challenges from the ambitions of Islam.

Eastern Church, Councils of Constantinople and Trullo

There were more Christians in the East than in the West and the structure of the Church there was more settled. But it was the Eastern Church which first felt the threat of Islamic fervour spreading from Arabia.

Two councils were held in Constantinople towards the end of the 7th century which were important to the Church, the Sixth Ecumenical

Council in 680 and the Trullan Council of only Eastern prelates in 692.

The Sixth Ecumenical Council, **Third Council of Constantinople** was convoked by Patriarch George I of Constantinople in 680 to address concerns regarding theological disputes of the previous century with origins in the east. Byzantine Emperor Heraclius (reign 610-641) had spent a good part of his reign in a long war to regain territory that had been lost to the Persians, which had begun before he became emperor and lasted from 602 to 628. In the course of this he encountered the Oriental Christians there who had followed Nestorian thinking, which ran counter to Chalcedonian Christology. In an astute bid to keep them on side, he came up with a compromise fudge definition called monoenergism (that while Christ had two natures, one divine and one human, he had one energy, both divine and human). After debate, the council evolved this into monothelitism (the same two natures but with only one will, so there was no conflict between his human will and his divine will).

This may all seem rather 'technical', but monothelitism proved acceptable to Byzantine Christians, which was important in the short term. However it was vehemently opposed by delegates from Jerusalem and Rome in whose favour the Ecumenical Council ruled.

Heraclius' grandson Constans II (emperor 641-668), outlawed any discussion on this subject, seeing it as a threat to the stability of the empire. Since the Roman Church saw monothelitism as denying the full humanity of Christ, Pope Martin I (649-655) and a monk called Maximus called a synod in Rome to condemn both compromise Christologies. Both were tried for high treason and found guilty. Maximus was executed and Martin exiled but died soon after.

The **Council of Trullo** endorsed a number of previous synods and the six ecumenical councils held so far. As an exclusively Eastern Church affair, it went further, reflecting particular feelings of the Eastern Church not matching those of the West. It aimed to address some differences that had developed between East and West in practiced rites and clerical discipline and banned some festivals and practices with possible pagan origins. Some practices of the Armenian Church were condemned, such as eating eggs and cheese at weekends during Lent, not adding water to the communion wine at Mass and ordaining the children of clergy. These were now punishable by rescinding the priesthood of offending clergy and excommunicating lay people for what could be considered rather minor contraventions. The same penalties were applied for following the Western practice of fasting on Saturdays in Lent and any ban on married clergy.

There were many more canons of which those relating to the Eucharist are worth noting here. The Eucharist should be received in the hand, with the hands forming a cross. It should never be administered to a dead person and in Lent it should only be celebrated on Saturdays and Sundays.

As to prohibitions applied to the clergy, these included adultery or any improper relationships with women, simony, charging for the Eucharist, entering public houses, usury, gambling , attending theatre or horse races and wearing unsuitable clothing. Conducting liturgy in a private home required the approval of a bishop. Abortion was forbidden.

As a Byzantine council, it satisfied the expectations of the Eastern Church but did not please Rome. Pope Sergius I, of Syriac origin, found it unacceptable and refused to sign off the canons, so he was arrested on the orders of Emperor Justinian II and would have been taken to Constantinople but for the intervention of the militia of the Exarchate of Ravenna. (As mentioned in the 6th century, the Byzantine Emperor's power in Italy was delegated to his representative, the Exarch of Ravenna.)

Church Music

The Eastern Church proudly guarded its own direct links to the apostles and its services of worship followed the early liturgy of St James, using only the human voice for music without instruments, as had the Jews since the destruction of the Temple. So from the early days of the Church, psalms and prayers were sung in a monophonic plainchant inherited from Jewish and Greek traditions. Basil the Great encouraged the use of music in prayer to attract the young, saying, perhaps with tongue in cheek, "For when the Holy Spirit saw that mankind was ill-inclined toward virtue and that we were heedless of the righteous life because of our inclination to pleasure, what did he do? He blended the delight of melody with doctrine in order that, through the pleasantness and softness of the sound, we might unawares receive what was useful in the words according to the practice of wise physicians who, when they give the more bitter drafts to the sick, often smear the rim of the cup with honey. For this purpose, these harmonious melodies of the psalms have been designed for us, that those who are of boyish age or wholly youthful in their character, while in appearance they sing, may in reality be educating their souls." The Orthodox Churches always resisted instrumental music.

The Roman Church had followed suit for some centuries, but without the same strength of resistance. Pope Vitalian is believed to have encouraged the introduction of the organ to western Churches about the middle of the 7th century and this gave birth to a whole new field of polyphonic choral music with instrumental accompaniment which could take the soul "soaring to the very heavens".

Plainsong had been used since the very early Church and it was customarily used in singing Psalms and other prayers adapted for the purpose. It was widely adopted in monasteries and developed into the less monotone Gregorian chant, probably by Pope Gregory II around the 9th and 10th centuries.

China

Following the 5th century Nestorian schism when the 'Oriental' Church split from mainstream Christianity, Persia's existing trade links by land, including the Silk Road, helped their missions bring Christianity to the Far East, including Mongolia, China and Korea. The schism had lent added impetus to their efforts, which seemed fortunately timed to bring new success.

The Chinese people followed old traditional customs into which were randomly woven the three main religions, Buddhism, Confucianism and Taoism, all popular in the region. People seemed to pick and mix from these to make up their own syncretic faith. So the exclusive nature of Christianity was not easy for them to adopt and there is scant evidence of missionary success until the 7th century. Christianity finally met a welcome in the Tang period (618-906) as recorded on an important limestone monument or stele about 2.8 metres high discovered in Xian in 1625. This dates from 781 but seems to have been buried for its protection around 845, during a period of suppression. The Xian area is also where the buried Qin Tomb with its terracotta army was unearthed in the 1970s.

This Nestorian Monument has inscription in Chinese and Syriac script recording about a century and a half of Christian communities in northern China, with the names of a bishop, 28 presbyters and 38 monks inscribed on it, some of whom were known Assyrian Church clerics. It refers to a Christian missionary Alopen winning the interest of Emperor Tai Tsung, second emperor of the Tang dynasty (ruled 626-649), in 635. This emperor was open to foreign trade and learning and ordered translation of the sacred writings that Alopen had brought, and encouraged the spread of their message. Christianity was described as the 'Religion of Light' and Emperor Tai Tsung supported the building of a monastery, which was followed by one in every province built under his successor Kao Tsung, who also respected Christianity. During his reign, Christian books were published in Chinese, spreading its reputation.

The Church enjoyed mostly good times during the Tang dynasty, although there were periods of set-back. One such period was under Empress Consort Wu, an ardent Buddhist, who assumed power when her husband, Emperor Gao Tsung was disabled by a stroke. Christian fortunes recovered soon after her rule.

North East Asia

Branches from the Silk Road by then also reached Korea, as well as Japan and what is now the east coast of Russia as other missionaries had ventured along these routes. There are records of Christianity in Korea from the 7th century, when they had representatives at the Tang court in Chang-an. So the seed was being sown here also.

CHAPTER 10

8th Century

Popes

701-705 John VI
705-707 John VII
708 Jan-Feb Sisinnius
708-715 Constantine
715-731 Gregory II
731-741 Gregory III

741-752 Zachary
752-757 Stephen II
757-767 Paul I
768-772 Stephen III
772-795 Adrian I
795-816 Leo III

Emperors

698-705 Tiberios III
705-711 Justinian II
711-713 Philippikos
713-715 Anastasios II
715-725 Theodosios III

717-741 Leo III
741-775 Constantine V
775-780 Leo IV
780-797 Constantine VI
797-802 Irene

This century saw a change in political power balance between Eastern and Western Europe as the emperors in Constantinople became preoccupied with threats from the south and east and as a result lost territories further west. Potential and actual divisions between East and West were widening. The nominal Roman Emperor of the East, became more detached from Rome as the Franks proved their undisputed leadership in the West over the Lombards. This rendered the papal role even more complex and demanding as it increased potential conflict between his spiritual and temporal responsibilities. Meanwhile the Eastern Churches became preoccupied by pressure from Islam's expansion.

Pope Gregory II (715–731) and Rome

Pope Gregory II was a much-needed strong, energetic and thoughtful pope, regarded by many in the Church as perhaps the best defender of the faith in the 8th century. He repaired and strengthened the Aurelian wall around Rome, which included the 7 hills and the Campus Martius. Work was interrupted by the River Tiber bursting its banks in 716, flooding parts of Rome for over a week, so he also further strengthened the river banks.

In 716, Theodor I, the Duke of Bavaria visited Gregory seeking more preachers to bolster conversion work. Gregory sent delegates who were instructed to support the duke, and to establish a local church hierarchy with an archbishop. Gregory maintained this interest in Bavaria and in 726 he sent Corbinian, a monastic, to be Bishop of Freising there. He also widened his support of the Church in Germany following an approach by Devonian missionary Winfrid, whom Gregory renamed Boniface. The pope followed Boniface closely as he became a renowned evangelist, eventually consecrated him bishop in 722 and then appointed him the first Archbishop of Mainz, where he drew the attention of Duke Charles Martel, Prince of Francia.

Other notable visitors received by Gregory were ex-king Ina of Wessex and Abbott Ceolfrid who presented him with the Codex Amiatinus, a highly regarded and huge example of the Latin vulgate translation of the Bible in the finest mediaeval calligraphy, considered the truest witness to Justin's original. It is kept in good condition in the Laurentiana Library in Florence, its aged pages still fresh and clear today.

Pope Gregory opposed the iconoclastic views of Byzantine Emperor Leo III the Isaurian, which some historians see as the basis for subsequent schisms and wars that led to the eventual acquisition of Papal States and political and temporal powers for the popes. Leo was disliked in Italy for his earlier attempt to impose taxes there and Gregory was respected for his opposition to this. Gregory also rejected Leo's attempts to interfere in ecclesiastical affairs, which gave the Lombards a chance to exert their authority as their leader Liutprand decided their best interests were served by supporting the pope. They exercised pressure on Ravenna, home of the Exarch, whose job it was to persuade the pope to obey the Emperor. The Lombards would prove unreliable allies after Gregory's papacy and in spite of their differences on tax and iconoclasm, Gregory was loyal to Leo as emperor.

Italy

With Islam to the east and Lombards to the west and the fall of the Exarchate of Ravenna to Lombards in 751, the Byzantine Empire was under pressure. The 'Middle Ages' were approaching.

The Lombards in Northern Italy had developed following the Roman era from being mainly pagans and Arians to gaining Catholicism during the 7th and early 8th centuries. But Balkan Slavs nibbled away at their eastern borders, pushing the Lombards back to the current border with Slovenia during the reign of King Aripert II (701-712). Lombard fortunes recovered under King Luitprand, whose long reign (712-744) followed. He was a committed Catholic and keen supporter of new monasteries.

About 722, Pope Gregory II's relations with Byzantine Emperor Leo III became strained first by the latter's attempt to impose more taxes on the papal patrimonies to replenish funds for wars against the Arabs. Gregory refused to comply with Leo's order, arguing that the income was needed to feed Romans. It resulted in the people of the city driving out the imperial governor. In view of the Lombard pressure on Ravenna, Leo could hardly dispatch an imperial army from there to enforce payment. After a failed assassination attempt on Gregory in 726, Leo issued an edict banning possession or display of any icons or statues of saints the following year. Gregory refuted this ban, restating that the images only serve as remembrance and encouragement rather than worship, adding "The dogmas of the Church are not a matter for the emperor, but for the bishops". The people of Ravenna were equally dismissive and together with the army billeted there, they rose against the emperor. Exarch Paul of Ravenna was killed in the battle. Loyalists of the emperor in Naples marched to attack Rome, but were routed in defeat.

Meanwhile, King Aistulf had become the Lombard leader in 751 when his brother abdicated to become a monk. Aistulf took advantage of the chaos in Ravenna and led the Lombards in conquest of the city, only for the Franks to gain it a couple of years later. The Lombards also took some of Istria from the next Byzantine Emperor Constantine V, whom the previous Pope Zachary had criticised for his part in the iconoclasm.

Franks, Pépin, Charlemagne

The Franks had grown further in stature and influence. As related in the 7th century, they had links with England, with some Frankish princesses marrying English royals, bringing their Christian faith with them. Their craftsman brought new construction, masonry and window glass techniques to England, notably in ecclesiastical projects. Since the Romans had withdrawn, the Franks had progressed and their own imperial ambitions helped drive them to become the most powerful empire in Europe.

The Franks' tradition of dividing inheritance equally between sons was a measure of their quest for *égalité,* albeit only among males, but it undermined the widespread unity they had managed to achieve as it led to generational fragmentation of the empire. This inevitably resulted in the king's role becoming more ceremonial than active and Childeric III (reign 743-751), the last Merovingian king, was no exception as he accepted the 'figurehead' role. With the agreement and support of Pope Zachary, Childeric was deposed by Pépin the Short, son of a Carolingian prince whom he succeeded as Mayor of the Palace, effectively the manager of the king's household. With his brother Carloman, Pépin had been successful in protecting the empire by suppressing revolts by Bavarians, Aquitanians, Saxons and Alemanni, all of which helped acceptance of Pépin's elevation. Pope Stephen II had succeeded Pope Zachary and Pope-elect Stephen I in 752 and foreseeing no chance of support from Byzantine Emperor Constantine, he travelled to visit Pépin seeking help in quelling the Lombards. Receiving a helpful response, Stephen blessed Pépin and his two sons at St Denis abbey near Paris in 754, effectively introducing the Frankish Carolingian dynasty.

Having been educated at St Denis, it came naturally for Pépin to support the papacy, and he duly invaded northern Italy later that year, securing assurances from the Lombards. In time these proved worthless, so he was obliged to reinvade in 756, driving the Lombards from Ravenna. Emperor Constantine claimed his right as previous owner of these lands, but the Franks countered that as the conquerors, the territory was theirs to do with as they wished. They handed it to the pope and his successors. The Roman Church would retain ownership of these states for over eleven hundred years, which would prove a mixed blessing.

This was part of a significant transformation in the balance of power taking place in Europe. Pope Stephen II led a shift from the Byzantine Papacy to the Frankish papacy. The 'Donation of Pépin' committed the pope to exercising temporal leadership over some states in addition to his universal spiritual leadership duties. This introduced an incentive for secular leaders to interfere in papal succession. The Byzantine Emperor made overtures to Pépin, recognising the need for peaceful co-existence.

The Carolingian empire proved to be no more solidly united than the Merovingians before it, being similarly weakened by that Frankish inheritance tradition and consequent internecine quarrels. They were only held together by their common Roman Christianity and external threats. Since each state had a different leader, they developed increasingly different cultures and natures. The empire needed somehow to be reunited and this would finally happen under the next leader. The eldest son of Pépin the Short was Charles, who would become known as Charlemagne, meaning Charles the Great (c745-814), a more regal title. His brother Carloman I was co-heir, so the Empire was split between them. Their relationship was lukewarm and one of mutual suspicion, perhaps envy.

Charlemagne (c745-814) was a natural and gifted leader. Under him the Frankish Carolingian Empire grew to its peak early in the 9th century. It was not uncommon for royals to take a pragmatic approach to marriage and Charlemagne did so in 770, when he married Desiderata, a daughter of Desiderius. This brought him into alliance with the Lombards, thus surrounding his brother's lands in southern France, Alsace and southern Germany. Charlemagne then repudiated Desiderata, who returned to her father, while he married a very young Swabian princess Hildegard, whose family owned substantial territory within Carloman's share of the Frankish Empire. She died in 783, following the birth of the last of several children. On his brother Carloman's unexpected death in 771, Charlemagne reunited the Franks and became their overall ruler, accepted by the people in Carloman's territories.

The Iconoclastic Controversy

Christianity had initially followed Jewish rejection of figurative religious art as being too close to idol worship (Ex 20:3). But once it became the official religion of the entire Roman Empire under Constantine, the Roman tradition of portraying and honouring their gods in art soon entered Christian practice. A difference in the art culture grew between Western and Eastern Churches, with the West adopting pictorial representations of saints and biblical scenes versus the Eastern use of two-dimensional icon imagery; just two different approaches, each intended to provide a focus for intercessionary prayer. Then Franks about the 7th century developed stained glass images in church windows as a new craft.

So the iconoclastic controversy was really an Eastern Church issue, with their general use of icons, which had not caught on in the west. The Western Church was generally more relaxed and found paintings of biblical scenes and saints as helpful to their followers' focus for prayer and understanding of the Christian message. The bishops in the West had also realised that the beauty and grandeur of a church could be enhanced by mosaics, frescos and paintings.

The controversy centred on Constantinople with iconoclasts versus iconodules who favoured the use of icons in churches. At the heart of the argument lay the second Commandment forbidding veneration of 'graven images', with the 'clasts' interpreting this as all images and the 'dules' offering incense, candles and even prostration before icons. The distinction between veneration and worship is that the first is the limit for saints and the second is reserved strictly for the divine. St Basil the Great said of veneration, "The honour given to the icon is referred to the prototype." Iconoclasm was the banning, removal or sometimes destruction of all images to which iconoclasts object.

The Byzantine iconoclasms occurred in two periods bridging the eighth and ninth centuries. The first lasted from about 726 to 787. There was a background in the east of Islamic military successes in the 7th and 8th centuries that led some Byzantine Christian authorities to adopt the Islamic prohibition of any images of creatures, human or animal. The controversy also had a social element as the poorer regions to the east could suffer Arab raids and punishment for any images found, so wanted to eliminate the risk. Wealthier, safer people in Greece and the Balkans for example, firmly opposed Iconoclasm, as did the Italians.

Icons were replaced in many churches by simple representations of the cross, often in mosaics. This removal of the artistic 'gateway to God', as the icons had been regarded, caused some riots to break out in protest, but Emperor Leo was determined and had some support among people who were uncomfortable at the very idea that art could even come close to enhancing the glory of God.

He banned images of Christ and the saints from churches, on the basis that no artist could do justice either to the divine or to the glory of Mary and the true saints. In parts of the East, there was a purge on icons by ardent iconoclasts, who destroyed a valuable heritage of ancient Church art over a wide area. Perversely, those areas which were by then under Muslim control were largely protected from this destruction.

In the West, Pope Gregory III held two synods in Rome and condemned Emperor Leo's actions, and in response Leo confiscated papal estates in Calabria and Sicily, bringing them as well as Illyria under Constantinople's governance, much of which would last for some time.

Emperor Leo's successor, his son Constantine V (741–775), was also an iconoclast and he called the Council of Heiria in 754, the first council to deal mainly with religious imagery. He was closely involved in proceedings which found in favour of iconoclasm, but the legitimacy of this council is disregarded by both Eastern and Western Churches as there were no Roman bishops, Eastern patriarchs or their agents present. Most Western monks were opposed to iconoclasm and John of Damascus, a monk regarded by some as the last of the early Church Fathers, proposed that in becoming man, Jesus showed us the human face of God and thus authorised portraits of God, so why not saints as well? The same logic applied to statues, which emerged in Church decoration later as sculptural skills developed. It was always made clear these were not to be subjects for any worship, which would contravene the first two commandments.

Constantine's son, Leo IV (775–80) was less rigorous, and for a time tried to mediate between the factions. When he died, his wife Irene became regent for her son, Constantine VI (780–97), then became Empress when her son died in 797.

Since the death of the last Western Roman Emperor in 480, popes had accepted that the Eastern Roman Emperors convoke councils of the Church. However, now that a woman was in that position, the papacy could not recognise her as ruler, considered the role vacant and Pope Leo crowned Charlemagne, King of the Franks and King of Italy as Roman Emperor, successor to Constantine VI.

In an attempt to repair relations with Rome regarding iconoclasm, Irene initiated a Council of Nicaea (797) soon after Leo's death but asked Patriarch Tarasius to convoke it in order to avoid a clash with the pope and to allow Western Church participation. Patriarchs and papal delegates attended the council and its canons were approved by the Pope so this is regarded by the Church as the Seventh Ecumenical Council. The Eastern Orthodox Church regards it as the last genuine ecumenical council and icon veneration was re-adopted, reversing the decrees of the previous iconoclast council for the time being.

Popes Paul I, (757-767) Stephen III (768-772) and Adrian I (772-795)

Paul I succeeded his brother, Stephen II as pope. The Lombards continued to pose a threat and moved into some of the duchies that Pépin had given to the papacy. Paul tried to keep the Lombard King Desiderius, the Byzantine Emperor and Pépin all on side while covertly asking Pépin's help in restoring the lost duchies, Spoleto and Benevento as well as some disputed cities held by the Lombards. Pépin held some Lombard hostages and negotiated with Desiderius the return of Benevento and some land in Tuscany and Spoleto.

Paul's reign clearly demonstrated how political responsibilities distracted from the spiritual as he paid scant attention to the latter. Following Paul's death in 767, King Desiderius tried to install a monk as antipope Philip, but Philip was ousted within a day and never recognised. He was replaced by a Benedictine monk who took the name Stephen III.

With a number of rival traditional Roman families of influence vying for the new powerful papacy, it took a year of quite brutal conflict before Stephen III was finally elected in 768. Added to this, Toto of Nepi, supported by Desiderius and an armed Tuscan group installed Constantine II in the antipope role for twelve months from June 767, but he was finally deposed from his assumed position with some Lombard support. Stephen called a council and wrote to Pépin asking him to send bishops with knowledge of canon law to attend this. Pépin died before he read the letter and Frankish rule passed to his sons Carloman I and Charlemagne. Charlemagne sent a dozen bishops to the Lateran Council in 769.

The two most significant canons arising from this council were new rules regarding papal election and the condemnation of iconoclasm. The first included a ban on the election of a layperson as pope; a ban on laypeople voting in such an election with only cardinal deacons or cardinal priests being eligible; and all ordinations of antipope Constantine were deemed void. Regarding iconoclasm, the findings of the Council of Hieria were condemned and the veneration of icons and images was permissible and desirable, confirming the canon from the Council of Rome in 731.

Pope Adrian I (772-795), the son of a noble Roman family, was elected on Stephen's death. The Lombards, under King Desiderius (756-774) continued to threaten Papal Lands. When Desiderius asked Adrian to declare Carloman's sons the rightful heirs to the southern Frankish territory, the pope turned to Charlemagne, who was deeply involved in the matter.

Charlemagne Defeats the Lombards

On his brother's death in 771, Charlemagne seized the rest of the Frankish Empire. Carloman's widow Gerberga fled to join Desiderius at his court in Pavia to seek his support for her sons' claim to Carloman's inheritance. So Desiderius approached the new Pope Adrian to request his backing for such a move in exchange for peace. In the absence of any help from Constantinople, so reliant on Frankish support, Adrian declined, leading Desiderius to resume attacks. So Adrian turned once more to Charlemagne.

Charlemagne knew he had offended Desiderius by rejecting his daughter soon after marrying. Realising that Desiderius' inferred alliance with Carloman's sons meant that he posed a threat to Charlemagne's occupation of Carloman's share of Frankish territory. Charlemagne left a battle he was leading at Paderborn and took an army south to invade and lay siege to Pavia. The Lombards surrendered to save their lives and Desiderius was captured and held in an abbey in France, while Charlemagne became King of the Lombards, further extending his empire.

Having dislodged the Lombards from power in Northern Italy, he assumed the role of protector of the papacy. The Moors had by then occupied the southern two-thirds of Spain and Portugal and even part of South Western Francia, as the Emirate of Cordoba. Charlemagne led an army into Spain as far as Barcelona, although its success was fairly short-lived. He was more successful in driving the Moors from Corsica, Sardinia and the Balearics, leaving behind strengthened garrisons and fleets to repel frequent attacks by the Moors' Saracen pirates.

To the north east, Charlemagne pursued a vicious campaign against the pagan Saxons, forcing Christianity on them on pain of death, including the infamous Massacre of Verden, where allegedly 4,500 were killed on his orders in 782 AD. The borders swung to and fro in ensuing battles, but

Charlemagne triumphed in the end, building abbeys and places of education where his victory endured. Such a means of spreading the faith by force and at a high cost of lives would have been unconscionable in the time of Jesus and during the early centuries of Christianity. But in Charlemagne's terms, the policy succeeded in the end as Saxony produced some able leaders for the German territories, who would become significant players in later extending Christianity further north into Denmark and Sweden.

Further south and east, Charlemagne sought conversion of the Slavs. This developed into a race between Eastern and Western Christianity, creating friction with the Orthodox Church and Constantinople. Missionary opportunities in the West were now limited to North Eastern Europe due to the Islamic hold on North Africa and parts of Iberia, while the Orthodox Churches embraced Eastern Europe and Asia. Overall, with such competition within and the violence of the northern campaign, this was a period of questionable evangelism and consequence for the Church that had been founded to help believers follow the uniting, loving and pacific example and teaching of Jesus Christ.

Pope Adrian I's Long Reign

Adrian's 23-year reign was the longest since Jesus had appointed Peter as leader of his Church. This offered some stability to the Western Church in turbulent times, but achieved little by way of rapprochement with the Eastern Church. The iconoclast controversy was only superficially resolved and revival of the long-standing *filioque* controversy over the Nicene Creed still simmered. The lack of forthcoming support from the Eastern Emperor led Adrian to appoint Charlemagne as Protector of the Church in recognition of his help for the Church against the Lombards and with an eye to the strength and scope of his empire.

In England, King Offa of Mercia (reign 757-796) secured the support of English bishops in persuading the pope to make a new archdiocese centred on Lichfield.

Pope Adrian died at the end of 785 and was succeeded by Leo III, who saw the Church into the next century.

Filioque and the East-West Divide

Over the next few centuries there would be several measures taken in an attempt to maintain unity between Roman and Eastern Orthodox Christians. The failed proposal of marriage between Charlemagne and the Byzantine Empress Irene around 790AD was just one of these.

But Charlemagne proved unhelpful in resolving the issue of unity in terms of the contentious matter of the *filioque*. No doubt meaning well, he hardened the Frankish view that the Nicene Creed should include the *filioque*, "and the Son". The practice of chanting this version of the Creed in the Mass spread in the Frankish Kingdom and by the end of the 8th century was common throughout it and into northern Italy, but not as far as Rome. This presented a considerable challenge to Popes Hadrian I and Leo III in finding a way of limiting the growth of this potential creedal rift between Eastern and Western Churches.

In 787, following the second Council of Nicaea, Charlemagne accused Tarasios, patriarch of Constantinople of infidelity to the first Council of Nicaea in accepting the Holy Spirit proceeded 'through the Son' rather than 'from the Son'. At Charlemagne's command the *Libri Carolini*, a series of four books, were published against the advice and wishes of Rome, clearly supporting the view that the word *filioque* was essential to the Creed. Theologians of the time declared it erroneous and Pope Leo III (reign 795-816), acknowledging the danger, rejected and forbade the *'filioque'* version of the Nicene Creed.

For the rest of Pope Leo III's reign, and for another two centuries, there was no Creed at all in the Roman rite Mass, whereas the Frankish Mass included it, usually sung and including the *filioque*.

In responding to a further call to help Pope Leo III in 799, Charlemagne was acclaimed by the pope as emperor, calling him 'Charles, most serene Augustus, crowned by God, great and pacific emperor, governing the Roman Empire'. This set the scene for the Holy Roman Empire which would be established formally in the 9th century. So Charlemagne had united much of Europe and become the first recognised Western European emperor since the fall of the original Roman Empire.

Islam Continues to Expand, New Caliphate

Islam continued its own expansion by conquest, natural to Arabs if contrary to Mohammed's teaching, just as Charlemagne's strategy in Saxony had contravened that of Jesus. Although the early Christians had spread faith peacefully, many of the activities and arguments that developed among Christians including schisms had over the centuries come to involve violence, contrary both to Christ's way and to his expressed wish for unity. Unlike Christianity, after Muhammed, Islam never adopted an ongoing central spiritual leadership to enforce such principles. Their Qur'an was as ambiguous on the matter as the Bible, though Jesus did arrange succession. Islam would in time experience division as did Christianity.

Once Islamic conquest and occupation of an area settled down, they usually afforded to indigenous Jews and Christians tolerance, courtesy and freedom to worship. They all shared the Pentateuch, Abraham and more, but the Christian belief in the Trinity gave rise to serious Muslim suspicion as they could not accept it as compatible with 'One God'. They opposed any use of images and banned proselytisation or mixed marriage. In unconquered Christian countries, there was no reciprocal tolerance of Muslims, who usually had to either embrace Christianity or face expulsion. However, comparison is far from simple. In Islamic territory there was much pressure brought to bear on the other faiths and once anyone converted to Islam they could not change their minds as apostasy incurred the death penalty. Furthermore, non-Muslim individuals were heavily taxed and suffered prejudice, which was a strong incentive to adopt Islam.

The Rashidun caliphate had come to an end following the first Muslim civil war of 661, in which the first caliph of the Umayyad clan was chosen. He was Muawiya, who had been a longstanding governor of Syria and whose family laid claim to dynastic descent from the family of Mohammed. When he died in 680, there was a family argument over the succession which sparked the Second Civil War, which resulted in Marwan, from another branch of the same family becoming the new caliph. This Umayyad dynasty continued the caliphate's aggressive expansion, venturing east of Persia and further westward along the whole Mediterranean fringe of North Africa to Morocco and eventually up into Spain. They had moved their capital to Damascus.

The Second Siege of Constantinople took place under the Umayyads, beginning in 717 with an attack by land and sea following a succession of assaults on the fringes and some years of internal strife within the Byzantine Empire. But strong city walls, a hard winter, rough seas, the Imperial navy and help from sympathetic land neighbours repelled and largely defeated Arabian forces. The Byzantines had been deceived by Emperor Leo III who claimed that he was supporting their cause, but in 725 he seized the Byzantine throne from Theodosius III for himself. This marked an end to Islamic expansion for some time.

The Umayyad dynasty was considered by some Muslims as too secular and was eventually overthrown by the Abbasids in 751, though the Umayyads retained control in Spain.

This third caliphate after Mohammed descended from a paternal uncle of Mohammed, Abbas ibn Abd al-Muttalib. They built a new capital city, Baghdad in Iraq, near the ancient city of Ctesiphon. After they moved there, Baghdad became a serious centre of culture, science and philosophy as scholars were welcomed and helped translate western studies and papers into the Arabic language. Prosperity grew, ushering in the Islamic Golden Age which lasted at least until the Mongol raids in the 13th century.

Spain

The Islamic Umayyad expansion into the Visigoth's Kingdom of Spain began with their mainly Berber army landing in Gibraltar. From 711-788 they ruled over the area known as al-Andalus, even occupying a strip in south west Francia beyond the Pyrenees until 759. After their defeat elsewhere by the Abbasids in 750, the Umayyads settled in Cordoba, forming an emirate then in 756, a caliphate as the Abbasids' attention was drawn elsewhere. Christianity remained the majority religion, with a sizeable Jewish population as well.

Islam's Effect on Monastics in the East

When Islamic forces moved into Egypt in the 7th century, many desert monks and hermits were motivated to seek alternative solitary enclaves. Some were set up in the opening of a gorge near the foot of Mount Sinai where the monastery of St Catherine had been built in the 6th century. They installed a library that now claims to be the oldest working library in the world with many unique documents. The monastery is a UNESCO World Heritage Site. John Climacus (c.579-649), an ascetic hermit in the gorge, became abbot there at the beginning of the 7th century. He published 'The Ladder of Divine Ascent' about the same time. It is a book on monasticism, outlining 30 steps of vice to be overcome and virtue to be embraced to achieve full spiritual fulfilment. It is still read in Eastern Orthodox Churches especially during Lent.

Other desert monks moved out of Egypt altogether after the Islamic wave and eventually settled in monasteries on Mount Athos.

Mount Athos Monasteries

Accounts of monasticism would not be complete without mention of Mount Athos. As Islam swept into Egypt in the 7th century, many desert monks sought alternative havens of tranquillity. The Athos peninsula in north east Greece was naturally suited for this. It is accessible only with difficulty, an inhospitable rocky land with steep cliffs, mountains and clefts. It was ideal terrain for solitary living and many hermits settled there from about this time. The landscape was also attractive to outlaws, so the religious occupants had to organise defences against bandit raids and initially tended to concentrate their settlements for mutual safety around the even less accessible Mount Athos near the peninsula's southern end. It is known to have been inhabited before 726 as contemporary Theophanes wrote in his 'Chronicle' that the eruption of the Thera volcano in that year was witnessed from Mount Athos. There is also a record of monks from Mount Athos taking part in the 7th Ecumenical Council of Nicaea in 787. It suffered invasion by Saracens from Crete about 829, but some thirty years later, a well-known monk Efthymios the Younger moved to Mount Athos and was followed by others. Basil the Confessor built a monastery where the Hilandariou monastery stands today. This was followed by a monastery at Megali Vigla, built by Joannis Kolovos, then others.

Mount Athos grew as a powerhouse of prayer, attracting devotees from all over Christendom. Benedictines arrived there in the late 10th century as did monks from distant Georgia, which had earlier founded the Megisti Lavra monastery, which still stands on the south-eastern foothills of the peninsula.

Vikings

The Romans had never reached Denmark or Scandinavia and there had been little religious progress there since. With large coastlines and a high dependency on fish for food, the inhabitants developed sophisticated boat-building and sailing skills. Being tribal societies with local chieftains, they used these skills to make boats suited to coastal raids. As their boats increased in size, sailors ventured further afield and the Vikings arrived on the international scene late in the 8th century. The Norse were a strong and aggressive seafaring people of mainly Germanic descent who set sail from the coasts of Denmark and Norway westward to raid coastal communities in North Sea Europe, Britain, Ireland and elsewhere up to the 11th century. In the course of the attacks on the east coast of Britain some monastic communities were affected in Northumbria, including Whitby.

The Vikings were great seamen, navigators and explorers. They established settlements in the volcanic island of Iceland in the 10th century, reached Greenland and landed as far away as North America led by Lief Eriksson some 500 years before Columbus' and Cabot's transatlantic voyages. Ericsson landed in Newfoundland, which they called Vinland and also in New Brunswick in Canada.

Norse beliefs followed a variation of the old Germanic pagan religions and recognised Odin (English Wodan) as their 'chief' God; his wife Frigg, Goddess of their home Valhalla; Thor, the God of thunder symbolised by a hammer; Loki, their 'devil, a beguiling handsome giant and his Valkyries led by Brunhilda. The men idolised Thor, the strong God and pursued glory and honour in this world, with no thought of an afterlife. They were not passionate about any faith attached to these gods and proved surprisingly accepting of other faiths, which they encountered in the places they raided. They often took a syncretic approach to absorbing parts of new beliefs into their own tradition, which over time resulted in significant conversions among their ranks.

Viking raids and adventures would continue. They were just one of a number of influences that arose or continued in this century which changed power and culture balances in Europe and North Africa.

CHAPTER 11

9th Century

Popes

816-817 Stephen IV

817-824 Paschal I

824-827 Eugene II

827 Aug-Oct Valentine

827-844 Gregory IV

844-847 Sergius II

847-855 Leo IV

855-858 Benedict III

858-867 Nicholas I

867-872 Adrian II

872-882 John VIII

882-884 Marinus I

884-885 Adrian III

885-891 Stephen V

891-896 Formosus

896 Apr 15 days Boniface VI

896-897 Stephen VI

897 Aug-Nov Romanus

897 Dec 19 days Theodore II

898-900 John IX

Roman Emperors

A long sequence of German monarchs, sometimes co-monarchs, beginning with Charles I, Charlemagne, were recognised and crowned by respective popes as Emperors of Rome. Modern convention has the Holy Roman Empire beginning with the coronation of Otto I in 962 as Roman Emperor by the pope, though the title Sacrum Imporium Romanum is not recorded until the 13th century.

Carolingian dynasty:		Charles III (the Fat)	881-888
Charles I (Charlemagne)	742-814	Widonid dynasty:	
Louis I (the Pious)	813-840	Guy I	891-894
Lothair II	823-855	Lambert I	892-898
Louis II	855-875	Carolingian dynasty:	
Charles II (the Bald)	875-877	Arnulph of Carinthia	896-899

The 8th century had seen the Roman papacy quite suddenly assume significant political and economic roles and dependencies. The Vatican had been ill-prepared for this and found it a serious diversion from its main purpose of leading and propagating the united faith as Christ had originally asked of Peter. It lacked the requisite civil government infrastructure, officers and experience for such roles. Under these circumstances and given the embedded culture in the region, it was open for corruption to creep into the process of grooming and appointing popes as well as the behaviour of some of them. Outside pressures on the Church came variously from emperors, powerful families and other influential groups. In spite of this, there were some well-respected and devout Popes, but even they could not always resist being distracted from their main purpose by such temporal issues.

The Franks had gained considerable influence in Church matters through Pépin's donation. Within Italy, the new breadth of power and influence of the papacy led to noble families pressing to provide papal candidates who could bring financial support and further estates to add to the Church's wealth. This was not harmful in itself so long as the resulting incumbent could remain dedicated to his primary role. But it proved over time to be too challenging a balance, diversionary and so open to abuse that popes of the forthcoming 'Dark Age' period will feature more prominently in the unfolding story of the Western Church than had their forebears. It was helpful that Pope Leo III followed Adrian, the longest-serving pope to date, with another lengthy reign of over twenty years to assimilate the effects of this transformation.

This still led to a rather unproductive 9th century as the distraction of further tensions between Rome and Constantinople arose and there was some capricious decision- and match-making by Roman Emperors and their families while a succession of numerous brief papal reigns all led to little advancement spiritually, politically or socially. This all makes for tedious reading so the period is recordeded quite briefly.

Pope Leo III (795-814)

Leo's election was hastened, probably either to avoid noble Roman families jostling for contention or to complete the process before news of Adrian's death reached the Franks. He was elected on the same day as Adrian was buried. Leo was a cardinal-priest from an ordinary family in southern Italy. He confirmed Charlemagne as the protector of the Holy See and in return received the emperor's good wishes and a generous gift of captured riches, which he used diligently to support churches and charities in Rome as well as to improve the city's beauty.

In 799, Leo was seriously attacked by a group of armed men sent by some Roman families who believed him unfit to succeed the high-born Adrian. He was rescued by the imperial militia and after a period of recovery hosted by the Duke of Spoleto, he was escorted to Charlemagne's camp in Paderborn. He was warmly received there with full respect. The following year, Pope Leo III crowned Charlemagne as Holy Roman Emperor at St Peter's in Rome. This annoyed Constantinople, but Eastern Empress Irene surely recognised that they no longer had the strength or reach to protect the papacy in Rome.

In 803, Leo helped settle some differences in England between the Archdioceses of York and Canterbury and demoted Lichfield back to a normal diocese. Then in 808, he handed Corsica over to Charlemagne's control, the better to oppose the Saracen raids to which it was vulnerable.

The *filioque* controversy rumbled on and Leo forbade the inclusion of the term in the Nicene Creed. In 809, he stressed the point by placing two silver plaques in St Peter's basilica inscribed with the creed, one Latin, one Greek without the term. Roman Catholicism and Eastern Orthodoxy held together for the time being.

Pope Leo died aged 66 in 816, two years after Charlemagne's death. Charlemagne's only surviving son by Hildegard, co-emperor since 813, inherited the empire and became known as Louis the Pious.

Charlemagne's Empire Divides

The Franks' were confident of a role in Church affairs following Pépin's donation, which was confirmed in 813, when Charlemagne decreed for reform councils to be held at key cities throughout his empire. Sixty six abbots and bishops gathered at Chalon-sur-Saone demanded clerical training schools, condemned simony and suggested that all monasteries adopt the Rule of Benedict. They also recommended the restoration of public penance and private confession to God and a priest, who would assign an appropriate canonical penance and required that all Christians receive Holy Communion on Maundy Thursday the day of the Last Supper of Christ with his apostles.

The empire established by Charlemagne collapsed two generations after him about 855, whereupon the Franks divided into distinct cultural entities – the various German States and the Kingdom of France, which included some semi-autonomous kingdoms in the east of present-day France.

Clouds Gather for Papacy, Popes Stephen IV and Paschal I

Meanwhile, Italy fell into disarray. The pope lost the support of the powerful and stable Francia and his successors lost the reassurance of a coherent and consistent rule of law. Both Rome and the papacy lay in the hands of dubious elections and sometimes corrupt or criminal gangs. The next few centuries would see the 'Dark Age' of the papacy with popes of widely varying calibre, some meeting violent ends.

Succeeding Leo III, **Pope Stephen IV** (816-817) came from the noble Marinus family which would also produce future popes Sergius II and Adrian II. He was raised at the Lateran Palace, ordained in the time of Pope Leo III and became well known and liked in Rome.

To avoid misunderstanding with Frankish King Louis the Pious, Stephen ordered the Roman people to swear loyalty to Louis and sent envoys to Louis' court to give news of his election. Louis invited Stephen to visit him in Rheims, where the new pope anointed Louis as Emperor of Rome. This act was seen as confirming the role of the Pope in the establishment of an emperor. But Stephen's reign lasted only 7 months before his death at the beginning of 817.

Pope Paschal I (817 to 824) was another aristocrat, from the Massimo family, which had produced Pope Anastasius I at the end of the 4th century. Paschal became pontiff amid turbulence in Rome and is known for encouraging the first serious but failed attempt to spread Christianity to Scandinavia, described below.

Paschal offered sanctuary to monks escaping persecution in the Byzantine Empire for opposing iconoclasm. He offered work decorating Roman churches to mosaic artists emigrating from the reduced demand for their skills, a move which prompted Byzantine Emperor Michael to complain to King Louis.

Missions to Scandinavia, Bishops Ebbo and Ansgar

Scandinavia was still regarded as missionary territory in spite of Charlemagne's efforts to spread the gospel there by violence. The natives were proud of their physicality and showed little spiritual commitment even to their pagan gods and when Christianity came knocking their reception of it was lukewarm.

Louis appointed his close friend Ebbo Archbishop of Rheims (reign 816-851) whom he then chose to lead a mission to Denmark. Pope Paschal I blessed Ebbo and made him his legate to the North. He made three brief missions with limited success but may have prized open the door for Ansgar (801-865), who would follow later and become known as the 'Apostle of the North'.

Ansgar's mother died young and he was educated by the Benedictines. In 822, he helped set up an abbey at Corvey in Westphalia, where he taught and preached. About five years later, the Swedish King Björn at Haugi asked King Louis to send a mission over to Sweden and Louis chose Asgar to lead this. Together with friar Witmar he travelled to Birka, which was an important trading centre on an island in Lake Mälaren, west of present-day Stockholm. This was a wealthy community and they were hosted by Mor Frideborg, an influential and wealthy woman, supported by one of the king's stewards, Hergeir. Both these helpers were converted quite early and Frideborg especially became known for her piety. They soon built up a small Christian community, the process being accelerated by the presence there of foreign slaves who had known or practised Christianity in their countries of origin.

Ansgar was ascetic and wore a hair shirt, gave much of his income to the poor and ate little but bread and water. In 831, Pope Gregory VI consecrated him bishop of Hamburg with a mission to evangelise his diocese, missionary territory itself, in addition to Scandinavia. Ansgar asked Archbishop Ebbo to look after Sweden, while he himself concentrated on Denmark and Norway.

Danish Vikings raided Hamburg in 845, destroying all the Church contents, including books and treasures, so Ansgar effectively had to rebuild the diocese from scratch whilst continuing his Nordic mission. The Danish civil war meant he had to build good relations with royalty, which proved helpful in gaining tolerance of Christianity there. A church was built in Schleswig in southern Jutland, an important trade bridge between the North Sea and the Baltic.

Through all this, Ansgar continued to support the mission in Sweden and stayed there from 848-850 successfully heading off a threatened pagan revolt. He returned there again when King Olof gained the throne in Birka and he found Olof sympathetic to Christianity.

When Ansgar died in 865, he was succeeded in Hamburg by Rimbert, who had accompanied him on one of his missions to Scandinavia and wrote Ansgar's biography.

Iceland

Continuing the spread of the faith northwards, some Irish monks are believed to have taken Christianity as far north as Iceland, having landed there possibly unintentionally in the 8th century, predating by at least a century the Norse settlers who arrived there about 870. The Norse brought their own heathen polytheistic religion, but Christianity spread rapidly in the island during the 10th century and was adopted as the national religion by the chieftains gathering at their early democratic National Assembly about the year 1000 AD. At the future Reformation, given its close links to Denmark, the Lutheran wave would sweep across Iceland and become entrenched as the predominant Christian denomination there.

Iconoclasm Returns

Leo V (813-820) succeeded Irene as Byzantine Emperor and his army was defeated by the Bulgarians in a number of battles. His generals took the view that Icon veneration was turning God against them. Leo had apparently observed for himself that all the emperors who took up images and venerated them had met their death either in revolt or in war; but those who did not all remained in power until they died a natural death. So he sympathised with the iconoclast view, and replaced the icon of Jesus Christ on a main gate into the Palace of Constantinople with a cross. A synod held in the Hagia Sophia confirmed the re-imposition of iconoclasm, ushering in the second Byzantine Iconoclastic Period (814-842) which saw further destruction of valuable works of art.

Leo V's successor, Michael II (820-29) wrote to the Frankish king Louis confirming he held Leo's views on icons, but this view was reversed as Michael II was succeeded by his son, Theophilus, who died young, leaving his wife Theodora regent for his young heir, Michael II. Theodora restored icon veneration in the East in 843. She, with Michael and Patriarch Methodios, convoked the Synod of Constantinople and following the first session, processed in triumph to Hagia Sophia and restored its icons. This event has been celebrated across the Church in the east on the first Sunday of Great Lent ever since.

Popes Gregory IV, Sergius II, Leo IV, Nicholas I

After Paschal, two popes followed with brief reigns before **Pope Gregory IV** (827-844) was consecrated. His pontificate was notable more for what occurred in Paris than for anything he achieved. Emperor Louis the Pious faced arguments with and between his sons. There was an original deed of 817 that on his death, his empire would be divided between the three sons by his first marriage – Lothair, Pépin and Louis. He planned to change this in 829 by adding his youngest son Charles. Pope Gregory made an indirect criticism of this decision and the emperor and his sons reached reconciliation, which was not to last long, as in 833, hostilities broke out once more. Lothair sought the pope's intervention for peace and Gregory travelled to meet Lothair, which upset the pro-Louis Frankish bishops. They suspected him of favouring Lothair against his father and refused to obey him.

Gregory IV saw this family strife as giving him increased independence from the emperor and he claimed primacy of the seat of St Peter over that of the emperor. The Frankish bishops countered that their combined opinion carried more weight than that of the pope. The failure of Gregory's visit was compounded by its disastrous effect on the diplomatic balance which saw Lothair topple his father. Louis was eventually restored to a weakened throne in 834, while Lothair retained a title as King of Italy.

Louis died in 840 and Lothair became emperor, leading to war between the brothers. This was settled by the Treaty of Verdun in 843, which separated Charlemagne's empire from the Carolingian dynasty, leaving Lothair as Emperor and King of Italy.

Gregory avoided any further involvement in diplomacy and turned to Church work. He organised some urban improvement work in Rome and appointed a number of bishops, including Ansgar as Archbishop of Hamburg, before his death in 844.

The next pope, **Sergius II** (reign 844-847), a noble cleric himself, was selected by nobility against popular preference for John, a deacon. People seized the Lateran palace and installed John there, but nobility prevailed, declaring John Anti-pope. Sergius was rapidly consecrated to avoid further insurrection, leaving no time to obtain the approval of the Frankish King, as had been agreed in 824. The Lateran palace was retaken and John arrested with some pressure for his execution. Sergius intervened to save his life, and John lived out the rest of his life far from public notice in a monastery.

Lothair I was disturbed that once more a pope had been appointed without constitutional ratification, so he sent his son Louis with an army to re-establish his authority. There was negotiation between Louis and Pope Sergius with advisors, probably including his brother Benedict, which calmed matters and resulted in Louis being anointed and crowned King of Lombardy by Sergius. The need for mutual approbation illustrated the importance of the role of religion to the people and their support of leaders.

Sergius completed the major urban development works started by his predecessor in Rome. That achievement may have been tainted by simony which some accounts suggest flourished under Sergius' reign. Simony is condemned by the Church, involving the sale or exchange of favours for spiritual benefits, indulgence, forgiveness or positions of influence in the Church. Much of the cost of the development works may have been covered by such income.

Towards the end of Sergius' life, Rome was attacked by Saracen raiders in 846. The city walls were held, but the Saracens caused considerable damage to buildings outside them including St Peters and St Pauls.

Pope Leo IV (847 –855) was a Roman and educated in a monastery before being noticed and ordained by Pope Gregory IV, then made cardinal by Sergius. He organised the repair of the churches that had been damaged during the raids on Rome, at the same time improving Rome's defences by adding a wall around the Vatican Hill and St Peter's.

Leo sought and prayed for resistance to the Saracens. He blessed a league of Italian cities which formed a navy to face the Saracens at the battle of Ostia. Half way through the battle, a storm intervened and the Italians were able to shelter in the port, returning after the storm to find the Saracens scattered and having sustained heavy damage, so they were easily defeated, many being rescued and imprisoned.

Following decades of relative inactivity by popes on the spiritual and canonical fronts, Leo was followed briefly by Pope Benedict III before **Pope Nicholas I**, (858-867), also known as Nicholas the Great.

Papal Authority, East-West Strains

Born in 800 of a noble Roman family, Nicholas' election took place in the presence of the Holy Roman Emperor, Louis II, who stayed for his enthronement. Italy was suffering Muslim incursion in the south and Viking attacks from the north. Nicholas was known for his deep piety as well as generosity, intelligence and eloquence. In his nine-year reign he renewed and consolidated papal spiritual authority, and believed that in matters of faith and morals, the pope transcended state rulers. He actively confronted three headline issues among others:

- Dissident archbishops in Ravenna over his ambition and oppression of clergy
- Trier and Cologne who tried to support the remarriage of King Lothaire II to his mistress Waldrada
- Rheims where the archbishop had deposed a bishop without reference to the pope.

All these disputes were eventually solved albeit with some difficulty.

In the second case, Lothair II's marriage to Teutberga had been a union enforced by his father. When she proved unable to bear children Lothair sought the freedom to marry his mistress, Waldrada. A synod in Metz of Frankish bishops approved annulment, but this was over-ruled by Nicholas who stood by his decision throughout a siege of Rome by Lothair's army, which ultimately failed. Lothair had by then married Waldrada but faced with the failed siege, the threat of excommunication, an attack by Teutberga's brother Hucqbert and suspecting the possibility of fellow kings, his uncles Charles and Louis, dividing the empire, he yielded and took back Teutberga in 865. Nicholas insisted that marriage is inviolable.

Pope Nicholas continued to consolidate his spiritual authority. The Byzantine Emperor and Orthodox Church opposed his claim to suzerainty on issues of faith and morals as going further than the 'first amongst equals' understanding. Both Emperor and Patriarch changed in Constantinople between 858 and 879, a period that spanned all of Nicholas' reign and beyond. There was a prolonged tussle over the Patriarchy with the interested parties backing either Photios or Ignatios for the post, while Emperor Michael III (842-867) was assassinated for his successor, Basil I (867-886). Tensions ran high between Rome and Constantinople, with old differences being resurrected, for example the lands in Southern Italy, Sicily and Illyria that Constantinople had annexed during the iconoclasm dispute; the *filioque*; and contests over to which centre the spiritual allegiance of some Slavic and East European states should be directed.

Lothair's reign had also seen a decline in relations between the Frankish and Byzantine Empires due to his support for Ignatios who was deposed as Patriarch by Emperor Michael III (r. 842-867) in 863. Michael had been concerned that the Franks were approaching too close to his Empire's borders and he arranged for the appointment of a layman, Photios as Patriarch, with undue speed supported by one discredited and some minor bishops. This led to inevitable further disputes between Pope Nicholas and Emperor Michael. Photios called a synod in 867 which accused Nicholas of heresy and declared him deposed, regardless of the synod's weak authority.

In September 867 Basil I usurped Emperor Michael, who was assassinated in the process. Although he was of simple peasant stock and in spite of his ruthless and violent route to accession, Basil would prove to be a highly respected historical leader. He was seen as one of the greatest Byzantine Emperors and reigned for 19 years, bringing his family into rule, initiating the Macedonian Dynasty and enhancing Constantinople's power and standing. His financial administration was prudent and he completed a major revision and codification of Byzantine law, which earned him the reputation of a 'second Justinian'. He also oversaw a revival of Byzantine art and one of the most enlightened and prosperous periods of their Empire.

Pope Nicholas was also active in encouraging Christian missions in Northern Europe and the Slav territories. He died in November 867, just two months after Basil's coup. The next pope was **Pope Adrian II** (867-872).

Basil I's ecclesiastical policy was to seek alliance with both the Pope in Rome and the Western Emperor. He initially established a good rapport with elderly Pope Adrian II who came from a noble Roman family. Following an Ecumenical Council in Constantinople in 870, Basil exiled Photios in favour of the return of Ignatios as Patriarch, a step that pleased Rome. But Basil always conducted the relationship with Rome on his own terms and when Boris I of Bulgaria chose to attach the new Bulgarian Church to Constantinople rather than Rome, there was undisguised disappointment in Rome. In fairness, the Byzantines had defeated the Bulgarians in battle earlier and their Khan Boris had accepted Christianity and persuaded much of the population to convert. He wanted a new patriarchate for Bulgaria, but Photios had refused this in 867, whereupon Boris invited missionaries from Rome. Rome denied Boris his wish to have Formosus as the Bishop of Bulgaria, which led him to turn back to Constantinople. Ignatios died in 877 and Basil recalled Photios to be Patriarch, rather chilling relations with Rome once more.

Evangelism, Violence and Unity

There was anguish among both the faithful and the clergy at the levels of violence being used in spreading a faith that upheld mercy, peace and justice. The early Christians had foresworn violence in any form, whilst submitting to extremes of violence at the hands of their detractors up to and beyond the time of Constantine. Another concern was that many of the bishops who were sent to shepherd these new Christian territories also held state office on the lines of the German prince-bishops. So the debate on Church involvement in states, already initiated by the new Papal States, was acquiring an extra dimension.

Nevertheless, Christianity was a broadly uniting force in European politics for some time. The Germanic tribes brought their Rome-based north, from Bavaria to Norway and Britain, also east to Slavs, Slovaks and Czechs, though many Slavs had already accepted Greek Orthodox influence. Charlemagne's empire was Latin-speaking and he looked to Rome for a pope to crown its emperors. Language created more division, which became further complicated in 862, when Moravian Prince Ratislav invited Byzantine Emperor Michael III to send Christian missionaries to spread the gospel to the Slavs. This was an overtly political move on his part to demonstrate his independence from the Franks.

Slavic Missions

Constantinople responded by sending missionaries Cyril and his elder brother Methodius to Greater Moldavia, a large part of Slavic central Europe. They achieved widespread conversions there, but on hearing of the appointment of Photios, they sided with Rome against him. Their wide success had been partly due to their use of the local language rather than Greek or Latin. They trained local assistants and set to work translating the Bible in the course of which they developed a new alphabet more suited to the language of the Slavs, which was the origin of present-day Cyrillic script, used there and notably in Russia.

Tensions were building between the brothers' highly successful mission and the claims of the Frankish kings to that same territory. Cyril and Methodius wanted no friction between Christians, and Cyril had studied in Rome, so the brothers went there and obtained the blessing of Pope Adrian II.

Fate and politics intervened as both Cyril then Ratislav died and the latter's successor Svatopluk did not support Methodius. Although he had been appointed Archbishop of Moravia and Pannonia by Pope Adrian, Methodius was deposed by Frankish King Louis' bishops in 870 and imprisoned for over two years. Adrian's successor, Pope John VIII secured his release but insisted that he drop the vernacular Slavonic liturgy, which had been so successful. In 878, Methodius was summoned to Rome to face charges of heresy and continuing to use the Slavonic language, but he defended his case so convincingly that he was freed to return to his duties with permission to use the local language.

When Methodius died in Greater Moravia in 885, a disciple called Gorazd succeeded him. Pope Adrian again insisted they revert to Latin, effectively pushing Moravia back into the arms of Constantinople. This sense of competition accentuated the growing differences between Constantinople and Rome, none of which had much to do with the teaching of Jesus, but more to do with institutional inability to reach accommodation on what in the grand scale are arguably side-issues. Nevertheless, such episodes had more far-reaching consequences than anyone could foretell at the time as Rome's 'fatherhood' role in Christianity of first among equals was being challenged.

Councils of Constantinople

There were two lengthy Ecumenical Councils held in Constantinople exactly ten years apart; the first was 869-870, the second 879-880, both running from October to February.

The first was called by Emperor Basil I and Pope Adrian II. Photios was deposed and Ignatios reinstated as Patriarch of Constantinople. Photios was later canonised as a saint in the Eastern Orthodox Churches which did not recognise this Council, whereas the Roman Catholic Church regarded it as the Eighth Ecumenical Council.

The second Council was also called by Emperor Basil to endorse the reinstatement of Photios as Patriarch. Pope John VIII sent legates to approve this together with the gift of a Pallium (a vestment with a narrow woollen ring resting on the shoulders, with short vertical hangings front and back), signifying the Pope's blessing. Somehow, a condemnation of the *filioque* as heretical was included. The Roman Church later disregarded this council, whereas the Greek Orthodox Church regards it as the Eighth Ecumenical Council. Both Constantinople and Rome accepted all seven previous ecumenical councils as ecumenical.

Following Pope Adrian's death, **Pope John VIII** was appointed. He was more of a diplomat and sought non-confrontational accommodation with the east. He sent representatives to the second of these councils in Constantinople, who agreed acceptance of Photios as Patriarch. In return, Photios conceded to Rome nominal authority over Bulgaria, with actual jurisdiction lying with Constantinople. Bulgaria continued to be autocephalous. In 927, it became a full Patriarchate by agreement with the Byzantine Empire.

Otherwise, Pope John VIII was heavily preoccupied with blocking and reversing Muslim gains in southern Italy, which were damaging the economy of the Papal States. His papacy was briefly followed by that of Pope Adrian III, who was in office for just over a year, mainly preoccupied by the Saracen attacks on Southern Italy and the onset of a drought.

Famine and Saracen Wars

Pope Stephen V (885-891) came from a noble Roman family, was educated by the Church and showed outstanding piety. He too was elected without prior approval from the emperor, but when Charles the Fat (Roman Emperor 881-888) learned how overwhelming the vote had been, he kept his counsel.

In the six years of Stephen's reign, there was famine in Rome due to the ongoing drought and a plague of locusts. Since the treasury was depleted Stephen had to use family funds to help feed the poor and continue to rebuild infrastructure and churches damaged in the Muslim wars. With the Saracens still invading by sea, relations with Constantinople were sufficiently good for Stephen to persuade Byzantine Emperor Leo VI, successor to Basil I, to send army and navy forces to help overcome this mutual enemy. By 886, the Saracens were cleared from southern Italy, but some of the Byzantines settled themselves into those parts ostensibly as defenders.

Ecclesiastically, Pope Stephen V felt himself and the Roman Church under attack from Patriarch Photios. He resisted these jibes and copied Emperor Leo VI into his responses, resulting in Photios becoming once more exiled in 886. For good measure, Stephen nullified all ordinations that had been made by Photios.

Pope Stephen also took issue with some senior Western clergy including the Archbishops of Lyons, Bordeaux and Ravenna who in his opinion, were making arbitrary and uncanonical decisions regarding various Church matters including bishop appointments.

Pope Formosus (891-896), who succeeded Stephen had a turbulent reign, mainly related to political matters in which he unwisely became involved. He is possibly best remembered for the Cadaver Synod, a post-mortem trial for which his body was exhumed.

An earthquake struck Rome near the end of the century, causing some structural damage which included Church buildings.

Communion Bread

It was about this time that the Roman Church adopted the use of unleavened bread for the Eucharist. The Last Supper was held on the Feast of the Passover at which Jews customarily used unleavened bread, marking the Jews flight from Egypt which was so sudden yeast was left behind. Jesus probably used unleavened bread at the Last Supper, respecting this tradition. Early Christians shared the more available leavened bread in their Eucharistic services, the celebrant breaking the loaf into pieces onto a large plate or paten for distribution. Those receiving would pick a piece up by hand before putting it in their mouth. There is no inferred New Testament instruction as to which bread should be used in Holy Communion – yeast is praised in Matthew. There are some Old Testament comparisons of leaven with sin or evil, but as so often, there are also contrary references. For example, in Leviticus 7:13 there is reference to leavened bread as part of the communal offering or sacrifice and it contains others in 23:16 and 17.

Celtic Faith and Plainsong Music

Plainsong was used in the very early Church and became customary in singing Psalms and other prayers adapted for the purpose. Plainsong was widely practiced in monasteries and developed into Gregorian chant around the 9th and 10th centuries. Plainsong is a monophonic form of singing that became common in worship over subsequent centuries. Although a similar form of chant was also used in the Eastern Church, they do not usually refer to it as plainsong.

The monastic Celtic Christians were geographically distant from the influences of the struggles of the Church, so the practice of their faith continued as before. They managed to preserve their own traditions of Celtic culture and art, including those originally imported from Greece and Mesopotamia by their forefathers. Irish monastics played an important part in using these traditions to bring them back to Europe to help feed Carolingian art in the 9th century and what evolved from it.

CHAPTER 12

10th Century

Popes

900-903 Benedict IV
903 July-Dec Leo V
(903-904 Antipope Christopher)
904-911 Sergius III
911-913 Anastasius III
913-914 Lando
914-928 John X
928 May-Dec Leo VI
929-931 Stephen VII
931-935 John XI
935-939 Leo VII
939- 942 Stephen VIII
942-946 Marinus II
946-955 Agapetus II
955-963 John XII

(963-964 Antipope Leo VIII)
964 Feb-May John XII
964 May-June Benedict V
964-965 Leo VIII
965-972 John XIII
973-974 Benedict VI
(974 30 days Antipope Boniface VII)
974-983 Benedict VII
983-984 John XIV
(984-985 Antipope Boniface VII)
985-996 John XV
996-999 Gregory V
(997-998 Antipope John XVI)
999-1003 Sylvester II

Roman Emperors

Until this century, the Frankish Emperors, though always elected, often ran in Germanic family dynasties, the incumbent being crowned Roman Emperor by the pope of the day. From Otto I in this century, the title Holy Roman Emperor applied.

Louis II (the Blind)	901-905
Berengar I	915-924

Holy Roman Emperors

Otto I (the Great)	962-973
Otto II (the Red)	967-983
Otto III	996-1024

The period from the appointment of Pope Sergius III in 904 until the death of Pope John XII in 964 was generally known as the *Saeculum obscurum* or Dark Age of the Papacy. It can reasonably be argued that it started in the 8th century following Pépin and Charlemagne's donation of Papal Lands and ended later than 964, as powerful Roman families exerted heavy influence well beyond the 10th century. In this period members and relatives of corrupt and powerful families competed in holding particular influence over the papacy and exacted 'rewards' while some even became incumbents. The practice of simony, which is the sale or exchange of honours, benefits or positions in the Church, became quite widespread, often at the behest of the families as a means of accessing Church funds or position. In terms of tracing the history of Christianity, it was a low point that did little to honour or reflect the enormous sacrifices already described, freely suffered by so many of the faithful in the building phase of the Church. It would also lead to weakening of trust and even outright rebellion from within the ranks of Christians over several centuries.

There were various invasions and struggles over the Papal Lands, due to the attraction they held for the Saracens, or to Byzantine ambition or else just finding themselves in the way of the to-ing and fro-ing of other warring powers. These were beyond the realistic power of the popes to address, especially in a period of so many short papal reigns, with two dozen popes in this century, as well as five anti-popes.

These factors all led to lengthy periods during which spiritual leadership from Rome fell far short of Christ's set purpose for it. Over such times, the devotion of the faithful supported by committed clerics, missionaries and perhaps monasteries maintained continuity of Western Christianity, which had gained widespread critical mass and momentum which had seen it through several generations of patchy leadership. As for the Eastern Church, tensions with Islam continued and Christian leadership was more distributed to the regions, though generally maintaining its conformity with the Council of Nicaea.

Influence of Families in Rome

This decline was in part due to the merging of spiritual leadership of the papacy with temporal and political power, which could be self-conflicting and overwhelming for one person. This was hardly surprising, as the two roles required entirely different training, skills and experience. The door had thus been opened to two-way traffic, allowing outside influences to enter the Church hierarchy, from among foreign leaders, royalty and especially around these times, powerful and often feuding Italian families. Corruption was also entering the heart of the Roman Church. Two such families at this time were the Tusculani (Counts of Tusculum) and their rivals the Crescentii. The Tusculani would put a good number of popes on the throne and their family tree included something like that shown (which ignores some less relevant members):

The family's intimate involvement with the papacy began with Theophylact, who inherited the title Count of Tusculum, and commanded a force of soldiers for Emperor Louis III, to protect Rome as Louis returned to France in 902. Theophylact played a part in dethroning Antipope Christopher, who had seized the papacy in 904, deposing and murdering Pope Leo V. He supported Alberic I of Spoleto in appointing Sergius III to the papacy, for which Sergius III helped Theophylact become the leading official of the city of Rome.

Theophylact's wife Theodora was a powerful senator and influenced his selection of several popes who were appointed by the couple during their lives. Sergius III was followed by Anastasius III, Lando and John X, John allegedly being romantically close to Theodora, or one of her relatives. The daughter of Theophylact and Theodora, Marozia, was another powerful aristocratic beauty who knew how to dispense her charms with purpose. She allegedly had a relationship with Pope Sergius III resulting in an illegitimate son, who would also become pope – John XI. If the suggested family tree is right, there cannot be many women who could match Theodora's claim to have shared DNA with seven popes over five generations. Hearsay all this may have been, but it conveys some understanding of influences on selection and behaviour of the papacy in those times. The current prevailing family had effective control over the pope and senior management of the Church at some cost to its spiritual wellbeing.

In Italy, such large, corrupt and violent 'families' formed and one such family which grew to be a serious threat to the dominance of the Tusculani during this century were the Crescentii. It is not certain that they were all from the same biological family origin, but they all embraced the common interest so the word family applied in the gangster sense, with known sub-groupings within, such as the Stefaniani and Ottaviani. The Crescentii were dominant in the Sabine Hills outside Rome, whereas the Tusculani were well established within the city.

Otto (912-973), Duke of Saxony and King of the Germans, having seen off invasions from Hungary by the pagan Magyars, conquered Italy through the Lombards attacking Rome in 961. The treaty then signed between Otto and Tusculani Pope John XII, guaranteed control of the Papal States donated by Pépin and clarifying the relationship between emperor and pope, but was not welcomed by the ambitious Crescentii. These families were huge concerns, as illustrated by the Crescentii stronghold of Castel Sant' Angelo.

This general picture is important in conveying an understanding of the context within which the leaders of the Church were selected and some of the influences that affected the mission of Jesus Christ to which they were sworn. They played an important part in the future direction, or perhaps directions of travel of Christianity, especially in the Western Church. It saw a sequence of suspiciously brief papal reigns with varying commitment or freedom to do God's work. It raised serious questions over their individual involvement in dubious activities, the degree to which they may have been distracted by temporal responsibilities or manipulated by others, and whether they followed Christ's model of a good shepherd.

Popes and the Church

Feudal upheaval and violence affected central Italy during **Pope Sergius III's** reign. Opinions differ widely on him and knowledge is limited and blurred by the prolific gossip and rumour around him, including his suggested complicity in the murder of two predecessors and his alleged fathering of an illegitimate child.

It is certain however that he rebuilt the Lateran basilica, which had been destroyed by an earthquake at the end of the 9th century. He refurbished it and had new frescos painted on the interior walls. His relationship with Constantinople was at best arms-length and he approved a number of new bishoprics in Britain. He was succeeded by **Popes Anastasius III**, then **Lando**, both supported by Theophylact and Theodora. Neither achieved much ecclesiastically, their leadership being so weak that the Saracens attacked and settled along the river Carigliano in southern Italy during their time.

Pope John X (914- 928) was generally regarded as a good and valiant pope. He was related to Theodora and she helped ensure family support for his candidacy. He enjoyed the longest reign of the century at 14 years, his cause being furthered by his support for Senator Theophylact's aim to unify and secure the imperial base in Italy under Berengar of Friuli, whom Pope Sergius III had been reluctant to support against Louis, King of Provence. But Louis had been succeeded and in 915, Pope John X brokered an alliance with Italian rulers so they helped drive the Saracens from southern Italy. Berengar did not send troops, but John X personally led a force of Christians into the Battle of Carigliano in 915. The Christians routed the Saracen fortresses along the river, eliminating their threat to Rome and central Italy which had lasted for too long. John then crowned Berengar as emperor in Rome at the end of that year.

Theophylact's death in 924 left his daughter Marozia and her husband,

Guy of Tuscany in positions of control in Rome and they used it to have John X deposed, imprisoned and murdered.

Pope Leo VI had a brief reign of only a few months but in that time he completed John X's work on the jurisdiction of bishops in Dalmatia, over the Adriatic. He appointed Archbishop John and ordered all the bishops of the region to obey him. Some had been overly ambitious and he counselled them to restrict their activities to within their diocesan boundaries.

Pope Stephen VII (929- 931) was selected by Marozia to fill the position for a couple of years until her teenage son John would be ready. There are few records of Stephen VII's activities as pope but he was known to be insistent on moral behaviour by the clergy and to have punished miscreants severely. The manner of his death is uncertain, but came at a convenient time for Marozia whose son was then aged 20.

Pope John XI (931-935) became pope aged 20. His paternity is still unclear. His mother was certainly Marozia, but his father was either Pope Sergius III or Alberic I of Spoleto. Since his mother was ruling in Rome, she arranged his appointment and exerted control over his pontificate.

When Marozia was deposed around 932, John XI's younger brother Alberic II took her place and pulled the strings of this puppet pope. Alberic arranged for him to give the pallium to Theophylact of Constantinople, confirming his consecration as bishop, which helped East-West relations both in Church and politics. He also conferred privileges on the Benedictine community at Cluny, which eventually proved to be perhaps the most enlightened decision of this chapter of the papacy.

Cluny was an abbey in France (Saone et Loire), founded in 910 by William the Pious, Duke of Aquitaine. He put Abbot Berno in charge to implement a more austere form of the Benedictine rule in a number of respects, including centralised governance, which ran counter to Benedictine tradition. Duke William endowed the abbey with his entire estate and over three hundred monasteries under Cluny's oversight would be founded by the 12th century, from Scotland to Italy. The Cluny offshoot of the Benedictines would have a strong influence within the Western Church. It remained for several centuries as a form of sub-order of Benedictines and was a cradle of learning for Church leaders, including Popes Gregory VII, Urban II, Paschal II and Urban V, so significantly influenced some reforms within the Church.

Pope John XI died in his early twenties in 936. This might not have raised suspicion were it not for the number of the popes under the Tusculani regime in Rome who had brief reigns ending in early deaths.

Alberic II sought a successor to John who would be malleable under his control, so he chose a priest in Rome, who had no personal ambitions beyond the service of God. He became **Pope Leo VII**, (936-939), arriving on the scene during an ongoing feud between Alberic II, ruler of the Roman Republic and his stepfather, Hugh, King of Italy. Leo VII called in Odo, the Abbot of Cluny as mediator. He succeeded by arranging the marriage of Hugh's daughter Alda to Alberic II.

During yet another brief tenure of office, Leo VII appointed Frederick as Archbishop of Mainz in Germany. Frederick wanted to expel Jews refusing baptism, but Leo VII restrained him from enforcing their baptism.

Pope Stephen VIII (939-942) another appointee of Alberic II, succeeded Leo VII. Stephen was a Roman, educated partly in Germany. As pope, he achieved little ecclesiastically, but he became embroiled in the politics of Western Europe, almost certainly at Alberic's behest. Hugh the Great, Duke of the Franks and Herbert II, Count of Vermandois had sought help from Otto the Great in Germany with their rebellion against King Louis IV of West Francia, the last of the Carolingians. Stephen threatened them with excommunication if they continued their rebellion. This threat may not have changed their hearts, but it did achieve the withdrawal of the bishops' and nobles' support from Hugh and Herbert. The pope also appointed Herbert's son, another Hugh, as Archbishop of Reims.

Pope Marinus II (942-946) reigned for just four years and had neither time nor effective authority to do much.

Pope Agapetus II (946-955) followed Marinus, both chosen by Alberic II. Agapetus, a genuinely pious man, impressed with his ability to promote his spirituality in such difficult times, though it is fair to say the Papal lands were somewhat out of his hands, which helped concentration. He supported Emperor Otto in spreading Christianity north into Scandinavia

Political unrest in Francia

A complex political power struggle was taking place in Francia. The principal players were ultimately English-speaking King Louis IV in the west and the German King Otto I in the east. There was also Herbert II of Vermandois on behalf of his son Hugh, effectively Regent. The Church became involved over a disputed appointment of an Archbishop of Reims. Herbert II had forcibly displaced the incumbent Archbishop Artald in 740 after Artald had anointed Louis IV as King of the West Franks. Alberic II had an interest in the outcome and Pope Agapetus II was probably acting under Alberic's instruction in favouring the re-installation of Artald in 946 and securing Otto's support of Louis' choice for this. This move was sealed at a synod in Rome in 949 when Herbert was excommunicated for his action.

Otto I, Duke of Saxony sought to achieve his father's ambition to unify the various German states, also to make some changes to the diocesan structure in Germany. He revised his plans following input from his son, Archbishop William of Mainz. Pope Agapetus II had shown support and following a request from King Frode of Jutland, he also sent missionaries there authorising the Archbishop of Hamburg to consecrate bishops in Denmark and other Northern European countries.

While restrained from achieving much on his own initiative because of Alberic's control, Agapetus II still gained a reputation for care and piety before his death in 955, a year after Alberic, who wished for his son to be pope. So Agapetus was succeeded by Octavianus, Alberic's son.

Octavianus became **Pope John XII (955-964)**. He had been leader of Rome in 954 then Head of the Western Church in 955 and led an army against the Lombards in an attempt to win back some of the lost Papal States, but the project failed as the Lombards made local alliances. Meanwhile there was unrest in Rome as John was not the leader his father had been and Berengar II, King of Italy was emboldened to attack other Papal States then Rome itself, so John turned to Otto I, King of Germany, for support. Otto was already in southern Germany, having just defeated the pagan Magyars who had been attacking from the east and he crossed the Italian border with a regathered force in late 961, whereupon Berengar withdrew his siege of Rome, leaving Otto free to enter the city in January 962. After meetings with John and Roman nobility, Otto swore solemnly that he would to the best of his ability uphold the Holy Roman Church and John, its leader and that he would remain loyal to both. He further committed to return any past territory of St Peter that he might win back and that anybody to whom he or his successors may entrust the kingdom of Italy would be covenanted to swear to defend Church lands.

So Pope John XII crowned Otto I Holy Roman Emperor, following the example of Charlemagne's coronation and filling a vacancy that had existed for some forty years since the death of Berengar I. Pope John XII and his nobles swore to support the emperor and never to provide any assistance to Berengar II or his son Adalbert, who was co-ruler of Italy. Accordingly a formal agreement was signed by both parties recording this and declaring the emperor as guarantor of independence of the Papal States. It also confirmed the free elections of popes subject to ratification by the emperor before their consecration.

John XII showed little interest in spiritual or ecclesiastical matters apart from fulfilling some of Otto I's wishes regarding German bishops. Otto I himself observed that John lived a life of vanity and adultery and suggested the pope should mend his ways. Otto left Rome to take on Berengar II, remove him from the Papal States and absorb Italy into the Holy Roman Empire. Meanwhile, perhaps unhappy with Otto's parting shot, John broke the vow to support the emperor by approaching the Magyars and Byzantine Empire with a view to garnering support against Otto I. He also met Bishop Adalbert of Prague, missionary to the Hungarians. In fairness, John had also heard that Otto was exacting vows of fidelity to himself from the leaders of the Papal States he overcame, which also contravened their agreement. Otto I learned of John XII's scheming and having almost completed his victory, with Berengar behind bars in 963, he returned to Rome, which was by now split into pro- and anti-John camps. Adalbert was also in the city having talks with John and the two of them fled east to Tivoli, taking papal treasures with them.

Receiving no response to his calls for John to explain himself, Otto declared him deposed and with his council, elected **Leo VII** (963-4), a layperson who had been rapidly ordained. John in his self-imposed exile, had allegedly been hunting, hawking and enjoying pleasures of the flesh, but when he heard that Otto I had left Rome, he returned, confident in the support of a good part of the population there. He expelled Leo, who fled the city. John resumed his rule, tortured and maimed some of his enemies and called a council to declare his deposition by Otto uncanonical (which it was). John XII died in May 964.

The Romans rapidly elected **Pope Benedict V** (May-June 964), but without seeking Otto's permission. In response, Otto I returned and laid siege to Rome. When he destroyed the crops around it the population soon yielded. Benedict V was deposed in June and **Leo XII** re-installed. He was known for his energy and reliability, but soon died in March 965. The Roman nobles asked for the return of Benedict, but Otto could not accept this and a compromise candidate, John Crescentius was selected. He was a member of the Crescentii family who would control the papacy for much of the rest of this century up until 1012.

Pope John XIII (965-972) installed Crescentii family members into positions of authority in Rome to curb the nobles he distrusted. He also strengthened ties with Otto I. Otto was keen to return to Germany and when he did so, disgruntled Roman nobles took John XIII captive within two months of his consecration, sending him to a castle in Campagna in the winter 965-6. Otto assembled a large army in response and in the summer of 966 they marched south. Meanwhile, there had been two developments. Pope John XIII had escaped from Campagna into friendly Sabina, where his brother-in-law Benedict pledged his help. Also, his nephew had led supporters to rebel in Rome and the two leading dissident nobles were killed. Otto's arrival ensured that influential opponents were removed, some by execution or blinding and others exiled to Germany. It was clear the papacy was disposed more towards political than spiritual matters and was by then hardly concerned with religion.

Once John XIII, known as John the Good, had been reinstated, he worked with Otto I on some ecclesiastical housekeeping issues, mostly related to new dioceses, but also secured the return of some papal lands, including Ravenna and its territory. At the end of 967, John anointed Otto I's son Otto II as co-emperor of the Holy Roman Empire. The cool relationship between the Eastern and Western Empires continued with the Byzantine Emperor casting doubt on the legitimacy of the Holy Roman Emperor's right to the title. Otto I tried a conciliatory move, suggesting a marriage between young Otto II and a Byzantine princess. Pope John supported this in a letter to Nikephoros II, who took offence at being addressed as Emperor of the Greeks rather than Emperor of the Romans as well. Otto I perhaps revealed his true ambition when asking for a dowry of those Byzantine-held territories in the south of Italy. Nikephoros II took a hard line and when the negotiations failed, he took matters further by appointing Patriarch Polyeuctrus of Constantinople in ecclesiastical charge of those Italian territories as well as requiring services there to be held in Greek language rather than Latin.

Nikephorus died in 969 to be succeeded by John I Tzimiskes, who was more amenable to discussion with Otto I so the proposed marriage alliance was revived with the ultimate result that Otto II married John I's niece, Princess Theophanu. The marriage ceremony was conducted by Pope John XIII in Rome in 972 shortly before his death.

Meanwhile, Pope John XIII had met a brilliant young monastery student, Gerbert d'Aurillac, who had been to Catalonia to further his mathematical studies and been fascinated by the Arab leaders in Spain, who were learned in maths, astronomy and natural sciences. John XIII was impressed enough by Gerbert's scholarship suggest him to Otto I as a tutor for his son, Otto II around 970, a position he took up to good effect. Gerbert subsequently went to study at the Cathedral School in Reims and was spotted, soon being appointed head teacher there.

The year 973 was one of change which would lead to probably the deepest of the Dark Age in the papacy. **Pope Benedict VI (973-974)** was elected thanks to a majority of pro-Otto electors, running counter to the interests of local Roman aristocracy. He was installed in January, but never ratified by Otto I, whose death came soon after the election, leaving Otto II as sole emperor. The death of Otto the Great encouraged Crescentius I, brother of John XIII to attempt to revive his family's status among the nobility of Rome. Benedict found himself imprisoned in the Castel Sant'Angelo and replaced by **Antipope Boniface VII**. Otto II sent Sicco as imperial envoy to Rome to release Benedict, but in mid-974 the Pope was strangled to death in defiance of Otto II.

Sicco consequently took control of Rome and oversaw the election of **Pope Benedict VII** (974-983), nephew of Alberic II of the Tusculani family. Anti-pope Boniface VII rejected his authority but fled to Constantinople, taking with him some of the Church treasures. Otto II backed Benedict VII, who then had the confidence to issue a papal bull condemning simony and followed a number of his predecessors in supporting and enhancing the status of monasticism in the Church,

Otto II also had an interest in Monasteries, stoked by John Philagathus, who had accompanied Theophanu, Otto's fiancé, from her native Constantinople prior to their marriage in 972 and became her chaplain. Otto II also appointed him Abbot of Nonantola Abbey near Modena.

Pope Benedict VII was concerned by the plight of Christians in North Africa who were overrun by Islam, but still practicing albeit in reduced numbers, dioceses and organisation. He consecrated a priest named James as bishop of Carthage to help. Probably less helpful was his dissolution of the diocese of Merseburg in Central Europe, in that it weakened the potential of the Church to grow in the Slavic region.

In 982 the Saracens defeated Otto II's forces in southern Italy. Soon afterwards, the Slavs arose against his rule as he was preparing to counter-attack the Saracens, forcing him to abandon that territory. The following year would see the deaths of both pope and emperor.

Following Pope Benedict VII's death, Otto II chose Bishop Pietro Canepanova of Pavia, to succeed him. Pietro took the name **John XIV** (983-984) to avoid the presumption he associated with the name Peter. Otto II died shortly after making this appointment, while his son was only three years old. The current leader of the Crescentii, John I, took over the title of patricius of Rome. Anti-pope Boniface VII, was still in Constantinople, convinced of his rightful destiny with the backing of the Crescentii family. Emboldened by his family's return to favour in Rome, he returned there and arranged for John XIV to be incarcerated in Castel Sant'Angelo. Without imperial backing, John soon died in prison probably from either starvation or poison. With Crescentii backing, Boniface was re-installed in August 984.

Meanwhile, Theophanu, as regent of her son Otto III had appointed Abbot John Philagathus to be the child emperor's tutor. Back in Rome, Antipope Boniface VII was not popular and when he died suspiciously suddenly in July 985, his body was paraded publicly, abused and dragged through the streets, its remains being left by the statue of Marcus Aurelius near the Lateran Palace. Early the following morning priests retrieved the body and gave it a Christian burial.

John Crescentii seems to have used his influence as patricius in the subsequent election of **Pope John XV** (985-996), helping the Crescentii family regain some of the prestige lost by the killing of their puppet antipope. Empress Regent Theophanu ratified this appointment. The Crescentii held control over John XV, occasionally modified by intervention from Theophanu, sometimes at John's own request. On the whole, though, John XV was shackled by the politics and limited in his freedom of spiritual initiatives, although he showed little interest in such matters, leaning more towards Church politics. With encouragement from Theophanu in 988, John XV appointed Abbot John Philagathus as Bishop of Placenza, which was raised to an archbishopric.

Another dispute arose over Reims in 993 when the monarch in Eastern Francia, Hugh appointed Arnulf, Bishop of Orleans as Archbishop of Reims. Arnulf was a nephew of Charles, Duke of Lorraine, who opposed Hugh's reign, so Charles overcame Reims and imprisoned Arnulf. Hugh in turn invaded Reims and imprisoned both Charles and Arnulf. Believing that Arnulf had betrayed him, Hugh called a synod at Reims in 991, deposed Arnulf and replaced him with Abbot Gerbert d'Aurillac.

Arnulf was furious and being frustrated by a succession of unworthy popes, he issued a passionate critique of John XV, which was declared uncanonical by a synod in 995 led by a legate of John XV. But in 996, after Hugh's death Arnulf was freed from prison. Pope John XV was patron and protector of the monks of Cluny and he followed the practice of a number of his predecessors, conferring many privileges on monasteries and convents, earning recognition of at least some token spiritual activity during his papacy.

First Papal Canonisation

One significant spiritual event in John XV's papacy was the first recorded canonisation of a saint by a pope. He solemnly canonised Bishop Ulrich of Augsburg in 993 at Otto III's request. Prior to that, saints had generally been declared as such by bishops and accepted as such mainly just within their diocese or region.

Theophanu, regent and mother of Otto III died in 991. Since Otto was still a child, his grandmother stepped in as regent for three years. In 995, young Otto asked his godfather, Archbishop John Philagathus to arrange for an eligible Byzantyne Princess as a match in marriage. He chose

Philagathus because he was born in Byzantine territory and having spent time in Constantinople, had the contacts there.

Otto III was on his way to Rome in 996 for his formal imperial coronation blessing, when Pope John XV died just before Easter. Otto continued his journey, so he played a major part in the selection of John XV's successor, his cousin Bruno of Carinthia a great-grandson of Otto I. Bruno, the first German pope took the name **Pope Gregory V** (996-999). He was also chaplain to Otto III. Gregory V was only 24 years old on election and within three weeks anointed Otto III as Holy Roman Emperor. While Otto was still in Rome, a synod was held to reinstate Arnulf as Archbishop of Reims, declaring Hugh's appointment of Gerbert invalid. Gerbert moved to Magdeburg to become a lead teacher of Otto III.

Once Otto had left Rome following Gregory's installation and his own anointment in 996, Crescentius II, a relative, perhaps brother of John Crescentii, connived with some fellow Roman nobles in making a rival appointment of his own choice for pope, in defiance of Otto III. His surprise choice was none other than John, Archbishop of Placenza, who had recently returned from his assignment in Constantinople for the Royal family. It seems that his main allegiance to the family had been to Theophanu because he met Crescentius II and agreed to join the plan to unseat Gregory V. Crescentius drove Gregory V out of Rome in September 996 and appointed **Antipope John XVI** (997-998) in his stead.

Following the council of Pavia in 997, which declared John antipope and excommunicated, 15-year-old Otto marched on Rome with his army and defeated Crescentius, who barricaded himself in Castel Sant'Angelo. Antipope John XVI fled but was captured then maimed, blinded and humiliated in front of Otto and Pope Gregory V. Crescentius was eventually captured, executed and his body hung from the Castel walls in 998. Antipope John was spared death and either imprisoned or confined to a monastery for the rest of his life. He is believed to have died in obscurity about 1013.

After his re-instatement, Pope Gregory V subsequently made Gerbert Archbishop of Ravenna in 998. As for the Crescentii family, Crescentius' son John II would become patricius following Otto's death in 1002 and was the lead figure in Rome until his death in 1012, the last of the Crescentii run of leadership.

Gregory V died suspiciously suddenly in early 999, bringing to an abrupt end this unsavoury century of the papacy, true to form. He was succeeded by Gerbert, who became the first French pope, his candidacy being supported by Otto III. Gerbert took the name **Pope Sylvester II** (999-1003) and was close with Otto, who stayed in Rome.

Otto declared the Donation of Constantine to be a forgery. This was the supposed official document by which the Emperor Constantine was believed to have transferred authority over Rome to the pope and is now believed to have been forged about the 8th century.

Sylvester II, a recognised cleric and talented mathematician, was soon even more widely recognised as highly intelligent, devout and responsible, a suitable leader of the Church. He actively campaigned against simony and concubinage which he knew were quite widely practised among the clergy. Any members with such a record would be barred from becoming bishops whom he insisted should demonstrate spotless character. Sylvester II re-confirmed the validity of Arnulf's position as Archbishop of Reims. He also established new dioceses in Poland and Hungary and in the year 1000, granted the title of king to the Hungarian ruler, at the same time appointing him papal vicar of Hungary.

In 1001, there was an uprising in Rome against Otto III, from which he and the pope escaped to Ravenna. Otto led two failed military attempts to retake the city and was killed in the course of a third in 1002, just as the second daughter of Byzantine Emperor Constantine VIII was travelling to their intended wedding as a result of John Philagathus' diplomacy. Pope Sylvester II returned to Rome following Otto's death, in spite of the rebels still being in control. He died the following year.

Salerno Medical School

The monastery in Salerno, a seaside city in southern Italy, established a dispensary in the 9th century, which became the seed of a medical school as the Lombard's power waned in the latter half of the 10th century. With support from Archbishop Alfano I of Salerno its fame spread rapidly and the city earned the title 'Town of Hippocrates'. It attracted the best international medical experts and practitioners, male and female, including from Arabia and it accumulated a superb library which included writings of Hippocrates, Galen, Dioscorides and Arab physicians. Salerno soon became the top source of medical knowledge, learning and practice in the known world – a medical university before universities as such existed. People flocked to the 'Schola Salernitana' both for treatment and to learn the latest in the science of medicine.

Ukraine and Russia

In 998 the Christian Church in Russia and Ukraine began, when Prince Vladimir, his sons and many aristocrats were baptised into the faith in the River Dnieper, followed by the residents of Kiyv, the Ukrainian capital, known as the 'Baptism of Kiyvan Rus'. This was carried out by clergy from the Ecumenical Patriarchate of Constantinople, so the Kiyvan Church became subsidiary to the Patriarchate of Constantinople and its Metropolitan was usually a Greek.

The eastern Slavic territories had begun to be influenced by the Eastern Roman Empire's Christian culture in the second half of the 9th century when Greek Macedonian Saints Cyril and Methodius first translated parts of the bible into the Slavonic language, a move that Rome had opposed. It had opened the way for missionaries to spread Christianity to the Balkans, Eastern Europe, Ukraine and Southern Russia, where paganism had hitherto been the norm. Legend has it that they were preceded well beforehand by the Apostle Andrew, who is believed to have travelled to the north coast of the Black Sea and even as far as Kiyv where he may have erected a cross on the site where St Andrew's Cathedral now stands. By the mid-10th century, a substantial core of Kiyvan nobility had become Christian and Princess Olga of Kiyv had become the first ruler to convert. But it was her grandson Vladimir who proclaimed Christianity as the state religion around 988. After he was baptised by missionary priests, he issued an order for his people to follow suit.

Epilogue to Christianity's First Millennium

Christianity had spread impressively in the western part of the known world in these first thousand years, but in many ways unsatisfactorily. According to the gospels, Jesus Christ had preached the faith with beliefs, personal disciplines and demands at a level his simple, artisan followers could understand. He promised that they would never be tested beyond their physical and mental capacities, but they needed to follow his two principal commandments – to love God above all things and to love their neighbours as they loved themselves. In human terms, it was a recipe for peace, harmony and spiritual fulfilment. Christ had illustrated his supernatural powers in several events recorded in the gospels, culminating in demonstrating God's power over and beyond human life through the crucifixion, resurrection and transfiguration. God also apparently fulfilled an aim to demonstrate the emergence of the faith relevant to the world in the post-biblical era through the example and teaching of Jesus, his son and earthly manifestation. As he handed leadership over to Peter, Jesus said that the Holy Spirit would ensure the survival of Christ's Church against adversity for all time. This seemed to signal that the age of prophets was then over and Jesus might be the last direct tangible intervention of God in the world prior to its end.

However, the consequent human institution called 'the Church' seemed to aim higher than Christ himself, with extreme reclusive and physical practices of self-punishment or abstention being accepted by a zealous few as helpful in achieving God's blessing. It also supported highly intellectual theological and Christological studies. All of this was understandable, especially given the Greek reverence for Philosophy, which appealed widely to the intellectual elite. But it went over the heads of most people, who looked to the local presbyter or bishop to guide them in their faith. Yet in the early days, all members could be subjected to the most dreadful cruel persecution, the vast majority of them displaying inspirational bravery and fortitude in defence of their faith and those two commandments of Jesus. Through all this they valued human life as sacrosanct and the taking of another human life was absolutely prohibited.

In the wake of Emperor Constantine's support and gifts with the subsequent inevitable involvement of the Church in Roman and international politics, the institution gained in influence, wealth and power, opening its hierarchy to human ambition which drove competitive quests for seniority and power within its structures. Observers may have been forgiven for wondering at times where the Holy Spirit was. It is important to remember how much of the effective work on the ground is done by the vast majority of clergy members who work only for good and of committed lay people, who all too rarely make the news, yet are beacons of hope and light. That remains the case today.

In the Eastern Mediterranean, the Eastern Orthodox Church with its autocephalous regions, liturgy and some practice developed in different directions from Rome, without straying from the guidance of Jesus in its core doctrine. The pragmatic ambiguity of some of the results of the Council of Nicaea was unhelpful in this and would be made worse by a future papal decision in the heat of a moment.

It was becoming clear that human hands alone are inadequate caretakers of God's Church. How will it fare in the following Millennium, when the rest of the world will be discovered, travel develops, the written word will be broadly available, literacy and education become widespread among ordinary folk, science leads to industrial and social revolutions and war involves use of mechanisation and the ability to deliver deadly explosives beyond the battlefield and the direct combatants?

CHAPTER 13

11th Century

Popes

1003 May-Nov John XVII

1003-09 Sergius IV

1012-24 Benedict VIII

(1012 June-Dec Antipope Gregory VI)

1024-32 John XIX

1032-44 Benedict IX (Tusculani)

1045 Jan-Mar Sylvester III (Crescenti?)

1045 Mar-May Benedict IX (Tusculani)

1045-46 Gregory VI

1046-47 Clement II

1047-48 Benedict IX

1048 24 days Damasus II

1049-54 Leo IX

1055-57 Victor II

1057-8 Stephen IX

1058-59 Antipope Benedict X

1058-61 Nicholas II

(1061-72 Antipope Honorius II)

1061-73 Alexander II

1073-85 Gregory VII

(1080-1100 Antipope Clement III)

1085-87 Victor III

1088-98 Urban II

1099-1118 Paschal II

Holy Roman Emperors

Otto III 996-1002

Henry I 1014-1024

Conrad II the Elder 1027-1039

Henry III the Black 1046-1056

Henry IV 1056-1106

The 11th century opened with Christianity still strong in Europe and would see it continue spreading north and eastwards, mainly thanks to many dedicated bishops, priests and religious people who saw it as their mission to work as Jesus had asked. But the Church was not without its internal clerical and leadership faults. The good bishops had to be particularly strong as many of their clerics and colleagues continued to achieve positions and influence by simony or other questionable means, while the higher echelons of the Church had not really emerged from its 'dark age' as papal appointment was based on political as much as spiritual criteria. This is covered further in this chapter under Gregory VII.

The militarisation of recent centuries had distanced Church practice and mission from the original exemplary non-violent and passive missions of early Christianity. Tension between the Churches of East and West ran high, though the beliefs of the Eastern and Western Churches were still consistent albeit with some disagreement in fine theological detail. Differences in practice and architecture were visible and there were political and ecclesiastic disputes between leaders. It was about the year 1000 AD that the double-headed eagle motif was adopted by the Orthodox leader as a sign of facing both east and west.

Islam presented an ongoing challenge to Christianity in North Africa and Arabia, but there were sufficient strong people to continue to make Christian faith attractive enough to continue its spread. The Saracens had made inroads by conquest into fringe territories and islands on the north Mediterranean coasts, including Sicily, Sardinia and parts of Southern Italy while also penetrating well into Spain.

Another Crescentii Pope

In May 1003 Pope John XVII succeeded Sylvester II but he died in November. Since John XVI had been declared anti-pope, the new John should have been so designated. This was never corrected, the first of a couple of such anomalies in papal numbering in this century. He was succeeded by Pope John XVIII in January 1004. Both Johns were appointed by John Crescentius II who ruled Rome and were expected to serve his political demands. **Pope John XVIII** took the easier option of attending to Church matters mainly outside Italy, including strengthening the Slavic Church and at a Roman synod in 1007 he authorised a new diocese in Bamburg to provide a base for local missions. He also improved relations with Constantinople, briefly bringing East and West closer together. He abdicated in 1009, and died within a month.

Sergius IV, John's successor was a cardinal monk, son of a shoe-maker. Although still subject to Crescentius' over-riding power, he apparently gave some help to the German King Henry II, but his main efforts were directed at supporting the poor in Rome who were suffering badly from famine. In 1012, soon after the death of John Crescentius II, Sergius died amid rumours he was murdered. The Crescentii family supported a hastily appointed Gregory VI, who found little backing and was soon declared anti-pope and left Rome for Germany where he sought the approval of King Henry II. Henry asked him to stand down.

Revival of the Tusculani

Then Benedict VIII (1012-1024), of the Tusculani family, was elected as a result of their renewed ascendency over the Crescentii. Henry II supported Benedict, who later anointed him as Holy Roman Emperor.

The Saracen attacks on Italy's west coast continued from their established bases on nearby Sicily and Sardinia. Norman forces, descendants of Vikings who had settled in Normandy, travelled to Italy and vanquished the Saracens on the mainland, then going on to remove the Saracens from Sardinia.

Benedict helped the cause of peace in Italy by allying with the Normans, a move which strengthened his control over the troublesome Crescentii in Rome, although unwittingly leaving a problematic legacy for some later popes. But one decision he made at Henry II's request would prove to be the root of the Great Schism between the Roman and Orthodox Churches. In 1014, when Henry came to Rome to be crowned Holy Roman Emperor, he was surprised at the absence from the Creed of 'Filioque' which had been adopted in Germany. In gratitude for Henry usurping the Antipope Gregory VI, Benedict VIII had the phrase included in the chanted Creed from then on, the first time this had happened so officially and publicly in Rome. It was of course a significant and controversial move in the eyes of the Eastern Orthodox Church.

Benedict VIII is regarded as having been a strong and effective leader of the Church. Being related to the senator and consul of Rome who would become his successor, and friendly with the emperor, he enjoyed powerful backing. He travelled to Germany in 1020, consecrated the cathedral at Bamburg, visited the Fulda monastery and persuaded Henry II to confirm the status of the Papal States, the donations of Charlemagne and Otto. The emperor joined him in a synod at Pavia in 1022 to emphasise the Church's condemnation of the sins of simony and clerical incontinence and also to support the changes being promoted by the great Benedictine monastery of Cluny. Benedict VIII died in 1024.

Filioque and Tense Relations

Benedict VIII added the *filioque* to the Nicene Creed by Rome in 1014, and it has been part of the Catholic (and most Protestant) Creed ever since. The circumstances were quite bizarre in the light of the seriousness of the consequences. The Orthodox Church had always contended that the term denigrated the standing of the Holy Spirit within the Trinity in declaring his subordination to the Son. It arguably implies numerous anomalies and runs counter to the common and much recited prayer "Glory be ..."

Matthew's Gospel (1:18) says that Mary had a child through the Holy Spirit, so in earthly terms, where the dimension of time exists, the Spirit predates Jesus Christ, though not the Logos, which would become Jesus the Son of God. However, as the Trinity including the Logos always existed, God selected a moment in earth's time to experience human life on earth and refresh his message through his Son.

The Catechism of the Roman Catholic Church says in clause 485: 'The mission of the Holy Spirit is always conjoined and ordered to that of the Son. The Holy Spirit, "the Lord, the giver of Life", is sent to sanctify the womb of the Virgin Mary and divinely fecundate it, causing her to conceive the eternal Son of the Father in a humanity drawn from her own."

Benedict VIII's successor, another Tusculani, his brother Romanus, took the name **John XIX** (1024-32). He had been senator and consul in Rome, so was another layman who became pope. He too would play a part in the forthcoming schism as he rejected a proposal, backed by generous gifts from the newly elevated Byzantine Emperor Basil II, that the pope recognise the Patriarch of Constantinople as the Ecumenical Patriarch, leader of all the Eastern Churches. John XIX was tempted to agree, but when the proposal was leaked, public opinion and especially that of supporters of ecclesiastical reform ensured its rejection.

The Patriarch Eustathios erased the pope's name from the diptychs in Orthodox churches, yet another sign of growing distance between Constantinople and Rome, but with this succession of 'sponsored' popes with political responsibility, neither side of the Church was receiving much spiritual commitment from either of its leaders during this period. Pope John was more political than religious by nature anyway. He was also spending heavily to retain the support of the Romans. Communications with Eustathios were not severed and a reciprocal agreement was reached whereby the Byzantine Rite or Orthodox form of Mass in Greek language was allowed to continue in Italy after the re-annexation of the Bari diocese to Rome in return for the freedom to establish Roman Rite Churches in Byzantium. This was the conception of the distinction between 'Roman' Catholic, 'Greek' Catholic and Eastern Orthodox Rites as they stand today.

Emperor Henry II died in 1024 and Pope John XIX offered his support to Conrad II when he was elected to succeed as king. In March 1027, Pope John and Archbishop Heriberto of Milan invited Conrad II and his consort to Italy. Heriberto presented him with the iron crown of Lombardy in Milan before Conrad moved on to Rome and was crowned in a grand ceremony in St Peter's basilica at Easter, 1027. Kings Rudolph of Burgundy and Canute of Denmark, England and Norway made the journey to attend both this high profile ceremony and a synod in the Lateran basilica two weeks later. Pope John XIX and King Rudolph agreed a request from King Canute to allow his subjects passage to Rome without hindrance of tollgates and levying of tolls on them either along the roads or at borders.

John XIX offered his protection to Cluny Abbey but reprimanded Abbot Odilo for rejecting his own appointment as Bishop of Lyons. The pope also retained his office's rights to appoint a number of specified bishops in France.

Truce of God

The Truce of God (Treuga Dei) differs from the Peace of God, which came later, in that it is a temporary rather than a permanent cessation of hostilities. It had its origin in the sanctification of the Sabbath and became a necessary measure to empower lay authorities to pacify the frequent events of feudal anarchy in the 11th century. Numerous wars between land-owners with private armies of servants and tenants led to many castles being built for their defence against incursion by armed bands of men who held respect neither for sanctified days and people nor for the right of sanctuary. The Council of Elne in 1027 agreed a canon regarding the sanctification of Sunday prohibiting hostilities between Saturday night and Monday morning. Later, holy weekdays such as Ascension, Lent and Advent were included in the Truce, violation of which was punishable by excommunication. This was initiated in France and soon spread to Germany and Italy, then the whole Roman Church in an Ecumenical Council of 1179.

Worst Pope Ever?

Pope John XIX died late 1032 to be followed by his and Benedict VIII's nephew, Theophylactus of Tusculum, who at about 20 years of age was placed in the Chair of St Peter thanks to generous donations by his father Alberic. He was perhaps the youngest pope ever and took the name **Pope Benedict IX**. He is generally recognised as having been a disgrace to the office, not only for the dissolute life he led. Archbishop Heriberto of Milan thoroughly disapproved quite vocally and when Benedict IX went north for a meeting with Conrad II, he excommunicated Heriberto.

Emperor Conrad II died in 1039 and was succeeded by his son Henry III. Benedict IX showed little interest in a working papacy. A secular group formed in Rome which was hostile to Benedict's lifestyle expelled him in 1044, installing a member of the opposition Crescentii family, Bishop John of Sabina as Antipope Sylvester III. Public unrest led to Benedict returning and expelling Sylvester within months, but having done so and to free himself to marry, he actually sold the Papacy to a senior priest John Gratian, who was summarily elected, becoming **Pope Gregory VI** in mid- 1045.

Shortly afterwards, Benedict IX appeared to regret his deal with Gregory IV and sought to depose him. News of this reached the emperor, who travelled to Italy, where his friend Heriberto had recently died. Henry III called a Council at Sutri in 1046 at which all three 'popes' Benedict IX, Sylvester III and Gregory VI were deposed and German Bishop Suidger of Bamberg was appointed **Pope Clement II** (1046-1047).

Clement II was consecrated on Christmas day 1046 and in turn he crowned Henry III and his wife Agnes as Holy Roman Emperor and Empress. The people of Rome were clearly relieved at the orderly outcome and they presented Henry III with the golden chain of the patricius which conferred on him the powers previously held by the Crescentii and Tusculani to nominate popes when their members respectively filled this post. It remained an anomalous situation to have a non-ecclesial civil power selecting the head of the Church even if he did also hold political responsibilities. But if it had to be so, Henry III, an ardent opponent of simony was a reasonable choice. He immediately imposed his rule on Frascati, home of the Counts of Tusculum and took over all the castles of the Crescentii.

Another anomaly was that Pope Clement II continued in his role as bishop of Bamberg in spite of then also being pontiff. Clement initiated a number of reforms through a synod in January 1047, including a serious crackdown on simony which would thenceforth incur excommunication. He settled a long-standing rivalry between the dioceses of Milan, Ravenna and Aquilea, ruling in favour of Ravenna. But he then travelled back to Germany with Henry III to attend to duties in Bamberg. As he was returning to Rome in October 1047, he died near Pesaro of suspected poisoning by supporters of Benedict IX. Clement II is the only pope buried in Germany, in the Cathedral of Bamberg. Tests carried out on his remains in the 20th century proved the presence of lead acetate poison. At the time, suspicions gained strength as Benedict IX, who was living in Tusculum, used some of his stored wealth to raise a following and with the added help of the resurgent Tusculani seized Rome in November 1047. He made a brief return, moving into the Lateran palace and reclaiming the papacy.

Henry III only heard of Clement II's death in December and was advised by the Bishop of Liège and some clerics in Rome to reinstate Gregory VI, who was held in his custody, but he was not willing to reverse Gregory's dismissal. He appointed Bishop Poppo of Brixen, who had attended the synod in Sutri and became **Pope Damasus II** in July 1048, while Benedict IX was yet again unseated. Damasus was enthroned to the jubilation of the Romans but died from suspected malaria, only 23 days later.

Benedict IX eventually went to Grottoferrata Abbey, after another brief but unsuccessful attempt against the next pope in 1049, apparently repenting of his sinful life. He died there about 1065, still quite young.

Alsatian Pope with Gravitas, Golden Rose

The papacy remained vacant until the following February 1049, when an Alsatian aristocrat, Bruno of Eguisheim-Dagsburg, whose father was first cousin of Emperor Conrad, was selected at a meeting in Worms. He had been Bishop of Toul in France for over twenty years, during which this frontier town had known famine and war. He exercised strong diplomacy and helped maintain durable peace. He avoided the limelight, so insisted that he would take the papacy only if elected by the clergy and people of Rome. Hugh, then Abbot of Cluny, whom he met at Besançon on his way to Rome supported him. Hildebrand, a young Benedictine following the strict rule of Cluny joined him in the journey to Rome. He was recommended as a good administrator, of which the hierarchy was in sore need. A namesake, Bishop Bruno of Sengi spoke on behalf of many Christians when he said the world was "lying in wickedness; holiness had disappeared, justice had perished and truth had been buried". The Church needed a good leader.

When Bruno and Hildebrand arrived in Rome, Bruno received a rapturous welcome and was elected and enthroned, taking the name **Pope Leo IX** (1049-54). He appointed Hildebrand administrator with the primary task of restoring Church finances and the Patrimony of St Peter. As pope, Leo IX was impatient, driven to restore clerical holiness and discipline and ensure reform of the Church. As some before him, Leo IX sought to combat simony and 'clerical incontinence', which covered more than mere lax celibacy. He held a Paschal synod on these in Rome in April confirming simony as a sin worthy of excommunication and insisting on celibacy being practised by any member of the clergy above the rank of sub-deacon.

Leo IX believed in face-to-face persuasion and had a reputedly powerful presence. So with Hildebrand based in Rome, he arranged to travel around his vast constituency. In May 1049, he held a synod in Pavia on his way north to meet Emperor Henry III in Saxony. They travelled together to Cologne then Aix-la-Chapelle (now Aachen), where they settled a peace in Lorraine, which involved excommunication of a rebel leader. They moved on to Reims where the pope had been invited to consecrate a new Church and had arranged a council of senior clergy. King Henry I of France objected that he had not been consulted about this being held on his soil and retaliated by demanding the presence of French clergy at a feudal levy event, which he hastily arranged to coincide. About one third of French invitees attended Leo IX's synod, while others obeyed the king. Bishops and abbots travelled from Britain, Spain, Ireland and Brittany together with clergy and lay followers to Reims. Pope Leo IX took a hard line and excommunicated the absent French clergy members. Some of those attending, including senior clerics and some nobles, were also found guilty of serious crimes such as simony, clearly in breach of Church laws. Leo IX took no immediate action on these offences, but kept them in suspense for a decision on penalties after his return to Rome.

In this way, Pope Leo IX stressed beyond doubt the weight of authority that lay in the papacy more strongly than any of his predecessors had done. He was helped in this by weakness of French King Henry I and a supportive Emperor Henry III, with whom he worked well. Leo IX then held a synod at Mainz, still aimed at clerical reform and making the most of his natural charisma to influence public opinion regarding the clergy abusing their vows. He had a meeting with Adalbert, Archbishop of Bremen, who was also responsible for the Scandinavian countries, Greenland and Iceland and agreed that Adalbert could consecrate the first local bishop in Iceland.

The golden rose seems to have become a recognised part of Catholic culture during this visit. In return for privileges extended to her order following Leo IX's visit there, the Abbess of Wolfenheim undertook to send a golden rose to the pope every year before Laetare Sunday, which is the half-way point of Lent and has also become known as Rose Sunday, so the pope could wear it that day. To this day a skilled crafted rose ornament in pure gold is blessed by the pope each year on Laetare Sunday and sometimes conferred upon deserving individuals, groups or churches in recognition of special service, devotion and loyalty to the Roman Catholic Church. It is the only Sunday in the year when priests wear rose-pink vestments for Mass

Leo IX returned to Rome at the beginning of 1050, but soon left for the south of Italy, where there were reports of people suffering under the Norman occupation. He was given comforting reassurance by the Normans at Spoleto, which would soon prove to be rather worthless.

The Nature of the Eucharist, Transubstantiation

Leo IX returned to Rome and held his Paschal Synod there which included feedback on the progress of his reforms of clerical behaviour. Also, reports led him to condemn the respected theologian Berengarius of Tours for his opinion on the nature of the Eucharist. This addressed what remains a point of difference between many Protestants and Roman Catholics – whether the bread and wine of the Eucharist is transformed during the Mass physically into the body and blood of Christ. Was Christ talking literally when he said at the Last Supper of the bread and wine respectively, "This is my body …." and "this is my blood…"? (Luke 22:19,20; Mark

14:22,23; Matt 26:26,27). Berengarius was regarded as highly intelligent and strongly opinionated from an early age and he was clear in his belief that the body and blood of Christ are present in the sacrament at both intellectual and spiritual levels rather than in substance. He was firmly of the opinion that his belief tallied with those of august predecessors such as Jerome, Augustine of Hippo and Ambrose. This was not good enough for Leo IX or the Church, which held that at the consecration, the bread and wine on the altar were transformed into the true and real body and blood of Christ, an apparent denial of reality which was and is seen as a true test of faith. The 'process' is now known as 'transubstantiation', a term coined in the following century by Hildebert of Lavardin.

Towards the end of 1050, Leo IX travelled north once more, first to Toul to collect relics of the late Archbishop Gregory, whom he had just canonised, then on to Germany to meet Henry III. One result of the meeting was that the emperor persuaded Archbishop Hunfrid of Ravenna to cease acting as independent ruler of the Ravenna district and submit to the authority of the pope. Leo IX returned to Rome before Easter 1051 to hold the regular Easter synod at which he considered the question whether priests ordained by simoniacs should be re-ordained. He then went south to Benvento, where the people wished to submit to the pope's rule rather than continue suffering harassment from their Norman enemies. Since he was in that area, the pope tried to persuade the Normans to honour their earlier agreement, but his efforts were frustrated by resident Lombards killing some Normans in Apulia as he travelled. This left the native Normans unwilling to talk of compromise. His further effort at diplomacy the following year also failed.

Leo IX thus became heavily distracted by territorial and inter-ethnic conflict which did not improve when he was called to intervene in a dispute between Henry III and the Hungarians, where the best peace proposals he could extract from the Hungarians were rejected by Henry III, who then renounced an earlier promise to help subdue the Normans in Southern Italy. When he then returned to Rome early 1053, the situation in the South had deteriorated. The ethnic Greek communities were afraid of being expelled and begged his assistance. As his diplomacy failed, his family raised a small army of Swabians to help and he led an expedition against the Normans. It was a failure as the Normans first defeated the Greeks then, reluctantly as devout Christians, met and vanquished the pope's German forces in a fierce battle at Civitella in June 1053. Leo IX surrendered himself and was afforded honoured captive status, but would always be haunted by feelings of guilt at the fate of his supporters which he had witnessed in the battle.

Having lost appetite for such conflict, Leo IX found greater success lay in persuasion. The Normans gave him full backing as sovereign pontiff, escorted him back to Benvento with full honours and became faithful supporters of the See of Rome, to which they donated the territory of Benvento.

The Great Schism of 1054

Despite these distractions, Leo IX with Hildebert's help, still managed a heavy ecclesiastical workload. An ambitious and aggressive Patriarch of Constantinople, Michael Cerularius had taken office in 1043. He sought priority over Rome and sole leadership of the whole Church. Probably a member of a group that sought to reverse the settlement of the Photian schism of 801, he had already removed Leo IX's name from sacred diptychs and condemned the Roman Church's use of unleavened bread in the Eucharist. Early in the 1050s, he began a violent campaign of closing Latin Rite churches in Constantinople. Pope Leo IX sent a strong protest letter to Michael Cerularius in 1053. Byzantine Emperor Constantine was disturbed by this dispute given the recently weakened Greek interests in Southern Italy and foresaw danger Norman retribution there in support of the pope. He called for more respect for the pope, insisting that Cerularius join him in conciliatory letters to Leo, who replied early 1054 objecting to Cerularius' arrogance and demanding that he accept papal primacy and drop the full title of Ecumenical Patriarch. He tasked senior Cardinals Humbert and Frederick to convey the replies in person. Cerularius rejected papal primacy, so the cardinals excommunicated Cerularius, an action of questionable legal validity, as unknown to them, Leo IX had died in the meantime. It is debatable whether such ready use of excommunication devalues the tool or even the Church itself. Cerularius remained unmoved and the Great Schism of 1054 had been triggered.

This precipitation of the schism was another study in the difficulty of balancing political power with leading doctrine and theology. Finding a genuinely 'Christian' approach to resolving secular differences often felt unworkable. Patriarch Michael Cerularius, ordered the closure of all Latin Rite churches in his area in 1053, aware that this posed an obstacle to conciliation. All bishops were equal in the first millennium, though the Bishop of Rome was afforded a special place as direct successor to St Peter. But the Bishop or Patriarch of Constantinople was naturally equally revered by all the Eastern, Greek speaking Christians and differences had grown between East and West. The Western Church had persistently equated disagreement to heresy and taken a hard line. The disagreements centered partly on doctrine, albeit in reality only on fringe issues, but exacerbated by liturgy, translation and Greek versus Roman cultural tensions. Then a key factor had been that decision in 1014 AD to change the originally agreed text of the Nicene Creed, to which the West added filioque, 'and the Son', by which the Roman Church had arguably exceeded its authority in overriding the Ecumenical Councils of Nicea and Chalcedon. The Eastern Christians believed the decision undermined the concept of the Holy Trinity but they were also dismayed to observe that Mary and the saints were at the same time being promoted as intermediaries in prayer petitions to God.

The Eastern Orthodox Church held to the original agreed interpretation of the doctrine of the Holy Trinity and rejected Western insistence on primacy of the pope in Rome. With added concerns such as the alleged undue reverence of Mary and the saints and the use of unleavened bread for Holy Communion along with a few other concerns of detail, the Orthodox Church formalised the schism and thereafter the two Churches ploughed separate but parallel furrows, each side being confident that they were following Jesus more faithfully than the other. This result still remains – two huge Christian Churches with so much in common, both able to trace direct descent from Jesus Christ himself – Roman Catholic and Eastern Orthodox, still completely separate organisations; not at all as Jesus wanted.

And yet, to this day the Western Christian Churches all say the prayer *"Glory be to the Father, the Son and the Holy Spirit*, as it was *in the beginning*, is now and forever will be. Amen."

The strain of the schism was perhaps most felt then by the Orthodox Church, still under such pressure from Islamic forces, but the schism meant that Moravia had to make a choice and it opted for Orthodoxy. This was encouraging to Orthodoxy as it spread north-east to Kiyv in the Ukraine and thence to Russia.

Following Leo IX's death, another German, Schwabian Bishop Gebhard of Eichstätt was proposed. He refused the honour in September 1054 when Cardinal Hildebrand travelled to Mainz to ask the emperor to appoint him pope. He finally agreed in March 1055 on condition that all the possessions that had been taken from the See of Rome by emperors be returned, to which Henry III agreed. Bishop Gebhard travelled to Rome with Hildebrand and was enthroned in April, taking the name **Pope Victor II** (1055-57). He energetically followed the ecclesiastical policies of Leo IX, whilst enjoying better support from the emperor than Leo. This enabled Victor II to move against those guilty of simony and clerical incontinence and at a major synod in Florence he also persuaded King Ferdinand of Spain to accept Henry III as Roman Emperor.

Then to reinforce Leo's clerical reforms, he sent Hildebrand back to France in 1056 to pursue these reforms in the north and instructed the archbishops of Arles and Aix-en-Provence to do the same in the south. Later that year, Henry III called him urgently to Germany where he was present as the emperor died, leaving instructions that his six-year-old son succeed him. Henry entrusted Pope Victor with the care of his son and made him advisor to the king's mother, Agnes as regent. After Henry III's funeral, Pope Victor had young Henry IV formally enthroned at Aix-la-Chapelle and then elicited the fealty of the Frankish princes at an imperial diet in Cologne in the December. Victor II left for Rome in February 1057 and died there in July.

Pope Victor II's successor, **Pope Stephen IX** (1057- 58), often referred to now as Stephen X, was Frank, brother of Godfrey the Bearded, a rebellious Duke of Lower Lorraine. Made a cardinal by Victor, Frank had been papal legate to Constantinople and latterly abbot of Montecassino, where he had been impressed by monk Peter Damian, a good friend of Hildebrand. He made Peter a cardinal.

As another clerical reformist, Stephen X directed Hildebrand to join Bishop Anselm of Lucca as papal legates to Milan in 1057 to try to suppress endemic breaches there of papal policy on clerical discipline. Their success was minimal and they would be dispatched again two years later with the addition of Peter Damian on a similar mission by Stephen's successor. Milan presented serious challenges for the Church.

Stephen was only in post for 6 months before he died, so he never had time to fulfil his plans to drive the Normans out of Italy or to help his brother become emperor.

Following Stephen's death, another Tusculani **antipope, Benedict X,** youngest brother of Benedict IX, was installed in April 1058. Some cardinals who deemed the election non-canonical were forced to leave Rome. Hearing of this as he returned from business in Germany, Hildebrand obtained the approval of Stephen IX's brother, Duke Godfrey of Lorraine and the blessing of the emperor to elect Bishop Gérard of Burgundy. He called a meeting of cardinals and senior clerics at Siena where Gérard was elected, becoming **Pope Nicholas II** in December. On his way to Rome Nicholas held a synod at Sutri attended by Duke Godfrey, which excommunicated antipope Benedict. The Normans helped Hildebrand drive Benedict from Rome.

Rules for Papal Elections

A significant Paschal synod was called by Pope Nicholas II at the Lateran Palace in 1059, attended by over 100 bishops. Its main business was papal election, a process which had cried out for reform for a couple of centuries. It was clearly wrong that secular interference whether from Roman civic leaders, families or the emperor should determine the selection of a Church leader. Perhaps unsurprisingly, consensus on the conclusions of the synod was at best unclear and the final texts ambiguous. The papal bull, (an official, sealed papal decree) In Nomine Domini was published in April 1059 confirming the new election process. The main decisions are now believed to have been along the following lines:

1. On the death of a pope, the cardinal-bishops shall confer privately to select a candidate. Following agreement on one name, they are to proceed with other cardinals to an election.
2. The candidate should be selected from the See of Rome unless a suitable person cannot be found, in which case one from another diocese may be elected.
3. The election is to take place in Rome except when a free choice is impossible there, in which case it may be held elsewhere.
4. If war or other circumstances prevent the solemn enthronement of the new pope in St Peter's Chair, the one elected shall nevertheless exercise full Apostolic authority.
5. Due regard to be paid to the right of confirmation or recognition conceded to King Henry IV, the same deference to be afforded those of his successors who have been granted personally a like privilege.

Thus a new law was established which also ensured the legitimacy of Nicholas' papacy. The imperial right of confirmation was thus relegated to a courtesy privilege.

Other matters covered were the prohibition of both ordination involving simony and the right of priests involved in concubinage to say Mass as well as setting limits on the property-owning rights of clergy. Also the theologian Berengar of Tours, who had been berated for his view by Leo IX, was made to modify his view and sign up to the accepted Church doctrine regarding the real presence of Christ in the Eucharist.

Feeling these matters had been resolved, Nicholas II travelled south in July 1059 and with the Normans, signed the Treaty of Meifi, whereby the Normans through their leader Duke Robert Guiscard, acquired the sovereignty of Apulia and Calabria as well as Sicily, subject to them dislodging the Saracens from Sicily. Nicholas travelled on to reach a similar accord with Prince Richard of Capua. In return, each leader would pay an annual tribute to the See of Rome, hold his lands as the pope's vassal and ensure protection of the Holy See of Rome and of the freedom of future papal elections according to the new rules.

Pope Nicholas II then called in on Benvento for a synod. He gathered a Norman army that retrieved the Holy See's control of the Tusculani family home and Numentatum, forcing Benedict X to capitulate in the autumn. Nicholas had moved rapidly and decisively, while Hildebrand, who had prepared the ground for the decree of election as well as the alliance with the Normans, remained at the heart of the pontificate and was made archdeacon. As matters became more settled in Rome, it became clear that the new election rules had not gone down well in Germany, given the downgrading of the emperor's right to approve the selection. As a first step, Cardinal Stephen was sent to France to secure support for those rules in synods over which he presided at Vienne in January and Tours in February 1060.

With Norman support assured, Nicholas II confirmed the electoral rules and the prohibition of simony and concubinage at the Lateran synod in 1060. Cardinal Stephen was again dispatched, this time as papal legate to see the Regent Empress in Germany but was refused an audience for some days after his arrival. He returned empty-handed to Rome. Then a German synod was held at which all Nicholas' ordinances were declared void and he was deemed to be deposed. Nicholas simply confirmed the electoral decrees at a 1061 synod in Rome, then died in July. He had achieved much in his short incumbency and the next pope would be the first to be elected solely by a gathering of cardinals without the Emperor's formal approval.

Bishop Anselm of Lucca was chosen in that first election under the new rules and took the name **Alexander II**. He was known to be in favour of clerical reform since his time at Cluny with Hildebrand, and was installed in October 1061, though not in St Peter's since the Roman nobles, were against the election as were the Germans. Regent Empress Agnes had convened a council in Basle, where Bishop Cadalus of Parma was elected as Pope Honorius II. Cadalus went to Rome with supporters but was never allowed to take the seat from Alexander II. When the imperial court in Germany lost interest as Anno of Cologne supplanted Agnes as regent, Cadalus' candidature was formally annulled by a council in Mantua in 1064.

In 1063, Alexander II expressed the need of a *Reconquista* in Spain to expel the Muslim occupiers. With probable support from Hugh of Cluny, whose brother led the Burgundian army, Alexander encouraged the assembly of an international force, a 'pre-crusade' of French, Burgundian, Italian Normans and Spanish to lay siege then take Barbastro in North West Spain from the occupying Moors. It was successful, but contrary to the surrender agreement, the crusaders massacred the Muslim men and abused the women. The incensed Moors retook Barbastro ten months later.

In 1065, Alexander signalled that Jews should be respected rather than attacked, with no innocent blood shed and nor should they be converted by force or threats.

In 1066, William the Conqueror, descendant of Rollo, the first Viking leader in Normandy, visited Rome seeking the pope's blessing on his imminent invasion of Britain. Alexander II gave his blessing as well as a papal ring and the standard of St George. He asked in return that William secure agreement to the pope's edict that the independent clergy of Britain submit to the Roman Church. After the conquest of England, Lanfranc of Bec, a former teacher of Alexander II and known to be a keen clerical reformer, was appointed as Archbishop of Canterbury and Primate of England in 1067. He found the clergy and most bishops there corrupt and undisciplined. The bishops were eventually mostly replaced by Norman appointees.

In another step Alexander II removed the 'Alleluia' from the Mass or other worship during the season of Lent. He was also relentless in his campaign for clerical reform, banishing many priests and imposing penance on senior figures, not least Abbo, his protector. For acts of simony, the bishop of Constance and the Abbott of Reichenau had to return to the king the rings and croziers they had been gifted.

When Alexander II died in 1073 it was the overwhelming view of both the clergy and the faithful that the most influential person behind the Church's strategy of cleansing and reform as well as its quest for independent sovereignty should take the helm – the good, long-serving and faithful Hildebrand.

Spiritual and Moral Decline and Violence

Hildebrand had rebuffed all earlier soundings, but this time the pressure was overwhelming. He had felt he was of more use to the cause of the Church when supporting its figurehead, being freer to apply diplomacy and manoeuvre effectively away from the limelight. Also, he was as aware as anybody that it was a time of massive challenge for the pontificate. Christianity and its leadership and clergy had descended to a nadir in the previous century and in spite of repeated campaigns by recent popes, many bishops and priests still lived extravagant and depraved lives, setting deplorable example for their flocks.

Several factors had led to the decline. First the 'gift of Pepin' in the 750s which brought significantly more temporal power to the Church leaders, radically unbalancing their spiritual role, although there had been an increasing element of politics in their survival and authority before that. No candidates were ever suitably trained for fulfilling both political and spiritual roles expected. As Emperors and Roman families became involved in the appointment of pontiffs, the criteria for their selection became quite detached from the need of their key role.

Then around the time of Charlemagne, military force had been adopted to spread the faith, in stark contrast to the wish of Jesus, his apostles and early Christians. The mutual interdependence of pope and emperor with reciprocal approbation on election meant that little was done to limit the use of force. At the regional operational level, the clergy seems to have included a proportion of power- and pleasure-seekers, while some bishops, had used irregular means to secure their appointment.

Monastics were vocationally more ascetically oriented, but not entirely; not all monasteries followed their own rule strictly. But they were generally on a tighter lead and under closer oversight than the broader clergy. Any lapses among them caused community upset which led in some cases to the establishment of stricter levels of discipline such as seen and respected at Cluny. Thus, recent popes had granted privileges to many monasteries and convents, while always struggling to keep bishops and secular clergy in check. Central control on all branches of the Church was not helped by slow transport and news transmission of the age. As well as the ongoing challenges in Rome itself, the Eastern Church had become similarly lax, thus rendering itself more vulnerable to the ever-present Muslim competition.

Hildebrand's reluctance to assume leadership was understandable but, pressed to accept the candidature, his election was a formality and he chose the name **Gregory VII** (1073-85). In order to strengthen his position and also as a matter of courtesy, he would not accept full consecration until he had the approval of Emperor Henry VI. In the meantime, he was ordained as a priest. Knowing Hildebrand's zeal for reform, the German bishops expressed concerns to Henry VI, but on receipt of a favourable report from his legate in Rome, the emperor approved the appointment. This was notable for being the last papal election ever ratified by an emperor; it became an internal Church matter. Gregory was consecrated in June 1073.

The pope complained to Abbot Hugh of Cluny that wherever he turned bishops were in place through simony and their lifestyles and conversation did not reflect their sacred calling. Their work was motivated more by worldly gain than the love of Christ. He asked where the princes of the Church were who would put God's honour before their own ends or place righteousness above their own ambition.

Gregorian Reform

Gregory VII decided to make a determined effort to nail those elusive goals of ridding the Church and society of simony and permissive behaviour. First step was to secure popular support for his pontificate, so he toured the south and gained pledges of support for himself and the pontificate from the leaders there. The Norman leader at the time, Robert Guiscard, was not trusted and was ultimately excommunicated for activities against the interests of the Papal States.

Gregory embarked on his mission of reform and at a Lent Synod in 1074, issued the following canons:

- Clerics who have obtained any grade or office of Holy Orders by payment should cease ministry.
- No purchaser of any church role should retain it, nor should future ecclesiastical rights be traded.
- All clerics who are guilty of incontinence should confess and cease to exercise their ministry.
- The people should reject the ministrations of clerics who fail to obey these injunctions.
- All clerics should obey their bishop only so long as he obeys the pope.

Although several of his predecessors had issued similar edicts, the realisation that Gregory VII was far more determined and dedicated to this cause raised a storm in the Church, as the abuses were known and widespread. Papal legates and bishops who tried to enforce the rules were often threatened, stoned or received death threats. Although not clear from the text above, priestly celibacy was included in the prohibitions and there were many married priests who declared openly that if it came to a choice between Church and spouse, the latter would be the choice. The inclusion of priestly celibacy in the reforms was unfortunate as it caused a whole body of clergy to rise against the edicts on this issue alone, whereas the real evil lay in the issues of simony and concubinage. There was a genuine debate to be had on celibacy, about which scripture is ambiguous. Jesus was never apparently preoccupied with that issue. He certainly supported marriage itself and actually appointed a married man to lead his Church.

Sex, Marriage and the Bible

The gospels make no mention of Christ condemning marriage or sexual intercourse. Paul could be quoted in support of either side, rather akin to the Old Testament. There were already ascetics, hermits, monks and some priests who voluntarily adopted vows of celibacy to which nobody objected.

Proverbs (18:22) say "He who finds a wife finds happiness, receiving a mark of favour from the Lord." Genesis (1:26-28) is clear that God created human beings male and female in his image and told them to "be fruitful and multiply" and everything he had made "was good". Matthew's gospel (19:5-6) repeats this and goes on to say "that is why a man leaves his father and mother and becomes attached to his wife and the two become one flesh." Like Luke and Paul, Matthew goes on to say that anyone who divorces his wife and marries another is guilty of adultery. God blesses marriage and Jesus says that what he has joined together should not be separated by people.

In Mosaic Law, adultery was regarded as a sufficiently serious sin to merit the death penalty. In John 8, Jesus saved an adulteress from being stoned to death by suggesting the first stone should be cast by the one without sin, at which the accusers melted away. In this demonstration of his forgiveness, Jesus told the woman he did not condemn her but told her to go and from that moment to "sin no more".

In the Sermon on the Mount (Matt 5:27-30) Jesus not only warned against adultery but also a man nurturing lust as he looked on a woman, saying that if your eye or hand cause you to sin it is better to gouge out the eye or cut off the hand as it is better to lose one part of your body than have the whole body go into hell.

As today in that part of the world, the women then tended to be held more responsible than the men in cases of adultery, which some believe refers back to Eve's role with Adam in Genesis. But in Christ's time, pre-marital sex was hardly an issue as families were strong, youngsters were chaperoned and parents generally arranged for daughters to be married soon after they reached puberty.

As part of his reform, Gregory took an important step towards improving the educational and training standards of clergy. Although a long-term aim, he saw this as urgent and the move led to the first ever universities. The first one in Europe was established in Bologna in 1088, majoring in law, although arguably the renowned medical school in Salerno which preceded it should claim the title as it also offered courses in philosophy, theology and law. (The world's first university was probably Al Quaraouiyine in Fez, Morocco, established in 859 AD). Bologna was followed by Paris (theology) in 1150 and Oxford in 1167 with a wider curriculum.

The universities attracted the best teachers and the degrees they conferred qualified graduates to teach. Thanks to pope Gregory VII, the Church was closely involved in this growth in learning and would in time put it to good use as explorers and missionaries venturing ever further were usually followed by monks and nuns who also brought teaching and medical experience, setting up schools and hospitals for the indigenous people and encouraging them to help their own communities towards a better, longer life in Christianity. Thus Church sponsored education and health services became powerful missionary tools for forthcoming centuries.

Another priority of the pope was to mend the Great Schism and reunite Eastern and Western Christianity. Byzantine Emperor Michael VIII had conveyed his wish for this to Gregory in 1073. The plight of Eastern Christians under the Turks was something Gregory believed that the West could help alleviate. So he tried to rally an early crusade, with little success. Young King Henry in Germany offered his full support for the pope, but he was known to be capricious.

The encouragement and support for clerics to graduate gave them clear advantage over congregations and enabled them to offer qualified pastoral support. This strengthened Church mission and observance, as well as raising levels of knowledge, enhancing the spread of informed Christianity. The fact of linking faith to intellect in addition to the social and spiritual messages of Jesus Christ, gave faith a stronger base and wider acceptance. It also gave clerics community power.

Violence and '*Pax Dei*'

Concern within the Church at the use of violence infecting its mission had led to the beginning of a movement called *Pax Dei*, Peace of God in France in 989. This spread widely in this century in an effort to replace violence with spiritual sanctions applied by the Church.

At first it related to consecrated people, places and times; clerics and monastics; churches, monasteries and cemeteries; Sundays and designated holy or ferial days. The Church declared all these to be protected from violent activity and any transgressors using violence against such people or places or on designated days would be subject to excommunication. The range of persons covered was soon extended by councils to the poor, pilgrims, travelling merchants and even crusaders. The Pax or 'peace' of the places offered the right of sanctuary and eventually asylum. As to the peace of times, this confirmed and extended the 'Truce of God', since Sunday had always been a day on which battle and legal dispute were suspended. Pax Dei lasted into the 13th century and had a social effect in villages with churches, for example, offering a public space for gatherings with immunity from violence.

It did not really tackle war-like activity itself apart from promoting a pause on certain days. Indeed, Gregory VII's final years were embroiled in battle with Henry IV helped by the Normans, which involved such disagreement with the Romans that he was obliged to move to Montecassino. Gregory VII died in Salerno in 1085, his reforms remaining as work in progress. He had built a base for forward movement.

Pope Victor III (1085-87) was consecrated pope in 1085 for a brief reign which allowed no time for any reform. He was a good choice, being from Lombard ducal stock and having been a strict monk from a childhood ambition. When he became a monk, he took the name Desiderius and after several moves to introduce ever stricter rule for monasteries, including a spell advising Pope Gregory VII, he had made his name as Abbot of Montecassino, a post he held from 1058, for achieving major reform of discipline. He was also recognised for tireless improvement work and building new or rebuilding much of the infrastructure, including a new church. He was supportive of Gregory VII's reforms, but always maintained that he would have chosen a gentler approach in applying them. Gregory obviously respected him as he nominated him as his successor.

Victor III was another reluctant pope and it took two years after Gregory's death for the cardinals to almost force him to accept consecration in May 1087. Part of his reluctance related to poor health, as he even had difficulty in getting through his initial Mass. He died in September. One notable action while he was pope lay in sending a military expedition to Tunisia under the flag of St Peter, which forced the Muslim ruler in Tunis to free all Christian prisoners and give respect to Rome, perhaps a precursor to the crusades.

Pope Urban II (1087-1098) followed. Born as Otto in 1042 into French nobility, he studied at Rheims under Bruno, who would become founder of the Carthusian Order and be canonised. In 1070, Otto joined Cluny Abbey under Abbot Hugh and became prior. Gregory VII made him cardinal-bishop of Ostia in 1078 in thanks for all the help he had given the pope and he was proposed as an alternative candidate for the papacy when Desiderius at first refused it. Urban II espoused the reform policies of Gregory VII but, being an accomplished tactician and with understanding of human nature he followed Victor II's more finessed approach, though never left any doubt as to his determination.

However, Urban II's installation on the throne of St Peter in the Lateran

Palace was delayed some six years after his consecration because an **anti-pope, Guibert** of Ravenna, who took the name Clement III, had earlier been unconstitutionally appointed by Emperor Henry IV.

As well as the emperor's support, Guibert also enjoyed the backing of the Romans and drove Urban II into deep poverty and debt. Urban, was greatly helped throughout his reign by a monk at Cluny, Pietro Pierlone, son of a wealthy Roman family. Pietro's family gave Urban II refuge by protecting the approach to the island of St Bartholomew on the river Tiber while he lived there in a miserable existence of poverty and debt. The Frangipani family also helped Urban, hosting him in their fortified home in Rome when Guibert was occupying St Peter's. Henry IV was leading such a dissolute life that even his second son Conrad was appalled by his behaviour and sought rebellion, which offered Urban II a chance to retrieve his position. Urban II supported Conrad, Duke of Lower Lorraine in his rebellion against his father and facilitated his marriage to Maximilla, daughter of wealthy Count Roger of Sicily. The dowry helped finance Conrad's ongoing campaigns.

Urban II's moment of securing lasting fame came in 1095 when he convened a huge Council at Clermont in the Auvergne at the Church of Notre Dame du Port. 13 Archbishops, 225 bishops, nearly 100 abbots attended and many nobles and knights followed proceedings. It began normally enough with reiteration of Gregory VII's decrees regarding clerical reform, then went on to declare King Philip of France excommunicated for adultery – he had forsaken his wife Bertha for Bertrade, wife of Fulk of Anjou.

First Crusade

The next item on Urban II's agenda was the critical question of the Eastern Church, with Constantinople still threatened by the Seljuk Turks, a Sunni Muslim empire of Turkey and Persia based in Isfahan founded in 1037. Urban II had received representation from Alexis, the Eastern Emperor beseeching him to provide help. Christian pilgrimage was tolerated by the Muslim rulers of Palestine and Sinai until this century, but it had recently become dangerous there with attacks, especially by the Turks upon pilgrims while they were travelling the last stages of the route. This raised the highly anticipated issue of an armed Crusade. The council decreed that those who joined a crusade were freed from all obligations relating to penance.

The idea of a crusade was most keenly received in France and the first result was a 'People's Crusade' of thousands of mostly ordinary citizens led by a priest 'Peter the Hermit', who set off in 1096. Few of them had any military training, but they were an aggressive bunch, short on discipline, gratuitously attacking and killing many Jews on their way through Europe. Having crossed Byzantine territory, they entered enemy ground in Anatolia soon to be ambushed by the Turks and routed.

Meanwhile, word had spread with enthusiasm beyond France for a crusade during 1096 and attracted nobles and knights in their thousands, still with a French majority, to Clermont. The focus of the debate settled on Jerusalem and the Middle East, rather than direct conflict with the Seljuk Turks. So the decision was taken to assemble an army of horsemen and foot soldiers to retrieve Jerusalem from Islamic rule as well as the churches Muslims had taken in the Middle East. Urban II roused those present with a famously eloquent speech, urging them to follow that First Crusade, which began in November 1096.

Having reached Anatolia, this force of nearly a hundred thousand laid siege to Nicea from land while the Byzantine navy blockaded the sea port, capturing it in June 1097. Having secured Nicea it took a difficult year of advance with poor supplies of food and water together with developing disease and Turkish attacks before they captured Antioch in June 1098. Jerusalem was reached a further year later and a month-long battle ensued, during which the defenders were massacred. This crusade resulted in the establishment of four crusader enclave states in Edessa, Antioch, Tripoli and Jerusalem, which would be held until near the end of the 13th century. The main body of the crusade returned home after the capture of Jerusalem.

Mission for Clerical Discipline Continues

In the meantime, Urban II had travelled throughout France in his mission to exact tighter discipline from their clerics and bishops. Antipope Clement had reoccupied Rome, but had soon left as some of the crusaders, who supported Urban, gathered there. Urban II then went south once more to hold a large council at Bari in an attempt at reconciling the regional Orthodox with the Latin Rite Christians over the question of the '*filioque*' and the use of unleavened bread in the Eucharist. The council succeeded with these Orthodox settlers, but went no further towards repairing the Great Schism. Another item addressed at the Bari Council II was the expulsion of the reforming Archbishop Anselm of Canterbury from England by the 'Red King', William II. The king was condemned but no further action ensued.

Urban II's papacy was regarded as mostly positive. He was clearly a leader with eloquent and persuasive rhetoric, a good organiser, tactician and strategist, a holy and committed Christian, though he was not averse to violence in achieving his objectives. He was leading a Church under violent threat from the Saracens, while concurrently the Eastern Church suffered from land-based Islamic forces. The leaders of these Churches in the 11th century had to decide whether turning the other cheek was a viable choice, given what had already happened to the embedded Christianity in North Africa.

Roman Curia, Carthusian Order

Another noteworthy achievement of Urban II was his reorganisation of Church governance in 1089. He set up a form of cabinet of local bishops on the model that bishops elsewhere held colleges of clerics for debate and advice on running their dioceses. He held three cabinet meetings a week for general administration in Rome. Pope Urban II then formed committees led by cardinals to examine and report back to him on specialised subjects as an effective way of managing the complexity of matters spiritual, practical, financial, social, political, local and international that now lay before the Church. Perhaps understandably, Rome had previously been shy of delegation, one dilemma having always been the additional opportunity for corruption that such a body offers. This was the first recorded time the term Curia was used and it was not far removed from the basis of the 20th century Roman Curia, which is a central body to control the administrative and policy functions of the Roman Catholic Church in the Pope's name.

The Carthusian Order was originated in 1075 by Bruno of Cologne, chancellor of the church at Rheims. He and a few of his colleagues had been yearning to exchange their secular life in the Church for a solitary or cenobitic life of devotion to God. Bishop Hugh of Grenoble offered them a location in the remote Alpine Chartreuse Valley, so in 1080 they built a small monastery there with cloisters and cells, all separate from each other. Half a dozen fellow clerics and two lay monks took up an ascetic life of deep prayer, devotion and poverty in isolation from one another reminiscent of the Desert Fathers, albeit closer together in the remote Alps. They were all highly learned men but spoke rarely, even using signs for communication where possible. There was no communal meal, but food was distributed once a week and each member cooked for himself in his cell. All was well until 1090, when Pope Urban II called on Bruno's advice and help with clerical reform. He reluctantly left the community for a while accompanied by a couple of fellow monks. After his project for Urban II was finished, he persuaded the pope to allow him to resume the solitary life. The pope agreed, but subject to that life being closer to Rome. A local nobleman provided a site in the Calabrian Mountains in 1091, in which grew a second Carthusian community. **Pope Paschal II (1099-1118)** succeeded Urban in August 1099, beginning the longest papacy of the next century, though heavily challenged by antipopes in its course.

Islam

The tide of Islam had begun to turn in this century with the beginnings of a retreat from the European continent, notably Spain and latterly Sicily.

Middle Ages

As the universities in Europe grew and their range of subjects widened into arts and technical spheres, the era of the High Middle Ages was being born.

CHAPTER 14

12th Century

Popes

1099-1118 Pascal II
1100-01 Antipope Theodoric
1101-02 Antipope Adalbert
1105-11 Antipope Sylvester IV
1118-19 Gelasius II
(1118-21 Antipope Gregory VIII)
1119-24 Callixtus II
1124-30 Honorius
1130-43 Innocent II
(1130-38 Antipope Anocletus II)
1143-44 Celestine II
1144-45 Lucius II
1145-53 Eugene III

1153-54 Anastasius IV
1154-59 Adrian IV
1159-81 Alexander III
(1159-64 Antipope Victor IV)
(1164-68 Antipope Paschal III)
(1168-78 Antipope Callixtus III}
(1179-80 Antipope Innocent III)
1181-85 Lucius III
1185-87 Urban II
1187 Oct-Dec Gregory VIII
1187-91 Clement III
1191-98 Celestine III
1198-1216 Innocent III

Roman Emperors

1056-1106 Henry IV
1111-1125 Henry V
1133-1137 Lothair II

1155-1190 Frederick I Barbarossa
1191-1197 Henry VI
1198-1215 Otto IV

The High Middle Ages began in the 12th century and saw development of the long roots of the coming Renaissance movement that would introduce renewed intellectuality to Western Europe with a bias to philosophy, science and mathematics, laying the literary, artistic and scientific base of the later Italian Renaissance as well as subsequent scientific and industrial revolutions to follow much later in this millennium. Translations were becoming available of past Greek and Arabic studies of sciences which opened to the west and its universities new avenues of research in these fields, bringing with them social, political and economic ideas. More distant trade links grew such as with the Hanseatic League in Northern Europe and Marco Polo's exploration of the Silk Road as far as China. This mattered to Christianity because its mission was never far behind trade.

Important developments in technology also ensued. One of the most important was the manufacture of paper, invented in the far distant past by wasps for building their beautifully complex nests and picked up for development by the Chinese as a writing and painting material, which came west via the Silk Road before the Moors introduced it to Spain about 1100 AD. Its use then spread east to France and Italy during this century, encouraging the growth of learning materials. Other innovations to Europe included harnessing the power of wind by the first recorded windmill in Yorkshire, England; the astrolabe returned to Europe, an instrument for measuring angles or inclination, so useful for establishing latitude if the time is known, for marine navigation, identifying stars or for triangulation in land surveys. These and other pre-industrial ideas would become fashionable and begin to power the advance of improvements to standards of living and learning.

The curious mix of political and ecclesiastical intrigues in Rome and further afield, together with the shifting shape and demands of the empire over the past two or three centuries had made the job of running a 'universal' Church almost impossible without the requisite administrative structure and skills in place. Urban II had reorganised the inner cabinet, but the breadth and demands of focus upon local issues in Rome and Italy alone were such that they really required their own dedicated unit of administration. Another such unit attending to the wider international mission and ecumenical issues could have run in parallel with the first with both reporting to the top. The absence of a suitably broad and robust structure led to more cracks developing. Lessons were not being learnt in Rome even after the recent Great Schism.

Urban II's cabinet had been an essential step in helping to spread the load and maintain continuity through transitions of leadership. There were countless difficulties in selecting the right people to form a cohesive team in the Curia, avoiding personal agendas, feuding parties, the power-hungry and the greedy to ensure a reasonable degree of teamwork and integrity. A series of brief papal reigns by diverse characters and policies, plus the outside unrest, influences and power of family and other interests in the Roman cauldron undermined the potential stability a sound cabinet could provide. In order for the Church to become more cohesive and effective, it needed to take further the administrative reforms that Popes Gregory VII and Urban II had begun and improve its governance in this new century. It should manage the challenge of handling the temporal in parallel with ecclesiastical matters, including cleansing copious suspect front-line clerics of their leanings to temporal rather than spiritual indulgence.

Managing the Church on earth had become a gargantuan task in itself. Human failings, gluttony, greed, power, lust and more all thrived around and within it. It truly needed the help of the Holy Spirit through the core of holy and dedicated people working within the Church to bring it back to protecting and promulgating the message and ethics of Jesus Christ, which is its true mission. Over the next few centuries there would be a resurgence of philosophy and some influential thinkers thanks to the growing number of universities and the respect that they engendered. Assimilating the results would present new challenges.

England, Rome and Politics

Ranierus became a monk at Cluny Abbey when still very young, then at twenty he went on monastery business to Rome, was spotted and retained by Gregory VII, who made him cardinal-priest of San Clemente basilica in Rome in 1073. After Urban II's death in 1099 he was elected pope **Paschal II (1099-1118)**. Having limited administrative experience, he opted to continue the policies of his recent predecessors.

In 1102, Archbishop Anselm of Canterbury in England held a Council in London where he introduced a prohibition of marriage for priests in England. Henry of Huntingdon wrote in his 'History of the English People 1000-1154' that while celibacy was accepted by some as "the greatest purity", others warned of "a danger that if they sought a purity beyond their capacity, they might fall into horrible uncleanness, to the utter disgrace of the Christian name." That was almost identical to the argument by Paphnutius, a fourth century celibate Bishop of Egypt, who argued that apart from being too rigorous, insistence on clerical celibacy would be unwise as such a rule would serve no better purpose than to create many sinners among the clergy and thus damage to the Church. Nevertheless, this policy was fully adopted by the wider Church at the 2nd Lateran Council in 1139. It laid to rest historic doubts on the matter, but history since proved the realism, prescience and perception of Paphnutius' and Henry's counsel regarding its dangers.

Pascal II inherited an ongoing disagreement in England between King Henry I and Archbishop Anselm over the right of investiture of the primate. Agreement was eventually reached in 1106 that the pope retained that right together with the right to appoint bishops, while the king held the right to approve lesser appointments and benefices.

Holy Roman Emperor Henry IV died in 1105, to be succeeded by his son Henry V, who had already rebelled at his father's depravity and asked Paschal II for forgiveness for having associated with him. The son was intent on re-gaining the imperial right of papal investiture. The pope's resistance led to a stressful distraction for much of his long papacy. It was settled unsatisfactorily in a hectic year of 1111, which culminated in Henry V travelling to Italy, partly to enforce his right to investiture and also to hold his coronation as Holy Roman Emperor. A meeting between the pope and emperor resulted in a compromise, the Concordat of Sutri. In this, Henry V dropped imperial claims to investitures, while the pope would compel all prelates and abbots in the Empire to yield all worldly rights and privileges they had received from the emperor. This caused deep indignation and disturbance in Rome, where the agreement was first announced on the day of the expected coronation of Henry V. The protests were led by the prelates who had accordingly been threatened with transformation from princely to basic living, while the Holy See remained immune from these strictures. As rioting began, Henry IV and his entourage escaped from the city, taking Paschal II and the Cabinet members with him as captives.

After two months of harsh captivity and a failed rescue attempt by the Normans, Paschal II acceded to Henry's demand regarding investiture and they returned to Rome for the coronation of Henry V. On the promise that there would be no reprisals, Henry and his party returned to Germany. However, nearly a year later at a council in 1112, the investiture accord was declared null and void on account of the forceful coercion used to extract it and Henry V was excommunicated for good measure.

During this time, the Byzantine Emperor Alexios I tried hard to mend the schism between Eastern and Western Churches. Paschal II was also keen, but the continued stipulation that the pope be recognised as the ultimate leader of the Church worldwide remained the stumbling block. The Eastern clergy simply would not have it, however hard the Patriarch tried to persuade them. This remains the case today, but that was an important missed opportunity for both sides at the time, not helped by the many other local and international calls on Paschal II's intervention, with an inadequate cabinet structure.

Cistercians

With a desire among some of the clergy to return to early Church values and the simpler life, yet another religious order was founded in 1098 by three Benedictine monks. Formed in the village of Citeaux near Dijon for stricter adherence to the Rule of Benedict, they were joined in 1110 by Bernard of Clairvaux (1090-1153) with thirty colleagues, who gradually went out and helped the new Order spread widely. It clearly satisfied an appetite among monks for the original discipline with emphasis on seclusion and prayer along with the option of some menial work and self-sufficiency with horticulture and agriculture. This was felt to re-establish people's connection with God and direct feel of the beautiful and bountiful earth that he gave them. This Order adopted a white habit to distinguish them from the black of the Benedictines.

The Cistercians eventually made significant contributions to beauty in architecture as well as advancing agricultural techniques, metallurgy and engineering. Despite being an enclosed Order, they were happy to share advances to the benefit of all. They established their only English charterhouse, St Hugh's in Parkminster, Sussex, which has a full kilometre cloister.

Politics Continue to Intervene

Problems over pope versus monarch arose once more in both England and Italy in 1115. In England, Henry I was moving bishops without Paschal II's approval so the king was threatened with excommunication. Matilda of Tuscany died and Emperor Henry V immediately claimed her lands, which the Church had expected to inherit. Henry V entered Rome, forcing Paschal to flee from the city.

Spain also needed help in resisting the Moors. In 1116, Paschal II ordered a Crusade to recapture Tarragona from the Moors. Further afield, Paschal II also created the first bishop for America as discovered by the Vikings, offering the See of Greenland and Vinland (Newfoundland) to Nordic bishop Erik Gnupsson. Paschal returned to Rome just before he died in 1118.

Paschal II's successor was Giovanni Caetani, who had been a monk at Monte Cassino before being drafted in to the Vatican by Urban II, whom he helped greatly in reforming Church administration. As Chancellor of the Church from 1089 to 1118, Caetani installed a permanent staff of clerks to replace outsourced lawyers for writing up papal documents. The tradition of always appointing a cardinal as Chancellor and holding the post until death or elevation to the papacy began with him. Caetani was rapidly and unanimously elected to succeed Paschal II, taking the name **Pope Gelasius II** (1118-1119), but he only lived for a further twelve months. It proved a turbulent year in office with more fighting, attempts at installing anti-popes and expulsion over Henry V's persistent quest for investiture rights, so Gelasius ended his days in Cluny. His main achievements for the Church had been made as Chancellor.

When Gelasius II died, the ensuing conclave of cardinals was called at Cluny because Henry V's forces still occupied Rome and were looking to install another anti-pope there. In February 1119, the nine cardinals present elected Guy of Burgundy to the papacy. Born of an elite aristocratic family, with relatives in the royal families of France, England, Germany and Denmark, he was Archbishop of Vienne and a known supporter of the pope's position in the investiture conflict.

Guy of Burgundy took the title **Pope Callixtus II** (1119-24) and immediately sought direct negotiations with Emperor Henry V, sending a legate to Strasbourg. They agreed withdrawal of the proposed antipope from Rome and a face-to-face meeting between Callixtus II and Henry V in the autumn at Chateau de Mousson, near Rheims. When Callixtus II arrived in Rheims, word came that Henry had arrived at the Chateau with a force of 30,000 men, so he prudently stayed in Rheims and conducted papal business from there while negotiating with Henry by proxy and notes. Henry V would not compromise on the investiture issue, so at the end of October, Henry and his anti-pope, Gregory VIII were excommunicated.

Callixtus II returned to Italy, intending to make for Rome, but imperial forces and their local allies guarded Gregory VIII and Rome. Callixtus engaged the help of Normans and prevailed with underlying popular support. The antipope was captured and Callixtus II was installed as pope.

One of Callixtus II's early moves was to declare in 1120 that Jews should be free to enjoy their lawful liberty, echoing the policy of Pope Gregory I. He expressed regret at the killing of thousands during the First Crusade. As a corollary to this declaration, Christians were prohibited from harming or taking property from Jews, interfering with their festivals or cemeteries, or forcing them to convert to Christianity, all under pain of excommunication. Reiteration of his bull would prove necessary by many popes over the following three centuries.

Callixtus II was by now well established in Rome and still anxious to resolve conflict with Henry V who sensed the danger of his own obduracy splitting the empire. Callixtus sent three cardinals to Germany in 1121 seeking final settlement regarding the investiture. Negotiations began in Wurzburg where agreement was reached to proclaim a general truce between the emperor and subjects who had rebelled against him. The emperor agreed to allow the Church free use of its own possessions, to restore the confiscated lands of those in rebellion and to reach a peace agreement with the Church as soon as possible.

A synod was called at Worms in September 1122 where Callixtus was represented by Cardinal Lambert of Ostia who helped formulate the agreement known as the Concordat of Worms. Henry V conceded his claim to the investiture of the pope and freedom of election of all bishops. The Church allowed imperial oversight of elections and right to the investiture of bishops and abbots in Germany but their election would be by canons of the cathedral or monks respectively. Also, to avoid impropriety or suspicion, any imperial donation of properties to dioceses involved should take place in Germany prior to a new bishop's consecration and the habitual levy on such appointments by the Emperor would not be allowed. In Burgundy and Italy, imperial investiture would come after the consecration ceremony, while in the Papal States, the pope had sole right of episcopal investiture without interference from the emperor. Thus Henry V saved face by retaining influence at least in the case of German bishops, but had only ceremonial involvement in Burgundy and Italy and none in the Papal States.

The First Lateran Council was convened in March 1123 to ratify the concordat, clarify the jurisdiction of bishops over clergy and reaffirm past decrees against simony, clerical concubinage, people violating the Truce of God, forgers of ecclesiastical documents and church robbers. The council was well attended, by almost 300 bishops and 600 abbots from all over Europe.

Callixtus II died near the end of 1124, having succeeded where predecessors had failed in cementing the authority of the Church in appointing its officers and ending lay appointment of clerics. The bishops wielded political influence and often great wealth, especially in Germany, so he could be satisfied he had treated Henry V fairly by yielding him the privilege of investing some new bishops. His aim had been to ensure the Church authority in the world matched its spiritual responsibility as far as possible.

Despite Callixtus' successes regarding investiture, the election of his successor was not trouble-free. Cardinals elected an Italian who adopted the name Celestine II. But the power and unity of the Frangipani and Leoni families in Rome were at a peak and they proposed Lamberto Scannabecchi, cardinal of Ostia. He was a man of humble birth but deep faith and high intellect who had connections with the Frangipanis.

Although this arose after the election of Celestine, it was of such strength and backing that the cardinals reassembled to consider the challenge and accepted the new candidate. In a new ballot they elected Scannabecchi, who took the name **Pope Honorius II** (1124-29) and was confirmed pope following a dignified withdrawal by Celestine late December 1124.

When Emperor Henry V died mid-1125, Pope Honorius II lost no time in dispatching legates to Germany to join Archbishop Adalbert of Mainz in a mission to protect the Church's position as agreed in the Concordat of Worms. The election of Lothair II to succeed Henry V was welcomed as he recognised the supremacy of the pope even in temporal matters. He requested formal papal approval of his elevation, a precedent which the pope was happy to grant. Conrad of Hohenstaufen challenged Lothair's position, supported by Archbishop Anselm of Milan but he failed and was excommunicated along with his supporters.

Honorius had to intervene in the monasteries of Cluny and Montecassino when excommunicated abbots at both establishments defended their tenure using armed supporters. He removed the Abbots and installed trusted replacements to restore monastic discipline. Honorius II retained a suspicion of Benedictine abbeys as a result and always favoured the more recent orders such as the Cistercians and Augustinians.

Britain and Denmark

Henry I, King of England, habitually interfered with the Church in England and had long resisted visits from papal legates, claiming that the Archbishop of Canterbury, over whom he felt he could exercise local control, already held that role. So, when Honorious II sent Cardinal John of Crema to England as legate, Henry I ordered him to be detained in Normandy. When he was eventually given permission to enter England, the cardinal first visited King David of Scotland to understand the latter's dispute with the Archbishop of York, who claimed that Scotland should fall within his jurisdiction.

Cardinal John called a synod at Westminster to enforce the celibacy of clergy and declare against simony. William, Archbishop of Canterbury, accompanied the cardinal back to Rome with instructions from King Henry I to secure his rights as legate to England and ensure the pope would send no others. He was successful in the first, but not the second. Meanwhile, the King of Denmark asked Honorius II to send a legate there to call a halt to clerical abuses in Denmark.

Knights Templar, Early Bankers, Saladin, Knights Hospitaliers

Following the successful but bloody capture of Jerusalem by the First Crusade in 1099, most of the crusaders had returned home, leaving some to lead a partly local defence force. The flow of pilgrims grew quickly over following years and soon ran the risk of attack and robbery by all sorts of bandits both on their way and within the Holy Land. This led to the creation of the Knights Templar, a religious order of warrior monks with rule, hierarchy and a code of ethics geared to growth. The order was founded about 1118 by Hugh of Payens, a noble knight from the Champagne region with eight knighted relatives who took their oath to protect the pilgrims by 'holy war' in the presence of the Patriarch of Jerusalem.

King Baldwin II of Jerusalem, had given the Templars permission to set up their headquarters on the Temple Mount, believed to be on the site of Solomon's Temple. Their initial title 'Poor Soldiers of Christ and the Temple of Solomon', became shortened to 'Knights Templar'. There was naturally concern in the Church at the very idea of religious men carrying swords, but Bernard of Clairvaux a rising influential churchman and nephew of one of the knights wrote cogently in their favour. He pointed out that this mission was solely for defence of pilgrims and crucial to the Church which had long held to the theory of just war, which allows use of the sword to protect the innocent or the Church from violent attack. Honorius II gave papal approval to the military order of the Knights Templar in 1128.

At the Council of Troyes in 1128, which Bernard attended, the Knights Templar undertook to follow the strict Cistercian version of St Benedict's Rule, taking their white habit and adding a red cross. All aspiring members had to swear those vows of obedience, chastity, piety and poverty, surrendering to the cause all their material possessions, which in addition to wealth, lands and property included servants, livestock and business. The community soon amassed considerable wealth, supplemented by gifts and donations from as far as Portugal. In 1139, they were given a major boost by Pope Innocent II directing that Knights Templar were subject to no authority other than the pope and could pass through any border freely, without tax.

In addition to military-style protection, pilgrims were assisted by the monks who became early bankers, despite themselves being committed to personal poverty. Pilgrims to the Holy Land often carried large sums of cash to cover their food and shelter on the long journey, so they provided ripe pickings for bandits. The Templars set up offices in major centres in countries of origin and on the way where pilgrims could deposit their cash in return for receipts, effectively banker's drafts, by means of which they could draw cash as needed at offices on their way, thus limiting any losses to robbers. It is not certain how they validated the drafts and pilgrim identities, but there was probably a system of codes, demonstrating an ingenious and practical start to international banking and currency security and exchange in Europe.

The Knights Templar became formidable warriors, offering help to the kings of Jerusalem and elsewhere in repelling frequent attacks by Saladin and others. Saladin would eventually become the first sultan of Egypt and Syria (1174-93). He rose quickly through the ranks as a talented military leader of Kurdish descent and he introduced the Sunni Ayyubid dynasty to the region. He was a frequent thorn in the side of the Crusaders culminating in his decisive victory in 1187 at the Battle of Hattin, following which he gained control over much of Palestine, including the city of Jerusalem before his death in 1193.

Back in Italy, there was a dispute between Honorius II and Count Roger of Sicily over the will of Roger's cousin, William of Apulia, when the latter died. The Church believed William had bequeathed his lands to the See of Rome. Roger tried to sequester the lands and armed conflict ensued, but the matter ended with a compromise in 1128 by which Roger kept Apulia but renounced his claims to Benevento and Capua.

In the previous century, around the time of the monastic reform movement, a group of hospital workers in Jerusalem dedicated themselves to St John during the 11th century with the aim to provide care for sick or injured pilgrims to the Holy Land. Following the conquest of Jerusalem by the First Crusade, they became a military religious order as Jerusalem still needed to be defended from future possible attacks. Paschal II had issued a Papal Bull in 1113 confirming the Hospital of St John of Jerusalem as a religious order under papal protection, which included their property and donations. They became known as the Knights Hospitalier then later the Sovereign Military Order of Malta as they are known today.

Papal Election Chaos

The death of Honorius in 1130 led to further election chaos, with the election of two rivals – Innocent II and Anacletus II. Prior to the death of Honorius II, his chancellor, Haimeric who aligned with the Frangipani family, proposed Cardinal Gregory Papareschi of the Guidoni family as candidate and he was quickly elected by a gathering of eight cardinals in accordance with the rules laid down by Pope Nicholas II. He was consecrated as **Pope Innocent II** (1130-43) the day following Honorius II's death.

The cardinals who had not been included in this election process protested and on the same day elected another candidate, Cardinal Pietro Pierlone from an equally powerful Roman family, which held no love for the Frangipani. Innocent II's election was declared invalid by this faction and Pierlone was consecrated as **Pope Anacletus II** on a wave of popular support powerful enough to oblige Innocent II to escape from Rome. He sailed to France where he found strong allies among senior clergy, who introduced him to the king. Innocent would spend most of the following two years in France, during which he went on to gain the support of Emperor Lothair III and the German bishops. His election was ratified at an 1131 synod in Wurtzburg, at which the royal family declared their allegiance. Innocent II crowned Emperor Lothair III and Queen Richenza in Liége cathedral soon afterwards then attended a great synod in Rheims where he crowned the young prince who would become Louis VII of France. He also met King Henry I of England.

By the end of 1131, Innocent II had won support from central and northern France, Germany, England, Portugal, Castile and Aragon. In contrast southern France and most of Italy and Sicily as well as the Patriarchs of Constantinople, Antioch and Jerusalem gave their backing to Anacletus II. In 1132, Lothair III raised a force that travelled to Italy with the dual aim of dislodging anti-pope Anacletus and enabling Innocent to crown him Emperor in Rome. When they arrived, Anacletus II and Rome were too well defended, so the first objective could not be achieved, but Lothair's coronation by Innocent was held in the Lateran Basilica, outside the walls of Rome in 1133. A later attempt to take Rome also failed, but death overtook Anacletus II at the beginning of 1138, whereupon Innocent took his seat in St Peters.

In April 1139 a second Lateran Council, which the Roman Catholic Church regards as the Tenth Ecumenical Council was held. It was a huge international Council with over a thousand bishops, abbots and other prelates present. The papal election rules were changed to prevent a repeat of the 1130 anomaly and all rulings of Anacletus II quashed together with most of the ordinations he had carried out. This Council also excommunicated Roger of Sicily, who had consistently opposed Innocent. Malachy, Bishop of Armagh was received by Innocent He wished to join the Cistercian community of Bernard of Clairvaux, but Innocent would not accept his resignation as bishop and appointed him papal legate for Ireland.

Innocent II is remembered as a dedicated pope who upheld the standards of Christianity. He died in September 1143 and was followed by a pupil of Peter Abelard, **Pope Celestine II**, whose election was straightforward. Celestine II only lived for five and a half months to be followed by **Pope Lucius II**, another brief reign of just 11 months. These brief tenures allowed considerable unrest to grow in Rome and Roger of Sicily became increasingly aggressive in his ambitions to take more of Southern Italy whilst efforts at rapprochement with the Eastern Church had to be deferred. In 1145 **Pope Eugene III** arrived, who was elected as the first Cistercian pope and held the post for over eight years.

Peter Abelard and Héloise

Born in the family castle at Le Pallet, near Nantes, son of the local lord and destined for a military future, Peter Abelard (1079-1142) chose instead to study dialectic, a branch of philosophy, which led him to travel around France as a peripatetic student and debater. Around 1100 AD, he joined the Paris Cathedral School of Notre Dame to learn dialectic then rhetoric, studying under William, a disciple of Anselm of Laon. He moved on to Laon in 1113 to study theology (biblical exegesis and Christian doctrine) under Anselm. He became widely renowned as a teacher in Paris, being appointed master of Notre Dame and a canon at the metropolitan cathedral of Sens, which also covered Paris. His looks, manner, sonorous voice, argument and rhetoric were all assets, but he was abrasive and vain, claiming to be the only true philosopher alive. Such pride precedes a fall and his whirlwind love affair with Héloise d'Argenteuil soon initiated that.

Héloise was the niece of a fellow-canon, Fulbert, under whose care she stayed at Notre Dame as a teacher of languages and literature in Latin, Greek and Hebrew. Fulbert discovered the affair with Peter and forbade it, only driving it into secrecy. When Héloise fell pregnant, she fled to the care of Peter's parents in their castle in Le Pallet. There she gave birth to their son Astrolabe before joining a convent near Argenteuil. Peter held an olive branch out to the furious Fulbert by offering to marry Héloise in secret and although she was initially reluctant, they were married. Fulbert decided to damage Peter's career progress by publicly announcing the marriage, which Héloise equally publicly denied. Peter arranged for her to return to the convent in Argenteuil and though never taking the veil, she lived with nuns there in refuge from Fulbert, whose fury was such that it is thought he hired thugs to attack and castrate Peter.

After this attack Peter joined the Benedictines at the Abbey of St Denis in Paris, deeply affected and intending to spend the rest of his life in such confinement. But his arrogance led him to offend fellow-monks with his doubts regarding their founder, St Denis. The enraged Abbot Adam sent him to a branch priory where he responded to popular demand and began teaching philosophy and theology once more.

Peter soon attracted unfavourable notice again for proclaiming his particular theory of the Holy Trinity that many saw as Monarchianism or Sabellianism, which had been declared heretical in the third century. He seemed to view the Father as having created the Son and Holy Spirit. Having accumulated so many adversaries as a student, many of whom now held positions of authority, Peter was summoned before a Council at Soissons in 1121 at which a papal legate presided. He was instructed to burn his book on the Trinity and to recite frequently the Athanasian Creed, focusing on the Trinity and Christology. He was also to be detained in the Abbey of St Médard. But Peter was soon released and he accepted the invitation of Abbot Suger, who had been appointed at St Denis following Adam's death, to return as a monk.

Peter grew restless and went to a wilderness in the Champagne area to live as a hermit in a reed hut, but eager students flocked there as his location became known. It led to the restoration of his reputation as a teacher and the construction of the Oratory of the Paraclete on the site of his frustrated solitude.

Around 1126-7, Peter Abelard was invited to become Abbot of St Gildas of Rhuys, near Vannes on the Southern Brittany coast. At the time this was a wild, lawless and inhospitable place and he found the community itself little less daunting. In a neat twist of fate, Héloise's community at Argenteuil was disbanded as Abbot Suger wished to take the buildings for expansion of St Denis. Héloise gladly joined then became Abbess of the Oratory of the Paraclete. Peter collaborated with her and established a rule. He composed hymns and they worked together in writing a compendium of their love letters and religious correspondence with each other.

Peter remained as abbot at St Gildas, but his disciplinary ambition was too challenging and over time his monks rebelled and he left the monastery, moving close to his place of birth. Around 1136 he returned to Paris and resumed a teaching career, his pupils including Arnold of Brescia and John of Salisbury.

Bernard of Clervaux, such an influential member of the Church of the time, regarded Peter with deep suspicion, believing some of his teachings, especially regarding the Trinity to be heterodox. Bernard's concern was magnified as Peter's reputation grew, so he warned Peter privately. When this had no effect, he asked the French bishops to intervene. Peter was so confident in his abilities in debate that he requested a council before which he and Bernard could argue their cases. This was called at Sens in 1141. Bernard met the bishops the evening before the council was due to start and shared some of the writings of Peter that he felt were verging on the heretical and gained their agreement with his own view.

Peter Abelard got wind of the evening meeting and when the council assembled to condemn him, he claimed appeal to Rome. He was given leave to do so and Bernard wrote to members of the Curia along the lines he had presented to the bishops. As Peter journeyed to Rome, on reaching Cluny, he learned that Pope Innocent II had confirmed the Council of Sens condemnation of him in July 1141. The papal bull excommunicated him and demanded his silence on theological matters. The Venerable Peter, Abbot of Cluny pleaded with the pope on Peter Abelard's behalf and won mitigation, then persuaded Bernard to let the matter lie. Peter was offered ongoing hospitality at Cluny as a respected guest, where he spent many of his remaining months of life, before moving to the priory of St Marcel near Chalon-sur-Saône in 1142, where he died. His body was buried at the Oratory of the Paraclete near that of his ever-beloved Héloise.

Arnold of Brescia

One student and follower of Peter Abelard who gained notoriety was Arnold of Brescia (1090-1155), who opposed the wealth, land ownership and possessions of the Roman Catholic Church. He became an

Augustinian canon then prior of a monastery in Brescia, which was the subject of dispute between local government and the diocese over the ownership of some land. He had been brought up as a disciplinarian and witnessed the great wealth and lax ways of some monasteries and secular clergy. He maintained the Church should be above such worldly ambition and proposed drastic measures to strip all monasteries, sees, their prelates and indulgent clergy of their riches, which should be distributed to the needy faithful. Arnold made public his views, which attracted supporters to him, but he made the mistake of being especially critical of the Curia, leading them to persuade Innocent II to condemn Arnold and order his silence and exile.

So loud were Arnold's protestations at this that he was exiled from Italy at the Second Lateran Council in 1139. He went to Paris and joined Peter Abelard's criticism of Bernard of Clervaux, the darling of the Church. Following Bernard's win at the synod in Sens and Peter Abelard's excommunication and silencing on theological matters, Arnold continued to speak out. Pope Innocent II demanded his silence also and since he could not accept such a penalty and Bernard continued to have him hunted down, Arnold moved to Bavaria and Switzerland, continuing to speak and write promoting apostolic poverty. He eventually ended up in Bohemia where he befriended a papal legate called Guy in 1143. Through Guy, Arnold arranged an audience with the new pope Eugene III in 1145 at Viterbo. Although he made his peace with Eugene III and went to Rome, he was encouraged by the rise of the Roman citizens against Eugene and so again spoke out, even stating that any member of clergy owning possessions should be denied the right to confer sacraments. Arnold was part of the conspiracy to drive Eugene III from Rome in 1146, for which he was later excommunicated. When Adrian subsequently restored the papacy to Rome, he exiled Arnold, who was seized by Imperial forces and executed. Arnold's writings were ordered to be burned, but a group of his followers remained faithful to his beliefs and grew into the next century, becoming known as the 'Arnoldists'. They were condemned by the Church as heretical.

Gratian's Decretals, Early Canon Law

During this century, an expert researcher in jurisprudence called Gratian studied and collected as many pronouncements and declarations as he could find from records since the early times of the Church. As well as canons from synods and councils, he referenced the Bible, other writings of Church historians and commentators, Roman Law, papal bulls and decretals. Gratian wished to distil them into a systematic legal textbook for the Church to the date of its publication, probably during the 1140s. Originally known as Decretum Gratiani, it was added to over time and proved an important base for Canon Law. This was used until it was completely revised and updated in 1918 for Pope Benedict XV.

Bernado Pignatelli had entered the Cistercian order at Clervaux influenced by Bernard of Clervaux. In 1140, Pope Innocent II appointed him Abbot of the monastery *Santa Anastaio alle Tre Fontane*, built on the site where St Paul was martyred outside Rome. Bernado was still abbot there when Pope Lucius II died. In view of civil unrest in Rome, the cardinals planned to gather immediately in a monastery some way out of Rome to elect a new pope. Their haste was aimed at pre-empting the Roman Senate, which they were sure would seek to have someone appointed who would swear allegiance to the Senate. The conclave swiftly elected Abbot Bernado as **Pope Eugene III** (1145-1153). He was enthroned in St John Lateran then consecrated as bishop at Farfa, another remote monastery about 25 miles from Rome before settling for the while in Viterbo, a proven reliable and hospitable refuge for popes. Expressions of support and homage flowed from many Western European countries.

Eugene III's old teacher, Bernard of Clairvaux, who had been an influential mentor to several recent popes, was not sure Eugene had the steel to perform his duties in Rome's political turmoil, then on the brink of anarchy. But Bernard was pleased and offered his support in a rather patronising letter, notable for the comment "Who will grant me to witness before I die, The Church of God as in past times, when the apostles put out their nets for a catch, not of silver and gold, but of souls?" No doubt regarding Eugene III as much his disciple as pope, Bernard then wrote a guide for popes, '*De Consideratione*'. In reality, Bernard became the power behind the papal throne, exerting a strong influence on policy.

Arnold of Brescia came expressing deep penitence and Eugene III believed he was sincere, so absolved him subject to him avoiding repetition of his sins, making a pilgrimage to the shrines of the Apostles and fasting. When he went to Rome on the first part of the pilgrimage, Arnold encountered an atmosphere of rebellion as the Senate and the people sought ascendancy over the temporal power of the Church. He could not resist joining in and he gained a leading role. As the violence grew, cardinals' palaces and Church property were robbed and destroyed, as were mansions of some noble supporters of the pope. Anarchy reigned in the city under Arnold's new 'democracy'. As so often happens in such 'revolutions', the mob were blindly destroying their very livelihoods and future prospects. Eventually many powerful Roman families and their supporters united and persuaded the people that Rome was not viable without the papacy. This resulted in talks and a weak treaty between the senate and Eugene, by which the senate would be maintained, but would be subject to the pope. Eugene III entered Rome to loud but fickle acclaim in December 1145 but the treaty soon proved unworkable. As public disorder grew anew, Eugene moved to the safety of Castel San' Angelo then left and headed north to France early 1146. He could not address the wider needs of the Church while Rome persisted in self-destruction whatever steps he took.

These wider needs included the serious Islamic threats to Christian interests, particularly those established by the crusaders in Palestine and Syria. The crusaders' merciless aggression had lowered the level of tolerance of Christians in the Islamic controlled parts, some assuming licence to Islamic forces to muster against Christian areas. The region of Edessa had already fallen in 1144 and Eugene III had expressed to Bernard of Clairvaux the need for a Second Crusade while they were in Viterbo. Bernard had acted on this and his pleas had led to an impressive gathering of two armies led by the kings Louis VII of France and Conrad III of Germany. These armies made the mistake of travelling separately in 1148 and were each picked off by Seljuk Turks on their way. The kings and the depleted forces reached Jerusalem, but failed again in an attack on Damascus. The Muslim armies had decisively won this round. A further separate crusader force from North Sea coastal countries and Britain travelling to the Holy Land by sea, were persuaded by Portugal to liberate Lisbon from the occupying Moors. They laid siege to the city and took it in October 1147. Some of the crusaders settled there or went on to Spain, leaving a reduced force to continue to the Holy Land to support the other parties there. The only lasting achievements of this fragmented crusade were the victories in the Iberian Peninsula.

Eugene III was a pious and humble man and accustomed to hard work, which he applied in France in propagating the Faith, continuing the campaign for discipline and challenging cleric's over-indulgence in dress, comfort, food and immorality. To this end he organised synods in Paris, Trier and the best known in Rheims in 1148, which threw the responsibility for enforcement onto bishops under threat of suspension. To underline his intent, he dismissed the Archbishops of York, Metz and Rheims, which surprised many and shook them out of their complacency, for Eugene was reputed for his gentleness. His time in France was well-spent and enhanced public regard for him and the Church.

Cardinal Pullen and Oxford University

In teaching and theology, Eugene III encouraged notable scholars with the help of his English chancellor, Cardinal Henry Pullen, a philosopher who played a major role in establishing Oxford University, becoming skilled in the organisation and administration of centres of learning. Peter Lombard was one such scholar, who sowed the seed of a new intellectual movement at Notre Dame Cathedral School in Paris.

Henry Pullen had refused Henry I of England's offer of a bishopric in favour of pursuing philosophy in which he became an early master. He was Archdeacon of Rochester in 1134 then took leave from that position to teach in Paris for some years, where he encountered Peter Abelard and vehemently opposed details of his theology. Pullen came to the notice of Bernard of Clervaux, who wrote to the Bishop of Rochester apologising for keeping him in Paris so long but requesting more of his time there so that he could explore further his doctrine. Pullen stayed in Paris, though still nominally archdeacon at least until 1143-4, when he was invited to Rome by the pope and made cardinal. Pope Lucius II appointed him Chancellor and when Bernard's protégé Eugene III succeeded to the papacy in 1145, Bernard wrote to Pullen expressing the need of his support and counsel for the new pope.

Peter Lombard

From humble origins in Italy, Peter Lombard (1100-1160) showed impressive intellect and under the patronage of Bishop Odo of Lucca, he studied at Bologna University. Bernard of Clervaux then underwrote his further studies at Rheims and Lombard went on to Paris, where he met and attended lectures by Peter Abelard around 1136. His own reputation as a theologian grew and he was invited to join the elite canons of Notre Dame on merit alone, becoming professor there about 1144 and publishing the first of his eventual quartet of 'Book of Sentences' which became important theological references.

Lombard became a sub-deacon in 1147 and met Pope Eugene III the following year at the Council of Rheims. He rose fast through junior clerical ranks, was conferred with a prebendary in 1152 and ordained priest about 1155. He was respected for his self-discipline and theology and around 1158 was consecrated Archbishop of Paris, but he died a couple of years later. His successor, Maurice de Sully oversaw the building of the great cathedral of Notre Dame.

Eugene III returned to Rome in 1149 after imaginatively inviting King Conrad III to have a fortified residence in Rome and provide protection for the papacy. Eugene died in July 1153, to be succeeded by **Pope Anastasius IV**, who had been vicar of Rome and a strong opponent of Antipope Anacletus while Innocent II was in France. He was Dean of the College of Cardinals when Innocent II died. Anastasius IV's pontificate of just over a year was too brief to make much impact.

English Pope Adrian IV

Nicholas Brakspeare was born in the English parish of Abbots Langley about 1100 AD. He was possibly educated at the Abbey School, St Albans, where his relatively poor father became a monk. Nicholas went to Arles and then joined St Rufus monastery near Avignon where he was appointed Abbot around 1145. On a visit to Rome, he was noticed by Pope Eugenius III and made bishop of Albano. He stayed in Trondheim from 1152 after setting up an archdiocese of Norway as papal legate. Helped by another English priest, Henry, whose surname is not known, but who is believed to have become bishop of Finland, they established cathedral schools, which remained famous in Scandinavia beyond the Reformation. In 1154, Nicholas became a cardinal then was elected as **Pope Adrian IV** (1154-59), the only Briton ever to become pope.

Welcomed back to Rome as 'the Apostle of the North', Adrian IV's immediate priority on consecration as successor to Anastasius IV was to confront Arnold of Brescia, who was hostile to the papacy and stirring turbulence in Rome. Outside Rome there was opposition from King William of Sicily and his friend Roman Emperor Frederick Barbarossa. In addition the barons in southern Italy were feuding between themselves and against the pope, raiding and robbing isolated hamlets, homes and travellers, as well as pilgrims heading for Rome, whose stays were a valuable part of the Roman economy.

When unrest in Rome resulted in the death of Cardinal Gerardus during Lent 1155, Adrian IV withdrew to that reliable haven, Viterbo. He placed Rome under a firm interdict, an unprecedented ecclesiastical step. The Church previously just banned specified people and groups from participating in Church services but in this case it rendered invalid the rites and services of a swathe of churches in Rome pending resolution of the unrest. The financial and material effect on Rome was to reduce greatly the number of pilgrims arriving for Easter seasonal services, which heavily impacted the economy, leading the Senate to banish Arnold, the rabble-rouser, who was eventually executed.

Later in 1155, Emperor Frederick came to Rome to be crowned by Pope Adrian IV as Holy Roman Emperor. There was an uprising of the citizens of Rome, which was held back on the day of the coronation by the Imperial Guard. Frederick then travelled back north, leaving Adrian IV and his supporters to fend for themselves against the hostile Romans and Normans. The Byzantine Emperor's forces soon invaded southern Italy, defeating the Normans, which Adrian did not regard as a problem as he soon negotiated an alliance with Byzantine Emperor Manuel, who was keen for a re-integrated Roman Empire. Adrian IV seized the opportunity to make it clear that re-integration could only happen if the Great Schism between Eastern and Roman Churches was repaired. Negotiations on this soon began.

Sadly, that ray of hope was soon extinguished, first by a major victory for the Normans over the Greeks under the new King William of Sicily at the battle of Brindisi. Then the Eastern Church negotiators absolutely refused to accept Adrian's precondition that any agreement would have to include recognition of the pope in Rome as supreme authority of the Church. The talks failed, as did Manuel's invasion.

Adrian IV moved to Benevento. With the help of his chancellor, Cardinal Roland, he negotiated with King William, agreeing that the Normans keep the territories they had conquered, which comprised most of southern Italy. William agreed to pay an annual tribute to the pope and to protect him and his possessions from aggressors.

During his stay at Benevento, John of Salisbury visited Adrian in 1156 for several months and asked him to gift Ireland to King Henry II of England, to which Adrian agreed. According to Constantine I, all such islands of 'ancient right' belonged to the Roman Church, so it was regarded as theirs to give. The gift was sealed with a gold ring set with finest emeralds for Henry II's investiture as governor of Ireland.

Adrian IV subsequently moved back to Viterbo and soon negotiated with the Romans his return to Rome early 1157. Meanwhile, Frederick was furious at the loss of southern Italy from his empire and hostilities broke out between him and Adrian IV's supporters, including the Lombards. Conflict was ongoing when Adrian died in 1159.

John of Salisbury (1115-1180)

This intellectual prodigy born in Salisbury went to Paris aged about twenty to study Arts and Philosophy under top teachers, including Peter Abelard. After a spell at the school at Chartres, he returned to Paris to complete theology and history. John became accepted in top church and social circles as a distinguished scholar and writer, spending some years in Pope Eugene III's entourage in Rome before travelling with the pope to the Council of Rheims in 1148, where he was introduced by Bernard of Clairvaux to Theobald, Archbishop of Canterbury.

Returning to England, John became private secretary to Archbishop Theobald, in which role he visited Rome and the Holy See five times over the following eleven years, gaining good insight to the Vatican and its cabinet workings. He met King Henry II and his chancellor Thomas Becket, being much impressed by the latter. He fell out with Henry II in defence of the Church in 1159, in spite of his success over Ireland, and turned to writing. After another spat with Henry in 1163, he went back to Reims, joining an old friend Peter de la Celle who was by then abbot at the monastery of Saint Rémi. In 1162, Thomas Becket became Archbishop of Canterbury but he too incurred Henry's wrath and had to move abroad.

The dispute in both cases was about ecclesiastical independence. Henry held that Church clerics should be subject to civil law in the case of any malfeasance whereas Thomas and John supported the Church view that it alone was responsible for disciplining all members of clergy. John took up the cause of reconciling Henry and Thomas but it took until 1170 before Thomas and John could return to England. At the end of that year, John was a witness to Thomas' murder in Canterbury Cathedral. John moved to Exeter Cathedral for a while then in 1176 he became Bishop of Chartres. He died in 1180, a year after attending the third Lateran Council, which confirmed the requirement of priests to be celibate. John was one of the most accomplished philosophers and Latinists of his time and a copious writer.

Donation of Ireland

Henry II accepted his investiture as governor of Ireland, but the Irish found this unacceptable and in any case, Henry was in no position to enforce the matter at that stage. He was just twenty two years old, facing fractious barons in England, unrest in Wales and similar difficulties in his French dominions.

But Henry was forced to take early action by an internal dispute within Ireland when Dermot McMurrough, King of Leinster was unseated and appealed to him in 1169 for support. Henry arranged this through Richard de Clare, 2nd Earl of Pembroke, who gathered a force led by Norman knights, who were promised the prize of land. When they succeeded, Henry II became concerned that they may form an autonomous state, so when he was more settled as king he raised a large force in 1171 to assert his right and won the fealty of the Norman knights and the Irish kings and leaders with the backing of Pope Alexander III.

Pope Alexander III (1159-81) had succeeded Adrian IV in 1159. Born Roland of Siena to an aristocratic local family, he taught theology and became professor specialising in canon law at Bologna University. Roland was made cardinal by Pope Eugene III and led Church opposition to Emperor Frederick Barbarossa, which would eventually lead to a dispute during his election to succeed Adrian IV as pope. A majority of the cardinals voted for him, while a vocal minority of Frederick supporters chose Victor IV. Given the strength of imperial forces in Italy, Alexander

III was obliged to live outside Rome for many years of his papacy. Nevertheless, Alexander gradually built strong support from the monarchs of Hungary, France and England, adding to those of Spain and Portugal who had been on side since his election. But it still took a defeat in battle for Frederick to agree to recognise Alexander III as late as 1177.

Alexander III was known for paying unprecedented attention to missionary work in the Baltic States and Scandinavia, particularly strengthening the Church in Finland and Estonia. He also canonised two English Saints – Edward the Confessor and Thomas Becket. Alexander had been close to Thomas Becket and wanted penitence for his murder from Henry II, one of the most powerful of the Western monarchs. He castigated Henry for this in 1170 and combined steely determination with his powers of diplomacy to obtain Henry's agreement to everything that Thomas had died in seeking. But Alexander still showed magnanimity and confirmed Henry as Lord of Ireland two years later. His firm political stances and negotiations did not prevent him from attending closely to social and spiritual matters.

Alexander III called the Third Lateran Council in 1179, regarded by the Roman Catholic Church as the 11th ecumenical council. Attended by over 300 bishops, many abbots and learned people, its canons involved a number of improvements to Church affairs including the exclusive right for a two-thirds majority of cardinals to determine the election of future popes, which still applies. Soon after this, republicans forced Alexander III to depart Rome once more. He would never return. One of his last acts was to excommunicate King William I of Scotland and impose an interdict on his kingdom over William's appointment of the Bishop of St Andrews over Rome's objection to it. Alexander died in 1181 and has received acclaim for his qualities down through history, including from Voltaire, who felt he did not receive sufficient recognition in his own time for abolishing slavery; overcoming the dominant violence of Frederick Barbarossa; demanding Henry II's admission and request for pardon for the murder of Thomas Becket as Archbishop of Canterbury; also restoring rights to people and splendour to many cities.

Massacre of the Latins

Born around 1100 in Lucca of a distinguished local family, Ubaldo Allucingoli became cardinal deacon in 1138 then Dean of the College of Cardinals under his predecessor Alexander III. **Pope Lucius III (1181-85)** resided in Rome on his election in November 1181, but by the following March republican disturbances forced him to leave, just as they had Alexander III. Lucius III also resisted pressure from Emperor Frederick to withdraw the Church's claims to an inheritance of substantial lands in Tuscany. This led to political conflict.

1182 was notable for the 'Massacre of the Latins', a campaign of slaughter of Roman Catholics in Constantinople by resident Eastern Orthodox Christians. This had its origins in the predominance of the fleets from the Italian port city states of Venice, Genoa, Pisa and Amalfi, which had been given concessions in Constantinople for the powerful Italian merchants, who had set up branches there earlier in the century. Unable to compete and losing market share, local merchants suffered. Their growing resentment was aggravated by sectarian distrust between the Orthodox and Roman Catholics, each suspicious of the others' beliefs, all adding up to serious tension that only needed a trigger for violence to break out.

This came when Andronikos I ousted the regent, Maria of Antioch, mother of the young emperor, in 1182 to public acclaim. Celebrations deteriorated into an alcohol- and hatred-fuelled Christian upon Christian massacre. Aware of looming trouble, many of the merchants had ships at the ready for a quick departure, forfeiting their possessions in Constantinople, which were in any case looted. Tens of thousands of innocent resident Latins who remained were slaughtered, including women, children, the elderly and the hospitalised. This led to a popular western view of the Byzantines as barbarians, although trade and diplomatic links were soon pragmatically re-established. The incident laid the ground for a further disaster.

Hostility hardened, so in 1185, William II of Sicily led a seaborne attack to sack Thessalonica, the second city of the Byzantine Empire. There were continuing threats from German kings, first Frederick, then Henry VI against Constantinople and then in 1204, the Fourth Crusade would actually sack the great city, destroying any remaining chance of healing the schism between Eastern and Western Christianity. Thus a high price was paid for the earlier failures of the respective Church hierarchies to find a Christian accommodation, leaving the dispute to descend into this tribal-style conflict, so far from the apostolic vision.

Heresies in South West Europe

For a few decades there had been some distortions of the Faith arising in northern Italy, southern France, and Spain which were regarded by the pontiff as heretical and the Emperor joined Pope Lucius III in condemning these. Both leaders threatened serious sanctions including excommunication and interdiction for any community, nobles or officers failing to suppress the heresies.

The heresies were debated at a council in Verona in 1184 (also notable for raising matrimony to sacramental status), which anathematised groups such as Cathars, Waldensians, Paterines and Arnoldists, together with any who supported them. The seeds of Inquisition were thus sown, though action was initiated only at diocesan level. This may have been due to growing points of dispute between Pope Lucius and Emperor Frederick, such as disagreement over control of bishops' appointment in Germany and refusal to crown Henry of Hohenstaufen as designated successor to the Imperial throne. Some bishops acted to denounce or punish leading heretics and this phase became known as the Bishops' Inquisition.

Rome considered two groups, the Cathars and Waldensians, particularly heretical and subjected them to heavy suppression, which was only the beginning of their stories, which developed in the next century.

In the 1140s, the Cathars in southern France believed that everything spiritual was made by God and everything worldly by the devil; they believed in reincarnation and that heaven could only be gained by self-denial. This had echoes of Gnosticism and certainly did not suit the overtly indulgent clergy of the day.

The Waldensians were founded by Peter Waldo in Lyons in 1173 as the Poor Men of Lyons. He was a wealthy merchant and gave away all his property, practicing what he preached – that poverty like that of the apostles was the way to perfection.

Fall of Jerusalem, New Popes and Challenges

While so much was happening in Western Europe, King Baldwin of Jerusalem appealed for help in holding back the tide of Islam and preparations had begun for the Third Crusade when Pope Lucius III died in 1185.

Pope Urban III (1185-87), successor to Lucius III, was pope for just under two years and never resided in Rome. A Milanese graduate of Bologna university, Uberto Crivelli was Cardinal Archbishop in Milan when elected pope. He unusually retained that Archbishopric after his election and continued the struggles with Emperor Frederick I Barbarossa and then his son, Henry. It was a personal matter as Frederick had earlier sacked Milan, affecting some of Urban's friends and relatives. Urban III also refused to anoint Henry as successor designate to Frederick. When Henry married Constance, the daughter of the king of Sicily who would inherit that kingdom, Urban was caught in between Frederick in the north and Henry in the south. Moreover, the marriage nullified the hard-earned support of the Normans, which included their protection of the Papal States. Urban III lived in Verona, whose burgers restrained him from excommunicating Frederick I, fearing inevitable reprisals, so he moved to Ferrara, but died there in 1187 before he could carry out the threat. News had probably reached him of the rout of the crusaders by Saladin at the battle of Hattin, but news of the fall of Jerusalem in October, the month of his death probably had not.

Urban III's was succeeded by **Pope Gregory VIII** (Oct-Dec1187), who achieved plenty in his brief reign of just 57 days. As legate of Pope Alexander III, he had brought an offer of reconciliation to Emperor Frederick in 1163 and when he was later appointed Chancellor of the Holy Roman Church in 1178, he pursued a conciliatory role again, so he and Frederick were on amicable terms from the time of his election. On hearing the news of the fall of the kingdom of Jerusalem to Islam, Gregory VIII set in motion another Crusade, asking the faithful to support with donations, prayers and fasting. To this end he went to Pisa with the aim of negotiating an end to hostilities between the rival ports of Pisa and Genoa to enable a joint fleet of both their navies to carry troops, supplies and equipment for the Crusade, but he was overcome by a fever and died in Pisa in December.

Roman born **Pope Clement III** (1187-91) followed, bringing the papacy back to the Lateran in Rome by agreeing a treaty early 1188 with the citizens' representatives allowing them to elect magistrates, while leaving the appointment of the governor in the hands of the pope. It seems surprising that such an apparently simple solution had taken so long, but Clement III was known as a man of peace and maybe it needed a Roman; it probably also needed a less contentious relationship with the Emperor and the Normans, which his predecessor had achieved.

Clement III strengthened the College of Cardinals, who numbered only twenty on his accession. He appointed a further thirty in his time. In 1188, he re-established relations with King William of Scotland by resolving the dispute over the appointment of the Bishop of St Andrews and by replacing their subjection to the Archbishop of York with direct control from Rome. Clement II also resolved a similarly contested right of election in the diocese of Trier in Germany.

In 1190, Holy Roman Emperor Frederick 1 died. His son Henry VI, who had married Constance the daughter of Norman King Roger II of Sicily, took the German throne and was made Holy Roman Emperor in 1191, ruling until his death in 1197. Early in this time he invaded Sicily to enforce Constance's claim to inheritance of the Kingdom of Sicily, which included the foot of mainland Italy (Apulia and Calabria) had been taken in 1189 by her nephew, Tancred, illegitimate son of her brother, Roger III. That invasion was cut short by an epidemic, but Henry VI repeated it successfully in 1194, funded by a ransom for the release of Richard I of England.

Third Crusade

Clement III had maintained peaceful relations with Emperor Frederick I before the emperor's death and in April 1189 he persuaded King Philip II of France and King Henry II of England to support actively the Third Crusade. Clement's legates helped the kings make peace with each other and they agreed to lead the crusade together. In the event Henry died that same year and his successor Richard I 'Lionheart' joined Philip II at the head of the Crusade. Frederick raised a German force intended to join the crusade and led it by a northern route through Anatolia, but he drowned in a river on the way in June 1190. His death led many of the Germans to return home, but Leopold, Duke of Austria, took his place and regathered the remnants. The crusade was partly successful in that it won back from Saladin the cities of Acre, Arsuf and Jaffa. After the fall of Acre, Richard I argued with Philip II and Leopold over who should be left in charge of the city and when Richard's choice prevailed, the other two leaders returned home in summer 1191, leaving most of their crusaders and delegate leaders. The remaining Crusaders then needed to take the city of Jaffa before any attempt could be made on Jerusalem. Clement III died in the Spring of 1191.

At Arsuf on the way to Jaffa in September 1191, Saladin's army attacked the Crusaders, but was heavily defeated. Victory raised the European morale and Jaffa was soon taken and became Richard's base, but the Crusaders never won back their main target Jerusalem. The low morale of the inhabitants should have facilitated victory, but an impatient winter assault was aborted by bad weather. Several months further delay arose as the English and French leaders, Richard I and the Duke of Burgundy argued over tactics. Saladin made a last attempt to regain Jaffa with temporary success, until a surprise seaborne attack by Richard I with two thousand troops sealed a victory which opened the way to negotiation.

Richard I reached an accord with Saladin in September 1192 whereby Jerusalem remained in Muslim hands but unarmed Christian pilgrims and merchants would be allowed free access. Neither side could be totally satisfied with this, which both regarded as unfinished business, but that third crusade had established safe enclaves along the Syrian coast and in Cyprus. Trade flourished in the area and the Crusader kingdom based on Acre grew to be wealthy, while Christianity was restored to the Levant.

Clement III was succeeded by another Roman pope from the noble Orsini family, **Pope Celestine III** (1191-98). He was 85 when elected, and no diplomat. Immediately on election, he completed an essential item of unfinished business that had been left since the death of Gregory VIII, in crowning Henry IV as Holy Roman Emperor after Henry agreed to the

Romans' demand that he hand over Tusculum to them. Celestine seems to have set aside diplomacy in favour of threats of excommunication to enforce his will over kings: first, Tancred of Sicily, to make him release Empress Constance, his aunt and Henry IV's wife; second, Henry IV of Germany, to achieve release from prison of English King Richard Lionheart who had been seized by the Duke of Austria on his way back from the Crusade and handed over to Henry; finally Alfonso IX of León who had planned to marry a close relative. He then sued for peace with the Muslims and attacked Castile. Celestine III also placed Pisa and León under interdict for defying his authority. He died aged 92, having wished to resign earlier but failed to secure the cardinals' agreement.

Celestine III's battles to have royals accept the position of the Church may have laid the ground for his far younger and more energetic successor, **Pope Innocent III** (1198-1216), to use his authority to take the Church into the 13th century on a more positive note than Paschal II had left it a century earlier.

Angelus, Purgatory and Praying for the Dead

In terms of religious belief and practice, it was around the 12th century that Angelus prayer became more widely and publicly practiced. Also, the theological concepts of purgatory and indulgences assumed wider recognition, study and use.

The Angelus midday call to prayer stemmed from the monastic practice of reciting three Hail Marys during the Compline bell, signalling the evening prayer, which was in use by the 11th century. Catholics now associate it more with the midday bell, calling for a pause for prayer, but in its complete form, it is repeated at Prime bell, the call to 6am morning prayer, noon and 6pm Compline bell. The Angelus prayer is a set form recalling the incarnation, when the Angel Gabriel announced the conception to Mary.

Benedictine Monks had developed a tradition of praying for the dead during the 6th century. They related this tradition to 2 Maccabees 12:46, "It is a holy and wholesome thought to pray for the dead that they may be loosed from their sins." This came later to spin around the idea of purgatory, although the term probably did not appear until the 12th century. The Benedictines thought that human bonds may traverse death. The concept is behind the celebration of All Soul's day, put aside for prayer that the dead may know the mercy of God. The date 2nd November for this was suggested by Odilo at his abbey in Cluny in 998 and adopted by Rome in the fourteenth century.

The word purgatory (Latin purgatorium) relates to a state or place for cleansing, purging a soul of unforgiven lesser sins of its earthly life prior to entry into paradise. The idea of contributing to a reduction of their time or experience in purgatory provided reason to pray for the souls of the dead. The concept is generally accepted by both Roman and Eastern Churches and some Jews already had an equivalent, as did some Buddhists, who make offerings for their dead. The doctrine was developed at a number of subsequent Ecumenical Councils – Lyon I (1245), Lyon II (1274), Florence (1438-45) and Trent (1545-63).

Indulgences

An indulgence in the Church sense is a remission of temporal sin awarded through the Church on behalf of God. In effect it means that via specified acts of self-denial or penances, one can reduce the debt to be repaid in purgatory either for oneself or on behalf of one who has died. It is clearly a Church-led process but claims New Testament backing from John 20:23, where Jesus delegated his apostles and their successors with powers on his behalf, saying to them before the crowd on Pentecost "whose sins you forgive, they are forgiven; whose sins you retain are retained."

Herein lay opportunity for some. Given the corruption that existed among some members of the Church hierarchy in spite of the efforts of many popes, it was not long before money or favours became involved in the 'granting' of indulgences. Such malpractice would reach a point at which it would discredit the belief in purgatory and the value of prayers for the dead to the extent that some Christians would perceive it just as a convenient source of benefit to the clergy, which devalued it as serious doctrine, whether valid or not.

England

Tension had existed for years between monarchs and the Church based on the relative power of each. It was certainly true in England in the appointment of the primate and senior bishops, as well as control over the clergy who held considerable sway over their congregations through the pulpit.

Henry II was no exception in his resistance to papal authority but in the 12th century a sequence of popes had pushed with some success for increased autonomy for the Church and more limited royal influence. There were cases where the Church protected errant clergy from the civil authorities, which raised reasonable suspicion of closed ranks. It was an ongoing conflict, as had been seen earlier by King Stephen (1135-64) exiling Archbishop Theobald of Canterbury. Theobald's successor Thomas

Becket was then murdered for Henry II. But Henry was also king of significant lands in North Western France and there were far fewer such tensions there, where the clergy seemed to be more accommodating towards the secular authorities. After the murder of Becket, Henry II had needed a boost to his image and he relaxed his drive towards monarchical control as he supported some monasteries and abbeys in England and also founded and endowed a number of monasteries in France. He also helped the Church build hospitals in England as well as in France. His successor, Richard 'Lionheart' I changed none of this, concentrating on crusades and France and spending only a few months on English soil, almost seeing this century out with Anglo-papal relations in good shape.

So the twelfth century had seen some emergence from the papacy's 'dark age' thanks to a few strong popes who pushed to improve clerical standards and regain senior Church appointment rights from secular leaders. Some resistance to the former persisted at senior clerical levels, with stronger resistance to the latter from monarchs, particularly in Germany and England. Closer to home, the pope also had to tread carefully to maintain Church relationships with the Roman senate and citizens. Advances made by the effective pontiffs were prejudiced by so many all-too-brief weak tenures of the post. Its many complexities continued to distract those in office from their primary goals of spreading the true word of Jesus Christ and holding his Church in unity. The Roman Church had become an unwieldy institution and difficult to manage.

CHAPTER 15

13th Century

Popes

1198-1216 Innocent III	1276 Jan-Jun Innocent V
1216-27 Honorius III	1276 Jul-Aug Adrian V
1227-41` Gregory IX	1276-77 John XXI
1241 16 days Celestine IV	1277-80 Nicholas III
1243-54 Innocent IV	1281-85 Martin IV
1254-61 Alexander IV	1285-87 Honorius IV
1261-64 Urban IV	1288-92 Nicholas IV
1265-68 Clement IV	1292-94 Interregnum
1268-71 Interregnum	1294 Jul-Dec Celestine V
1271-76 Gregory X	1294-1303 Boniface VIII

Emperors

1198-1215 Otto IV

1230-1250 Frederick II

An eventful century in prospect with a refreshed assertion of papal power and the emergence and brutal suppression of zealous groups which arose partly from dismay at clerical laxity in the Church, but had also developed some beliefs and practices that the Church regarded as heretical. An important Fourth Lateran Council was held during this period. A disastrous Fourth Crusade failed to free Jerusalem.

In terms of progress in the mission and unity with which Jesus Christ had charged the Church, the end of term report would not impress, not least for the infamous sacking of Constantinople by the 4th Crusade. Weakened Eastern Orthodox Churches pleaded in vain for help against Islamic pressure. Western Church preoccupation with worldly politics resulted in funds raised for crusades diverting elsewhere. Brief papal reigns, especially in the latter half of the century, and inter-family or Franco-Italian conflicts over their selection and location distracted the leadership from its true mission. Every time an initial East-West agreement seemed possible, it fell at the final hurdle of Roman insistence on absolute papal primacy, meeting with popular Eastern refusal regardless of incumbent.

On the positive side, this century produced some good and gifted people such as Francis of Assisi and Thomas Aquinas who would leave lasting legacies of enhanced understanding and appreciation of Christian faith and practice. A new form of pragmatic order in the Church appeared which bridged the monastic and secular preaching life – Franciscan and Dominican orders of friars. Friars were to live generally ascetic rule-driven lives but reached out preaching and working among the public rather than being reclusive.

Europe became subject to a new unforeseen threat in the form of the aggressively expansionist Mongol Empire, while the Vatican would still persist in its myopic disinterest in the Far East and China.

Papal Authority

Pope Innocent III (1198-1216), nephew of Clement III, had been taught by Benedictines then studied theology in Paris and jurisprudence at Bologna. He reigned long enough to become arguably the most powerful and effective pope of the era, covering a range of organisational achievements. He claimed supremacy of the papacy over all heads of state, basing this on the Donation of Constantine which conferred such power, even though it was most likely a fraudulent document forged about five hundred years after Constantine.

Innocent III developed guidelines to the rights and relationships between the pope and West European heads of state. An example of this was his ruling regarding Germany:

- German princes have the right to elect their king, who would become emperor, in line with the transfer from Greeks to Germans when Charlemagne was king.
- The pope has the right to check and decide whether the elected king is worthy of office and he is empowered to anoint, consecrate and crown the choice if worthy.
- If the pope finds the elected king unworthy, the princes must elect a new king. In the case of refusal, the pope will appoint another king as emperor for patronage and defence of the Church.
- In the case of two claimants to the throne, the pope will ask the princes to reach agreement. In the event of delay or failure in this, the pope will arbitrate and use his office to decide which claimant should be king and emperor on the basis of his suitability.

In his aim for acceptance of papal power, Innocent was assisted by the death of Emperor Henry IV of the Hohenstaufen dynasty just prior to his own election and the fact that the regent for young Frederick II, Henry's widow Constance of Sicily was keen to free Sicily from German rule. Before her death, she made Innocent guardian of the young king and he thus achieved the reinstatement of the Papal States' rights to Sicily that had been surrendered by Pope Adrian IV.

Another matter of administration begging for improvement was that of centralising control of sources of Church income and calls for expenditure. It was no simple task but Innocent III laid some useful early groundwork, for his successor to take further. He began moving towards a centralisation of widespread census mechanisms and accounts for the Church. With various forms of Church dues from different countries, the clergy taxes towards a crusade, struggles with the Hohenstaufens, not all bishops being amenable to paying diocesan dues and widely varying efficiencies of collection, this needed much work.

Fourth Crusade, Sacking of Constantinople 1204

Innocent III regarded the fall of Jerusalem to the Muslims in the 1180s as a failure of earlier Church leadership and called for the Fourth Crusade against Muslims first in the Holy Land then in Spain in 1198.

The Fourth Crusade seemed fated from the beginning. It took time to get off the ground in the face of reluctance from Germany, already in dispute with the papacy, while England and France were fighting each other. Eventually a few French and Italian nobles raised an army, which found an Italian leader in Count Boniface. They had decided to attack via Egypt, first to defeat the successors to Saladin as leaders of the Abbayyid Sultanate, who held Jerusalem. This meant journeying by sea, which also avoided the hostile land traverse of Anatolia. They had assembled a force of over 33,000, mostly French, including 4,500 knights and their horses. It was a huge undertaking, requiring a fleet for which many new ships would have to be built. So Count Boniface set about negotiating protected transport with port states such as Genoa and Naples, though Genoa and some others showed little interest.

Probably unknown to Boniface, Naples had designs on Constantinople, to whom they were already contracted for naval support, so if they could build a large fleet and train the crews largely at someone else's expense, it suited them well. It took well over a year to complete preparations and the fleet sailed in June 1203 with Pope Innocent III's blessings and his prohibition of any violence against Catholic states. In the event, only about 12,000, one third of the anticipated force arrived to set off. The Venetians had stretched their economic and human resources to the limit and foregone other profitable business to honour their side of the bargain, but the fewer crusaders could barely raise half the agreed money. The Doge Dandolo threatened to intern the crusaders but that would not have solved Venice's problem and the solution they came up with was to use the crusader force to capture Zara, a Catholic Dalmatian port, which the Hungarians had won from Venetian control in battle in the previous century. So Zara was sacked and its defences demolished. The pope excommunicated the crusaders for this forbidden attack against Catholics.

Boniface had left the crusaders before they sailed for Zara to meet his cousin Philip in Swabia, where he also met the 20-year-old Prince Alexios IV, son of deposed Byzantine Emperor Isaac II. Recent poor and corrupt governance of Constantinople, had led to instability and impoverishment of the treasury. Alexios III had unseated his brother Isaac II in 1195, but proven no better and indulged in hedonism as well, leading to public unrest. The young prince wanted to take what he regarded as his rightful inheritance of the Byzantine throne and to this end he promised to pay all crusader debts to the Venetians plus adequate funds and supply thousands of troops and protection of the navy for the crusade if Boniface would first lead them to usurp Alexios III. The empire and certainly its navy were in no position to fulfil such extravagance, yet the Doge of Venice and most of the crusaders agreed. The main fleet set sail from Zara, picked up Boniface and Alexios IV on the way, while some crusader forces decided to travel direct to the Holy Land via Christian held parts of Syria. The invading force took Constantinople by surprise, but its defences ensured it was not a walk-in victory. After over a month' fighting, Emperor Alexios III fled, taking with him valuable gold and treasures to help ensure safe asylum. The citizens replaced him by bringing back Isaac, which was a surprise blow to the Crusaders' ambition, who then negotiated co-emperorship for his son Alexios IV to fulfil their mission and qualify for their rewards.

Alexios IV realised he could no longer raise that amount but asked the crusaders and Venetians to give him until April, 1204 to raise it. He then ordered that all icons in churches be removed and their gold and jewels handed over to the Imperial treasury, causing revolt. Isaac II died soon after, then Alexios IV was killed and the throne awarded to a leader of defending Byzantine forces who took the name Alexios V.

The crusaders and Venetians realised their only hope of the reward was to overwhelm the city, which they did from separate fronts. The crusaders sacked it for all the treasures they could find, involving the ruination of many churches and a mosque then set fires, leaving tens of thousands homeless. Alexios V escaped. The Venetians were paid off in full, leaving the crusaders with plenty for themselves and to finance ongoing operations. But some left with those spoils and the crusade fragmented. Measured by the pope's intention to recapture Jerusalem, it was an unmitigated failure.

The Byzantine Empire was divided between the crusaders and Venetians and the Latin Empire of Constantinople resulted, with the aim of re-establishing dominance there of the Roman Catholic faction. Baldwin of Flanders was crowned emperor of an empire with its defences against the Turks seriously weakened by the sacking.

Pope Innocent III rather pointlessly excommunicated the leaders and key participants in the Crusaders' sacking of Constantinople. In terms of Christian unity, the pope realised the act and the manner of the Christian against Christian conflict had created a wound that may never heal.

Carmelites

Since biblical times, Mount Carmel had been regarded as quite sacred and the 'Sons of the Prophets' community from the time of the Book of Samuel is believed to have been there, their most famous superior having been Elias. They lost their prominence as Jerusalem fell, but hermits probably continued their presence on Mount Carmel. It became a place for pilgrimage and a chapel was built there soon after Christ's time in honour of Saint Mary.

A number of important new religious orders were consecrated in this century. The first of these was the Carmelite order, officially formed between 1206 and 1214, when Albert, Patriarch of Jerusalem enabled the hermits on Mount Carmel to collect together into a community. They had originally come to the Holy Land as independent pilgrims, settling on Mount Carmel for lives of prayer, penance and poverty.

In the early 13th century, a few members of a Crusade had gone to Mount Carmel for individual retreats then representatives of the community asked Albert of Jerusalem to provide an outline rule for it. Albert was the Latin Church Patriarch of Jerusalem and legate of Pope Innocent III. He wrote for them a rule with sixteen headings which included commitment to living in individual cells, a life of constant prayer, poverty and hard work, attending daily Mass, silence overnight between vespers and terce (about 7pm-9am), eating no meat and fasting from mid-September to Easter.

Pope Honorius III agreed the rule and approved the Order of Carmelites in 1226. Due to the Great Schism and other pressures in the Holy Land, they moved off Mount Carmel and settled far away in England with two communities at Aylesford, Kent and Alnwick, Northumberland. From here they thrived and spread, including establishing a community in the south of France from which they grew throughout continental Europe. A couple of major new Orders of friars would also be founded which brought members out into public ministry rather than taking the option of seclusion. These were the Franciscans and Dominicans.

Hohenstaufens

After Emperor Henry IV died in 1197, Otto IV faced a rival claim to the throne from his uncle, Philip of Swabia, so was not installed until 1208. He was anointed Holy Roman Emperor by Pope Innocent III but soon he overturned his earlier promises and aimed to regain imperial power in Italy and Sicily contrary to his late mother's wishes. The pope excommunicated him, supported to his ward, King Frederick II of Sicily and aimed to restore the Hohenstaufen dynasty to the Holy Roman court. Otto IV and his ally King John of England were opposed by French King Philip II. Otto was defeated in the Battle of Bouvines by Philip's forces in 1214 and after his death in 1218, Frederick II became emperor. King John of England, meanwhile lost French possessions and had to accept Pope Innocent III's choice of Stephen Langton as Archbishop of Canterbury. The issue of papal supremacy within wider Christendom would soon be formalised unilaterally in favour of Rome in the canons resulting from the Fourth Lateran Council in 1215.

England, King John, Magna Carta 1215

In England, there had been changes since Henry II had died. King John, youngest son of Henry II and Eleanor of Aquitaine succeeding his brother Richard as English king from 1199 until his death in 1216,.

John verged on atheism, regarded as a serious matter at the time. It aggravated an already tense relationship with Pope Innocent III, which had arisen from conflict over the appointment of a new Archbishop of Canterbury. There were three key interest groups in England – the king, the Chapter of Canterbury Cathedral and bishops of the province of Canterbury, each of which championed a different candidate, while Pope Innocent III was determined to pursue his claimed right to make the choice. Innocent selected Stephen Langton, but John refused to accept this, believing it abrogated his regal right. He began to take over papal property in Canterbury. Relations deteriorated as the pope issued an interdict on England, prohibiting the clergy from conducting any services other than child baptism or confession for the dying. In reply, John confiscated the lands of any clergy refusing services and arrested the concubines commonly held by clerics, fining the clerics heavily. Monasteries and other institutions also had to pay in negotiating their freedom and Christians who fled abroad had their lands confiscated by the crown.

Innocent III excommunicated John in 1209, which the king regarded almost as a badge of honour, matching the same imposition on Emperor

Otto IV and Count Raymond VI of Toulouse. Excommunication remained an over-employed and devalued sanction and the pope misjudged the English. John gained financially, his appropriations being worth about 14% of the previous income of the Church. As there was no sign of the uprising against John he had anticipated, Innocent III relaxed some of the interdiction. Monasteries could celebrate Mass again. As John's concern at the possibility of an attack by France grew, he reached a resolution with Innocent III in 1213, which involved accepting Stephen Langton as Archbishop, restoring Church property and committing England to an annual payment as a feudal state of the pope.

When John allied with Otto in an attempt to regain lands in the north of France, they lost in the Battle of Bouvines, additionally losing Anjou and the east of France. On his return to England, King John was confronted by rebel barons. Despite Innocent III's support, John was losing domestic sympathy and when London was taken by the rebels, he called on Archbishop Langton to arrange peace talks. Langton drafted a charter guaranteeing the rights of the Church, of free men to be protected from illegal imprisonment and have access to rapid justice and of barons to consent or object to any proposed new taxes. The charter introduced the principle of all people, aristocrats and royalty being equally subject to the law. This is an essential element of God's natural law – all people are equal in the eyes of God. It also allowed for a council of twenty five barons to monitor adherence to these conditions. This was all subject to the barons returning London to the king and the baronial army standing down. John had no choice but to sign this charter, which became known as the Magna Carta.

The charter did not last long as it ignored the recent installation of the pope as the feudal lord of England. Innocent III poured fuel on the fire by confirming his support of John, excommunicating the rebel barons and declaring the Magna Carta null and void since it had been signed under duress. This led to the war of the barons who found support from Prince Louis of France who provided them with much-needed armaments. John's disaster-prone reign came to an end when he died of dysentery in 1216 during this war.

The Magna Carta was later modified to be acceptable to all parties and signed by John's 10-year-old son, King Henry III and his protector, William Marshall in 1217.

Albigensian Crusade from 1208

Proscribed heretical groups of this time included Cathars, Waldensians, Paterines and Arnoldists, as below.

Cathars – The name is from Greek for 'Puritans'. Cathar beliefs drew from the ancient Paulensians named after Paul of Samasota, a dualist sect based on Manicheanism (see 2nd century). They developed from ascetic clerics in the 1140s in Albi in the Languedoc region of southern France, so Cathars are sometimes known as Albigensians. They spread east and west into northern Italy and parts of Spain between the 12th and 14th centuries. Their radical Christian beliefs included elements of Gnosticism which saw spiritual as good, material as bad, with a dualistic 'good' god and 'bad' god. They saw the New Testament god as creating the spiritual world and therefore good, while the Old Testament god as creator of the physical world was bad. Among other practices, they supported suicide and preached against all sexual intercourse. These practices were underpinned by their belief in re-incarnation and an understanding that heaven could only be attained through self-denial. The latter did not suit some of the comfort-loving clergy.

Waldensians – This 1170s pre-Reformation Christian reform movement, founded by Peter Waldo in Lyon, soon spread over the Alpine border with Italy into the Piedmont valleys. Waldo, a successful merchant, gave away his considerable wealth and property, practicing his belief that apostles-like poverty is the route to perfection. He believed in the use of lay preachers and strict adherence to the New Testament. The sect survived inquisition and persecution and can still be found in some pockets of the region today.

Paterines – This eleventh century religious movement was born of the Gregorian reforms to the morality and status of the clergy, supporting condemnation of simony, clerical incontinence and concubinage. It opposed lax discipline in some monasteries and those landowners and aristocrats who had gained wealth through dubious means. The movement was centred on Milan diocese, where clerical rights had been robustly protected, and it spread in northern Italy. They particularly opposed the vast difference between some genuine but impoverished local clergy and the visibly well-fed and wealthy senior ranks of clergy.

All three groups were deemed heretical by the Church as well as the **Arnoldists**, followers of Arnold of Brescia in the 12th century, mentioned in the previous chapter, whose influence had spread northwards.

Back in 1147, Bernard of Clairvaux had encountered a group of zealous Cathars in the Languedoc region who believed that the Roman Curia had strayed from the true Church by shunning manual work. They refused to revere the Cross as it represented the death of Jesus. He reported them as heretics, but no immediate action was taken. In 1207 Catholic clergy engaged these Cathars in theological debates at Montréal and Fanjeaux, birthplace of St Dominic, but reached no resolution, so committed were the Cathars to their beliefs. Their spread and intensity was partly in reaction to the evident dissolute lifestyle of the clergy in the region, factors which had already contributed to the establishment and growth of influence of the strict Rule of Cluny Abbey.

The apparent murder of his legate, Pierre de Castelnau by the Cathars in 1208, sufficed to harden Pope Innocent III's resolve in setting up a localised Albigensian crusade to stamp out this now threatening heretical group. King Philip of France offered his support as he also perceived the opportunity to win over some of the region, especially around Toulouse, from Spanish influence.

French nobleman Simon de Montfort was chosen to lead the Albigensian Crusade in 1209, taking Béziers in infamous circumstances. The military hesitated to slaughter the population on account of many Catholics being among them. There is one account that when consulted on this before the final assault, the Papal Legate replied after a moment's thought, "Kill them all, the Lord will know His own." If there is any truth in that account, it is another case for stark comparison both with the teaching and practice of Jesus in the New Testament and an excerpt from Genesis 18:20-32 describing Abraham's pleas on behalf of Sodom and Gomorra to which God replied that if there were only a few good men there he would spare the towns from destruction. The entire population of Béziers, in the high teens of thousands was slaughtered and news spread quickly, as did escaping refugees desperately seeking shelter. Villages surrendered to the passing crusader forces who then laid siege to Carcassonne, which was well fortified, but by then bulging with refugees, so resistance did not last long once the water supply was cut off. After this, several towns fell quite easily including Albi, Montréal and Fanjeaux. Minerve presented solid resistance but when it fell, the populace was offered the chance to re-embrace Catholicism and given what had happened to Béziers, most did so. 140 refusers were summarily burned at the stake, reviving an ancient penalty for heretics.

This crusade was slowed down as some conquered territories reverted, requiring violent settlement. There had also been a counter-attack from Raymond of Toulouse, after the Cathars secured the reluctant assistance of Peter of Aragon, the neighbouring kingdom in Spain. Peter was a respected

Catholic, but his sister had married Raymond of Toulouse through a past alliance so Peter felt duty bound to support him. Peter led the alliance forces, far outnumbering the Crusaders, into the battle of Muret in 1213, but they lost and Peter was killed. The Crusaders, still led by Simon de Montfort, thereby gained the northern part of Toulouse, while Raymond escaped to England. His lands were taken and gifted to King Philip II by the pope, ensuring some support from Philip. The crusade moved west in 1214 to Périgord and took the castles of Domme and Montfort. Simon's forces entered the city of Toulouse in 1215, which he was then given.

Pope Innocent III died in 1216 during a revival of Cathar forces as Raymond returned from England with his son. They re-took Toulouse with little resistance from the inhabitants as Simon was away in 1217 quelling disturbances in the Pyrenean foothills. He returned and early the following year put Toulouse once more under siege but he was killed by a rock projectile from a siege machine.

The Cathars gained initiative as leadership of the Crusade passed to Philip II, whose real interest lay in Toulouse. In 1222, Raymond de Toulouse died and the reigns passed to his son Raymond II. The next year saw the death of Philip II who was succeeded by Louis VIII. Simon's son Aumory de Montfort had inherited the lands around Carcassonne from his father and offered them to Louis VIII as a gesture of solidarity. He accepted. In 1226, Aumory revived the Crusade with considerable success and by 1229, Raymond was ready to sign the Treaty of Paris that ended the Albigensian Crusade. But Catharism was not dead and most Cathars gravitated towards Montségur, though some stayed under cover at Carcassonne and elsewhere.

Fourth Lateran Council 1215

This is often considered to be the most important ecumenical council up to this point and was attended by well over a thousand bishops, abbots, priors and nobles from all over Europe and the East. It was called by Innocent III to apply and record his reading of the papal powers over royal and imperial appointments, thus formalising, within the Church at least, the over-riding authority of the pope of the day. It also served to clarify and apply some consistency to the structure of services and sacraments; to define doctrines including the nature of the Eucharist; and to determine the requirement for at least annual confession of sins and the absolute secrecy of the confessional, however grave the sin. It also detailed the procedures for electing bishops.

Although called by Pope Innocent III in April 1213, the council was not held until November 1215, allowing for thorough preparation in drafting canons for discussion and a huge attendance of over 70 Patriarchs (including Constantinople and Jerusalem) and Metropolitan bishops, 400 bishops, 900 abbots and priors as well as representatives of royalty. It began under Pope Innocent III, but after his death, Pope Honorius III took charge from his installation in July 1216.

The council published over 70 canons, subjects including transubstantiation, confession, procedures for the election of bishops, papal powers over royal and imperial appointments and endorsement of the proposed Fifth Crusade. Significantly, it also laid down strict lifestyle disciplines for clergy and forbade their participation in any judicial process that could result in inflicting pain or death on the accused.

Key elements of the canons selected for note here, using their official numerations were:

1. A compulsory condition of receiving Holy Communion is to believe in transubstantiation, the transformation of the Eucharistic bread and wine into the body and blood of Jesus Christ.

3. Defined procedure and penalties for heretics.

4. Exhorted the Greeks to reunite with the Catholic Church – "one fold, one shepherd".

5. Outlined the extent of papal primacy.

11. Re-iterated the requirement of each cathedral to have a school and a seat of theology.

13. Forbade new religious orders – any new house was to adopt an existing approved rule.

14-17 Covered detailed aspects of required discipline of clergy. Marriage and celibacy were not mentioned.

18. Clerics were not to perform surgical operations.

19. Clerics were prohibited from pronouncing sentence of death or partaking in judicial tests and ordeals, e.g. blessing water or hot iron. (This signalled the end of trial by ordeal.)

21. Every Christian over the age of discretion had to confess their sins at least once a year in their parish.

50-52. Ruled on marriage impediments, limitations and publishing banns.

53-54. All Christian landowners obliged to pay tithes which must take priority over other taxes and dues.

64. Related to simony, monks and nuns should not seek payment from applicants for entry to religious life.

67-69 Covered the obligations on Jews and Muslims; Jews not to charge extortionate interest on loans; both to be distinguishable by their dress so that no Christian would unknowingly marry them; Jews barred from holding public office.

Quite contrary to early Christians, actual reception of Holy Communion had become uncommon due to a belief that had grown among the laiety that they were unworthy to receive it. The Church ruled that every Catholic should take communion at least once a year at or near Easter. Failure to do so was considered to be a sin. For most Catholics, this became a maximum until the 20th century, when more frequent reception became the norm once more.

Fifth Crusade

Pope Innocent III died in 1216 and was succeeded by **Pope Honorius III** (1216-27) who was a popular choice as he was a Roman and widely known as a warm, holy and kind man. He inherited preparations for and oversight of the Lateran Council reported above.

Honorius III's priority was to send the Fifth Crusade to regain the Holy Land. He tried to persuade Emperor Frederick II finally to launch the Crusade in 1217. But circumstances in war-torn Europe and prevarication by Frederick II frustrated his ambition, even after crowning him as Emperor as late as 1220. Honorius thought he had forced the issue when he helped arrange Frederick's marriage to Queen Isabella II of Jerusalem, but still the Emperor hesitated. Honorius would not live to see the Crusade to fruition.

Another aim of Pope Honorius III was to achieve the clerical reforms which had proven resilient to previous popes' efforts. His natural way was to employ kind persuasion to achieve his ends as opposed to the more direct approach of Innocent III, although he did authorise the use of forceful persuasion where needed.

Being a man of learning himself, Honorius III believed that much of the issue of clerical discipline could be helped by making improved theological education a necessary qualification for clerics. This fitted with his aim of establishing theological schools in every cathedral and he endowed privileges on the great universities of the time at Paris and Bologna to help achieve the best education in theology for those who would in their turn instruct the diocesan teachers.

In the meantime, following the Lateran council, Honorius III focused his efforts on overcoming those heresies around the south of France and beyond. He accepted the right of Simon de Montfort, Earl of Leicester, to the lands of Raymond of Toulouse and scored a diplomatic victory in involving French royalty in the conflict on the side of the Church. He also helped Louis VIII, King of France (1223-23) in the capture of Avignon, both of them ignoring Emperor Frederick II's claim to it.

Honorius III supported Spanish efforts to drive back the Islamic occupiers. He saw the spread of Christianity along the Baltic coast and tried to strengthen the fading Latin Empire in Constantinople. He also effectively became proxy ruler of England after the Regent, William, Earl of Pembroke died before Henry III was of an age to rule. He authorised excommunication of the rebellious barons and demanded their allegiance to Henry rather than Louis of France, to whom many had turned.

He approved three new religious orders – the Dominicans in 1216, the Franciscans in 1223 and the Carmelites' Rule of St Albert of Jerusalem in 1226.

Pope Honorius III died in 1227, leaving **Pope Gregory IX** to press for action on the Crusade. Gregory would perhaps be best known for the Papal Inquisition which lasted twenty eight years, with repercussions for centuries to come.

Episcopal Inquisition (1183-1230s)

The Inquisition arguably sprang from the previous century about the time the Albigensian Crusade was launched in the 12th century. When the extent of the spread of the Cathars had been realised, some institutions within the Roman Church were tasked with countering heresy where it arose. Apart from the active part played by the crusade, responsibility for implementation of this task was mostly delegated to bishops so this phase was called the Episcopal Inquisition. In 1173, Pope Boniface VIII had declared null and void any inquisitional judgement of guilt unless it carried the free and informed support of the bishop.

An added pressure was imposed when Innocent III in 1205 prohibited lawyers and notaries from "assisting in any way, including counsel or support, all heretics or their followers nor render them assistance or defend them in any way." The Church had thus far regarded as worthless the evidence of apostates, heretics or excommunicated persons, but this took matters much further. Even in those early days, there was public unease with these restrictions and soon the right of a defendant to a lawyer was acknowledged so long as the lawyer was a man of impeccable character and committed to the Catholic faith. But even with this acknowledgement it must have remained questionable as to whether the appointed inquisitor could have taken a neutral view of any defence witnesses, should he even have the courage to appear.

Church courts before the Inquisition had also often withheld the names of witnesses for the prosecution, but Boniface VIII changed this towards the end of the 12th century. The inexorable tightening of the terms of reference for defence and the procedure of tribunals was no doubt forced by the concerns of the faithful at the reliability of conviction, severity of the sentences and excessive zeal of some inquisitors. It had become a campaign of terror that bore little relationship to the teaching of a merciful and loving God.

Early on in the Roman Empire there had been a practice of executing condemned Manicheans by fire at the stake. In the Albigensian Crusade, the practice was revived following the siege of Carcassonne, and mob rule sometimes took over to drag suspected heretics to a fiery death. In the 1220s, Emperor Frederick II put in place legislation to sentence a proven heretic to prolonged imprisonment or death at the stake.

Papal Inquisition

Pope Gregory IX is seen by the Catholic Church as the initiator of the Papal Inquisition in 1234. It is likely that Pope Gregory, an excellent lawyer, was acting partly to prevent Emperor Frederick II's creeping encroachment on ecclesiastical territory, with his Hohenstaufen dynasty's historic penchant for claiming God-given control over the Church as well as the State.

Gregory IX set up a new court system for the inquisition. He was determined to hold the line so well established by Innocent III of Church control of doctrinal matters. A religious court would safeguard such control and ensure that judges of good repute and learning, appointed by the Church for their integrity, could protect its doctrine. Most popes of this century tried to set rules to limit abuse of the accused, but must have been aware that this was frequently unsuccessful.

The task of judgment was transferred by Pope Gregory IX from local clergy to the new appointees. Most of the new inquisitors were members of one of the new orders of friars, Franciscans or Dominicans described below, predominantly the latter who had been at the forefront of visiting those areas affected by heresy and preaching bravely against those beliefs. These were selected and acknowledged to be holy men, well versed in theology and without interest in possessions, so they should have been able to apply dispassionate judgement, even though few of them were legally trained.

Pope Gregory IX meanwhile died in 1241 and his frail successor, **Pope Celestine IV** only survived for 17 days, to be followed by **Pope Innocent IV** (1243-54). While Innocent IV's principal aim was to remove Frederick II, mainly for his refusal to accept Church precedence over empire or to concede reinstatement of Lombardy to the Papal Lands, his appointment did not change the course of the inquisition.

When it became a matter of a potential sentence of death, Canon 19 of the Lateran Council prohibited clerics 'from pronouncing sentence of death or partaking in judicial tests and ordeals' The term 'tests and ordeals could also be considered to cover torture. They were of course aware of the option of handing those they found guilty to the secular courts for sentencing. The potential penalty for heterodoxy was such that the responsibility of judgement should have lain heavily on the inquisitor, yet question marks will always hang over this due to the known nature of the ecclesiastical courts.

The general procedure was that on arrival of the inquisitor in a town, a month's period of grace would be announced to the population, during which they would be invited to meet the inquisitorial panel. This gave them an opportunity to confess and if they did so, they would be awarded a penance, which would not involve punishment by the civil authorities. The meetings and interviews could also provide useful intelligence to the inquisitor regarding where to look for culprits as disclosure was equated to remorse. The resulting suspects were called before the inquisitors. If they freely admitted their beliefs but indicated remorse, they would be given a relatively light penitential sentence such as a pilgrimage.

Most suspects pleaded innocence. They could sometimes be bailed or freed on oath that they would not abscond, as the proceedings could take some time to come to full trial. The oath may not have meant much to a heretic, but the court saw it as a serious obligation and breaking it earned severe punishment. At a point before trial, they were subjected to one or more of the following levels of persuasion: a reminder of the type of death they faced if found guilty; detention in a small cell for some days with minimal food, sometimes followed up with an apparently friendly visit by someone already sentenced, who would try, in return for a promised benefit, to elicit an unwary admission; or ultimately, torture.

In those cases pleading innocence, the delay was due to a rule requiring at least two witnesses to be found and prepared. These witnesses were rarely for the defence and it was also unusual for the accused to be represented by an advocate, as anyone speaking in defence of a heretic knew they would be suspected as a sympathiser or a heretic themselves, which even applied to lawyers who were just doing their job.

If there was a defence lawyer, his first action was to discover the names of the defendant's enemies. He would pass these to the court and if the accusers were among them, the case should have been dismissed. Perjury was viewed as a more serious crime than it is today because an oath on the Gospels was a serious matter. There were examples of life sentences plus repeated scourging for perjury in false witness.

As an intended further safeguard for the accused, Pope Innocent IV declared that no action should be taken that might lead to punishment such as life imprisonment or death at the stake without first securing agreement of the local bishop, who was to have full and free access to the court records.

Pope Innocent IV issued almost incidentally, the papal bull *Ad Extirpanda* in 1252 authorising the use of torture in certain circumstances to extract confessions from accused heretics, whom he described as "robbers of God's sacraments and of the Christian faith". He imposed limits on the use of torture, including that the inquisitor must be virtually certain of the validity of the evidence against the accused, the torture should be used no more than once per suspect and it should not be applied to the extent of loss of limb or life. Apart from confession of guilt, the torturer should also obtain details of accomplices, sympathisers and anybody who has offered the accused lodging, support or defence.

The bull also stated that in the case of conviction, a share of the property confiscated from the heretic would be passed to the state, which hardly encouraged a neutral approach once the accused was handed over for sentencing.

Present-day criteria, would judge such events as barbaric, especially the cruelty of execution at the stake and torture, which often meant the rack. There were some attempts by the hierarchy to ensure justice, but again, by today's standards the checks and balances left enormous loopholes and made unfounded assumptions regarding the fair intent of all parties. For example, the torture was to be used only once if deemed necessary and not to be used as a punishment, but as a means of yielding the truth. It is difficult to imagine a truly compassionate person becoming a torturer or any confession thus achieved being considered free and true. It is a recorded fact that many were tortured more than once.

While the Fourth Lateran Council canon denied the Church courts the power to impose the death penalty or prolonged imprisonment, it was clear that handing the guilty party over to civil authorities for sentence usually amounted to the same thing. Influential people including the Emperor made use of the opportunity to settle scores, eliminate opposition or at least gain some land.

Spain

The full Spanish Inquisition would not take place for a couple of centuries yet, but King James I of Aragon, son of Philip II became aware of the spread of Cathars from neighbouring Languedoc, so he proscribed them and asked the pope for assistance. In 1232, Pope Gregory IX instructed the Archbishop and Bishops to engage the help of Dominicans in searching and punishing the heretics. The Council of Lérida in 1237 confirmed the appointment of Dominicans and Franciscans to establish the Inquisition in Aragon. It was slow to be implemented, delayed further by the killing of two senior inquisitors and the wish of the Dominicans to do it strictly according to the rules defined by successive recent popes.

Overall, Spanish Catholics were proving to be proactive in defence of their religion and though much of Spain was a Muslim Caliphate, a start had been made to drive the Muslims back in preceding centuries as Spain's northern kingdoms had helped overpower some of the occupied territories, such as Toledo in 1085. A renewed effort in 1236 regained Cordoba for the Christians and the re-introduction of Christianity in the South accelerated with a corresponding decline of Muslim power in Spain. Granada became part of the Kingdom of Castile in 1238 but the Emirate of Granada would remain in Muslim hands until late in the fifteenth century. As the Christian faith edged back into the south, diplomatic negotiation enabled Jews and Muslims to practice their own religions in the occupied lands.

Francis of Assisi (1181-1226), Franciscans, Poor Clares

St Francis came from a wealthy family in Assisi and was taken prisoner during the 1204 city war with Perugia. After his release, he took refuge alone in the ruined church of San Damiano and caves near Assisi, spending all his time in prayer, whilst suffering intense spiritual anguish as he observed people's crude behaviour, at the same time struggling to subdue his own human urges and conform to the will of God as he had learned it. He made a pilgrimage to Rome, where he joined beggars outside St Peter's, an experience that led him to adopt a life of total poverty in imitation of Christ. As he prayed in front of the crucifix in San Damiano, he heard God calling him to rebuild his house, "which was falling into total ruin". Initially thinking this meant the church of San Damiano, he later realised that God had meant the Church itself. The original crucifix is today in the Basilica of Santa Chiara, St Clare. As an early follower of St Francis, Clare had established a convent near Assisi where she founded the Poor Clare sisters, an order inspired and protected by St Francis which followed a similar life of poverty, work and prayer.

Despite Francis humility, which led him never to seek ordination to the priesthood, his fame spread. He gathered 3000 followers likewise imitating the life of Christ. They multiplied at least tenfold over the next 100 years. One of his celebrated instructions was to "preach the gospel at all times and when necessary, to do so using words". Adopting the same grey habit of Francis, they became known as the Grey Friars (friar, meaning brother, as *frère*). The term friar came to be applied to men of a religious order who worked and sometimes lived among the public while practising a holy calling. This distinguished them from monks, who lived enclosed in a monastery, though some orders of monks sometimes mingle in public.

In 1209, Francis of Assisi sought Pope Innocent III's permission to establish a new order to be known as the Franciscan Order. Perhaps with the 11th century Waldensians, the 'Poor Men of Lyon' in mind the pope gave only provisional approval subject to later ratification to be based on their performance and the canonical correctness of their preaching. The fact that they were tonsured helped in that it was visual testimony to their acceptance of Church authority. They also foreswore all possessions and preached on the streets. They gained Innocent's full approval as early as 1210 then adopted the familiar brown habit.

Saints

Apart from Mary, Peter and Paul, the first saint to gain universally popular celebrity for their life was Francis of Assisi in the 13th century. Many saints had been determined by local bishops in the past. About this time the pope took on sole responsibility in the Western Church for confirming and canonising saints and the practice of placing the relics of a saint in the altar of a church began. The patronage of a saint for particular activities or needs was also adopted and saints became patrons or the focus of prayers, not to be worshipped but to intercede for those causes, such as St Christopher for safe travel.

As in national honours systems, people respect shining examples and many such appointments are deserved. But it is unsurprising that there are sceptics of this whole business considering the history of corruption that had sullied those institutions at times. Only God knows all about anyone and makes the only judgment that matters. This all led to one condition of canonisation being the proof of at least two miracles being attributable to the saint when alive or through prayers to the proposed saint after death.

Christmas Crib

Francis of Assisi is well known for his love of animals, but it is not so widely known that he arranged the first Christmas nativity scene. There may have been word-of-mouth description of the crib with the ass and oxen present over the years. Francis of Assisi had asked Giovanni, an ascetic living in nearby Greccio, to prepare a scene at Christmas recalling birth of the infant Jesus in a manger bed of hay in a Bethlehem stable, helping many to join in truly celebrating the birth of Christ. When Francis with townsfolk, children and friars came to Giovanni's crib in the forest, they carried torches and led an ass and an ox and brought hay to complete the scene. A sung Mass was held there in the forest and Francis sang the Gospel then preached in his usual inspiring manner, centring on the baby Jesus in the manger. The idea of re-enacting the nativity scene soon spread to towns, villages, churches then homes. A basic similar picture of the Nativity scene was rediscovered in 1877, depicted in a wall decoration in a Roman catacomb, the burial chamber of a Christian family.

Dominicans (Order of Preachers)

This new order of friars was also founded to break out of the totally monastic life and to take God's mission to people in the street. Somewhat contrarily, this seemed to qualify them to be chosen to take the lead in judging heretics during the inquisitions.

Dominic, the founder was born in Spain in 1170 of noble parents, his mother being particularly devout. He had two brothers and they were all taught up to the age of about fourteen by a maternal uncle, who was a priest, assistant to the bishop with special responsibility for the poor. The boys were greatly influenced by their uncle and all devoted their lives to the service of God. Dominic went on to study the arts and theology in the college at Palencia, soon to become a university. When he was twenty one and still a student, a devastating famine hit Spain and he surprised his peers by selling his books and giving away most of his money and spare clothing to the hungry.

Dominic became known to Bishop Martin de Bazan of Osma, who appointed him to membership of the chapter of the cathedral of Burgo de Osma, which the bishop wished to reform. Dominic showed a leadership of such humility and passion such that most members became canons regular, a category of ordained priests who vowed poverty, chastity and obedience but were generally attached to a group who may live communally. They usually accepted the Augustinian Rule but were not enclosed as were monks, who were not ordained. When Martin was replaced as Bishop of Osma by Diego d'Azevedo, in 1201, Diego recognised Dominic's contribution to the reform of the chapter by making him prior.

Alfonso VIII, King of Castile charged Bishop Diego with a royal task in Denmark, which eventually proved abortive. The matter was of such importance that Diego asked Dominic to travel with him and they passed through Languedoc on the way where they were both horrified at the Cathar heresy they encountered. So having done with the king's task, they travelled to Rome where Diego asked Pope Innocent III to relieve him of his position as bishop in order that he could work on the reconversion of the heretics. The pope refused Diego's request, but asked the two of them to support the Cistercians, his chosen crusaders for this mission. When they arrived back in Languedoc, Dominic soon realised the relatively indulgent lifestyle of the Cistercians denied them the credibility to open the Cathars' minds to theological discussion. He believed that only truly devout, ascetic and humble Catholic preachers stood any chance of winning the Cathars back to the Church. This way Dominic persuaded senior Cathars to engage in debate. He also felt that women were an important factor in any attempt at conversion. With the permission of Bishop Foulques of Toulouse, he set up a convent in Prouille in 1204, with rules based on those of Saint Augustine.

In 1208, Raymond of Toulouse's forces killed Pierre de Castelnau the papal legate, who had become a Cistercian and had led the mission to reconvert the Cathars. This sparked off the full military-supported Albigensian Crusade under Simon de Montfort. Dominic never became involved in the armed conflict, though he continued his preaching and he did befriend Simon. Before the Battle of Muret he is said to have used the rosary in his prayers for Catholic success there, which duly ensued.

Around 1214, Dominic returned to Toulouse, still nurturing a desire to set up an order that would preach Christ's true faith, practice, moral living and overcome heresy. He had a group of about fifteen disciples and Bishop Foulques supported his idea as well as organising a channel of income for Dominic. A house in Toulouse was gifted to the Order by Pierre Seilan, a wealthy local man, who would become a fellow-friar. The Order of Preachers was thus formally established there in April 1215. Bishop Foulkes provided them with a church as a base. Dominic had wider ambitions, having dreamed of fulfilling Christ's instruction to take his message and way of life to the ends of the earth. He and the bishop attended the Fourth Lateran Council in November 1215 as its main aims tallied with those of Dominic's order – 'the improvement of morals, extinction of heresy and strengthening of faith'. Those aims were approved by the council, but it was also reluctant to countenance any new religious orders or new rules, holding that public preaching should be overseen by bishops, otherwise Rome would find it difficult to control – the pope had learned from previous orders to think beyond the lifetimes of trustees such as Francis and Dominic.

Canon 13 stated that any new order had to adopt an existing approved rule, which led to Dominic adopting the Rule of Saint Augustine, considering it general enough to be sufficiently adaptable for his purpose. Having written this in, Dominic returned to Rome and gained papal approval of his new order at the end of 1216. He preached there during his stay and was appointed to be 'Master of the Sacred Palace', effectively the pope's theologian, which is an office that has since always been held by a Dominican.

In August 1217, Dominic and his group agreed an ambitious plan to grow their order throughout Europe, the first step being for each of the seventeen original members to travel and set up in a different country. Pope Honorius III asked all bishops, priors, abbots and other clergy to encourage and support the Order of Preachers and he gifted them a church in Rome, enabling them to found their first monastery. In return he asked Dominic to help bring the women of Rome closer to the Church and its disciplines. Dominic's success in this led to further support from the pope and as the community in Rome grew rapidly, so Honorius III donated a larger basilica. Dominic believed education of his fellow friars and disciples was the key to ultimate success and he encouraged them to establish foundations first at Paris, then Bologna followed by other major universities. This was all well under way by the end of 1218. He left Reginald d'Orléans as his leader in Italy while he took a party towards Spain, a couple of whom stayed at Lyon to set up a convent. In early 1219, the first monastery of the order in Spain was commissioned near Segovia, followed by convents near Madrid and Palencia, then one in Barcelona. On his journey back to Rome, Dominic established at least five new houses throughout France, so fast was the order now growing.

In 1247, Pope Innocent IV approved a modification of Augustine rule drafted by Dominicans to suit better the European conditions.

The Rosary

Repetitive prayer or chant has long been recognised by many faiths as a helpful aid to meditation, prayer that seeks to open a personal channel for the mind and soul to God or to receive a message or inspiration from him. The Desert Fathers had knotted prayer ropes in the third and fourth centuries AD, for counting repetitions of the Jesus Prayer – 'Lord Jesus Christ, Son of God, have mercy on me, a sinner'. The final two words may have been added since their time, but this prayer became the Orthodox Church's equivalent of the Roman Church's rosary. The First Council of Ephesus in 431 sparked the growth of prayer to Mary, the mother of God, rather as children often find their mother a helpful intermediary with their father. The use of this prayer accelerated during the Middle Ages and the 'chain of prayer' that is called the rosary is believed to date from the thirteenth century. There are historic references to the 'Vita Christi' rosary since the thirteenth century, which may suggest its use also for the Jesus prayer as in Orthodoxy.

Marco Polo was surprised to find that the King of Malabar in south west India had a rosary of precious stones in the thirteenth century, but the use of prayer beads by early Eastern religions in India is now known to have existed as early as the third century BC. Islam has also been using a bead string they call the Tasbih with 33 beads or a multiple for at least as long as Catholics have used the rosary and St Francis Xavier found the Buddhists in Japan widely using a form of rosary in the sixteenth century.

Crusade Procrastination, Council of Lyon

Pope Gregory IX (1227- 1241) was a nephew of Pope Innocent III and a graduate of both Paris and Bologna universities. His involvement in the Inquisition has already been mentioned above.

Gregory IX held Church diplomatic posts prior to his accession, so was well versed in the complex politics in Europe and the evasive guile of Emperor Frederick II. Gregory felt that Honorius III had been too tolerant of Frederick's procrastinations, so one of his first acts was to press Frederick II on the overdue Crusade. Frederick duly gathered forces and departed, but returned after two days claiming the death of a key leader and his own illness. So annoyed was Gregory IX by this latest excuse, that he excommunicated Frederick II, who claimed that the pope had acted unjustly. The leader of the imperial party in Rome supported Frederick by calling an insurrection, which forced the pope to flee to Viterbo then Perugia.

Frederick II aimed to prove he had been wronged by continuing the Crusade, but the pope said a Crusade could not be led by someone who had been excommunicated and released the knights from their oath of allegiance to Frederick. After an appeal to the pope failed, Frederick II returned to Italy in 1229 and led a crushing defeat of papal forces, taking papal lands and Sicily. There was a timely disastrous flood of the Tiber in Rome the following year, which led the superstitious Romans to call Gregory IX back to the city.

Eventually, Gregory IX and Frederick II were partially reconciled so the captured lands were returned and Gregory lifted the excommunication in 1230. But neither would concede supreme rule so tensions remained, re-surfacing later in the decade. Frederick was camped with his forces near Rome when Gregory died in 1241 at nearly one hundred years of age.

Gregory IX was responsible for codifying past established canon law and recent additions in a work entitled *Decretales Gregorii* IX, published in 1234. He was extremely close to Francis and Dominic and held mendicant orders in the highest regard, seeing their avowed life of poverty as ideal examples to the more over-indulgent members of the wider clergy, so afforded them, the Carthusians and others substantial privileges throughout his reign. Gregory IX also hoped for reconciliation with Orthodox Churches, but was frustrated at an Orthodox council by the Greek refusal to accept the *Filioque* in Roman creed.

Gregory was succeeded by **Pope Celestine IV**, who died after only three weeks. The Curia meanwhile split into two parties over dealings with the Emperor. This and the reluctance of the cardinals to return to the city where they had suffered maltreatment during the recent conclave led to a delay in the election of a new pope, resulting in **Pope Innocent IV** (1243-54), perhaps the leading canonist of his day, in 1243.

Innocent IV studied canon law before being ordained then was chosen by Honorius III to join the curia then made cardinal by Gregory IX. He and Frederick II got on well together before his election, but their talks foundered on the issue of Lombardy being reinstated to the patrimony of St Peter. Imperialists fomented feelings against the pope in 1244, leading to yet another pope having to flee Rome. Innocent IV headed home to Genoa and was greeted warmly. He was safe from Frederick there. He began preparing for an ecumenical council at Lyon, which he opened in 1245 with a sermon stating his five main concerns –poor behaviour of Catholic clergy and laity; occupation of the Holy Land by the Saracens; the Great East-West Schism; the Mongol-Tatar threat to Hungary; and Emperor Frederick II's hostility to the Church.

While these issues were discussed, the key actions emerging from the council were to depose and once more excommunicate Frederick and to raise another Crusade to the Holy Land under Louis IX of France. The pope had no means of physically deposing the Emperor and the only result of Frederick II's excommunication was turbulence throughout the continent until Frederick died at the end of 1250. Innocent IV was advised to remain in Lyon for his own safety.

Then from out of the blue, Europe's turmoil was exacerbated by a huge threat from the distant east. The second Mongol 'storm from the east' had swept through Russia and silk-route countries, allied with the Tatars then entered Eastern Europe. Their invasion now threatened Poland, Hungary and further West, so Innocent IV despatched envoys in 1245 to seek a cessation of the Mongol aggression. He held that as God's vicar on earth he had rights even over non-Christians and could exact punishment should they transgress the non-God-related elements of the Ten Commandments. Güyük Khan, son of Ogedai Khan sent an unyielding response in 1246, demanding the submission of all European leaders, including the pope. In 1248, Mongol envoys arrived at the papal court in Lyon to demand submission and that the pope travel to Karakorum for direct instructions but he repeated his call for the Mongols to cease killing Christians.

Mongols

The Mongols were mostly nomadic tribes from in and around Mongolia with a proud tradition of expert horsemanship and fierce fighting skills on horseback. They built a formidable empire and Genghis Khan (1162-1227) was voted in as the first Khan by a council of tribal leaders. He brought the tribes together and gathered an invasion force to spread their empire that would grow to twice the size of the Roman or Ottoman Empires at their height, in fact second largest empire ever in the history of the world. As occupiers, they put most resistant people to death, enslaving the rest while conscripting their able-bodied men. In Genghis Khan's lifetime the empire grew through much of China and central Asia. After a sudden pause at the news of his death, the unified Empire continued under the leadership of Ogedei, his third son.

After a due period of mourning, Ogedei (reign 1227- 1241) resumed expansionist hostilities. Wherever battles were lost, extra troops were sent back to reverse the loss and deliver harsh punishment. As this huge empire expanded, logistical and leadership challenges arose, leading to family tensions, although these did not result in action during Ogedei's life. His nephew Batu, with new Tatar allies, pushed the Western front further into Eastern Europe, invading Hungary and Poland. The Hungarian and Polish national armies gained the help of Christian Knight Orders as well as some forces from Western Europe and the Balkans, who sought to halt the advance of these fearsome warriors as far east as possible. Batu's forces broke through within Hungary and were moving towards the prize of Vienna when news of Ogedei's death came through at the end of 1241. There was an immediate cessation of hostilities and the Mongol Princes left their forces' leaders to secure and hold their gains up to determined lines some distance back from the front. Those princes descended from Genghis attended a council called to elect the next leader.

After a number of rather ineffective and short-lived reigns of regents and elected leaders, a grandson of Genghis Khan called Mongke came to the fore. He was the son of Tolui, brother of Ogedei, although Ogedei's sons were not supportive of him. But Mongke held the respect and support of his cousin Batu, who had become an influential general under Ogedei and Mongke was duly installed as Khan.

The spread of the empire during the reigns of Genghis and Ogedei fostered interchange of learning and practice between east and west in such areas as trade, science, philosophy and ideology, though there remained tension among the Mongols between their traditional nomadic lifestyle and the western settled and cosmopolitan way of life. Nevertheless, their capital embraced imported architecture and culture, with many Europeans, especially French, spending time there. The Mongols' tolerance of different faiths allowed the construction of Buddhist monasteries, Christian churches, mosques and temples.

After Mongke died in 1259, family divisions surfaced again, mainly between other descendants of Genghis' son, Tolui, father of Mongke. Brothers, Ariq Boke and Kublai were each elected as Khan by competing councils, leading to the Toluid Wars 1260-64 to settle leadership. These were lengthened by other family claimants pitching in during its course. Kublai won the war and he managed to expand the empire in new directions. As the Toluid wars began, the Mongols suffered their first defeat in battle not quickly to be reversed, in Galilee. While some further growth took place in the Levant, Persia and China, by the time of Kublai's death family rifts had split the empire into at least four Khanates, weakening the Empire. Decline had begun which would eventually lead to backlash from the Yuan Dynasty in China as well as elsewhere.

Religious Position of the Mongols

Genghis Khan surprisingly urged religious tolerance in the conquered countries. In common with a majority of his compatriots, he was a Shamanist which encourages people in aiming for higher levels of transcendental consciousness through meditation tapping into a spirit regime that they believe in, so bringing their energies into this world. Genghis also invited a Chinese Taoist to give him spiritual support, showing a personal flexibility on which his policy of tolerance may have been based.

But Nestorian Christianity, 'Church of the East' from Persia via China, had earlier reached Mongolia, gaining a significant minority following resulting from active proselytisation around the 7th century. Some Mongol tribes were predominantly Nestorians, but suffered no serious prejudice and Genghis' sons married Christian wives from the Keraites tribal group. Under Mongke Khan, Christianity was the principal faith. Franciscans, Dominicans and other missionaries came in from the west to convert the Nestorians to Roman Catholicism as Nestorian Christianity was still regarded by other Christians as heretical in its Christology.

Once the Mongols conquered further and encountered Jews and Muslims, their tolerance was challenged. They could not abide Jewish and Muslim butchery practices or their fasting, especially to the extent of Ramadan, nor circumcision, so these practises were prohibited, faiths being otherwise accepted.

The Mongols conquered much of China and Mongke Khan put Kublai in charge in 1251. Kublai made Shangdu in Inner Mongolia his capital, reformed education, agriculture and commerce as well as introducing paper money, all of which improved Chinese standards of living. He also revived Nestorian Christianity in that country. There were occasional uprisings and in 1264, Kublai built another capital that is now Beijing. He proclaimed the new Yuan dynasty in 1271, the first under which all of China would be ruled by a non-Han dynasty. This was the year he met teenage Venetian Marco Polo, son of Niccolo, whom he had met earlier with Matteo Polo when he had sent them back west to ask the pope for a hundred Christian missionaries to convert the idol-worshipping Chinese. Marco returned with his father but without the missionaries. Niccolo and Matteo operated as envoys while Marco stayed for seventeen years as a civil servant of Kublai, respecting his beneficent government for the people. He called Shangdu, Kublai's summer capital, Xanadu.

Having missed that great opportunity in the 13th century to bring Christian missionaries to China, it would not be until the 16th century and arrival of the Jesuits that another chance would arise, which Rome would again squander.

Papal Conflict with Hohenstaufen Emperors

Following Frederick II's death in 1250, Innocent IV felt able to return to Italy. He and his court stayed in Perugia for two years and while there, he issued his 1252 bull Ad Extirpanda, which included authorisation of torture in direct contravention of Jesus' teaching. He returned to Rome in 1253 and pursued with passion his conviction that the pope should have precedence over temporal kings and emperors, opposing the house of Hohenstaufen and the German possession of Sicily and Papal States.

In England, Henry III, a pious king, attended Mass every day and gave copious alms to the poor. He still faced some opposition from the barons and bishops, especially in 1240 for his support of Pope Innocent IV's fund-raising for his war with Frederick II and again in the 1250s when Henry demanded tithes to help the crusade. Before he died, Innocent IV granted the papal fiefdom of Sicily to Henry's son Edmund, having previously offered it to Henry III's brother Richard of Cornwall and Charles of Anjou. The catch was the need of force to remove the incumbent Conrad IV and Manfred. The price that Innocent IV's successor put on this was high and would be a factor leading to the second barons' war in England in 1261.

Innocent IV's deep involvement in politics came at the expense of spiritual and compassionate leadership and underlined perhaps more than ever the risks and difficulties of combining spiritual and temporal leadership. He died in December 1254.

Pope Alexander IV (1254-1261), Pope Gregory IX's nephew, succeeded Innocent IV and continued political conflict with the Hohenstaufens, but failed to garner sufficient support for a crusade against the dynasty.

Manfred, the illegitimate son of Frederick II was his representative in Italy, while his legitimate half-brother Conrad had been heir to the kingdom of Germany and therefore the empire. When Conrad died in 1254, Manfred became regent for his infant son Conradin. Manfred remained King of Sicily, which included some of the southern states of Italy including Naples. To all of these the papacy had a claim, but insufficient means to reconquer as Manfred could always call on support from the all-too-willing Saracens.

There were ongoing Hohenstaufen family disputes between the Ghibellines, who sided with Manfred who supported their Tuscan communes, in taking Florence, and the Guelfs who were less reliably pro-papal. Due to their confrontations in Rome, Alexander IV moved his court to Viterbo, that proven safe haven for some past popes. Though a peace-loving man, he was politically weak.

On the ecclesiastical front, Alexander IV pursued the Papal Inquisition against the Cathars in France, but opposed its involvement against witchcraft, which he felt was a state matter. He pursued Innocent IV's quest for Orthodox-Catholic conciliation, supported the mendicant orders and tried to raise a further crusade to confront the Mongols, who were attacking Poland for a second time.

As well as financial support to friars' orders during his rule, Alexander IV canonised St Clare and confirmed St Francis as the first known stigmatic. That is somebody who displays wounds or scars such as the wounds Christ received to his hands and feet when he was crucified.

Alexander IV was followed by his Latin Patriarch of Jerusalem **Pope Urban IV** (1261-64), who was a French cobbler's son. He was hard-working, reliable and self-reliant and studied theology and law at Paris University. When Pope Alexander IV died, he was in Viterbo seeking help following the fall within the past few days of the Latin patriarchate of Constantinople to the Byzantines. Urban IV was hoping another crusade could be called, so on his surprise election, over which the cardinals haggled for three months (he was not a cardinal), addressed the task, but soon realised that more domestic issues had to take priority. He had the political acumen and nerve to do it, but it would be a long process.

Urban IV is considered to have been potentially one of the greatest popes, but sadly did not live long enough to see the completion of his task list. He was forceful, energetic, politically astute, strategically sound, a good judge of people, pious and attentive to his flock. He appointed fourteen new cardinals, seven of them French in the first year of his papacy, thus ensuring majority support and a team that would carry on his work beyond his own reign.

It was clear that he had to deal first with the Hohenstaufens and take back Sicily and then he had to re-establish respect for the Holy See that his predecessor had lost. Charles of Anjou had the power to help achieve these priority objectives and Urban IV inherited Alexander IV's unfinished negotiations. King Louis IX of France could see that Sicily would be an important coup and would also provide a good launching pad for a crusade, but he hesitated to confront Manfred, partly because he was Regent Emperor but also because he could still summon the Saracens' help. Also, Manfred could at any time head north to topple the pope militarily, although Urban IV held him in discussions. The pro-Manfred Ghibellines were becoming daily stronger and richer in Italy. But from this perilously weak position, Urban kept his nerve and insisted that in the event of Richard of Cornwall retrieving the Kingdom of Sicily, the pontificate's suzerainty over Sicily should be restored and a further crusade should be launched to the Holy Land.

By 1264, Urban IV's position was on a knife-edge and he sent a French cardinal envoy with powers to concede some points of negotiation to Charles and his brother Louis, which included removal of an obligation to a further crusade in the short term. Louis agreed some more compromises and the papal envoy had also secured agreement of French clergy to tithes in support of a campaign to dislodge Manfred, so all was set. Meanwhile, the Ghibellines had defeated the Guelfs in the south and also taken Lucca so the pope's security in Orvieto was under threat. He moved to Perugia in September 1264, but soon died there.

Urban IV had set in motion a process which would end the Hohenstaufen's and Germany's Imperial hold for good, give France the opportunity for leadership in Europe and restore respect to the papacy in Italy.

Through all this, he had not been idle in ecclesiastical matters either, having initiated the building of a large basilica in Troyes, the city of his birth and among other things instituted the feast of Corpus Christi in 1264. He asked Thomas Aquinas, a Dominican theologian to write the Mass text and the Office for this, which included the well-known hymns *Pange Lingua*, *Tantum ergo* and *Panis Angelicus*.

Augustinians

There were a number of groups of hermits living in the Tuscany region, who got together and approached Pope Innocent IV in 1244 to ask permission to unite under a common rule of life with a single Superior

General, similar to other orders. The pope gave his blessing on condition that they accepted the Rule of St Augustine, which aims to follow directly the teaching and lifestyle of Jesus Christ, and that they form a chapter with a leader from each group to elect a single overall leader as Prior General under whom they should unite. In time, they grew so they spread throughout central Italy, developing a Grand Union of the Order of St Augustine in 1256. The solitary or eremitical life of the original members changed into one of contemplation mixed with pastoral ministry as the Church called on the Augustinians to bring evangelisation to the public arena, strengthened by their prayerful discipline.

Conflict in Italy, French and Italian Popes

Pope Urban IV was followed by another French pope, **Clement IV** (1265-68), recently the papal legate to England. His history was colourful, having begun his working life as a soldier then studying law. He became a distinguished advocate then advisor to King Louis IX. When his wife died, he took Holy Orders and was sponsored by Louis, helping his rapid rise to cardinal. Clement was elected after a lengthy conclave during which there was much discussion over Urban IV's plan with Charles of Anjou. Clement IV was a deeply pious man and begged not to be given the burden of the pontificate, but the cardinals insisted. Once elected, Clement IV also foreswore nepotism, so no relatives or friends would benefit from his investiture.

Charles of Anjou had a claim to the throne of Naples, for which he was willing to recognise the pope as feudal overlord. Charles was crowned by cardinals in Rome in Clement IV's absence at Viterbo on account of the Ghibelline clan's control of Rome. Charles marched into Naples in support of the pontificate and then in 1266 he met Emperor Manfred's army in the Battle of Benevento, where he was victorious and Manfred was killed. Charles went on to take Sicily with relative ease and when he went to Rome to be crowned, he was made a senator and consequently also became well involved in Roman politics.

Clement IV was respected for his asceticism and anti-nepotism. He asked the famous polymath Franciscan Roger Bacon to write his Opus Magnus, recording his thoughts and works, covering seven subjects – the obstacles to wisdom; philosophy and theology; the importance of the four biblical languages; mathematics; optics and sight; experimental science (which included alchemy, astronomy and forecasting developments, all of which would take place, including optical instruments, steam engines, hydraulics, and flight) and finally moral philosophy and ethics.

Clement IV died in 1268 in Viterbo and his death sparked the longest ever debate in what is sometimes claimed to be the first conclave between cardinals regarding a successor. So it was not until 1271 that Gregory X filled the shoes of St Peter.

Gregory X (1271-76) was an Italian, Teobaldo Visconti who spent a lot of his formative years in France and helped Innocent IV in setting up the Council of Lyon in 1244, where he met Thomas Aquinas. Clement IV sent Teobaldo to England in 1266 to assist his legate there in supporting Henry III in his struggles with the rebel barons. While in England Teobaldo befriended Prince Edward and joined him in the ninth crusade led by Louis IX of France in 1268 to Tunisia, reaching Acre in May 1270.

Teobaldo was elected as Pope Gregory X in September 1271, when the cardinals finally reached agreement. The cardinals had been equally divided between French and Italian members, with each faction supporting a candidate of their own nationality from within the College of Cardinals. The citizens of Viterbo became so frustrated by their delays that they eventually locked the cardinals into the building, which established a precedent for all future conclaves, then even reduced their food supplies. In the end Teobaldo, who could be identified equally between the two factions and whose nephew was Archbishop of Aix-en-Provence as well as a supporter of Charles of Anjou, was deemed an ideal compromise choice. It came as a complete surprise to him as he was in Acre with the crusade at the time and not even a priest.

Teobaldo reluctantly left the crusade at Acre and arrived at Viterbo in February 1271. The following month, he was taken to Rome, ordained and consecrated bishop before being crowned in March. The Ghibelline power in Rome had been overcome by Richard, so the papal court could now safely return there.

One of his first challenges was the arrival of the two explorer brothers Niccolo and Matteo Polo fresh from Kublai Khan's court with that message to the pope, requesting the dispatch or 100 missionaries and some oil from the lamp in the Holy Sepulchre. With little idea of the scale of this missionary opportunity, the new Pope Gregory X decided he could only spare two friars and the oil. So the Polo brothers and Niccolo's 17-year-old son Marco returned to Mongolia with the oil, but the friars dropped out and returned to Italy after a few days. This was neither the first nor last huge opportunity lost by the Church in Asia.

Gregory X set his priorities as seeking peace between Christian nations and leaders as well as between the Ghibellines and the Guelfs in Tuscany and Lombardy; achieving stability in the German Empire; improving the moral standards of clergy and people; liberating Jerusalem and the Holy

Land; and seeking reconciliation between Greek and Roman Churches. He called the **Second Council of Lyon** within days of his election. It eventually took place in 1274 with another good attendance of well over a thousand bishops and prelates including Germanus, Patriarch of Constantinople. Representatives of royalty including envoys from Byzantine Emperor Michael VII Palaeologus attended as well as over a dozen from Khan Aqaba of the Ilkhanate – part of the Mongol/Tatar Empire around today's Iran, Iraq, south-west Asia and parts of Turkey, Afghanistan and Pakistan, conquered by Genghis Khan, destined to convert to Islam in the 14th century.

A key item addressed by this council was reunion of Eastern and Western Churches. Byzantine Emperor Michael VIII's envoys tabled a letter from him expressing his desire for an end to the Great Schism. At a Mass celebrated by Pope Gregory X, the Eastern contingent recited the creed, including the controversial '*Filioque*' clause, which discomforted Eastern clergy. Agreement was reached accepting the clause and progress towards re-unification, but most of the Orthodox faithful could never really accept this, so when Michael's son Andronicus II was crowned in 1282 he reversed this. So near yet so far.

Discussion on raising a further Crusade to the Holy Land concluded that it should be financed by a tithe applied to all clergy, while the Mongol representatives were requested not to interfere with this battle against Islam. It transpired that the main objective of the Mongol delegation was to make an alliance with the Christians. There was a dramatic moment when two of them, including the lead envoy were baptised. Gregory X declared the Crusade would begin in 1278. He granted indulgence to participants, imposed the tithe to fund it and was assured of non-interference from the Mongols; prohibition of any trade with the Saracens; naval support to Italian ports; and an alliance with Byzantium. However, western monarchs proved not to be wholeheartedly in favour and reluctant to supply troops, so the Crusade never materialised. Gregory X died in 1276.

Other decisions made at the council included:

- Dismissal of some senior clergy, abbots and bishops as unworthy, following investigation.
- Full approval was given to Franciscan and Dominican orders, but not to some other mendicant orders.
- Rudolf I of Habsburg was declared King of the Romans with a view to becoming Holy Roman Emperor.
- In view of recent gaps in the papacy and to prevent outside influence, it was decided that in future, the Electoral College

cardinals should not be allowed to leave the conclave until a decision had been made.

- The doctrine of purgatory

Thomas Aquinas (1225-74) and Thomism

Thomas Aquinas was and remains one of the greatest philosophers and theologians in the history of Christianity. His was distinguished by his realism and pragmatism. Not calling much on scripture, his 'Thomism' relied on natural law and acceptance of the truth of what one experiences in the world and life, which ran contrary to the stoics. Many texts from Aristotle and his contemporary followers were discovered in the Middle Ages and these impacted on Christian philosophy and theology. Important influences in Thomas' thinking were Aristotle's philosophy as well as the basic Neoplatonism of Plotinus and his successors from the third to sixth centuries AD, many of whose texts were only translated into Latin in the early Middle Ages. (Aristotle's ideas had also influenced early Islamic theology.)

Thomas was born to Landulf, Count of Aquino and Theodora, Countess of Teano in the mainland part of the Kingdom of Sicily. Landulf's brother, Sinibald was abbot of the original Benedictine monastery at Montecassino. Aged 5, Thomas went to school there for about 9 years until it was occupied during hostilities between Emperor Frederick II and Pope Gregory IX. Thomas then went to the recently established university in Naples where he studied a range of subjects, favouring philosophy and theology, under the influence of a Dominican preacher John of St Julian. Thomas thus worked towards becoming a Dominican friar rather than a Benedictine, which disappointed his parents, who brought him home and detained him there in spite of pressure from the Dominicans. While at home, he read scripture, Aristotle's 'Metaphysics' and Peter Lombard's 'Sentences'.

Aged 19, Thomas was released and went to Rome, where he met Pope Innocent IV and the Master General of the Dominican order and he took his vows. The Dominicans sent him to the University of Paris the following year to study and he was noticed by a senior Dominican theologian, Albertus Maximus, who was sent to teach in a new university in Cologne. Thomas had also caught the eye of Pope Innocent IV, who invited him, although a Dominican, to become Abbot of Montecassino. But Thomas chose to follow Albertus to Cologne, where he taught and wrote a few commentaries on the Old Testament. Archbishop Conrad ordained him a priest around 1250. Thomas returned to Paris in 1252 to study for a higher degree in Theology, during which time he wrote a major commentary on

'Sentences' and other works. He received a doctorate of Theology together with Bonaventure, future bishop, saint and Doctor of the Church, and in 1256, was made Regent Master Theologian back in Cologne, writing copiously on philosophy and theology. He also began work on his 'break-through' book – *'Summa contra Gentiles'*, a book on 'Truth of the Catholic Faith against Errors of Unbelievers', probably intending to help missionaries to counter doctrinal arguments from Judaism and Islam.

Thereafter, Thomas spent his life praying, teaching and writing about his over-riding passion to explain, argue and promulgate the truth of Jesus Christ's teaching. He read from scripture and from John Cassian's 'Conferences' every day as part of his personal rule. He declined another papal invitation when Pope Clement IV wished to appoint him Archbishop of Naples in 1265, but Thomas was intent on his research and writing, leading to his most famous work *'Summa Theologica'*, not quite finished by the time he died.

Pope Gregory X called Thomas to the Second Council of Lyon in May 1274, asking him to be sure to bring his book 'The Errors of the Greeks'. He set off on foot but fell on the way and was taken in and cared for by Cistercian monks amongst whom he died. As the Last Rites communion was administered he said "If in this world there be any knowledge of this sacrament stronger than that of faith, I wish now to use it in affirming that I firmly believe and know as certain that Jesus Christ, True God and True Man, Son of God and Son of the Virgin Mary, is in this Sacrament ... I submit all to the judgment and correction of the Holy Roman Church, in whose obedience I now pass from this life." His school of philosophy is commonly known as Thomism, notable for taking theology back to its basis, the teaching of Jesus.

Thomas Aquinas' saintliness was beyond doubt and Pope John XXII canonised him just under fifty years after he died. *Summa Theologica* was a huge work in three parts. The 1960's English version fills 60 volumes. Happily, an abridged version in modern English has since been written by Timothy McDermott.

Pope Pius X more recently underlined Thomas' importance in his 1914 encyclical *Doctoris Angelici* in which he said that a true understanding of the Catholic Church's teachings relies on the philosophical foundations of Thomas' main theses. *Summa Theologica* is a central reference point on this. His writings were prolific, among which his commentaries on Aristotle and *'Summa contra Gentiles'* are probably the best known.

Natural Law

Thomas identified four types of law – eternal, natural, positive divine and positive human. Eternal law is God's plan which all created things follow – 'a natural tendency to pursue whatever behaviour and goals are appropriate' to them. As reasoning humans, we have some appreciation of this and can to some extent plan things for ourselves and the natural world around us. This is what Thomas means by Natural Law.

He contended that all practical reasoning depends on a notion of the 'good'. Good is to be pursued and evil avoided, where good means whatever a human naturally aims for. He split these aims into three groups:

- First, the aims we share with all created living things; anything that exists seeks to continue to exist and perpetuate its line.
- Second, the aims we share with all animals; to mate and to nurture their young.
- Third the ends we share only with fellow humans; our rational nature inclines us to seek truth about God and live in an ordered social structure.

He extrapolates from these some specific examples of secondary elements of Natural Law. So for example, from the first group, taking another human life except in self-defence is against natural law; from the second group, rules may arise regarding sex and family such as forbidding adultery; from the third group, acts and drives such as theft, greed and narcotics abuse. All these work against natural law. He regarded the first group as absolute and unchangeable. The others bear some flexibility depending on circumstance and local culture, which leaves them open to debate, so they may vary from human law.

His Positive Divine Law covers that which is in the Scriptures. Divine law is usually related to the Ten Commandments, but there are other laws, such as those about preparation of food and eating, not all of which were observed by Christ according to the Gospels. There are plenty of contradictions if one reads the Bible closely. We are all familiar with Positive Human Law. Thomas contended that human lawmakers should always take into account natural law, but there are numerous examples from all three primary groups that seem to be opposed by human laws, perhaps especially in the most 'wealthy' nations, which include capital punishment, euthanasia and same-sex marriage.

The Catholic Church has since Thomas been heavily guided by natural law in its doctrines and approach to social change. It's reluctance to endorse some legal policies that society sees as progress can be better understood in this light. However, natural law became the basis for developing international law and human rights legislation, influencing social teaching, workers' rights, political subsidiarity and international development. It is noteworthy that these too developed under Catholic Social Teaching in the 20th century, in which the topic of Natural law will be considered further. The span of Thomas' perception and articulacy is truly impressive, the more so when considering the era within which he lived.

Virtue Theology

The original meaning of virtue in Greek thinking was a quality of excellence related to purpose. Thomas Aquinas followed Aristotle and accepted Ambrose's qualification (below), while adding from his own studies of Greek philosophy that these virtues are only complete if directed towards a goal. The Greeks believed that life must have a reason, an end or goal (*telos*), i.e. teleology. It took more than 800 years for Christian virtue theory to be taken further by Thomas as he was developing his theory of Natural Law.

Plato (427-347 BC) defined the cardinal human virtues as courage, temperance (moderation), prudence and justice. He contended that one cannot be virtuous without having all these and in the right balance. His student, Aristotle (384-322BC) agreed and differentiated between intellectual virtues such as intelligence, understanding and mathematics versus moral or character virtues, which include courage, self-control and generosity, which are acquired from upbringing, example and practice.

Ambrose of Milan (339-397 AD) imported Plato's four cardinal virtues into Christian thinking and added St Paul's three theological or supernatural virtues of faith hope and love (1Cor, 13:13). Augustine of Hippo (354- 430) posited that virtue can only be good if supported by a knowledge and love of God, the source of goodness.

Limbo

In the previous century, Peter Abelard had argued against the commonly held Augustinian view of Limbo as described in the 5th century. He could not accept the justice of a punishment when there was no personal guilt as is the case with original sin. He did however accept that those with only original sin who had not been baptised could suffer no pain except that of the loss of the presence of God, which they had never experienced anyway. This view had met with general acceptance, including that of Pope Innocent III.

That is until Thomas Aquinas addressed the matter. He referred initially to the Greek Fathers, whose philosophy was that the fall in Genesis had no effect on human nature itself. He initially accepted a state of limbo existed for unbaptised children, *limbus infantium*, but that it was a state of natural happiness. His thoughts developed in the belief that infants souls were unaware of the God they were missing, which suggests their limbo was separate from those of adults who had died with original sin. Thomas suggested limbo could also accommodate non-Christian children of God, amongst whom there are many good people whose souls deserve a place. There is indirect scriptural support from John's gospel 14:6 in which Jesus says "No one can come to the Father except through me" but most of the theory of limbo was supposition for which there was no scriptural support. While the Catholic Church largely followed it and continued to inter the unbaptised in separate unblessed ground, the idea of limbo faded out during the 20th century.

Short-lived Successors to Pope Gregory X

Pope Gregory X died as a result of a hernia in January 1276 and was succeeded by a series of short-lived pontiffs: Peter of Tarantaise, a Dominican abbot, with whom Gregory X had worked closely, lived for 5 months, Adrian V for one month and John XXI for 8 months before dying under the collapse of a roof in an extension to the papal residence in Viterbo, that hitherto safe sanctuary for popes. None of these pontiffs were in post long enough to achieve much, though efforts continued to effect reconciliation of Rudolf, the Habsburg king of the Germans with Charles of Anjou, now King of Sicily.

After John XXI died, the election endured for six months because Adrian V had loosened the rules set by Gregory X. Added to that, due to the rapid procession of popes and passage of time, only seven cardinals remained. Eventually Giovanni Gaetano Orsini, made Cardinal Deacon by Innocent IV, emerged as **Pope Nicholas III** (1277-80) and headed for Rome, to be ordained, consecrated as bishop then crowned. Charles of Anjou was unimpressed, as he had tightened his Angevin grip on the papal lands and this pope had openly expressed the view that Charles held too much influence over Rome and the Papal States.

The new Pope was intent on strengthening the standing of the papacy and Rome, the latter having suffered repeated swings of imperial and local interference and influence. He spotted an opportunity in German King Rudolf, who was anxious for a belated coronation. Nicholas III showed a will to proceed on this with conditions including Rudolf's acceptance of Church claims which Nicholas had enhanced for the purpose of negotiation. A concordat was agreed in 1278 then approved by the Habsburg princes, whereby the northern territories of Romagna, Ravenna and the city of Bologna came under papal control. This gave Nicholas III leverage to persuade King Charles of Sicily and Naples to retire from his posts as Senator of Rome and Papal Vicar of Tuscany. Having achieved these aims, Nicholas III soon changed the constitution of Rome to deny any foreigners senatorial or civil office, regardless of their rank or title.

He was an effective if manipulative pope, though prone to nepotism in appointing relatives to lucrative positions of authority in the newly acquired territories. He did attend to ecclesiastical aims although the nature of the papacy then still necessarily involved politics and he was adept at using them to the benefit of the Church as well as of his noble family. He was behind an agreement in 1280 in which King Charles, who was also Count of Provence, allowed Provence and Forcalquier to become imperial fiefdoms of Rudolf and also encouraged the engagement of Charles' grandson to Clementia, a daughter of Rudolf.

Nicholas III made efforts to retrieve and drive further the brief reconciliation between the Greek and Roman Churches achieved at the Council of Lyons. He did what he could to limit the power of Charles in the South Eastern 'heel' of Italy and sent envoys to Byzantine Emperor Michael to secure his confirmation of the oath sworn by his legates at the council. Nicholas a tough negotiator, sought more stringent conditions controlling the Greek Rite and the need for their clergy to seek absolution for transgression of Roman wishes. He gained the Emperor's support, but optimism for success was doomed by the fact that the population and the faithful simply would not accept renewed Roman dominance.

Further east, Nicholas III sent five Franciscan missionaries to Khan Aqaba in 1278 to spread the Gospel in Persia then move on to China. It proved challenging missionary territory and tangible results were to be slow in coming.

He redressed the serious shortage of cardinals by appointing ten more, strengthening the Roman contingent and diluting the Angevins, weakening further Charles' influence within the Church.

Nicholas was conscious of the recent peripatetic nature of the papacy and the difficulties of managing a Church from temporary bases. So having made Rome a safer operational base, hopefully for the long term, he moved the papal court back to where Saints Peter and Paul were buried. He enhanced the palace and acquired more property around the Vatican. He built the Chapel of St Nicholas in St Peter's, where after his death in 1280 he was buried, having taken some significant steps in his reign of less than three years.

Nicholas III had died while in the diocese of Viterbo, so the next conclave was held there, where King Charles had more influence as many members of the supportive Annibaldi family lived there. There were disturbances during which the Governor of the city, a nephew of Nicholas III, was expelled.

The conclave reached a stalemate as neither the Angevin nor Roman factions could muster a two-thirds majority. In February 1281, two pro-Orsini cardinals were captured and held, so Cardinal Simon de Brion was elected, taking the name **Pope Martin IV** (1281-85). Viterbo was put under an interdiction for the successive disruptions of recent conclaves and Rome duly refused to have a French pope crowned in Rome, so Martin was crowned in Orvieto, living there until Ghibelline v. Guelf feuds forced his move to Perugia.

As pope, Martin IV was a virtual puppet of Charles, even though Charles lost control of Sicily to Peter III of Aragon, in spite of excommunication and other sanctions by Martin IV against Peter. Martin IV also fell out with the Byzantine Emperor Michael, effectively putting an end to the Lyons accord. He refused to crown Rudolf as emperor and misguidedly placed Venice under interdiction for failing to launch an attack on Sicily in support of Charles following its defeat by Peter of Aragon.

Martin IV appointed seven more new cardinals, mostly French. He died after a brief unexpected illness shortly after Easter in 1285, bringing to an end an ineffective, even damaging papacy.

Giacomo Savelli, from that wealthy Roman family was elected four days after Martin IV's death, becoming **Pope Honorius IV** (1285-87). He was a graduate of Paris University made cardinal deacon by Urban IV, so underwent the same process as Nicholas III before his coronation. He moved the Curia to Rome where he was known and welcomed. After a while living in the Vatican, he moved to the newly built family palace, being elderly and chair- or bed-bound. He championed peace and justice in Sicily and also repaired relations with Rudolf, agreeing to crown him as emperor, but war in Northern Europe prevented Rudolf from travelling to Rome.

Like Martin IV, Honorius IV inherited the desire for a Crusade, and received an encouraging letter in 1285 from Arghun, a Mongol ruler, who proposed co-ordinated attacks on the key Muslim lands of Syria and Egypt from two directions. But war-weary European leaders never took up the opportunity so the tithes established at Lyons just accumulated in the bank. Honorius IV died two years after his accession.

Girolamo Masci was one of four Franciscan friars who had been selected for the mission to invite Greek representation to the Council of Lyons. He was appointed leader of the Franciscans in 1274, then sent with

John Vercelli, Master General of the Dominicans as pope's envoys to Philip IV of France to encourage him to make peace with Alfonso III of Aragon, but without success. He became cardinal bishop in 1281 and when Honorius IV died in April 1287, the election was delayed. Ten of only 13 cardinals attended the council but failed to agree on a successor. Seven of them died of a fever during an adjournment before **Pope Nicholas IV** (1287-92) was finally elected in February 1288, the first Franciscan pope.

He soon appointed one new French cardinal and five Italians, including an Orsini. He also notably awarded the cardinals the generous income of half that of the Holy See split between them, which would come to cause future serious financial problems for the Church. In Rome another powerful family had come to the fore, the Colonnas, who also held influence over the pope.

During the papal interregnum, Edward I of England had mediated a treaty that awarded Sicily to James II of Aragon. Pope Nicholas IV annulled the treaty and crowned King Charles II of Naples and Sicily, who acknowledged the papal suzerainty over Sicily, a move that In practice resolved nothing.

Nicholas IV met Nestorian Christian Rabban Bar Sauma from China and sent missionaries to China, also to Mongolia, the Tatars, Bulgaria and Ethiopia.

The election that followed Nicholas IV's death was the last one without a conclave as it is known today and had been specified by Gregory X and resulted in another impasse. **Pope Celestine V** (1294) was an extreme ascetic and hermit who had founded a new order, the Celestines around 1264. They followed Benedictine rule with added disciplines. His papacy only ran from July to December 1294 and although an exceptionally devout man, he made some awful decisions in that brief period. Against the cardinals' wishes, he moved the papal court to Naples to show support for Charles of Naples. He made twelve new cardinals, seven of whom were French and the rest mostly Neapolitan, which would lead to the troublesome Avignon papacy. He reinstated Gregory X's rule covering future conclaves, which annoyed the cardinals. He then abdicated a week after issuing a decree that popes should have the right to retire, his only lasting decree. He wished to return to the life of a hermit monk, but his successor insisted he live in a castle in Ferentino. It was believed to ensure he did not change his mind and become an anti-pope, although with his nature and history that was unlikely, his retirement more plausibly being the result of realisation and regret at some of his unpopular decisions, some of which would soon be reversed. He died a year later aged 81.

This next election was in conclave and rapidly concluded. **Pope Boniface VIII** (1294-1303), who had been born near Rome with maternal connections to a couple of past popes, was elected on Christmas Eve then crowned early 2095. He immediately returned the papal court to the Vatican. Like Gregory IX he had considerable knowledge of canon law. Since so many changes and additions had been made to canon law, including a good many of his own since the publication of *Decretales Gregorii IX* he authorised a new, expanded edition including a glossary of legal rules or principles called *Regulae Juris* which should underlie the formulation of canon laws.

Boniface VIII mixed sharp political instincts with quite an overbearing style with little subtlety, holding extreme views on the total supremacy of the papacy in both ecclesiastical and civil matters. He summed these up later in his own Papal Bull (*Unam Sanctam* in 1302), "it is absolutely necessary for salvation that every human creature be subject to the Roman pontiff". He applied this as much while interfering in civil political matters as he did with ecclesiastical issues, inevitably building tension with both Albert I of Germany and Philip IV of France. He also became the butt of some works by the literary giant of the time, Dante Alighieri, who wrote *De Monarchia* against Boniface VIII's claims to such broad power. Fourteen new cardinals were appointed during Boniface VIII's reign, none of them French, but three of them members of his family.

Decline of the Colonna Family, International Tensions

During this period, the fortunes of the Roman Colonna family also took a steep decline. It began with Cardinal Jacopo Colonna declaring his three brothers disinherited from their lands, which he planned to pass to his nephews. The brothers appealed to the pope, who ordered the Cardinal to restore their inheritance, as well as to restore the papal treasure that Stefano Colonna had seized on its way from Anagni to Rome and to give their stronghold towns of Colonna, Palestrina and Zagorolo to the Church. The cardinal restored the treasure, but he refused the rest. He was soon deposed and excommunicated together with his nephew, Cardinal Pietro Colonna for their dealings with James II of Aragon and Frederik III of Sicily, enemies of the pope. The Colonnas posted a declaration on Church doors and the high altar of St Peter's that Boniface VIII's election was non-canonical. The pope moved from Rome to Orvieto as warfare broke out between the Colonna family and the pope's army, led by Landolfo Colonna, one of the brothers the pope had helped regain his inheritance. Papal forces won in 1298, destroying the towns Jacopo had refused to hand over, sparing only their cathedrals. The Colonna ex-cardinals begged forgiveness and their excommunications were lifted but they were not re-appointed. Colonna property was distributed between Landolfo, the Orsini family and relatives of the pope.

Boniface VIII failed in several attempts during his reign to make peace between the Genoese and Venetian republics in northern Italy as they vied for control of trade with the Levant. The pope regarded the importance of these port cities as lying in their potentially vital role in any crusade towards the east.

Hostilities continued with Sicily, which Boniface placed under interdict; with the King of Aragon; and with Florence, where Dante Aligheri was among the leaders. When Florence was invaded, the leaders were all exiled. In the case of Dante this led to his literary revenge on Boniface VIII in his 'Inferno', the first canticle of 'The Divine Comedy'. Although not an anti-Catholic work, it would be claimed as support by Thomas Cromwell, lawyer to Henry VIII of England in a later century in its supposed questioning of Marian intercession and purgatory, that non-biblical concept that became accepted in mediaeval orthodoxy as an intermediate state between heaven and hell where lesser sins are purged before a soul's acceptance into heaven. Dante adopted a pauper's view of Christianity that assessed the Church by the standards set by Christ and his Apostles in contrast to those of the pope. The protagonist in The Divine Comedy, experiences the nine circles of Hell before ascending the summit of Mount Purgatory to enjoy the revelation of God in paradise.

Meanwhile, Philip IV of France was preoccupied with wars against England, which were draining his resources as well as those of England's Edward I. While resisting clerical interference in his government and legal systems, Philip IV noted the wealthy Church could bear some taxation such as had been approved in the past, but only on a temporary basis to fund crusades desired by the Church, not wars between states. When Boniface VIII responded with refusal and hostility in 1296, Philip banned the export of all money and valuables to the Papal States, cutting off a major source of income for the Vatican, forcing Boniface to back down. This allowed French clerics to contribute to the national need. So Philip IV eased the sanctions, allowed collections for a proposed crusade and used the pope in a mediation or arbitration role on several occasions, though tension still simmered between them.

In England in 1294, following Philip IV's unexpected seizure of Gascony, Edward I also badly needed funds to retrieve the territory. He began by demanding even higher taxes than the French on clerical incomes and went so far as to sequester the contents of the treasuries of all Churches and monasteries found by his agents. At the end of 1296, during the convocation at Canterbury the king demanded a fifth of clerical income in tax to support the wars with France. Archbishop Robert of

Winchelsea said he would consult the pope as the higher authority. This response enraged Edward I, leading to him outlawing all clergy and seizing their incomes, goods and chattels.

England invaded the Scottish borders in 1296, and forced their King John Balliol to abdicate. The Scots looked to Rome for support, claiming that they were historically a Papal fiefdom, which Boniface VIII accepted, but Edward I refuted. Thus began the first wars for Scottish independence with William Wallace and Andrew Moray famously leading the Scots to victory at the Battle of Stirling Bridge in 1297. The troublesome English barons also refused the pope's appeal in 1301 and Boniface VIII, hearing reports of violent internecine conflict among the Scots, decided to let the matter lie.

The year 1300 was widely proclaimed in advance as a Jubilee Year in Rome. The resulting masses of pilgrims to Rome for the celebration helped top up funds that had suffered from a drop in income. Pope Boniface VIII became involved in further conflict with Philip IV of France, paving the way to dramatic developments between France and the papacy in the following century.

CHAPTER 16

14th Century

Popes

1303-04 Benedict XI	1352- 62 Innocent VI
1304-14 Clement V	1362-70 Urban V
1314-16 Interregnum	1370-78 Gregory XI
1316-34 John XXII	1378-89 Urban VI
1328-30 (Antipope Nicholas V)	(1378-94 Clement VI French rival pope)
1334-42 Benedict XII	(1394-1423 Benedict XIII French rival)
1342-52 Clement VI	1389-1404 Boniface IX

Emperors

1312-1313 Henry VII
1314-1347 Louis IV the Bavarian
1346-1378 Charles V

This century is generally regarded as the beginning of the Late Middle Ages which would see continuing misfortune and turbulence for the Church lasting through this century and beyond. The Church had already seen the effects of attempts to combine ecclesial and political leadership, something never suggested by Jesus Christ. The Church structure had already been proven to be unsuitable for the dual role, there being a sense that during recent centuries the Church had survived rather than thrived in its pastoral role. But the pain of this next period would spread wider than the Church as another devastating plague would spread through most of Europe.

The Spiritual-Temporal Conundrum

Europe was an unstable and troubled place whose political ills and strife spilled into those lands that had been given to the Church and should have provided much of its wealth. So popes for some time now had been so preoccupied with political and financial distractions that they were unable to protect the faith from its enemies, promote its great mission and maintain its unity. Spiritual leadership was weakened with many members of the clergy lax in their discipline, devotion and mission. It was no wonder that the faithful felt frustration with a Church that had become a body less inspirational, more worldly and with leadership increasingly seen to be self-serving, putting its own ends before those of God. Many popes were wise and pious men, but the politicised conclaves that elected them, the external influences on their administration and conflicting demands of their responsibilities, led to some promoting trusted allies or family members, only compounding the distrust, a situation was now to be aggravated by a persistent Avignon papacy.

Roman Family Feuds and Popes

The **Colonna** and **Orsini families** were both of long-standing Roman nobility who had regarded each other with ambitious suspicion and mistrust, resulting in frequent feuds in defence of their influence in the city. They were equally competitive in ecclesiastical affairs, both families having provided a number of cardinals and popes over several centuries. The Colonna's traced their roots and Church connections back before the Tusculani, who featured in the 10th century and with whom they were related through marriage. The Colonnas were lead members of the Ghibelline party, politically opposed the Orsini-supported Guelph's. In the Middle Ages, the senior Colonnas tended to side with the Empire, while the Orsinis leaned towards the Roman Church, although some individual members of both were exceptions to this generality.

The expatriated Colonna family approached King Philip IV of France, who had been tutored by a Colonna in his youth and was himself no friend of Pope Boniface VIII.

Turbulence Persists, Church versus French King Philip IV

The 13th century had been a difficult time for the papacy due to instability within Rome and the ongoing bitter feud between the Colonnas and Orsinis making it a dangerous place. Popes had frequently been forced to set up their bases in other cities such as Viterbo, Orvieto, Agnani and Perugia, so there had been little surprise at a French Pope choosing to settle in Avignon, but nobody had foreseen the huge consequences this would have for the Church. The frequent transience of the papacy prejudiced the ongoing authority of the Church which even had to resort to leading missions of violence within Italy, such as a fierce battle to retrieve Venice led by Cardinal Pélagrue in 1309. These were unruly, violent times in which ambition and greed rendered peaceful paths to resolution almost impassable. The Church further undermined its own influence by visible internal indulgence, excesses, hedonism and corruption, as well as some behaviour of crusaders and Knights Templar.

This set a difficult background for the genuinely good clerics who could only keep praying and working for the good of people and the glory of God.

The relationship between Pope Boniface VIII and Philip IV had been deteriorating towards the end of the previous century and reached its nadir early in this one as Philip openly campaigned against the pope's claim to supremacy of power over all earthly leaders. Philip IV had levied taxes on clerics and tried them in the courts, which Boniface opposed as breaching the liberty of the Church.

The king had tried to force the pope to hold a council in France, but he had refused because of the risk of interference with the agenda and discussion. He called a council in Rome in 1302 and a large number of French prelates attended regardless of Philip's prohibition and confiscation of their property. Following that council, Boniface confirmed in a Papal Bull the popes' claim to overarching spiritual and temporal power, to which monarchs were subordinate. French Chief Minister, Guillaume de Nogaret had discreetly visited enemies of Boniface VIII's Gaetano family in Italy. He denounced Boniface as a heretic and in 1303 Philip sent de Nogaret with Sciarra Colonna, relatives and allies to invade Boniface in his birthplace, the palace at Anagni with the objective of bringing the pope back to France. Boniface excommunicated Sciarra and Guillaume but the attack went ahead, initially successfully. Nogaret restrained Sciarra Colonna from killing the 73-year-old for his defiance. Two days later, sympathetic locals raised enough men to confront and expel the invaders. Boniface VIII was released and escorted by cardinals to Rome where he soon died.

The cardinal electors wisely sought a successor who would take a more conciliatory line with King Philip IV, choosing another Dominican, Pope Benedict XI. Benedict quickly lifted Philip's excommunication, but not that of de Nogaret, because of his part in the attack at Anagni. Benedict XI also brokered an armistice between Edward I of England and Philip IV of France. He then died suddenly mid-1304 at Perugia with a finger of suspicion of poisoning pointed at Guillaume de Nogaret, but never proved.

Avignon Papacy

Benedict XI's eight month rule was followed by nearly a year of interregnum due to difficulty reaching a two-thirds majority for proposed candidates as a result of the Franco-Italian balance of cardinals. A French candidate who had been Archbishop of Bordeaux and chaplain to Boniface VIII was eventually elected and took the name Clement V. He chose to have his coronation at Lyons in November 1305. King Philip IV attended and saw an opportunity to exert enough control over Clement V to attenuate recent tensions between the papacy and his own rule. Not long after Clement V's consecration the king asked him to declare Boniface VIII a heretic, remove him from the official list of popes, disinter his body for cremation and scatter his ashes widely. Clement V chose to play for time, attempting to pacify Philip by offering favours. So in 1306 the pope rescinded Boniface VIII's claims to temporal supremacy of the pope as well as his prohibition of taxing the clergy. Clement also appointed more French cardinals.

The following year 1307, King Philip IV, still struggling financially, was in debt to the Knights Templar. He had hundreds of Knights arrested in France, including their Grand Master. Philip IV had for some time accused them of abuses, including usury, fraud, heresy and immorality and he took this as an opportunity to avoid repayment of substantial sums owed to them. Although Clement V was unhappy with this situation, he took no decisive action in the Knights' favour, seeing the issue as secondary to Philip's attack on Boniface VIII and in any case the Knights had alienated much of French aristocracy by their attitude.

A peace treaty was signed the same year between England and France at Poitiers, reducing the drain on both treasuries. Philip IV still pressed his demand that Boniface VIII be tried posthumously as a heretic.

Clement V was content to be persuaded against any move from Lyon to Rome, which was not considered a dramatic choice at the time. Colonna and Orsini family feuds continued to foster turbulence in Rome and recent popes had become accustomed to living elsewhere. But this was the first time the court had been in France and in 1309, a new Papal Palace was built in Avignon with Philip IV's help, although at the price of demanding that posthumous trial of Pope Boniface. Clement said it was up to complainants to make a case and asked the Bishop of Paris and a senior French Dominican to see that any such complainants fix place and time of trial such that the pope could be present. There was powerful opposition to this from leaders of Italy, Aragon, Castile, Germany and the Netherlands and Clement prayed for a distraction which may give time for the matter to subside.

In April, 1310, in another peace gesture to Philip, Clement V lifted the excommunication of Nogaret and pardoned his actions at Agnani and against the Church, subject to Nogaret travelling to the Holy Land and serving with the next military expedition there. But the Colonna cardinals kept the pressure on by supporting Philip in the accusations building against Pope Boniface VIII. A preliminary judicial examination took place in autumn 1310. Clement V was convinced the evidence was dubious and probably corrupt and announced his conviction that Boniface was quite innocent. Accusers left one meeting to discuss further proceedings, in the face of gauntlet challenges from knights supporting Boniface, so Philip IV eventually yielded to Clement V's wish to determine the matter of judging Boniface at a forthcoming council to be held in Vienne, a relatively neutral location, being outside Philip IV's control. This Council was delayed until the end of 1311.

The Council of Vienne was attended by twenty cardinals, four patriarchs and well over a hundred archbishops, bishops, abbots and priors. The main item on the agenda was that of the Knights Templar and its lands. The need for a commission to gather evidence and report back resulted in the council spreading over several months. The drawn-out process and ultimate decision to disband the Knights, which was to Philip's advantage, seemed to have diverted Philip's intent on the issue of the past pope.

Other items raised at the council were the need for a new crusade to the Holy Land; the King of Aragon's request for a crusade to help attack the Muslims in Granada; the Beguine lay spiritual revival movement; also the age-old matter of reforming ecclesiastical morals. Working parties were to report back on these.

The debate regarding Boniface VIII did not last long after three cardinals attested to his rectitude, orthodoxy and moral integrity and the council declared the matter closed.

By the close of the council in May 1312, decisions included the following:

- The Order of the Knights Templar was disbanded
- King Philip IV dropped the issue of Pope Boniface and was absolved of blame for his actions against him.
- Philip IV would organise a crusade to the Holy Land within six years and would be replaced by his eldest son if he died in the meantime.
- There would be no crusade to Spain for the time being
- The unregulated 'Beguine movement' of lay religious orders would be disbanded.
- No decisions were made regarding reform of ecclesiastical morals.

It was ruled that the lands of the Knights Templar be passed to the Hospitaliers, but in fact much of it ended up in Philip's hands. Clement V died in 1314, soon after Philip IV. It was a reflection on the complex relationship of Church and Royalty in France as well as the strains among cardinals that it took two years before the new pope was finally elected at a conclave in the Dominican monastery in Lyons, facilitated by the newly crowned King Philip V, the younger brother and successor to Louis X, who had meanwhile briefly succeeded Philip. IV.

The new Cahors-born French pope chose to stay in the papal palace at Avignon rather than St Peter's and followed Clement in that he enjoyed the luxury of the palace whilst working to maintain the central power and revenue of the Church. **Pope John XXII** (1316-1334) was clearly not convinced of the need for clerical orders to adhere to absolute poverty with no possessions as a way of life, and declared as suspect Pope Nicholas III's bull on the subject. He agreed with Clement V's view that there should be no compulsion on spiritual orders to forego ownership, be it individual or joint. Most orders tended to accept this to the extent of leaving it to leaders and individuals to decide according to their own consciences whether poverty was a necessary part of reflecting the life of Jesus Christ.

The question arose as to whether this argument really merited such determined pursuit. Both Popes Clement V and John XXII thought so. Perhaps it had occurred to them that if the rejection of all worldly goods were a condition of holiness, then the papal possessions, riches and lands would be difficult to justify and they regarded these as vital to running and sustaining the church. This suggested confusion between personal, 'papal' and 'Church' possessions as well as conflating spiritual and temporal leadership.

Some Franciscans refused to accept John's insistence that there was nothing wrong with ownership and that Jesus had never required such absolute poverty. In 1317, John XXII ordered the dissenting friars, mainly in Italy and the south of France, to accept the softer line on clerical poverty. The argument rumbled on until in 1323. Pope John denounced as heretical the view that Jesus and the Apostles had no possessions themselves or as a group. Leaders of the Church still made liberal use of that word 'heresy' and its partner 'excommunication'. By this time, the general of the Perugia chapter, Michael of Cesena, who supported the stricter Franciscan view, was summoned with two supporters, William Ockham and Bonagratia di Bergamo to Avignon to explain themselves. When threatened with imprisonment, all three accepted sanctuary in Germany offered by Louis IV of Bavaria.

During the interregnum between Clement V and John XXII, there had been a dispute in Germany over its vacant throne. Two claimants had been separately crowned – Louis IV of Bavaria in Aachen and Frederick of Austria in Bonn in 1314. When Pope John XXII was elected, both of them sought his blessing, but he said he had no preference and suggested they reach agreement. Meanwhile, Church income was being severely reduced by the both the absence of a pope in Rome and turbulence in Italy, not least in the Papal States.

Pope John XXII was a good administrator. Inefficient collection of Church dues and significant papal loans taken out under Boniface VIII led Pope John to take much further the earlier attempts by Popes Innocent III and Honorius III to improve central financial controls. He adopted a uniform system of book-keeping and raised the status of financial management, or Camera in the Curia. The chief officer or '*camerarius*' now reported directly to the pope regarding policy and its application. Second in line was the treasurer, responsible for safe-keeping of money and its distribution as well as accurate record-keeping. The auditor was responsible to the camerarius and had a legal team. The hitherto disparate international network of dues collectors was formalised and although independent, they reported directly to the camerarius with detailed accounts to help secure better returns. There had been a considerable shortfall, far in excess of reasonable collection costs, between amounts collected from the public and those reaching the treasury.

In another step to improve security of finances, selected Italian bankers replaced the Knights Templar as more reliable collection records were needed. Merchants became necessarily involved in currency exchange as tax was levied and expenses incurred in various nations and currencies.

King Louis caused friction by appointing a vicar of Italy in 1315 and supporting the anti-pope Ghibellines. Pope John XXII claimed that imperial jurisdiction rested in him since there was no single king of Germany, and overrode Louis' choice by appointing Robert of Sicily as Imperial Vicar in 1317. A further irritant between them was Louis IV's rejection of John XXII's approach to clerical poverty.

When, in 1322, Louis IV advised Pope John XXII that he prevailed as king, Pope John wrote a friendly reply, but there was no reciprocal warmth from the king, who continued supporting the Ghibelline party. John XXII reminded Louis that his coronation as Holy Roman Emperor lay in the pope's hands and he was doing himself no favours by acting as if he were already emperor and supporting the enemies of the Church. The pope asked Louis IV to attend at Avignon within three months. Louis sent an envoy requesting a further two months to arrange travel and used that time to promote opposition to the pope in Germany. He also sought theologians who would confirm his view that his authority should not be subject to that of the pope, which he argued was surely a constitutional matter rather than a theological one. John XXII excommunicated him in 1324, having obtained his own learned theological support.

By 1327, Louis IV felt sure enough of his position in Germany to travel to Italy and hold meetings with the Ghibellines at Trent then move on to Milan, still a problem city for the Church. Pope John announced the forfeiture of all Louis IV's rights to the German and Bavarian crowns or to the fiefs inherited from his predecessors and the Church. John XXII also issued a summons for Louis to meet him in Rome, which Louis ignored, but proceeded to Milan where he was crowned emperor by two deposed Archbishops. He appointed several new bishops for good measure. After this, he proceeded to Rome where the Guelphs had been overthrown, including their senator, King Robert of Naples. In January 1338, Sciarra Colonna crowned Louis IV as Holy Roman Emperor, setting in motion an extraordinary chain of events.

Louis IV, who had been excommunicated, declared Pope John XXII deposed and a heretic and followed this up in May by appointing Pietro Rainalducci of Corbaldo, a strict Franciscan as Antipope Nicholas V. To most Italians this was clearly untenable and as Louis IV burdened them with heavy taxation, his popularity declined and many Ghibelline followers and territories swung behind Pope John XXII. In 1330, the antipope repented and came to Avignon to beg forgiveness and confirm his support for John and the cardinals. John gave him absolution, but detained Pietro in Avignon in penance for the last three years of his life. Meanwhile, Louis IV had lost almost all his support in Italy as Italians aligned with Pope John XXII, so he returned to Germany. Finding the Germans had lost their ardour for the conflict between their king and the pope, Louis IV put out some conciliatory feelers through German bishops to which the pope responded with insistence on Louis IV renouncing his imperial claims. It took until 1333 for Louis IV to accept this.

This prolonged dispute with Louis IV overshadowed other aspects of Pope John XXII's papacy. He was also known for his views, expressed even before his elevation, that souls of the dead will not see the 'Beatific Vision', the sight of God in Heaven, until after the Last Judgement. In this he was opposed by many theologians, but he held to the view for some time.

He also issued a papal bull in 1326 in which he warned against learning or teaching magic and strictly prohibited its practice, which he called witchcraft. He declared witchcraft to be a heresy and authorised the ongoing inquisition to use any means to seek out witchcraft and eliminate it. The guilty were to be treated in the same way as heretics.

Jacques Fournier came from an ordinary family near Foix and became a Cistercian monk, rising to abbot and gaining a reputation as an intelligent and gifted organiser. He became a bishop in 1317 and organised the hunt for Cathars with notable success which helped him to the cardinalate by 1327. He succeeded Pope John XXII in 1334, as **Pope Benedict XII** (1334-42).

He wished to return the papal seat to Rome and planned the restoration of St Peter's and the Lateran. The cardinals, mostly French, counselled that the move would be unwise given the ongoing factional feuding in Italy.

They also advised against his compromise suggestion of Bologna, so he remained in Avignon.

Benedict XII acted against clerical greed, such as expecting payment or favours for awards of benefices, high charges for episcopal visits and corruption generally, which included the papal staff exacting a price for their countersignature on referrals for decisions from the pope. Benedict XII's simple solution to the latter was to establish a Register of Supplications. As a Cistercian, and in contrast to John XXII, he promoted restraint among monastic communities, with limited success and he began to repair papal relations with the Spiritual Franciscans. He opposed nepotism and was quite active in beginning to improve organisation and discipline in the Church, but successes in the latter were rather diminished by his own obesity and the grandeur of his plans in 1339 for the *Palais des Papes* in Avignon. There was some disappointment among the faithful in Rome at his failure to move back where they felt he belonged.

Benedict XII had little political experience and his overtures to the Eastern Church and Emperor Andronicus made no progress. He tried to hold out a hand of peace to King Louis IV. King Philip VI of France astutely used the predominance of French cardinals to apply restraints, including that desired return to Rome, and to manipulate the pope on matters that affected Philip.

Benedict had neither the guile nor political support to counter this manipulation effectively, so he was humiliated on a number of fronts. For example, Philip VI diverted money collected for another crusade to support his war with England. The so-called Hundred Year War began in 1337, and would last until 1453. Eventually an alliance was reached between Philip VI and Louis IV with some of Benedict XII's enemies. Then Louis IV's declaration that the marriage between John Henry of Bohemia and Margaret Maultasch was null and void, freeing Margaret to marry Louis' son, was a clear contravention of papal prerogative.

Benedict was deeply interested in theology and enjoyed debating it with leading scholars of the day. He disagreed with a number of his predecessors' theories, especially concerning the Beatific Vision and he issued an Apostolic Constitution – as high a declaration as a pope can make, outranking an encyclical, declaring that anybody who died in a state of grace would immediately enjoy that ultimate reward.

Pierre Roger from Aquitaine entered a Benedictine monastery aged 10 and grew to be a capable bishop and Archbishop before being made cardinal aged 47 by Pope Benedict XII. Having succeeded Benedict as **Pope Clement VI** (1342-52) he soon created twenty five cardinals, most of whom were French and a fair number his relatives. He did not share

Benedict's sensitivity to nepotism, becoming so famous for it that after his death over 40 statues of relatives were placed round his sarcophagus. Fiercely French, he rejected a Roman delegation's plea to return the papacy to Rome and underlined this message by subsequently buying the sovereignty of Avignon for the Church from Joanna, Princess of Naples and Provence, to whom it belonged. Part of the price for this seems to have been his declaration of her innocence of arranging the murder of her husband, for which she had been accused. This move suggested his desire for permanence of the papal seat in France.

Clement VI gave generous gifts to all visitors in the first two months of his papacy, which is said to have attracted about 100,000 clerics. He enjoyed the high social life and exotic banquets, so funds soon ran low. He attempted to replenish them by levying taxes and reserving many monastic and diocesan appointments to himself, for which he charged heavily. He overrode many protestations from close advisors, feeling that the palace at Avignon needed more lavish comforts and design befitting a pope who was superior to all earthly authorities. He added impressive facades, new towers and a grand staircase to a new Papal Chapel, while upgrading many rooms. He confirmed his intention to establish Avignon as the permanent Papal Seat by adding extensions intended to accommodate parts of the Roman Curia.

Edward III of England's antipathy toward the French was magnified by this flagrantly Francophile pope, so he resisted the proposed increases in Church taxation and exerted his own right to make senior Church appointments in England.

Clement made the then customary approaches to Greek Christians as well as the Armenians, who were also threatened by the Turks, to reunite with the Roman Church. They replied in encouraging vein but it was based on their main aim to win support in repelling the Turks. A crusade in 1344 achieved little more than an attack on Smyrna from the sea, so the matter was left pending once more.

In 1345, Clement VI encouraged King Casimir III of Poland to ease his oppression of senior clergy and to make peace with King John of Bohemia. Clement had received complaints about the over-authoritarian handling of German clergy by Archbishop Henry III of Mainz and Prague. Knowing he was also a staunch follower of Louis IV, Clement VI replaced him with a younger man, created the new archdiocese of Prague, and gave its Archbishop the right to crown future kings of Bavaria.

King Louis IV was fast losing support from the Germans, due to his manipulation of Church matters in freeing Margaret Maultasch from her marriage so she could marry his son. Thus weakened, he adopted humility and approached Pope Clement VI offering to renounce all his imperial actions, but asked for ongoing recognition as King of the Romans. Clement VI agreed on the following conditions:

- no imperial or even royal decree in Germany could be enacted without papal approval
- all abbots and bishops appointed by Louis IV should be returned to their former office
- Louis IV return sovereignty of the Papal States of Sicily, Sardinia and Corsica to the papacy

The German princes would not allow Louis to accept these conditions', His time as king was clearly limited, so the German panel of Royal and ecclesiastical electors chose Charles of Luxembourg in 1346 as future successor, which met the pope's approval. The German people were divided, but on the sudden death of Louis IV on a boar hunt, opposition to the election of Charles IV soon evaporated.

Clement IV called 1350 a Jubilee Year in Rome and as usual, pilgrims flocked there from far and wide for the plenary indulgence such pilgrimage would earn. Those from Britain found a sad lack of accommodation and had to pay extortionate rates for overcrowded, filthy and damp quarters a long way from St Peters. This spurred the English community in Rome to acquire a building which they dedicated to the Holy Trinity and St Thomas and converted into a hospice for poor, sick and needy English travellers to Rome in 1362. It would later be converted into a seminary as the English College in Rome in 1579.

In 1352, Clement VI sent Abbot Guillaume de Grimoard to sort out turbulence in Northern Italy caused by the ambitious Visconti family of Milan, with Giovanni Visconti, Archbishop of Milan a lead figure. They had invaded much of Lombardy and were threatening Florentine territory. In an astonishingly ill-judged move, Pope Clement VI authorised Grimoard to make the archbishop his Vicar of Genoa on condition that he return this Papal City to the pope. Grimoard made the deal and also persuaded the archbishop to renew an expiring treaty with the King and Queen of Sicily.

When the **Bubonic Plague**, known as the Black Death struck in the south of France in 1347-9, Clement IV showed his wiser and kinder side in offering a safe refuge to Jews in the sovereign state of Avignon. They had been subject to widespread attack and massacre as many people quite illogically blamed them for the pestilence. Clement VI died in 1352, without succumbing to the plague. His extravagance had largely spent the wealth that his predecessors John XXII and Benedict XII had carefully built for the Church.

The Bubonic Plague was brought to Europe by a trading ship from China in 1347 and spread rapidly, taking only a year to reach Britain. It was passed on by fleas from small rodents and produced pustules on lymph glands in the armpit, neck and groin, with death following three or four days after their appearance.

The plague killed a third of the population in Europe and so many workers died that the shortage of labour led to rapid wage inflation. In England a law was passed to fix maximum wages, but ran into problems in its implementation. Eventually, when young King Richard II tried to impose a new poll tax in 1381, this proved the last straw for the discontented poor and led to the first popular rebellion in England – the Peasants' Revolt, or Wat Tyler's Rebellion, which lasted only a month but ensured there would be no poll tax.

Pope Innocent VI (1352-62) was yet another French Pope. Soon after his election, he revoked an earlier agreement that the College of Cardinals was superior to the pope. He repealed some of Clement IV's appointments and reservations he had taken on monastic and other benefices.

Innocent VI then set about restoring order to Rome, through two legates, a cardinal and a Roman citizen, Cola di Rienzi, who had successfully done this between 1344-47, but only temporarily. Rienzi had always dreamed of achieving harmony in Rome and uniting Italy. But after defeat and expulsion by the Colonnas, he had sided with Charles IV in 1347 against Pope Benedict XII regarding temporal supremacy, resulting in his imprisonment in Avignon. Once in office, Innocent released Rienzi and appointed him senator before the latest mission in 1355. The Colonnas were successfully replaced and Innocent VI agreed to King Charles IV being crowned Holy Roman Emperor on the condition Charles left Rome immediately afterwards.

The Byzantine Emperor John V Palaeologus offered the submission of the Greek Orthodox Church to the Roman See on condition the latter supported his conflict with challenger John VI Kantakousenos. Such a solution to the schism had been the treasured objective of many popes, but Innocent was in no position to accept. The costs of wars in Italy and recovery from the plague were draining the meagre Church finances left by Pope Clement IV. Avignon's lack of funds and Innocent's continued insistence on temporal authority meant that Emperor Charles IV was unlikely to help without unacceptable conditions.

Abbot Guillaume de Grimoard was asked once more to travel to Rome in 1354 to resolve some disputes in St Peter's basilica. Then Innocent VI summoned him again to help his legate Cardinal Albornoz who had been in Italy for about seven years and faced intransigence from the nephew and successor of now deceased Archbishop Giovanni Visconti, Bernabo Visconti of Milan, who was invading Bologna. Grimoard encountered such hostility that he reported back to Avignon. Pope Innocent VI sent him back with further authority to Italy only to find that Cardinal Albornoz's forces had crushed the Viscontis near Bologna.

Innocent VI also played a significant diplomatic role in facilitating a peace deal between King Edward III of England and King John II of France through the Treaty of Brétigny in 1360, which saw the English release King John II in return for a ransom and some adjustments of territorial right on the part of both parties.

The Black Death returned to southern Europe and at least 9 cardinals died of it in 1361. Abbot Grimoard returned to France to take refuge from the resurgent plague in his castle at Auriol. But within months, he was on his way back to Italy. King Louis of Naples had died, so the pope sent Grimoard to represent his interests as feudal overlord of the realm. While there he visited the Benedictine abbey of Monte Cassino and found its structure and piety distressed due to earthquakes and diocesan neglect respectively.

Historical judgement is largely favourable to Innocent VI's papacy as he greatly improved policy and practice compared with recent predecessors and promoted peace and justice. He might have tried a little harder to make more of the opportunity to reunite with Orthodoxy. Regarding ecclesiastical matters, Innocent was harsh in his treatment of the extreme Spiritual Franciscans and other orders, who gained the generic name *Fraticelli* and opposed the Church having any possessions. Innocent VI died in 1362, of natural causes but not the plague, to be succeeded by the trusty Grimoard.

Guillaume de Grimoard was born in 1310 and joined the Benedictines aged 17, was ordained a priest in 1334 and went to Toulouse University. He gained a doctorate in canon law in 1332 and soon became Prior of Notre Dame du Pré in Auxerre. He had been back and forth to Italy on behalf of the last two popes and was papal nuncio in Italy when Pope Innocent VI died in September 1362. He was elected pope in his absence and recalled to Avignon late October. He accepted the papacy and was consecrated bishop before being crowned with the name **Pope Urban V** (1362-70).

Once installed, Urban V continued to wear the Benedictine habit and follow the Rule. As a lawyer and living by the Rule, he established codes to guide the clergy and monastics in improving their discipline and commitment. His aim was to reduce lax timekeeping, simony, immorality, food and comfort, all of which reduced respect and discipline among the laiety. He encouraged further development of universities in France and abroad and he strictly forbade interference or enforced conversion and baptism of Jews.

King John II still owed Edward of England a considerable part of the ransom agreed in the Treaty of Brétigny and asked permission to levy a tax on the clergy to help pay this. The pope refused. Nor would he support the match John II desired with Joanna of Naples, as she was also Countess of Provence and Forcalquier, which surrounded the small Papal state of Avignon.

Urban V wished to return the papacy to Rome, but the city was still regarded as unsafe. First, Bernabó Visconti, his family and others would have to be forced from Papal Lands and to drop their claim to rule in the city. Urban's brother, Cardinal Angelicus Grimoard, was his only family appointment and accepted by all as well merited. He was sent to open discussion with the Visconti in 1362. Urban V excommunicated Bernabó for theft of Church lands and went on to declare him a heretic, but in 1364, he had to send the recently promoted Abbot of Cluny, now Cardinal Androin de la Roche as Apostolic Legate to Italy to seek peace. Charles IV, Holy Roman Emperor, mediated the lifting of Bernabó's excommunication. Bernabó exacted a high price in gold for Bologna, while still holding the Papal Lands.

Meanwhile, Pope Urban V was keen to set up a crusade against the Turks. He persuaded King John II of France, to invite King Peter I of Cyprus to Avignon in the Spring of 1363 to discuss this. Peter I greeted the idea with enthusiasm. King John II's Treasury and forces were still reeling from the 100 Years' War, so his support was lukewarm but he was soon captured again by the English. The Apostolic Legate to the crusade died, so King Peter I decided to do his best alone. His army overcame Alexandria, but as the Turks regathered and brought in reinforcements, the Cypriots withdrew after sacking and burning the city. In 1365 another crusade was raised by Kings Amadeus of Savoy and Louis of Hungary but met with a similar lack of success in that they captured Gallipoli, but the Turks forced them too to retreat. King Peter I continued to make forays against the coasts of Egypt and Syria before being assassinated in 1369.

Urban V was still conscious of the need to help his own diocese of Rome, which had not hosted its bishop for sixty years. Italy continued to be wracked by feuding, but his mind was made up by earnest pleas from the poet and scholar Petrarch as well as Bridget of Sweden for him to come to Rome. His vicar and enforcer in Italy, Cardinal Albornoz had helped ease the way through hard work and strength, but he had died in 1367, before his work bore fruit. The Emperor and most of Christendom except the French king agreed with the pope's plan. Urban V travelled to Viterbo, where Emperor Charles joined him in 1368 and they travelled to Rome together to a joyful welcome. Urban V crowned the Empress Elisabeth, Charles IV's fourth wife in a display of friendship inconceivable in the past hundred years and more.

Once back in Rome, Urban V refurbished churches and palaces and received such leaders as King Peter I of Cyprus, Queen Joanna I of Naples and the Byzantine Emperor, John V Palaeologus, but he became conscious that his presence had gained no power for him in Italy. Indeed, several cities within the Papal States still resisted. France and England had resumed hostilities and the French cardinals were pressing for his return to Avignon. He had yearned for his home country and felt needed there, where his succession could probably be more freely decided, so he began preparations. Bridget of Sweden was in Rome to seek pontifical approval for her new Order of the Most Holy Saviour, a monastic order of Augustinian nuns now commonly known as the Bridgettines. Urban approved it in 1370 and she predicted his early death if he left Rome. Urban V left Rome in September, fell ill and died three months later.

The conclave of 1370 unanimously elected Cardinal Pierre Roger de Beaufort, who had been present when Bridget foretold his predecessor's death. Beaufort had been made a cardinal deacon by his uncle Pope Clement VI in 1348, when only 18 and took the name **Pope Gregory XI** (1370-78).

In 1372, Gregory XI confirmed a treaty that brought together the feuding Papal State kingdoms of Naples and Sicily and oversaw peace settlements in Castile, Aragon and Navarra. He also had ambitions to bring Greek and Roman Churches back together and organise a further crusade. Like all the Avignon popes he appointed many French officials and leaders in Italy, where the French were generally despised. They all seemed blind to the fact that favouring French appointments and the pope's having a French base gave rise to popular Italian opposition to the Church. Gregory XI was no exception and this self-imposed challenge would demand his close attention for much of his papacy.

Gregory XI was a learned, sensitive and pious man who knew the papacy really belonged to Rome. He tried to keep peace and deal with heresy, with limited success, but his reign was another clear example of the difficulty in combining spiritual with temporal aspects of leadership. The conundrum was clear to many, including clerics but none knew where to draw a line between politics and religion. There was a tendency to include Church reform in their reformist theories and that was to grow. An early example would be John Wycliffe in England, regarded as an important initiator of future reform who influenced his contemporary Johannes Klenkok in Germany. Wycliffe and Klenkok published books describing proposed ecclesiastical reforms, Gregory XI condemned them and their followers.

Italy suffered severe shortage of food in 1374-5 and the pope was advised to embargo exports of grain, which upset influential merchants and leaders of port cities. Florence, helped by Milan formed a league of affected cities against the Holy See. Robert of Geneva, papal legate in upper Italy, was instructed to raise a force to regain control over these cities. Robert needed reinforcements and received Pope Gregory XI's clearance to engage Breton mercenary assistance. Thus began the three-year 'War of Eight Saints' in 1375. The city of Florence was placed under interdict and in return it withheld all clerical taxes.

Pope Gregory XI was at least partly influenced by Catherine of Siena in deciding to return the papacy to Rome. Staff and offices were moved in preparation for his arrival in January 1377. As a French pope in the Roman spotlight, the Italian people's opinion on this was divided.

The War of Eight Saints was still raging and in 1377 there was an uprising of people in the small city of Cesena, so Robert of Geneva led a mercenary force which massacred some 3000 citizens.

Florence and Catherine of Siena (1347-1380)

Not long after Gregory XI's election, Duke Bernabó Visconti of Milan had once more shown his hostility to the papacy. All other avenues failing, Gregory again excommunicated Bernabó in 1372 and declared war on him. Bernabó was successfully defiant at first, but when the Hungarian king, the Queen of Naples and some mercenaries aligned behind Gregory XI, he bribed papal staff members to help him achieve a truce in 1374. Florence felt threatened by the resulting increase in the pope's power so the city state offered Bernabó support in the struggle, encouraging him to resume. The grain issue would soon arise again.

The Florence interdict was applied in 1376 and Catherine of Siena soon arrived at Avignon as Ambassador of Florence to offer peace between Florence and the Papal States and plead the case for lifting the interdict. The pope refused since the Florentines continued the War of Eight Saints against the Papal States. Catherine was relieved of her post but while in Avignon, she continued her campaign for the pope to return the Papal Seat to Rome. This may not have been the only influence on him to move back there, but move he did, entering Rome in January 1377. This did not end the fighting and news of the Cesena massacre in February 1377 did not help. The Romans held no great respect for the French pope and rioting forced him out of the city in May 1377, although he returned in November and died while there.

Catherine of Siena, born into a large and poor Siena family at the height of the Bubonic Plague, was a most remarkable woman, holding a deep faith and love for Jesus Christ from an early age. She became attached to the Dominicans against her parents' wishes and was a religious author famed for her holiness and influential at the highest levels in the Church. She yearned for a crusade to retrieve the Holy Land from Islam and reunite Christianity. She also prayed for the conversion of Muslims, whom she admired deeply for their diligent religious practice and prayerfulness, which she felt could shame and set an example to over-indulgent Christians. Catherine died at 33, the same age as Jesus Christ and canonised the following century. She was one of the first women doctors of the Church, the other being Teresa of Avila.

England, John Wycliffe, Lollards, Geoffrey Chaucer

Wycliffe (c1325-1384) was ordained a priest in 1351. He held the plague from which disproportionately high numbers of monks and priests died, had been God's vengeance on unworthy clergy. It may have had more to do with their public caring roles exposing them to frequent close contact with the sick, added to which monks lived communally. Professing absolute loyalty to Christianity, the Church of Christ, Wycliffe campaigned strongly against aspects of the Roman Church, including its abuses of wealth and power. He advocated the Bible in English, predestination and the right of a monarch to be the supreme head of both State and Church in the realm ('caesaropapism'), with rights over all Church wealth and property. His views gained a following among ordinary people and many members of the clergy and aristocracy, including John of Gaunt, Duke of Lancaster, the third surviving son of Edward III. Wycliffe, Rector of Lutterworth became an Oxford professor, philosopher, theologian, Biblical translator and reformer. He probably met Johannes Klenkok, who was at Oxford from 1357-61 and wrote '*Decadicon*', on Church reformation.

Wycliffe wrote a book 'On Civil Dominion' which included his proposed articles of reform, nineteen of which Pope Gregory XI condemned in his 1377 bulls. In this book, Wycliffe expanded on his views, for example attacking Church practices and beliefs, such as veneration of saints, sacraments, transubstantiation, requiem mass, monasticism, clerical celibacy and its hypocrisy of abuse, purgatory, sale of indulgences and the papacy, which he regarded as 'imperialised'. Many of his initial followers, including John of Gaunt, drew the line at the denial of the sacraments, especially transubstantiation, and withdrew their support. Those who remained committed supporters became known as the 'Lollards', a derisory adaptation of a Dutch word for 'mumblers'.

Geoffrey Chaucer(1340s-1400), also a friend of John of Gaunt, would become known as the father of English literature. He travelled to northern

Italy and was influenced by writers there, including Petrarch and Boccaccio, writer of *'The Decameron'*. Both were deeply concerned at the excesses and corruption of clergy, bishops and cardinals of the Roman Church and accused the popes of forgetting that they were successors to Peter, a humble fisherman whom Christ had chosen to spread his gospel, which hardly compares with the greed, fine attire, palaces and power etc. sought by some Church leaders. In 'The Canterbury Tales', Chaucer conveys this message but also features the good parson, illustrating that among all the corruption and abuses of the institution of 'the Church', there remained good and holy ambassadors of Christ who were doing what he had asked of Peter. As this was written, there was a schism between Avignon and Rome with two claimants to the seat of Peter. The widely known behaviour of the Church institution's officers was beginning to devalue its teaching, though both Chaucer and Boccaccio subsequently intimated concern and regret at any chance that their words had undermined Christ's message and the many good clerics who lived according to it.

Transubstantiation

The Roman Catholic Church believes that when the Communion bread and wine are consecrated during Mass, they are miraculously transformed into the body and blood of Christ. This belief is based on Jesus' words at the Last Supper as he broke the bread (Matt 26:26; John 22:19; 1Cor 11:24), "This is my body", which is given for you; do this in commemoration of me", and similarly, as he poured the wine "This is my blood ..." Since the altar bread and wine do not visibly change texture, John Wycliffe proposed his theory of 'consubstantiation', positing that at the consecration, the body and blood of Christ become present together with the physical bread and wine.

But Wycliffe's legacy would revive in central Europe where, early in the next century Jan Hus (1369-1415), a Bohemian priest, philosopher and dean at the Charles University in Prague, was greatly influenced by his ideas. Regarding transubstantiation Jan Hus would put forward a similar proposal that became known as 'empanation', by which the real presence of Christ's body comes into the bread and his blood into the wine, neither of which change in substance. The Catholic Church dismissed both consubstantiation and empanation theories, as heretical.

Julian of Norwich (1342-1416)

A female anchorite, or religious recluse, Julian lived in a cell attached to what is now St Julian's Church in Norwich. Norwich was a concentrated religious centre, hosting many churches, monasteries and other religious houses as well as being a prosperous centre for the wool and worsted trade. During Julian's life it was also one of the places more affected by the Peasants' Revolt and the suppression of Lollards. A native of Norwich, Julian lived through turbulent times but is known for being the first English woman to have written a book in the English language, 'Revelations of Divine Love'. She was also a mystic and had apparitions while she was seriously ill when aged thirty, some six years before the Black Death swept into the city killing a quarter of its population. She made an apparently miraculous recovery after which she either began or resumed a solitary life of devotion and writing. The apparitions she had seen whilst ill were of Jesus' passion and Mary, his mother.

Papacy Back in Rome

The successor to Pope Gregory XI was an Italian, Bartolomeo Prignano, born in the Kingdom of Naples and a committed monk who studied Moral Theology in Avignon, later becoming Bishop of Bari in 1377. The conclave was held in Rome while rowdy demonstrations took place outside demanding a Roman pope.

The Italian cardinals were well aware of the urgency and importance of their responsibilities as the French were equally strongly demanding another French pope. The majority of cardinals were French, but disunited and it seems the candidate's education in Avignon facilitated a unanimous vote in Prignano's favour, even though he was not a cardinal. Both the Roman and French factions outside would be disappointed, but at least the new pope was Italian and had the patronage of figures such as Queen Johanna I of Naples. He took the name **Pope Urban VI** (1378-89).

This man of simple and humble life was expected to be a fair and capable manager, but his new and unaccustomed power seems to have created a transformation of character as he became arrogant, ill-tempered and of questionable judgment. He soon alienated French cardinals, who queried the validity of his election and brought three Italian cardinals to their side in a meeting in Fondi. King Charles of France had his doubts, strengthened by a wish for the papacy to remain in Avignon. Meanwhile, Urban IV's patroness Johanna was tiring of his inconsistency. Urban IV refused an invitation to join the cardinals in Fondi, so they felt free to declare his election void and vote for a replacement pope. Robert of

Geneva was elected as the Italians abstained. With the name Clement VII he moved into Avignon, triggering the Great Western Schism, which would divide Christianity even further for the next forty years.

The true reason for the schism at that time is difficult to pin down, most likely being due to a combination of factors. Its foundation was laid in the length of time the supposedly temporary earlier move of the papacy to Avignon endured, to which the ambitious French had grown accustomed for over a generation. It was now aggravated by Urban IV's behaviour. Support for Clement came from France, the Iberian Peninsula, Scotland and western parts of Germany, while England and its dominions in France, most of Germany, Ireland, Flanders and Northern Europe remained loyal to Urban IV. Catherine of Siena was a firm supporter of Urban, as was the Chancellor of Florence.

Urban IV made peace with Bologna with the return of Church possessions in 1377, whilst Florence paid a price for him to lift the interdiction in 1378. Florence had been suffering badly from the cost of its wars, the resulting loss of visitors and the income they brought and also from the interdiction at a time when the Italian Renaissance was taking hold there in its birthplace and offering huge commercial opportunities to the city. The Chancellor of Florence, Collucio Salutati, who was a leading figure in the Renaissance, provided invaluable support to Pope Urban against antipope Clement.

Urban IV continued to alienate many of the people with whom he had personal dealings. He deposed and excommunicated Queen Johanna, replacing her with Charles of Durazzo on a promise that Charles would cede some southern territories to the pope's nephew, Francesco. Urban's unpopularity grew to the extent he had to flee from Rome. Ignoring his cardinals' advice, he went to Aversa, only to be imprisoned by King Charles III. The cardinals negotiated his release, whereupon he misguidedly moved to Nocera where Charles' wife Margaret gave him a cool welcome. He stayed there with some recently appointed fellow-Neapolitan cardinals, who supported him. Most of the older cardinals were tired of his foolish and capricious ways and plotted to depose him, probably supported by King Charles III and Queen Margaret, so he excommunicated Charles and Margaret and imprisoned six of the cardinals involved. Those who refused to confess were tortured. The King responded by laying siege to Nocera and Urban's army resisted for some months. He eventually escaped with his prisoners by sea to Genoa. During the voyage, one of the cardinals was executed. Revulsion at this and the treatment of the others was so strong that a serious plan grew to get rid of Urban IV by any means.

When King Charles III of Naples was murdered abroad in 1386, Urban

IV wanted to take back the kingdom of Naples. When he could no longer afford his army and his diplomatic inadequacy once more let him down, the supporters of Clement took the kingdom so the Papal States fell into disarray. This totally inadequate pope died in 1388, while recovering from a fall, amid rumours of poisoning.

Next in line was **Pope Boniface IX** (1389-1404), another seemingly spiritually ineffective pope. Boniface was born in Naples and he supported Ladislaus, the heir of Charles III in expelling the French Angevines from the kingdom of Naples. Also, he did at least benefit from the quelling of Roman independence and was able to exercise temporal power over the city. There were times, though when he was safer staying in Assisi or Perugia. He also saw the return of the Papal States to Church control.

Pope Clement VII died in 1394 but was succeeded in Avignon by another French bishop, Benedict XIII, who came under considerable pressure to step down in the interests of unity, but clung firmly to office.

In England, John Wycliffe supported King Richard II in resisting Boniface's insistence on granting benefices and levying a fee, or '*annates*' of half a year's income at the outset. Parliament was a strong supporter of the papacy, but this demand led them to vote to strengthen the king's power of veto over papal appointments. Nonetheless, the English bishops held a synod in London in 1396 to condemn Wycliffe.

Pope Boniface IX supported seats of learning and was a pragmatic politician, but in a world that sought money for most things, including loyalty and support, he was hampered by loss of revenues resulting from the schism and having to hold together the Papal States as well as fortifying Rome. He ramped up the opportunities for income from benefices and no doubt indulgences and saw his family comfortably looked after, but he was unable to fund or win sufficient support for another crusade that was so desperately needed by the Byzantine Emperor Manuel II Palaeologus, with Constantinople under such threat from Sultan Bayezid I. Although a devout man and supporting several new universities, he was able to achieve little on the ecclesiastical front before he died in 1404.

Prayer, Theological Questions in the Eastern Orthodox Church

Earlier in the 14th century, a controversy arose which involved prayer and relationship with God.

Gregory of Palamas was an Orthodox monk and theologian on Mount Athos who became Bishop of Thessaloniki. He promulgated the practice of *hesychasm*, an already-recognised deeply spiritual way of inner personal prayer in close communion with God, where in solitude one becomes one alone with God at a level far higher than language or physical experience.

It does begin with the simple but important Jesus Prayer – "*Lord Jesus Christ, Son of God, have mercy on me, a sinner.*" But from there, solitary isolation and intense spiritual concentration is needed to join with Christ's 'energies'. The theology of Gregory, known as Palamism involves an important distinction between Christ's essence (non-transmissible) and energies (transmissible), which he associated with the light mentioned in the three synoptic gospels in the Transfiguration of Christ (Matt 17:2; Mark 9:3; Luke 9;29). So in really deep prayer it is possible to achieve '*theosis*', the union with God through these energies. It became an important and aspirational practice in orthodoxy, not only among clerics.

This was attacked as heresy by Baarlam of Calabria, a cleric and theologian from a part of Italy with people of mostly Greek ethnic origin, language and sentiment, but his own over-riding influence was Western learning. He contended that the essence-energy concept raised questions on the Trinity.

Two Orthodox councils ruled in favour of Palamism, which was included as dogma in the Eastern Orthodox Church and is looked upon more kindly by some Western theologians today. Gregory was subsequently canonised in the Orthodox Church.

Renaissance

The Renaissance began in Florence in the early 14th century as a cultural and political rebirth on the intellectual foundation of 'Renaissance Humanism', a modified revival of classical moral philosophy. The movement, affecting art, architecture, science, literature and politics, was enhanced by the arrival of numerous scholars from Greece, who brought their philosophy, language, literature and translation skills back to the west. The origins of the Renaissance are uncertain, but explorers such as Marco Polo were bringing back to Europe new science, mathematics, art and cultural discoveries from China and countries along the silk route. Papal and other patronage encouraged students and practitioners in these fields to develop and in the following century, the Ottoman invasion of the Greek Byzantine Empire led to a large influx of many more Greek scholars to Italy, which seems to have provided fertile ground in spite of it still seething with feuds, power struggles and fickle loyalties between influential families and states.

In the early 1370s, Florence had offered support to Bernabó Visconti in Milan, who opposed Pope Gregory, leading to an interdict being placed on Florence and its people. Such a sweeping move penalised many totally innocent people, but perhaps they channelled anguish into creativity. The Chancellor of Florence, Collucio Salutati played a crucial role in building a city and republic attitude entirely supportive of cultural and political renewal and growth. He personally enjoyed strong literary skill and was legally trained but he was also politically and diplomatically astute and had a natural grasp of public relations.

Any accommodation with the Viscontis of Milan was short-lived and they remained a challenge. Pope Urban VI released Florence from the interdict, though demanding a high price. They helped him by opposing the anti-pope Clement as perceived by Rome. They would soon find wealthy support in their burgeoning Renaissance, not least from the Tuscan Medici family, who would rise to regional prominence in the following century, while the movement spread to other north Italian city states including Venice, Bologna and Milan.

Monasteries

The mediaeval period saw monasteries in Britain revive and thrive following centuries of deterioration and new ones had sprung up bringing their total to over 500. The nature and public perception of the monks had matured as monasteries became important centres of learning, creativity and research into science, chemistry, medicine, agriculture, horticulture and theology, continuing the twelfth century Renaissance in Britain. Literature, art and music were also beginning to be encouraged by the new Renaissance from Italy. Added to their important spiritual role, they encouraged wider social development with modern hospitals and schooling as well as new cultural opportunities in the fields of music and art.

This success was laying valuable foundations for future missionary work, but there were also downsides for the monasteries. The loss of reclusion and tight discipline that arose from them dealing so broadly with the outside world led to temptation and 'worldliness'. In fact these Orders and their members running the monasteries who had vowed poverty came to own more than a quarter of the land in England.

CHAPTER 17

15th Century

Popes

(1394-1423 Benedict XIII French rival)
1404-06 Innocent VII
1406-15 Gregory XII
(1409-10 Antipope Alexander V)
(1410-15 Antipope John XXIII)
1415-17 Interregnum
1417-31 Martin V
(1423-25 Antipope Benedict XIV)
(1425-29 Antipope Clement VIII)

1431-47 Eugene IV
(1439-49 Antipope Felix V)
1447-55 Nicholas V
1455-58 Callixtus III
1458-64 Pius II
1464-71 Paul II
1471-84 Sixtus IV
1484-92 Innocent VIII
1492-1503 Alexander VI

Emperors

Sigismund	1433-37
Frederick III The Peaceful	1440-93
Maximilian I	1493-1519

For some seven centuries before this one dawned, the Western Church had supported or participated in violence in wars, crusades and inquisitions, while some clergy and leaders openly practiced nepotism, simony and corruption. All of this was contrary to its founder's message in the Gospels that they continued to preach from the pulpits. Congregations were becoming better educated and more discerning, while many conscientious members of clergy rebelled inwardly in their discomfort, some being brave enough to display such feelings. There was no clear balance of responsibility or accountability of clergy and officers of the Church. Papal reigns were mostly of short duration due to age at election and sometimes suspiciously sudden deaths. The popes and leaders of the Church continued to be distracted from their spiritual duties by jockeying for positions and their governance of the states around them, tasks for which they had little experience and no training, which also applied right down the hierarchy.

Given these conditions, together with apparent inability to overcome the papal schism as the century began, the Church was struggling to maintain credibility and loyalty in its spiritual and missionary role.

The Council of Constance succeeded in ending the Western schism, but failed in its aim to clean up clerical corruption, so it laid a base for informed protest. The availability of faster and wider dissemination of knowledge, news and education thanks to the recent arrival of paper into Europe and early developments in machinery to produce multiple prints of documents, leaflets and even books was bringing education to a wider population. The introduction and rapid spread of the printing press thus heralded the world's first real information and communications revolution, which it soon became clear the world was unprepared to handle. Nearly all nations, autarchies and organisations of the time, including the Church, had guarded and sought to control information and inconvenient truths. This control was now undermined and led to political ructions and the Thirty Year War as well as preparing the ground for the forthcoming Reformation, which would arise first among the clergy who had already been enjoying the benefit of education and informed dialogue and now had this freer access to information.

End of the Western Schism

Coming from an ordinary family, Cosimo De Migliorati became a teacher of civil and canon law before he joined the Curia and was chosen by Pope Urban VI as collector of papal revenues in England, where he lived for around ten years. He was made cardinal-priest by Pope Boniface XI in 1389, and from his parish of Santa Cruce near Rome, he was sent as papal legate to Lombardy and Tuscany.

When Boniface XI died in 1404, the College of Cardinals in Rome asked the legate of the anti-pope, Benedict XIII whether he would abdicate if they refrained from holding an election. All cardinals, including Migliorati were sworn to do everything in their power to settle the schism. His response was firmly negative, so the election proceeded and Migliorati was unanimously elected, taking the name **Pope Innocent VII (1404-06)**. The Ghibellines and their supporters in Rome rioted on hearing the news, but King Ladislaus of Naples helped restore order. In return Ladislaus asked for the new pope's assurance that he would not co-operate with Avignon in any move to endanger Ladislaus' rule of Naples. Innocent VII agreed, having no intention of any accommodation with Avignon.

Innocent VII was another nepotist pope, installing nephew Ludovico as head of his Papal Militia. Ludovico had been a senior mercenary for Gian Galleazzo Visconti. Innocent appointed Ludovico as Rector of Todi in 1405. These turned out to be disastrous appointments as Ludovico took it into his own hands to murder some adversaries of the pope as they returned from a civilised meeting with Innocent. As a result the Romans chased Innocent VII and his court out of their city, killing several family and party members on the way. King Ladislaus calmed things enough for the pope and his followers to return to Rome. Ladislaus tried to extract further power for himself, without success as the pope was wary of his ultimate motives.

In fulfilment of his vow as a cardinal to try to settle the schism and with pressure mounting in Germany and France for him to do so, Innocent had proposed a Council in Rome, but the 1405 turbulence provided a reason to postpone it on the basis he could not guarantee the safe passage of Benedict XIII. Innocent VII rejected a proposal that both of the popes should resign, but died suddenly at the end of 1406.

Angelo Corraro from a noble Venetian family, was made a cardinal-Priest by Innocent VII in 1405 and later spent three years as Apostolic Administrator of Constantinople. He was elected pope by a College of just fifteen cardinals on condition that if Benedict XIII renounced all claim to the papacy, then he would do the same to end the Western Schism and enable a new election to take place. He took the name **Pope Gregory XII** (1406-15).

His papacy was notable only for years of attempts to resolve the schism, manoeuvring of cardinals on both sides and his nepotism in appointing several more Carraro family cardinals to consolidate his position.

In 1409 a group of well-meaning cardinals called the Council of Pisa to resolve the schism, inviting both papal claimants. Neither would appear and in their absence, by the fifteenth session, the Council declared both of them deposed and elected Alexander V as the one and only pope, though in reality Rome and Avignon continued as before. Alexander died the following year and the conclave of cardinals elected John XXIII to replace him (yes, but read on). So the end result of the Council of Pisa was to aggravate rather than solve the schism, now with three claimants to the papacy, each with a limited following of Catholics.

The original two claimants to the papacy in the Western Church each had support, split as follows:

Avignon Papacy (Benedict XIII) – Kingdom of France, Corsica, Scotland, Kingdoms of Aragon, Castile and Léon (Spain), Kingdoms of Naples and of Sicily (Southern Italy), Sardinia, Cyprus.
Roman Papacy (Gregory XII) – England, Ireland, Flanders, Denmark, Scandinavia, Northern Italy, Poland, Hungary.
Swing support – The Holy Roman Empire and Kingdom of Portugal swung between the Avignon and Roman papacy over time.
Pisan Papacy – This changed the balance above. Support naturally came initially from the cardinals present at Pisa who believed in their right to appoint the pope, but it did not take long for most supporters

of the Roman papacy and a few more to transfer their backing from the conditionally elected Pope Gregory XII to the Pisan choice, now John XXIII. These included France, England, Portugal, Bohemia, much of Northern Italy, including Venice and Florence, and parts of the Holy Roman Empire.

Avignon's Benedict XIII still held the support of Spain, Sicily and Scotland, while **Rome's** Gregory XII could count on Naples, Bavaria, Poland and some of Germany.

John XXIII proclaimed a crusade in 1411 against King Ladislaus of Naples, the powerful supporter of Gregory XII. John XXIII appointed the Medici Bank as bankers to the papacy, which would bring wealth and prestige to the family. It would also help fund-raising for the crusade. In order to raise further much-needed finance, he appealed to his supporters and offered indulgences in return. These were promises of forgiveness of some sins, involving 'reduction of sentence' in purgatory after judgment in the afterlife, which caused much discomfort among the faithful and derision by others as providing another Church practice wide open to corruption. His ambition failed and the crusade never took place.

Council of Constance (1413-1418)

Sigismund, King of Hungary, Bohemia, Germany and Croatia was keen to resolve the schism and persuaded John XXIII to convoke a council at the cathedral in the south German border city of Constance which gives its name to the Swiss lake. Pope Gregory XII endorsed this, thereby legitimising any ensuing election. The council ran from late 1413 until 1418, involving 29 cardinals, over 180 bishops and archbishops and over two hundred abbots and recognised theologians from all over Europe. Unusually, votes were cast by nations rather than individuals in attendance, illustrating national partisanship on the matter and the political interests in the outcome. Three topics were on the agenda:

1) to restore unity in the Church, ending the schism,
2) to eradicate heresy
3) to reform corrupt morals in the Church – yet again, the last item.

John XXIII fled from the council in March 1414 down the Rhine with the help of Frederick IV, Duke of Austria. John could sense that the proceedings of the council could spell trouble for him. His flight annoyed Sigismund of Hungary, who was also King of the Romans and he sent a squad to catch up with Frederick and John XXIII in Freiburg, Germany.

John XXIII was put on trial on numerous charges including heresy, simony and immorality. He was found guilty and imprisoned, having meanwhile been deposed and wiped from papal records by the council. His title would not be claimed until the 20th century.

Avignon Pope Benedict XIII was asked to resign but refused, so he was excommunicated and also wiped from the records. Gregory XII, the Roman pope resigned voluntarily and was given the post of Dean of the Sacred College of Cardinals while all his cardinals were retained, satisfying the Carrero family. The papal seat was left vacant, so the Curia ran the Church until Gregory XII died in 1417, when Pope Martin V was elected as sole pope, fulfilling the first topic on the agenda, effectively to end the schism. Aragon still recognised Benedict XIII, his successor Benedict XIV and his successor, Clement VIII. Clement VIII eventually resigned in 1429 to recognise Martin V, thus concluding what had become the Avignon antipapacy.

The Catholic Church now recognises the Roman popes as the legitimate line and it was decreed by Pope Pius II later in the 14th century that only the elected pope could reverse a decision of a legitimate conclave.

A concept raised from the floor at this council was that of 'Conciliarism', a movement claiming that such Councils should have superiority over the pope. This was understandable at a time when three 'popes' had all claimed legitimate rights to the papacy. To avoid the old danger of the institution becoming an end in itself, turning a convenient blind eye to the perceptions of its followers, it was felt that over time it would be more important to ensure an indisputable single legitimate means of electing the true successor to St Peter who would be vested with the power of the Holy Spirit in guiding the Church.

The second agenda topic, heresy, was aimed at three principal alleged heretics of the time, John Wycliffe from England, Jan Hus and Jerome, both from Prague in Bohemia (see below). All were found guilty. Wycliffe was already dead but his bones were ordered to be exhumed and destroyed, Hus was burned at the stake during the proceedings and Jerome was excommunicated. They all left an enduring legacy, enhanced by the third agenda item.

The third item, to rid the Church of corrupt practices, was deferred as ever, being claimed as too lengthy a matter following such detailed consideration of the previous two. Whatever the underlying reason, it was seen as a case of Curia self-interest overcoming social and natural justice. This historic omission would soon prove to have been one of the utmost significance.

There was little will in the higher echelons of the Church to tackle corruption or change their established power and income structure as over the past few centuries it had become accepted that first-born men from influential and powerful families in Italy would be appointed to senior positions within the Church hierarchy or even the papacy. These families would frequently intermarry to consolidate their positions and were able to buy into local authorities, estates, land and even regions around Italy and elevate relatives to positions of considerable power and wealth with titles such as Marquis, Duke and Prince often with support from papal influence and money. Having a Pope as a relative could see quite ordinary merchant or farming families elevated rapidly. At the same time, already wealthy families could purchase curial positions for their male offsprings. Powerful families arose and consolidated their own power bases.

The terms 'meritocracy' and 'social mobility' did not exist in any language at the time. It was normal for the vast majority of people to accept their situation, expecting to remain at the same social or wealth level from birth. Those who progressed in power and wealth usually did so by seizing opportunity quite ruthlessly. Church Leaders were often there by family influence, not always being wise, learned or caring in their decision-making and enforcement of Church rules such as might be expected.

The principal accused 'heretics' of this century and the next were often genuine students of philosophy and theology who observed the workings of the hierarchy with disdain and if their views contravened or threatened interpretations of the least of the Church's beliefs, the reaction was decisive and the sanction firm. This was an age of 'black and white' as defined by those in power, leaving no room for debate. Of course there were also theologians and philosophers of equally strong conviction in the membership of the Church. As these gained senior positions in the Church, some would have their ambitions aroused by opportunities of secular power. Genuine questioning theologians were incensed and rebelled, at some risk to their own safety, against repression of academic freedom, convinced that it weakened rather than strengthened the Church as a divine creation and messenger of Christ.

Many accused of heresy then were people genuinely endeavouring to do God's work in a time and places where self-interest, corruption and greed were rife throughout society as a whole. A gap existed between what the Church preached and what its officers practiced. More was expected of the governed than of the governors, who were deemed to rule by divine right and with the guidance of the Holy Spirit, a concept always promoted by the Roman Church but sometimes used as a shield. Society itself was organised on the flat triangle structure of a few masters and many servants and the Church reflected this. Since there was little chance in such a society of honestly earned upward social mobility, the plight of the servant was hardly considered by those in power in their decision-making, regardless of Jesus' teaching to the contrary. The Church reflected that society in its ways.

The foundation for the Protestant Reformation was being laid within Western Christianity.

Jan Hus (c1369-1415), Hussite Wars

Jan Hus gained a degree in arts at Prague University, was ordained in 1400 and within two years was preaching the need for serious Church reform. He found common ground with John Wycliffe's thinking, much of which had been condemned by the Church. He translated some of Wycliffe's works into Czech and preached critically of Church practice, fellow clergy and even the papacy as well as espousing 'empanation', that alternative theory to transubstantiation of the bread and wine in the Holy Eucharist. Archbishop Zajic tolerated this and gave him an opportunity to address a Czech bishop's synod, but when Pope Innocent VII heard of this, the archbishop was ordered to oppose such preaching and obeyed.

In 1406, two students returned from Oxford with a document praising Wycliffe and Hus read from this during a Mass. In 1408, Pope Gregory XII told Archbishop Jadic that he was aware of the heresies of Wycliffe as well as of King Wenceslaus' sympathies for the non-conformists who were gaining traction in his country. As a result, all Wycliffe's written works in the country had to be surrendered to the Archdiocesan chancery for correction. Hus complied and publicly renounced the errors they contained.

King Wenceslaus was lobbying to be crowned Holy Roman Emperor at this time, while there were two popes during the Western Schism. He ordered the clergy to observe neutrality between the claimants, Gregory XII in Rome and Avignon's Benedict XIII, and asked the University to do likewise. The Charles University in Prague had become a highly respected international establishment and the students were grouped into four 'nations' – Bohemian, Bavarian, Saxon and Polish. Jan Hus led the Bohemian students into neutrality, but the other three groups were faithful to Rome against Avignon. The King therefore decreed that the Bohemians would have a weighted vote to ensure their dominance, which led to a mass exodus of foreign students and staff, who helped set up new universities in Leipzig and elsewhere. With the favour of the king Jan Hus was appointed Rector of Charles University.

By now, the Pisan 'third pope' John XXIII had been announced and he asked Prague to support the crusade by buying indulgences. This was anathema to Jan Hus, who once again condemned the Church's sale of indulgences and use of violence. The university would not fully support him in this. He made an address, which was almost word-for-word the last chapter of Wycliffe's *De Ecclesia*, condemning indulgences and also preaching that no pope or bishop had the right to resort to bloodshed in the name of the Church, but rather should pray for his enemies. Also, sins can only be forgiven by true repentance, certainly not a cash payment or grant of favour. It caused a major stir, but he rebuffed the entreaties of papal legates and the archbishop to exercise more restraint while all this time his fame and following in Bohemia was growing. The king called a synod to seek reconciliation to no avail. To protect Prague from the threat of an interdict, Hus left for the countryside in 1412, but before doing so he announced that he could not trust the judgment of king, pope or synod, so put all his trust in Jesus Christ as the supreme judge.

Given recent history, this chimed with public sentiment and was regarded as a reasonable view. Details of his hypotheses relating to prevailing Christian worship and practice, the behaviour of the hierarchy and political involvement of the Church may have been open to challenge, but his claim to follow Jesus Christ before the Church institution found huge support in the Bohemian community. The two should be in absolute harmony, but self-evidently were not. The wider spread of his ideas was only delayed by the limited means of mass communication at the time, but his thoughts would bear early fruit.

His time in rural Bohemia was an eye-opener to Hus in terms of how uneducated were the priests, their ignorance only exceeded by that of the people who looked to them for guidance. Many country priests knew little Latin, so Hus began to write down in the Czech language some basics of the faith as he saw them, to help priests improve their message. The problem was that these works were heavily based on Wycliffe's books and when their dissemination reached Prague they came to the notice of Church leaders. At a general council in Rome in 1413, it was ordered that all such books be collected and burned. But by then their message had already been preached into Austria, Hungary, Poland and south as far as Croatia.

King Sigismund, brother of Wenceslaus, yearned for a solution to the schism in the Church and to limit growth of any further divisions foreseeable from Jan Hus' preaching. He supported the call for the Council of Constance which began in November 1414. He not only gave permission for Hus to attend but also offered his personal guarantee of safe conduct. Unsure of his safety, Hus wrote his will then left for Constance, where he stayed in lodgings and preached in a local church, although notices had been posted on church doors, then a common means of spreading news, saying action was to be taken against him.

Hus was eventually imprisoned against strong protests from Sigismund and put on trial in a Church court, with an appointed prosecutor. Without representation for his defence against multiple accusations, he took the line of refusing to confess unless it was shown by the Inquisition's prosecution that any of the deeds of which he was accused were contrary to the teaching of the Holy Bible. The Polish contingent at the Council supported Father Hus against his accusers. But in July 1415, the bishops condemned this priest and fully aware of his fate, they handed him over as a heretic to the civil authorities who burned him at the stake in Constance. None of them ever imagined the scale of the actual conflagration they were igniting.

The knights and nobles of Bohemia and Moravia were outraged, to the annoyance of King Sigismund, whom the council had calmed by convincing him of Hus's guilt. Although a crackdown was threatened on all who still followed Wycliffe or Hus, public resentment at the clear injustice dealt to him led to wars in central Europe that lasted nearly thirty years, with lasting effect on the global Church.

Jan Hus' ideas found a large following in Bohemia and Moravia. The Church excommunicated many, including some nobles, who regarded its treatment of Father Hus as dishonourable and therefore sheltered Johann of Jesenic, one of those who had been condemned. This led to Prague being put under interdict. That was a step too far for King Wenceslaus, who would accept no more interference in his domain from the Curia and ordered a reversal of their dismissal of all Christian ministers and the restoration of their incomes.

Pope Martin V (1417-31) was appointed to the papacy on the death of Gregory XII in accordance with the council's resolution of the Western Schism. He was Otto Colonna, from that powerful Roman family and yet another pope who had studied law at university. Promoted to cardinal-deacon in 1405 by Pope Innocent VII, Cardinal Otto was a member of the Council of Pisa in 1409 and supported the Pisan popes Alexander V and John XXIII. He was elected on St Martin's day, November 1417.

Martin V stayed at Constance until the council officially closed in May 1418, then moved to Florence, where he made some diplomatic moves to regain some Papal Lands. In particular he recognised Johanna II as Queen of Naples and persuaded her to withdraw her 'enforcer', Muzio Attendolo from Rome. Martin returned the papacy to its traditional home, also his family's home city, in 1420. He set about major reconstruction works, involving some masters of the Tuscan school of art, so setting in motion the Roman Renaissance. During his tenure, he showered his family and relatives with gifts of land and castles, thus consolidating their wealth and power in and around Rome.

Meanwhile, things were not going well for the Church in Wenceslaus' kingdom following the execution of Jan Hus. His treatment had become a *cause celebre* and his supporters in Moravia and Bohemia became known as the 'Hussites'. They divided into two main groupings – the Ultraquists and the Taborites. The Ultraquists were more moderate but insisted that the sacrament of Holy Communion be taken in both forms, i.e. bread and wine, contrary to Roman convention. The Taborites, centred on the town of Tabor, were more extreme reformist and militant, recognising only two sacraments – Baptism and Communion. There were demonstrations and some civil disturbances between the factions.

King Wenceslaus tried to quell the Hussites and their leaders began to leave Prague until a priest leading a protest was struck by a stone thrown from the Town Hall, whereupon the demonstrators invaded the building and threw senior officials out of the first floor windows, killing several. King Wenceslaus died shortly after this event, sparking widespread war over most of Bohemia between Hussites and Catholics.

King Sigismund of Hungary remained faithful to the Church of Rome and was supported by Pope Martin V, who issued a bull in 1420 proclaiming a crusade to destroy all Wycliffites, Hussites and other heretics in Bohemia. Following the failure of a siege of Prague by a huge international crusader army, Sigismund entered negotiations with the united Hussites, who issued the 'four articles of Prague' as conditions for peaceful settlement:

1. The word of God shall be preached freely in the kingdom of Bavaria by the priests of the Lord.
2. The sacrament of the most Holy Eucharist shall be freely administered in the two kinds, bread and wine, to all the faithful in Christ who are free from mortal sin, according to Our Saviour's wishes.
3. The clergy shall yield the secular power which they hold contrary to Christ's precept, over riches and goods of this world and they shall return to the evangelical rule and apostolic life such as led by Christ and His Apostles.
4. All mortal sins, public and other disorders which contravene God's law shall be prohibited and extirpated by relevant officers, regardless of the rank of the offender.

The first two articles represent the earliest formal public demands specific to Church practice, while the last two reflect similar sentiments to earlier personal or group expressions of impatience with the involvement of the Catholic Church in secular matters and its elitist selectivity of sin and its punishment. Sigismund rejected these demands on the papal legate's advice that they undermined papal authority. The Hussites then defeated his army on a hill outside Prague and soon gained domination over all of Bohemia.

A second crusade against the Hussites in 1421 failed following which internal strife arose in which the mainly Ultraquist Bohemian estates, rebelled against Habsburg rule, partly aggravated by the theological dispute. In this the Hussites lost one of their leaders, but they were supported by the Poles and invited Vladislav II, the Polish king to take on the regency of Bavaria, but he sidestepped and proposed his cousin Vytautas of Lithuania. Vytautas agreed to appoint the younger Prince Sigismund Korybut as regent in 1422, subject to the Hussites reuniting with the Catholic Church. He was accepted by most Bohemians, but they did not re-embrace the Church of Rome. Eventually, under pressure from Sigismund of Hungary and the pope, young Sigismund was recalled home. Hussite infighting then broke out between the mostly Prague-based Ultraquists and the Taborites, in which the latter prevailed.

An attempted third crusade failed to gain sufficient support then the Hussite factions made peace between themselves in 1424, facilitated by the return of Sigismund Korybut with about 1,500 troops. Sigismund stayed and became a Hussite leader. They saw off invaders including a fourth crusade and later, during the Polish-Teutonic war (1431-35), the Hussites helped the Poles and in 1433, some 7000 Hussites went through Prussia, captured Dirschau on the Vistula and followed the river all the way to the Baltic Sea.

The Hussites had been immensely successful against a number of crusades and no political body was willing to take them on. One of their strengths was their open democracy that deterred neighbours from intervening for fear of failure which might allow such ideals to spread across their borders. An ecumenical council in Basle was convoked by Pope Martin V in March 1431 to discuss the Hussite heresy, the concept of Conciliarity and the increasing Ottoman threat. Rather than enter peace negotiations, the pope decided to mount a fifth crusade against the Hussites. Given the religious nature of a crusade, support was forthcoming and the crusaders entered Bohemia in August, but they were routed and withdrew once more a couple of weeks later. The Ultraquists tended to sympathise with the people of Bohemia, who were becoming weary of war, but the resolve of the Taborites remained committed.

Joan of Arc (1412-1431)

During all this, the Hundred Years' War (1337-1453) was continuing between England and France and a young girl called Joan came onto the scene. She claimed visions of St Michael the Archangel and St Margaret and St Catharine telling her to help the Dauphin Charles VII to rescue those parts of France under English rule. She duly enrolled in the army and was sent to Orléans with a relief force which aimed to lift a siege on the city. The force was successful within days of arrival. Still a teenager, her incongruity and involvement in successful campaigns gained her prominence on both sides. Charles VII was duly crowned at Reims, but Joan was captured by allies of the English. The nineteen-year-old was tried by a pro-English bishop and a tribunal packed with pro-English clergy, ignoring ecclesiastical law. She was found guilty of heresy and dressing as a man and burned at the stake in 1431. Twenty-five years later, a court authorized by Pope Callixtus III demanded a posthumous retrial, pronounce her innocent, and declared her a martyr. She was canonised in the early 20th century.

Exploration and Mission

State-funded exploration of other continents really began in the fifteenth century, mostly led by navigating explorers from Italy, Spain and Portugal. One of the first was the third child of King John of Portugal. Henry, Duke of Viseu (1394-1460), better known as **Henry the Navigator** was a principal initiator of the forthcoming 'Age of Discoveries' which would also open missionary opportunities. He explored the west coast of Africa and learned of the trans-Saharan trade routes. In 1415 he persuaded King John to invade and occupy Ceuta, a centre of such trade just over the Straits of Gibraltar, for the benefit of Portugal.

Towards the end of the century, **Christopher Columbus** (1451-1504), set off across the Atlantic. Columbus was born in Genoa and became a passionate explorer early in this era when trade routes by sea offered help in expanding commercial markets. There were considerable delays and dangers in trading with India and China overland, partly through uncharted and unpoliced land. Columbus nursed a hope that there could be a sea route to the Indies by heading west across the Atlantic Ocean, so he sought government backing to finance such a venture. Having failed to obtain it in Genoa, Venice and Portugal, he eventually found the favour of Queen Isabella I of Castile through his introduction by Cardinal Mendoza. She and Spain would be well rewarded for her generous support. Columbus was able to fit out and crew three caravels and set sail from

Palos in south-west Spain 3rd August 1492. As the fleet made its first landfall which he named San Salvador on 12th October, Columbus believed he had reached the Indies by the Western route. This eventually led to the discovery of a new continent and America itself with its native population and all manner of riches and potential – a momentous event in European colonial history.

It should not be forgotten that at least one earlier landing had taken place on continental America. Lief Erikson led a Norwegian fleet to land in Newfoundland and the St Lawrence estuary in the 11th century. John Cabot, a Venetian navigator commissioned by Henry VII of England sailed from Bristol and landed on the North American mainland in 1497.

Isabella, mother of Catherine of Aragon, recognised the need to protect the natives whom Columbus had called Indians so she set up the Secretariat of Indian Affairs for this purpose. Even though not the India they had hoped for, this would turn out to be a rich source of trade and materials. The governance of Ferdinand II of Aragon and Isabella II of Castile, the 'Catholic Monarchs' who married in 1469, uniting Spain, heralded a golden age for their nation, which thrived in producing cloth, silks, leather goods, fine steel swords, glass, silverware and the first paper in Europe, into and beyond the 16th century.

Then Portuguese **Vasco da Gama** discovered an easterly ocean trading route to India and the Far East via the southern tip of the African continent, the Cape of Good Hope. His voyage lasted from 1497-99 and helped West Europe become the centre of world exploration, discovery, trade and colonialism for centuries to come, while also spreading Christianity throughout the world as Christ had directed.

Renaissance Papacy, Dowries and Convents

The earlier Middle Age has been referred to as the Dark Age of the Church for reasons that have been mentioned, including violence, inquisition, war, nepotism, simony and clerical indulgence. The Western Schism then having been resolved, the Church was entering the Renaissance Papacy period. There would be little evidence, if any of the badly needed change of direction or growth of serious piety, humility and mercy from its leadership. Mission by religious orders was not always a savoury process either.

Debate and disagreements continued as to the role and direction of the Church, but these matters were largely resolved within the College of Cardinals, although this was unbalanced by the number of cardinal-nephews recently appointed by successive popes, crown cardinals elevated at the demand of Catholic monarchs and cardinal members of powerful

Italian families. Popes were normally elected from the ranks of the College and in this period there were two popes from each of the houses of Borgia, della Rovere and Medici. The family wealth that accompanied their installation helped fund their patronage of Renaissance art and the refurbishment of Rome's glorious buildings, whereas issues such as poverty and social justice were left to society to sort out or fend for themselves. The pope and Curia were far more involved in and concerned with state politics than social justice or ecclesial or theological matters and it is significant that unusually none of these popes were beatified or canonised. So while there must have been recognition of dysfunctionality, little or nothing positive was done to improve matters.

An interesting social development affecting the wider Church occurred during the 15th century in that dowries escalated sharply to the extent that it became difficult for a family to afford to secure a 'good' marriage for more than one daughter. So the practice grew of putting second and further daughters in a convent which required a lesser dowry, although any dowry at all for this was contrary to canon 64 of the 4th Lateran Council. So convents thrived on good incomes of both money and recruits.

Council of Basle and the Conciliar Movement

Pope Martin V died in 1431. Cardinal Gabriele Condulmer, from a wealthy merchant family in Venice and nephew of Pope Gregory XII, who had appointed him cardinal, was elected to succeed him as **Pope Eugene IV** (1431-1447). He had signed a pledge before the election to continue allocating half of all Church revenues to the cardinals and to involve them fully in all matters of the Church, be they worldly or spiritual.

At the beginning of his papacy, Eugene IV, who was no diplomat, managed to alienate the powerful Colonna family, by trying to recover some of the gifts that Colonna Pope Martin V had given to his relatives. He was obliged to back down in the interests of peace in the city of Rome, but the relationship remained strained, as did that with the Duke of Milan of the Visconti family.

Eugene IV confirmed the need for the Council of Basle, having considered the factors that led Martin to convoke it in the first place. The Council of Constance had demonstrated the potential effectiveness of councils in having been the key to resolving the Western schism that had so seriously weakened the papacy. Near the end of the Constance Council, it had been resolved that councils should be more frequent than in the past, suggesting the next in five years' time then at least one every ten years. As a result, Pope Martin V proposed convoking the Council of Basle, carefully selected as a 'neutral' city, to avoid accusations of national favour – French, German or Italian. The view that a general council was every bit as important to the wellbeing of the Church as the pope, if not more so, gave rise to the concept of 'conciliarity' and what became known as the **Conciliar Movement**. So Eugene soon found himself in the front line of a battle which arose in a prolonged **Council of Basle** (1431-39) which opened in October.

The principal aims for which the council had been called were to:

1) reform the Church "head and members"
2) establish peace among nations including the Hussite Wars
3) seek reunification of Western and Eastern Churches.

At the initial assembly, which was fairly sparsely attended, the pope's legate opened proceedings and reported back to the pope quite negatively. So Eugene IV declared it dissolved, promising another council in Bologna later. The council rejected this, in so doing reviving the Conciliar Movement and thus initiating a battle for supremacy between pope and council, which delayed the re-starting of the council.

Eugene IV reluctantly decided to invite the Hussites to participate. Negotiations took over a year and the council firmly rejected the Hussite suggestion that the Eastern Orthodox and other Christian Churches should also be invited. Both factions of the Hussites arrived in Basle at the beginning of 1433, led by prominent Taborites, concerned that the Ultraquists would accept peace too cheaply. Agreement proved elusive, leading to a break in proceedings, during which Eugene IV, in spite of their differences, crowned King Sigismund Holy Roman Emperor in 1433.

The tension between the Hussite factions led to another civil war and this time the Ultraquists won a decisive victory in 1434 at the Battle of Lipany, where the Taborite leaders were slain. With the more moderate Hussites now in charge, it was felt worth another attempt at the peace they wanted, so they submitted a revision of the original four articles of Prague. The Council of Basle reconvened and after negotiation, the Church accepted these articles with modifications, as 'the compacts':

1. The Holy Sacrament is to be given freely in both kinds to all Christians in Bohemia and Moravia, and to those elsewhere who adhere to the faith of these two countries. It is also valid under either kind alone.
2. All mortal sins shall be punished and extirpated only by lawful tribunal.

3. The word of God is to be freely and truthfully preached by the priests of the Lord, and by worthy deacons but subject to the appropriate ecclesial authority.
4. Clerics to retain possessions only subject to bestowing the surplus according to the canons.

Cardinal Louis d'Allemand led firm insistence on stricter discipline and control of papal income. A majority of lower ranks of clergy voted with him, so the disputed canons from the Council of Constance were pushed through. Discussion began on further Church discipline leading to agreement on decrees against concubinage and over-use of excommunication and interdiction. But when all annates and papal taxes were abolished without proposals for alternative means of income for the Church, this was a step too far for the papacy, leaving irreconcilable differences.

The Hussite compacts were agreed and signed by all parties in Moravia in 1436 although the Church of Rome refused to recognise the Archbishop of Prague, John of Rokycan, a theologian and active supporter of the Hussites. He would become leader of the Bohemian Brethren who grew from the remnants of the Taborites, largely located in the east of the country. The Hussites in Poland were effectively closed down following defeat by the Polish royal army. Some dispersed Ultraquist groups continued to practice together in that part of Europe, later becoming a cradle for a following of Martin Luther. Their Hussites had achieved much for their founder, having challenged Rome and extracting its agreement to those compacts.

The three broad aims of the Council of Basle had resulted in the following:

Church Reform

There had been a succession of popes and councils who had given lip service to Church and clerical reform, but it had always been put to the back of the list then dropped as being too thorny a problem.

The need for Church reform was driven by the broad population and secular powers becoming impatient with some of the Church's dubious ways of raising funds, its open laxity, abuse of position and privilege by its clergy and its ready use of extreme punishment. Funds were raised through sometimes quite arbitrary bestowal of benefices and imposition of papal taxes, annates and so on. These were especially resented by the faithful in England and Germany, who were offered little say in the matter and few reciprocal benefits. Congregations sought Church discipline, clergy and leaders whom they could respect, an end to simony, concubinage and extravagance as well as excessive use of interdicts, excommunication and Church complicity in torture and executions in the ongoing inquisition.

Need for Peace in Europe and Unity against Threats from the East

France and England had been at war since 1337, straining both their financial and military resources while also distracting them from wider European concerns. The Church was worried by the extent of support for Wycliffe's ideas in England and the power of the Hussites in central Europe, while Emperor Sigismund's treasury was being severely stretched by the costs of wars to suppress the latter.

Meanwhile, the Ottoman Turks' threat to the Eastern Empire was growing apace. In the past century they had entered Bulgaria and the Balkans and by the 15th century, with the extreme zeal of Islam they posed a potential danger to the rest of Christian Europe. The whole Western Empire felt an urgent need to drop their differences and work together for reunification with the Greeks in the face of this, which had been foreseen by so many popes and emperors over the past century.

Council of Basle to Ferrara/Florence

Pope Eugene IV had tried to have the Council of Basle moved to an Italian city, but could not raise sufficient support in the struggle as to which party had the supreme power, even after Eugene settled differences with Sigismund and crowned him Holy Roman Emperor in 1433. His position was weakened by his disputes with the Colonnas and the Duke of Milan. Eventually he cancelled all his previous reservations and decrees against the council and declared it valid. While the pope's legates were accepted as presiding over the council, they were in reality toothless and allowed no jurisdiction over the decisions reached.

The Greeks had been invited in 1434 to take part in the initial discussions on the agenda item of reunification, but the Eastern Emperor, while keen to progress towards re-unification of Eastern and Western Churches, showed little appetite to join a gathering that had engendered such controversy and he discussed alternative venues with Eugene IV, ideally at a port city to facilitate their travel. Eugene issued a bull in 1437 transferring the council to Ferrara, which most Christian states in Europe supported.

Germany remained neutral for longer than France, but Cardinal Louis d'Allemand still led a majority in the council, which responded by excommunicating Eugene IV, employing a sanction which they themselves had already condemned as being over-used. They installed anti-pope, Felix V whom few outside d'Allemand's group recognised. Eventually, Pope Eugene IV made an agreement with the German princes, known as the Concordat of Vienna. This allowed for papal annates and reservations to continue in Germany, contrary to the declaration of the council of Basle and for the princes to appoint their preferred bishops, but importantly gave the pope the right to confirm their selections or replace any he deemed unfit for office. This was signed in 1449 by the next pope after Eugene died in 1437.

Tomasso Parentucelli was the son of a doctor and had graduated in Theology at Bologna University in 1422 then ordained the same year. His bishop sent him to England, Germany and France and he was made a cardinal in 1446 by Eugene IV, whom he succeeded a year later as **Pope Nicholas V** (1447-55).

Pope Nicholas held a Jubilee in Rome in 1450, raising sufficient income and donations to fund his personal desire to bring the Renaissance to Rome and promote it as a cultural centre of literature and art. He also upgraded the city's fortifications and restored ancient Roman viaducts for a decent water supply. But his dearest wish was to restore glory to the papacy and its home the Vatican, rebuild St Peter's basilica and refurbish the Lateran Palace, for both of which marble salvaged from the old colosseum had been stored.

The new Emperor Frederick III banned from Basle what had become regarded as the schismatic assembly. The council had changed location but had lost any serious standing and after a few desultory sessions at Lausanne, anti-pope Felix V stepped down, accepting the new lawful pope Nicholas V. The Council of Basle was dissolved in 1449. It had finally been a failure in its primary aim, the urgently needed reform of the clergy and hierarchy of the Church, matching earlier failed efforts, all of which the Church would soon live to regret. Progress had been made however regarding the Hussites and the Greek question had been opened in Eugene's choice of location, Ferrara in January 1438 following his death.

The Greeks fielded an impressive delegation of about 700 at the Ferrara council, including the Patriarch of Constantinople, Joseph II with twenty metropolitans and Byzantine Emperor John VIII Palaeologus. The following January, the plague reached Ferrara, so they all decamped to Florence. A further six months discussion with the Greeks under enormous pressure from John VIII Palaeologus to heal the great schism and achieve agreement on doctrinal differences including filioque, purgatory, transubstantiation of the Eucharist and overall papal primacy. Both parties signed a decree of union in July 1439.

Other decisions made at Florence included the following:

- The Roman pontiff as successor to Peter, appointed by God, is the supreme leader of the Church. This closed the Conciliar issue.
- Infant baptism was encouraged in the light of the latest thinking on Limbo.

However, any joy regarding the end of the Great Schism was cut short as on returning to Constantinople, the Greek party still could not win the support of the monasteries and the people so the decree was never ratified. It did, however, form the basis of agreements between Rome and some other Eastern Churches, though these were by now much weakened by the Islamic occupation, so many were short-lived.

The eventual outcome, a dreadful blow for Christianity, came in 1453, adding to the abject failure of the Councils of Basle and Florence. Constantinople fell to the Ottoman Empire. The city had been devastated by the Black Death between 1346-9, which killed nearly half its population. It had petitioned Rome for assistance which had opened a real opportunity for re-unification. Byzantine Emperor John VIII Palaeologus had meanwhile died to be succeeded by his brother Constantine. Progress towards re-unification was not eased by long memories of the mutual excommunications in 1054, the Massacre of the Latins in 1182 and the sacking of Constantinople in 1204, all still leaving dissenters on both sides. Pope Nicholas V was keen to raise a new crusade to support Constantinople, but West Europe's preoccupation with its local differences (the costly Hundred Year War between England and France was just reaching its end), deafened it to the pleas from Rome and blinded it to the immediacy of the huge threat from Islam and the East.

In April, 1453, the new young Ottoman Sultan Mehmet II the Conqueror laid siege to Constantinople, having effectively closed off the northern end of the Bosphorus with a castle on either side, while also blocking any likely help from the Peloponnese, which were ruled by Emperor Constantine's brothers. He made military history by using gunpowder, which had travelled the silk route from China, and canons, which enabled his army to breach the traditional defensive city walls and enter the city after only seven and a half weeks. Thus the great Byzantine Empire ended, leaving no buffer between the Ottomans and Christian Europe, which was still otherwise preoccupied. The huge church of Hagia Sophia became a mosque, but although most churches had been ransacked in the victory, once things had settled down, Christians were allowed to continue practicing their faith.

Roman Renaisance

One fortunate outcome of Constantinople's fall to the Ottomans was a wave of emigration to Italy of Greek scholars bringing with them ancient Greek manuscripts and a wealth of traditional literature and historical texts as well as their own translation capabilities, helping to fuel the Italian cultural Renaissance. Among the literature were many great neo-Platonic and Christian works especially on the New Testament, which injected fresh enthusiasm and insights into Christian studies. While this strengthened the Western Church, it weakened the defensive boundaries it had drawn around itself against intellectual development and new ideas that it often regarded as threatening, even heretical. The timing of the arrival of such documents was ideal as Gutenberg's printing press of 1450 was beginning to spread and make its mark.

Being a highly learned man, Pope Nicholas V encouraged this learning opportunity and provided funds and scholars to support it, even tolerating humanism with all the heretical dangers it posed, in the interests of the Renaissance of Rome. In the event this did no harm as many neo Platonists and Humanists embraced Christianity and there was an explosion of Renaissance art dedicated to it.

Towards the end of Pope Nicholas V's life, a certain Stefano Porcaro planned to replace papal governance of Rome with a republican government. The intended insurrection was discovered in 1453 and put down. This event left a deep sadness in Nicholas, who died in early 1455.

Alfonzo of the ruthlessly powerful Borgia family was elected as **Pope Callixtus III** (1455-58), regarded as a relatively neutral candidate in preference to either the Orsini or Colonna faction. He was actually second choice after a Greek Orthodox convert Basilios Bessarion had been rejected, partly on account of his beard, which was considered non-canonical for any priest at that time.

Though he did not reign for long, Callixtus III is known for having appointed two nephews as cardinals and holding a review of Joan of Arc's trial at which she was exonerated post-mortem. He also interrupted Nicholas V's project for the renovation of Rome's buildings and infrastructure so that the money set aside for it could be available to the defence of Europe against the Ottoman Turks.

Callixtus III sent legates and missionaries throughout Europe to convey the need for a crusade against the Turks. Churches were to ring their bells at midday to call people to pray for the crusade. Hungary, under threat on the front line of likely action, responded and defeated the Turks at Belgrade in 1456. This great success did little to detach other leaders in Europe from their domestic focus – Germany, Hungary and Tyrol, concerning the Habsburg family; France versus England; Aragon and Sicily's expansion ambitions, which inhibited the Genoese fleet from joining and leaving their city vulnerable.

When Callixtus III died in 1458, he had little to show for his pontificate, having minimised expenditure on Rome, made little ecclesiastical impact and failed to galvanise Western Europe against the Islamic threat. The same issues continued during the reign of his successor, *Pope Pius II* (1458-64), who was learned but similarly limited in achievement, also failing to raise a crusade against the Turks. He did persuade Vlad III, 'the Impaler' of Wallachia, in Rumania to wage war against Sultan Mehmed II of Turkey, to little avail. Pius II became perhaps best known as the only sitting pope to have issued his autobiography, 'Commentaries'.

Pope Paul II (1464-71) was the nephew of Pope Eugene IV through his mother and a member of the Barbo family in Venice. He studied business but joined the clergy when his uncle became pope and was soon made cardinal in 1440. Paul II was quite a reclusive and inaccessible pope, often at odds with his cardinals in some of the many appointments he made, including at least three of his nephews. One notable action was his introduction of the cardinals' red biretta. Paul II enjoyed luxury and built San Marco's Palace in Venice, his city of birth and often stayed there. Venice was by then an important centre for printing and Paul II introduced a printing press to the Vatican, so dispensing with handwritten manuscripts.

The Printing Press

The first printing press in Europe, known as the metal movable type printer, was the innovation of Johannes Gutenburg, a goldsmith in Mainz who used his experience of mould-making and coin punching to develop the hand mould. This was a simple compact and versatile means of casting at low cost repeated individual metal letters like those in a typewriter which could be positioned as required on a plate to make up a page for printing. The recently available paper was an ideal substrate, so his team also developed suitable oil-based inks to avoid the spreading that occurred with the water-based inks hitherto used to write on the less porous parchment. His first press was installed in Mainz in 1457, but they soon reached Venice and by the end of the decade were all over Europe. This development gradually gained immense importance in the spread of information and education, raising a challenge to the authority of those members of clergy who fell short of sound religious knowledge and practice.

Francisco della Rovere, became a Franciscan at an early age, and studied philosophy and theology at Pavia University before lecturing widely at various universities. As a senior Franciscan, he was made Cardinal in 1467 by Paul II, whom he succeeded as **Pope Sixtus IV** (1471-84).

The new pope first tried to raise another crusade against the Turks, but with little success. Like Paul II he opposed French King Louis XI's insistence that any papal decree required royal approval before taking effect in France. He also tried to reconcile the Russian Church with Rome. Being inexperienced in diplomacy and having failed in international matters, he turned to more domestic issues, but his ambitions lay mainly in politics rather than more spiritual areas. Sixtus IV was another nepotist, making at least one nephew a cardinal and supporting his family with favours and wealth.

His nephew, Cardinal Rafael Riario planned the 'conspiracy of the Pazzi' in 1478, in an attempt to displace Florence's leading Medici family in favour of his own. After a failed assassination attempt in 1478 by another nephew, Girolamo Riario on Lorenzo de Medici in which Lorenzo was injured and his brother Giuliano killed, the city rebelled. Pope Sixtus IV had endorsed the plot, but not assassination. As a result of the rebellion he excommunicated Lorenzo and placed Florence under interdict. He then went even further by declaring war on Florence and persuading the Venetians to join with his own Neapolitan forces in attacking the city as he wanted it for Girolamo. Sixtus IV totally overestimated the influence of his family and papacy as virtually all of the rest of Italy rose in support of Florence. This included the d'Este family from close to Ferrara, which held such wide power and influence under the astute Ercolo d'Este that it would become a princely dynasty throughout Europe reaching as far as England and Russia.

The pope was forced to make peace. This learned philosopher and theologian had strayed from his skill areas, seeming oblivious to the real demands of papacy and politics. This was becoming the tendency of Renaissance Church – family interests represented in the College of Cardinals with the pope a virtual prince of the Papal Lands which required defending against growing ambitions of Italy's republics. The Church's aspirations and practices were being dominated by the temporal at heavy expense of the spiritual.

Sixtus IV's generous support for Rome did have some ecclesial benefits, his greatest achievement being the Sistine Chapel. The first foundling hospital was established and several churches were repaired or built. Rome was transformed to a Renaissance city under his papacy and he supported or commissioned some great artists of the time including Sandro Boticelli.

As to spiritual matters, he established a Holy Day celebrating the Immaculate Conception, i.e Mary was conceived without original sin. He also formally annulled the Council of Constantine decrees and while he appointed a number of inquisitors in Spain in 1482, he condemned the excesses of the Spanish Inquisition.

When Sixtus died in 1484, his nephew Giuliano della Rovere realised he was not yet ready for candidacy, so he supported Cardinal Cybo, who had helped him become a cardinal, as he felt Cybo could be influenced to help him further. Giovani Cybo was from Genoa, his father of Greek descent and his mother from a respected local family. He was educated in Padua where as a wayward youth he fathered two children, then Rome where he was ordained. He was appointed cardinal by Pope Sixtus IV. Giuliano used some of his wealth for bribery in that cause and following a stormy conclave, riven by family factions, Cybo was elected as **Pope Innocent VIII (1484-92)** and appointed Giuliano as his closest advisor.

Innocent VIII's tenure began with the now almost obligatory attempt to gather a European crusade against the Ottoman Turks. It was another failure, this time due to his own dispute with King Ferdinand I of Naples, in which he was helped by King Charles VIII of France. This led to a prolonged dispute and created difficulties for most of Italy for some time and renewed family feuding in Rome. During and before all this, a power rivalry developed between Cardinal Giuliano della Rovere and Cardinal Rodrigo Borgia, renowned as another beneficiary and practitioner of nepotism and for having a number of children by various mistresses. Innocent VIII sent Giuliano once more as Papal Legate to France.

Innocent VIII then enjoyed a stroke of luck from the Ottoman Sultan Bayezid II, whose brother Cem contested his throne. After defeat in battle, Cem took refuge on Rhodes with the Knights of St John. Bayezid paid a large sum to the Knights to keep him captive and in 1448, when Cem was transferred to the pope's custody the sultan paid the Vatican and also refrained from attacking Christian lands in the Balkans which he had been threatening.

When Innocent VIII died the College of Cardinals was wary of Giuliano's French sympathies and this led to another stormy election, surrounded by rumours of bribery by three main contenders. It is fairly clear that following the first round of votes, Borgia bought off the candidate from Milan, Forza, who had rivalled him in that round. It is also true that by this stage, nepotism and either royal or noble family 'influence' had severely unbalanced the composition of the College of Cardinals to the extent that of the twenty seven cardinals only four were clerics with no worldly sponsorship. So Giuliano's rival Rodrigo Borgia of that prominent Spanish family was elected as **Pope Alexander VI (1492-1503)**. He had graduated in law at Bologna University before ordination. He was made cardinal by his uncle Pope Callixtus III and was soon serving in the Curia, where he used his influence to increase family wealth. He had a mistress with whom he fathered four illegitimate children and astutely supported successors to his uncle's papacy to retain his position and his own eventual election. He brought his family history of ruthless ambition and corruption to the papacy, where it dominated for most of his reign so his contribution to the spiritual health and reputation of the Church leadership was mostly negative.

In 1497, his illegitimate second son Giovanni was murdered and the pope's grief was such that he withdrew into seclusion for a while and resolved to improve the morality of the Church thenceforth. He declared a Jubilee year in Rome for 1500. At Christmas 1499, he introduced a practice in St Peters that still exists, of opening the Holy Door on Christmas Eve and processing through for a period of penance and reconciliation. He was a patron of the arts with active interests in architecture, painting and theatre.

Spanish Inquisition and the 'Reconquista'

During Pope Innocent VIII's rule he had confirmed the appointment of Tomas de Torquemada as Grand Inquisitor of Spain in 1482 at a time when many Jews and Muslims had converted to Christianity to escape the persecution and expulsion that was going on there during the feared Spanish Inquisition. Many of these were superficial converts of convenience only for family, economic or personal safety reasons and all were therefore seen as a possible threat to the integrity of the faith. The monarchs of Aragon had for some time enforced the Inquisition and had chosen Tomas. He descended from Jewish converts to Christianity but was a devout and learned Dominican monk.

The Inquisition in Aragon during the 14th century had been led with excessive zeal by Dominican Nicolas Eymeric from the middle of that century, which led to discomfort in the hierarchy of the Church and a lull in its application. There had been a similar dwell in the *Reconquista*, a Christian backlash that had driven the occupying Islamic Moors southwards. The Jews had lived beside these Muslims and enjoyed their protection but now they faced direct hostility from the Christians, who not only still regarded them as 'Christ killers', but suspected their loyalty as it was still remembered that they had helped the Muslim invaders into Spain back in the 8th century. Most Jews therefore moved south into the Muslim-held region of Granada. Some of both remained and converted to Christianity, enabling them to keep their homes and jobs, but there were inevitable suspicions about the true sincerity and allegiance of these converts.

Ferdinand and Isabella who reigned, faced two concerns. First the restlessness of the nobles of Castille and second the danger to the Catholic Church in Spain of being undermined by these converts of convenience from Judaism (*Marranos*) and Islam (*Moriscos*). They astutely recruited the Castilian nobles to a revived Reconquista to free Granada, the last region in Spain still in Muslim hands. This had the effect of hardening both public loyalty to the crown and hostility towards suspected pseudo-converts and in 1478, Pope Sixtus IV had given them the green light to revive the Inquisition to root out uncommitted converts.

The ideal opportunity to resume the *Reconquista arose* when the Emirate attacked the border town of Zahara just before Christmas 1481. A force of Castilians and their nobles was raised and supplemented by Catholics from other countries along with Swiss mercenaries. The Granada war began in 1482 when the Spanish captured the town of Alhama de Granada. The Muslim rulers were distracted at the time by a dispute over succession of the House of Nasrid, but a ten-year war of attrition ensued. The Spanish eventually reached the city of Granada and besieged it in 1491. Terms of surrender were eventually agreed and at the very beginning of 1492 the last Muslim ruler there, Muhammed XII agreed to withdraw all his forces. There followed a mass migration of Muslims from Spain. In the same year King Alfonso III of Portugal likewise recaptured the Algarve from Islamic control. Those Muslims who remained in the peninsula found themselves faced by intolerance, leading to an uprising in 1500, which was brutally suppressed and followed by further expulsions and migration. A point worthy of note here is that Christianity was at that time of about the same age since it its foundation that Islam is today.

Islam in the East

Islam recognises Jesus as an important prophet even though it does not accept him as the Son of God, so Muslims tolerated Eastern Christians, though the Roman Church was regarded as an enemy as it supported Islam's enemies. Orthodox churches carried on quite normally under the Ottomans, though reduced in membership because some became Muslims through conviction or marriage as conversion to Islam took place among the population. Once a Christian converted to Islam, they could not revert as Islam punishes apostasy by death. Despite being tolerated, Christians were treated as socially second class and were forbidden to carry weapons or ride horses or to criticise or ridicule Islam.

Orthodox Church administration, canon, hierarchy and practice continued to function, though the patriarch's influence over the court and secular affairs naturally receded as it was no longer the state religion. His authority was expanded in other ways as all Orthodox Churches within the Ottoman territory came under the control of the Patriarch of Constantinople, who held both civil and spiritual leadership over them. This tended to unite Eastern Christians as a broad society spanning borders and languages, in spite of Eastern Orthodoxy's autocephalous structure tending to promote nationalism. The East European community based on Constantinople was known as the Rum Millet and this situation remained until the 19th century when re-emerging nationalism forced change. In Constantinople and Greece, Mehmet the Conqueror allowed the election of a new patriarch, Gennadius Scholarius. The famous Hagia Sophia and the Parthenon were converted to mosques, having been churches for the best part of a thousand years.

Islam in the West

As the Islamic tide west ebbed in the 11th century, Christian regimes had begun to regain lost territory beginning with Sicily and Spain. At first, they allowed Muslims to practice their faith, but in the final years of the fifteenth century Ferdinand and Isabella declared that all Muslims had to convert or leave the country. Hospitality to guests was paramount in Moorish culture, so by expelling them Spain created a bitter enemy.

Stations of the Cross

Christians in the Holy Land preserved and passed on through generations the memory of the stages on Christ's journey from Pilate's residence, where he was tried, scourged and crowned with thorns then on to crucifixion at Calvary before being entombed. Once Constantine had legalised Christianity, the Church marked key points in this journey of Christ's passion. In 1343 the Franciscans became official guardians of the shrines in the Holy Land. The 'Way of the Cross' became a focus of pilgrimage, and over time it was replicated in various forms in several places in Europe. An English pilgrim called William Wey in 1462 is said to have applied the word 'Stations' to the key stages of Christ's journey to death and resurrection. He recorded fourteen stations, some of which differed from those usually recognised today.

Given the difficulties of a pilgrimage to the Holy Land in the face of Muslim hostility, Pope Innocent XI gave the right to all churches to install figurative Stations of the Cross in 1686 and allowed the Franciscans who used them the same indulgences as for the original pilgrimage. These indulgences were extended to all by Pope Benedict XIII in 1726.

Though there are some variations, fourteen traditional stations are now commonly accepted:

1. Pilate condemns Christ to death;
2. Jesus carries the cross;
3. The first fall;
4. Jesus meets His Blessed Mother;
5. Simon of Cyrene helps Jesus carry the cross;
6. Veronica wipes the face of Jesus;
7. The second fall;
8. Jesus speaks to the women of Jerusalem;
9. The third fall;
10. Jesus is stripped of His garments;
11. Jesus is nailed to the cross;
12. Jesus dies on the cross;
13. Jesus is taken down from the cross;
14. Jesus is laid in the tomb.

A fifteenth station is sometimes now added commemorating the resurrection in recognition of its importance to the passion and death of Christ and to the Christian faith.

CHAPTER 18

16th Century

Popes

1492-1503 Alexander VI

1503 Sept-Oct Pius III

1503-13 Julius II

1513-21 Leo X

1522-23 Adrian VI

1523-34 Clement VII

1534-49 Paul III

!550-55 Julius III

1555 April-May Marcellus II

1555-59 Paul IV

1559-65 Pius IV

1566-72 Pius V

1572-85 Gregory XIII

1585-90 Sixtus V

1590 12 days Urban VII

1590-91 Gregory XIV

1591 Oct-Dec Innocent IX

1592-1605 Clement VIII

Emperors

1493-1519   Maximilian I

1519-56   Charles V

1556-64   Ferdinand I

1564-76   Maximilian II

1576-1612   Rudolph II

The sixteenth century in Europe is notable for huge religious and political upheavals and global maritime exploration. Key figures were the Holy Roman Emperor (Charles V 1500-1558) and successors, Reformation leaders, popes and in England, Henry VIII (1491-1547) and successors. Reformation activity centred mainly on Germany and Central Europe. The disruptions in Britain seem almost parochial in scale, but would also leave a lasting legacy which in time would affect a far wider world than Europe, as Britain would build the largest empire the world had ever known. Russian Orthodoxy also flexed its muscles as a similar royal situation arose to that in England.

Emperor Charles V sat at the head of three huge European dynasties including the House of Habsburg and thus ruled over much of central, South and West Europe. Plenty of exploratory and colonial activity was taking place following the ventures of Columbus and da Gama in the late 15th century. European, particularly Iberian influence was extending to Asia and the Americas. Emperor Charles V became the first monarch of a united Spain as King Charles I and his reign was relatively peaceful. He encouraged exploration. Ferdinand Magellan organised the Portuguese exploration of the East Indies, which would lead to the first crossing of the Pacific Ocean by Europeans and circumnavigation of the earth.

The Roman Catholic Church remained reluctant to confront its evident internal problems, while persisting with an unyielding attitude to genuine protest against the abuses which it had continually made only half-hearted efforts to address in councils and failed. It was difficult because the abuse was so widespread, shared by many recent popes and aggravated by the extra distractions and demands on a Church which also had sovereign territories to defend. Members were losing patience with the elitism, arrogance and corruption in its higher echelons which led to its confrontational defensive approach, so distant from Christ's way. Its leaders no longer held their monopoly on learning and understanding, thanks to wider access to education, mass publishing and more universities. When top-down leadership visibly falls short in such demanding situations, a bottom-upward pressure usually ensues, which it is dangerous to ignore. Rapid escalation and diversity of dissension occurred, including some of the Church's own clergy. Lollards and Hussites bred successors who were now finding wider support that was more difficult to extinguish.

Troubles within Italy and Rome encouraged leaders of the Church, in their worldly aloofness and myopic resort to the worn but now utterly devalued response to reformists – accusations of heresy and threat of excommunication. The Church leadership was deaf to the gospel of Matthew (7:4,5) relating the hypocrisy of the man with a "plank" in his own eye who comments on the splinter in his brother's eye.

Pope Alexander VI had laid a poor foundation for this momentous century for the Church.

New Pope from a Noble but Nepotist Family

Born in 1443 of the della Rovere, a family that had gained nobility largely through papal nepotism, Giuliano followed his uncle Francesco, (Pope Sixtus IV) into the Franciscan Order in Perugia. He was made cardinal priest in 1471 by his uncle who showered him with lucrative benefices, including the new Archdiocese of Avignon in 1475. Sixtus IV also sent Giuliano to lead several military and diplomatic missions in all of which he was successful, returning to Rome in 1482. One of these missions was as Papal Legate to France to help build a peace between French King Louis XI and Emperor Maximilian I of Austria, secure a significant contribution to finances for a crusade that never took place and win the release of two cardinals accused of treason. **Pope Julius II** expelled the rival Borgias from

Italy and furthered his safety in Rome by effecting reconciliation between the Colonna and Orsini families. He fathered three illegitimate daughters, one reportedly before achieving high office, one as a cardinal and one as pope. One daughter, Felice, married into the Orsini family in 1506. He was also reputedly adept at the judicious distribution of bribes

On the death of Alexander's short-lived successor, Giuliano entered into discussion with the other cardinals. They agreed that the new pope they were about to elect should aim to do the following:

1. Continue the war against the Turks, whom the Hungarians warned had their sights on Italy.
2. Convoke a general council within two years to secure ecclesiastical discipline
3. Take no measures in matters of importance such as declaration of war with another nation or appointment of new cardinals without a two thirds majority of the Sacred College.
4. The pope would determine the location of the next general council subject to the support of such two thirds majority.

Giuliano de la Rovere was then elected as **Pope Julius II** (1503-1513) in the briefest conclave in history. With his impatient and aggressive nature, he knew the two-thirds majority only applied to the election of the pope and he had no intention of bowing to such restrictions of his power. It soon became clear that his personal objective was to restore temporal power for the Church. The Papal States of Perugia and Bologna, had each been taken over by a local powerful family, so Julius II, led a force that won both back.

In 1506, Julius II laid the foundation stone for the new St Peter's basilica. it had been a frustrated dream of Pope Nicholas V in the mid-1400s to demolish the rather dilapidated St Peter's and build a grand new basilica in its place. Pope Julius II picked up the idea and the architect Bramante won a competition to take it forward. It was in the same year that Julius summoned Michelangelo to Rome and commissioned him to paint his renowned frescoes in the Sistine Chapel, which he completed just before Julius died.

In terms of temporal challenges facing the pope, a significant occupier of Papal States at the time was Venice, a powerful and ambitious state with a strong naval heritage that had enabled it to encroach on other continental territories outside Italy. Emperor Maximilian I and King Louis XII of France formed the League of Cambrai to contain further incursions. Since his forces were insufficient alone to conquer the Venetians, Pope Julius II reluctantly joined the League in 1509 and together they prevailed. Having thus achieved full control of all the Papal States, Julius II left the

League. In 1510 he set his sights on ridding Italy of all French rule. After much diplomacy, negotiation and dealing with the French cardinals, he gained support from Spain, England and Switzerland as well a measure of commitment from Maximilian I. The French were driven out and the cities of Parma, Piacenza and Reggio were added to the Papal States.

Julius II was a 'worldly' pope and a gifted military leader, but he also gave some attention to his spiritual duties. He did not indulge family members as several predecessors had done, and although he had not been above dispensing bribes prior to his election, he preached against simony. He established dioceses in the newly discovered islands of Haiti, Puerto Rico and San Domingo and secured missionary successes. He was also a major patron of the arts and provided the means for Michelangelo and Raphael to create some of their most famous works. He commissioned Bramante to link St Peter's with Villa Belvedere via a huge courtyard, and he was party to an inspired concept which would influence courtyard and piazza designs around Europe for centuries to come, but Bramante died in 1514. Bramante's successors changed the plans of the basilica to the form of a Roman cross by extending the nave, but eventually Michelangelo, who was an architect as well as a painter and sculptor, took control in 1548 and was so impressed with Bramante's original concept that he reverted to it as far as he then could, readopting the Greek cross. He strengthened the central piers so that they could support his envisioned grand dome.

Mission and the Russian Orthodox Church

The rise of Islam had curtailed and partly reversed the missionary growth of Christ's Church, but Eastern Orthodoxy had recently spread north to Ukraine and Russia, while the Roman Church was again actively evangelising as it followed explorers and traders to newly discovered lands in the Americas and Asia.

The Russian Orthodox Church had quickly grown to consider itself spiritually superior to the rest of Christianity. In 1515, an old and scholarly monk Philotheus of Pskov told Tsar Basil (*Vasili*) III 'The Adequate' (reign 1505-33), of his vision based on the Book of Daniel (2:44), that the Russian Tsardom would be the final kingdom of God's people on earth. It was the 'third and final Rome', the first Rome having fallen to heresy and the second, Constantinople, to sin, but this third "would stand forever". This statement of politico-religious ideology, couched in servile language with the backing of biblical reference, laid the ground for the argument that God willed the closest alliance between Church and State.

But this was about to be tested as after twenty years of marriage, Basil III's wife Solomonia Saburova was barren, with no prospect of sons to succeed to the throne. Basil sought a divorce to free him to remarry and provide an heir to the throne. Patriarch Varlaam refused this because the Russian Church did not recognise such a reason for divorce. However, many in the Church led by a monk metropolitan of Moscow called Daniel felt an exception should be made to maintain close relations between Church and State and achieve peaceful succession. Varlaam was forcibly deposed in 1521 and confined to a monastery, where he died in 1522, while Daniel became Patriarch of Russia (1522-39) and subsequently celebrated Basil's marriage to Yelena Glinskaya, who bore him a son – Ivan, whom history would mark as 'the Terrible'.

By this time, the Russian Orthodox Church was the only one outside Ottoman control and has regarded itself as the superior Orthodox Church ever since. It is now by far the largest, despite lengthy Communist suppression. Outside Russia, the Greek Metropolitan is still regarded as the senior cleric in Orthodoxy.

Islam, Corsair Raids and Slavery

Following the expulsion of Muslims from Spain, Islamic communities in North Africa nursed a keen desire to take revenge on Christendom. Slave-raiding of Christians by Muslim corsairs had begun and they now built more ships. Using such North African ports as Algiers, Tunis and Tripoli they sailed out to pillage settlements along the north Mediterranean coast and take Christian slaves for whom there were lively markets in North Africa and Arabia. It was an effective weapon that undermined the morale of coastal communities, some of whom moved inland, though most depended on the sea for their livelihood.

North African Muslims using slave-raiding as an economic and ideological weapon gained the tag Barbary pirates. European Christian seafaring powers became equally active in taking Islamic ships and using their crews as slave labour. As the Barbary pirates learned from captives and defectors more advanced design, ship-building and handling techniques, with well-armed square-rigged ships, they widened their activities beyond the Mediterranean into the North Atlantic, south along the West African coast and north as far as Iceland. The south and west coasts of Ireland were particularly subject to raids, the most famous being the sack of Baltimore in 1631, with over a hundred people taken for a life of slavery in Africa. The occurrence of red-haired Arab and black African people dates from this period. The pace of this activity declined beyond 1650 due to improved European navies, but continued sporadically for a further two centuries.

Exploration and Mission

European exploration grew as trade opportunities became more widely recognised and public appetite for exotic crafts, materials, food and spices grew. The opportunity for spreading the gospel was also seized.

There was a dark side to the commerce in the form of a new slave trade mainly involving England, Spain, Portugal and Holland, all with colonies in the West Indies. A triangular trade developed in which traders benefitted from the endemic tribal rivalries in Africa. Alcohol and trinkets were shipped to West Africa as currency for the purchase of slaves, usually captives from enemy tribes of coastal clients there. These unfortunates were packed tightly with no sanitation into ships which then took them across a frequently stormy Atlantic to the West Indies. Many died on the journey but survivors were exchanged there for sugar and rum, which fetched good prices back in the home country before the lucrative cycle was repeated.

New trade routes and destinations were discovered. Ferdinand Magellan, a noble Portuguese explorer had reached Malaya via the eastern route between 1505 and 1512. Like Columbus he felt there must be a western route, so with Spanish backing he set sail in 1519 with five ships to southern Patagonia and discovered the navigable Straits of Magellan between Chile and Tierra del Fuego to a relatively "peaceful sea" now known as the Pacific Ocean. They reached the Moluccan "Spice Islands" in 1521. Magellan died in a battle in the Philippines the same year, but having come so close to them from the opposite direction in the past, he is recognised as the first circumnavigator of the globe.

The Spanish *conquistadors* in their planned expansion in the Americas based themselves on a few Caribbean islands, spreading from Hispaniola from which they launched many expeditions to Central and Southern America. They overcame the great Aztec Empire with its interesting alien architecture and much evidence of gold. The locals presented no military match for the invaders who were appalled by their pagan idolatry which involved human sacrifices. The Spaniards, so far from home restraints, ruthlessly slaughtered these people in their greed for gold and glory, claiming justification from the indigenous pagan practices. Missionary Franciscans introduced Christianity to the population.

Pope Alexander IV had given broad powers to Spanish and Portuguese royalty including the right to appoint bishops in their conquered territories. The first Bishop of Mexico was a Basque Franciscan friar, Juan de Zumarraga who was given special priest status and the right to administer sacraments. He conducted an inquisitional drive to eliminate idolatry. This involved torture and ultimately death by burning at the stake. A call for more missionary friars was answered by Franciscans and Dominicans.

Bartolomé de Las Casas (1484-1566), a Dominican friar initially participated in the military-supported inquisition but soon became appalled by the degree of violence and opposed it. He wrote about it graphically and returned briefly to Spain and succeeded in influencing King Charles I to reduce royal support to the conquistadors, which left them disillusioned given the riches they had sent back. Las Casas returned and as the persecution subsided, he was recalled. He opposed the destruction of pagan temples but prayed for the conversion of their worshippers.

Spain set up a group of territories in Central America, Mexico, the Inca Empire, Argentina and much of Western South America having accessed it via the Isthmus of Panama. They then took the Philippines as 'New Spain' in 1535. Portugal succeeded similarly on the Eastern side in Brazil.

This 'Age of Discovery' became an ingrained part of European culture as new lands with tradeable commodities were explored, occupied and colonised, with missions introducing Christianity, education and medical care, an effective base for evangelisation.

Reformation of Churches in the West

Popular Church reform continued to gain ground, the work of its activists being fertilized by widespread disaffection with the behaviour, stance and responses of Roman Church leaders and their apparent lack of compassion. "Heresy" was still the leadership's standard response to dissension and excommunication was liberally applied – heavy-handed justice instead of mercy. Had the Church been more open, dissidents may have preferred evolution to revolution, but with doors to dialogue firmly closed, the latter resulted. The first of a spate of new community churches was the Brethren's Unity or Moravian Church, based on Jan Hus' teachings, an extension of the earlier views of John Wycliffe and the Lollards in England. But the serious beginning of the Reformation is usually linked with a German Catholic monk and Professor of Theology, Martin Luther whose desire was change in the Church rather than this turmoil.

The eventual Lutheran Church would become the largest new international Church, spreading quite rapidly in its early stages through northern Germany, Scandinavia and the Baltic States. In challenging Rome it would compete with the Reformed Church, which followed Jean Calvin, a French Catholic priest. The latter spread more in Central Europe – parts of France, Switzerland, southern and western Germany then the

Netherlands and Scotland. An academic and religious rivalry was forming in a quest for new theological propositions for a Christian Church that might rediscover Early Church-style practice of Christ's message with the humility, holiness and pastoral guidance of the early disciples and evangelists. World events and tests of faith added to the mix – Black Death, first Great Schism, demise of the Eastern part of the Roman Empire, paper and the printing press improving dissemination of knowledge and news. Rivalry soon grew into open conflict which spread, leading to the Religious Wars across those parts of mainland Europe which would not culminate in the Peace of Westphalia until some 130 years later in 1648.

Rome's use of Indulgences played a conspicuous part in the Reformation, so an understanding of them may be helpful. They are a difficult concept to grasp from outside the Church and had been another subject of abuse by clergy and leaders, providing more fertile ground for protest. Some wise leaders including Cardinal Ximines in Spain and Duke George of Saxony forbade their 'sale' in their regions.

Indulgences

Indulgence is seen by some as a benefit that can be earned to gain partial or total (plenary) remission of sin. The Roman Catholic Church regards itself as having the God-given power to distribute these benefits from the treasury of merit which was accumulated by Jesus Christ's sacrifice on the cross and the sacrifices and penances of saints. It is intended as a purely spiritual transaction.

During the mid- to late Middle Ages, some members of the Roman Catholic Church hierarchy misused indulgences, treating them as marketable commodities. Critics objected to the wealthy apparently being able to purchase relief from God's punishment due for their sins by contributing to Church causes.

Protest swelled in the 16th century when Pope Leo X promoted the sale of indulgences as a means of raising funds for building the new Basilica of St Peter's. Martin Luther stood out against this. His background and part in the sad drama is expanded below as his role became so important, whether by chance or by divine design. The need for drastic revision of clerical behaviour had been building for ages and Pope Leo X was a key figure in the prologue to the main drama.

Giovanni di Lorenzo de' Medici, became cardinal at the age of thirteen due to the influence of his father, Lorenzo the Magnificent, leader of the Florence Republic. He was elected **Pope Leo X** (1513-1521), the last unordained pope elected. Soon ordained priest then consecrated bishop before being crowned, he began with ambition to secure his family standing and tried to raise forces to counter the Turks. His poor financial planning combined with political jousting between France, England and Spain left the Holy See's finances in a poor state. Leo X appointed thirty one new cardinals after learning of a plot to kill him. These new appointments were calculated both to raise money and secure Curia support.

A major catalyst of the Reformation was the thirst in Rome for funds to build the new basilica of St Peter's. Germany felt the effect of this because the Archbishop of Mainz, Albrecht von Brandenburg was already in debt to Rome for benefice fees or simony and the extra charge for St Peter's stressed him further. During this time a Dominican friar, Johann Tetzel, caught the eye of the Archbishop through his gift of persuasive oratory and his success in raising funds through his preaching of indulgences. Tetzel was made general commissioner for the diocese then called to Rome to become papal commissioner for indulgences. He returned to Germany in 1516, when Pope Leo X gave permission for Archbishop Albert to sell special plenary indulgences for funds towards the construction of St Peter's and agreed that half of the funds raised in his diocese could be put towards the benefice debt. Tetzel proved successful but somewhat over-zealous in his promotion of indulgences and many people bought them on behalf of deceased friends and loved-ones, believing they may escape purgatory. One of his sayings was "As the coin in the coffer rings the soul from purgatory springs", clear distortion of the teaching of the Church.

This was too much for Martin Luther and many others who struggled with the theology of indulgences, open simony, the claim of pope, bishops and priests to have the power to erase sin all seen against the background of overt lack of clerical discipline.

On 31st October 1517, Martin Luther wrote to Archbishop Albrecht protesting at the sale of indulgences. He attached a summary of his views, derived from intensive study, discussion and thoughts with the title 'Disputation of Martin Luther on the Power and Efficacy of Indulgences'. It is now known as his 'Ninety Five Theses' and was probably the legendary 'nailing to the church door' event. Many scholars doubt that he made such a public protest at the time, though this is not certain as a contemporary printed placard version can be seen in the Berlin State library. However published, it was intended as a scholarly view on indulgences, the outcome of agonised Socratic self-dialectic. Luther abhorred the idea that God's forgiveness could be bought by those who could afford it and even more that it could be applied to those already dead. Not only was this prejudicial to the poor, whom Jesus loved, but he believed that the very idea was in danger of encouraging people to relax in their duty always to repent their sins and strive to live and work well in the cause of their own salvation. To his mind, only God could grant such forgiveness.

Leo X was worried by the dissent arising in Germany, much from Martin Luther's theses against indulgences. He failed to persuade Luther to come to Rome and dispatched his legate Cardinal Cajetan to argue his case with Luther, which also failed. Pope Leo X relaxed in the belief that Luther would follow a similar path to history to Wycliffe and Hus. His shortage of funds, his family and Italian politics plus the war with France diverted his attention and he totally misjudged the long-term threat.

Leo X went on to take his quest for funds for St Peter's to the wealthier parts of Northern Europe, sending a strong nuncio who was not well received. The nature of this financial pressure from the Church opened the door to Lutheran activists in Denmark and Norway, followed by Sweden in 1520, the population of this region already being antagonised by evident clerical abuses in their wealthier benefices.

When Emperor Maximillian I died in 1519, Pope Leo X would have preferred Frederick the Wise of Saxony to take the position but Charles I of Spain was the natural successor, becoming Holy Roman Emperor Charles V, since he was heir to three large European dynasties. Leo X spent many of his final years dabbling in Medici and Italian politics, securing the help of Emperor Charles and Henry VIII of England, while also spending heavily on Swiss mercenaries to strengthen his forces.

Martin Luther (1483-1536)

Luther was brought up in a tough mining community with strict parents, his father being a mine leaseholder and town Councillor. His joyless early childhood seems to have continued at school, where he was frequently punished. His parents supported his further schooling away from their village. Although he later called his schooling "purgatory and hell", he achieved and went on to graduate in philosophy at Erfurt University, which he also did not enjoy, but stayed on to gain the higher Master's degree there in 1505. He continued his studies to begin a course in law as his father wished, but soon dropped out of that, preferring theology and philosophy which he felt could bring him closer to God. Philosophy failed to do that and he formed the opinion that the only route to a love of God was through divine revelation.

He surprised family and friends by suddenly joining the Augustinian monastery in Erfurt. His father regarded this as the waste of a good mind. Debate surrounds Martin's decision, some seeing it as a consequence of his severe childhood and others the result of a terrifying thunderstorm during which his friend Alexius was killed by lightning. Realising he dreaded death and judgement, he made a vow to St Anna that he would join a monastery. He wrote to his father, "I made an involuntary and forced vow in terror, overwhelmed by the fear I was about to die." It was known that he suffered from a brooding and troubled mind and displayed sudden and violent outbursts of anger, perhaps as a consequence of a lack of sense of self-worth arising from his strict upbringing which is believed to have involved some violence.

His monastic life began as a further trial as he fasted and spent ages in prayer and frequent confession, but felt no closer to God, even seeing him as more of a judge than a saviour. His mentor, Johann von Staupitz pushed him to regard true repentance as a change of heart rather than needing punishing penances. He claimed never to have seen a Bible until he came across one in the monastery library and became firmly attached to it in his quest for divine revelation. He was ordained in 1507 and at the end of the following year, he was called to the new Wittenberg University by von Staupitz, by then its first dean, to lecture in theology and begin studies for his doctorate. He was recalled to the monastery late 1509 and reportedly was sent to Rome a year or so later, staying for about five months. During an act of penance there, the phrase came to him "the just shall live by faith", which he adopted for guidance. The impression he took back from Rome seems to have left its mark on his future life.

Luther returned to Wittenberg University and gained his doctorate in 1512, becoming lecturer in Bible studies in 1513. A further appointment as district vicar made him so busy that he felt his own spiritual life suffered. He still maintained stringent asceticism and the pressure told on him, especially after being appointed vicar-general for Saxony and Thuringia in 1515. The responsibility further aggravated his tortured mind and his deep anxiety as to whether anybody was able to match up to God's required standards. Despite this he stayed on at his post through the plague which swept Wittenberg in 1516.

Did his fruitless search for forgiveness and perfection, his short temper, constant need to clean the soul by penance, inescapable anxiety and bursts of anger suggest what we now know as obsessive compulsive disorder? Not an uncommon condition, it was unrecognised then, so lacked treatment or sympathy, the battle being his alone. His conclusion that faith rather than penance may be the key to salvation could have helped him in this. From his personal doctrine 'justification by faith alone', he concluded that a faith that entails charity and moral behaviour brings 'grace', God's blessing that leads to salvation.

Luther believed that all humans, clergy and lay people, carried the indelible flaw of original sin. He strongly contended that the clergy have no claim to fast-track salvation. Therefore no human authority could dictate doctrine, which left the Bible as the only valid source of God's teaching. He extended this argument, claiming that only death could erase original sin and it did so, leaving no need for purgatory, prayers for the dead or indulgences. Furthermore, there was no point in the ascetic life or monasteries.

This line of thinking was hardened by Pope Leo's offer of indulgences to people who contributed to funding St Peter's basilica. It led to Luther's 1517 protest letter to Archbishop Albrecht including his 95 theses, which Albrecht forwarded to Rome. The hierarchy of the Catholic Church demanded that he recant. As the full list of those famous theses is readily accessible, a brief summary suffices here.

The Ninety Five Theses

In the first thesis, Luther stated that when Jesus told his followers to repent, he meant them to spend all their lives in penitence. The next three theses dwell on the Christian's whole life involving an inner struggle with sin and penance which he believed inevitably involves some form of physical self-mortification, rather than the external sacrament of confession and token penances; not quite in line with his "faith alone".

Luther moves on (5-8), to consider the pope's power regarding forgiveness of sin. The gospel reference is clear "If you forgive anyone's sins they are forgiven; if you retain anyone's sins, they are retained." (John 20:23). This was addressed not just to Peter, but to the assembled disciples, so was read by the Catholic Church as the power to forgive or not to forgive sin being transferable to their successors, the priests. Luther argued that it was neither in the popes' nor the Church's gift to forgive the guilt of sin, as that belonged to God alone. He would only go so far as to accept that indulgences could relieve the penitent of any punishment imposed by the Church itself, a concept that has never been recognised in the Church.

In theses 9-19 Luther seems to debate the concept of purgatory or the need for it, suggesting that the agonies of death may suffice as the final trial in itself; also that the Church cannot impose or ease any penalty that would apply beyond death, leading to the following six theses which reflect his views on indulgences and in particular plenary indulgences, the erasure of all past sin. He suggests that the indiscriminate and alluring promise of release from all penalty is deceiving the faithful, then continues (26-40) with his thoughts on whether the pope has the power to offer relief to the dead and he questions the value of indulgences for those already paying the debt for their sins in purgatory, arguing that contrition must surely precede absolution. In these, belief in purgatory seems implicit, though he had denied it.

In 41-50 Luther further examines payment for indulgences and suggests money is better spent in bringing up a family and any surplus is best used in helping the poor and needy. Love grows by acts of love, not money; the value of prayer and good works in the cause of God's grace and pardon cannot be surpassed by distribution of money, which is selective in giving advantage only to those who can afford it. 51-55 speak of 'letters of pardon' and propose that far more preaching time should be given to the Gospel than to penance and pardon. Theses 56-65 speculate as to the nature of 'the treasures of the Church' and lead into 66-81 covering the treasure of indulgences and the need for care in their promotion and handling.

A series of questions follow, for example why the pope does not empty purgatory for compassion rather than gain if this is within his power; why prayers are said for the dead etc., most of them rephrasing earlier points. The document tended to ramble through circular arguments, some seeming to retract earlier theses, such as purgatory or faith, but contained a number of well-argued propositions worthy of debate.

Response to the Theses, Andreas Carlstadt, Johann Eck

Luther wrote lengthy letters to his mentor Staupitz and to Pope Leo X with copies of his 'disputation', begging them to consider the issues he raised. Such a disputation was a common means of stirring debate among academics or within a university and church doors were commonly used as 'notice boards', so it would not be too surprising or confrontational if Luther did nail it there on 17th October 1517. However it was done, the depth of his convictions on the matter are beyond doubt.

The incident would have passed without too much notice had it received a more considered response from Leo X. January 1518 began a year of inflammatory exchanges, with an academic response to Luther's theses from Texel and Conrad Wimpina, Luther's teacher at Leipzig. When an opportunist tried to sell hundreds of copies of their quite dogmatic refutation of Luther's theses, students grabbed the lot and burned them publicly. Luther disapproved this action but responded to the refutation by circulating his condensed thoughts in the vernacular via a leaflet 'Sermon on Indulgences and Grace'. He forwarded a more formal Latin response to his bishop, Scultetus of Brandenburg, who replied advising Luther to say or write no more on the subject for the time being. Being a monk, Luther obeyed.

One of the inevitable consequences came from Johann Eck, Vice-Chancellor of the University of Ingolstadt, a respected Dominican Friar, one of the day's foremost theologians. His bishop commissioned him to read and comment on Luther's theses. He reported privately in manuscript form that some carried a hint of Hussite heresy and some undermined the established power structure of the Church hierarchy, a few cases being almost seditious. A limited number of internal copies of this report were transcribed for internal study but Luther and Andreas Carlstadt, an older colleague and supporter of Luther's theses saw one copy. They were as incensed as Eck was embarrassed at the indiscretion and tried to pacify them for the sake of damage limitation, imploring them to keep his private report out of the public arena. Carlstadt argued directly with Eck then Luther issued a new public disputation, supported by a conscientious young disciple Philipp Melancthon, who was likewise offended by the sale of indulgences.

Since the dispute was now in the public domain, Eck challenged Carlstadt to a debate in Leipzig about free will and grace, then following Luther's latest publication, Luther and Melanchthon were invited to join. At Luther's request, further subjects were added, including the existence of purgatory, the sale of indulgences, requirement and forms of penance and the extent of papal authority.

This debate took some time to organise and meanwhile, the pope had a Dominican theologian examine Luther's theses. He drafted a case of heresy from some of them which led to the Pope issuing a summons for Luther to attend Rome. Knowing he had influential sympathisers in Germany and preferring to seek judgment there, Luther claimed ill health with the backing of Emperor Maximilian and the Elector Frederik. Pope Leo X sent as legate Cardinal Thomas Cajetan, Master of the Order of Preachers, head of the Dominican Order and the top theologian of his day, having gained a PhD at the age of 20. Cajetan was given a twofold mission as the pope's legate. He attended an imperial diet at Augsburg in October 1518, called to seek the support of Emperor Maximilian and the King of Norway, Sweden and Denmark in the war against the Turks. Then Cajetan met Luther, whose hearing began the day after they first met in Augsburg. In the course of it, Luther displayed inconsistency in his attitude to the pope, varying from passionate condemnation to humble praise as well as moments of fiery anger as Cajetan probed. Regardless, Luther held to his view that the pope had no right to issue indulgences as he was now doing. Cajetan failed to secure a recantation by Luther, but he did not arrest him as the Pope had asked.

Luther returned to Wittenburg on the anniversary of posting his theses and still buoyed by the support of Princes and many students and other followers, he continued preaching and writing. Nobody seemed to have a realistic sense of the gravity of what was happening. The Cathars, Waldensians, Lollards and Hussites had come and gone; could the outcome be any different from this introspective Augustinian monk who was so lacking in empathy and public appeal?

The well-advertised Leipzig debate, on a subject which commanded so much public interest that the attendance was too large for the university, was held at Pleissenburg Castle. It coincided with the appointment of the new young Holy Roman Emperor Charles V. Although not regarded as of Imperial importance, Duke George of Saxony attended the mid-1519 debate. Eck lived up to his reputation as a formidable debater, quickly defeating Carlstadt on the subjects of divine grace and free will. He then faced up to Luther, who argued that scripture alone is the basis for Christian belief and since there was no mention of either purgatory or pope in the Bible, the pope had no God-given authority and purgatory did not exist. Luther saw these as valid reasons to condemn the sale of indulgences and their implied ability to relieve the souls in purgatory. But this proved too thin an argument to hold up in the face of such a learned Christian theologian and by the end of the debate Eck had inflicted a clear and humbling defeat on Luther.

Pope Leo X issued a papal bull mid-1520 forbidding the preaching or writing of Luther's theories, ordering the recantation within 60 days of forty one sentences from these and other writings he had distributed and threatening Luther and Carlstadt with excommunication. Luther burned this bull in public protest in December, having rejected diplomatic entreaty from the papal nuncio Karl Militz, so at the beginning of 1521, the exasperated Pope Leo X finally excommunicated him.

This did not affect the German people much as they were concerned by more mundane matters arising from the aftermath of plague, the effects of developing new industries and decline of the agrarian economy. Knights and lower nobility were fast losing position and wealth as new methods of warfare and Roman law were introduced, while land values fell.

But the frantic nature of the Catholic Church's excommunication of Luther had the effect in some unexpected quarters of making him a populist figure as he became regarded more as a revolutionary than a reformer. His celebrity attracted some dubious followers. Ulrich von Hutten, a brilliant but unscrupulous leading humanist and Franz von Sickingen, an ex-mercenary who had ruthlessly and criminally gained great wealth, power and influence, latched on to Luther's side. Sickingen was a much-feared figure even at government level in a Germany that was suffering widespread dissatisfaction and civil disturbance through its socio-economic stress. These men and their cronies were not at all interested in religion, but disliked the pope and resented Church ownership of valuable property so they saw Luther as a useful tool. Luther in return was pragmatically aware that he may need help and protection, but it was not to last long as Sickingen died in 1523 of battle wounds after a serious defeat and Hutten died young about the same time.

With his uninvited fame, Luther wrote and preached copiously with no problem in finding willing publishers who recognised that he now had a wide audience. He began translating the Bible into German from Jerome's Latin vulgate version of the 4th and 5th centuries. His translation could now be printed and circulated, with accessibility for less educated people in mind. It would by no means be the first as nearly 20 editions were printed in German and more in French in the early 1500s, but the quality of his translation ensured wide circulation. The Church feared errors in translation or interpretation from this man, but his version inspired various later translations, including into English by William Tyndale.

Luther also wrote some hymns and introduced singing, which would become a forte of the 'Evangelical' Churches as they became known in Germany, 'Reform' in Switzerland and 'Huguenot' in France. He also saw no biblical-based reason for the clergy not to marry and he set the example by marrying a former nun. Luther was personally anti-Semitic though this did not transfer to followers of the Lutheran tradition.

Diet of Worms

The imperial Diet of Worms was called to involve the recently crowned Emperor Charles V in discussion on a number of national political and social issues. Given the continuing importance of the Church and its influence in society, the effective trial of Luther became the top item on the agenda. The diet began at the end of January 1521 with Emperor Charles presiding and Johann Eck, now a senior papal appointee, representing the pope and the Emperor on the floor. Elector Frederick 'the Wise' of Saxony guaranteed Luther's safe passage to and from the court. Some of Luther's books and theses were laid on a table and Eck asked two questions: Were the books his work? Did he stand by all their contents in the light of events? Luther said they were his work but asked for a recess to consider his response to the second. He consulted and prayed before returning the next day with the prepared reply "Unless I am convinced by the testimony of the Scriptures or by clear reason, (for I do not trust either in the pope or in councils alone, since it is well known that they have often erred and contradicted themselves), I am bound by the Scriptures I have quoted and my conscience is captive to the Word of God. I cannot and will not recant anything, since it is neither safe nor right to go against conscience. May God help me."

Eck replied that resort to scripture is a common basis of heresy, quoting from Pelagius and Arius through to Huss. Following the process, there were private consultations and in May 1521, Charles V issued his **Edict of Worms,** including declaring Luther an outlaw who should be arrested, receive a heretic's punishment and his writings banned. Nobody should offer him shelter or comfort. But Luther was snatched by sympathetic armed men posing as highwaymen and taken to Wartburg castle at Eisenach for sanctuary.

While there Luther worked to translate the New Testament from its original Greek into German vernacular, edited to reflect his own views. It was published in 1522. He also continued writing and condemning the sale of indulgences to such effect that Archbishop Albert of Mainz ceased this money-raising practice in his dioceses. Luther went further, criticising most of the seven sacraments and making it clear he regarded the ascetic or monastic life as an evil concept contrary to God-given human nature, though he seemed mainly opposed to just one of its aspects, the vow of celibacy. Luther regarded concupiscence as invincible so suggesting celibacy as a route to salvation is to devalue the essential, constructive and saving role of marriage. He also wrote an ill-judged bitter response to Henry VIII of England's defence of the seven sacraments, effectively alienating a valuable ally for Germany in the Reformation at that time.

The Diet of Worms had also condemned all innovation in practice and preaching of Christianity, which drew protest from the evangelical group. Luther, unabashed, also developed his new theology, refuting the possibility of earning God's forgiveness by good works, self-denial, indulgences or pilgrimage, contending that God made us sinners without free will and we can only find salvation by having trust in Christ stronger than the strength of our sins. He challenged the Church's teaching by suggesting that any action to curry favour with God was a sin. He said that monks and nuns vows were a sinful way of seeking God's favour, so should be broken and he also posited that the only sacraments were baptism, the Eucharist and penance.

Radical Reformation and German Peasants' War

Meanwhile, Carlstadt was attacking the use of fine vestments for priests, overelaborate altar decoration and imagery such as statues, pictures, icons and Stations of the Cross as idolatrous and contravening the second Commandment. Another reformer turned up in the person of Gabriel Zwillig, who had followed a similar educational path to Luther and also been an Augustinian. Zwillig left the order to return to Wittenberg and join Carlstadt, becoming an ardent iconoclast. On Christmas day 1521, Carlstadt celebrated the first reformed communion service at Wittenberg, wearing secular clothing and avoiding reference to sacrifice. During the consecration, he said the consecration aloud "This is my Body ... This is my blood..." in German instead of Latin and the Communion was distributed as both bread and wine. The city council allowed these changes to continue and at his request authorised the removal of imagery from churches. Then in January 1522, Carlstadt emphasised his denial of the requirement for clerical celibacy as he married fifteen-year-old Anna von Mochau. The Pope and Emperor both ordered Elector Frederick to reverse the changes to the Mass, which Frederick passed on to the Council of Wittenberg, while signalling some compassion for Carlstadt. These orders were mostly implemented.

Another radical at this time was Nicholas Storch, who came from Zwickau in Saxony. He was an unordained lay preacher and leader of the 'Zwickau Prophets' who were expelled from Zwickau and moved to Wittenberg in 1521, having heard of the reforms there. They encouraged Carlstadt to go even further in his reforms, which took them well beyond Philip Melancthon's comfort zone and led to civil disturbances.

Pressure grew on Luther to leave the sanctuary of Wartburg Castle for Wittenburg. He sought Frederick's blessing, saying the Devil had crept into the parish and his work could only really be repaired by Luther's personal presence and preaching. On receiving this blessing, which would have included some protection, Luther arrived in Wittenberg in March 1522 and preached eight sermons denouncing the Zwickau Prophets and Carlstadt as extremists. The 'Prophets' soon left and Luther's preaching swung the congregation back behind his less extreme reforms as it did Zwillig, who publicly confessed his errors. It naturally turned out to be a period of division between Luther and Carlstadt.

Thomas Müntzer (1489-1525), another priest and theologian who met Luther in Wittenberg and supported his stand against sale of indulgences, believed that although not everybody could read the Bible, God intended it to be accessible to everyone as the route to God. He gave a sermon during 1521 that replicated quite faithfully the Sermon on the Mount. Müntzer proved to be as radical as Carlstadt and left Wittenberg to keep in touch with the Zwickau Prophets. They and the Swiss Brethren are often seen as forerunners of the Anabaptists, who regarded infant baptism unscriptural, insisting on re-baptising converts only in adulthood. Rejected and persecuted by both Catholics and reformists, the few that remained eventually emigrated to America, from whom emerged later the Amish, Mennonite and Hutterite communities.

In 1523, Luther helped twelve young nuns escape from a Cistercian convent in Nimbschen. One of them was Katherine von Bora whom he married two years later. They had six children, two of whom died as youngsters, while they lived a very frugal life. He continued his writing and preaching but fell out with Erasmus, Dutch philosopher and foremost Humanist thinker of the time. The Humanism movement grew out of the Renaissance and its main spiritual home was Basle University.

Carlstadt became pastor in the town of Orlamünde in 1523 and was allowed the freedom to follow the personal views he had developed. He continued to preach and lead services in everyday dress; with no music or imagery; preached against clerical celibacy and infant baptism; accepted the spiritual presence of God in the Eucharist but denied trans-ubstantiation. He also allowed the regular congregation a large say in the planning of services and running of the parish in the manner that would become associated with Jean Calvin and the Congregationalists. Carlstadt was a significant figure in the Radical Reformation.

Ulrich Zwingli (1484-1581), another important figure in Church reform, studied at Vienna then graduated in 1504 in Basle. Zwingli, also musically gifted, was ordained as a Catholic priest in Zurich in 1506. He had been impressed by the theology lectures of Thomas Wyttenbach and soon developed disdain of corruption and simony in the Roman Church, which led him to question other aspects of the Church and become a leader of the Reformation in Switzerland. Zwingli could see no reason for prohibiting clerical marriage and found some practices such as Lent fasting and imagery in churches discomforting. Luther and Zwingli shared much common ground but they disagreed on consubstantiation in the Eucharist.

The rapid spread of challenges to such long-accepted norms led to a sense of freedom, rights and justice that baulked at the inequalities in society and led to the German Peasants' War in 1524-5. It was always an unequal war and destined to failure as the peasants were carried on a wave of frustration and passion but had neither the organisation nor weaponry to match the nobles. They were brutally suppressed with many villages burned, monasteries destroyed and about 100,000 dead by the end. The nobles associated Carlstadt with the uprising although he was an avowed pacifist, He took safe secret refuge with Luther for some months and could not preach or write for a while. Thomas Müntzer, on the other hand, was openly involved in leadership of the Peasants' War.

Luther continued to preach Christian values, sympathising with the peasants' poverty and suppression, but he was clear from the outset that they should employ peaceful protest. On seeing in his travels the destruction they wrought and burning of monasteries, libraries and other valuable Church property, he lost sympathy and sided with the nobles, encouraging their repression of the uprising. This persuaded many of the rebels to lay down their pathetic arms, soon ending the uprising in their defeat at Frankenhausen in May 1525, followed by Müntzer's execution. In large parts of Germany Luther was beginning to be accepted as almost conventional and although still excommunicated and vilified by the Church of Rome, he was gaining influence and acceptance in Saxony and other parts of Northern Europe, where the Reformation was finding fertile ground for its growth. This was fed by fast-moving social and economic changes, rising prices and poverty in the countryside coupled with wider access to education and the diminishing power of nobility. In the south and Austria, the Lutherans were strong in the towns while the Anabaptists grew most in villages and the countryside especially among peasants.

German nobles themselves had felt severe impact from both Church and state taxes and could see a growing difference between their standard of living and that of the monasteries, bishops and cardinals of the Catholic Church. Little surprise then that they added to the damage and losses already inflicted by the peasants on Church property, whilst contriving for the blame to fall on the peasants. The civil authorities also eagerly took their opportunity to seize much property and wealth from the Church and relieve the population of despised Church taxes.

Luther worked tirelessly through the chaos and Melancthon helped set up a management and regulatory structure for a new Church and compiled and distributed a simple German language catechism. Concerned at the social upheavals, especially the loss of Church schools and other buildings, Luther cultivated the support of princes and encouraged hymn singing in the vernacular, which became popular. He reversed his original plan to maintain a Latin Mass, converting all to the German vernacular. He made some changes to its format, including eliminating references to sacrifice, distributing communion as both bread and wine and leaving the use of vestments and candles optional. He won active support from Elector Frederick, who confiscated the benefices of resistant clergy and forced recalcitrant landowners to sell up and move from the state. The Lutheran Church was soon predominant in Saxony and spreading. Frederick died in 1525, still a Roman Catholic but supportive of Luther's reforms and was succeeded by his like-minded brother, John 'the Steadfast'. Luther concentrated his efforts on Saxony, helped by funding from John which was essential as he could then expect none from Rome, which had seen a change of papacy.

Adrian Boeyens, from a poor Netherlands family, became doctor of Divinity and was chosen by Emperor Maximilian as tutor for his grandson, who would become Charles V. Adrian was a notably pious, ascetic and humble professor but with imperial support he was swept into a series of promotions in Spain then made cardinal. Nobody was more surprised than him when aged sixty three, news of his election as the only Dutch pope ever came through in January 1522, taking the name **Pope Adrian VI** (1522-23).

He had never set foot in Italy and knew he would be resented as a 'barbarian', but he prepared for the job with a daunting, almost impossible list of necessary objectives:

- To rid the clergy of long-established abuses.
- To rein in Italy's testosterone-charged expansionist rival princes.
- To reverse the rising tide of Reformation in Germany and Central Europe.
- To raise an international army to protect Hungary and Rhodes from the Turks.

Laudable though these ambitions were, he never stood any chance of success. Predecessors had left papal finances in a sorry state; his courtiers refused to rein in their expenses; the Curia resisted any reform or cut-backs on the basis of established rights and practice; his appointed nuncio to Germany was scorned and Adrian VI's open accusations of the Church leadership and court corruption only served to fuel the Reformers' justification of their apostasy; his appeals for a combined effort against the Turks was ignored and Rhodes fell, thus giving the Turks control of the Mediterranean Sea.

Adrian's highly influential friends in central Europe, counted for nothing in Rome. He was a good, humble and holy man but without the wholehearted support of his Curia or the local princes and politicians his ambitions for Church reform and protection were doomed. It seemed more a Roman than a universal Church. He died broken-hearted in September 1523 and no future popes would come from outside Italy again until Polish Pope John Paul II over four centuries later.

Although from the powerful Medici family of Florence and in the post for longer, **Pope Clement VII (1523-34)**, achieved no more success than Adrian VI before him. As the Italian Renaissance ended, he came with an excellent record as a man and cardinal, intelligent, learned in science and theology, respectable and devout and with recognised gravitas and powers of rhetoric. His reign was dogged by many pre-existing handicaps, with his Church almost bankrupt with further challenges about to arise. He had been advisor to both his immediate predecessors, so he came to the post well aware of what confronted him. For all that, he appeared surprisingly oblivious to the real changes that had taken place in the position of the Church in its relationships with society, regimes and Christians in Europe.

As he took the throne, the two most powerful kings in Europe, Emperor Charles V and Francis I of France were at war with each other on Italian turf. Francis I conquered and took control of Milan in 1524, whereupon Pope Clement VII decided at the beginning of 1525 to ally with Francis I and the Italian princes. He was keen to secure a return of Medici control over Florence and the return of Parma and Piacenza to the Papal Lands, which would give Francis I a route to Naples and the southern part of Italy controlled by Emperor Charles V. He thus alienated the Spanish-German axis and Charles V turned his interest to the rising fortunes of the Reform movement in Germany. It was not long before there was an uprising of the Roman barons, forcing Clement VII to seek mediation from Charles V, who seized the opportunity and his forces rapidly defeated Francis in the Battle of Pavia and took him prisoner.

Clement VII found the Imperial German and Habsburg rule oppressive and when Francis was released in 1526, Clement VII allied with France, Venice and Milan. Charles V was offended and threatened a council on the Lutheran Reformation. The Pope's vacillation gave rise to an Imperial faction in the Curia, led by Cardinal Pompeo Colonna but Colonna's subsequent departure from Rome meant that Clement VII could only stay with the French. As Italy swung behind the Emperor, Rome could do nothing to prevent a force of Imperial soldiers attacking and taking control. Clement VII took refuge in the Castel Sant' Angelo, but soon had to submit. He was imprisoned there and his life was spared subject to payment of a huge fine and handing over some Papal Lands. Enemies of the Medici threw the family out of Florence. Clement escaped from the Castel and found sanctuary in Orvieto, but returned to Rome in 1528 only to find the city in ruin. Peace was restored at the Treaty of Barcelona mid-1529, by which the Papal States had some of the lost lands restored and Charles V undertook to support the return of the Medicis to Florence. Thereafter, Clement VII remained faithful to the emperor, pressing him to oppose the spread of Lutheranism while himself continuing to evade pressure for a council.

Clement VII died in 1534, having achieved little progress for the Church on account of the obstacles he faced, his lack of determined focus on ecclesiastical goals and poor political judgment. His Medici family weakness for nepotism did nothing to improve the finances of the Church while it saw favours dispensed. A couple of his legacies are worth noting. He accepted Copernicus' theory of heliocentrism in 1533, that the planets, including earth, spin around the sun, which soon became controversial. Clement VII flouted the Canon Law that required clergy to be clean-shaven, growing a beard as Rome was sacked, which he never shaved again, beginning a trend. Regarding Church matters, though the Ottomans had taken Rhodes, the base of the Knights Hospitaliers during his watch, he acquired Malta for them and they were re-constituted as the Knights of Malta. He also approved the Capuchin Franciscan Order. Wider events in Europe during his papacy help to put his reign in context.

The Ottoman Threat

Suleiman and the Ottomans overtook Buda and much of Hungary in 1526, then were repulsed by the Habsburg's Charles V and Ferdinand I of Austria, but retook it in 1529, advancing to the walls of Vienna the following year. The attackers retreated due to poor weather and stretched supply lines, returning with the aim of laying siege to Vienna once more in 1532 but did not even get their forces that far for similar reasons. In the next couple of decades, the Ottomans were distracted by wars on their eastern front with the Safavid dynasty of Persia, relieving pressure on Europe for a while. Then in 1542, King Francis I of France sought an alliance with the Ottomans against their common foe, the Habsburg dynasty. Suleiman consigned a hundred ships to Barbarossa to support the French in attacks and pillage along the Western Mediterranean coast. This was short-lived as Francis I and Charles V signed a peace treaty in 1544.

First Diet of Speyer 1526

The wave of Reformism was making nonsense of the Edict of Worms, contributing to the need for the imperial Diet of Speyer. Charles V had intended to head it, but other international matters diverted him, so his younger brother and regent, Archduke Ferdinand I of Austria presided as his delegate at the meeting with instructions to bring the Reformist and Catholic sides together. It soon became apparent that the Reformation had advanced to the point where many imperial cities outside Germany had swung against Catholicism. This combined with tension between Emperor Charles and Pope Clement VII, who had given support to Francis I, emboldened those German Princes who favoured Luther to declare openly their embrace of the Reformist cause. The extent of the conversion surprised the Catholic contingent, which was also conscious of the imminent threat from the Turks. The Catholic Church therefore found itself in a far weaker position than expected.

Emperor Charles V, still a committed Catholic, hoped that the Edict of Worms would be enforced and rebellion suppressed until a council could be arranged, hopefully to reach peaceful accommodation between the parties. Ferdinand I agreed an outcome by which the Edict of Worms was suspended temporarily until such a council took place, which he thought was imminent. Meanwhile every state was to exercise religious tolerance, living and practicing according to its belief in the wishes of God and the Emperor. In his spat with the pope Charles V neither signed nor condemned the edict of Speyer 1526, which suspended the edict of Worms until another diet was called to settle the Church question. This was ambiguous enough to be taken as reprieving Luther from the charge of heresy, resulting in people and Reformist states doing as they chose.

This introduced a new concept of sovereignty whereby the state ruler also determined and ruled the religion within its borders, which gave a huge boost to anti-papist Reformists. But given their lack of a clear leader and wide disparities in reformist views among the new, relatively untrained clergy it also opened the flood gates to disunity of faith, contrary to the expressed wish of Jesus Christ. Nonetheless, new Reformist sects would continue to proliferate without control.

Sack of Rome 1527

The French had control of Milan, Venice and Florence and the support of the pope, who wished to avoid imperial German and Habsburg dominance of Rome and papal lands. When Charles V's army had won a victory in northern Italy and Rome's funds had run out, a large force of about 34,000 men under Duke Charles of Bourbon decided to plunder Rome's riches, defacing the splendour of the Roman Renaissance.

Second Diet of Speyer 1529

A second meeting was called firstly to determine action against the Turks who were now threatening Vienna and secondly to halt the advance of Reformism. Senior Catholics and notable Reformists attended, but the Emperor once again delegated the presidency to his regent Ferdinand. Ferdinand's opening address deplored the interpretation of many German princes of the conclusion of the 1526 diet. He declared that the Catholic faith was to be followed by all states within the Holy Roman Empire. The edict of Worms was to be enforced, there was to be no further reform. The Zwinglian and Anabaptist variations were proscribed until a council could be held which was promised within a year.

The followers of Luther and Zwingli joined under the leadership of John of Saxony to oppose this existential threat to them with a legal appeal issued in April 1529, quoting the 'Word of God', their consciences and the result of the previous diet in their defence whilst asking for an objective German judge or preferably a general council. This was known as the Protestation, from which the name 'Protestant' grew.

Augsburg Confession

Philip I of Hesse, a Protestant political strategist, called a conference at Marburg Castle in 1529. Philip I was sure that disunity among Protestants would weaken them, so he arranged this 'Marburg Colloquy' with the aim of maintaining unity between Luther and Ulrich Zwingli in particular. Philip Melancthon also participated. Although Zwingli and Luther agreed on many points of criticism of the Roman Church, they could not find common ground on the Eucharist. Luther contended that at the consecration, the real presence of the body and blood of Christ were united with the bread and wine. Zwingli believed that Christ made his sacrifice on the Cross once for eternity so he saw the bread and wine of the Eucharist as simply a symbolic memorial of this. On such a key point of doctrine, full unity was thus out of reach. Nonetheless, this colloquy laid the ground for the Augsburg Confession to be signed at the Diet of Augsburg, called by Holy Roman Emperor Charles V in 1530 and the formation of the Schmalkaldic League by leading Protestant German nobles including Elector John Frederick of Saxony and Philip I of Hesse.

The Augsburg Confession was a list of Protestant articles of faith which summarised the main items of their common creed.

Augsburg Confession Articles of Faith:

1. **God.** Christians believe in the Triune God and reject other interpretations regarding the nature of God.
2. **Original Sin.** Lutherans believe that the nature of man is sinful, without fear of God, without trust of God and with concupiscence. It is redeemed through Baptism and the Holy Spirit.
3. **Son of God.** Lutherans believe in the incarnation, that is, the union of the fully human with the fully divine in the person of Jesus. Jesus Christ alone brings about the reconciliation of humanity with God.
4.* **Justification by Faith.** Humans cannot be justified before God through their own abilities. We are wholly reliant on Jesus Christ for reconciliation with God.
5. **Office of Preaching.** Lutherans believe that to ensure that the Gospel of Jesus Christ is proclaimed throughout the world, Christ has established his office of the Holy Ministry.
6. **The New Obedience.** Lutherans believe that the good deeds of humans are the fruits of faith and salvation, not a price paid for them.
7. **The Church.** Lutherans believe that there is only one holy Christian Church and it is found wherever the gospel is preached in its truth and purity and sacraments are administered according to the gospel.
8. **What the Church is.** Despite what hypocrisy may exist in the Church (and amongst men), the Word and the Sacraments are

always valid because they are instituted by Christ, no matter what the sins may be of the one who administers them.

9. **Baptism.** Lutherans believe that Baptism is necessary and that through Baptism is offered the grace of God. Children are baptised as an offering to them of God's grace.

10. **Lord's Supper.** Lutherans believe that Christ's body and blood are truly present in, with and under the bread and wine of the sacrament and reject those that teach otherwise.

11. **Confession.** Lutherans believe that private absolution should remain in the church, though a believer does not need to enumerate all of his sins as it is impossible for a man to enumerate all of the sins for which he should be forgiven.

12. **Repentance.** Repentance comes in two parts: in contrition for sins committed according to the Law and through faith offered through the gospel. A believer can never be free from sin nor live outside the grace of God.

13. **Use of the Sacraments.** The Sacraments (Baptism and the Eucharist) are physical manifestations of God's Word and his commitment to us. The sacraments are never just physical elements but have God's word and promises bound to them.

14. **Ecclesiastical Order.** Lutherans allow only those who are "rightly called" to publicly preach or administer the sacraments.

15. **Ecclesiastical Usages.** Lutherans believe that church holidays, calendars and festivals are useful for religious observance, but that observance and ritual is not necessary for salvation. Human traditions (such as observances, fasts and distinctions in eating meats) that are taught as a way to "merit" grace work in opposition to the gospel.

16. **Civil Affairs.** Secular governments and vocations are part of God's natural orders; Christians are free to serve in government and the military and to engage in the business and vocations of the world. Laws are to be followed unless they command to sin.

17. **Christ's Return to Judgment.** Lutherans believe that Christ will return to raise the dead and judge the world; the godly will be given everlasting joy the ungodly will be "tormented without end". This rejects notions of a millennial kingdom before the resurrection of the dead.

18. **Free Will.** Lutherans believe that we have free will in the realm of "civil righteousness" (or "things subject to reason"), but that we do not have free will in "spiritual righteousness". We are free to choose and act in every regard except for the choice of salvation. Faith is not the work of men, but of the Holy Spirit.

19. **The Cause of Sin.** Lutherans believe that sin is caused not by God but by "the will of the wicked", turning away from God.
20. **Good Works.** The Lutheran notion of justification by faith does not somehow condemn good works; faith causes them to do good works as a sign of our justification (or salvation), not a requirement for salvation.
21. **Worship of the Saints.** Lutherans keep the saints, not as saviours or intercessors to God, but rather as examples and inspirations to our own faith and life.
22. **The Sacrament (Eucharist).** It is proper to offer communicants the consecrated bread and wine, not just the bread.
23. **Marriage of Priests.** Lutherans permit their clergy to enter the institution of marriage, for the reasons that the early Church bishops were married, that God blesses marriage as an order of creation, and because marriage and procreation is the natural outlet for human sexual desire.
24. **The Mass.** Lutherans retain the practice of the Mass, but only as a public gathering for the purposes of community worship and the receiving of the Eucharist. Lutherans reject the practice of using the Mass as a "work" for both salvation and worldly (monetary) gain.
25. **Confession.** Lutherans uphold the need for confession and absolution, but reject the notion that Confession should induce guilt or anxiety to the Christian. Absolution is offered for all sin, not just sins that can be recounted in a confession, as it is impossible for a man to know all of his transgressions.
26. **Distinction of Meats.** Human traditions that hold fasting and special observances with dietary restrictions as a means of gaining the favour of God are contrary to the gospel. While fasting and other practices are useful spiritual practices, they do not justify man nor offer salvation.
27. **Monastic Vows.** Man cannot achieve purity in community or isolation from the rest of the world, and perfection cannot be attained by any vow taken or actions of man alone.
28. **Ecclesiastical Power.** The only power given to priests or bishops is the power offered through Scripture to preach, teach and administer the sacraments. The powers given to the clergy in issues of government or the military are granted and respected only through civil means; they are not civil rulers of governments and the military by divine right.

* Article 4 is often regarded as the one by which the Lutheran church stands or falls.

Martin Luther had also developed his own thoughts on sacraments. He did not regard all the sacraments as sources of grace and argued that there were only two genuine sacraments – Baptism and the Eucharist, which he argued were the only ones to promise salvation and convey the grace to believe in it. He demonstrated flexibility in discussion but in his opposition to papal authority he was unyielding on account of his negative views on the behaviour of so many past popes.

Philip Melancthon worked closely with Luther, but for all its faults he simply loved the Catholic Church, its services and most sacraments. He was not alone in his reluctance to see ties cut. Melancthon criticised but could not reject the papacy and continued to work and pray passionately for Christian unity, though this was fast becoming a distant prospect, to both the east and north of Italy. He played a major role in composing the 'Augsburg Confession' hoping to prove that Protestants still had the right to be part of the Catholic Church in spite of the Edict of Worms because the 'innovations' to which the latter referred were simply well-intended corrections of abuses which had been introduced into the Church since Christ.

Changes made to the articles during the meeting sessions were accepted by Luther and theologians from all the evangelical groups. Rome's eventual refutation of these articles was unclear to the extent that Charles V decided not to publish it. However, Melancthon saw their response and felt obliged to write an explanation of the Confession, still appealing for reconciliation and unity within the Catholic Church.

During this period Lutheranism became dominant in northern Germany and Scandinavia, while other Protestant reform groups continued to grow and proliferate more widely elsewhere. While the Protestant movement was spreading, there was justifiable concern for the future of Christianity due to the variety of strongly held conflicting views growing within it. This was seen as potentially self-destructive, as was the total absence of a unifying leader. Luther ceased wearing his friar's habit but still prayed for a change of heart in Rome in 1532. In contrast, Ulrich Zwingli declared in 1534 that he could no longer be a Catholic.

In 1537, Luther published his Schmalkald Articles which include many of his beliefs, for a meeting of the Protestant Schmalkaldic League, held to prepare for an expected general council. He believed that after death the soul was separated from the body and remained in a peaceful sleep with God, which was the heavenly state. He rejected the concept of any penitential suffering in purgatory or punishment by eternal torment in hell. This put him at odds with Melancthon and Calvin, as well as the Catholic Church. Luther also doubted whether non-Christians could share this heavenly state (suggested in Augsburg Article IX), but Zwingli, as an admirer of Augustine of Hippo, believed that Heaven was accessible by all good people.

As Luther aged and his health painfully deteriorated, he became increasingly mentally wracked by resurgence of the torments of his youth. He was uncompromising in the face of any disagreement with his beliefs, which hardened and broadened in their span. For example, his approach to Jews became quite conciliatory around 1523 on the basis that Jesus was born a Jew, but when efforts to convert them failed, Luther lost all sympathy with them and by 1543 condemned them for having rejected the Christ's divinity and crucified him. While supporting a secular war against the Turks, he believed God would not countenance a religious war against Islam, seeing it as an Old Testament type scourge sent by God to punish the anti-Christ, meaning the papacy and Roman Church. Luther had a large following and his writings were widely read, especially in Germany. He continued to preach right up to his death in 1546.

Luther nurtured a hope that the Catholic Church would accept what he saw as the right reforms and that he could help these from within, but he misjudged its immovability. He may have been disappointed by the level of division his actions caused, but such reformation rarely remains a binary choice. Different moral and political views grew, although in his lifetime the extent of the spread was limited by political support only for either Lutheran or Reformed Protestantism and no one could then imagine the extent to which Christian sects would proliferate. Luther would have been warmed had he known that a number of his proposed changes would in due course be adopted by the Catholic Church, such as celebrating the Mass in the vernacular, less ornate altars, or communion under both kinds

Jean Calvin (1509-64)

Jean Calvin was as active and passionate as Martin Luther in his demand for reform in the Catholic Church. His activities were in different regions and culminated in different outcomes. Calvin grew up in a middle-class Catholic French family and studied theology at Paris University with a view to priesthood. During his course, he encountered Renaissance Humanism, having already been wrestling with his concerns about the elitism and corruption in the higher echelons of clergy and what he regarded as the Church's limited commitment to humility, holiness and pastoral guidance and its poor representation of the life and message of Jesus. This led to a change in direction and he went on to study law at Orléans and Bourges before returning to Paris to resume his deep interest in theology.

Back in Paris, Calvin developed his theology, around his conviction that radical reform was essential in the Roman Church. His views had evolved, now including a belief in predestination, which questions the idea of free will. He moved to Basle in Switzerland, which had grown as a reformist centre and more tolerant than France of questioning Church doctrine and practice. He gained prominence with his well-argued new Protestant theology and ideas on Church structure, favouring decentralised authority and liturgy even at parish level. He also maintained correspondence with Philip Melancthon and other reformers.

Calvin's book 'Institutes of Christian Religion' records his views. A principal tenet holds to the absolute sovereignty of God in religious and mundane matters, which argued for limiting clerical authority and a more direct relationship of individuals with God, thus reducing the scope for clerical corruption. These ideas would lead to Calvinism or the Reform Churches then to the Congregational (England, America) and the Presbyterian (Holland, Scotland) Churches, while the Baptists also grew from his theology.

Subsequent disunity and branching of Western Christianity continued as academic competition for new theological propositions gained pace, becoming a virtual free-for-all. Foundations of this lay in wavering confidence of lower-order clergy and public in the Roman Church as well as wider world events.

Alessandro Farnese was from a wealthy family, his mother being a Caetano, the family of Pope Boniface III. A graduate of Pisa University, he trained as an Apostolic Notary at the court of the Medici before joining the Roman Curia in 1491 and being appointed cardinal deacon in 1493 by Pope Alexander VI, of whom his sister Giulia was reportedly a mistress. As a young cleric, Alessandro had taken a mistress himself, by whom he had three sons and two daughters.

As **Pope Paul III** (1534-49), he was the first pope of the Reformation era to take the reform seriously and attempt any meaningful counter-measures. In 1536, he had set up a committee of nine senior prelates to examine Church reform in preparation for a general council in Mantua in 1537. They reported on abuses, especially in the administration and practice in Catholicism and suggested approaches to reform. Pope Paul was supported by Charles V's impatience for reform and both of them believed a general council, which was well overdue, was the only effective way to achieve this. Opposition from most cardinals and the inability of the Mantua authorities to guarantee civil order and safety led to its deferral.

In 1538, Pope Paul was more decisive in excommunicating Henry VIII of England following a campaign there against perceived idolatry, which had culminated in the destruction of a statue to Saint Thomas Becket. It was in Paul's power as pope to make this decision alone.

The council for which Charles V was so impatient was finally called by Paul III in 1537 against the wishes of nearly all his hierarchy. Concerned for their lifestyle, they helped ensure delay, though other events added to it. After a false start in 1537 in Vicenza, it had to be postponed due to the Franco-Italian war. Charles V was the most persistent leader of the age in seeking peaceful accommodation with German Protestants. His determination eventually resulted in the appointment of a nuncio in 1540 and a meeting in Regensburg in 1541 seeking an attempted compromise with Luther. With unanimous opposition from the cardinals, it came to nothing.

Paul also effectively went to war with his own people in 1540 in securing a dukedom for his grandson by usurping the incumbent by force against the popular will. His nepotism was conspicuous as he appointed two other grandsons as cardinals, one when aged just fifteen, and did much to advance the influence and wealth of his family while in post, all serving further to underline Protestant concerns with the papacy.

Paul III did oppose slavery. Then, with the settlements taking place in America, the plight of the indigenous people came to his attention which moved him to issue an instruction that as human beings they were God's children and should not be robbed of their freedom or possessions.

In 1540 Paul III gave approval to the new Society of Jesus, founded by Ignatius Loyola, which was probably unwittingly his most important contribution to the counter-reformation, as shall be seen.

In 1542, Pope Paul began a significant administrative reform in establishing the Holy Office, the first congregation to address Catholic doctrine in the face of Reformation. It replaced the Office of the Inquisition and became known as the Congregation for the Doctrine of the Faith of the Roman Curia. Congregations covering other areas of administration would follow.

The Council of Trent finally took place, but became spasmodically interrupted and prolonged, during which period, life and administration had to continue. Pope Paul agreed to provide men and money to support Charles V in fighting the Protestant princes and the Schmalkaldic League cities. By 1547, Charles V had won that war and managed to re-establish a Catholic majority in most of Germany. But the pope had withdrawn much of his support because Charles V had resisted his plans to install Paul's son Pier Luigi as Duke of Parma and Piacenza. When Pier Luigi was assassinated later that year, Paul III sought alliance with Francis I of France, but Francis was dying and Paul had to endorse the Emperor's successes. Pope Paul III died in 1549 leaving his family stronger but the Church little changed.

Cardinal Alessandro Farnese (1520-89) was the namesake and

grandson of Pope Paul III and by far the wealthiest cardinal bishop. He was a collector and patron of the arts and sponsored a young Augustinian friar called Onofrio Panvinio, to whom he was drawn by the fact that Onofrio researched the history of the papacy in great detail at such an early age. The cardinal was accompanying him on a research tour in Sicily when the young friar was taken by a fever and died, only 38 years old. In spite of the cardinal's wealth, Panvinio's copious manuscripts had never been published as they concerned extremely delicate matters and therefore carried potential danger for the writer or publisher.

Farnese kept these locked in a series of trunks, which were subsequently passed through successive cardinals, including some in charge of the Inquisition. It took a papal commission to order their opening which revealed a rich collection of history of the Church and its leaders as well as of Rome and its emperors. Orders were issued to remove from them any false or dangerous dogmas but Panvinio's records of papal election history represented such detailed research, they stretched to 10 volumes, covering all papal appointments back to St Peter. It included reference to the interference of emperors in the election process and criticism of prelates for their ambition, materialism and lax morals. They were so unsparing as to the truth that the Inquisition rejected them. A loyal Spanish lawyer, Francisco Peña, when asked to censor them, was in no doubt as to what was required of him and his report is in the Vatican Library as are most of Panvinio's volumes, still unpublished. Peña's summary included that the work was "imperfect, jumbled and confused, some of it useless and dangerous". His report would have been as intended, a tool for a convenient edit of history, but there was a keen sense of the dangers of taking this any further, so this extraordinary historian, Onofrio Panvinio remains uncredited for his most important work.

Franco-Italian War

In 1542, hostility between Emperor Charles and French King Francis had grown into the Franco-Italian war over various territorial claims in Italy, the Netherlands and France. Charles allied with England's Henry VIII as Francis did with Suleiman to add an eastern front, splitting Charles' defence resources. This was largely resolved in 1544 by the treaty of Crépy by which Charles V dropped his claim to the Duchy of Burgundy and Francis yielded Naples, Flanders and Artois. In a secret side-agreement, Francis agreed to help Charles V in resisting Protestantism, by force if necessary and to join him in pressing for a general council of the Church. The war between England and France continued.

Council of Trent

Eventually the council's first proper session began at Trent in 1545, just before Luther died. A plague led to another lengthy pause from 1547 until May 1551 when the council restarted under **Pope Julius III** (1550-55), only to be suspended by the surprise victory of Maurice of Saxony over Charles' imperial forces, allowing Maurice's army to enter Tirol, adjacent to the state of Trent. By then **Pope Paul IV** (1555-59) was in place. He was implacably opposed to Protestants, to Philip II of Spain and to the Habsburgs. At long last, under another pope, **Pope Pius IV** (1559-65), the council reconvened in January 1562 and closed in December 1563. None of the popes had attended in person, but were represented by legates.

The principal objective of the council had been to define the doctrines of the Church and prepare a counter-reformation from within. Charles V was supportive, wishing to deal with the hostile Schmalkaldic League and the spread of Protestantism southwards. It would be difficult to exaggerate the importance of this council to the Church, but it started late, was over-long and fragmented, spanning eighteen years and the reigns of four popes. The most important decrees that came out of it were the following:

- Confirmation of the validity of veneration – not worship – of saints, relics and images. This level of honour is called *dulia*, (to Mary, *hyperdulia*) whereas the worship of God is *latria*, the two being as different in degree as created and creator.
- Reform to the status and behaviour of monks and nuns.
- Reform of the lifestyle of cardinals and bishops; approvals for suitability of ecclesiastics; conditions for Mass; administration of ecclesiastical benefices; prohibition of clergy concubines, requiring celibacy and guidelines on their behaviour.
- Dogma on indulgences
- Fasts and feast days
- The Pope would organise revision of the Missal, Breviary (book of the Divine Office, canonical prayers for the hours of the day) and preparation of a catechism and a list of forbidden books.

There were some decrees affecting lay people, including the sacrament of marriage, which would have quite serious effect on the faithful from the 20th century, when divorce and remarriage became more commonplace. The Church strangely more or less defined when God may provide his grace to people.

The Council of Trent was notable in accepting the Roman Catholic Church's shortcomings and showing the wider world that in spite of these faults, it still held genuine religious strength and commitment to Christian principles and values. Trent provided some basis for countering dissent but most of the decrees related to internal Church reforms. It did not bring back many Protestants but served to take momentum out of their geographical spread, especially southwards. The fifteen year delay then the eighteen year length and discontinuity of the Council were unhelpful, diluting the effect and compromising clarity and definition of the decrees. It could fairly be regarded as too little, too long, too late.

Too late indeed, for it was almost a thousand years since Pope Gregory I (590-604), known as Gregory the Great and regarded by Martin Luther as 'the last good Pope' had condemned simony, the purchase of sacramental grace as well as ordination for money or favours.

A second congregation of the Curia was established by Pope Pius IV in 1561 to interpret and apply the canons of the Council of Trent, to be followed in 1571 by one for the Index under Pope Pius V (1566-72).

Censorship of books – Index Librorum

Following the Council of Trent and no doubt with the Augsburg confession in mind, the Tridentine Catechism was issued under the Papal Imprimatur in 1566, soon followed by the breviary, the Missal then eventually the Vulgate Bible in 1590-92.

There was now better literacy and so a wider potential readership. Together with the Reformation this contributed to suspicion in the Church leadership of the potential dangers of pernicious books. So a decision had been made at Trent to control the list of books that Catholics should be allowed to read. Such censorship was not new as it had been applied in some dioceses in Germany in the 1480s and led to a Bull by Pope Innocent III in 1487 authorising bishops to make diocesan lists of prohibited books. Censorship of books had been proposed at the Lateran Council, but a catalogue of the Inquisition of 1559 was the first intended for the whole Church and the first to be called the Index. A congregation was set up to keep this updated as new material was published.

Japan

Portuguese Jesuits began missionary work in Japan in the late 1540s with sufficient success for Pope Gregory to add Japan to the diocese of Macao. In 1588 Japan became a separate diocese based in Nagasaki. Early in the 17th century, English and Dutch traders brought Protestant missionaries but as Japan did not prove a lucrative trade market, the English withdrew, leaving it to the Dutch.

Japan had been traditionally mostly Buddhist or Shinto whose beliefs bore no resemblance to those of Christianity, which was an entirely new spiritual concept there. Listeners had first to grapple with a God who created the entire universe and most had difficulty in confronting the possibility of hell, particularly related to their ancestors. Missionaries faced added challenges from ongoing civil war between followers of the Japanese Emperor and those of the Shogunate, military leadership. Toyotumi Hideyoshi (1537-98) had risen from being a peasant to succeeding his master, senior samurai Oda Nobunaga in seeking to unite Japan. Toyotumi was profoundly suspicious of Catholics following attacks on Buddhist temples and saw them as parties to European expansionism in the East. There were some executions of Catholics.

Regardless of political and cultural difficulties, by 1590, the Jesuits had recruited some seventy Japanese to their order, doubling their active presence in Japan. As the sixteenth century closed, Catholicism had spread throughout the nation albeit sparsely, though the majority of citizens of Nagasaki were baptised Catholics, earning the city the tag 'Rome of Japan'. The suspicions of the national leadership persisted and around 1614, conscious of the Spanish take-over of the Philippines, Tokugawa Ieyasu banned all Christian Japanese activity on threat of execution and expelled foreign missionaries. A few continued to practice underground with lay leadership of services. It was not until 1853 that the country reopened to foreigners in a limited way after the American navy had opened dialogue. Missionaries of all denominations piled in despite the ban still applying on Christianity and proselytisation. In 1865, a French priest discovered that under cover of great secrecy, the underground Church had courageously continued with ministers following the lectionary and baptising children and recruits during those ten generations. Governments from Europe and the USA eventually persuaded the Japanese government that their interests would be best served by removal of the ban on Christianity and they finally did so in 1873.

English Reformation

Luther's German Bible inspired translations elsewhere, including one in English by William Tyndale (1494-1536. Tyndale translated directly from Hebrew and Greek sources which pre-dated the vulgate, augmenting Tyndale's claim to authenticity. It introduced God's name as Jehovah, derived from the Hebrew Yahweh, into English scripture. Tyndale's translation made him a leading figure in the English Reformation in spite of the death penalty applying since the time of Wycliffe to anyone caught in possession of an unlicensed Bible in English.

Tyndale's Bible challenged that law and the Catholic Church that was behind it, so he went to the continent to find publishers, settling for a while in Hamburg to work on revisions and other books. He antagonised King Henry VIII by writing in his 1530 book 'The Practice of Prelates' that the annulment of Henry's marriage would be contrary to scriptural teaching. However his book 'Obedience of a Christian Man' gave support to Henry's mooted plan to separate the Church of England from the Roman Church in 1534.

While Tyndale was in Hamburg in 1531, the English courts asked Emperor Charles V to extradite him, but Charles refused on the grounds of lack of evidence. He opposed Henry VIII's wish to divorce his aunt, Catherine of Aragon. Tyndale was arrested in 1535 in Antwerp, at a principal publisher of his translation. He was jailed near Brussels for a year before being executed at the stake for heresy in 1536. His last prayer was answered when in 1538, Henry authorised publication of his Bible for use by the Church of England.

While Pope Clement VII was prisoner near Rome in 1527, Henry VIII petitioned him to annul his marriage to Catherine of Aragon. They had a daughter Mary, but two sons died in infancy and Henry VIII was desperate for a male Tudor heir. Catherine had been his brother's widow when they married and this was cited as a reason for annulment, although Pope Julius II had given dispensation for the marriage. Clement VII refused Henry VIII's request, perhaps influenced by his captor Emperor Charles V, Catherine's nephew. Henry VIII's situation was similar to that of the Russian Tsar whose similar request was refused by Patriarch Vaarlam.

Since William Warham, the Archbishop of Canterbury was a friend of Pope Clement VII, Henry VIII held a meeting of clergy and lawyers, led by Thomas Cromwell in 1530 to see what could be done, but they counselled against Parliament trying to press Archbishop Warham to gainsay Pope Clement VII's decision.

Church taxes were paid directly to Rome and the final say on appointment of bishops lay with Rome, which meant that bishops looked to the pope for authority, so this issue replicated the familiar old political dispute over ultimate sovereignty. When Archbishop Warham died, Henry VIII persuaded Clement VII to appoint Thomas Cranmer in his place. Cranmer was a friend of the Boleyn family and he agreed to annul Henry VIII's first marriage, allowing Henry to marry Ann Boleyn towards the end of 1532.

With help from Thomas Cranmer, Archbishop of Canterbury and lawyer Thomas Cromwell, Henry VIII split from Rome by establishing a national Church of England with the sovereign at its head. Some advisors advocated a congregational-style church nearer Calvin's Reform concept but Henry felt more comfortable with a path closer to that of Luther as more akin to the familiar Catholic way. Pope Clement VII responded by excommunicating both Henry VIII and Thomas Cranmer from the Catholic Church. The personal and political argument had become a religious one, while the decline of feudalism in England, growing usage of common law and rising nationalism combined to provide fertile ground for the spread of Protestantism

Parliament countered the pope's decision by passing two Acts – First Fruit and Tenths, which diverted taxes on Church revenue and Peter's Pence from the pope to the crown, making it an offence for landowners to pay the annual levy to the pope, claiming that England had no superior authority beneath God, so no longer accepted the pope's right to appoint its bishops. Then in 1534, there came a third, the Act of Supremacy, which separated the Church of England from the Roman Catholic Church and declared the monarch as its supreme governor.

Henry VIII then dissolved the monasteries in 1536. It was estimated that some 2% of the total male population were directly affected by this, which involved 900 religious houses in all. Many abbeys and priories had their roofs removed to render them unusable for worship. Apart from effectively bringing to a halt daily recitation of the Divine Office and making lay people of the monks, nuns and friars, the spiritual objectives were limited. The main benefit to the crown was the funds received from the use, sale or rent of the properties plus much of the art, stained glass, lead and building materials such as tiles and stone. Some of this funded modest provision and pensions for the personnel affected and the rest was used in support of military campaigns in the following decade against France and Scotland.

The social and cultural effects of the dissolution were enormous and a heavy burden on the state and affected members of the population. Losses included:

- Libraries, valuable books and manuscripts, including manuscript Church music.
- Religious hospitals which had provided widespread care for the public, including poor, disabled and special care for the elderly. Some of these were re-founded by the government.
- Free food and alms to the destitute.
- Schooling and colleges at universities; again some were re-founded.
- 8,000 square kilometres of land with tens of thousands of tenant farmers.

It took half a century for overall charitable giving in England to regain pre-dissolution levels.

On the spiritual plane, there was a huge decline of contemplative spirituality and prayer arising from the dispersal of the religious personnel. Only a few of them regrouped in Catholic lands on the continent, some of whom would return temporarily during the subsequent brief reign of Queen Mary.

On Henry VIII's death in 1547, his son Edward VI took the throne aged just nine but only lived for another five years, during which he was pressed to condemn Catholicism and confirm the Church of England as the established national Church. In 1549, the precursor to the Book of Common Prayer, edited by Thomas Cranmer, was published. Aware that he was dying, Edward VI and his Council named his cousin Lady Jane Grey as heir, excluding his half-sisters Mary and Elizabeth, to prevent England reverting to Catholicism. When he died in early 1553, powerful opposition to this order led to Jane's reign lasting only a few days before she was replaced by Mary Tudor. Once on the throne, Mary renewed communion with Rome so reversing Edward VI's Protestant Reforms, but by now the country was confused and divided in faith.

Mary died five years later in 1558 to be succeeded by her sister Elizabeth I who moved rapidly to revive the Protestant Reforms in England and reaffirm the Church of England (C of E)'s independence from Rome. The following year, Parliament debated a Reformation Bill aimed at formalising this independence. The resulting Act also removed the concept of transubstantiation from Holy Communion, banned elaborate vestments, forbade images in church, allowed clerical marriage and re-confirmed the monarch as Supreme Governor of the Church of England. The House of Lords, which included Catholic peers and bishops, blocked the Bill. Parliament then introduced two new Bills, the Acts of Supremacy and Uniformity, which would have similar effect. The first superseded one of the same name during Henry's reign and confirmed Elizabeth as Supreme Governor of the C of E. The Act of Uniformity defined the bases of structure and worship of the C of E and confirmed that services would be based on the Book of Common Prayer. Various members of the House of Lords had been removed and replaced to prevent further blockage there.

After the Council of Trent, the intellectual leaders of Protestantism were as likely to find further grounds on which to disagree between themselves as to extend the quarrel with the Catholic Church. This soon led to further divisions in the Protestant side of Christianity, which lacked the firm leadership of Catholicism. The divisions were greatest in those new Protestant Churches where sound constitutional foundations had not been laid, often intentionally so. England was perhaps unique here in that due to Henry VIII's dispute with the pope over the issue of his divorce he had welcomed the opportunity afforded by Protestantism so he made sure that the Church of England was given a sound legal constitution. Then in 1563, the Thirty Nine Articles of Religion were adopted as the defining doctrines of the Church of England, distinguishing it from Roman Catholic and Calvinist beliefs and practice.

In 1570, Pope Pius V declared Queen Elizabeth I a heretic and excommunicated all who followed her orders, relieving her subjects of any obligation of allegiance to their monarch, leaving the faithful confused. With fault-lines exposed in old and new Churches alike and with the rise of persuasive choices, English people were fast learning to exercise their own discretion and judgment. Having little time to settle itself, the Church of England suffered a rise in internal disagreement and polarisation. Antipathy between the emerging factions would lead to civil war in England in the next century.

Puritans, Robert Browne (1550s-1633) and the Congregational Church

Puritans was the name given to a large group of members of the Church of England who felt that its Protestant reforms had not gone far enough and still reflected too many Catholic practices. They leaned towards Calvinist reforms, rather than Henry VIII's preferred Lutheran option. The Puritans spanned a wide spectrum of opinion and never became a specific faith, rather like the Cathars. As in all society, a minority tending to the extreme can make the news and lead to break-away groups.

In 1572, Robert Browne graduated at Corpus Christi College Cambridge, strongly influenced by the Puritan theologian Thomas Cartwright. Cartwright was eventually levered out of his fellowship at Trinity College and went to Geneva for the freedom to pursue his beliefs, then to Antwerp. In 1581, Browne was the first minister with Puritan principles to go so far as to set up a Separist church that wished to dissociate itself from the Church of England. These reformist Separists spawned the Congregational Church. Browne was arrested but then released on the advice of William Cecil, statesman and counsellor to Queen Elizabeth. Browne then moved later the same year to Middleburg in the Netherlands, where he set up a similar church, according to his take on the New Testament. Dissensions existed between these passionate Puritan pioneers, Cartwright being more Presbyterian and Browne Separist.

Browne wrote a couple of books on his principles and practice which were banned in England, at least two people being hanged for circulating them. But Browne only remained an active Separist from 1579 to 1585 when he returned to the Church of England, leading to recriminations with steadfast Separist followers who scorned him as a turncoat. He became a schoolmaster in the East Midlands then was ordained in 1591. His seven years of separation saw him imprisoned many times for his views and he had started an enduring movement. He is still regarded as the founder of the Congregational Church and the pilgrims of the Mayflower in the next century were Puritans who followed his movement. From them would emerge numerous further branches of Reform Christian practice in what would become the USA.

Scotland and John Knox

Meanwhile, Scotland was still a separate nation and John Knox (1513-72) emerged as a leading figure of Church reform there. He was associated with the murder of Cardinal Beaton in 1546 and eventually exiled to England in 1549 where he worked in the Church of England and became chaplain to Edward VI.

When Queen Mary came to the throne and re-introduced Catholicism to England, Knox moved to Geneva in 1554. He met Jean Calvin there and was impressed with his Reform Church ideas. He made a brief return to Scotland late 1555, but returned to Geneva the following year to accept an invitation to minister there to the many English Protestants who had emigrated. He was an extreme and unashamed misogynist, which was not unusual then and wrote a famous pamphlet on those lines. Queen Elizabeth I had now taken the English throne and was deeply insulted by his writing. Her accession and embrace of Protestantism led many English refugees to return, depleting Knox's congregation, so he returned to Scotland in 1559.

Knox's powerful rhetoric against Catholic practices and a fiery sermon in Perth in 1559 led to disturbance and attacks on churches and statues. Stained glass windows in churches and cathedrals throughout Scotland were smashed as this spread, with the loss of priceless 13th century glass. Significant buildings were left wrecked while others were subsequently repaired and glazed with plain glass. The Scottish Reformation followed in 1560 and parliament passed acts that within days abolished the jurisdiction of the pope there, outlawed all practice and doctrine other than that of the reformed Church and prohibited the Catholic Mass. The formalities of establishing the new Church of Scotland, or Kirk, were set in motion.

What emerged was a Church run on democratic lines, with a pastor chosen by each congregation and each congregation aiming to be self-sustaining. Instead of bishops, there would be 'superintendents' with lesser, mainly administrative powers. Overall control lay with a General Assembly and a national system of education would be open to all. Funds would be appropriated from Roman Catholic patrimony, much of which was held by nobles, who were disinclined to cooperate. However, this did not become law then as Mary Queen of Scots returned from France in 1561 after the death of her husband, Francis II, the King of France and declared there would be no change to the religious status quo.

The relationship between Knox and Mary was stormy until Mary was imprisoned by Protestant rebels and forced to abdicate in 1567. Her son and heir James was baptised a Catholic and became King of Scotland when only thirteen months old, so regents ruled in his stead until 1583. Knox delivered the sermon at his coronation as King James VI of Scotland the following year.

King James VI of Scotland

In 1584, James VI ordered the Scottish Parliament to pass the 'Black Acts', bringing the Kirk under Royal control with two bishops leading it. This was so vehemently opposed by the Calvinists that James VI had to retract, allowing control to return to the General Assembly. He signed the Treaty of Berwick in 1586, a peace treaty with Queen Elizabeth I of England, which he saw as preparing his way to succession to her throne and she saw as easing her path to executing his mother a year later. When Elizabeth I died, he duly became King James I of England in 1603 and left Edinburgh for London.

Ignatius Loyola (1491-1556) and the Jesuits

Ignatius was the youngest of a family of thirteen children in Loyola in the Basque country. He became a brave knight displaying distinction in battle and a proud, swashbuckling ladies' man with qualities as a leader and diplomat. He came to the notice of the royal court and spent time working for an administrator in the royal palace of Ferdinand and Isabella where he relished fine clothes and a rather dissolute life. All this came to an end when his left leg was splintered by a French cannonball at the siege of Pamplona in 1521. This took many greatly painful months to mend, having to be reset twice without anaesthetics. It left him with a limp as this leg was then shorter. In the months of confinement as it mended, he read from the limited choice then available and found the lives of Jesus and the saints more compelling and life-enhancing than romantic novels of knights, damsels and derring-do which he found frivolous.

Ignatius was particularly impressed with 'The Life of Christ' by Ludolph of Saxony, a 14th century Carthusian monk, as well as accounts of St Francis of Assisi. This led him to his principle of Ignatian discernment, i.e that God communicates directly with each of us directly through our hearts, mind and soul. This would guide his future life and faith decisions and he resolved to live a life of poverty and devotion and to make a pilgrimage to the Holy Land. Once he could walk again, Ignatius went to the Benedictine monastery Santa Maria de Montserrat in Catalonia and after reflecting on his earlier life, he made a humble confession. His penance was a fine for charity which he chose to give to poor people he met. He laid his sword and dagger on the altar and took to wearing rough clothes. He then walked to a nearby town and begged for subsistence, eventually working at odd menial jobs in the local hospital in return for a bed and food.

In 1523, he embarked on his pilgrimage to the Holy Land and on returning to Barcelona, he took up study in Theology and Latin for the next ten years. In the later stage of his time at university, he did some preaching and was once arrested for questioning by the Inquisition then released. During this time he developed his 'Spiritual Exercises' and went on to study in Paris, where he met six companions of like mind. Two of them, Peter Faber from the Savoy region and Francis Xavier, a fellow-Basque shared a room with him. In August 1534, all seven of them gathered in St Peter's church in Montmartre to make solemn vows of poverty and chastity and to work together for life on the project they had agreed.

In 1539 the three ex-room-mates founded The Society of Jesus, who became known as Jesuits – "soldiers of God working for the defence and propagation of the faith." Their stated aim was 'peacefully and intellectually to counter Protestantism'. After they had added a vow of obedience to the pope in matters regarding mission, direction and assignment, the Society was blessed and approved by Pope Paul III in 1540 which boosted their numbers. Ignatius was the Society's first Father General. He took a long-term view of mission and sent their followers throughout Europe to set up schools, colleges and seminaries, stressing the importance of spiritual education.

In 1544, the Jesuits gained the valuable support of Francis Borgia, grandson of Pope Alexander VI, a duke and senior aide to Emperor Charles V. After his Portuguese wife Eleanor, a noblewoman died in 1546, Francis made provision for their eight children and trained as a priest. Once ordained he joined Ignatius as a full member. When Francis heard that Pope Paul intended to make him a cardinal, he 'disappeared' into the Basque country to avoid this whilst his evident talents as an administrator soon earned him the leadership of Spanish Jesuits. He set up a number of colleges and then took on some overseas missions.

In 1548, Ignatius published his book 'Spiritual Exercises'. He was interviewed again by the Roman Inquisition who examined this before clearing it for further publication. This book is the basis for a 28-30 day silent retreat with guidance on meditation about the purpose of life and the life of Christ. It helps the participant discern God's will for their lives and to follow a life of commitment to Jesus and remains as relevant and popular today as it was then. Having been founded as the Council of Trent stuttered along, the Society of Jesus was to become a major player in the counter-Reformation and late Renaissance. By the time Ignatius died in 1556, it already had over seventy colleges across three continents.

Ignatius Loyola was succeeded by Diego Laynez and on Diego's death nine years later, Francis Borgia became the third Father General. In spite of living in humility and asceticism, his management and academic skills maintained the high reputation of the Society of Jesus and one of his achievements being to found the forerunner of the Gregorian University in Rome. His counsel was sought by popes and monarchs, and all the time he was maintaining control and discipline in the Society as it rapidly expanded its membership, activity and geographical reach whilst gaining serious stature within the Church.

The effectiveness of the Jesuits was the greater for their freedom from the daily rule and asceticism of many orders of contemplative monks and friars. Though following strict disciplines, the Jesuits were positive 'achievers', deeply committed to their primary objectives of mission and education. Their schools adapted Renaissance humanism into Catholic scholasticism and their curriculum emphasised Latin, Greek, modern languages, including non-European languages and science as well as literature, philosophy, theatre and the arts. Rhetoric was also encouraged, so they produced superb missionaries, lawyers, linguists and people quite comfortable attaining public office and influence. As they spread, they brought many back to Catholicism, including from some Protestant strongholds in northern Europe, notably Poland and the Baltic States. At the same time, they were widening the boundaries of Catholicism in Asia and the Americas.

Francis Xavier travelled to Goa in 1541 and worked his way east through southern India and Macao, into China where fellow Jesuit Matteo Ricci (1552-1610) would follow some forty years later to spread the faith widely and to people of influence. He was probably the first European ever to visit China's Forbidden City. Since missionary rights were closely tied to trading rights, there was some dispute between Spain and Portugal over whose missionaries should aim to convert Japan. In 1575, Pope Gregory XIII declared that Japan belonged to the diocese of Macao, a Portuguese colony. Thirteen years later, the diocese of Nagasaki was set up under Portuguese protection. Two of Jesuits' real strengths were their mastery of languages and teaching ability. Other Jesuit colleagues followed into those countries and penetrated further north into Lhasa, Tibet and also down to South-East Asia.

Colonialists in North America considered the Jesuits a nuisance for their defence of natives from slavery, also becoming the case in South America, particularly in Brazil and Paraguay. But this work helped pacify the indigenous people. The Jesuits were no ordinary order as they spread the word peacefully and as Jesus commanded 'to the ends of the earth,' more than matching early Christians in its spread and effectiveness. The Jesuits' relationships would become strained with the Vatican Curia and other orders.

Witchcraft

This was still an era of widespread superstition and unexpected natural events were often blamed on witchcraft or wizardry, on devil-worship rather than vagaries of weather or health. Some individuals made fraudulent claims to practice witchcraft, offering to overcome such misfortune. Governments legislated against this and in 1542 the British Parliament passed the first Witchcraft Act which included the death penalty for such practitioners. Such trials were therefore transferred from the Church to state legal systems as similar penalties were applied in Europe.

Tridentine Creed

Published under Pope Pius IV (1559-65), this was the longest creed and is hardly used today. It contained most tenets of the Nicene Creed and aimed to respond to Protestant challenges, so included mention e.g. of the seven sacraments, presence of the true body and blood of Christ in the Holy Eucharist, the validity of indulgences, veneration of saints through their images, purgatory, the supremacy of the Holy Catholic Apostolic Roman Church, the need to observe its canons and the infallibility of the Pope's teaching.

Action on Catholicism Limited by Brief Papal Reigns

When Pope Julius III (1550-55) died, his successor **Pope Marcellus II** only lived for 22 days, then **Pope Paul IV** (1555-59) was an austere and authoritarian character and a diplomatic disaster. He came to office unsupported by Spain and Germany, having already alienated the Habsburgs and soon made an enemy of England, briefly under Catholic Queen Mary. Paul IV also built a wall round the Jewish quarter in Rome and locked the gate during hours of darkness. He produced an Index of Prohibited Books applying especially to Venice to deter the growth of Protestantism there, the only region of Italy seriously affected by it.

Pope Pius IV (1559-65), a Medici, succeeded Paul IV and resumed the Council of Trent for the final time. He applied political skill and some compromise to restore relations with key nations of the Empire and he oversaw publication of the Tridentine Creed. His patronage kept Michelangelo busy in Rome and improved the water supply to combat endemic typhoid and malaria. He wanted his nephew Ferdinand made a cardinal aged thirteen but faced implacable opposition from his eventual successor.

Pope Pius V (1565-72) followed, a Dominican who kept many of his order's daily disciplines as a deeply pious pope, banned luxury from his office, gave alms to the poor and physically embraced lepers. He worked hard on his own discipline, and took some measures supported by his own example, to restore discipline and morality among clerical leaders and reduce costs in Rome. It fell to him to put into effect the canons of Trent, the Council having closed in 1563. This included the Tridentine Catechism followed by a new missal for the Tridentine Mass, new breviary and the vulgate Bible. He blocked Emperor Maximillian II's wish to abolish clerical celibacy and made the late Thomas Aquinas a Doctor of the Church.

Pius V focused on resisting the Ottoman and Protestant threats to Catholicism. He set up the Holy League of States to oppose the Ottomans and helped finance the Knights of Malta in strengthening their defences and fortifying their port of Valetta. The League's forces won a great victory at the Battle of Lepanto off Crete in 1571, the last naval battle to use oar-propelled vessels, which was the turning point of Ottoman expansion if not their ambitions. The League was led by Austria with mainly Spanish and Venetian forces.

Pius V also worked to prevent Protestant incursion into Italy and sought to clear Huguenot influence from the Catholic Church, dismissing a cardinal and several bishops. As he became pope, Protestantism had swept all of England and Scotland, half of Germany, Scandinavia and Baltic States and part of France. Spain had remained Catholic, having already reversed their earlier accommodation of Islam for five centuries, now pressing all Muslims either to convert or leave the country. Pius V excommunicated Elizabeth I of England as she assumed leadership of the Church of England, declaring her a heretic while supporting Mary, Queen of Scots. The consequence of these actions was the persecution of Catholics in England.

After Pius V, **Pope Gregory XIII** (1572-85) was elected with strong Spanish support. After a worldly youth and fathering an illegitimate child, he was a brilliant lawyer and manager. He implemented the canons of Trent regarding clerical disciplines and reined back the power and luxuriant lifestyle of the cardinals with a corresponding increase in the power of the papacy. He set up a committee of cardinals to complete the Index of Prohibited Books and set aside one day a week to be accessible to all for an audience.

Gregory XIII strongly supported the Jesuits as an effective missionary force spreading the Catholic faith overseas and countering the spread of Protestantism in Europe. He funded the opening of many Jesuit colleges and seminaries including the expansion of their Roman College, which adopted his name as the Pontifical Gregorian University. He also funded other colleges to help train priests for countries that were now Protestant, such as the English College in Douai and the Scottish College in Pont-á-Mousson.

In 1575 Gregory XIII officially recognised the **Congregation of the Oratory.** This was set up initially in 1556 by Fr Philip Neri with a group of lay people of like mind who would gather for prayers, hymns and readings followed by a lecture. Musical selections based on scripture were often performed and became known as oratorios. A church was donated, which they expanded. Other Oratory branches formed which Neri decided should be autonomous and the movement became well established internationally.

Gregory XIII's best-known legacy is his new calendar, which came to replace Julius Caesar's Julian calendar (45 BC), in which the years were about 6 hours too short. The **Gregorian calendar** was put into effect in Rome in 1582, when Thursday October 4th was followed by Friday October 15th, but it was not adopted by Protestant states for more than a century and Britain changed in September 1752. The Orthodox Churches still use the Julian calendar for determining their feast days, which consequently differ from their Roman equivalents. Gregory also changed the time of the New Year from 25th March to 1st January.

Although the Ottoman threat had diminished over the years, the main antagonists, Spain and Venice had signed treaties with the Turks while other European nations had their own different priorities. So Gregory XIII was able to turn his attention to the Protestant challenge. He encouraged Philip II of Spain to invade England and depose Elizabeth I. The invasion did not take place until the next papacy in 1588, but the infamous outcome for Philip II's armada is well known and the result in England was even greater suspicion and suppression of Catholics. In 1580 English Jesuits persuaded Gregory to soften Elizabeth's excommunication and he told all British Catholics to obey the queen in civil matters.

Church finances suffered during Gregory XIII's time as he spent unstintingly on education, mission and defence. He started building the Quirinale Palace, commissioned as a summer residence for popes away from the overpowering stench of the River Tiber and the Lateran Palace. One issue that Gregory XIII failed to address was that of thriving banditry and corruption in the Papal States. But in thirteen years reign, he did plenty of good work and he achieved much, both spiritually and temporally.

Colonna and Orsini Families

The Roman families of Orsini and Colonna had frequently feuded in Rome through the Mediaeval and Renaissance periods. They were called to order by a Papal Bull *Pax Romana* of Pope Julius II in 1511. A kind of unity was then initiated by the future heads of both families marrying nieces of Pope Sixtus V in 1571, prior to his election as pope, though tensions remained between the families.

Felice Piergentile came from a family that had emigrated from Dalmatia to escape the Turkish threat. He became a Franciscan in his youth and rose rapidly through the ranks of the Church, having caught the eyes of some influential cardinals. He held his counsel while Gregory XIII, with whose politics he disagreed, occupied the papacy. On election, he took the name **Pope Sixtus V** (1585-90) and wasted no time in trying to improve order in the Papal States and improve Church finances. He emerged as a real hard-liner, using any measures to restore peace and safety to papal lands, with many brigands being executed.

Sixtus V sold assets and raised punitive taxes to restore finances, building up a large treasury surplus. He spent some of this on ambitious urban reform, including roads, bridges, water management, reclaiming marsh and other land for agriculture and industry. He refurbished many churches and completed St Peter's dome, rebuilt the Lateran Palace and added a wing to the Vatican Palace for popes' quarters and finished the Quirinale among many other buildings. His energy was such that he even dreamed of relocating the Church of the Holy Sepulchre from Jerusalem to Rome. Surplus money raised was held in reserve for future emergency. The economic effects of the taxes which removed so much liquidity from the economy were recessionary and aggravated popular resentment among those whose lives had been disturbed by the civil works as well as those who resented the destruction of many antiquities.

Sixtus V's ecclesiastical work concentrated on a re-organisation of the cardinals and their functions and he set a limit of seventy on their number. He also revised the Curia in 1588, creating fifteen permanent congregations of cardinals, a couple of which already existed. Each had a defined function, such as Doctrine of the Faith; Index; Inquisition; Press; Public Welfare; Rites; Ceremonies (liturgy) and Apostolic Signatura (to become the highest legal body in the Church, covering spiritual and some temporal duties of the Church at the time). He was wary of the Jesuits and intended to limit their freedom, but never found time to implement action on this. He achieved impressively for his less than six years in office.

Sixtus V renewed the excommunication of Elizabeth of England and offered a large subsidy to Philip of Spain for the armada, payable only on a successful landing in England. As history shows, it was never due.

Pope Urban VII succeeded Sixtus for the shortest reign thus far of 12 days, followed by **Pope Innocent IX** (1591) for 2 months. But the next pope would see out the century and more.

Pope Clement VIII (1592-1605) was from Florence's Medici family and a canon lawyer, Pope Clement VIII proved to be a wise pope and a statesman with all the thoroughness to be expected of a lawyer.

He intervened in a theological dispute between Jesuits and Dominicans regarding the relative importance of 'efficacious grace' and free will. He sought resolution by asking the opinion of a congregation of cardinals, whose reply was ambiguous, so he discouraged further disagreement or debate on the matter.

Henry IV of France had been excommunicated as a Protestant. Clement VIII's representative reconciled him so effectively that he embraced the Catholic Church in 1593. This was a shrewd move in Clement VIII's strategy to clip Spanish influence in the Curia. It also proved invaluable as Henry IV supported the pope's move to take influential Ferrara into the Papal States as the Este family line ended on the death of the childless Duke of Ferrara. Henry IV's support deterred intervention from Emperor Rudolf and Philip of Spain and Clement went on finally to broker a peace between France and Spain.

Pope Clement VIII mirrored Sixtus V's containment of lawlessness and hostile nobility in the Papal States. The nobles' resentment of Sixtus V's heavy taxes had led them to encourage much of the lawlessness for their own benefit. One notable execution in 1592 was that of a member of that extremely wealthy and powerful Roman Savelli family, who had built up a large debt to the Church. Clement VIII dealt with cases of heresy in his lands equally severely before he died in 1605.

Castel Gandolfo

The Savelli family discharged their accumulated debts to the Church by transferring their estate at Castel Gandolfo to the Pope in compensation in 1596. It was in an area of the Alban Hills renowned for its healthy climate and in the 17th century, Pope Urban III would build a villa there to which he and subsequent Popes could retreat from the heat of Rome as a summer residence when not using the Quirinale Palace.

Contemporary Church Design and Art

Until about this time, nearly all members of the congregation had been expected to stand for the duration of a church service. There were just a few benches around the nave walls for elderly, frail or sick members attending. In the Protestant churches, sermons began to lengthen so they introduced more benches.

The Reformation brought with it a virulent resurgence of iconoclasm in some Protestant areas, again related to the second commandment forbidding graven images, perhaps overlooking its reference to 'other gods'. Carlstadt, Zwingli and Calvin in particular encouraged the removal and destruction where possible and painting-out where not, of all 'graven images' in churches, even including crucifixes. Statues and crosses were smashed or burned and frescos were painted out with lime wash. The introduction of more decorative Baroque and Rococo architecture in new churches offered some compensation. They also discouraged use of the habitual 'sign of the cross'.

CHAPTER 19

17th Century

Popes

1592–1605	Clement VII	1655-67	Alexander VII
1605 (26 days)	Leo XI	1667-69	Clement IX
1605-21	Paul V	1670-76	Clement X
1621-23	Gregory XV	1676-89	Innocent XI
1623-44	Urban VIII	1689-91	Alexander VIII
1644-55	Innocent X	1691-1700	Innocent XII

Emperors

1576-1612	Rudolph II	1637-57	Ferdinand III
1612-19	Matthias	1658-1705	Leopold I
1619-37	Ferdinand II		

The seismic upheavals of the Reformation and societal development would take time to settle down, if they ever would. As far as Jesus Christ's wish for one Church was concerned, disarray was such that it was now hard to see any return to earlier norms, although the Roman Catholic Church would not accept that. God was no different but his Church on earth was. As a human organisation the Church could never be perfect. State rulers would take time to adapt to dealing with numerous Church leaders, to allow freedom of personal faith while still ensuring civil loyalty. Jesus himself had faced tests on this more than once, such as saying "Give unto Caesar that which is Caesar's; give unto God that which is God's" and by his ultimate submission to civil authority in his crucifixion, after the previous evening showing his human nature by pleading with God to relieve him of his destiny, then accepting, "… but thy will be done."

The new century would see widespread colonisation and mission as well as the proliferation of new reform Churches. Since Britain provided a particularly interesting case-study in this, it is focused upon below.

King James I of England and VI of Scotland

On the death of the childless Queen Elizabeth I in 1603, King James VI of Scotland inherited the thrones of England and Ireland, claiming to be King of Great Britain and Ireland. When he travelled from Edinburgh to accept the crown in London, a large group of Puritan ministers of the Church of England, prepared the 'Millenary Petition' to lobby him. Since Puritans regarded the Church of England as only partially reformed, they wanted it to go further in purging Catholic practices. James found their demands distasteful but the number and weight of signatories was such that he suggested a meeting of all relevant interested parties to debate the matter, resulting in the 1604 Hampton Court Conference.

The Puritans wanted to abolish the sign of the cross at Baptism; Baptism by lay people; the sacrament of Confirmation; wedding rings; bowing the head when the name Jesus was uttered; clergy wearing surplice and cap; and making any payments for various ecclesiastical roles. They also objected to some Catholic titles and terms, such as priest or absolution and pressed for tighter observance of the full Sabbath day. James I carefully managed to sidestep these demands but launched a review of the different translations of some books of the Bible to eliminate discrepancies that had been subject to complaint. He employed over fifty experts to hasten this, which resulted in production of the now famous King James Bible in 1611.

In 1605 James, his wife Anne of Denmark and "the whole body of state" survived the plot of Irish Catholic dissident Guy Fawkes who was discovered with 36 barrels of gunpowder under the Houses of Parliament the night before Parliament's state opening, which they were due to attend. Apart from inevitable executions, even tighter control over English Catholics followed. Pope Paul V wrote a very belated letter of congratulations to James three years after his accession to the throne, beseeching James I not to blame and punish innocent Catholics for the few criminals that were responsible for the gunpowder plot. He would instruct all Catholics to be submissive and loyal to James. Nonetheless, James I passed the Popish Recusants' Act of 1605 which required Catholics to swear an oath of allegiance denying the pope's authority over the monarch. Catholics were also barred from certain professions such as law and medicine, they could not act as guardians or trustees and they had to take Holy Communion at least once a year in their local C of E parish, or either pay a heavy fine of £60 or forfeit two thirds of their land.

These new laws gained Protestant acclaim, but James astutely realised that he might need Catholic support, so he tended to be satisfied by the oath of allegiance and not to persecute those who kept their heads down and caused no trouble. But as well as Catholics he also aimed to bring the Scottish Kirk as close as possible to the Church of England and re-introduce the episcopy, a step that Presbyterians vehemently opposed. He made his only return to Scotland after the one to accept the throne in London, in 1617 hoping to resolve this dispute. His bishops pushed through the Five Articles of Perth, which covered confirmation by a bishop, convention for receiving communion and baptism and the observance of Christmas and Easter. These articles were eventually accepted with reluctance by the General Assembly and ratified by the Scottish Parliament, but then largely sidelined to remain a subject of controversy within the Scottish Church well beyond James VI's death.

Plantation of Ulster

This was a plan devised by King James and others to achieve compliance of the ethnic Gaelic-speaking and almost entirely Catholic population of the totally rural Irish province of Ulster that had been stolidly hostile to English control. The plan was to colonise Ulster with 'British tenants', who had to be English-speaking and Protestant. The British confiscated land principally from the troublesome O'Donnell and O'Neill families and offered packets of it to approved emigrants. The English tended to be Church of England, while the more numerous Scots were mostly Presbyterian. The new tenants arrived in numbers and many of the Irish were deprived of land they owned, leaving a long-term legacy of sectarian resentment and hostility. Many of the Gaelic chieftains affected had fled to continental Europe following the recent failed nine-year war against English rule in Ireland. The official plantation began in 1609, preceded by some private investment by wealthy English landowners all over Ireland. It continued until 1690.

Colonisation of the Americas, Puritans and Pilgrim Fathers

King James I set up by Royal Charter The Virginia Company of London as a vehicle for establishing colonial settlements on the East Coast of North America. Their first expedition landed in April 1607 at Jamestown, from which settlers gained control of Virginia and developed tobacco plantations. In 1612, a captured Portuguese slave ship was brought to Jamestown and the fifty surviving African captives were put to work. Slavery was not formalised in America until 1640. Other colonial settlements followed initially as 'charter colonies', whose Royal Charter defined their rules of governance. King Charles II later changed this system which in time developed into that of crown or royal colonies, which were the property of the monarch and run by his appointed governors.

Other nations set up colonies on the east coast at about the same time, notably the Dutch who eventually established 'New Amsterdam' in 1624, which was later taken over by the British and called New York after the Duke of York, the future James II.

In England, the Church of England had ruled out many of the Puritans' suggested extreme measures to 'purify' the faith from Catholic practices. The Puritans were regarded as anti-establishment and were still persecuted in some quarters, leading many to leave for the sanctuary of Holland. But some were not satisfied there and were concerned that they might lose their English cultural identity if they remained in the Netherlands, so they arranged with English investors to help them establish a new colony in North America. In September 1620, a substantial group of them from England and the Netherlands set sail for America. The English ship, the Mayflower left from Plymouth with about 102 mostly Brownist pilgrims and a crew of between 30 and 50. September was not the ideal timing for the crossing in terms of weather, but a first attempt earlier in the summer had to be aborted due to their Dutch companion ship springing a leak just west of Land's End. Sea conditions were indeed appalling and the seasonal headwinds meant the voyage took over two months. Two people died during the journey and after a harsh winter at Cape Cod, mostly spent in the relative security of the boat but ravaged by disease, just 53 pilgrims and a slightly higher proportion of the crew survived and established the second successful English settlement in North America at Plymouth, Massachusetts before some of the remaining crew sailed home.

A year after landing, the Pilgrim Fathers and indigenous Wampanoag Indians had a joint feast in November 1621 to celebrate and give thanks to God for the harvest – the first Thanksgiving Dinner, which became an annual national holiday and celebration of the landing in the USA.

English and Scottish colonisation of North America expanded, as Dutch and other claimed territories were ceded to them in this 17th century so they grew to rival the military and economic strength of the Spanish conquests in Central and South America.

Baptists

In 1609, an English-ordained Anglican priest, John Smyth, set up as an independent pastor the first known Baptist Church in Amsterdam. The Baptists believed that only practising Christians should be baptised and that this should be by immersion in water similar to St John's practice and they rejected the baptism of infants. Furthermore, they believe in salvation by faith alone and at the outset would not allow scriptural readings in worship. Their only ritual practices were baptism and the Last Supper. To emphasize the sovereignty of God, they had no officers above Deacon and Pastor and each congregation was autonomous, resulting today in huge variations of practice especially in the USA. Baptists reached America in

1638 and their practice was especially embraced by the African slaves in the southern states, who introduced their own iconic Gospel musical tradition. The Baptists were strong missionaries, now having a world-wide presence.

Catholics

In the early years of colonisation in North America, there was a small minority of Catholic immigrants from different national cultures of Catholicism. There were some tensions between the practice and theology of Irish, Polish, German and French Catholics, though these more northern Europeans tended to find common ground in frowning upon the ways of their Latin counterparts. However, the prejudice of the developing majority Protestant establishment against the Catholics tended to encourage basic unification of those Catholics. However, significant differences would later become apparent and endure in attitudes to such matters as slavery and the death penalty as the Catholic Church in America grew fast in numbers, mainly through immigration gaining social acceptability and influence.

Japan

In 1615, a Japanese ambassador visited Pope Paul V in Rome to present a letter from Date Masamune, an influential regional leader in Japan. It asked for more Catholic missionaries and a trade agreement with 'New Spain'. The pope agreed the first request and referred the ambassador, Hasekura Tsunenaga to the King of Spain for the second. The king recognised Hasekura as an intrepid traveller, having come from the west and traversed New Spain on his way to Europe. But since he had word that the suppression of Christianity was beginning in Japan, he refused the trade agreement. The ambassador returned to his homeland which was politically increasingly isolationist.

Arts and Literary Strength

King James I/VI was a gifted scholar and writer and ruled during part of the period often referred to as the Golden Age of British literature, poetry and drama, in which the likes of Christopher Marlowe, William Shakespeare, Sir Francis Bacon, Ben Johnson and many others flourished. They were able to travel and learn from Renaissance ideas as well as current literary and dramatic works of comedy and tragedy.

Galileo Galilei (1564-1642), Science and the Church

The Catholic Church continued to denounce any discoveries that challenged its established views even on studied matters in which the curia had little expertise, so suppressing some genuine scientific research and development of thinking. A classic example was Galileo Galilei (1564-1642), gifted mathematician, physicist and astronomer, who improved strength and clarity of the telescope, facilitating major astronomical advances. But one of his many discoveries and inventions was to change his life. He confirmed irrefutably by observation that all the planets including the earth spin around the sun, so the earth was not the centre of the solar system, confirming Copernicus' theory of heliocentrism. Galileo wrote his findings accordingly.

A priest felt Galileo's writings re-interpreted scripture and possibly indicated Protestant leanings, so he reported Galileo to the Roman Inquisition, which in 1616 declared his writings to be heretically contrary to the Bible. Although Jesuit scientists openly agreed with his findings, Galileo was tried and ordered by Pope Paul V to recant his opinion and sentenced to house arrest for the rest of his life, nor could he publish any of his recent or future works. Copernicus' writings on the subject were also banned together with any other literature promoting heliocentrism. The Church could not abide challenge to its thinking even on matters of the universe of which they knew little but perceived as a threat to their image of creation theology, a weakness that was bound to occur again in the future. During his confinement, Galileo produced some of his best science. He wrote up work he had done when much younger on two new scientific areas, kinematics and strength of materials and he circumvented the ban and the censor by having them published in Holland. Blindness sadly overtook him by 1638.

Thirty Years War (1618-48)

Meanwhile, in continental Europe the Catholic counter-Reformation following the Council of Trent had gathered momentum and now included the broader populace and clergy with far more passion than during the earlier post-conciliar Catholic Movement, so religious sectarianism was intensifying. By 1610, the concept of the Holy Roman Empire as a unified entity was utterly undermined by divided internal loyalties and interests. A citizen could face conflict of loyalty in choosing empire, nation or religion, any one of which could be seen to be contrary to either or both of the others, depending on the issue. The empire would be the least likely first loyalty of the individual; it had lost authority in many of its territories, notably Switzerland, Bohemia and south-west Germany. Its difficulties encouraged other West European nations' ambitions, especially those of Spain and its ally the Netherlands, who consolidated their hold in neighbouring Rhineland during a truce. The added element of religious sectarianism helped cloud some of the underlying territorial ambitions in the Thirty Years War. While religion had been an important factor in its foundation, its disturbance of delicately balanced political equilibria led to this war becoming primarily a political conflict between the Habsburg and Bourbon dynasties, drawing in most of Europe's nations.

The German Elector of the Palatinate, Frederik V was a leading Protestant and married to King James I of England's daughter Elizabeth. Bourbon King Henry IV of France was assassinated in 1610, forestalling planned French involvement in a regional succession dispute in the Rhine border area, which boiled down to a Catholic-Protestant quarrel. The Danes wanted a share of control of the newly Protestant neighbouring dioceses of North Germany, which would importantly gain them some control over the Elbe estuary. Sweden also displayed interest. All of these countries had strong national interests in the Thirty Years War countered by internal pre-occupations which in many cases limited any direct involvement. Add into this the rival ambitions of the French Bourbons and the ubiquitous Habsburgs who ruled in Spain and the Austrian provinces, also having footholds in the Netherlands and Germany. Germany's long land borders were physically ill-defined in places and challenging to defend. High taxes to sustain their defence finally drove the nobles and aristocrats to rebel throughout these regions of central and northern Europe, providing further destabilisation. They had no problem recruiting equally hard-pressed locals as soldiers with the prospect of some pay and possible plunder.

This volatile political-religious-social mix lay behind the Thirty Years War, mainly centred on Germany, but affected the whole of Europe. It caused massive destruction and loss of life, estimated at 8 million, with Germany suffering a 25% reduction in total population, some of their towns losing up to 40%. The war ended with the Peace of Westphalia, comprising a series of treaties which also established the superiority of national sovereignty over empire and became an early basis for future international law, at the same time sacrificing the aim of broader union within an empire in Europe. *Plus ça change!*

British Isles – King Charles I (1625-49), Civil Wars, Republic

On James II's death in 1625, his son Charles succeeded to the three thrones of England, Scotland and Ireland.

James II had attempted to make a marriage between Charles and Habsburg Princess Anna Maria of Spain, to help achieve peace in Europe early in the Thirty Year's War since James feared its potential spread. A Protestant rebellion in 1619 led to Anna Maria's uncle, Archduke Ferdinand of Austria, King of Bohemia being toppled in favour of Charles' brother-in-law, Frederik V who led the Protestant Union, in his place. But Ferdinand was elected Holy Roman Emperor. In 1620, Frederik was defeated in battle near Prague and the Spanish-Netherlands Habsburg army took over his lands.

James II's efforts to marry his son to a Spanish Catholic had caused much consternation and opposition from the English and Scottish public. Charles had made a covert visit to Spain in 1623 in an attempt to court Anna Maria, but the Spanish insisted that no such match could take place unless England agreed to tolerate Catholicism and reversed the penal laws. Charles realised it was a futile aspiration and returned home to a warm public welcome and tried to persuade his father to declare war on Spain.

Charles I went on to marry the young Bourbon French Princess Henrietta Maria, another Catholic, before opening his first Parliament in 1625. The news of this marriage met popular opposition and was not a good start to his monarchy. Parliament suspected him of planning to move to more tolerance of Catholics, as indeed he had secretly agreed to do with Henrietta's brother, Louis XIII in the the firm belief that his monarchy was divinely ordained. The Relationship between Charles I and Parliament was strained for a couple of years, with his subjects hostile to his attempts to raise taxes without the approval of Parliament to fund war with Spain. In 1629, Charles I dismissed Parliament. This lasted for eleven years, although legal limitations on the tax he could raise left him little hope of waging any successful war in Europe. The resultant peace he made with Spain increased British suspicion of his Catholic tendencies.

Politically naïve, Charles I showed himself too supportive of high Anglican figures such as Richard Montagu, which alienated Puritans in England and Presbyterians in Scotland. In 1633, he appointed William Laud as Archbishop of Canterbury and a series of reforms ensued to establish more uniformity with liturgy based on the early Book of Common Prayer, more focus on sacraments in the Church and permission for some activities on a Sunday of which the non-conformists disapproved. He made his first visit to Scotland as an adult for his coronation there the same year, insisting on an Anglican service. Without reference to the Scottish Parliament or the General Council of the Kirk, he ordered that a new prayer book very similar to the Book of Common Prayer be adopted in Scotland. Following public outcry the General Council rejected the prayer book and the authority of Episcopal Church bishops, adopting instead the Presbyterian Church led by elders and deacons. Presbyterians disliked 'smells, bells, bishops and priests' as being too close to the Catholicism they despised. A state of war resulted with Scotland advancing to occupy Northumberland and Durham and Charles I, without a Parliament or sufficient finances could only prevaricate with peace talks beginning with the Treaty of Ripon in 1640. Eventually Charles I was obliged to recall Parliament and agree to their broader control of taxation and that in future Parliament had to be summoned at least once every three years with or without royal approval.

In Ireland, 1641, rebellion loomed with religious differences simmering and the English Parliament seeking to subjugate its own Parliament. With insufficient funds to sustain the army in Ireland, Charles I disbanded it, leaving trained troops unemployed. The Gaelic Irish Catholics rebelled against the mainly Protestant New English and Scottish. A third faction, the Old English, who were mainly Catholic and loyal to the king, supported the Gaels in this Irish rebellion. In England, anti-Catholic sentiment grew as Charles I made some rash and unsuccessful moves against Parliament, weakening his support in the House of Lords and in the country whilst strengthening Parliament's hand. Fearing that Charles I may recruit Irish Catholic soldiers to his cause, Parliament entered into an agreement with the Scottish in 1643 – The Solemn League and Covenant. This guaranteed primacy of the 'reformed religion' in Scotland as well as reform of the religion in England and Ireland, including the elimination of 'popery and prelacy'.

Charles I arranged for his wife to escape to the Continent and headed north with an armed group. The first English Civil War ensued, for a while indecisively then the tide began to turn, notably at Naseby in 1645. Parliament's New Model Army with mainly Puritan leaders and supported by the Scottish defeated the royalists. Charles I sent his teenage son and heir Charles from England to join his mother in France in 1646.

Charles I was eventually tried and beheaded in 1649 and England became a republic under Oliver Cromwell known as the English Commonwealth.

Charles II (1649-51 & 1660-85), Restoration

Charles II succeeded to the throne at this difficult juncture. The triumphant English Parliament left the Scots out of their negotiations, frustrating Scottish ambition for predominance beyond Scotland for the reform style Church over the episcopal Church of England style. Given mutual interest in each other's support, Charles and the Scots signed the Treaty of Breda during his exile. Having failed to prevent his father's execution and aware the Scottish Parliament needed help to reassert their authority, he wanted to take up his throne and the Scots price of allowing Charles II's return to Scotland was his acceptance of the terms of this treaty. He returned and was crowned at Scone in 1651 but soon regretted signing the Treaty of Breda as this perceived betrayal of the Church of England seriously undermined his support in England.

Charles II and the Scots engaged Cromwell in battle at Worcester in 1651 and lost. So Charles II, an unusually tall man in those days at over six feet, famously hid in the Royal Oak Tree at nearby Boscobel House before escaping to the continent. Cromwell became Lord Protector of England, Scotland and Ireland, now effectively a military dictatorship. Cromwell's death in 1658 was followed by unrest and disturbances which led to a Scottish army entering London and the first General Election for 20 years. In the resulting so-called Convention Parliament, the House of Commons was fairly evenly split between Parliamentarians and Royalists as well as between Presbyterians and Anglicans.

Charles II was restored to the thrones of England, Ireland and Scotland and travelled back from Holland in May 1660, arriving on his 30th birthday. After the coronation in England, the Convention Parliament was dissolved and replaced by the Cavalier Government, which was heavily Royalist and Anglican. A number of successive Acts were passed to ensure Anglican dominance, together known as the Clarendon code:

- The Corporation Act 1661 required civil office appointees to swear allegiance to the Church of England.
- The Act of Uniformity 1662 declared the use of the Book of Common Prayer as compulsory.
- The Conventicle Act 1664 forbade non-Anglican religious assemblies in excess of five people.
- The Five Mile Act 1665 excluded non-conforming clergy from coming within 5 miles of the parish from which they had been banished.

Puritanism consequently waned in England, while north of the border the Church of Scotland was returned to the Anglican vision of King James I, which would last as such only until the Revolution of 1688.

The Restoration gave the Anglican majority a new sense of freedom, leading to social changes. Literature revived and theatres that had been closed during Cromwell's joyless Commonwealth were reopened and more risqué and bawdy comedy developed. But theatrical Charles II frowned upon cross-dressing, so boys could no longer play female parts as had been common in the past.

Charles II was wary of the London coffee houses, seeing them as crucibles of discontent. They certainly fostered gossip but most of those attending were London businessmen exchanging news and views mainly relating to their business. Each one provided the London Gazette for reading government announcements and were forerunners of the gentlemen's clubs of the following century, whose exclusivity attracted the wealthy aristocracy. Each coffee house gradually developed a specialist clientele who met for business and spawned some famous businesses such as Lloyds of London for shippers and merchants discussing insurance from Edward Lloyd's Coffee house and the London Stock exchange from Jonathan's, where commodity and stock prices were listed. Some were linked to auction rooms from which the likes of Sotheby's and Christie's evolved. There grew to be over 500 coffee houses in London before mid-century.

Natural disasters then played their part. The Great Plague struck London in the summer of 1665, killing several thousand per week. The royal court moved to Salisbury and Parliament to Oxford for the winter after which plague subsided. Following a dry summer in 1666, a fire that started in a London East-end bakery rapidly spread for four September days through the close-packed, mainly timber buildings. Fanned westward by winds, it destroyed over 13,000 houses and dozens of churches, including St Paul's Cathedral, within the old Roman walls. The inevitable hunt for culprits alighted on an alleged Catholic conspiracy. A simple-minded man, who was later proved to be away at sea during the fire, was hanged for causing it. The monument constructed by Charles, who some suspected as a closet Catholic sympathiser, being married to Catharine of Braganza, carried for some time an inscription that included "… by the treachery and malice of the Popish faction …"

In the later years of Charles II's rule, concerns arose regarding his succession. Since he had no legitimate children, but more than a dozen by mistresses, including the Duke of Monmouth, his rightful heir was his Catholic brother James, Duke of York. In 1679 the House of Commons introduced the Exclusion Bill designed to deny James the right to succession on account of his religion. Those opposed to the Bill were called Tories after Irish Catholic bandits who had been dispossessed, while those in favour were nicknamed Whigs after persistent Scottish Presbyterians. When it looked likely the Bill would be passed, the king dissolved Parliament. This happened four times between 1679 and 1681. The mood in the country changed in his favour over the following years as Charles II ruled directly without a Parliament.

Early 1685, Charles was seized by sudden illness and died four days later. James arranged his death-bed reconversion to Catholicism and agreed to provide for Charles' mistresses including 'Nellie' Gwyn.

Catholic James II took the throne early 1685, generally welcomed by the public who remembered the British Civil Wars. But he soon faced rebellions in Scotland and England, the first led by the Earl of Argyll and the second by his nephew Duke of Monmouth, both originating in Holland. Both uprisings failed and their leaders were executed and many of the defeated English rebels were either executed or transported to American colonies under heavy sentences by Judge Jefferies after the battle of Sedgemoor. James augmented his army, dismissed the hitherto supportive Parliament and threatened repeal of laws that penalised Catholics and reform Protestants and upheld established Churches of England, Scotland and Ireland. He proposed tolerance for Catholics but harsher treatment of hard-line Presbyterians in Scotland.

Sir William Penn, admiral and MP supported James as he had done Charles, with interesting consequence. Penn's son, also William and an early Quaker, accepted from Charles II in 1681, considerable land in North America in lieu of money owed by the Crown to his father. This became known as Pennsylvania, where he started another colony.

James II appointed several prominent Catholics to senior offices of state and court to the extent that their representation became disproportionate to the population. In 1687 he made his Declaration of Indulgence. This was on the face of it designed to grant freedom of religion in Britain, removing the penal laws that had been in force and allowing people to worship as they pleased. The king began losing the support of many Anglicans who were disturbed by this, looking over their shoulders at the Catholic minority, but also fearing the possible growth of non-Christian religions and paganism arising. He planned to reopen a Parliament packed with supporters of the Declaration of Indulgence and to repeal the Test Act of 1673, which required commitment to the Church of England for any public office. He was clearly pushing the limits of his powers by gerrymandering government and the judiciary.

In 1688, consternation grew among Anglicans as a son was born to James II. Five days later, the prosecution began of seven Anglican bishops, who were soon acquitted. Hitherto Anglicans had been relaxed in the belief that James' Catholic era would be only temporary as his only two children thus far had been daughters, both Protestant girls. One of them, Mary was married to James' Protestant nephew William III of Orange. A group of influential Anglican nobles, now confident they would be well-supported by a majority of the population, invited William and Mary from Holland to England with an army sufficient to pose a credible threat to King James II's tenure of the throne.

Glorious Revolution 1688

William landed in England in November 1688 relatively peaceably and allowed James II to escape to the sanctuary of his cousin Louis XIV of France. James' overthrow was called the 'Glorious Revolution'. In 1689, William called the 'Convention Parliament' which decided that James II had effectively abdicated and appointed his daughter Mary as queen and joint ruler with her husband William as king. Parliament also passed the Bill of Rights 1669 declaring that no Roman Catholic could ascend the throne of England and no future monarch could marry a Roman Catholic. The next in line to the throne would be one of James II's daughters so to cover for the event of that line of succession dying out, it was declared that in such a case the monarchy would pass to Sophia, Elector of Hannover, granddaughter of James I and IV or her issue.

Queen Mary died of smallpox in 1694, James II died in 1701 and when William III died the following year, James II's daughter Princess Anne of Denmark inherited the throne. Queen Anne died in 1714 without surviving issue, so due to the Bill of Rights 1669, over fifty Catholic relatives with superior hereditary claims were bypassed as Sophia's son George I brought the House of Hannover to the English throne.

Jansenism, Sacred Heart of Jesus, Tensions with Louis XIV

Meanwhile in Europe, Dutch Catholic Bishop Cornelius Jansen (1585-1638) proposed a theology that emphasised human weakness and original sin, asserting that people are individually responsible for their sins and therefore must work hard to earn God's necessary mercy, forgiveness and grace, while suggesting the likelihood of predestination. He was in other words a kind of 'Puritan' or extremist of the Catholic faith. When he died in 1638, his friend Abbot Jean Duvergier de Hauranne carried forward these ideas which spread through the Low Countries, France and Italy. 'Jansenism' was regarded as heresy by the Catholic Church but remained popular until the late 18th century, although actively opposed by Jesuits. The Jesuits seized upon a concept promoted by Margaret Mary Alacoque (1647-90), a nun who claimed apparitions of Jesus including the Sacred Heart at Paray-le-Monial, leading her to believe in Jesus as foremost a source of love, mercy and forgiveness. She used the imagery of the Sacred Heart to illustrate this and the Jesuits adopted this to counter the Jansenists who lay at the opposite end of the spectrum of Catholic theology. **Pope Alexander VII** (1655-67) supported the Jesuits in this argument.

Tensions existed between the papacy and Bourbon King Louis XIV of France (1643-1715) over taxation and rivalry with the Habsburgs. This continued under **Pope Innocent XI** (1676-89), but evolved into an argument over primacy of the Catholic Church. Louis tried to please the pope by persecuting the Calvinistic Huguenots, a French Protestant group who followed Jean Calvin's theology. But Innocent XI thought Louis XIV took it to extremes. Innocent's successor, **Pope Alexander VIII** (1689-91), reduced the tension and during his brief papacy restored a reasonable relationship with Louis XIV.

Amish, Mennonites and Hutterites in America

The Amish, Mennonite and Hutterite groups grew from the few remaining Anabaptists who had migrated to North America following severe persecution from both Catholics and Protestants in Europe. To this day they live in something of a time bubble, in tight communities eschewing many modern developments.

Hutterites settled mainly around the American-Canadian border areas, particularly Alberta, Manitoba, and Saskatchewan in Canada and Montana in USA. Amish are further west, mainly in Pennsylvania, Ohio and Indiana as well as over the borders in Canada. The Mennonites' territories mingle with those of the Amish.

Quakers, Friends Church

The Quakers formed in England in the mid-17th century as the 'Friends Church' from a group of mostly farmers and tradespeople in Lancashire, known as the Valiant Sixty. Led by George Fox, they were largely Anglicans with some Non-Conformists and Baptists. Believing there is a bit of God in everyone, they travelled and proselytised throughout Europe and North America, preaching the importance of a direct personal relationship with God through Jesus Christ. They believe in the universal priesthood of all believers, so had no ordained ministers or formal theological training. They were pacifists and strove to live and speak reflecting emotional purity and the light of God. When brought before magistrates on a charge of religious blasphemy, Fox referred to a passage from Isaiah (66:2), which included "tremble at the Lord", leading one magistrate to ridicule him as a 'quaker' and the name stuck. In standing against the established Church, they were outlawed in England and many suffered imprisonment and beatings. This subsided when King James II, influenced by William Penn in America, issued a declaration granting them religious freedom. In the meantime, many had left for Holland and America.

When King Charles II had given William Penn the State of Pennsylvania, Penn had envisaged a state with complete religious liberty. So Quakers moved there and were initially predominant in its government. When it came to matters of defence and funding for essential military activities, they faced a moral problem and subsequently left government, whilst continuing benevolent work. Some who had prospered as merchants in Philadelphia generously funded philanthropic work such as schools, hospitals and asylums. The Quakers developed their concerns for slavery and mental health as well as proving supremely successful as benevolent leaders in trade and industry, with exemplary staff and worker welfare schemes and they initiated international caring and environmental charities.

Trade and Missionary Spread

While Catholic Portugal and Spain were exploring and expanding westwards seeking to build Empire, Britain, Holland, France, and to some extent Germany and Russia ventured to colonise Africa and parts of the Far East and India. Trade was usually followed by religious orders bringing education, medicine, hospitals to support their mission. Results for the natives were mixed as the benefits of education and improved living standards came at the cost of heavy loss of life through the introduction of diseases to which indigenous people had little resistance as well as the slave trade already described in 16th century.

Jesuits, China and Inculturation

Like some earlier popes, Pope Urban VIII disliked enslavement of indigenous people in missionary territories and issued a bull *Commissum Nobis* in 1638, forbidding it. The Jesuits had a policy of providing safe sanctuary for natives where they could use their crafts and skills for commercial benefit while also being proselytised, though the practice seems to have been open to abuse.

Though not the first, Jesuits were the most celebrated early missionaries to China, led by Francis Xavier. Indeed the Nestorians from Persia had long since visited the advanced nation of China in the 7th century via the Silk Road. The Jesuits were also the best prepared as in the late 16th century, Alessandro Valignano realised that they would not get far in their mission without first learning the language and culture of the Chinese, so he had set up a Jesuit college in Macao for this purpose.

The breakthrough came in the early 17th century by a team including Matteo Ricci and Michele Rugieri. Ricci employed the strategy of converting the ruling and upper classes who mainly followed Confucius, so that their influence would encourage the spread of Christianity through the wider population. Rugieri mainly targeted the non-aristocratic population, who mostly followed either Taoism, regarding Confucius as a deity, or Buddhism.

The European Jesuits arrived at a time when China's active period of scientific discovery and development was ebbing and helped revive it by translating some Western works on Mathematics and astronomy. Their cartographers also made the first modern maps of the country. The order caught the eye of the Emperor who saw their potential and appointed them as mathematicians and astronomers to the court then allowed them to open the first church in Peking in 1650. Their missionaries took Christianity further east into Korea. The Jesuits brought back to Europe new knowledge of Chinese science, culture and philosophy, including that of Confucius, whose ideas would have some influence on the 18th century Enlightenment.

Confucius (551-470 BC) was an early Chinese philosopher who stressed the importance of personal and state morality, social justice and sincerity. He recognised family loyalty and cohesion as an important basis for society and model for government, also respect of children for their elders and wives for husbands. His version of the 'Golden Rule' was "Do nothing unto others that you would not have done to yourself." Confucius' teachings became widely accepted and respected throughout the world.

Confucian rites were important to the Chinese and embedded by tradition. The European Jesuits, always pragmatic, adapted their practice in China to allow continuation of some of these, such as honouring family ancestors, judging that these were secular cultural practices. This assimilation of local culture in Christian services and practice became known as 'inculturation'. The Dominicans, who arrived later having done less groundwork disagreed, regarded these as religious practices. Distant Rome sided with the Dominicans in 1645, then after appeals, reversed the decision in 1656. There followed a dispute between the orders as to whether these rites could be compatible with Catholicism. Rome's further guidance was sought and in 1704 Pope Clement XI decreed that they were idolatrous, superstitious and therefore not permissible. The Chinese emperor would not allow any change to practice, resulting in an uncomfortable stand-off which countered much of the Jesuit missionaries' good work.

Trappists

In an example of history repeating itself, a group of Cistercian monks sought return to a simpler, more menial lifestyle at La Trappe Abbey in France. Abbot Armand de Rancé introduced the reforms in 1664 and they spread. The group became known as Trappists, reflecting the original formation of the Cistercians in the 11th century. They would grow into Trappist congregations within the Cistercian Order then were eventually constituted as an offshoot Order in their own right in the late 19th century.

Church Music

Music had not played a significant part of Church worship before this time. There had been some singing of Psalms (Greek *Hymnos*) and more text in monophonic plainchant, which had spread from its original use in sung Divine Service in the early monasteries. This had transferred and eventually developed in the Roman Church into Gregorian chant, often polyphonic but without harmony or instrumental accompaniment. The organ had first appeared in churches about 900 AD, being used mainly for ceremonials. By the 15th century, it had become an established church instrument and an essential component of cathedrals built from that time. Hymns as known today were adopted as part of Christian worship from the 17th century, mainly in Protestant Churches. The inclusion of the organ and harmony attracted gifted composers and lyricists so hymn singing came to play an important part in church services and worship.

One of the first recorded professional church organists was a young Catholic French virtuoso. Francois Couperin (1668-1733) followed his father and older brother as organist in a Paris church. He was paid a salary from the age of seventeen. Since then, many great composers composed their own Mass, musically covering the essential parts of the Eucharistic liturgy, including specifically the Kyrie (penance), Gloria (praise), Credo (creed), Sanctus (Holy) and Agnus Dei (Lamb of God). They were not all written with their inclusion in the Mass itself in mind, but rather as a musical spiritual exercise that would stand alone as a performance. Several such composers also produced the music for hymns, many of them still popular.

Musical instruments are still not used in Orthodox worship, which mainly uses traditional chants.

Russian Orthodox Church

Christianity was followed with great devotion by most of the population in Russia. The Russian Orthodox Church had become a force for unity and motivation, a people's religion, which the Tsars regarded as a powerful tool as Moscow pressed its claim as the 'third Rome'. It developed a distinctive Russian character in its church architecture and liturgy as well as eventually recognising the Tsar as God's representative on earth, as referenced with Ivan the Terrible in the 16th century. They encouraged beard growth, believing Jesus had not shaved and adopted the use of two fingers in the sign of the cross, representing the two natures of Christ – God and man – instead of three elsewhere for the Trinity.

Tsar Peter the Great (1672-1725) was not a religious man and with an eye to Rome he was suspicious of the political ambitions of the bishops. Many citizens regarded the office of Patriarch as superior to that of Tsar, so when Patriarch Adrian died in 1700, Peter forbade his replacement.

Russian society was even then highly controlled within a rigid and legal caste system and the clergy was one of those castes with priests quite low in the pecking order. The Church had its own schools, so a family tradition of a religious career was difficult to escape.

Monastic religious orders were more open and accessible than many in the west, which meant that the more educated and intellectual youngsters with a vocation tended to go to monasteries to develop their knowledge of the faith. Russian Christians followed up these opportunities in numbers.

Church Architecture

In the Western Church, the congregation would sit and kneel for parts of the worship, with the installation of pews and kneelers or hassocks. These were arranged in rows with aisles dividing the width to ease access and procession.

There are various shapes of Orthodox building, always more centre-focused than the usually elongated churches of the West. They may be cruciform, star-shaped or round or an elongated oval, symbolic of Noah's Ark. Orthodox churches were usually domed, though in colder climates, they developed steep conical or the familiar onion-shaped domes, to shed snow, which may over-stress a dome.

So regions developed their own architectural styles and over future centuries, churches joined public buildings and grand palaces as significant subjects of architectural design. Church design reflected the greater glory of God and was to provide a valued source of local employment and skill development.

The significance of easterly orientation was that the sun rose in the east. Sun and light are important to the Christian Church – God the light of the world; light is good, dark is bad; Sunday; and Christmas dated near the rebirth of the sun, the Winter solstice.

CHAPTER 20

18th Century

Popes

1700-21 Clement XI
1721-24 Innocent XIII
1724-30 Benedict XIII
1730-40 Clement XII
1740-58 Benedict XIV

1758-69 Clement XIII
1769-74 Clement XIV
1775-99 Pius VI
1799-1800 Interregnum

By the 18th century, the Catholic Church, while having been spread and strengthened by missionary and imperial expansion overseas by Catholic countries had also been weakened by the Reformation, with governments of the major powers in Europe seeking to control the Church within their territory. So even though the 18th century saw longer papal reigns, secular powers were increasing in influence over religion.

In Russia for example, part of the Orthodox Catholic Church, Tsar Peter I abolished the Patriarchate in 1721 and created the Most Holy Synod, following the leadership pattern established by the Lutheran Church in Sweden and Prussia, with a synod of ten government appointed senior bishops and lay administrators under the control of a senior bureaucrat, the Chief Procurer. The Chief Procurer held cabinet status in the national government, while the Tsar himself appointed bishops and lay administrators of Church affairs. In effect, the Russian Orthodox Church was a department of government. Russia had gained a strong political grip on the Ukraine and the Kiyv Metropolitans also became subject to Russia. Peter favoured Ukrainians as leaders of the Russian Church, being more compliant with change.

New challenges arose in the Churches and society. In the Roman Catholic Church, papal dissolution of the Jesuit Order, arguably the Church's most effective arm, would cause considerable self-damage. The two 'Awakenings' of the Protestant churches in Europe and America and the beginning of the Industrial Revolution took place this century. Protestantism developed in America, tending towards the evangelical end of the spectrum with preachers introducing a more personal level of faith. The Enlightenment movement emerged and spread in France. The Reformation was maturing.

In this century Europe would see more devastating wars aggravated by religious disputes. France moved centre-stage on the continent in the latter part of the century, while Anglo-French rivalry was again a dominant factor overseas. France was the major land power on the continent, whilst newly united England, Wales, Ireland and Scotland, now known as Great Britain, became a leading commercial and colonial power. Great Britain and France both suffered financially from the American War of Independence (1776-83), in which French involvement contributed to Britain's defeat.

Having spent heavily on wars against England in the previous century, France was spending even more in America, covering deficits with loans that threatened to bankrupt the country, leading King Louis XVI to impose heavy taxes. Together with the visible tax-avoidance of the privileged and wealthy aristocracy, this only needed an extremely hard winter to fan the embers of revolution in the final quarter of the century.

The rest of Europe was also restless. Spain's King Charles II died in 1700 and his closest heirs were members of the French Bourbons and Austrian Habsburgs, which led to a war of succession between these expansionist dynasties and their respective supporters. Meanwhile Spain put huge effort and investment into its new fast-expanding colonies in Central and South America. Italy was preoccupied with its internal divisions and strife. The Austrian Habsburgs, in addition to their territories in Northern Italy, Germany and Holland also had to keep an eye further north-eastwards in protecting their interests against Frederick the Great's Prussia and Catherine the Great's Russia. The boundaries between French- and Austrian-dominated territories were neither clearly defined nor well patrolled, inviting incursion from either side.

Against this backdrop, changing moods in religion and philosophy were playing out. Novel lines of thinking and reasoning that had emerged towards the end of the 17th century, supported by scientific discoveries, would spread and dominate this century as information, education and dialogue became ever more accessible, even though only two thirds of men and even less women could sign their own name, let alone read by the end of it. Secular forces such as politics, science and industry provided the spur alongside rekindled philosophy and popular religious evolution.

Acts of Union in Britain

England and Scotland had shared a monarch since 1603, when King James IV of Scotland inherited the English throne. There had been several attempts to formalise a union between the two nations and Queen Ann was especially keen on such an outcome. She had lent the Scottish Court party substantial funds to develop a scheme in their Central American colony called Caledonia in the Gulf of Darien near Panama to establish Scotland as a global trading nation. The fanciful Darien scheme in the 1690s envisaged an overland route linking the Atlantic and Pacific oceans. In the face of competition from the East India Company and a blockade by the Spanish, the ill-advised choice of location led to it becoming a financial disaster that left Scotland so heavily in debt to England that it faced financial ruin. The Lowlands of Scotland suffered such devastation as a result of this that any opposition to union with England almost disappeared. Reciprocal Acts of Union resulted in the Treaty of Union which took effect in May 1707. England and Scotland were thus "united into One Kingdom by the Name of Great Britain", from which time the government of both countries took place in Westminster.

Reformation Aftershocks

Religious debates following the Reformation continued to give rise to various movements that swept across swathes of Europe and to America via migrants. The fragmentation of Christian leadership arising from the Reformation freed up individuals and groups of intellectuals to promote their own studied views on religion and its practice, resulting in various new 'isms', many finding enthusiastic disciples. Emphasis transferred from obedience to a defined doctrine to self-discovered inner piety, opening a sense of freedom and closeness to a personal God that led to a powerful grass-roots evangelical movement. This led to the formation of further reform groups such as Pietism and Evangelicalism, then the Enlightenment, Deism and in America, the Great Awakening. Profound theological discourse was eclipsed by promotion of personal conversion experience, so new liturgies and preaching styles were introduced as well as sects within or separating from existing denominations, such as Methodists from Anglicanism. Bible reading and active lay participation in Church affairs was encouraged by many such groups.

Protestant Pietism Movement

Pietism was a popular religious movement that grew in Lutheran Germany, originated in the late 17th century by Lutheran Philipp Spener

(1635-1705). Pietism stressed individual spiritual rebirth and renewal, leaning heavily on the Old Testament. It embraced personal piety and Christian commitment and offered laiety more active participation in Church matters. Pietism spread quickly into the mystic community in Switzerland then further into wider German-speaking Europe, Scandinavia and the Baltic area as well as across to North America, where Pietism played a part in the Great Awakening and wider Evangelicalism which was soon also being embraced by people of other ethnic origins there, leading to a lasting change in Evangelical Protestantism.

Pietism did not sit comfortably with the less emotional and demonstrative mainstream Lutherans so it peaked in the mid-18th century before declining and almost disappearing by the end of the 20th century. But it had left its mark on Protestantism including being one of the influences that led to the Anglican Priest John Wesley founding the Methodist movement within the Church of England and Alexander Mack doing the same in the Brethren within Anabaptism. It left its mark in Scandinavia too, where its stress on humility, frugality, orderliness and sense of duty sat well with the prevailing culture.

Evangelicalism and the Great Awakening in North America

People in the North American colonies, many of whom descended from quite fundamentalist Protestants, learned of a new wave of devout worship and behaviour brought in by German and Scandinavian Pietists. This was developed by some bright thinkers and eloquent preachers, such as Harvard theologian Jonathan Edwards who followed Calvin's view that people can only reach God through the Bible. What became known as the First Great Awakening took hold in Connecticut from 1733 and spread rapidly, reinforced by the visit in 1739 of Anglican evangelical leaning priest George Whitefield, who was a founder member of Methodism. He and Edwards were much sought-after inspirational preachers with complementary but differing styles that made religion more personal, emphasising individual responsibility, guilt and the redemption offered by Jesus. Followers became passionately and emotionally involved, in contrast with hitherto relatively passive acceptance of dry theological pronouncement.

The more emotional and zealous so-called Enthusiasts, who included Methodists, Baptists and Quakers welcomed this Great Awakening while Anglicans and the relatively few Catholics there at the time, held it at arm's length and were little affected. It certainly brought popular Christianity to the African slaves, who introduced new music and style to Christian worship and were part of a movement that left an enduring mark on American religion that remains evident today.

Evangelism had its critics in the general population. Some found the emotion-charged rhetoric too demanding, feeling they could never match up to God's requirements, even leading to suicides, including a relative of Edwards. It was distasteful to the more 'conservative' Christians, especially Catholics. As more people bought the Bible for their homes, reading and absorbing its message, it became a factor in decentralising Bible-reading, especially in the Southern States. This contributed to a move away from established Church services, ritual and doctrine and the introduction of highly emotive sermons, which alienated committed traditionalists and intellectuals but had most effect in the Reform Churches, e.g. Congregational, Presbyterian, Dutch and German reformed.

Methodism

Charles and his younger brother John Wesley, a lecturer led a small group of mostly Church of England students in the 1720s at Oxford University who met to seek a holier way of life through detailed study of the Bible. Fellow students teased them for their methodical study and quest for the holy life, calling them 'methodists', a name that John Wesley was happy to adopt. Following student life many of them evangelised and the Methodist movement spread within England and Wales. Music was an important part of their worship.

Later in this century, John Wesley built a large following that thrived in America. Following its War of Independence he ordained ministers in Britain and America to meet the urgent need to administer the sacraments, against the wishes of the Bishop of London. Wesley established legal status for the Methodist Conference in 1784 and made a clear break from the Church of England in 1795, with strong Methodist approval. They offered fresh compassionate piety, intensity and a strong tradition of music in their practice and worship which appealed to many at the time. They welcomed the poor and disadvantaged and it was not for nothing that some knew them as the "working class Anglican Church".

The Enlightenment

Philosophers were thriving in France, led by Voltaire (1694-1778), who mixed satirical wit with the writing and debating skills he brought to bear on the established Catholic Church and all Christianity. He supported freedom in religion and speech and clear separation of Church from State, passionately. This would become known as the Enlightenment movement, growing with the support of Diderot, Montesquieu and Rousseau in France, then others elsewhere.

The Enlightenment was a secular intellectual and philosophical movement. Recent scientific advances helped support arguments against prevailing repression of people's freedom and thought – 'despotism, feudalism and clericalism', and encouraged tolerance (including religious), fraternity, fair governance and the separation of Church from State. These were noble enough aims, but the reasoning soon veered towards self-interest, inviting opposition from authority.

Thanks to work by Keppler, Copernicus, Galileo and others, the universe was by then believed to be infinite, yet ordered and probably predictable according to rational laws which were judged to be capable of interpretation by human intellect once knowledge grew through further observation and calculation. The philosophers argued that all creation in the cosmos was similarly subject to rational laws which it would become possible for humans alone to deduce, including laws that regulated society, government, economics and morality. This opened up tempting vistas for the philosophers and their enthusiasm spread well beyond France. Early on in their studies, they concluded that most Western European Christian nations, with absolute monarchies, aristocracies and established Churches did not fit in with the vision. A little knowledge led to the growing feeling in some quarters that science may be able to explain everything, including creation, and help humans to do anything, in which case who needs God?

A philosophical approach known as Reductionism came into fashion in Enlightenment reasoning in which all phenomena were reduced to their simplest. It essentially claimed that it would become possible to explain even challenging physical and even psychological realities solely in terms of physics and chemistry, denying any need to turn to spiritual or metaphysical concepts. Thomas Nagel attempted to reduce all psychological phenomena to pure physics and chemistry, talking of 'psychophysical reductionism'. Others referred to physico-chemical reductionism explaining biological life. Some held that all 'inferior' live beings such as animals could be equated to automata. Enlightenment thinking seemed a way of effectively placing humans at the highest level of existence and stripping religion of its power. Those of a religious disposition argued that all animal and vegetable life is God's creation so of the utmost value, with humans distinguished from other animals by their soul.

Two of the fundamental assumptions underpinning much of the Enlightenment were:

a) autonomy of the individual – we are each in sole charge of our lives.
b) the power of unaided human reason – we need no supernatural authority to tell us what to do.

State censorship of printed works had been introduced around 1600 and was strictly applied in France, where it was illegal to publish any printed work without government permission. In 1757, the death penalty was introduced by royal decree for publishing anything critical of the government or religion. Discussion between philosophers was still free and those in France admired and envied British freedom of speech and press, no official power of arbitrary arrest, reasonable religious toleration and no absolute monarchy, which they felt made the monarchy stronger through the greater patriotism it engendered.

Voltaire's barbed satire was aimed at intolerance, injustice and absolute power in many countries as well as in the Catholic Church. Most of these original philosophers accepted that the universe was the deliberate work of an intelligent and rational creator, although they rejected literal interpretation of the Bible or any para-normal phenomena such as miracles.

Rousseau believed in the liberating and empowering effects of education and shared his colleagues' disdain of despotism, feudalism and clericalism. The Enlightenment laid the ground of '*Liberté, Fraternité, Egalité*' for the imminent revolution in France, though surely unaware of the extent it would assume.

Such forces as the 'rationality' of the Enlightenment could give rise to counter-forces such as would become the case in Europe later in this century with the emergence of 'romanticism'. This first appeared in Germany, spreading primarily through visual arts, music and literature, but also in religion and particularly Protestantism which was so open to fresh lines of thought. The disunity of Christianity indisputably weakened its message, allowing the opinion to grow that religion is a purely private matter irrelevant in public life, to the extent that discussion of it became regarded as socially suspect. It inhibited discussion of important moral issues, certainly any religious angle on them, which devalued the dialectic and drove further introspection regarding faith for some while perhaps relieving consciences for others.

A moral issue of the day was excessive pursuit of individual and national gain from colonial power. Any benefit for the indigenous people of these lands was outweighed by much suffering, which itself would result in unanticipated counter-forces in future centuries, when the colonialised communities would rebel and even flock to the colonist's own shores. Another issue was the effects of industrialisation, which will be examined later but would trigger other serious social challenges and changes.

Deism

Another prominent philosophical movement during the age of Enlightenment, mainly affecting Britain, France, Germany and America, was Deism. It appealed to those who could not accept the idea of spontaneous creation of life without external involvement, yet rejected Revelation and the concepts of a personal god, apparitions and miracles. Whilst accepting that there is a supreme being who causes all things and created the Universe, the Deists saw a perfectly ordered world upheld by natural law and divine providence, but without direct intervention by the creator. They believed that human reason and observation of the natural world were sufficient to deduce that a single entity created the universe. Followers of Deism were typically Christians who had become sceptical about the human-managed institutions of religion with unquestioning acceptance of the Bible.

A form of Deistic belief in France, known as the Cult of the Supreme Being suited well some leaders of the French revolution, such as Robespierre, who preferred it to the earlier 'Cult of Reason' as a potential replacement of the Roman Catholic Church. A sizeable secularist group in North America also found Deism helpful in promoting human reasoning as a basis for their ambition of revolution.

Latin influence in South America

Meanwhile, the Roman Catholic Church had played a significant role in the expansion of empires in Central and South America and in converting to Catholicism many indigenous people such as Incas and Aztecs.

Catholicism in Rome, Freemasonry

Pope Innocent XIII (1721-24) promoted clerical self-denial, clamped down on high spending and legislated against nepotism in a decree that forbade future popes from appointing family members to high office in the Church or granting them estates or income. Innocent XIII prohibited further recruitment to the Jesuits following a dispute over missionary methods in China, described further below.

Innocent's successor, **Pope Benedict XIII** (1724-30) was the third pope from the Orsini family. He had foregone his inheritance rights to join the Dominican friars at eighteen, but his father contrived for him to be made Cardinal by Pope Clement X when only twenty three. Too immersed in his spiritual and charitable activities to gain any experience in administration or politics, he was too unworldly to be suited to higher office, but was elected pope as a compromise candidate by a divided conclave. In office, he piously tried to introduce wide clerical reforms, from priests to cardinals and banned the Roman lottery as a source of income to the Church. Meantime, his trusted assistant, Cardinal Niccolo Coscia was covertly draining the treasury to the benefit of his own family and those of his assistants who effectively ran the papal office.

Benedict XIII's successor **Pope Clement XII** (1730-40) achieved little political success, being distracted by blindness and ill health during his papacy, but he improved Vatican finances by inviting restoration of generous donations made by his predecessor to some senior members of clergy and by fining some of them, as well as by drawing on some of his family's wealth and restoring the lottery. This enabled **Pope Benedict XIV** (1740-58) to set in motion a major building plan to improve the city of Rome.

Masons and carpenters had been held in high esteem by the Church in mediaeval times and when they were working in monasteries, the masters of the craft were often hosted at the top table for meals. As in many crafts, groups were formed with the common interest in mind and helped each other out when work was available, in times of low demand or on injury or bereavement. Groupings developed and the masons, who held themselves as superior craftsmen, formed local lodges in most European countries, including the French Compagnons de Devoir and Italian Roman Collegia and Comacine Masters. There is no clear common lineage between these and the Freemasons and written history is limited as the latter guarded their privacy. The earliest written records of them in England are from York Minster in 1352.

Freemasonry blossomed in the 17th century and by the early 18th had split into two factions, Jacobite (Stewarts and Catholic) and Hanoverian (Protestant). The latest Stewart, James was living in Rome as James III of England, as Jacobean king in exile. In 1737, when he heard that so many Catholics had joined the Hanoverian Grand Loge de France that they had surpassed the Jacobites, James III asked Pope Clement XII to condemn Hanoverian freemasonry in European Catholic countries. This was difficult for Clement XII because Cardinal Fleury was then Louis XV's chief minister and intent on maintaining peace with Protestant Great Britain. What is more, Jacobite sympathisers in France had formed a secret lodge of their own and pressed Fleury to support the Stewarts. Their base was raided and Fleury asked Clement to forbid Roman Catholics from taking part in Freemasonry on threat of excommunication.

In order to avoid conflict with either French or British thrones, Clement XII issued a purely religious-based constitution forbidding Catholics to join in or give house room to any known group or member of the

Freemasons. He made no reference to or distinction between Hanoverian or Jacobite, but decried the secrecy of the organisation, arguing that only if some of their intentions were evil or otherwise unacceptable would they avoid being more open, so they posed possible risks to states and the "salvation of souls". He thus astutely avoided direct offence to Britain, Louis XV and Cardinal Fleury. Some national and Church authorities had already become wary of the movement, concerned that its rules may override both civil and canon law in the eyes of individual members. This Catholic prohibition on joining masonic organisations would be reconfirmed in 1983 by the Vatican's Congregation for the Doctrine of the Faith.

China, Inculturation

The Jesuits continued their missionary work in China but there was no doubt the effectiveness of their efforts had been hampered by the stand-off following Pope Clement XI's decision not to allow Chinese traditional customs honouring Confucius and family ancestors to be represented in their worship because the Church regarded them as heretical, which the Chinese found insulting. When a legate confirmed Rome's unbending dogmatic insistence on such restrictions, the Kangxi Emperor responded by expelling all Christian missions in 1721, preventing the further spread of God's word further there. He told the papal legate "You destroyed your religion here and brought misery to all Europeans living here." It was for sure a diplomatic, Christian and missionary disaster, waste of good past effort and an enormous opportunity lost, raising a question of how Jesus might have taught there. He had told his disciples to 'go throughout the whole world' (Mark 16:15), to spread his teachings, but the Church was finding difficulty with how.

Innocent XIII (1721-24) confirmed Clement XI's prohibition of the Jesuits from their missionary work in China, and ordered that no new members should be received into the order. This encouraged some French bishops to petition him to rescind the bull condemning Jansenism, but he was unyielding in this.

Subsequent Popes Benedict XIII and Clement XII took no further action, Clement confirming the Church's opposition to Chinese reverence for Confucius and their ancestors. He did encourage Franciscan missions to Ethiopia.

Mixed Marriages, Orthodox Relations, Infallibility

In 1741 Benedict XIV (1740-58) condemned the mistreatment and slavery of indigenous people in new colonies, but perhaps his most noteworthy bulls were those covering the Church's own overseas missions. He issued a bull in 1742 with the same message as Clement XI regarding the purity of Christian teachings and traditions being upheld against all heresies, so forbidding any honouring of Confucius, ancestors or emperors. He thus clearly upheld the prohibition of 'inculturation' in its sense of adapting Christian language and practice to make them more understandable and acceptable to the very different cultures being encountered by the Jesuits, in particular in China, India and South America. These rulings virtually stopped the missions in their tracks, particularly in the Far East, and reversed many of their recent successes, dealing a final blow to the Jesuit aim to convert the influential classes in China, in which they had invested so much time for what had promised to be a highly successful missionary campaign.

[In 1939, Pius XII would authorise Christians to observe ancestral rites and take part in Confucian ceremonies, then in the 1960s the Second Vatican Council extended this, agreeing the principle of adapting some native ceremonies deemed suitable into the liturgy of the Church in such places.]

Whatever the judgment on him regarding inculturation, Benedict XIV was among the greatest thinking popes, having become a Doctor of Theology and Doctor of both Canon and Civil Law when only 19. He followed Thomist philosophy and his legal experience helped him clarify a number of ill-defined areas of doctrine or practice that had arisen since the Reformation. One of these was that of mixed marriages. The early extreme mutual antipathy between Catholics and Protestants had subsided somewhat and mixed couples often wanted similar ceremonies to the Roman Catholic marriages of the past, especially in north-eastern Europe. Benedict made it clear that mixed marriages could be celebrated in Catholic Churches provided that the couple agreed as part of the marriage contract to bring their children up as Catholics.

He was also one of several popes who promoted the concept of papal infallibility on the basis of God's promise of the Holy Spirit's guardianship. He held this as a reason for resisting ecumenical councils, believing they were contradictory to the concept of infallibility of the pontiff.

Benedict made conciliatory and welcoming gestures to the Orthodox Churches and achieved formal union with some of the Eastern patriarchies. He also specifically banned females from being altar servers.

His successor, **Pope Clement XIII (1758-69)** held an ambition to effect reunification of Protestants and ultimately full ecumenical reunion of them with the Roman Catholic Church, but he condemned it to failure by his blank refusal even to discuss compromise of doctrine or catechism. He was, however willing to accept the Hanoverian claim to the British throne against that of the Catholic Stuarts, which annoyed Cardinal Henry Benedict Stuart, who was the fourth and last Jacobite pretender to the British throne.

Catholicism, Jesuits and Governments

The power of the Catholic Church had waned in Europe since the Reformation as in many countries the sovereign or the state government now largely controlled the Churches. People within the Church consequently gained more personal freedom of belief, which posed additional challenges to the Vatican as 'competition' was introduced from various movements. The Enlightenment undermined and ridiculed the Catholic Church especially within France, its principal stronghold. Worse, the French Revolution would lead to the virtual closure of the Catholic Church in France as its property was seized for sale or sacked while monasteries and schools were closed down and Church leaders banished. Meanwhile, in the mainly Catholic Austrian Empire the government took over Church lands. Thus Catholic aristocracy lost much of its wealth and power, while the still devout peasantry remained powerless and largely voiceless everywhere.

The Jesuits had symbolised resourceful zeal and missionary strength and although their missionary work had been curtailed, the order of the Society of Jesus was still probably the most powerful order of the Catholic Church in the mid-18th century and symbolic of its independence and strength. It had 22,000 members, among them confessors for many sovereigns in Europe. This put them at odds not only with popes, but also with aristocrats and ministers who sought to reduce the influence of the Catholic Church on their leaders especially in matters of state.

As pioneering overseas missionaries with such experience and record of success, they had also been important to Spain, Portugal and France in consolidating their lucrative colonies across the Atlantic. Some powerful trade and government interests resented any Church influence on their monarchs or government and strongly opposed the Jesuits' defence of rights of the indigenous natives of North and South America. They pressed the Church, already disturbed by the inculturation issue, to act firmly against them. The Jesuits were expelled in stages between 1759 and 1770 by the governments of Portugal, France, Spain and Austria, resulting in the descent of thousands of destitute priests and brothers upon Rome.

Pope Clement XIII who was pope during these expulsions was a Venetian taught by Jesuits and he constantly had to resist pressure from within the Church to suppress them. Clement XIII was a realist, accepting obvious science and he lifted the prohibition on books supporting heliocentrism from the Index (*Index Librorum Prohibitorum*) soon after becoming pope.

His successor, **Pope Clement XIV** (1769-74), another Jesuit-schooled pope watched with sadness the expulsion of the Jesuits from the Bourbon-related countries during his predecessor's reign, but the leaders of Catholic countries in Europe were not about to lower their pressure, recognising the Jesuits as a serious potential obstacle to their authority over the Church. Louis XV of France was advised by a minister, Duc de Choiseuil, who had recently been the French ambassador to the Vatican, to strengthen his position by demanding not only total suppression of the Jesuits but also the renunciation of Vatican claims to territories in France (such as Avignon) and in Spain. Pressure on Clement XIV increased.

The pope relieved some of this by astute concessions. He gave dispensation to the young Duke of Parma, nephew of the King of Spain, to marry his cousin Amelia, daughter of Maria Theresa of Austria, relaxing tensions with both those countries. He appointed Paulo de Carvalho, brother of the troublesome Pombal in Portugal, to the Sacred College of Cardinals, a move that led to rescinding of the 1760 separation of Portugal from Rome by 1770. He also abolished the annual custom of publishing on Holy Thursday a list of papal censures on Catholic Princes, which had long been a point of contention.

Still none of this removed pressure to close down the Society of Jesus. Indeed at the height of the international pressure soon after his accession in 1769, Clement XIV had agreed in a letter to King Charles III of Spain to consider a scheme for "the absolute extinction of the Society". To demonstrate his intention, he took some hostile measures against the Jesuits, refusing to meet their superior, shunning their friends who had been close to him and expelling them from a few seminaries and colleges. None of this satisfied the new Spanish ambassador, who threatened a schismatic Spain which could probably include other Bourbon states such as recently reconciled Portugal. As reassurance, he offered the restitution to Papal States of Avignon and Benevento, currently in French and Neapolitan control, respectively.

Despite his discomfort at the intrinsic simony, Pope Clement XIV could not at that time countenance the potential Spanish schism so he agreed to King Charles' demands but prevaricated so the Brief of Suppression, less powerful an edict than a bull, was not presented until August 1773. The pope referred to it being a necessary step for peace in the Church without any hint of theological reasoning. It resulted in the immediate arrest and imprisonment of the order's general and his assistants. The general did not survive the trial, but the judge found in their favour and they were eventually freed under the next pope.

Meanwhile, before that judgment was announced, Jesuit priests could remain in ministry in Italy only by renouncing the Society of Jesus. Many who refused found a welcome in Catherine the Great's Russia, which profited from an influx of the outstanding educationalists and proselytisers of their time.

Clement XIV's successor, **Pope Pius VI** (1775-99) was yet another pope who had been schooled by Jesuits and regretted the hard anti-Jesuit stance of his predecessor. He acceded to Frederick II's request to allow their schools in Prussia to continue operating and approved all their work in Russia.

In Britain the Jesuits were theoretically banned, but excellent relationships between them and secular clergy remained. Ex-Jesuit teachers were so respected they were able to keep their college together in Belgium, eventually moving from Bruges to Liège then to Stoneyhurst in 1794, having carefully maintained and husbanded their valuable assets through all these setbacks.

Wolfgang Amadeus Mozart, Child Prodigy

The 14-year-old musical prodigy Wolfgang Mozart visited the Vatican in 1770 with his father Leopold. His fame went before him so he was received by Pope Gregory XIV, who witnessed an astonishing feat of musical memory. In the chapel, the 17th century work Miserere mei Deus was played for him. The composition was a closely guarded Church secret so no copies were allowed outside on pain of excommunication. Young Wolfgang heard it just once then transcribed the entire composition. The pope was so impressed that far from considering excommunication he awarded him a papal knighthood.

Turbulence in Europe

Rome had eagerly accepted its role as a central worldly power in mediaeval times with the result that its own spiritual leadership role had sometimes taken second place. The task of leading the Catholic Church had never been easy, but unaccustomed challenges had arisen in the past couple of centuries as ordinary people demanded recognition of their now better informed sense of discretion, while nations became more confident in their statehood and studies of science and philosophy provided cogent alternative approaches. So not only had Rome's hold on secular leadership been weakened but the Reformation had also undermined its spiritual leadership.

It was against this background that Pope Pius VI was drawn into most of the simmering disputes in Europe immediately on his election. Apart from friendly relations with Portugal, he was besieged by anti-ecclesial forces. The Habsburg Emperor Joseph II of Austria defied the Church in his country being in any way subject to Rome, confiscated several monasteries and ignored papal consent in appointing bishops. Joseph II planned to sever all ties between the German Catholic Church and Rome, but a Spanish diplomat eventually persuaded him against this. But from this position of strength he negotiated with Pope Pius VI the right to appoint bishops in his territories of Milan and Mantua in a concordat of 1784. His brother, Grand Duke Leopold II followed suit in Tuscany by appointing Bishop Scipio Ricci of Pistoia. At the Synod of Pistoia in 1786, Jansenism was sanctioned in a clearly anti-papal move. Spain, Venice and Sardinia followed Joseph II, whilst the greatest antipathy was evident in King Ferdinand of Sicily and Naples, the 'two Sicilies'.

French Revolution

Even worse pain was in store for the Catholic Church. The violent anti-clericalism of the French Revolution which began in 1789 arose from wars stripping the treasury bare and the Enlightenment calling for social fairness. Economic austerity led to heavy new taxes which fell disproportionately on the poor, justified in their outrage at the difference between their abject poverty in contrast to the luxuriant lives of aristocracy and clergy who took too much for granted, not least the loyalty of their followers. Then in 1783-4 a prolonged volcanic eruption in Iceland caused a haze over Europe that lowered temperatures by 3°C, reducing crops and bringing famine to the poor, who could not afford the raised prices of even basic nutrition. Meanwhile, the Roman Catholic Church's disproportionate wealth was evident to all, demonstrating how little they had learned from the Reformation. Similar conditions elsewhere accelerated the pace and hardened the secular movement throughout Europe. While pressure was intensifying the Church leadership remained inactive in addressing its internal abuses. Protestantism complemented this in providing an irresistible political opportunity for states to seize valuable land and property from the Catholic Church and suppress the power of its clergy over the people.

The effects of the French Revolution were catastrophic to the Church in France, including nationalisation of Church property; the state running the Church under law passed on the 'Civil Constitution of the Clergy';

dissolution of all monasteries and convents; and prohibition of clerical loyalty to any authority outside France. Legions of priests refused demands to take the oath of compliance to the National Assembly, leading to their exile and the Catholic Church being outlawed. The government set up a Church of Reason and a new Republican Calendar. Almost all monasteries were destroyed and 30,000 priests were exiled while many others were killed.

Most European nations were understandably opposed to the new French Republic, but following recent and ongoing wars each had its own agenda and ambition. With resources stretched, they failed to coordinate their efforts sufficiently in the First Coalition Wars between 1792 and 1797 to have a decisive victory in spite of their superior combined strength. The French had an excellent general in Napoleon Bonaparte who played astutely on clearly evident weaknesses in the coalition.

Pope Pius VI rejected the Civil Constitution of the Clergy in 1791, suspending those French priests who accepted it. When French revolutionaries responded by annexing a couple of small papal enclaves including Avignon, which popes had for over 500 years, Pius VI severed diplomatic relations with France. After King Louis XVI was guillotined in Place de la Concorde in 1793, Pius VI declared him a martyr and began to cooperate with those opposed to the revolution. Following the murder of the French attaché to Rome, Napoleon declared war and invaded the Papal States in 1796, the ensuing peace settlement costing Rome dearly in lands, works of art, money and prestige. Rome continued to resist the revolution, so the French took the city in 1798 and with the pope defiant, he was taken prisoner. Pius VI died the following year in custody in Valence aged 82 following which the seat of St Peter remained vacant for six months.

During his reign, Pius VI had suppressed Jansenism and encouraged growth of the Catholic Church in North America. He improved Church finances prior to the French invasion, restored works of art, completed some major road works including restoring the Appian Way and deepened some strategic docks to take new larger ships. In an attempt to restore some of its past grandeur to Rome, he resumed Benedict XIV's restoration of the city and succeeded in draining the marshes that some of his more ambitious predecessors had never really managed. But the century ended on an extreme low for Church finances and its srtanding in Italy and France although many of the latter's faithful were ruing the loss of spiritual support and sustenance of their religious structures. Some of them already showed restlessness.

Church of England, Broad Church

Church of England settled in to its reputation as conservative and respectable, very much a British middle- and upper-class institution headed by the monarch. Enthusiastic academic or social questioning or the merest suggestion of reform raised the unwelcome spectre of the previous century's Civil War in England as well as European Religious Wars. Bishops were selected as much for their political as their spiritual leanings, while at parish level, the vicar or rector held strong social status.

A group of Cambridge University theologians proposed a 'Latitudinarian' philosophy based on the belief that human reason supported by the Holy Spirit suffice for an individual to build a satisfactory relationship with God. They regarded a Puritan-style religious 'straightjacket' on doctrine and practice as unhelpful, restricting moderation and compromise, so true Protestantism should embrace a broad spectrum of belief and practice. Officially rejected by Anglican leaders, latitudinarianism was regarded as 'Low Church' or a 'Broad Church' approach and sat well with the Hanoverian monarchy's hands-off approach to Anglicanism.

Latitudinarianism was rejected by Pope Pius IX in the next century as giving freedom to individuals to discard or substitute well-founded and established Christian beliefs and doctrines.

Orthodox Church

Differences in emphasis had inevitably developed over many centuries of separation between the Roman and Eastern Churches to the extent that while each aimed loyally to follow the teaching of Jesus Christ, their philosophies and services would no longer have been familiar ground to the other.

Philokalia ('Love of Beauty') is a selection of texts from holy writers over the first fourteen centuries of the Eastern Orthodox Church, compiled by Nicodemus and Macarius of Corinth and published in 1782. They followed the mystical hesychast tradition, which covered a heritage of immersive contemplative prayer basing itself on Jesus' instruction in Mark's gospel (6:5-6) that believers should pray in private better than in public. Hesychasts thus aimed to pray deeply within themselves, dulling their senses in a quest to be closer to and better know God. This book enjoyed a special place as a highly influential spiritual text in the Eastern Orthodox Churches. The same name had been long used on mystical works of spirituality, including a 4th century anthology of Origen's writings by Basil of Caesarea and Gregory of Nazianzus.

The neo-Palamists sum up the division by suggesting that in Western theology rational philosophy is the dominant force, while Orthodox theology is based more on the experiential vision of God and ultimate truth. Palamism originated from a following of Gregory Palamas of Thessaloniki (1296-1359), who followed the hesychast tradition around the time of Thomas Aquinas. His central theological proposition in its support proved controversial, being that although God is inaccessible in his essence, he possesses energies through which he can become known, enabling the devout to share in his divine life. Roman theologians were uncomfortable with the Palamist distinction between the essence and energies of God, treating it as heretical because they saw it as endangering the concept of the Trinity, with suspicions of polytheism.

If it is surprising that the two early branches of the Church directly descending from Jesus Christ were now so unfamiliar to each other after 1800 years, one only had to reflect on what had happened over the past three centuries. The 18th century ended with Christianity embracing dozens of different forms, quite contrary to Christ's desire so clearly expressed in the Gospels and with no clear means or leadership to establish and agree the valid common ground related to Christ's teaching, which transcends, without denying the value of either rational or experiential philosophies.

.

CHAPTER 21

19th Century

Popes

1800-23 Pius VII

1823-29 Leo XII

1829-30 Pius VIII

1831-46 Gregory XVI

1846-78 Pius IX

1878-1903 Leo XIII

This century featured huge social and industrial changes in Europe while powerful nationalist and liberal secular movements gathered pace. Catholicism would see belated growth in North America.

In early 19th Century Europe, influences of the recent Enlightenment as well as scientific, social and cultural advances were maturing and leading to critical examination focused on the Bible, the Church in society and basic beliefs of Christianity, especially in the newer, more Bible-based Protestant churches. Concern at the proliferation of Protestant sects sparked some attempts to seek ecumenism, one early example being the London Missionary Society, begun by a Welsh Congregationalist in 1795 aiming to reunite the evangelical Free Churches. Intercontinental exploration raised awareness of previously unknown religions existing elsewhere, while scientific advance induced a sense of self-sufficiency in some people.

The Roman Catholic Church faced further tumult and loss of Papal Lands but a series of lengthy papacies helped steady its course, though it was slow to respond to the ministry needs of evolving society.

Industrial growth and mechanisation of agriculture led to migration from rural areas to cities, an increasing gap between rich and poor and serious need for fairer and freer societies and social policies, which proved troublesome to agree, establish and implement.

Napoleon

The new pope of the Roman Catholic Church for the new century was a Benedictine monk. The conclave, held at a Benedictine monastery in Venice, was fractious as the Habsburgs voiced loudly their opposition to two of the three favourites for the job and the Austrian cardinals opposed the third. A compromise candidate was appointed, who became **Pope Pius VII** (1800-1823). He appointed Ercole Consalvi, who had shown diplomatic skills as secretary to a testing conclave, to be Cardinal and Secretary of State.

Napoleon's mother was devout; his father more a child of the Enlightenment. He himself, although baptised and a declared admirer of Jesus, was not a church-goer. He was conscious of the unease of Catholics who composed the vast majority of his people, so set about rebuilding bridges with the Church. Reflecting on this during the lengthy conclave, he offered a ceremonial public funeral for Pope Pius VI.

Encouraged by this signal, Pius VII sent Cardinal Consalvi to France. He soon negotiated with Napoleon the Concordat of 1801, which gave the Catholic Church civil rights and sufficient recognition as the religion of the majority of French people. The state would pay clerical salaries to those priests who swore allegiance to the state, in return for which the Church would withdraw its claims to all lands that the state had taken over post-1790. Most of the anti-revolutionary exiled priests returned to their parishes while few of the compliant clergy were welcome to remain as far as the Church and congregations were concerned. Napoleon retained the right to appoint bishops and oversee Church finances in France.

The pope adopted a conciliatory co-operative stance towards Napoleon and attended his coronation as emperor in 1804. He supported Napoleon's Continental blockade of Great Britain from November 1806, which required all sympathetic and neutral countries to support an embargo on trade with Britain in response to the May 1806 British naval blockade of the French ports. The Continental blockade, aimed at crippling Britain's commerce, proved 'leaky' and ineffective as with a strong navy and good commercial links, Great Britain could ramp up its trans-Atlantic trade. Russia and Spain, each enduring their own wars of independence, also continued to trade with Britain, which led Napoleon to overstretch his resources by invading both those countries. France arguably suffered more than Britain by their loss of trade while smuggling between Britain and Europe thrived until the end of the embargo in 1814. Pius VII's support of the blockade was a hostile move against Britain and Cardinal Consalvi resigned in his opposition to it.

Regardless of their mutual respect, serious disagreement arose when Napoleon annexed the remaining Papal States in 1809 and Pius VII responded by excommunicating him. The pope was arrested in the Vatican and covertly transferred to the bishop's palace in Savona then in 1812, with failing health he was taken to Fontainebleau disguised in a priest's black cassock. After Napoleon's defeat at Waterloo in 1814, he abdicated and Pius VII was freed to return to the Vatican. Europe was on its knees economically and the Catholic Church at low ebb, but the end of the

Napoleonic wars brought fresh enthusiasm and respect for Catholicism and the papacy throughout Europe.

Napoleon was exiled to the South Atlantic island of St Helena, where his faith too seemed to enjoy a revival as he requested Mass "to rest my soul" and in 1819, two priests arrived there to attend to the spiritual needs of Napoleon and his entourage. He expressed regret at his spat with Pius VII.

Jesuits

Having almost been outcasts from much of Catholic Church territory for some time now, but still valued for their education and missionary skills, the Jesuits felt the time was right for a fresh start.

At the outset of his reign, Pius VII had given his full approval to the Jesuits in Russia and in 1803 he allowed thirty-five ex-Jesuits to renew their vows at Stoneyhurst under Marmaduke Stone as first head of the restored English Province. Following Napoleon's abdication and in need of support to reinstate Church structures, especially schools, Pope Pius VII soon reinstated the Society of Jesus worldwide. The Catholic Church had done itself only harm in banning and limiting their work and in reality had sorely missed them.

Russia

Regardless of continuing under tight state control, the Russian Orthodox Church maintained its integrity and mission and remained a valuable source of education, research and biblical study, also providing clerical and teacher training. Having established a theological academy in Moscow in the previous century they now built three more in other major cities. Their activity was confined to theological learning, and therefore restricted to priests and religious people in the Church, limited by what was effectively a caste system. People of wider educated and intellectual society took advantage of the openness of some monasteries where they could meet and learn from 'elders', known as '*startsy*', who lived exemplary lives and could advise or hear confessions. Some of these lived remotely in the many vast Russian forests practising the 'hesychast' tradition of contemplative prayer. Orthodox Christianity genuinely thrived among Russians in greater numbers than elsewhere in spite of the tight controls.

Century of Major Social and Cultural Change

In the leading nations of Europe, major changes were taking place in society as the industrial revolution gained pace. Nearly all Churches lagged in their awareness and organisation to spot and provide help to the social casualties of what was taking place. Consequently, a spiritual gap developed between industrial groups of workers and the Churches, aggravated by fatigue and shift patterns limiting their attendance at services. Deprivation, hunger and poverty that accompanied the industrial revolution cried out for practical help and support, which the Churches were not first in line to provide.

The social legacy from the Enlightenment and other developments was one of greater confidence and independent thinking, rationalism and questioning of hitherto accepted norms. Industrialisation and the consequent allure of urban living drew swathes of the rural population into cities where they seemed as reluctant to join churches as the urban churchgoers were to welcome them.

In Great Britain the industrial revolution flourished, the growth of industry offering hope of employment and potential improvement in people's circumstances. But for the majority of manual workers it turned out to be a curse and a poverty trap. There was an economic depression in the 1820s during which urban crime and squalor grew. Social mobility was still almost unknown.

Opportunity abounded for the owners of new factories and businesses and manual labour was cheap. With the exception of a few notable beneficent enterprises such as Port Sunlight on Merseyside and the Quaker-led chocolate dynasties of Bourneville near Birmingham, Fry in Bristol, Rowntree in York, workers and their families still suffered grim conditions. Few of the benefits of industrialisation reached them, apart from increased employment in the industrial areas.

For as agriculture became more efficient, demand for agricultural workers decreased, leading to mass migration to cities into ever more crowded slums with rising rents and living conditions ripe for spreading disease. This was in spite of settlement laws requiring parishes to take their migrants back if they became a burden to the state. Those who secured work in factories would find their livelihoods short-lived in the event of industrial injury or an outbreak of disease, common circumstances, which left families without any income whatsoever. Desperate people who stole vegetables or a loaf of bread to help feed a starving family could be hung or shackled on a boat bound for a penal colony in Australia. Without a breadwinner, older children would be forced to earn a living. Women had few rights or opportunities to earn a living wage, so widowhood usually meant abject poverty. A period of successive extremely hard winters did not help. In rural areas, the poor laws provided for relief via the parish, but these were paid for by taxes on landowners, who simply raised rents, bringing the hardship full circle back to the workers.

All this took place in a wealthy country with growing colonial and industrial riches. Very few ordinary people had any say in the government of the country, so saw little of the benefit. At the end of the 18th century less than 3% of men and no women had the vote. Many large cities were unrepresented in Parliament. Major social change was needed as resentment grew, leading to unrest sharpened by awareness of the French Revolution. This was all exacerbated by the Corn Laws, which introduced tariffs on cheap imported grain to keep cereal prices high in favour of land owners, who exercised disproportionate authority and franchise. Many protest meetings took place demanding reform of parliamentary representation. In one of these in 1819 in St Peter's Field in Manchester, the cavalry charged into a crowd estimated at over 60,000 people, killing eleven protesters. This became known as the Peterloo massacre.

In 1832, fearing revolution, Prime Minister Lord Grey pushed the first Reform Act through a parliament consisting almost entirely of aristocrats. It gave the vote allowing men occupying property with over £10 annual rent value, which was still such a high threshold it enfranchised only 366,000 adult men.

A protest group called The Chartists was then formed. The British establishment looked on in horror as a Charter was presented in 1839 by the self-taught radical leaders of London Working Men's Association, William Lovett and Francis Place. Born of a desire for democracy and signed by over a million people, this contained six demands:

- A vote for all men
- Voting by secret ballot
- Annual general election instead of one every five years
- Parliamentary constituencies to be of numerically equal population
- Members of Parliament to be paid
- Abolition of property qualification for Members of Parliament

The second was to prevent corruption, the third a clumsy way to ensure early accountability and the last two to help allow other than landed gentry to become representatives of the people.

The demands were rejected in full, as were two further Charters signed by over three million people. Civil unrest followed the first two, only to be put down firmly by force and arrests. Preparation of the military before the third ensured relative peace after that and the Chartist movement waned, but left a strong legacy. Its continued campaigning eventually led to subsequent Reform Acts in 1870 and 1884, bringing nearly 8 million men into suffrage, still only covering middle and upper classes. It also eventually gained the secret ballot which reduced intimidation and bribery.

The rural economy also suffered in the depression towards the early 1830s in which landowners reduced agricultural wages progressively. They were also investing in machinery that would reduce the need for such labour, thus eliminating their grounds for negotiation. In Wiltshire and Dorset, there grew a campaign of sabotage of new farm machinery such as threshers. Then in 1835 George Loveless, a Methodist preacher and seven Dorset farmers who were paid a pittance formed a secret friendly society of agricultural workers. They were charged with running an illegal union. Unions had recently been legalised but these men were convicted on the technicality of their secrecy and were transported to Australia. They became known as the Tolpuddle Martyrs and there was such a public uproar that they were pardoned and all returned alive by 1839. Meanwhile, over in Ireland the potato famine caused poverty, ruin and much starvation and death as absentee, mainly English, land-lords still exacted full rents. (see below)

Young German Prince Albert married Queen Victoria in 1840. He was a great enthusiast of railways and industrialisation. The industrial revolution had been producing a wealthier middle class and they were pushing for universities to offer a wider range of courses than just seminarian-style learning, to embrace at least science and modern history studies. German universities offered such a model and Prince Albert supported the move. One of the knighthoods he conferred was on geologist Charles Lyell, who had drastically revised the Church's estimate of the age of the universe. The Church calculated the world as having been created just before 4000 BC based on counting the generations of patriarchs of the bible back to creation in Genesis. A study of fossils alone showed their origins were many millennia earlier than that.

There was no formal police service in the United Kingdom until 1856 and judges had huge powers. Most parishes had an unpaid voluntary officer to find and arrest criminals, often on hearsay. Parishes were heavily dependent on contributions from their wealthier members, so religious ministers tended to lean towards their wishes while distribution of poor law money assuaged their consciences. It would have seemed natural for the poor to perceive the Church as of little help to them, but there were none as conservative as the poor who fear change as potentially destructive of livelihood, however meagre. Similar accounts and conditions of social stress applied equally in other European countries.

While Church leaders in Britain made efforts to help the destitute thanks to some ministers, individuals and benefactors at parish level, such efforts were relatively unheard of at national Church level, except for the Methodist Church, in spite of serious popular concern at social injustice early in the 19th century.

There were some exceptions to this, visionary Church individuals who grasped the need for caring mission. One such was Eugène de Mazenod (1782-1861), son of a wealthy French Catholic family who had to leave France and their fortune behind during the revolution when they escaped to Italy, living in much-reduced circumstances. He moved back to France in 1802 with the aim of helping rebuild the Church there. He became a priest then in 1816 he founded the non-monastic hard-working order of friars, Oblates of Mary Immaculate in Provence to reactivate the Church after the French Revolution by bringing the gospel to the poor. Friars took the usual vows of poverty, chastity and obedience together with a fourth one of perseverance in the order for life. Their stated objective was to grow close to Christ, with absolute respect for the dignity and sacredness of every individual, especially concentrating on those at the margins of Church and society. The Oblates' work was much needed in these times of hardship and deprivation. Their success grew to the extent that in 1831, they voted to spread and begin work with foreign missions abroad. One branch was set up with a base and church in London in 1864 which, in testimony to the extent of need, attracted huge congregations of up to 6,000 people. The order also became strong in Canada.

Much credit is also due to William Booth (1829-1912) for establishing the 'Christian Mission' in 1865 as a Christian humanitarian organisation set up on quasi-military lines and doing practical good work, openly and directly linking faith to social justice in the tradition of Jesus. This would become the Salvation Army which grew and endured world-wide.

Others strove to change further the churches from within, with some Protestants on the continent adopting Pietism. In Britain Evangelicalism thrived at the more romantic end of the Protestant spectrum, popular among the clergy and parishes, partly as a result of initiatives of John Wesley and others.

In the absence of concerted support from the mainstream Churches, these circumstances led to a movement of idealists seeking to understand the reasons for all the human suffering and how to alleviate it. Socialist thinkers made the distinction between the power of individual contract and that of a communal one and how to divide fairly the fruits of endeavour and production between the owner, any investors and the workers. They argued for a more equitable sharing of the benefits, which would lead to communal and individual gain. They called for the formation of workers unions to safeguard the fair rights and benefits of workers, a path the French had taken intuitively without the debate.

This became a century for floating and testing socialist theories, culminating with communism, as championed by Karl Marx, whose life spanned most of it. To his surprise, unlike more democratic European countries, Great Britain avoided revolution, perhaps thanks to its growing recognition of the wisdom of sharing more equitably the benefits of trade and industry and gradual if reluctant evolution of laws to loosen the shackles. Justification of capitalism, endemic in this successful imperial nation, was based on the belief that the nation as a whole is best served by the natural leaders being rewarded according to their achievements and that the benefits would work their way, or 'trickle down', to all. The contrary theory of socialism involved worker representatives in decision-making, including a say in the share-out of the benefits, which should encourage economic growth through improved incomes and incentives for the lower paid. The contest was simply one between the perceived greed of one system versus the need of the other. There were altruists in both camps and in between, but in reality, humans are naturally self-centred.

The national wealth flowing in from British colonial successes attenuated political pressure to make radical social changes at home during much of the nineteenth century. Token portions of it were allocated to minor social improvements in the vain hope of offsetting popular pressure for change.

Social awareness grew in Britain among the people themselves. Churches offered little and held limited power, helping in some local instances, but they were generally hostile to the Chartists. The Roman Catholic Relief Act of 1829 removed most of the restrictions on Catholics in Britain, but they had been a castigated minority for some generations so their confidence was low and considerable intolerance towards them remained which severely limited their professional and social progress and thus influence.

While the dominant and upper class Church of England stood largely aloof from social issues of the poor, intellectual groupings evolved, such as the Oxford Movement with John Henry Newman, Keble and Pusey who wanted to restore in it some values of Catholic tradition. Other intellectual trends such as critical approaches to the Bible, led to some divergent directions on Christianity for Europe and America.

Religion in Northern Europe and America

There were reported apparitions of Our Lady, the mother of God at Lourdes in the French Pyrenees and Knock in Ireland. Pilgrimage to these sites grew as word spread. There had been a few similar centres of pilgrimage such as that at Walsingham in England for well over 1000 years.

The Roman Catholic Church was struggling to recover from the aftermath of the Reformation, various wars, the French Revolution, loss of lands and hardening secularism and nationalism. It was late in becoming well established in North America, though it had flourished for some time in the Spanish and Portuguese colonies to the south.

Protestantism's divisions were exacerbated by new scientific and social developments as theologians, especially in Germany, sought to address the religious implications of modernism. A more critical approach to the Bible and the hitherto accepted norms of universal Christianity developed as did examination of the role of Churches in society. Meanwhile, atheism also grew. Some Protestant branches responded by adopting more fundamentalist approaches or intensified evangelism. People struggled to reconcile the lack of leadership from religions regarding moral imperatives in society, and followed their own consciences regardless of religion or scripture. There was wider awareness by then of other faiths throughout the world. These all followed the 'Golden Rule' – "treat others as you would wish to be treated" – so supported a sympathetic social approach

Following a good start, Protestantism was now facing its own obstacles outside its home territories of northern Europe and North America, in which it mostly enjoyed government support, with the trade-off of some government control over Church salaries, appointments and buildings.

The Catholic Church in America began a phase of rapid growth as greater numbers of Irish and Italians migrated, escaping from social hardship at home to better lifestyle opportunities. Tensions were already arising between the liberal and conservative camps within the American Catholic Church, hardening the two-party political system there. The 19th century also saw a spread of evangelical gospel singing in America.

The 'Latter Day Saints', were founded in New York State by Joseph Smith. Following his death they divided with the main offshoot, followers of Brigham Young becoming known as Mormons, centred on Utah. Between 1852 and 1904, they practised polygamy and built a strong reputation for proselytising. They eschew alcohol, tobacco and addictive substances as well as stimulants like tea or coffee.

Another new American Christian group appeared in 1870, led by Charles Taze Russell. Known as Jehovah's Witnesses, they take the Bible as their ultimate authority, believe in Christ but diverge from many mainstream Christian beliefs and are well known for their strong house-to-house missionary work.

Catholicism was following a different trajectory in Britain where 'nationalism' wore the conscience of a religion, Anglicanism being seen as the 'respectable' option.

Cultural, Social Issues and the Church

Through these times, foreign exploration fed the thriving sciences of geology and biology and opened new lines of research in anthropology which raised new questions about Old Testament stories. The messages drawn by people wrapped up in the devout differed from those closer to practical self-sufficiency or caring. Many of the latter group rejected atheism as too extreme but chose a closer, more personal relationship with Jesus Christ rather than institutional religion and formal repetitive church ritual. This was hardly surprising given government controls and the reticence of many Churches to active response to the social challenges of the era such as rank poverty, exploitation and slavery. These led to crime, alcoholism and brutality between people. This had not been a kindly era but awareness grew among the population on social involvement, health, sanitation and education, which might have been expected of the Churches.

The Oxford Movement, Tractarians, Newman, Wiseman, Manning

Within the Church of England, the 'Broad Church' concept, based on latitudinarian philosophy, had affected those clerics in its upper echelons who recognised the need to broaden the appeal of the Church. Meanwhile in Oxford and other universities, a movement was stirring to restore in the Church of England some pre-Reformation or contemporary Roman Catholic practices and devotions.

John Henry Newman (1801-1899), a gifted poet, theologian and churchman attended Ealing School, emerging as an Evangelical anti-Catholic. He went to Trinity College Oxford as an undergraduate at 17 and by 22 was a Fellow of Oriel College. He was ordained to Anglican priesthood and preached in his Oxford parish, where he attracted and joined then led the Oxford Movement, a group formed to address three perceived threats to Anglicanism – spiritual stagnation, state interference and doctrinal unorthodoxy. From 1833 into the forties they published a number of 'Tracts for the Times', earning the name 'Tractarians'. The tracts promoted their views, aspiring to bring more pre-Reformation practices into the Anglican Church. They proposed revival of monasteries, friars, and sisterhoods, which were gradually reintroduced under the Anglican banner, including the first woman to take Anglican vows, Sister Priscilla Sellon, who founded the Anglican Sisters of Charity. From the 1840s, religious orders for men and women spread nationally and in the colonies, bringing with them schools, laundry, publishing and soup kitchens to help especially those in poverty. At the more High Church end, the Church of England re-introduced vestments and incense to their services.

Tract 90, published in 1841, was quite controversial as shall be seen below. It impressed an intellectual young priest, Dr Charles Russell of Maynooth College, the famous seminary in Ireland, beginning a correspondence which built in Newman a strong sympathy with Catholicism.

Meanwhile, **Pope Gregory XVI** (1831-46) was elected at a fractious conclave. He had a mistrust of innovations such as gas lighting, seeing it as interfering with God's natural rhythm of day and night, also railways, fearing both would lead to empowerment of the middle classes which may result in liberalist challenges to the monarchical papacy. A weak leader with little political or financial nous, his extravagant patronage of favoured artists weakened Church finances still further. French interference led to conflict in Italy and there was restlessness in the Papal States throughout his reign. One redeeming stance was his opposition to the slave trade, which he formally condemned in 1839.

During 1835-6, a Father Nicholas Wiseman, was sent to London and delivered a number of lectures on the doctrine and practice of the Catholic faith. Wiseman (1802-1865) was a Catholic from Ireland, educated at Ushaw seminary in County Durham and the English College in Rome (which had only recently reopened following the Napoleonic wars). He became Rector of the English College at 25, a post he held from 1828-40, also holding other academic posts until asked by Pope Leo XII to preach to English speaking ex-pats in Rome. He delivered a powerful series of lectures on how scientific discovery had initially been thought to be in conflict with Christian doctrine, but when examined more closely to reach a genuine understanding of the science it could equally be argued that it did in fact serve to support belief. This made an impression as it denied the traditional Church scepticism, even fear of scientific discovery.

Andrew Dickson White, an American historian, academic and politician who co-founded Cornell University wrote 'A History of the Warfare of Science with Theology in Christendom' which supported the conflict view, but he acknowledged Wiseman in his book as a great Christian scholar, saying he "did honour to religion and to himself by quietly accepting the claims of science and making the best of them."

While Father Wiseman was in London to explain the Catholic faith in 1835 he came to Newman's attention. He wrote an article for the 'Dublin Review' in 1839 on the fourth to sixth century Donatist schism in Carthage. Oxford Movement members could see parallels between Donatists and Anglicans. Wiseman also delivered a sermon in the same year when opening a new church in Derby. The sermon included remarkably similar ideas to Newman's 1845 book 'An Essay on the Development of Christian Doctrine'. This supported the developments in doctrine as a credible progression traceable back through the early Church Fathers to Divine Revelation in scripture and traditions from the outset of the Church. Wiseman argued that Protestant objections to, for example, honouring Mary or believing in Purgatory were arbitrarily selected. They were no different in their development from other beliefs which Protestants accepted, such as the humanity of Christ or the Holy Trinity.

Newman's friend and fellow Oxford scholar Edward Pusey was impressed by Wiseman and persuaded Newman to attend some of these lectures, which he did and wrote favourable reviews in the 'British Critic'. In 1840, Father Wiseman had returned to Rome and was consecrated bishop that same year, then returned to England as coadjutor to Bishop Thomas Walsh, vicar-apostolic of the London district. He had been disappointed to find that most English Catholics and clergy had dropped devotions to Mary and cleared statues from their churches to avoid persecution during their suppression and the Marian tradition had rather been lost.

Newman was becoming gradually more 'high Church' and was a rising star, his influence in Anglicanism peaking just before 1840. But as he studied the early Church Fathers and was especially impressed by Athanasius and Augustine of Hippo, concern entered his mind that some Church of England doctrine as expressed in some of its 39 Articles came close to the rejected conclusions of some early theological controversies. His conviction grew firmly that the original aim of the Church of England had been to re-establish the early Catholic Church of the Church Fathers for England Henry VIII's time. Newman's problem lay in the 39 Articles, which he saw as politically designed to distance the Anglican Church from Rome rather than from Catholicism. In his controversial Tract 90, "Remarks on Certain Passages in the 39 Articles", published in 1841, he sought again to prove that the Church of England followed a Catholic ecclesiology rather than a Protestant one. He argued that if Anglicanism is a true continuation of the "Old Church", the doctrines must be the same and he believed they were. He identified the formulation of the 39 Articles as a "stumbling block"… "Man had done his worst to disfigure, to mutilate the old Catholic truth; but there it was, in spite of them, in the Articles still."

He decided that if that Tract 90 was rejected, he could no longer hold office within the Anglican Church. So when it was, he set up a small community and in 1842 he moved with some of his learned companions including Edward Pusey, John Keble and other academics to the village of Littlemoor, just outside Oxford where they lived semi-monastic lives, to avoid controversy.

The final straw for Newman came when the Church of England established a bishopric in Jerusalem agreeing to an alternating tenure by in turn Anglican then either Lutheran or Calvinist bishops. This deeply disappointed Newman, who saw it as Anglicanism identifying itself as just another Protestant faith, not as 'Catholic Reformed', as King James had claimed in respect for his mother. Newman converted to the Catholic Church, which was relatively scorned and sparse in England in 1845, but which he described as "the fold of the Redeemer". It was quite a step down from his recent highly respected and privileged positions as an Anglican priest and Fellow of Oriel College as he left Oxford, never to return.

Newman went to Rome to study for the priesthood, where he discovered and was attracted to the Oratory of St Philip Neri, founded in the 16th century. He was duly ordained and became an Oratorian. On return to England in 1848 he founded the first English Oratory in Maryvale, outside Birmingham. As it grew, he moved it to its present home in Edgbaston and in 1849, he sent Frederick Faber to open the London Oratory. Newman was invited to be the founding rector of a new Catholic university in Ireland, University College Dublin in 1851.

Catholicism in Great Britain

Bishop Wiseman was called back to Rome by **Pope Pius IX** to be made cardinal in 1850. The Pope issued a bull establishing a Catholic hierarchy in England and Wales.

New dioceses were established, now led by Westminster where Cardinal Nicholas Wiseman was appointed the first Archbishop. Although Wiseman was well respected, many English saw this as papal interference to exercise territorial rights, causing national resentment. The press reacted negatively and characterised it as an attempt by Rome to turn the clock back and impose jurisdiction in England. Lord John Russell, the Prime Minister wrote an open letter suggesting foreign interference. Public attitude became hostile with attacks on Catholic churches and clergy in the streets, accompanied by cries and slogans of 'No Popery'.

English Catholics had neither the will nor the power to resist physically, opting instead for dialogue and persuasion. John Newman cajoled lay Catholics to combine in response and argue intellectually and dispassionately in public, especially in towns, their case against this new persecution. He favoured public talks on faith and apologetics. In this, he led from the front and personally gave a series of nine advertised weekly lectures at the Birmingham Corn Exchange and distributed supporting leaflets. He was well qualified to convey the Protestant view of Catholicism, arguments for and against, myths and the truth of Catholicism, as he personally had lived and studied the issue from more than one standpoint.

Wiseman held his counsel but responded with a widely distributed leaflet 'Appeal to the English People' explaining the reasons for his appointment, explaining it was a natural consequence of the declared principle of toleration in England and stressing that his foremost concern was for the Catholics, now widely reduced to poverty. He worked with Newman, whose zeal as a convert may have been over-strong but most of the initial antipathy of the English population had been tempered.

In 1853, Charles Kingsley launched his heavily anti-Catholic book 'Hypatia'. Later that year, Cardinal Wiseman went to Rome and received Pope Pius IX's blessing and support for the work he was doing in Westminster. Encouraged, this gifted Briton started writing 'Fabiola', a fictional romantic novel set in the Church of the catacomb era. It was published in 1854 as an obvious Catholic response to Kingsley and enjoyed immediate success, selling widely.

Meanwhile an aristocratic but deeply caring figure had been developing a very personal take on early nineteenth century social conditions as he joined then rose in the Church of England and won the respect of many influential people. Henry Edward Manning (1808-1892) was the son of a Governor of the Bank of England and Tory MP and he was ordained as an Anglican priest in 1833. Some 6 years after Newman, he too converted and took Catholic Holy Orders. The Anglican community and the Oxford Movement were shocked at the loss of such a high-profile figure. He became the second Archbishop of Westminster in 1865 and Cardinal ten years later. Manning always held a firm belief in the social responsibility of the Church. He enjoyed a warm relationship with and good access to Pope Pius IX, which he used in trying to influence Rome in modernising its approach to social justice. He regarded as one of the benefits of stable and longer papacies that it enabled a pope to build relationships and understanding with the wider Church.

The Great Famine in Ireland (1845-52)

Sometimes referred to as the Irish Potato Famine, this was the second most costly disaster ever in life terms in the British Isles with over a million people dying. The Irish population was cut by nearly a quarter due to death and emigration during the period 1845-52. Ireland was run more or less as a British colony with many British landowners at the time. The potato crop was halved by blight in 1845, and reduced by 75% the next year, followed in the longer term. This prolonged hardship had dreadful effects on health and income. With heavy reliance on the potato for nutrition and many small plot growers depending on it for their living, already virtually at subsistence level, this blight was devastating.

Plenty of wheat, meat and dairy goods were produced in Ireland, but the poor could not afford these and most were exported to England. Landlords continued to demand rents and the British government initially took the view that the wealthy Irish should relieve the abject poverty in their country, but in January 1847, the government softened its line slightly, providing some relief funds on loan. Conditions were by then so poor that these were insufficient to change much, but soup kitchens were established. These were mostly concentrated in centres of population whereas the real need was widely dispersed in the countryside, so starving peasants poured into the towns and cities. Their packed and insanitary living conditions there led to epidemics of typhoid, cholera and dysentery which resulted in more deaths than the starvation itself.

By September, the British government cut the small relief fund stream and demanded that its place be taken by relief of the poor from the Poor Law rates – taxes on property from the landowners. This caused unrest and violence so 16,000 troops were sent from England to apply martial law in parts of Ireland. The potato crop failed again in 1848 and an epidemic of another strain of cholera arrived. The main escape routes were emigration to North America and Britain as earlier successful emigrants sent money back to help family members pay the fares. Through all this, devotion to Catholicism in Ireland remained solid.

Unification of Italy (*Risorgimento*), First Vatican Council

Much had been happening in Italy following European wars during the first half of the century. Nationalist General Giuseppe Garibaldi did good military work in Italy in support of the statesman Camillo Benso, Count of Cavour towards the vision of uniting the disparate, often feuding states and fusing them into a single nation. Negotiations between Austria, France and the Italian States facilitated this 'Resorgimento'. Italy was proclaimed a Kingdom in 1861 with Turin as its capital. Initially Austria still held Venice while France held the Papal States. Austria ceded Venice in 1866 and it became the new capital.

Pope Pius IX (1846-78) succeeded Gregory XVI and would become the longest reigning pope in the Catholic Church, introducing stability to its leadership in spite of some turbulence through the 1850s and 60s. French forces defending the Papal States left to help resist a rapid German advance in the ongoing Franco-Prussian war, which led to the capture of Emperor Napoleon III. The departure of these troops opened the doors to

Garibaldi's Nationalists who over-ran the Papal States, entered Rome in October 1870 and dissolved the Papal States. They did not enter the Vatican City within Rome, which had loyal troops including many French defending it. Pius had briefly left Rome after his Secretary of State was killed, but returned as the Vatican survived. He refused to negotiate with or accept the Law of Guarantees of the Italian Government, concerning the temporal power of popes within their civil territory, arguing that it would leave the Italian government free to alter the legislation at any time. In this impasse, Pius IX also refused to leave the Vatican City, coining the title 'prisoner of the Vatican'. Most of his staff remained with him in the Vatican. Pius IX was the last sovereign ruler of the Papal States.

[A negotiated settlement would not finally be agreed between united Italy and the Roman Church until as late as 1929, between Benito Mussolini and Pope Pius XI, when it was agreed that the Catholic Church retain a hundred acres of property in Rome including the Vatican of which the pope would be considered supreme ruler. That territory would be accorded valuable tax concessions and the compensation for all the land and property lost by the Church in the revolution was set at nearly one hundred million dollars.]

The First Vatican Council was perhaps the best prepared council thus far, with wide consultation of the Church's over 1000 bishops (about 750 of whom attended the council) and four years preparation. It was convoked in 1868 and opened at the end of 1869, continuing through the upheaval in Rome but was brought to a premature end without covering the full agenda, as the invading Italian Nationalists threatened. The Council rushed its declarations mid-1870 but had to leave some important pastoral issues pending for future action. Pius IX had wanted the Council to go further in at least formalising the threatened authority of the Church, but his hopes were cut short.

One religious benefit from ceding the Papal States was that Pius IX and future popes could concentrate their efforts on their main calling, ecclesial and spiritual matters. The dual role had proved conflicting in so many ways over the past thousand years, not least as regards the sanctity of life, which the early Christians had held so dear. Popes had supported and even led wars and inquisitions and effectively supported the death penalty, often applying it by proxy. All of these were quite contrary to the beliefs and teachings of the original Universal or Catholic Church that followed Jesus.

Two principal doctrinal matters which emerged from Pius IX's papacy were papal infallibility and the Immaculate Conception of Mary:

Papal Infallibility

Pius IX sought to maintain and consolidate the authority of the Catholic Church. He emphasised the term Magisterium, meaning the teaching authority of the Pope and his bishops, which marks a clear distinction between Catholicism and Protestantism. Put simply, Catholics believed that Christ conferred on Peter and the Church an ongoing apostolic teaching role in revealing God's truth in a changing world, whereas Protestant belief was that the truth is individually derived from the Bible with guidance available from their Churches. In reality there was a spectrum of opinion within both camps with some overlap. Pius IX went further, requiring that once a Pope had formally declared his magisterium on a matter of faith or morals, there should be no more debate and theologians should serve only to confirm that doctrine, not question it. A minority of bishops either accepted this in full or were strongly opposed, while most bishops simply supported what they saw as the pope reaffirming the authority of the Church.

The main driver of the papal infallibility issue was a defensive reaffirmation of the Vatican's centrality against its declining influence. Since almost the very beginnings of Christianity, the Roman Catholic Church was considered 'indefectible' because of its continuity, the importance it attaches to the apostolic succession and the Holy Spirit's guidance. It is still 'home' to over 60% of Christians. There has always been some pressure to reform from factions within and there is a broad spectrum of views among the faithful. Rather than start new denominations, some formed new religious orders within like Ignatius Loyola, which in spite of strains, added to its strength. For the Church as a whole to have survived and retained such global influence in spite of its officers' faults may be seen as witness to the Holy Spirit's support.

Infallibility remains an issue of contention, even ridicule for the Catholic Church today and is wide open to misunderstanding. In fact, it only applies when the pope speaks officially from the 'throne of St Peter' (*ex-cathedra*) on matters of faith and morals that lie at the heart of the Catholic faith. He is not infallible when he addresses crowds from his balcony or in his encyclicals. It is so restricted a claim that it is rarely exercised. For example, it applied to the announcement of the Immaculate Conception in 1854, pre-dating the Council declaration on infallibility, and again in 1950 regarding the Assumption of Mary. That such a level of importance be attached to these Marian declarations may raise eyebrows questioning how essential they are to core Christian belief, especially given the additional obstacle they pose in any serious quest for unity. Catholics themselves range from one extreme of accepting everything a Pope declares as infallible, which is technically plain wrong, to considering the concept of infallibility as fallible itself.

Infallibility remains the most remembered declaration of Vatican I. It was ripe for misunderstanding outside the Catholic Church and controversial inside it, never being fully explained, although Vatican II had a go at producing further clarification (*Lumen Gentium 25*), which still suffered the lack of clarity as might be expected of a committee-generated statement. There were opposing views regarding infallibility among Church leaders at the Council. For example, two English cardinals held differing views – Manning felt it appropriate in the face of the historical crisis facing Rome at the time, while Newman felt it was excessive. By 1861, Newman had come to fear that the Catholic leadership regarded the core Church as essentially consisting of the hierarchy and the humble or poor, viewing educated lay people rather as an irritant and widely 'heretical'. Newman strongly opposed the pressure to define papal infallibility at Vatican I, arguing that there was no threat to be averted and the move would create unnecessary dangers of its own. He consistently and publicly bemoaned the absence of open debate within the Catholic Church and the restrictive uniformity demanded by Rome. It still canonised him some 120 years after his death.

Amongst others, the infallibility declaration alienated a particular group in the Church. 'Old Catholics' was a description from 1853 of members of the See of Utrecht who did not accept papal authority as infallible. Their public influence spread, leading to a meeting in Nuremburg in 1870 at which the 'Old Catholic Churches' were founded by a group of Bavarians, Austrians and Swiss. They claimed episcopal succession in 1884 as a German Old Catholic Bishop was consecrated by a prelate of the Church of Utrecht. They accepted the first seven ecumenical councils and doctrine formulated before 1054 but rejected communion with the pope and some post-1054 Roman Catholic doctrines and practices. In 1925 they recognised Anglican ordination and have been in full communion with the Anglican Church since 1932.

To understand Pius IX and Vatican I, the historical context is important. Church and papacy had been facing increasing threats to their survival in Rome. The French Revolution was testimony to growing popular pressure through Europe for liberty and democracy. The Church had neither promoted nor embraced such values and was remembered for its past excesses and exercise of power. Early In the second millennium, the influence of philosophers and theologians had become a bulwark of the Church to the extent that theologians outnumbered bishops at the Council of Basle in 1439 and surely held influence beyond Christ's intention. Then post-revolutionary France condemned the Catholic Church, its priests were exiled, its vast health and educational systems dismantled and its property sold to fund the new regime. Napoleon's far flung forays had seen Church infrastructure elsewhere laid to waste. The Church of Rome having grown to behave as a 'supra-nation' was now suffering the consequences.

Communion, Eucharist

After the Reformation, Protestants were mostly relaxed about the use of leavened bread and this may have hardened Catholic allegiance to the unleavened variety, which had been adopted around the 9th century. The Orthodox Churches use unleavened bread. The practice of the communicant kneeling and the bread being distributed by a priest can only have developed since the adoption of unleavened bread and was a clear change from the tradition of a shared loaf between equals. Matthew 26:26 describes Jesus as blessing the bread, breaking it and inviting others, saying "take, eat" – altogether different from the 'sharers' submissively kneeling and having the bread placed on their tongues by a priest. The modern way of standing to receive the bread from the priest in a cupped hand for self-administration is a compromise.

Immaculate Conception

There had been a long-running disagreement between Franciscans and Dominican theologians over the question of whether Mary was born without Original Sin. This is a separate issue from that of the virgin birth of Jesus (Doctrine of Incarnation) and Pius IX favoured the Franciscan view that she was born without original sin, which he formalised as firm dogma of the Faith in 1858, the year of the first apparitions of Mary at Lourdes. Quite apart from its content, this was a controversial step for at least two reasons. First, in circumventing the bishops, it was seen as undermining their authority. Second, it ran counter to strong Protestant views, so disappointed those who were in favour of rapprochement with Protestants, though Pius IX was in any case no supporter of this.

Apparition of Our Lady at Lourdes

In 1858 a young French miller's daughter, Bernadette Soubirous (1844-79) reported sightings of 'a small young lady' in a white veil and blue girdle and rosary of pearls where Bernadette had been collecting firewood at a grotto in Massabielle, just outside the village of Lourdes in the Pyrenees.

The Catholic Church was initially dismissive of her tales but as the visions continued, they held a canonical investigation which decided in 1860 that they were 'worthy of belief'.

There were sixteen appearances in February and March followed by one each in April and July. After the first, it was clear her sister Toinette and a friend who were with her had not seen the vision so she swore them to secrecy. Toinette could not keep the secret and word spread, so after the 4th, she was accompanied by some family and friends. News spread and they grew to a few hundred by the 9th towards the end of February, who saw that day a spring of water appear below the rocks by the grotto, from which Bernadette was told to drink.

In early March, she was accompanied by a local woman, Catherine Latapie, who was nine months pregnant and had a paralysed arm due to past accidental damage to the ulnar nerve in her elbow. This was cured when she bathed her arm in the spring and she gave birth on the spot. After telling her doctor, Dr Dozous, he visited the grotto with Bernadette for the 17th apparition on 7th April and observed her rapture and saw that the candle she held in two hands with the flame playing on the fingers of one did not burn her. He kept a record of cures in the spring from then on.

The lady had told Bernadette earlier to ask the local priests to process to the grotto and build a chapel there. The parish priest refused as the Church had a policy of discouraging apparent visions. He told her to ask the lady who she was, which she did at every subsequent apparition. Eventually in March, when Bernadette asked her three times, the lady opened her arms and said "I am the Immaculate Conception". This was not the language of a simple working class girl who only spoke the local patois, Occitan. So Bernadette repeated it to herself all the way home so as not to forget it and reported to the priest. He went to tell the bishop at Tarbes, who told the priest to instruct Bernadette to cease her grotto visits.

Since nearly 10,000 people were by then coming from all around to these occasions, the mayor took preventative measures by boarding off the grotto. There was a final vision on 18th July. Napoleon ordered the grotto to be opened to the public in October. Churches and a large basilica were built nearby in subsequent years and Bernadette joined the Sisters of Charity in 1866. She died of tuberculosis at just 35. Lourdes has since become one of the most popular places of pilgrimage and cure.

Charles Darwin (1809-1882) and 'Origin of Species'

Charles Darwin came from a Unitarian, non-conformist family background but was baptised into the Church of England and went to Cambridge with the intention of becoming a priest, but his interest in natural science prevailed. On the Beagle, he was a committed Christian and held to the Bible, though as his theories developed, doubts crept in as to its accuracy. After his time on Beagle, he married devout Christian Emma Wedgwood in 1839 and continued to attend church with her on Sundays until 1849. Pain and cruelty in nature troubled him and he was devastated by the death of their eldest daughter Annie in 1851 which intensified his doubts of a loving God. In 1859, he published his well-researched and argued 'Origin of Species'. None of his writings reject God, though soon before his death he revealed privately to a few that he was not an atheist, but probably more an agnostic than a Christian and that he could no longer regard the Bible as a source of divine revelation

Darwin's theory of natural selection involving the transmutation of species shook all those who held to the absolute truth of the Bible. Their initial concern was the origin of man, which raised serious questions around the Book of Genesis. The Catholic Church raised no immediate comment, seeming to have tempered its tendency to condemn prematurely apparently inconvenient scientific theory. It was clear from quite early on that Catholic theology allowed for the Old Testament, which in places ran counter to reason and unfolding evidence, to be taken as allegorical rather than literal. Geological and other scientific research had already thrown doubt on parts of Genesis and Exodus – the creation of the world in six 'days', for example.

The Protestant faiths, being more attached to the correctness of the whole Bible, were far more concerned about the impact of The Origin of Species. But there were those among them whose religious philosophy had developed in the past century. Conservatives in the Church of England establishment voiced objection to Darwin's findings, while its more liberal children of the Enlightenment saw Darwin's evolution theory as part of God's design. In any case, the most learned Christian writers on science and religion had already accepted that some of the Old Testament could be read as metaphorical. Geology had developed into quite a sophisticated science by this time and it was clear that even the earth was far older than religion held the universe to be. Geologists were convinced that geological formation on earth alone must have taken countless millions of years although they could not give accurate estimates as carbon dating was then unknown and radioactivity would not be discovered until the turn of the century.

There was intense and emotional debate about Darwin's findings and creationists contest them to this day, but his publication did not register as highly on the Church Richter scale as is sometimes suggested.

Pius IX's successor **Leo XIII (1878-1903)** was an intellectual, socially aware pope who cared deeply about ordinary people and did much to update Church social teaching. His famous encyclical *Rerum Novarum*, published in 1891, stressed the right of workers to a fair wage, safe working conditions and the right to form trade unions. He overcame severe restrictions imposed on him to become a highly effective leader and made full use of his twenty-five years of papacy.

The restrictions he endured were persecution of the Church in Italy by legislation, vilification in education, expropriation of property and attacks on churches and other infrastructure, while the pope remained confined to the Vatican. Internationally, he built good relations with Russia and Germany and was the first pope to declare support for the French Republic. The two lengthy papacies in the second half of the 1800s helped further stabilise internally the Roman Church which was suffering and preoccupied by the ravages of Italian turbulence and aggression as well as the momentum of international secularisation.

Leo XIII made Newman a cardinal in England in 1879, re-established the Catholic hierarchy in Scotland and set up a new one in India. He decried the Plan of Campaign in Ireland which was an Irish government response to the eviction of tenant farmers during the great famine there as the mainly English absentee landlords were taking a hard line on rents and defaulters, of which there were many. Leo XIII forbade clerical participation in the disturbances in Ireland, which had been quite strong. He also declared Church of England ordination to be "absolutely null and void".

He opened Vatican archives to students in 1881, which was an uncharacteristic move of openness by the Church, allowing access to financial records among others.

In 1884, Leo XIII blessed the missions to Eastern Africa, largely operated by the 'White Fathers', Society of Missionaries to Africa. He initiated the first plenary council of the Church in South America and kept in touch with developments elsewhere in the world.

Leo XIII issued over 80 encyclicals on matters of faith and morals, the most notable being Rerum Novarum, below. In 1880, he firmly confirmed Church backing for Christ's message on marriage. This included the indissolubility of the marriage contract, which should protect it from polygamy and divorce. The Church regarded matrimony as a sacrament, sanctifying the married status. Other encyclicals ranged over subjects such as civil power, Freemasonry, human freedom. He revised the index of forbidden books in 1900.

Cardinal Manning, *Rerum Novarum*, Social Awarenes

During the great London Dock strike which began in 1889, Cardinal Manning held the trust of both sides, so was given the role of mediator. London's commerce approached standstill and the strikers' families were suffering even greater hardship than that they were striking to escape. 'The Cardinal's Peace' as it became known, brought an apparent end to both problems, but the Cardinal agonised over the profoundly unbalanced contract of the working poor with the new breed of prosperous industrial employer. This subject so offended his sense of fairness that he wrote with eloquence and passion about it in the Dublin Review in 1891. Later that same year, Pope Leo XIII wrote his encyclical *Rerum Novarum*, 'Of New Things', concerning the condition of the working classes, thought to have been linked with Cardinal Manning's writing and still regarded as the foundation of modern Catholic Social Teaching (see 20th century).

Since state secularism had become the norm, Christian hierarchies throughout Western Europe in this century had found themselves too preoccupied with internal and political challenges to do much that would have tangible effect on the social needs of the people, although some good individual clerics and orders were moved to do what they could locally. Towards the end of the century, encouraging indicators suggested that some of the hierarchies were at least recognising a need for responsible social action.

Social Revolutionaries, Karl Marx, Communism

Karl Marx (1818-1883), from a German middle class family studied law and philosophy. Initially a philosopher, economist and sociologist, he took up journalism and revolutionary socialism. On account of his political writings, he was made stateless and moved to London to continue his research. His impact on intellectual social, economic and political thinking was so huge that it became known as Marxism.

Marx contended that human society could only develop through confrontation between the bourgeoisie or ruling class, who control the means of production on the one hand and the proletariat or working class, whose labour operates those means in exchange for wages on the other. Marx was sure that capitalism would implode in the course of this clash, to be replaced by socialism. He argued that capitalism was inherently unstable since it leads to class distinction which creates tensions. Marx predicted that this, combined with the higher numbers of poor versus rich would result in an uprising and seizure of political power by the workers. They in turn would establish a classless 'communist' society. He actively promoted such revolutionary action by the working class as necessary to achieve social and economic emancipation.

In 1844 he met Friedrich Engels and together they published 'The Communist Manifesto' introducing the word into daily language. His other best known work was the three-volume tome '*Das Kapital*'.

Regarded as one of the most influential characters in history, Karl Marx catalysed wider awareness and consideration of social science. His rationale was idealistic, although many saw that communism lay at one extreme of the discussion, a view supported by world events in the subsequent century. George Orwell cleverly satirised the inescapable effect of human frailty on the ideology in his book 'Animal Farm'.

In response to this socialist movement, Pope Leo wrote one of the most influential and insightful papal encyclicals, *Rerum Novarum*. It covered the new strains in relationships and balancing rights and duties between owners and workers within the workplace; family and state framework arising from the industrial revolution; and issues surrounding socialism and the role of religion. Making frequent reference to Thomas Aquinas and Natural Law, it is a work of such relevance and importance to modern life that it deserves at least a brief summary of its contents below, divided under his own headings; as a précis, its non-inclusive language is of that age. Modern Catholic Social Teaching would grow from it in the next century.

Rerum Novarum (Of New Things)

The following is verbatim as the encyclical was translated:

"The Social Problem – Rights and Duties

Following recent scientific discoveries and rapid industrial expansion conflict arises in the new relations between employers and workers; in concentration of wealth among the few and the poverty of the masses; in the increased self-reliance and closer mutual cooperation of the working classes; and in a prevailing moral degeneracy.

Confusion exists about the relative rights and duties of the rich and the poor and about capital and labour, which agitators use to stir up revolt. Since the abolition of workingmen's guilds in the last century, a replacement relief is needed for the conditions of the working class. Institutions and laws have led to workers suffering from the competitiveness and greed of employers, compounded by usurious interest rates of lenders. Relatively small numbers of very rich men have been able to exploit the labouring poor masses with conditions akin to slavery.

Socialism and Human Rights

The Socialist remedy is to eliminate privately owned property, which would become the common property of all, administered by the government. They believe that by transferring property ownership from private individuals to the community, the current imbalance will be corrected as each citizen will then get his fair share of the benefits. But their proposals would rob the lawful possessor, distort the functions of the State and family and create public confusion.

When a man does paid labour, his ultimate motive is to progress and obtain his own property. If he lives sparingly, saves money, and invests his savings in chattels or land, these are his wages under another form, owned by him to use or dispose of as he pleases just as was the case with his wages. Socialists, by seeking to transfer the possessions of individuals to the community, strike at the interests of every wage-earner, since they would deprive him of the liberty of disposing of his wages as he wishes, and thereby of all hope and possibility of increasing his resources and of bettering his condition in life.

This 'remedy' is therefore manifestly unjust. Natural Law gives everybody the right to personal property. The animal has two main natural drives – self-preservation and the propagation of the species. The human also has reason, which gives him the right to have and to hold things in stable and permanent possession.

Humans apply their reason and choice regarding their welfare, present and future. God and nature have given them a source in the earth and its fruits from which he can draw continual supplies. People precede the State, and possess, prior to the formation of any State, the right of providing for their needs.

God has given the earth for the whole human race to use and enjoy which logically includes owning private property. God has granted the earth to mankind in general, not to any one in particular, to use responsibly but the limits of private possession have been left to be fixed by man's own industry, and by the laws of individual races. Those who do not own land contribute their labour. Human subsistence is derived either from labour on one's own land, or from work paid for either in the produce of the land, or in that which is exchanged for that product. The results of labour should belong in fair proportion to those who have given their labour.

In natural law the principle of private ownership conforms to human nature and is a clear basis of peaceful human co-existence, as accepted and enforced by just civil laws. Divine law also shows acceptance in the commandment forbidding us even to covet that which is another's.

These rights are stronger if we consider man's domestic obligations. All are fully free to marry with the principal purpose ordained by God: "Increase and multiply." Thus we have the family, a small but real society, older than any State. Its innate rights and duties are quite independent of the State.

In Natural Law a father should provide all that is necessary for family survival, which usually involves ownership of tools and productive property. The family, being a true society, has at least equal rights with the State, seeking to acquire things required for its preservation and liberty. The domestic household is antecedent to the community, thus society cannot work if operated contrary to the interests of domestic households of which it is composed.

While no civil government should normally intrude into the household, if a family is in extreme distress, public aid should be offered, since each family is a part of the commonwealth. Equally, if serious disturbance of mutual rights within the household occurs, public authority should intervene to enforce a fair settlement justly to safeguard them but go no further. Paternal authority can be neither abolished nor absorbed by the State. Socialists, therefore, in side-lining the parent and setting up State supervision, act against natural justice, and undermine the structure of the home. This is clearly against the natural order and would cause envy and discord. There would be no incentive in exerting one's talents or industry, so sources of wealth would run dry and that equality of which they dream would be in reality the levelling down of all to the lowest state. Thus the main tenet of socialism, community of goods, must be utterly rejected, since it would introduce confusion and disorder into society. The inviolability of private property must be protected.

Human affairs are naturally complex, so civil society cannot be reduced to one dead level; that is contrary to nature. Mankind displays many differences in capacity, skill, health and strength, resulting in inequality of fortune. As regards physical labour, even had man never fallen from innocence, he would not have remained idle, but after it his need to work became compulsory, the painful expiation for his disobedience. This is the lot of humanity. Nothing will succeed in ridding human life of all its troubles, so the world must be accepted as it really is.

The wealthy and the working men are not intended by nature to live in mutual conflict. In an orderly State, different classes should dwell in harmony as each needs the other, being mutually inter-dependent. Religion draws the rich and the working class together, by reminding each of its duties to the other, and of the obligations of justice.

The following duties bind the employer and the worker:

The **worker** must perform the work fully and faithfully as agreed, respect the property and the person of an employer and avoid resort to violence, riot or disorder in defending their own cause.

The **owner and the employer** must not treat their work people as their bondsmen, but respect every person's dignity. Natural reason and Christian philosophy regard working for gain as creditable, not shameful since it enables people to earn an honourable livelihood. To treat people as things in the pursuit of gain or to value them only for their physical powers is wrong. Religion and the good of a worker's soul must be considered, so the employee must be allowed time for his religious duties, protected from corrupting influences and danger, not be led to neglect their home and family, be pushed beyond their strength or employed in work unsuited to their gender and age. The employer's principal duty is to give everyone what is just. To defraud anyone of wages due is a serious crime. Lastly, they must refrain from reducing the worker's earnings, whether by force, fraud, or usury.

Riches in themselves do not bring happiness either here or in eternity, but can even be obstacles. "It is lawful," Thomas Aquinas had said, "for a man to hold private property; and it is also necessary for the carrying on of human existence." But as to how one's possessions should be used the Church refers to Aquinas again: "Man should not consider his material possessions as his own, but as common to all, so as to share them without hesitation when others are in need." True, no one is commanded to distribute to others that which is required for their own needs and those of their household, nor even to give away what is reasonably required to maintain their condition in life. But when what necessity demands has been supplied.... it becomes a duty to give to the indigent out of what remains over. It is a duty, enforced by human law, but also of Christian charity. In summary, whoever has received from the divine bounty a large share of temporal blessings, be they external and material, or gifts of the mind, has received them for the purpose of using them for perfecting his own nature and to employ them as the steward of God's providence, for the benefit of others.

As for the less fortunate, the Church teaches that in God's sight poverty is no disgrace and there is nothing to be ashamed of in earning one's bread by labour, as witnessed by Christ himself. Given this divine model, it is easier to understand that the true worth of a person lies in their moral qualities, their virtue. God displays his most tender love toward the lowly and the oppressed.

If Christian values prevail, the respective classes will not only be united in friendship, but also in brotherly love. For they realise that all men are children of God and that all have the same last end, God himself. The Church, practising the teaching of Jesus Christ, works for the poor and disadvantaged and has raised and supported institutions to help them.

Equality

All citizens are equal regardless of status or class. Benign rulers have a duty to apply justice fairly, regardless of class.

Although all citizens should contribute to the common good, it should not be supposed that all can contribute in the same way and to the same extent. Some must devote themselves to the work of the commonwealth, to make the laws or administer justice, or govern the nation in times of peace, and defend it in war. Such people do valuable work for community, but it is only by the labour of workers that states build industrial wealth. Justice therefore demands that the interests of the working classes should be carefully watched over by the administration, so that they who contribute so largely to the advantage of the community may themselves share in those benefits.

Rulers' primary role is to safeguard the community and all its members. Both philosophy and the Gospel require that the object of the State government should be the benefit of those it rules in precedence to the advantage of the ruler. As the power to rule comes from God, the highest of all sovereigns, it should be exercised like God's, with a fatherly solicitude which not only guides the whole, but reaches individuals.

The public authority must protect the general interest and that of all classes. Peace and good order should be maintained with all decisions being made according to God's laws and those of nature. Use of the authority of law should be proportionate and reasonable.

Rights

Public authority must respect peoples' rights wherever they exist, and it is the duty of the State to prevent and punish injury, and to protect everyone's possessions. Provision must be made for the poor, who are often unable to pay for justice, to be cared for and protected by the government. Private property must be protected by law, including during times of natural disaster or civil disturbance.

Workers too should be protected by the State. The authorities should forestall troubles by addressing in good time the causes of conflict between employers and employed, such as wages being too low, over-long hours, or the work is too hard.

Self-preservation is a natural law which gives everybody the right to procure what is required in order to live. The poor can only procure that through their work. Hours and conditions of work, including rest periods should conform to what is considered reasonable in the times. Their wages should suffice for the families' living costs and also to enable the prudent worker to put aside savings for security. If working people can be encouraged to look forward to obtaining tools and a share in the land, the gulf between vast wealth and sheer poverty will be reduced, and the respective classes will be brought nearer to one another with less resentment and risk of civil disturbance. People always work harder and better on that from which they also benefit. The law should favour ownership and enable many people to become owners.

There should be no work and labour on Sundays and certain holy days to allow people to follow their religious practices.

Employers and workers may gain through associations and organizations which provide aid to those in distress such as the ill or injured worker or his widow or orphans in case of sudden calamity, sickness or death.

Worker's unions would be a good development in the absence of artificers' guilds of old. Such unions should be suited to the requirements of this age of wider education, different habits, and more complex daily lives. The law should prevent any associations, whose purposes are evidently unlawful, or dangerous to the State. Some societies are in the hands of secret leaders, and are managed on anti-Christian principles and they try to force workers either to join them or to starve. Christian working men should rather unite and form their own associations.

Christian people should lead by example against those who adopt strife as a solution to their problems. Everyone should put his hand to the relief of social deprivation and injustice.

15th May, 1891, the fourteenth year of Our pontificate. LEO XIII"

Many papal encyclicals teach the results of moral examination of issues of faith and practice. This one was important in that it gave such moral guidance that was needed for governments and people in the recently industrialised world. Much of it seems obvious but to be heard, the Church relies on its acceptance and credibility in society to guide governments and individuals. No matter how important the message, only receptive open ears will hear it. The Catholic Church was struggling to achieve this in some areas in this era as it is today, when occasional equally clear and important encyclicals such as Laudate Si are being issued.

Biblical Manuscript Hunters

Many theologians and enthusiasts, especially Protestants who mostly laid clear emphasis on the Bible as the true, unchangeable word of God, were seeking hard evidence to support this. They had to overcome many challenges which they faced in the biblical parts of the Middle East.

Following a visit to Egypt, David Strauss had published a book which shocked Christianity with the suggestion that the Bible, including the New Testament was not the true word of God. Constantin Tischendorf, a Bible expert from Leipzig University was motivated to research Strauss' results and went on his own expedition, drawing blanks in the Coptic churches he visited. Eventually, at the Greek Orthodox monastery of St Catherine below Mount Sinai, he made some progress. This encouraged him to make a second visit in 1859 and he discovered the Codex Sinaiticus New Testament including the four canonical gospels in Greek dating as far back as late 4th century. Its 36,000 edits and corrections raised concern for the 'unchangeable' word of God. Also Mark's gospel ended at 16:8. Had 12 verses been added later? Later versions included reference to events beyond Christ's resurrection.

Agnes Smith Lewis and Margaret Dunlop Gibson, Scottish Presbyterian identical twins, had studied the New English Revised edition of the King James Bible and became bible hunters known as the Sinai Sisters. They went to St Catherine's monastery seeking an even older version than Tischendorf and in 1892 they found one in Syriac language, close to the Aramaic used by Jesus. It is still the earliest version known, and had palimpsest – previous writings partly erased by scraping or scrubbing with lemon juice, for preservation of the expensive vellum for over-writing. The over-written parts were later shown to be a Syriac 'Lives of the Saints' by John the Recluse from the 3rd century. It is known that the earliest Syriac translations were done in the 2nd century. When transcribed this one raised yet more questions as it had numerous corrections and still made no mention of Jesus' reappearance to the disciples after the crucifixion.

Orthodox Churches and Ottomans

The Islamic Ottomans allowed Christians within their empire to worship quite freely. They referred to the Eastern Orthodox Christians as Rum Millet (Roman nation). The Ottomans were all too aware of growing nationalism in the West, and that there were such movements stirring deep within the various ethnic groups inside their empire, but they seemed not to regard it as an urgent matter. Some Greek Orthodox intellectuals, alert to upheaval in Western Christianity, aspired to a fusion of all Balkan Orthodox Christians into a new kind of Eastern Empire. Their ambitions found wide appeal in Greece, while neighbouring supporters realised it would most likely become Greek-centric.

In 1821, Greek Orthodox Metropolitan Germanos III of Patras blessed the fighters and raised the standard of the Greek war of independence from the Ottoman Empire, thus displaying the Orthodox Church's support of such revolution. The Patriarchate of Constantinople was the formal body delegated by the Ottoman government to administer Christians. Its condemnation of this revolution fell on deaf ears, so to capture serious attention within the Church, the government held mass executions, destroyed many churches and hanged the Ecumenical Patriarch Gregory V in public from the gate of his residence on Easter Day, 1821 then there followed a purge of dissident clergy in Turkey.

As the Greek Church became isolationist, its bishops formed the synod of a new Orthodox Church, claimed autocephaly in 1833 and accepted strict government control similar to the Russian model. The Greek Revolution had by then gained the support of France, Britain and Russia, so it was reluctantly accepted as a fait accompli by the Constantinople patriarchate, which finally issued a charter of autocephaly to the new Orthodox Church of Greece in 1850.

The Ottomans finally woke up to the dangers of the western nationalism movement spreading eastwards and took belated steps to counter such pressures by planning their Tanzimât, a reorganisation aimed at making them more competitive with the western powers. So in 1839 they initiated a series of revisions to modernise their model of government, political and social structures and culture, allowing increased secularisation. Economies throughout their empire soon improved. They emancipated non-Muslim residents and embraced non-Turkish residents by enhancing their civil liberties and equality. The intentions were to nurture loyalty to Ottomanism, reduce internal nationalism and strengthen opposition to potential external aggressors. It encompassed a revised banking system, obligatory conscription in a modernised army, secular instead of religious law, decriminalisation of homosexuality and introduced an industrial strategy with modern factories. Opposition from the majority Muslim population slowed progress, but the reforms caught on and lasted until 1876.

None of this had suppressed the growth of nationalism and the Greeks had by then realised the difficulties of uniting all the various ethnicities under one umbrella. Having triggered the process of separation of their own Church as an autocephalous group as early as 1833 and with nationalism gaining traction in other local states, they saw their example being followed elsewhere as the Orthodox Church separated into a number of autocephalous national groups by the 1870s.

This led inevitably to profound ethnic and national rivalries throughout the Balkan states and their Orthodox Churches, ultimately resulting in conflict. A term used in the synod of Constantinople, 1872, was *phyletism* to describe the inclusion of ethnic or national distinctions in different Church constitutions. *Phyletism* was condemned at this council and it has remained a point of weakness from which the Christian Orthodox Church has suffered since and most recently in Russia and Ukraine.

The *Tanzimât* period came to an end in 1876 with the 'First Constitutional Era'. A group of Ottoman intellectuals who believed the

Tanzimât reforms did not go far enough had formed a secret society in 1865. Known as the Young Ottomans, they sought to preserve the empire by adopting a modern, Western style of constitutional democratic government, quite contrary to their ingrained leadership culture. In December 1876, Sultan Abdulaziz was dethroned and replaced by Abdul Hamid II. The constitutional monarchy, which had a parliament but no party system, only lasted about fifteen months, as the new Sultan suspended the recently established Turkish parliament and restored absolute monarchy. Democracy would not be reinstated until 1908 by the Young Turks Revolution.

The Russo-Turkish war in 1877-8 began to loosen the grip of Ottoman power over the Balkans. The multicultural Bulgarian (1870) and Serbian (1879) Churches became autocephalous as others followed suit. The Bulgarian Church split on ethnic and linguistic lines, so had two Orthodox Churches until the matter was eventually resolved in 1945. Each such step hardened the identification of ethnic nationality with Church attachment, which gave rise to deep rivalries and instability between and sometimes within Balkan states which eventually led to a series of armed conflicts around the region.

Pope Leo XIII was more sympathetic to ecumenism than his predecessor and extended a hand of friendship from Rome to the Orthodox Churches towards the end of the century.

Modernism in the Catholic Church

In the latter years of the 19th century, confidence was returning to the Catholic Church following some good conferences. This was interrupted by the emergence of a Catholic Modernist movement among French, British and some Italian intellectuals, with the Oxford Movement and some theologians from the Protestant Tübingen School of Theology as interested parties. Modernism embraced a rationalist approach to the Bible, many Enlightenment ideas, particularly secularism (clear separation of Church and State). It included a modern approach to philosophy and clearly challenged some Church teaching of the time.

The Church hierarchy reacted with defensive fury and required all Catholic priests and teachers to recite frequently a prescribed anti-Modernist oath. Modernisation as prescribed by the Modernists may have been a step too far but many practising Catholics became conscious of a need for the Church to update its rules and practice to maintain its relevance in the fast-changing world heading into the 20th century.

CHAPTER 22

20th Century

Popes

1903-14 Pius X

1914-22 Benedict XV

1922-39 Pius XI

1939-58 Pius XII

1958-63 John XXIII

1963-78 Paul VI

Aug-Sept 1968 John Paul I

1968-2005 John Paul II

As the 20th century dawned, Christianity in Europe faced accelerating secularism – in 1905, the French Parliament passed a law preventing Churches from holding any power or involvement in the state. There would be two major world wars, the second breaking new ground by involving entire populations, families and civilian infrastructure within the warring or occupied nations. The wars on a global scale included indiscriminate aerial bombing. There was recruitment and support by people from all over the empires then the loss of so many combatants and civilian casualties would leave devastated economies short of man- and now woman-power for rebuilding. It would be a century of technical, industrial, commercial and societal developments, all of which would affect religious faith and practice.

A Protestant ecumenical movement sought to bridge differences between its many denominations. The Catholic Church faced pressure to modernise and growing tensions with the Orthodox Churches. Due to missionary efforts, migration and increased travel, Christianity was spreading in other parts of the world, especially in the Far East, while competition came in the opposite direction.

This chapter will see more focus on Great Britain and the Catholic Church than has been the case since the Reformation as Britain, though not occupied, was closely involved in both the world wars. After these seismic events came a reforming Pope who called a second Vatican Council, which gave rise to briefly revived interest in the Catholic Church's activities. Ireland became an independent republic and the USA grew to capitalist super-power status, polar opposite to the communist bloc of countries that arose from the Russian Revolution. Nuclear weapons gave them both the power to destroy all life on the planet. Hope for lasting peace depended upon an apposite acronym – MAD, or Mutually Assured Destruction.

Diversity and especially women's rights grew as issues and achieved some success in this century, as did sexual and homosexual liberation.

After the Second World War Britain needed tens of thousands of workers for its new National Health Service. Resulting recruitment from across the colonies would bring major changes in ethnic and faith balances, as it had in the USA following abolition of slavery and absorption of African Americans and would in all European colonist countries as independence movements spread. Few countries had the time or foresight to establish welcome and support systems for these immigrants, whose help was so badly needed in recovering and fast-growing public service sectors such as transport, caring and health. Traditional suspicion of 'foreigners' was magnified by their visible characteristics of colour, accent, attire and faith as well as their consequent natural tendency to socialise and live together in pockets.

Finally, the long-standing issue of clerical discipline would rise again in the second half of this century as a self-imposed threat to some Christian Churches' suitability as channels for Jesus Christ's message.

Eastern Orthodox Churches

In the Eastern Mediterranean, the Young Turk Revolution took place in 1908, restoring the Ottoman Parliament, which the Sultan had suspended thirty years earlier. It proved a failure in terms of holding the old Ottoman Empire together as recent rulers on its fringes rebelled, then the Empire lost almost all its Balkan territories. This was just part of a regional transition which happened as follows.

The region was seeing a shift of national power from the religious hierarchies towards developing middle class and elites. The transition occurred initially in the Constantinople then Antioch Patriarchates, but stalled in Jerusalem and further south as the growing Arab national ambition among the middle classes of those countries compromised communal loyalty to religions.

Politicians seized the opportunity to appeal to religions for their own ends in government, so the hitherto homogeneous and firmly-based Orthodox community in so many countries in that region then split into various cultural and political groups, such as Arab (based on Antioch), Greek, various Balkan and others, as previous members of an empire took back their own national identities with confidence, carrying the 'ecumenical' structures of the Orthodox Church with them. So the Orthodox Churches' organisations became more related to nationality than the pan-national unity of the past. The result was a different kind of 'Reformation' from the Western Christian experience, which freed up the national Churches to establish their own separate bureaucracies and operate their individual autocephaly relatively unencumbered.

Russia was supportive of these developments in diplomacy, their Orthodox Church seeing them as helpful to their own ambitions based on their 'Third Rome' vision. Their government saw a gain in political influence in the region, including Ukraine, securing them more direct maritime access southwards.

Roman Catholicism

Leo XIII was succeeded by **Pope Pius X** (1903-14), who came from a poor family and won a scholarship to the Padua seminary, studying classics, philosophy and theology. As a priest he had become an advocate of Thomas Aquinas and pursued studies in canon law, while the poor health of his parish priest ensured he gained broad pastoral experience which he never forgot.

As Pope, he chose to live in poverty, piety and holiness. An ascetic and deeply caring man, he was conservative, vehemently resisting pressure to modernise the Church or adapt practices to modern life, though he sympathised in principle with the idea of using the vernacular in Mass. He presided over a low point of the Catholic Church's global influence, which was not of his doing, just the continuation of a long-term trend against which he was just another introspective leader having little outward effect. In 1907, he published an encyclical '*Pascendi Dominici Gregis*' in which he grouped all who pressed for modernisation as 'Modernists' and accused them of promoting heresy. Some of his consequent impositions included reform of seminaries and a review of studies for the priesthood with an emphasis on Thomism, updated breviary and the introduction of one catechism for all Roman Catholics. Priests and teachers were encouraged to repeat frequently an oath rejecting modernism.

In 1908, Pius X reorganised the Roman Curia, which only really needed to attend to spiritual and communication matters following the Church's loss of the Papal States in the last century.

Canon Law

Pius X's most notable contribution to Catholicism was collecting all the various laws of the Church into one document which was published in 1918 as the Code of Canon Law, a job entrusted to cardinals Eugenio Pacelli, Giacomo della Chiesa and Pietro Gasparri, the first two of whom were destined to be future popes. He also revised the rituals for betrothal and marriage. His focus was always directed inwards within the Church and he died just before World War I to be succeeded by **Pope Benedict XV** (1914-22).

In 1910, Pius X allowed communion from the age of 7, so Confirmation became the last of the initiation sacraments conferred on Catholics. Protestant Churches maintained a later first communion and this often coincided with Confirmation in the early teens. In the Eastern Orthodox Church, the three sacraments, Baptism, Eucharist and Confirmation were always included in one ceremony and remain so.

The current Catechism of the Catholic Church, quoting the Dogmatic Constitution on the Church, says, "by the sacrament of Confirmation, [the baptised] are ... enriched with a special strength of the Holy Spirit."

Ecumenical Initiatives

The Liturgical Movement had begun in the Catholic Church in the 19th century with a view to reforming worship, partly to refer back to the worship practices of the ancient Church. This had soon been replicated in the Anglican Communion as one of the aims of the Oxford Movement, who studied the history of Christian worship, how to use worship as a means of personal involvement and mission and how it may be helpful in bringing closer together those on either side of the Reformation.

In the broad Protestant community ecumenical conferences had been held in London in 1888, with 137 denominations present, then New York in 1900, followed up by the Edinburgh Missionary Conference in 1910, which yielded more decisions. The agenda was directed at agreeing tactics for overseas missions and the question of 'indigenisation' of Christianity, a topic that had presented earlier difficulties for the Catholic missionaries and hierarchy, who called it 'inculturation'.

A National Free Church Council had been formed in the 1890s, then a Federal Council of Evangelical Free Churches in 1916 which resulted in a statement of Faith and Practice from 1917 which continues to serve as its basis for membership. In 1940 the Free Church Federal Council was created from these two bodies, embracing also a number of smaller bodies. Rather than attend under the name of their denomination, local council representatives from all over England on the National Council collect under the banner of the Evangelical Free Church. The denominations include Baptists, Congregationalists, Methodists, English Presbyterians and Free Church as well as the Society of Friends, so nearly all the non-conformist Churches in England. The Free Church Federal Council advocates freedom of belief and conscience. It regards personal faith as integral to the Christian Gospel and seeks to create a safe, caring and equal society.

At its Moscow Council which ran from 1917-18, the Russian Orthodox Church had tabled on the agenda their desire for restoration of Christian unity, but then the October Revolution took place.

A series of five meetings in Malines, Belgium between 1921 and 1927, took place between French and German bishops of the Roman Catholic Church and 'High Church' representatives of the Church of England, which was not regarded by other Protestant denominations as fully 'reformed'. Referred to as "The Malines Conversation", their aim was to explore the possibility of a reunion between the two faiths. The conversations were respectful and probably helped each party understand better where the other was coming from but then as now, there seemed no sense of urgency to go further. The Church of England often struggled to reconcile the wide diversity of views of its membership, which stemmed partly from its intrinsic distribution of decision-making powers largely to each diocese, whereas the Roman Catholic structure was far more centred on the pope, who had been Italian for centuries. The latter's claim to infallibity was no help in encouraging understanding, particularly when seen in the light of history. Other sticking points included purgatory, transubstantiation and the Immaculate Conception of Mary. The exercise provided a foundation for future talks.

Following the First World War the International Missionary Council was formed, which then became the World Council of Churches in 1948. These were Protestant initiatives prior to the Second Vatican Council of the Catholic Church in the early nineteen sixties. So ecumenical movement had begun and would appear to gain further momentum during the second half of this century.

Fatima, Miracle of the Sun

Early 1917 in Portugal, three young Catholic shepherd girls who often prayed together during their duty claimed to see apparitions of an angel, followed in May by several apparitions of Mary, the mother of God holding rosary beads. In the last apparition, Mary apparently assured the girls that she would return in October and reveal herself and her identity in the same field to all present. Over 30,000 people attended on a wet day, making a quagmire of the ground. They included members of the public, press and clergy and witnessed a startling display of the clouds clearing and the sun dimming, radiating coloured light and 'dancing' in the sky, also at one point approaching the earth and drying the sodden ground.

The sheer number of witnesses was such that it is clear something remarkable took place and as a result Fatima, like Lourdes before it, became a centre for Catholic pilgrimage.

First World War

Back in the nineteen teens, tensions continued to harden between Eastern Orthodox and Roman Churches and arguably played a part in the start of WWI. Against this background in the Balkans between Orthodox Serbia and Catholic Croatia, the Catholic heir to the Austro-Hungarian Empire, Archduke Francis Ferdinand and his wife were assassinated during a visit to Sarajevo, a predominantly Orthodox city in July 1914. They were already key figures in complex political tensions and the event helped trigger a new kind of war.

Pope Pius X died soon after this assassination. His successor, Pope Benedict XV (1914-22) was a lawyer and diplomat, Cardinal Giacomo della Chiesa, one of the three cardinals involved in collating the Canon Law mentioned above. He was elected in September and headed the Church for the duration of World War I. He publicly confirmed the neutrality of the Roman Catholic Church and saw it as part of his role to work for peace.

As with Popes Pius X and Leo XIII before him, Benedict XV made symbolic protest at the Roman Question, an ongoing dispute with the Italian government regarding Papal civil authority arising from the Risorgimento, Italian Unification. This included his refusal to make the customary celebratory appearance on the balcony of St Peter's basilica for the *Urbi et Orbi*, city and world, blessing at Easter.

Foreseeing the 'suicide of Europe', Benedict XV called for a Christian truce, which was rejected by Germany and France. He continued tirelessly but in vain to press for peace and meanwhile turned efforts towards humanitarian work, organising a Vatican bureau to alleviate the hardship of prisoners of war, exchanging wounded combatants and helping feed the hunger-struck populations, with heavy emphasis on the plight of children. These all met with measurable success, accompanied by generous allocation of Church funds. Benedict also believed compulsory conscription was immoral and proposed its abolition

In 1917 Benedict tabled a 7-point peace plan. Great Britain gave it serious consideration but President Woodrow Wilson and the other Allies rejected it. On the other side, Germany and Italy remained dismissive of the Vatican, whilst Bulgaria and Austria-Hungary were favourable, so the plan was dropped.

His open struggle with warring state leaders did the moral and diplomatic standing of the Catholic Church no harm and it would become the basis of future Church responses to war, e.g. Pius XII in WWII, Paul VI on Vietnam and John-Paul II on Iraq. President Wilson included some of Benedict's 7 points in his subsequent 14-point peace plan and Benedict XV continued to work hard to bring relief to all those on both sides seriously afflicted by the war and to attempt changes in the rules of war.

Anti-Vatican sentiment in Italy, France and Germany as well as President Wilson's refusal to support Benedict XV's peace efforts, led to the Vatican's exclusion from the Paris Peace Conference. But Vatican feelings on the resulting penal conditions imposed on Germany in the Treaty of Versailles were made clear –they were excessive, likely to result in economic instability and could lead to a second such war.

Following resurgence of nationalism in Europe after the war, which threatened the Church, Pope Benedict XV issued an encyclical in 1920 arguing for moves towards European unification. He was deeply disturbed by the suffering from the Russian Revolution, subsequent famine and suppression of religion by Lenin.

Benedict achieved renewal of diplomatic relations between France and the Vatican in 1921, not long before his unexpected death. History remembers him as a caring, humanitarian and peace-seeking pope with political awareness who always sought reconciliation and harmony between peoples.

In 1914 Britain's first ambassador to the Holy See since the Reformation re-established diplomatic relations with the Vatican. This was a major step forward, signalling hope for more tolerance of Catholics, who had continued to face considerable discrimination in British society, including in employment, especially in public services and would do so for some time to come. British commanders in the war, among whom there were few, if any, Catholics were slow to learn the need to make Catholic chaplains available to the troops. They had not realised at first the importance of the sacraments to Catholics risking death daily. These are their principal source of absolution, grace and salvation and as soon as the chaplains arrived, officers noticed that these soldiers displayed a higher level of spirit and courage.

About 8 million combatants died in that war of attrition, while famine, malnutrition and epidemics killed around 9 million civilians. Dubbed The Great War, it only lived up to that in scale, death toll and individual bravery, not in any other sense, especially not in that of management.

Ever since the Reformation, the Church of England had forbidden the saying of prayers for the dead. The Reform Churches still discourage it, whereas most Catholics hold to the concept of purgatory and therefore the value of praying for the dead. They believe in the power of prayer for souls living or dead from any source to give benefit through God. The opposing view was that the dead were gone from this life, had faced the Last Judgement and been sent one of two ways. So what was the point in praying for them? During the Great War, however, that historical and theological stance began to crumble under the sheer weight of dead bodies in foreign fields, with many affected families never able to say a proper goodbye or be reunited with their loved ones, who could be offered little comfort other than prayer from back home.

Then in a cruel twist the so-called Spanish influenza pandemic which evolved from a bird 'flu, swept through the world in 1918 as the war ended. infecting many combatants, military doctors and nurses. One third of the world's population caught the virus and at least 20 million people died from it.

Peace

Following the armistice, there was strong allied pressure, especially from France to render impossible the repeat of such a war, eventually leading to the 1919 Treaty of Versailles. Among other demands it required Germany to accept their responsibility and that of her allies for causing all the loss and damage during the war, the so-called 'Guilt Clause'. Germany also had to disarm, make territorial concessions, and pay reparations amounting to a totally unaffordable cost. The British economist, John Maynard Keynes was a delegate at the Paris Peace Conference at Versailles and declared the reparation demand too harsh and likely to be counter-productive, but French Marshall Foch argued that it was too lenient. Neither side was thus satisfied by the resulting compromise, which left Germany feeling utterly humiliated. It is fair to say that the seeds of the Second World War were sewn at Versailles, a view fully matching Pope Benedict XV's expressed concerns. In 1932, the reparations were duly suspended at the Lausanne Conference.

The League of Nations was founded in 1920, born of the Paris Peace Conference at the end of WWI as an inter-governmental organisation. The aim of the League was maintenance of world peace, which apart from collective disarmament, security and channels for dispute settlement also included a code of social responsibility of each member nation towards immigrants, minorities and prisoners of war, labour conditions, drug trafficking and other issues.

Russia

In Russia, during the interim Petrograd government, it seemed that government control of the Church was all but over, so a council of the Russian Orthodox Church was called and held in the Assumption Cathedral in the Kremlin. It began in August 1917 and the head of the Provisional Government, Alexander Kerensky attended some of the sessions. A couple of months later, nearly five hundred years of Tsarist rule came to an abrupt end as Tsar Nicolas abdicated in the face of the October revolution in Petrograd (St Petersburg). Just three days after the Bolsheviks took control in Petrograd, the council agreed to restore the Moscow Patriarchy for the first time in about 300 years since Peter the Great deemed the emperor the head of the Russian Orthodox Church (ROC) instead of the Patriarch, as is the case in the Church of England. The ROC is monastically led, with all bishops being monks.

The new government of Soviet Russia declared the separation of religion from state and gave schools the right to follow any religion or none and freedom to attend services and sermons in designated church buildings, but denied the right of religious organisations to own property. When the authorities tried to force requisition of some churches and monasteries, there was popular resistance and bloodshed. Patriarch Tikhon of Moscow anathematised all perpetrators of such acts.

Civil war broke out later the same year and when the Bolshevik communists resumed power, they assassinated the immediate Royal family. In spite of the Church's efforts to remain neutral, the communist government regarded it and the clergy as anti-revolutionary. Following the Bolsheviks' success there was no place for God under the new communist leader Lenin, who oversaw severe suppression across the whole population including execution, torture, prison camps, labour camps and committal to so-called mental hospitals. Atheism was pressed on the people as the only scientific truth and it was illegal to criticise this diktat. The ideological aim of the newly established Soviet Union was to eliminate religion. Nonetheless, Russian Orthodoxy remained surprisingly strong and resilient underground.

Communism in Post-Lenin Russia

Under Lenin, an upper class autocracy had been replaced by a workers' totalitarian state which itself duly became stratified and rife with corruption, cruelty and privilege.

Lenin died in 1924 and his eventual successor was Joseph Stalin, an unfeeling and paranoid figure. Amongst other perceived enemies, Stalin targeted churches, clergy and worshippers as well as instigating a new round of iconoclasm and punishing religious dissidents by imprisonment or sending them to mental hospitals or the gulags. Then as World War II loomed, he realised the need for recruits to the armed forces and relaxed hostilities against the Orthodox Church. The 1936 Soviet constitution allowed for freedom of religion though more in theory than in practice as after the war ended there was another volte face. The endemic faith had lived on regardless, although driven underground. There were effectively two Russian Orthodox Churches, one underground and one obedient to the government with government-appointed leaders. The former was called the Catacomb Church or True Orthodox Christians. Unregistered worshippers gathered mostly in secret home groups. The latter was the Moscow Patriarchate or Soviet Orthodox Church. There was a third force, ROCOR, (Russian Orthodox Church Outside Russia), which publicly opposed the Moscow Patriarchate and supported the True Orthodox Church.

Women's Rights

In the late 19th and early 20th centuries, there were growing numbers of nations recognising the right of women to vote and stand for participation in government. Australia was the first nation to award them full franchise in 1902. Meanwhile in Britain, by 1918, all bar one of the Chartists demands had largely been met, the only exception being their rather unrealistic proposal for annual elections. The world was becoming a fairer and freer place. The Church of England took its 'pillar of the establishment' position of opposing the suffragette movement, though sympathetic members made their views known and some organised in favour of the suffragettes. There was much debate in the Catholic Church and Cardinal Francis Bourne, Archbishop of Westminster declared that Church members were free to vote with their own consciences, without guiding them in any particular direction. By 1920, women had gained universal franchise in most European countries and the USA. Notable European exceptions were France, Italy and Greece, where it was delayed until the 1940s and Portugal, Switzerland and Spain until the second half of the century.

Social Changes, USA

During the 1920s, following WWI, society hungered for relaxing leisure activities. They were supported by developments in recorded music and cine-films. This led to the establishment of dance halls, cinemas and popular entertainment, coinciding with ground-breaking changes in dress and behaviour, especially for women, so emancipated after gaining their franchise. Americans eagerly grasped and developed these freedoms further which led to a wave of open, often alcohol-fuelled over-indulgence while in the shadows crime and corruption grew and social problems rose as prisons and poor-houses became filled. This led the USA government to try the bold initiative of Prohibition in 1920, outlawing "production, importation, transportation, sale and consumption of alcoholic beverages". The aim was to reduce crime and corruption, reduce the tax burden of prisons and poor-houses and to improve social standards, health and hygiene in America. However, as well as limiting valued personal freedom, prohibition saw a spectacular rise in gangs, organised crime and corruption although its unmitigated failure was not recognised for a decade. It was repealed in 1933, by which time organised crime had made a fortune and was well placed to finance alternative ventures.

Another reaction to Prohibition among some sections of American society, was a wave of conservatism to revive old values, which resulted in a stricter kind of Christianity that became known as Fundamentalism. This spread through the 'Bible Belt', which includes Utah and a block of conservative south western states but excluding Florida, where the Bible was firmly and literally believed. These states passed laws including bans on short swimming costumes and gambling on Sundays and they were so affronted by Charles Darwin's theory of evolution that in six states it became illegal to teach it.

Meanwhile in some northern states there were still localised tight communities of Mennonites, Amish and Hutterites dating back to the 17th century, who rejected use of all modern equipment for transport, entertainment and in the home, which limited their available employment and led them to a high degree of self-sufficiency. The Hutterites took this to a Kibbutz-type level, whereby the whole community works together. The Amish also live in tight communities, but each family works its own farm or business.

When it came to modernity, the Amish were more extreme and to this day they will not connect to the electricity grid or run motor vehicles, so they have no domestic technology, television, or appliances and can daily be seen traveling to town in their horse- or mule-drawn buggies. The Hutterites and Mennonites do use powered vehicles and tractors as well as electricity in the home. They will also wear more modern, though modest dress, whereas the Amish still hold strictly to the distinctive full length 17th century style of clothing for both men and women.

Irish Independence

Pressure in Catholic Ireland grew for independence of the whole island from Britain, led by Michael Collins and Eamon de Valera with the occasional eruption such as the Easter Rising in 1916. The mainly Protestant northern province of Ulster opposed this, remained pro-union with Britain and formed the Ulster Volunteer Force with their regional leadership in Belfast. Contrary to the wishes of Dublin, Ulster dropped three of the historical nine counties to secure a 66% Protestant majority, anything less than which Belfast felt would have left them vulnerable to future all-Ireland unity. In a Dublin election at the end of 1918, *Sinn Féin* won a landslide victory and in 1919 open guerrilla warfare broke out between the Irish Republican Army (IRA) and British security forces. A treaty was signed between the parties at the end of 1921 creating the Irish Free State, which duly became the Irish Republic comprising 26 of the 32 counties in Ireland.

In retaining Ulster and continuing intolerance of Catholics, Britain was laying the ground for troubles ahead which would carry a heavy price in economics and lives. Roman Catholicism was the faith of the overwhelming majority in the Republic and became heavily influential in the government, being the principal national provider of education and hospital services, which were internationally admired for their excellence. The quality of their graduates, doctors and nurses was highly marketable and they continued to emigrate and spread widely in the diaspora, especially through the English-speaking world.

Orthodoxy, Istanbul, Mount Athos

Constantinople had been an important centre of Islam as well as the seat of the senior Patriarch of Eastern Orthodoxy for some centuries and following the First World War, a conference was held in Lausanne to agree an equitable division of lands, populations and rights between Greece and the new Turkish Republic before withdrawal of the Western powers' High Commissioners from the area. The Ottoman Empire was now defunct and the Treaty of Lausanne, signed in July 1923, determined a frigid peace between Greece and Turkey that involved an interchange of some territories and some Islamic and Christian communities, with an agreement to some remaining in place in both countries without disturbance or ill-treatment. The Greek Orthodox Patriarch would continue to have his seat in what was now Istanbul. In the spirit of this agreement, the beautiful Hagia Sophia, built in the 4th century as a great cathedral, then converted to a mosque in the 16th, became a museum some ten years later.

The autonomous state of Mount Athos has been associated with Christianity since at least the 3rd century and became an ideal monastic retreat from the 8th century. By the early 20th century about half the resident monks on the Athos peninsula were Russian Orthodox, swelled by emigration to escape communist pressure on the Church in Russia. The ban remained on access to the peninsula by women and beardless youths. All hermits and monks were attached to one of the twenty or so monasteries there and followed their rules. Their worship and services were close to those of the early Christians. Athos has been designated a World Heritage site and while still within Greece, it is named the 'Autonomous Monastic State of the Holy Mountain'. When Greece later joined the European Union, Mount Athos in its autonomy was excluded from the obligation of free movement of goods and people. There is some tourism nowadays but it is strictly controlled by the resident monks.

Stock Market Crash and the Great Depression

The carefree 'Roaring Twenties' came to an abrupt end in 1929 as America suffered its worst ever stock market crash. During 1928, all industrial shares made record advances, tempting many individuals to decide to invest. As the first half of 1929 saw even larger share gains, reported enthusiastically by the media, people piled onto the bandwagon, many of them borrowing heavily to invest and banks were happy to fuel the boom by lending up to two thirds of the face value of shares being bought. The bubble burst and the decline in share values began in September. London's Stock Exchange had suffered a crash the previous year. Huge numbers of shareholders began to panic and sell, fearing insolvency due to their heavy leverage. This caused share prices to drop. News travelled quite slowly, especially to outlying areas in those days, but over 28th-29th October, share values plummeted by 25% overall, a record to this day. Wheat stocks were high and the price plummeted, so farmers faced a serious income problem. This perfect financial storm resulted in a wave of suicides and worldwide unemployment and poverty resulted.

There followed a decade of austerity during which the two countries most affected were Germany, with its war reparations and USA, whose key great plains area farmers were then struck by the 'dustbowl' drought. There was mass migration west to California, but here too the depression had left widespread poverty, so not nearly enough jobs for the expectant migrants. Economies only improved as the international political situation declined. Governments multiplied capital expenditure and jobs in preparation for another war, which brought new challenges for families as many of their bread-winners were recruited into the forces.

With millions of people unemployed or having lost their life savings in America, the clergy hoped for a significant reverse of decades of decline in church worship between WWI and the depression. There was a bounce of about 5% during the thirties but a perceived drop in general piety especially among the struggling under-30-year-olds, who failed to see religion as relevant to them. The bulk of church attendance was accounted for by middle-aged women. One growth area in the USA was preaching by radio, with Father Charles Coughlan gaining celebrity status.

In spite of the depression, strong technical progress was made in bringing sound to the movies, long-distance commercial aviation, radio entertainment into homes, industrial and agricultural machinery and volume production methods in industry.

Authoritarian Regimes

To relieve the desperation of their citizens, some nations elected authoritarian leaders, including Italy with the fascist Benito Mussolini, Spain with General Franco and Germany's Third Reich. Weaker nations were being occupied, such as China by Japan and Ethiopia by Italy.

Political happenings in Germany in the thirties are noteworthy as the country sought a leader who may restore their pride and expunge the shame and privations heaped upon them in the Versailles Treaty. Consequently Adolf Hitler, who led the strongly nationalist socialist 'Nazi' party, became their leader in 1932. He soon demonstrated his wish to 'purify' the German people as well as his antipathy to Jews and minority ethnic people, through the Nuremburg Laws. He also set about rebuilding military strength and armaments. Germany annexed Austria in 1938 and threatened to invade Poland, claiming they needed lebensraum, living space. This brought Europe once more to the brink of war.

Roman Catholic Church

In November 1919, Benedict XV had appealed to Catholics everywhere to support generously the Catholic missions, also saying that the missions should foster local culture and not impose European norms. He died in 2022 to be succeeded by **Pope Pius XI** (1922-39).

In 1929, Pope Pius XI and Benito Mussolini finally achieved a negotiated settlement of the 'Roman Question' between the united Italian nation and the Roman Church. It was agreed in the Lateran Pacts that the Catholic Church retain a hundred acres of property in Rome including the Vatican of which the pope would be considered supreme ruler. That territory was accorded valuable tax concessions and the extra compensation for all the land and property lost in the revolution was set at nearly one hundred million dollars. Thus Pius XI became the Vatican State's first sovereign ruler. The estate at Castel Gandolfo also remained as papal property carrying extra-territorial status similar to Mount Athos in Greece. Meanwhile, Vatican Radio was established in 1931, broadcasting in many languages and for the first time giving the

Church leadership the opportunity to communicate directly with its global congregation.

During Pius XI's papacy after World War I, the German Weimar republic required careful attention and he appointed his erstwhile colleague from the work on the Canons, Archbishop Eugenio Pacelli, as Nuncio to Bavaria in 1917. In the absence of a Nuncio to Prussia, Pacelli acted effectively for all of Germany. He was a Doctor of Canon Law and learned the German language. After the humiliating settlement of WWI, the Protestant-leaning German government sought to assume greater control over faith schools in which the Catholic Church had a considerable investment. In order to protect its rights, the Catholic Church negotiated an agreement whereby they held strong influence in the schooling but in return agreed that clergy would refrain from future political involvement.

Pacelli was appointed Cardinal Secretary of State for foreign policy and relations in 1930. The Weimar Republic transmuted into National Socialist (Nazi), Germany as Hitler became Chancellor in 1933. Hitler was hostile to the Church and took aggressive action against Catholic organisations, schools and publishers. Cardinal Pacelli made representations and secured a further agreement, which would be sorely tested by violations over the next three years. German bishops felt the faithful were left in confusion by the apparent approval the Vatican seemed thus to give the Nazis. Pacelli wanted to correct this impression so with the help of the German bishops he wrote a letter condemning Nazis excesses and atheism.

Pope Pius XI, already a sick man, published Pacelli's letter as an encyclical, written unusually in German '*Mit Brennender Sorge*' (With Burning Anxiety), which was leafleted widely and read from all pulpits in Germany on Palm Sunday 1937, denouncing the Nazis' racism, extreme nationalism and profound hostility to Christ and his Church, which he saw as raising the possibility of religious conflict and carnage in Germany. The following year, after Kristallnacht, it is now known that Pius XI wrote strongly condemning Nazi anti-Semitism, but he was frail by then and this writing never emerged from the Vatican. He died in 1939 just before outbreak of the Second World War.

Forty years after Pope Leo XIII's encyclical *Rerum Novarum* on the condition of workers, defending private property rights and collective bargaining, Pope Pius XI had launched the Catholic Church's social strategy for the technological era in 1931, addressed anew the ethical aspects of social and economic interaction in the depth of the great depression of the thirties. As the Nazi party grew in Germany, the Church again raised issues around individual rights, dignity and freedom. One pillar of Pius XI's ethic was 'subsidiarity', a belief that decision-making should be made at the most 'local' level possible in hierarchies of State, big business, union, local authority, community etc.

Pius XI warned of dangers to individual liberty and dignity that lay in the opposite extremes of capitalism and communism. He concurred with Leo XIII's view that economic forces alone cannot create a just society. Just as class battle cannot unite human society, nor can free competition ever bring absolute economic order. Only if rights are balanced with duties can either begin to work properly. So Pius XI supported independent arbitration in industrial disputes. He had condemned radical left-wing politics in an earlier encyclical and when pressed to clarify whether this extended to milder forms of socialism he placed the Catholic position somewhere between free-market capitalism to the right and state socialism to the left.

Second World War

While the arms race to counter the threat of war in the second half of the 1930s helped reinvigorate economies it did nothing to ease the likelihood of conflict. A rapid succession of events ensued. The Nazis acted to create an internal atmosphere of national crisis and vulnerability which included clandestinely setting fire to the Reichstag, the seat of German government. This enabled them to take over with enhanced powers in the guise of protecting national security. Concentration camps were opened to imprison Jews, communists and political opponents without trial. An Enabling Act was passed with promises of peace and full employment which secured virtual dictatorship powers for Hitler.

A boycott was soon imposed on all Jewish shops, with storm troopers of the 'SA brown shirts', Hitler's intimidating *Sturmabteilung* posted outside them to dissuade sympathisers. This was followed by successive acts of legislation restricting Jews, such as allowing only Aryans to be employed in civil service, university or government posts, or as doctors and dentists with state insurance. Jews were also banned from public entertainment and cultural activities such as literature, art, concerts, theatre and cinemas. German university students burned 'un-German' books by hitherto revered authors such as Einstein and Freud, because they included ideas contrary to Nazism. Germany then left the League of Nations.

By 1934-35, the SA had become a lawless force lacking discipline, having developed their own revolutionary tendencies. Hitler was disturbed by this and used Himmler's SS to lead the 'night of the long knives' in which hundreds of SA leaders were assassinated or imprisoned for execution. His ruthlessness prepared Germans for the next steps. When President Hindenburg died, Hitler assumed the title of Fuhrer, outright leader of the nation. He stripped resident Jews of all rights then introduced conscription of young German men to the forces, running roughshod over the Treaty of Versailles. The rest of Europe looked on as the dark clouds gathered and while Mussolini's Italian army over-ran Ethiopia in 1936, General Franco in Spain replaced royalty as Head of State in 1939 during the Spanish Civil War.

German troops moved to re-militarise the Rhineland in another breach the Treaty of Versailles. Amid all this, the Olympic Games went ahead in Berlin. Then in a secret conference, Hitler shared plans to gain territory for *lebensraum* and protect borders by annexing at least Austria and Czechoslovakia by invasion. In 1938, Hitler announced Anschluss (union) with Austria. Neville Chamberlain, British Prime Minister, met Hitler in Munich with the aim of ensuring peace in Europe and returned with reassuring words which would prove unfounded. Hitler then took Czechoslovakia, first occupying its largely sympathetic Sudetenland region, home to many people of German origin.

The infamous Kristallnacht followed in November 1938, when the sound of broken shop-front glass echoed in many German towns as Jewish businesses were attacked and synagogues burned.

In 1939, the Nazis made an alliance with Italy and a peace pact with Soviet Union. Britain signed a Mutual Assistance treaty with Poland a week before the Nazis invaded it. Britain began evacuating civilians from London and together with France, Australia and New Zealand, declared war on Germany.

Taizé

In 1939, a Swiss Protestant pastor Roger Schütz (1915-2005) was recuperating from tuberculosis in the southern French hamlet of Taizé. When war broke out, France was soon invaded and divided in two, leaving Vichy France in the south under the puppet leadership of Général Pétain and German occupied France in the north.

Taizé was conveniently close to the demarcation line in the south-east of France. Schütz was moved by the plight of displaced people and he acquired a house in Taizé which he set up as a refuge with his sister, Généviéve, but they all eventually had to scatter when word came that the Nazis were coming. Once the war was over, Roger and Généviéve returned from Switzerland to Taizé with some young 'brothers' to help children orphaned in the war. On Sundays they sometimes invited German prisoners of war from a nearby camp to join a service and have discussion and refreshment. On Easter Sunday 1949, seven of the young brothers committed themselves to lives of celibacy and simplicity in the cause, creating an ecumenical community, one of the early returns of Protestants to monastery-style life. As the community expanded, over the 1952-3 winter, Roger wrote a Rule for them. It has since grown to over 100 brothers of Protestant and Catholic backgrounds from thirty nations. Some live in disadvantaged places in Asia, Africa and South America. Top religious leaders from many faiths have visited Taizé, including Pope John Paul II, Patriarch Bartholomew, Lutheran bishops and the Archbishop of Canterbury. Scottish Brother Thomas (1939-2019) established close links between the Taizé community and the ecumenical community on Iona in Scotland.

A thousand or so young people, mostly between 18 and 35, of many faiths from all over the world visit, camp or stay at Taizé every year when a wide programme of events and study groups is offered and services of chant and meditation attract large attendances.

Wartime Pope

Pius XI was succeeded by Cardinal Pacelli, who took the name **Pope Pius XII** (1939-58). He became the object of considerable criticism for a perceived sympathy with Fascism and Nazism before and during WW2. Given his earlier efforts as original author of his predecessor's encyclical 'With Burning Anxiety', this was perhaps unfair, although his lengthy posting in Germany had understandably left in him some affection for its people. He also had to tread a careful path back in Italy, a country allied to Germany. Mussolini was after all the Fascist ruler on whose good will the Vatican depended heavily.

Pius XII's own first encyclical, *Summi Pontificatus*, subtitle 'On unity of Human Society', issued in October 1939, opposed both racial prejudice and claims to superiority on the basis of every living person's common ultimate ancestry and supernatural destiny. These commonalities or unities demand mutual solidarity and charity, a demand sealed by Jesus' sacrifice on the cross for all sins. While observing the normal generality of judgments, when it went on to attack totalitarianism, the encyclical unusually makes specific mention of the attacks by Germany on Poland. Pius XII's view on totalitarianism was that it leads to violating the rights of other states and people, and works contrary the cause of peace.

During the war itself, he was accused of being a Nazi sympathiser and anti-Semitic, but the Nazis never saw him that way, describing him as a "mouthpiece for Jewish war criminals". Nor did his writings display any such leanings and at the end of 1940 he asked the Congregation of the Holy Office to put out a decree against the mass murders and the policy of Aryan racial purification. The German bishops though, held on to their positions of influence during the war due to their general acquiescence. With only one or two exceptions, they expressed no opposition either to the regime or its methods, or to the crimes of euthanasia and extermination against those with learning difficulties, Jews and Romany people, leaving front line Catholic troops and officers bereft of recourse to counsel or comfort from their Church. Pope Pius XII was criticised for not speaking out more often or more loudly against the Holocaust. There was no help from the Catholic Church to any German military personnel in its flock who had died in or lived through the conflict with troubled consciences for a cause they may have doubted. Pius XII never spoke out personally to an international public on the issue, though he did publicly condemn anti-Semitic acts on Vatican Radio. He held the Vatican in a strictly neutral role during the war which was no simple matter for a tiny landlocked state within Mussolini's fascist Italy actively at war on the Nazi side.

In 1943 Pius XII published his ideas on the role of the Church in the encyclical *Mystici Corporis Christi*, Mystical body of Christ, in which he described the Church as not just a bureaucratic institution but a live and active entity of which clergy and laiety are all members, a theme later to be developed by Vatican II. He followed similar lines to his predecessor in his social teachings, extending them to all occupations including politics, military and domestic as well as giving guidance in fields such as medicine, sport, media, science and law. He had an impressively wide span of technical interests and related all of them to Catholic ethical thinking. Medicine and health care was but one example and he presented many talks giving moral guidance to practitioners and researchers, covering their responsibilities regarding patient and family rights, mental illness and treatment, moral and medical responsibilities relating to terminal illness and honesty with information.

The war ended in 1945, with surviving active combatants slowly being demobilised and returning home, some with life-changing injuries or missing limbs, many to bombed-out houses. People on both sides were dazed and everything initially happened in slow motion, including the rebuilding efforts. European economies were in a parlous state with a shortage of manpower and many single mother families. So much had changed for ever.

Dead Sea Scrolls (1946-56)

In 1946, a Bedouin shepherd found an ancient earthenware jar containing a fragile manuscript scroll in a cave in Wadi Qumran near the West Bank of the River Jordan about a mile west of the northern shore of the Dead Sea. This triggered an excited search by scholars helped by local shepherds which unearthed from the cave complex many more old and sacred scrolls, which experts dated from about 300BC to 100 AD. There were also some coins issued between about 130BC to 70AD.

The texts had enormous value in terms of history, religion and linguistics. They included the largest find of such old manuscripts of the Hebrew Bible (Tanakh) and content of the Old Testament of the Christian Bible that had long been known and accepted as canonical from later manuscripts. There was also evidence of wider religious thinking in the years before the birth of Jesus Christ. About 40% of the decipherable scrolls discovered were copies of texts from Hebrew Scripture, while about 30% were from the period since the building of the Second Temple (c.500BC). Others cover the beliefs and rules of wider Judaic sects.

Most of the texts were written on parchment, some on papyrus or copper sheet. The language is predominantly Hebrew but with some Aramaic and Greek. When compared with the previous oldest manuscripts from over 1100 years later, their transmission was found to be almost flawless.

This find gave a welcome boost to understanding and authentication of the Bible at a time of growing scepticism. A much smaller but older (c. 600BC) find was since found on the site of Ketef Hinnom, south of Jerusalem in 1979, which had fragments from the Book of Numbers.

Post-World War II

Radical changes in society affected most of the countries involved in the war, so the following description of post-war United Kingdom was not untypical of other participants. The USA recovered more quickly on account of its size, wealth and demography and its distance from the theatre of war, so it continued to lead in production and commercialisation of the fruits of new technologies, propelling it to world leader. It also helped through the Marshall Plan to fund European and particularly German agricultural and industrial infrastructure recovery with the added aim of preventing the spread of communism.

During the war, governments had commandeered many large houses, public buildings, factories and valuable assets. Evacuees were forced upon owners of larger homes, who found themselves short of domestic staff. With men absent due to conscription or loss, the ladies of these houses had to turn to and do work in the home and cook, which many had never done before, having to learn as they went. The less well-off developed a wartime mentality of togetherness, looking out for and helping each other. As the war ended, it became clear that life could never again return to how it had been.

Women had also played a vital part in replacing men to keep production lines running during the war in addition to their family and domestic roles. This had introduced many of them to a first taste of employment who would press for its continuation after the war, a significant step towards greater participation of women in the economy and social work. Many men returning from the war needed new employment, so there was much jostling for scarce jobs. Domestic service opportunities had reduced because middle class families could no longer afford pre-war staff levels in their homes and householders had now learned to do these tasks themselves. This would create a market for new appliances.

Pre-war, in spite of the depression, strong technical progress had been made in bringing long-distance commercial aviation, sound to movies, radio entertainment into people's homes, industrial and agricultural machinery and volume production methods in industry, which would make domestic appliances more affordable, although initially only the wealthier could yet afford these.

Post-war, the pace of life increased as people became genuinely busier, packing more and varied activity into their lives. As prayers of thanksgiving for peace subsided, more pressing worldly matters arose. Weekends were less protected with round-the-clock operation of factories, which beneficially affected productivity more than church attendance. Employment in personal services had declined, such as tailoring on account of the growth of 'off-the-peg' suits and dresses. With the loss of manpower from war casualties and the need to rebuild the country's infrastructure and economy as well as to provide essential services, employment levels began to rise to the point where there was a shortage of labour. This was not helped by the requirement on all young men to serve two years of National Service in the forces after leaving school. This helped women's employment and the government turned to colonial countries to fill the gap.

So Britain opened its doors to immigrants from the Commonwealth, encouraging them to come and help provide labour to rebuild and man its services, industries and infrastructure, such as rail and bus transport. Early ones came aboard the ship 'Empire Windrush' in 1948, the same year that the National Health Service was launched, a major social advance, guaranteeing free health care to all according to their need, regardless of their means. This created a need for more qualified doctors and nurses. The population of Muslims in the Commonwealth was nearly double that of Christians, so numbers of devout members of this relatively unknown faith arrived, for whom there were few facilities for its practice in Britain.

As industry recovered and grew, the proliferation of relatively affordable vacuum cleaners, refrigerators, washing machines and other aids helped to reduce the burden in homes and allow more time for paid work or leisure for all adults.

1950s

In 1950, the Shops Act eased some restrictions on shops opening on a Sunday. It allowed a limited extension to what newsagents could sell on a Sunday, but pressure grew to include a wider variety of shops, leading to a 1992 Act against strong opposition from religious lobbies who knew this would only be the beginning of a process. With growing middle classes and increased social mobility, then with cheap package holidays abroad, more people discovered the freedom in other European countries for Sunday trading, sport and entertainment. As popular spectator sports began to include Sundays in their fixture lists in the UK, people also pressed for similar rules to apply to leisure and shopping.

Sunday sport spread to children, often involving parental support, which began a decline in regular church attendance on a Sunday morning. Children were becoming more assertive in family life, and pushing boundaries in a way not seen in Europe in the past.

With plentiful electric record players, popular music grew as an industry and welcomed Rock and Roll in the latter half of the 1950s, led by Bill Haley and the Comets. Youth embraced new freedoms as prosperity grew in most of the Western world.

The Churches had resisted the various laws that they saw as affecting Sunday worship, such as Sunday trading, but social pressure prevailed. Pope Pius XII was a thinking man of his time and fast-developing technologies including health and space exploration came under his scrutiny for their social implications. Even the biblically designated seventh day as a rest day had become one for family leisure and sports activities which clashed with Church attendance. The 1960s approached amid a wave of optimism, bringing even more unfamiliar challenges for the Churches to face.

Second Vatican Council, Pope John XXIII

Global post-war changes called for serious soul-searching within religious circles. Pope Pius XII died in 1958 and the ensuing conclave took 11 ballots to decide on his successor, reflecting the diversity of opinion on ways to tackle the prevailing challenges. The surprise choice was a 76-year-old Cardinal priest, Angelo Roncalli from a working family of fourteen children. His parents had been simple sharecroppers, living off the crops gleaned from working on a plot of land, whose owner accepted a share of the crops as rent. He chose the name **Pope John XXIII** (1958-63) and proved to be a refreshingly insightful and egalitarian pope capable of springing interesting surprises. He soon dispelled any idea that he was just a stop-gap pope due to his age by serving notice within three months from election of his intention to convene a Second Vatican Council. This caught the interest of a broad swathe of Christian Churches hoping for inspiration as to the way forward. Nor was John XXIII about to disappoint them.

In the meantime, John XXIII did not waste any of the precious time remaining to him in taking his vision for the Church as far as possible. He entered the international arena with particular focus on '*Ostpolitik*', addressing Communist countries in Eastern Europe. His ecumenical efforts included engaging with Eastern Orthodox Churches as well as promoting Christian unity with other denominations. He introduced some fresh thinking in formulating new policies regarding worship, social and political matters. He held a clear objective to modernise the Catholic Church and equip it for a more effective pastoral role in the context of the fast-changing society of the time, at the same time making it more credible in dialogue regarding affairs of state. He appointed several cardinals, taking the total number beyond the generally accepted maximum of 70 at the time to 85, also increasing their global diversity by appointing the first cardinals to come from Africa, the Philippines and Japan.

Back in 1845, John Henry Newman had referred directly to Jesus Christ's teachings in writing his 'Essay on the Development of Christian Doctrine'. He was far from alone in this, but his book played an influential part in the Second Vatican Council dealing with the role of the Catholic Church in the modern world.

Vatican II opened in October 1962, introduced by Pope John, who outlined its fundamental aim as imbuing all Christians with a new enthusiasm, joy and serenity of mind in the unreserved acceptance of the entire Christian Faith; also reviving evangelising mission so that the teaching of Jesus shall be more widely known, deeply understood and effective in people's moral lives. He also sought to soften the Church's centralised institutional tendencies as well as clerical self-aggrandisement, elaborate decoration and vestments, making it more relevant to developing nations and the poor – a poor Church for the poor, led by the gospel of Christ. He expressed a wish to "throw open the windows of the Church" and let in fresh air. Over 2000 people were present at most sessions, making it the greatest ecumenical council in history.

Many representatives of other Christian Churches were in attendance, with seventeen Orthodox Churches and most Protestant denominations sending observers. Over a dozen commissions were set up to study specific topics, each having 24 members. There was an initial delay following requests to rebalance the members, felt to have been too biased towards southern European cardinals. Once that was settled, the council was adjourned for the work of the commissions to take place with a view to reconvening in 1963.

This was delayed by the sad death the following June of this modernist Pope John XXIII from stomach cancer. In his brief tenure he had won many admirers and followers and made an enormous impact both within and outside the Catholic Church. He was seen to have something in common with Jesus and the apostles, with a passion for the equality of all people as children of God. His wide council agenda would have been better covered had he lived to see it through, as it ended leaving so much unfinished business.

Pope John XXIII was soon succeeded by **Pope Paul VI** (1963-71) who insisted that the council continue. He added to the list of invitees and removed the requirement for secrecy around the general sessions, in keeping with the council's pastoral nature. He also reduced the number of subjects on the draft agenda and saw it through three more years.

Pope Paul VI opened the second session of Vatican II, emphasising four objectives: to define more fully the nature of the Church and the role of bishops; to renew the Church; to restore unity among all Christians and seek pardon for Catholic contributions to separation; to begin a dialogue with the contemporary world. There would be four sessions in all and the broad outcomes were:

- Stressing the centrality of Easter and the 'Paschal mystery', i.e. the passion, death and resurrection of Christ. Some changes were made to the liturgical calendar.
- Changes to the liturgy of Mass, notably that it could use the vernacular instead of Latin, so all congregants could better participate, although Latin may still be used.
- Greater participation of lay people in parish work and in the liturgy such as readings and intercessions from the altar.

- The Council was a universal call to holiness. Whilst the Roman Catholic Church was the one directly descended from Jesus through St Peter as in its Creed, it acknowledged that "many elements of sanctification and truth are to be found outside its confines".
- The central role of divine Scripture should be revived in the Church's clerical and lay membership, with continuing work on and production of vernacular versions of the Bible.
- The collective collegial role of bishops under the leadership of the pope was revived in importance.

As a council it was unusual in what it did not do – there were neither new dogmas of faith nor prohibitions. But it offered a blueprint for the Church of the day, which was frequently referenced during the tenure of Paul VI, but then more or less rolled up and shelved for half a century.

The council decided that Mass would in future be held with the priest using the local vernacular rather than Latin language, which met mixed reactions from the faithful. Communion could be taken standing up rather than kneeling and served into the hand rather than direct to the tongue. Clerical vestments should be less elaborate than they had become and church altars which had tended to become more ornate than is strictly liturgically correct, had to be simpler and reconfigured to hold a 'table' behind which the celebrants would stand facing the congregation to say Mass or Benediction, making elevation of the Holy Sacrament more visible to the congregation. A more modern aesthetical atmosphere could also be introduced into the church with the use of contemporary liturgical music, instruments and art.

The changes in form brought services closer to those of the early Church, with greater sense of communal participation and enhanced feeling of welcome and access to Christ and the Sacrament.

As the council drew to a close in 1965, a group of bishops met together in the catacombs and made the 'Pact of the Catacombs'. In this they resolved to renounce excessive personal possessions, elaborate vestments, power and grand titles and to focus on the poor and needy. This was fully in line with some of the late Pope John XXIII's objectives for the council.

Clerical Vestments

The vestments priests wear in altar services mostly originate from the clothes of the Roman people, with some having roots in ancient Jewish vestments. Over the centuries the chasuble and stole have become of richer fabric and more highly decorated, far removed from the simple example of Christ. The question arises whether this was for the greater glory of God or aggrandisement of the clergy.

Cassock – neck to ankle length, long-sleeve base garment developed from that the Romans wore under their togas, usually black or red, worn by clergy and choirboys.

Alb – lighter ankle-length long sleeve tunic, usually white cotton or linen material with cincture, rope belt. This common every-day wear for 1st century Romans was adopted by Christian leaders for anonymity.

Surplice – an alternative or additional over-garment similar in colour and material to the alb, but only knee-length and with wider arms.

Stole – like a long scarf in silk or similar, worn over the back of the neck and hanging down the front of the surplice to below knee level. Senior Romans wore similar as a sign of authority.

Maniple was originally a type of handkerchief used by the priest.

Chasuble – outermost vestment worn over the alb and stole by the priest and deacons in Eucharistic services. It derives from a type of Roman coat, being more or less a long oval in shape with a hole in the centre through which the head protrudes as the ends hang front and rear to around knee length. Usually of fine silk material or similar, in different colours according to the liturgical season.

Cope – a circular liturgical vestment in similar material to the chasuble but larger, usually ankle-length.

Zucchetto – a skull cap commonly worn by bishops, cardinals and pope.

Pallium (RC and Eastern Orthodox only) – a narrow wool band decorated with six black crosses, with pendants front and rear. The pope wears one and traditionally gives one to Archbishops on appointment.

Preaching Bands or tabs (some Protestant clergy only) – two rectangular pieces of white cloth which hang, spreading downwards from the collar of the cassock.

Clerical collar – this is a fairly recent tradition. In the sixteenth century, it became fashionable for men to turn down their collars and clergy followed suit. The clerical collar was adapted by a Scottish Presbyterian minister in the 19th century as a starched cotton or linen strip, now usually plastic, joined at the back and worn with a cassock. It allowed easy fitment of preaching tabs. Cassocks now usually have a collaret with a gap at the front to display the clerical collar

There was still a large proportion of the public who held a fascination if not commitment to religion and Hollywood spotted mileage in this. In a 1963 Otto Preminger film 'The Cardinal' the lead role, an Australian cardinal, whose ministry it followed, was confronted by most of the noteworthy Catholic moral dilemmas through his scripted career in the Church, bringing them to the attention of a wider audience, though more as entertainment than proselytisation. There were other epic biblical films such as The Robe etc.

Paul VI's papacy continued to oversee comprehensive and far-reaching reforms in Church practice and worship. As early as August 1964 in his encyclical *Ecclesiam Suam*, "The Church in the Modern World" Paul VI outlined a novel and refreshing vision for the Church. It included stress on the importance of dialogue between the Catholic Church, the world and other faiths in its saving mission, also conveying supportive signals to the broader ecumenical work which was becoming a significant feature of this century.

The first oral contraceptives had been released to the public in 1960 amid growing concern about over-population, especially in poorer parts of the world. Pope John XXIII set up a commission in 1963 to consider the issues of birth control and population. Pope Paul VI augmented this and his resulting encyclical *Humanae Vitae*, On Human Life, in 1968 raised disappointment and controversy both within and outside the Catholic Church, as its ban on the use of contraceptives was perceived to run counter to the spirit of Vatican II. Many young Catholics were surprised and widely dismayed by this as they struggled to support growing families, having held hopes of a more tolerant and reliable approach than just approving the natural 'rhythm method'. This led to conscientious rejection by many who continued to worship as Catholics. Others felt unsupported by the Church in the challenges of the modern world and just drifted away.

There had long been prohibition of artificial contraception by all Christian Churches, but under social and membership pressure, some had yielded. The Church of England for example had given conditional approval at their 1930 Lambeth Conference.

The Catholic Church regards marriage as a blessed state with the principal objective of procreation, with which contraception or sterilisation interferes. The Church held that separation of procreation from marital sexual relations would lower moral standards, lead to infidelity and reduce womanhood to a mere instrument of man's desires. Contraception could also be misused by governments, as for example in Germany's Third Reich, India's transistor radio and China's one child per family policies. God has mastery over life and death, so it declared both contraception and sterilisation as wrong. Yet it approved the 'rhythm method', which involved self-control in avoiding sex during the wife's monthly fertile period.

Humanae Vitae also declared firmly that any intervention that puts life at risk between conception and natural death is contrary to God's plan, restating its condemnation of abortion.

1960s

The 'Sixties' became known as the 'Permissive Society' decade as they featured Hippies; sex with wider availability of contraception; and drugs with their accompanying psychedelia, influencing much of the art, music and fashion of the time. After four decades of austerity, war then ongoing food rationing and the privations of the early fifties, comparative relaxation brought improving prosperity and the music and social scenes were felt to be intensely liberating. The Press made much of 'decadent youth' 1960s.

The world scene held some serious contributing factors. From the 1950s, Russia, the United States and the UK built stockpiles of nuclear weapons, giving each of those nations the capability of destroying humanity. This led to a stand-off that became known as the 'Cold War', each arguing that the resulting 'mutual assured destruction' with its apposite acronym was the best insurance against future war. So life for the youth of this era could be perceived to be of very limited duration and the fault seemed to lie with their elders whose example they saw as unworthy of respect. Christian Churches were hardly vocal on the matter, although a few notable members of clergy joined protests. The Campaign for Nuclear Disarmament (CND), established in 1957, began the Easter Aldermaston Marchers in 1959. Aldermaston, home to the Atomic Weapons Research Establishment was 52 miles from Trafalgar Square, the route between them seeing the four-day marches. In 1960 it was particularly heavily advertised, attracting tens of thousands of marchers. These marches reflected realistic justified concern for the future of the human race.

Wider availability of reliable contraception for women helped liberate them further and the feminist movement for full equality rolled out seriously. With easy availability of contraception, consensual 'recreational' sex spread as did the use of mind-affecting drugs, with new synthetic varieties appearing, all adding to the atmosphere of escapism from depressing reality. Co-habiting as couples outside marriage, which had not really been an option before or soon after the war was increasingly practiced.

So the 'Sixties' was a decade of rapid change, with many adults in their twenties and thirties also taking part with at least equal vigour in its

'Permissive Society'. Some horrific events unfolded, including Hollywood's drug-fuelled Manson murders, the rise of cults capitalising on the hunger for some kind of 'truth' or reason for it all, amidst growing rejection of traditional Western religions which seemed at a loss for appropriate response. Some of the Beatles looked to India and transcendental meditation, sitar music (George Harrison), unleashing mass demand, upon which enterprising gurus lined up to cash in. There were others, such as the 'Moonies' from South Korea, with their mass weddings, then cults in the USA, many embracing and indoctrinating whole families while grasping their assets and wealth and cutting them off from their wider families and the world. A costly legacy was building for society and its services.

Peace and freedom became the bywords and the 'Hippies' developed in the mid-sixties from the 'beatniks', the 'beaten-down', suppressed youth, the beat music generation of the fifties in Greenwich Village, New York and Haight-Ashbury, San Francisco, as written about by Jack Kerouac. They spread throughout the Western world and were distinctive in their flowing, flowery dress, music and drug culture and alternative lifestyle. Placards promoted 'Love not War', and grand festivals included the Human Be-in in Golden Gate Park, the Summer of Love, Woodstock and the Isle of Wight. Some formed itinerant groups in convoys of counterculture New Age Travellers; others set up communes, while the movement also rubbed off and lingered on fringes of 'respectable' society as it gained fashionability.

Traditional Churches, never alert, were just not ready to meet such a challenge and looked on aghast. The Quakers were involved in setting up Amnesty International, Greenpeace and other such charitable movements.

There was a series of headline events over the period, with the Americans confidently taking over the Vietnam war from France; the assassination of American President John F Kennedy in November 1963; the 'Death of God' movement and growth of atheism in America, with a 1966 Time Magazine cover asking "Is God Dead?" following John Lennon's claim that the Beatles were more popular than Jesus; a steep decline in religion and church attendance in the Western world; violent anti-establishment protests with "Danny le Rouge" in France and the Bader-Meinhoff gang in Germany; Russia invading Hungary and Czechoslovakia; Civil Rights movement for African Americans in USA; legalisation of abortion in some countries; the increasing fragility of marriage with growing divorce rates; gay rights movements; an explosion in drug use then crime to support this expensively addictive habit. There were 'The Troubles' in Northern Ireland, a nationalist struggle that carried tickets of religion, which involved much violence and murder on which all the churches seemed remarkably reticent to comment. Their lack of leadership was interpreted by many of the faithful as lack of authority. The post-war 'baby-boomers', who had challenged previous norms of childhood had come of age to re-set social, moral, family and religious norms.

A further large influx of immigrants into Britain was called for in the early 60s to provide more much-needed staff for the NHS under Health Secretary Enoch Powell. In 1968, the same man, as a backbench Member of Parliament, delivered his famous 'rivers of blood' speech criticising mass immigration, which he had earlier encouraged as a minister of state. This contributed to the rise and organisation of racist nationalist elements in Britain such as the National Front and British National Party. Then in the early 1970s Idi Amin, President of Uganda expelled all Asian residents, of whom many had been successful tradespeople. Britain accepted them as British citizens in another surge of immigration.

British society's attitude towards Catholics was softening, as it did with other distinctions such as class, ethnicity and gender as the nation became more diverse. Some authorities feared this growing tolerance would lead to laxity, which it may have done to some extent, but there was a sense of liberation and a kinder world. At the same time, lay Catholics were becoming ever more questioning about moral and ethical issues, including new ones raised by advances in science and medicine then the Cold War and changes sweeping through society.

One region stood out as an exception to the atmosphere of tolerance – Northern Ireland, where memories were long and sectarianism ran deep. Catholics and Protestants, mostly Presbyterians of Scottish ancestry, lived in separate areas and had separate schools, each regarding the other with profound suspicion. Public structures and employment opportunities disfavoured the Catholic community, which led to 'the Troubles', serious flare-ups of violence between the sectarian parties supported and fomented by underground paramilitary organisations such as the Catholic IRA and INLA, in favour of a united independent Ireland and the Protestant UDF and UVF, supporting continued loyalty and union with the 'mainland' UK. Then serious institutional religious discrimination got out of hand and evolved into a war of ethnicity and nationalism so serious that it required the involvement of British military in their longest ever campaign.

Catholic Social Teaching

Catholic Social Teaching (CST) was an important but evolving body of thinking, still not in the form of a written code. Arising from Pope Leo XIII's encyclical *Rerum Novarum* in 1891, as the 20th century loomed, it had been developed and refined by subsequent teachings, encyclicals and then by Vatican II.

Christians are more grounded in the world than many non-churchgoers think. The gospels are about more than just providing a spiritual route to paradise. Believers must follow Christ's two great commandments: 1, Love the Lord your God with your whole heart and soul and 2, Love your neighbour as yourself. Pre-Christian philosophers examined social matters and Christian thinkers have continued the process, most notably through Augustine of Hippo's and Thomas Aquinas' concepts of 'human rights' and the 'just war'.

The role of Christianity in social matters had become far more complex with the industrial revolution and growing mechanisation of agriculture which raised new challenges regarding ethics of social and working relationships as well as justice and resolution of disputes, added to more recently by issues of safeguarding the natural world, our environment. Pope Leo XIII had laid the foundation of a modern Christian set of guidelines in his encyclical Rerum Novarum (19th C). Such documents are rarely written in a user-friendly way, but defy simple summary if they are to convey anything of value. CST was an important way for the Church to give informed spiritual guidance in helping governments and people make decisions regarding their behaviour, attitudes, relationships, ethics, work and politics. Some decisions are day-to-day issues as they arise, while others may affect the future direction of a life. Different commentators each stress their own take on the encyclical, but basically, it comprises the following broad themes, some of which overlap:

1 **Human Dignity** – every single human is created by God in his image, so all have human rights which any ethical society must observe. The sanctity of each human life is paramount from conception to natural death. In God's eyes all people are his children, with equal right to membership of the human family.

2 **Subsidiarity** – No higher level of government should get involved in managing matters that can be effectively managed at a lower level by individuals or groups who are closer to and better understand these matters. Governments should allow for unrestricted natural human individual, family and community development. Families are an important part of society's structure and their stability should be encouraged. People must be free to form and bring up their families, find employment or run legitimate businesses as they choose. Local and regional authorities that provide education, support services, police etc. to help constituents should likewise be free to organise their own governance to suit local conditions for the common good.

3 **The Common Good** – humans are made to live in harmony with each other. Each individual is valuable and equal in God's eyes, so society must be organised to offer each an equal opportunity to develop and use their personal gifts and skills according to Natural Law. A just society should be structured to ensure that people who are born or become disadvantaged, disabled, poor or vulnerable should be supported by sharing the common good. There is an obligation on more fortunate individuals within such society to be generous and charitable to those less fortunate.

4 **Social Justice, Dignity of Work, Labour and Capital** – Having human dignity, people take precedence over material things. Conditions of labour must reflect this dignity and capital must be used responsibly to serve people in the society. Businesses must help their employees fulfil their human potential and pay them fair wages. The basic rights of workers must be respected including the right to organize or join unions and the right to own property. Private property is derived from God's creation, so is in the care of the owner in their lifetime to use for their own benefit but not at the expense of the good of the community. Rights carry with them responsibilities.

5 **Solidarity** – The whole of society should be firmly committed to ensuring the welfare of every member within it. "Love your neighbour..." This strengthens the common good and lays the ground for peace and progress in society. Christian moral responsibility should not just be for individuals but for fairness in society as a whole and the Church calls on followers not just for charitable work but also to speak out in support of social justice.

6 **Stewardship of Creation** – Just as the dignity of human life derives from our creation by God, so must the rest of his creation be treated with care and respect. We have a moral imperative seriously to look after the environment.

This social teaching and the resulting guidance could usefully be incorporated in the Church doctrine for today's world. It seems entirely in accordance with the teaching of Jesus, which is the essence of Christianity. It is tangible applied belief that would lay down markers for world leaders and bring a powerful message to the whole of society as well as a valid framework for its operation and governance.

Ecumenism, Council of Churches

The question of reunification between Protestant Churches and even with post-Vatican II Catholicism arose from time to time, but never reached a point of real progress, fundamentally because the respective organisations remained at least in part, ends in themselves albeit with the common shared God in mind.

The encyclical *Gaudiam et Spes*, Joy and Hope, on the 'Pastoral Constitution of the Church in the Modern World' was issued by Pope Paul VI as the Second Vatican Council closed in 1965. It addressed the 'Dignity of Man, Community of Mankind, Men's activity and the Role of the Church' in the non-inclusive language of the time. It was notable for fostering peace, promoting the community of nations and influencing the social teaching of other Churches. The council had attracted wide publicity and interest and this document had given a boost to the ecumenical movement.

Pope Paul VI then made a ground-breaking visit to Canterbury where he famously took Archbishop Ramsey's hand and placed his papal ring on the archbishop's finger. This meeting brought to Anglican-Catholic dialogue wider attention, hope and even expectation. Archbishop Ramsey wore that ring until his death and his successors have always worn it when visiting the pope.

Various groupings of Protestant free churches had come closer together during this century. Methodists were supportive of the ecumenical movement throughout and became a founding member of the British Council of Churches which was formed in 1942 to provide a forum for the established Christian Churches of England and Scotland and the non-conforming churches with a view to moving towards unification. In 1948, the World Council of Churches was formed, based in Geneva for the same purpose on a more global scale and ultimately to seek unity in one faith and one communion together. Many Orthodox and a wide spectrum of Protestant Churches were members. The Roman Catholic Church agreed to be an observer.

There were some positive results in that the Anglican and Methodist Churches developed a plan for a two-stage reunion which was given mutual approval in principle in 1965. When the finished plan was put to the members in 1969, there was clear support for implementation among the Methodists but the Church of England could not rally a sufficient majority to seal it. A further attempt in 1972 also fell short, as did a 1982 proposal for a 'Covenant of Visible Unity', which was supported by the United Reform and Moravian Churches as well as Methodists. Peripheral discussions with Catholic representatives were held in an atmosphere of good-will which revealed a surprising overlap of issues on which they could probably agree.

1982 saw important progress in the UK, regardless of the earlier Anglican-Methodist setback. The report of the first-stage study of the Anglican-Roman Catholic International Commission, ARCIC I, was published and Pope John Paul II visited Britain that year, reviving interest in more general unity. In Glasgow he won hearts speaking to the wider community of believers in Christ, saying that all believers are pilgrims on this earth and posing the question "can we not make that pilgrimage together hand-in-hand?"

Those who sought unity realised that the British Council of Churches was not proving sufficiently effective because its member Churches were failing to commit to its good work and the Roman Catholic Church was not a member. Meetings between British and Irish Churches concluded that a complete re-think was needed, leading in 1985 to a huge consultation process which was named after Pope John Paul II's Glasgow address, 'Not Strangers but Pilgrims'. BBC radio was drawn in and played an important major part by broadcasting a Lent course 'What on Earth is the Church For' before Easter 1986. Over 60,000 church groups participated in this course, involving about one million people in Britain and Ireland, most of whom returned questionnaires from which the paper 'Views from the Pews' was collated. This was followed by a poll of the Churches involved, encouraging their understanding of Church mission. Christian Aid suggested that ecumenism should aim for a 'community of disagreement', effectively proposing that each keep its identity but should join together while reserving defined areas of difference.

Those involved in the 'Not Strangers but Pilgrims' process deduced that the gap between individual communities and a pan-British and Irish organisation were too large and there should be national groupings. So three national conferences were held in St Andrews, Bangor and Nottingham followed by an all-Britain conference with Irish observers at Swanwick, England in 1987. The big question here was how involved would the Roman Catholic Church become. There was relief all round when Cardinal Hume, the Benedictine Archbishop of Westminster conveyed that the Catholic Church should move "from a situation of co-operation to one of commitment to each other". At the end of that conference, a declaration on Christian unity was issued which included at its heart the following two paragraphs:

"We now declare together our readiness to commit ourselves to each other under God. Our earnest desire is to become more fully, in his own time, the one Church of Christ, united in faith, communion, pastoral care and mission ... In the unity we seek we recognise that there will not be uniformity but legitimate diversity.

It is our conviction that, as a matter of policy at all levels and in all places, our churches must now move from co-operation to clear commitment to each other, in search of the unity for which Christ prayed, common evangelism and service of the world."

In other words, it acknowledged that the Churches, although they were of different traditions and theologies, were committing themselves to a journey towards full visible unity. "Churches Together" resulted from this process, replacing the British Council of Churches with bodies that included a broader spread of churches, now also including the Roman Catholic Church as an active member. Churches Together emphasises that the Churches are in pilgrimage together towards full visible unity themselves rather than ecumenical institutions speaking on their behalf.

As a result, Churches Together in Britain and Ireland replaced the British Council of Churches in 1990. It comprises four national bodies – Churches Together in England, Action of Churches Together in Scotland, Cytun (in Wales) and the Irish Council of Churches. Within the British group, any community can adopt its own local title, e.g. Churches Together in Bristol.

Role of Women, Canon Law, Sex

Half way through the Second Vatican Council, Belgian Cardinal Joseph Suenens had posed the question of why they were discussing such important issues without at least half the Church being represented, there being no women on any of the committees. The eventual result of his question was the appointment of some twenty three women as auditors. Although auditors had no formal role in discussions, they participated in the sub-committees that worked to produce the resulting texts, especially those which dealt with lay issues. It was a modest start.

In the very early Church, a few women played an active part in ministry, although it was rare in Middle East society at that time for women to hold any leadership roles at all. Then for nearly 2,000 years, men alone ran and ministered to the Church. About the 11th century, the Church introduced a ban on married priests, which had already been a convention among monks and some priests for some centuries. The reason seems to have been to avoid distraction from prayer life and ministry. There had always been a concern that it was asking too much and human nature could not be changed by denial so there would always be cases of clergy yielding to temptation, be it concupiscence or greed for power or wealth.

Misogyny gradually assumed distorted proportions within the unequal religious society that prevailed, suggesting that it is wrong that men should be subjected to carnal temptation. This view is clearly unnatural as all humans have God-given drives. Christianity holds that God gave humans the power of choice and free will. Society is structured to take account of this, the Church is not. There is no harm in a hermit or monk choosing to seek to defeat his urges, but is it realistic and reasonable for the Church to impose absolute celibacy on anybody, man or woman, as a condition of serving God? The Western Catholic Church has struggled to maintain this unreality. Quite apart from abuse scandals, surveys show that a fair percentage of ordained men frequently break the vow of chastity. The lack of priests today is largely a self-imposed limitation to the Church's ability to carry out Christ's intended mission.

The Code of Canon Law provided clarity for Church judiciary. It had become part of a full legal framework within the Catholic Church, with lawyers, courts, judges and penalties, although it generally held no civil authority. The language used in Canon 230/2, of the Code commissioned by Pope Pius X and published in 1918, was revised following Vatican II and re-issued in 1983. It changed the usual reference to 'men' to become 'person' when referring to admittance to the role of commentator or cantor at Mass and in some circumstances that of lector (reader) or when conferring Baptism or distributing Holy Communion at the discretion of bishops. This was seen as covering gender and the use of females on such altar duties and as female altar servers over time became commonplace even though it caused controversy, not least in Africa and USA, which were home to many highly conservative Catholics.

However, the Catholic hierarchy ruled out ordination of women either as deacons or priests. The Anglican and Scottish Episcopal Churches ordained their first women priests in 1994, following a considered view by these Churches that there was no valid scriptural objection to such a move and it reflected appreciation of the positive part women played in the life of the Church. Conservative members of those Churches had long opposed the move, so it proved controversial and divisive. The conviction of some members, including a few clergy on this was so strong that it led some to convert to Catholicism.

A growing body of Catholic women had been pressing for more meaningful ways for women, who represented the majority in most congregations, to participate in the active life of their Church, rather than their traditional 'roles' of flower arranging, polishing brass and altar cleaning. Nuns, who were fewer in number by then, kept their counsel on such matters on the whole, though a few exceptions spoke out and most of these left their orders. Ongoing, there was the pressure from a high proportion of lay people for the Church to limit or abandon its opposition to the use of contraception for two main reasons – first to limit over-large families in a world heading for over-population and alleviate poverty caused by these and second, to reduce spread of sexually transmitted disease, especially following the new scourge of AIDS.

Some Christian Churches over time seem to have selected sex as an enemy, which is not a view supported by Jesus Christ according to the gospels, but an attitude developed since Christ's time. The following may offer some brief insight to their influencers and evolution:

- Plato's philosophy was admired in the early Church and he believed the mind was superior to the body, so passions should be controlled.
- Saint Paul, initially under the mistaken expectation of an imminent end to the world, advised people to stay celibate if possible, believing this to be a route to purity of body and spirit.
- Male physical strength being greater, by Christ's time society had evolved with them as leaders and guardians of families and tribes, with women having the role of mothers and supporters.
- Hermits and monks sought closeness to God by avoiding worldly distractions, including those of sex and opted for solitude and celibacy. Some suffered the consequent distraction of torment and anguish at the ensuing frustration of their natural drives.
- Even though there were female monasteries or convents, they were generally regarded as inferior. The view that women were 'occasions of sin' was perhaps introduced by Tertullian (160-220 AD), who called them "the devil's gateway" and this view seems to have endured among all-male Catholic clerics.
- Augustine of Hippo, a playboy in his youth, claimed that God's intention for sexual intercourse between a man and a woman was for procreation, the continuity of our species, but since the Fall of Adam and Eve it also became associated with original sin, leading to negative perceptions of lust associated with furtiveness and shame.

Such views were engrained in the Churches well into the 20th century. Yet human drives proved strong throughout the ages and the fact of their irrepressibility came into the light, eventually exposing a scandal of large scale clerical abuse involving women and children.

Towards the end of the 20th century and into the next, some outrageous revelations from the recent past were uncovered relating for example to Church establishments' treatment of orphans, unmarried mothers and their children since the Second World War as well as clerical sexual abuse of children among several Churches. Regardless of internal awareness of these events, they had long gone unpublicised. Recent examples included convent laundries in Ireland in which unmarried mothers were deemed as having no rights at all, including to their children, who were often sold for adoption abroad. When they died in infancy, they were buried in unconsecrated ground within Convent land. Such an actual event was well publicised by the film 'Philomena'.

Press freedom ensured publicity of a number of examples of clerical abuse. One was a senior Catholic bishop in Ireland who had an affair with a parishioner and had a child by her which he disowned. He later admitted that his main preoccupation after each illicit love event was to find a confessor before he took Mass the following morning. When his lover sought support and public recognition, the Church in Ireland belittled and supressed her while enabling the bishop's transfer to Central America. A well-known Anglican figure physically abused young boys, whose complaints were dismissed for years until he was uncovered dealing out excessive corporal punishment to boys in private. A highly respected Methodist leader, who became chair of a socially responsible bank, was found guilty of serial sexual abuse. These were but a few exposed examples. Silence from the highest Church levels prolonged these events, the main aim being to protect the reputation of the Churches and save the perpetrators at the total expense of the victims, who were typically discredited and left alone with their lives in ruins, self-confidence low, many with mental health issues, all without any support from the Churches responsible for their spiritual wellbeing.

As to women, Christianity was far from the only religion in which their roles were seen as inferior to those of men. In the second half of the 20th century, as women's drive for equality gathered pace and as their recognition and assertiveness in work, academia, society and government blossomed, so did their inclusion in official roles in an increasing number of denominations.

Faith in the City

In 1981, during an economic recession in Britain, with its first woman Prime Minister, Margaret Thatcher in power and high rates of unemployment prevailing, discontent was evident in deprived and minority communities. The police applied stop-and-search powers disproportionately to ethnic minorities, stoking their resentment. Riots broke out in Brixton then other areas including Birmingham, Manchester, Leeds and notably, Toxteth in Liverpool, where they reached an unprecedented level of destruction and looting, against which police used CS spray for the first time on the British mainland and required police reinforcement from numerous other forces from as far away as Devon.

Mrs Thatcher was urged by several of her Conservative ministers not to spend valuable resources in improving far-left Liverpool and Merseyside, which the Chancellor said would be "like raking water uphill", preferring a policy of "managed decline". She sent a more sympathetic minister, Michael Heseltine to study and report back on suggested action. He concluded the government should fund major regeneration.

A commission was set up by the Liverpool-born Archbishop of Canterbury, Robert Runcie to examine the Church's mission in Urban Priority Areas. Its aim was to examine the needs of seriously deprived urban areas and how the Church was equipped to help, then to make recommendations for positive help. It examined direct and indirect human consequences of unemployment, overcrowded and decayed housing, lone pensioners, single parent households, ethnic origins as well as sub-standard education and medical provision and social disintegration. The 1983 report, 'Faith in the City', was blunt and direct, making over 60 recommendations, two thirds for action by the Church and the rest for national or government action. In spite of the clear message from the riots, it noted that no adequate response had been forthcoming from government, nation or Church and little public discussion of the issues arising.

This met with strong resistance from government. Prime Minister Margaret Thatcher, herself a church-goer was quick to dismiss its conclusions, pointing out that it emphasised government action and did not refer to self-help, while some ministers were quoted referring to it as the "Marxist theology" of a Church led by "communist clerics". The Chief Rabbi Immanuel Jacobowits published a report stating that a Jewish approach would seek a more demanding and satisfying work ethic to build self-respect, ambition and enterprise which he felt would improve conditions and imbue respect for laws and the police.

The Faith in the City report stirred interest, consciences and awareness throughout the nation and led to the Church Urban Fund and eventually a government review of improvements in urban life on the report's 20th anniversary. In Liverpool, interdenominational relations strengthened as Anglican Bishop David Sheppard and Catholic Archbishop Derek Worlock formed a strong positive partnership, making joint initiatives to encourage social improvements in that city as well as a fresh dimension of ecumenism.

National Pastoral Congress, Liverpool, 1980

This was arranged by Archbishop Derek Worlock with the blessing of Cardinal Basil Hume, Westminster and was attended by 2000 delegates from all Catholic dioceses of England and Wales, dubbed 'The Easter People'. It was an expression of the concept of collegiality of bishops which was one of the aims of Vatican II, following which national bishops' councils were established, ostensibly to administer matters relevant to local Church communities. It had been realised, if not acknowledged that the Vatican did not have the capacity to manage local Dioceses to this extent. Encouraged by the progress achieved by Vatican II, a majority of Catholic faithful still expected and awaited important changes in practical areas of the Church's teaching. Vatican II had shaken things up but there remained a distinct 'unfinished' feeling and some of the issues needing to be addressed were outlined in the reports of this congress, including contraception, marriage breakdown, sacraments for remarried people, sexuality and parish support for all.

Marriage and family issues were considered at the meetings as just one part of an ambitious agenda. Delegates called for fundamental re-examination of the teaching on marriage, sexuality and contraception. Most felt that such an examination should leave open the possibility of change and development in the Church's teaching, a large minority feeling this was an urgent need.

The matter of broken marriages was acknowledged as a growing problem as the partners experience a sense of failure, hurt and rejection. They need reassurance, encouragement and acceptance from the Church as well as others. A study of the experience gained by the Association of Separated and Divorced Catholics in the USA was recommended to the bishops. They should re-address with compassion the exclusion of those who have divorced and re-married from the sacramental life and mission of the Church.

The reports included reference to the decline in Church attendance, calling for a structure for welcoming newcomers, recovering those no longer attending services, and providing appropriate help for needs.

They also covered a need to engage more effectively with younger members. More emphasis was felt to be laid on 'moral' imperatives that say little about Christ and his Good News, than was relevant to their own life style and concerns. Real dialogue, engagement and listening with the young at their own level were needed, helping them reflect on their own lives in the light of the Gospel. Many ultimately rejected the Church more on account of perceived lack of relevance rather than conviction. So every parish should provide opportunities, structures and encouragement to young people to take a part in the decision-making, work and liturgy of the parish. The engagement of priests and bishops with young people and provision for their growth was identified as a major priority into the future.

There were issues and conclusions of real substance here, but follow-up was so disappointing. As the Catholic Herald put it, "the Easter People were not very good at resurrection". In addition the new pope had settled into the Vatican by then, showing clear conservativism, which dampened enthusiasm for change among the national Bishops' Conference. The bishops, looking upwards, confined their response to the report to agreeing that the liturgy might become increasingly 'inclusive'. Results underlined that this was yet another opportunity missed as regular Mass attendance in England and Wales fell by more than a third in the ensuing 35 years, despite being boosted by tens of thousands of immigrant Catholic workers from Europe. This reflected what was happening over most of Western Europe.

Judaism, Zionism and The Holy Land

With increased immigration, as Europe became more multi-racial and sensitive to racism and xenophobia, society felt increasing discomfort with anti-Jewish sentiment.

Israel and Palestine was the ancient home of the Jews, the Israelites. Zion was the more eastern of two mountains outside Jerusalem, but the name became used for the Jerusalem area. It had been adopted by a nationalist movement called Zionism towards the end of the 19th century to recover a land around Jerusalem for the itinerant race that the Jews had become, without the anchor of a homeland. According to the Bible, God had covenanted their land to them, but after the crucifixion of Jesus Christ and losing the war against the Romans, most of them had severed their roots and left for the widespread diaspora, destined to lodge in other lands for two millennia. They would face many difficulties and much hostility over this time in spite of Paul's letter to the Romans (11:26-29) quoting Isiah (59:20-21) which referred to Zion and indicated that God's covenant with them was irrevocable.

The idea of Jewish emancipation surfaced during the Napoleonic wars and simmered until a recognised leader Theodore Herzl in the late 19th, early 20th century took the Zionists cause forward with a view to finding a homeland to which Jews could return. In 1904 he sought support for his project at a meeting with Pope Pius X. He declined, saying that Judaism was superseded by Christ's teaching, so it was not his place to grant it such validity. This was softer than the common view expressed in the past that had condemned Jews as killers of Christ.

During the First World War, the British government made a public commitment to helping the Jews create a national homeland. After defeat in that war, the Ottomans yielded Palestine and Trans-Jordan and the League of Nations granted a mandate in 1920 for the British to administer those territories for the purpose of creating a Jewish homeland. Israel was established and as Jews returned, native Palestinian Arabs were forcibly displaced, leading to inevitable tensions. In 1948, following the Second World War, Israel became so fiercely active against occupation that the war-weary British handed over independence and promptly departed. Palestinian-Israeli antipathy and mutual hostility continued.

By Vatican II, the mood in the Catholic Church had shifted. The declaration on relations with other faiths, *Nostra Aetate*, included a clear rejection of the view that Jews were guilty as a whole for what happened during the Passion of Jesus Christ.

While relations between Christianity and Judaism have become more relaxed, the Churches accept the rights of both Israel and Palestine as nation states but avoid any involvement in defining their borders. As to Jerusalem, they believe an international guarantee should ensure the freedom of Jews, Christians and Muslims to live and worship in that city which holds such importance to each of their faiths.

Long Reign of Polish Pope John-Paul II (1978-2005)

Pope Paul VI's death, followed by the very brief 33-day papacy of John Paul I, led to a surprise in the appointment of the next successor. The tall and relatively young Cardinal Wojtilla from Communist satellite Poland was the first non-Italian Pope since Adrian VI in the 16th century. He took the name **Pope John-Paul II** (1978-2005) in respect of his three immediate predecessors. He was to become a highly charismatic world figure, but being at the conservative end of the Church spectrum, he soon dampened any post-council expectations of rapid modernisation of the Church. He used his stature, personality and charisma to good effect in travelling worldwide as an ambassador of the faith. There was prescience in his selection as he was to lead the Church through an era of complete collapse of the Communist Soviet bloc. His very selection probably played a significant part in that political earthquake, by emboldening his strongly Catholic countrymen to show a lead in the protest movements.

John Paul II became the most travelled world religious leader to date, visiting 129 countries during his pontificate. His charismatic smile and personality won him many admirers as did his fortitude and forgiveness when attacked and shot as he greeted a crowd. He was a gifted missionary and had an ambition to bring the three great Abrahamic religions, Judaism, Islam and Christianity closer together. But many Catholics were disappointed and frustrated at how little, in the light of Vatican II, the Catholic Church progressed in those 27 years of his reign as serious urgent long-perceived needs remained unaddressed.

Communism and the Soviet Union

Communism's altruistic aims simply did not work out in practice. State control of everything disincentivised workers and the result was mediocrity, economic decline and defensively aggressive isolationism.

Mikhail Gorbachev was general secretary of the Communist Party from 1985-91. Although a committed socialist he believed the party and system were in need of reform, a view confirmed by the Chernobyl nuclear power station disaster in 1986. Following some years of poor economic performance with rising discontent in some states, he introduced policies of *perestroika*, economic restructuring, and *glasnost*, openness. As a socialist leader he got on surprisingly well with the free-marketeer leaders of USA and UK, President Ronald Regan and Prime Minister Margaret Thatcher. He worked with them to thaw the cold war, agreeing with President Reagan to reduce and limit their respective countries' excessive nuclear arsenals and openly implementing his side of that agreement.

At home Gorbachev loosened the shackles on the media and free speech and introduced some limited democracy. As people in Soviet satellite countries suffering similar privations observed his loosening of grip on the Soviet population they began to flex their own muscles in a rising tide of nationalism. Gorbachev held his counsel and declined to mobilise an army with low morale which he had recently withdrawn from the lengthy unwinnable war in Afghanistan. The breakthrough happened first in Poland, which was still strongly Catholic, where the anti-communist Solidarity movement was legalised, then in a free election, captured nearly every available seat in Parliament from the Communist in the summer of 1989.

This was the catalyst for a largely peaceful wave of revolution in the Eastern European states, the next step coming in that summer as over six hundred East Germans on a 'Pan-European Picnic' near the Hungarian border with Austria fled west for freedom. Others followed, loosening communism's grip on East Germany and Czechoslovakia, then other East European states so that Soviet communism had lost its strategic western buffer. The conceptual Iron Curtain and very real Berlin Wall separating East Europe from the West were dismantled and it was not long before the Soviet Union returned to its component states.

Religious practice in this region had been suppressed but had continued underground and was now free to rise again and flourish, which it did, as Russian Orthodoxy and Roman Catholicism in the main. So in this era Christians were hopeful but uncertain whether the collective opposition to Christianity would loosen or live on in Russia. Politics were quite chaotic under Gorbachev then Yeltsin, as was Orthodoxy which lacked a core or chain of proven and committed leaders who could claim apostolic succession. But the 'Iron Curtain' had collapsed and the new government showed democratic intent by allowing further freedom of speech and press, unfamiliar ground to all but a few living Russians. ROCOR helped build some churches to bring open worship to the hitherto underground Orthodox faithful.

It was a revolution lacking great enthusiasm and nobody in either Church or state appeared to be very good at managing the unfamiliar 'democracy'. The resulting government led by Boris Yeltsin from 1991 introduced a capitalist system in that he changed the state controlled economy to a market economy, but it was democratic in name only. Its lack of security and control allowed corruption to boom, so desperate poverty grew side-by-side with organised crime and extreme wealth in the population. Its Church was likewise understandably deficient in organisational and teaching skills, starting from its streams of Orthodoxy – official and 'true' underground Russian Orthodox Churches and ROCOR. That presented real challenges given the lengthy lack of religious education as well as emerging changes in social and cultural climates, which everybody had to get used to amidst economic stress. There was hunger for a spiritual dimension to add real meaning to a life that had been a controlled shared drudgery under communism for all but a favoured a few. The new-found freedom, seemed to promise no better for most people under the new regime. The new 'democracy' had opened the gates for alternative sects and religious interests to move in and capitalise on the chaos, complicating religious recovery under a leader who would be the first Russian head of state for well over a century to be buried with a Church service in 2006.

Patriarch Alexy II (reign 1990-2008) was now in place as leader of the Russian Orthodox Church, having been selected as the most pro-Soviet bishop in the Metropolitan Patriarchate. The now state-permitted religions of Orthodoxy, Catholicism and other Christian denominations, Islam, Judaism and Buddhism grew openly with a huge surge in building of new places of worship during the 1990s.

Yeltsin resigned his presidency on the last day of the 20th century, having ensured that a little known man hidden in Yeltsin's shadow, ex-Lieutenant Colonel of the KGB, Prime Minister Vladimir Putin would succeed him as president from the beginning of the next century.

Virtue Ethics

Virtue Ethics from early times returned to the fore in Christian philosophy from the late 1970s. It is worth summarising briefly here. Rather than asking "What should I do?" Virtue Ethics poses the question "What kind of person am I?" Catholic Scottish philosopher Arthur Macintyre published 'After Virtue' in 1981. He disagreed with Enlightenment thinkers, who wanted to maintain the moral values of an earlier tradition yet to abandon the tradition itself. Macintyre preferred reversion to Thomas Aquinas and Aristotle.

Plato (427-347BC), his teacher Socrates and pupil Aristotle, founding fathers of Western philosophy, saw the four cardinal virtues as courage, temperance, prudence and justice. The absence of any one of these renders a person non-virtuous. Aristotle added a distinction between intellectual versus moral virtues, such as intelligence and mathematics, versus qualities of character, like courage and generosity. Aristotle rated a good life as one lived virtuously with character, usually formed by upbringing, example, practice and habit. Good parenting and role models play important roles in one's formation.

The concept of virtue was embraced by other early Christian thinkers such as Ambrose of Milan (339-397AD). He adopted Plato's four cardinal or natural virtues and added to them Paul's three 'supernatural virtues' – faith, hope and love (1 Cor 13:13). Augustine of Hippo, who followed Plato closely, wrote that virtue can only really be good when it reflects the knowledge and love of God, the source of goodness. But some 800 years would pass before a comprehensive Christian virtue theory developed.

This fell to Thomas Aquinas, who drew from Ambrose's dual approach – cardinal virtues plus supernatural virtues. But he also pursued the teleological (*telos*, end or goal) approach, which blended well with his developing theory on natural law. In the latter he held three key tenets – that we humans naturally:

- seek to maintain our existence.
- are driven to continue our line, so mate then rear and nurture our offsprings.
- strive to live in ordered societies and seek the truth about God.

He said that to achieve the last, we need faith, hope and love because our supernatural goal is ultimately to find union with God.

New Theologies

In some colonised areas where the missions had taught the Bible to indigenous people, new biblical-based theologies had grown among those who felt oppressed or disadvantaged and sought resources that may help liberate them from their plight. These took various forms, each being influenced by local conditions. Noteworthy cases included South America,

Sub-Saharan and South Africa and USA. In the case of South Africa, the indigenous black people far outnumbered the governing whites, who applied the apartheid regime to maintain control. Among the black citizens, resistance groups formed to challenge and change the legal and political structures that imposed it. Just as the white Afrikaners drew their theology from the Dutch Reform Church, those they ruled found support from the Bible which lent legitimacy to their cause.

Elsewhere in sub-Saharan Africa, African Black Theology grew in those areas where colonists and missions had introduced Christianity. Once having embraced the Bible, the indigenous people studied it and applied their own contextual interpretation of its message, which did not always align with Western Christian teaching. So some breakaway churches had been built separate from the missionary churches, from the late 19th century into the 20th. Their theologians included a circle of African women formed in 1980, to study Christianity in relation to traditional African beliefs, from which they drew some links.

They pressed for the Christian Bible and theology to adopt the various local vernaculars which had long been demanded in the belief that versions in English and other European languages had grown to be refined and angled towards the benefit of original Western European colonial powers. They desired their own version to bring it closer to their traditions and people. Indeed, there were some clear divisions of conviction forming between the African Christians and for example Rome and Canterbury, in the issues of gender, sexuality and the sacraments, with Africans proving to be more conservative in such matters than Western Europe. Yet Christianity was still growing there while contracting in Western Europe.

The North American situation differed in that black people, mostly in Southern states, were a minority and socially disadvantaged because of the nature of their origins there as well as the strong racial prejudice prevailing in society at large. They retained a proud traditional connection and regard for their ancestral homeland. In the face of their past slavery, then severe prejudice, oppression and segregation, they had long turned to religion and developed their own lively, charismatic evangelical Baptist take on worship and fellowship, infused with music from their heritage. Some white Americans regarded this as an alien threat, while black worshippers drew on the gospels for their theology, which became known as Black liberation theology in the 1960s.

Martin Luther King, a Baptist minister from Atlanta, Georgia, became a leader of the civil rights movement from the mid-1950s, when he led the Montgomery Bus Boycott in peaceful protest against the segregation of blacks in modern America. He gained fame for his persuasive and moving rhetoric and non-violent campaigns, based on his Christian faith and inspired by the success of Mahatma Gandhi's non-violent protests in India. He was rewarded with the Nobel Peace Prize in 1964, but was assassinated four years later at a rally in Memphis, Tennessee.

The Second Vatican Council lent impetus to movements growing from extreme economic inequality in South American countries in the late 1960s, growing their own liberation theologies. The deprived communities saw local Church leaders as complicit with governments in their political and economic oppression. Groups formed deriving guidance from selective readings of scripture in challenging their situation, leading to them adopting concerted practical action towards social improvement. Capitalism was seen as the root of their oppression, so they drew on neo-Marxist social models.

When priests and Church leaders spoke out in support of the oppressed and the prevailing injustice, poverty, torture and assassination, many suffered the last two of those fates, the best known being the Archbishop of San Salvador, Óscar Romero, who was gunned down by a military death squad while celebrating Mass in a hospital chapel in 1980.

Rapid Technical Change, Social and Religious Consequences

At the beginning of the 20th century, Orville and Wilbur Wright made the first aeroplane flight and less than 70 years later, there were frequent scheduled intercontinental commercial flights, a few of these faster than the speed of sound, whilst men had walked on the moon and returned to earth. Entertainment had moved on from the scratchy clockwork phonograph to high fidelity electronic sound systems; from household radio to colour television; from flickering silent black and white silent movies to 360° surround sound and picture and even 3-dimensional life-like films. In the same period, wars had expanded, with civilian homes and families now targets for airborne destruction and death. Fearsome weapons had been developed, capable of destroying all known life. Electronic computers were conceived and developed then miniaturised for spacecraft, then personal computers became available to ordinary households; the telephone had become a pocket sized accessory, usable on the move anywhere; news in the making could be seen live on television as it unfolded from the other side of the world; the world-wide web provided full and instant information across all interests; huge strides had been made in our understanding of human genes, the science of the universe and the constituents of atoms. Medical science had advanced with antibiotics that could cure or relieve hitherto incurable or fatal diseases.

The speed and variety of technological advances had brought with them many advantages in health, mobility, leisure, cleanliness and standards of living but they brought deep social challenges as the hierarchical family dissolved and divorce and single parenthood became commonplace; many no longer regarded the family unit as the basis of society as homes became smaller; self-centredness, consumerism, loneliness and mental health issues grew. Social dialogue and contact had been totally changed and more distant while gender barriers had been shattered and human behaviour and mores were in a state of flux. Real happiness and personal satisfaction were eagerly sought but proving elusive as people grew in wealth and their ambitions became ever more impatient and superficial. Small wonder then, that slow-moving traditional religion was caught utterly by surprise and lagged well behind the unrecognised growth in need for spirituality as well as it did in learning and applying the means of communication now open to it.

All religions struggled with the new challenges as they always had. Change in the established Churches had probably been faster than in any previous century, but still fell far short of adapting to such revolutionary science and society. God, the ultimate architect of all this, is a constant, but religions had to understand and address new social and moral structures with guidance as to God's will, or lose their perceived relevance. There were questions in the Roman Catholic Church as to whether its all-powerful Curia was fit for this task. But the fewer faithful, who had their own lives to cope with as the clock ticked by, were left to make their own decisions according to their consciences and understanding of Jesus and the gospels, which many did. This widened the spectrum of opinion and practice within all Western Churches and especially the Catholic Church, including some divergence from Church teaching. There was a serious need for strong, clear and enlightened leadership, communication, clarity and transparency, in fact something like the Vatican II blueprint, which seemed to have been shelved.

The private and celibate lives of priests and monks in the sex-averse Church had for centuries been open to reasonable suspicion of misbehaviour, but towards the end of the 20th century, a global clerical sex- and child-abuse scandal was brewing which affected many Churches. Reports were emerging and the Church leaders, including Pope John-Paul II used their best efforts to suppress or ignore these to protect their reputations but would thus only exacerbate the sense of shock and betrayal when their deeply damaged but now emboldened victims helped bring it into the open over the turn of the century. Taking the Catholic Church as one example, this was aggravated by its conservative turn in the later decades of this century and the lengthy loss of momentum of Vatican II, which had raised such hopes of bringing the Church closer and more relevant to the modern world and its congregation. All Churches were losing members and regular worship at services, affecting some of the more recent offshoots far more than the Church of Rome, whose losses in the West were offset by expansion in Asia and Africa. They all needed leadership, trust and presentation into the modern era.

The hunger of populations for spiritual guidance was clear and the world looked to the Churches for that. They needed to address people as Christ would have done, at the level of the people and demonstrate an understanding of their needs in the world as it stood, not some past era. They are quite right when they say in their defence that God has not changed, but when the world changes so drastically they have to interpret and preach the true message of Christ in a way that makes sense in current conditions of society.

CHAPTER 23

Epilogue

Factors in modern life, politics and in religions themselves have decimated church attendance and Christian commitment in the developed world, calling time for all Christianity to revise and focus its approach to bringing Christ's message to the wider world. His love is already there, so a good start would be to work with intent and urgency for reunification as far as is possible without distorting his true message, as called for in Vatican II. Preconditions for this would have to involve reversing some of the practices and comforts that have again crept into the leadership of many branches, not least in the Roman Catholic Church. A return to the simpler way that Christ so successfully practised – including reduction of over-elaborate pomp, ceremony and dress as well as power structures, restrictive bureaucracy, intellectual pride, while listening to all of the laity, offering more varied liturgy for worship and opportunities to contribute to the Church's work.

Inter-faith dialogue in humility could start between Rome, where much of the responsibility for the divides lies and the too numerous, often nationalistic Orthodox Churches whose officers have also followed a path of aggrandisement. Orthodoxy itself is divided into Greek, Russian, Chaldean, Coptic and others, each with independent leadership, which adds to the difficulty as is also true with post-reformation protestants. There have been gestures, but nothing leading to meaningful dialogue towards unity so far. But if all worked with sincerity and in a manner to enlist prayer and selfless temporal support from followers, the power of the Holy Spirit could work. Human failings caused separation; can human need and good-will repair relations?

On the human level such change is never easy and sadly may not be too rapid as many of the faithful have inherited doctrines and ceremony which now give them comfort, but as this story demonstrates many of these are human introductions over the centuries as are the practices of the clergy and leadership that have diverged so far from the way of Christ. In following his mission, due consideration must be given to the multitude that has been alienated. The young are the future of churches.

Pope John XXIII started a process that Pope Paul VI continued but successors shelved. Now Pope Francis has reopened the opportunity and we have limited time to use it. He does not hold himself aloof. He identifies with all people, especially the disadvantaged. Yet he has a realistic broad view, innate empathy, perception and a natural dynamic open management style all of which bears visible similarity to that of Jesus. Francis gets it. He simplifies the message by focusing on the need to relate directly to Christ's teachings. He practices humility and approachability while showing the courage to confront difficult issues directly and personally. He is not a theologian, nor was Jesus or almost all of his flock, who appreciated the uncomplicated message. From the very outset, Jesus wanted all Christians in one body and Francis holds a similar vision, regardless of the formidable difficulties in its fulfilment.

Government leaders currently tend to the populist or the autocratic, with a swing to nationalist right wing in Europe and America, while Russians accept all-controlling autocracy, as do China, Middle-East, South America and parts of Africa. In some states, control over religion is part of this, reminding us of the dark ages and mediaeval times. True beneficence and moral direction are in short supply and populations seem to accept, some even welcome this. Technology has not helped and few efforts have been made by the Churches to grasp or adapt to it as with current transgender movements or with AI, artificial intelligence aspiring even towards 'transhumanity', with semi- or fully-automated beings envisaged. Serious and urgent adaptation and action in God's name is a crying need. Or is this how Armageddon will be?

So the story of Christianity faces an interesting new juncture as the speed, demands and complexity of life grow, yet most of us still have deep down a strong need for spiritual fulfilment. The twenty first century is already unfolding and Vatican II being revived and with it hope into the future. It is interesting how this story shows the Holy Spirit and the faithful have ensured continuity under prohibition, persecution and even risk of death. Remember:

- Early Roman Empire?
- England in the 16th-18th Centuries?
- France under Napoleon in the 19th?
- USSR under communism in the 20th?
- The Middle East and Africa today?

There is no shortage of food for thought and the story continues.

Finally with Acknowledgements

Over ten years research and writing I have looked into so many books, websites, encyclopaedias and sources that although I began recording them, I lost track after a few chapters. I was especially grateful early on for 'A History of the Early Church' by Hans Lietzman, which covered the first four centuries, about which I knew little beyond St Paul. His books were just part of an impressive personal library, kindly opened to me by Reverend Bill Lemmey, Anglican Rector of Porlock to whom I am deeply grateful on three counts. In a community ill-served by a stretched Catholic parish with one priest to cover nearly all the spread-out villages of West Somerset, my wife Elizabeth and I became involved in 'Churches Together in Porlock' which supported so much ecumenical community outreach, liturgies, prayer and study courses. Bill also introduced us to the excellent course 'Exploring Christianity' devised by the diocese of Bath and Wells, part of their preparation for Anglican readers licence and ordination which helped in ordering my thoughts for this project. Bill was also particularly helpful to us following a couple of family tragedies.

Thanks also to Elizabeth and our daughter Danielle, both historians, for helpful critiques of early drafts. I wrote this for my own benefit and to pass it on to our growing family as part of their legacy, but if it finds wider interest, well and good, though I have no commercial expectations. If it surprises, half of any net profit after costs will be donated to the Royal Marsden Cancer Charity (David Pinnington) in appreciation of their research and Mary O'Brien in giving our youngest son nearly two years extra quality life. As a determined non-celebrity, unknown in the worlds of Church, history or theology, I felt this book was a worth-while God-sent exercise worth paying to self-publish. I pray that Pope Francis live long enough to help show a path forward for Christianity as a basis of hope that it may provide inspired guidance for all people towards a true understanding of moral behaviour. Although he has already begun serious reform of the Curia and set in motion the synodal process in the Catholic Church, this may yet call for a third Vatican Council to follow up the second and take forward his drive for a global synodal Church. I would like to live to see this while I still have ability to record any encouraging signs for the future and who knows, another book?

If a pope and other Christian leaders could only find prayerful humility and resolve with the help of the Holy Spirit, could we even hope for a re-united global Christian Church albeit with tolerance of some divergent views on non-core theology, but a common worship of the Trinitarian God? Never let go of hope.

Glossary of Terms

Allegorical – the real meaning of such an account is open to interpretation.

Apologetics – arguments to support a theory or belief.

Autocephalous – a body run by its own appointed head or government, subject to no outside authority.

Autonomous – a body run by its own appointed head or government, possibly part of a greater authority.

Beguines – women's spiritual revival movement of 13th century.

Canon – item of Church law.

Catechumens – candidates preparing for acceptance into Church membership.

Christology – study of the nature and role of Jesus Christ.

Coenobitic – a communal closed religious order.

Dialectic – debate using entirely objective arguments and no subjective input in resolving good or justice.

Diaspora – dispersed population of people beyond their homeland.

Dogma – a belief held by an authority to be absolute truth.

Diptych – two panels with painting or writing on the inside, hinged to close like a book for safe transport.

Ecclesiology – study of the nature and structure of the Christian Church.

Eremitic – hermit or recluse.

Exegesis (exegetic) – critical examination and interpretation of scriptural text.

Gentiles – non-Jewish people or nations.

Glossolalia – seeming to speak 'in tongues', apparently unintelligible language, often in a form of trance.

Hermeneutic – relating to interpretation of the bible.

Incarnation – appearance on earth in the flesh.

Inculturation – adaptation of Christian liturgy to incorporate local cultural norms or practices.

Indulgences – spiritual benefits believed to gain partial or total relief of punishment for sin.

Logos – from Greek translation of the Bible – means 'Word' or 'Son of God'.

Paraclete – counsellor or advocate, meaning the Holy Spirit.

Pneumatics – gnostics highest order of humankind – spirituals.

Provisionality – current position but subject to possible change.

Syncretic – blend of more than one religious belief or practice.

Synod – assembly or council of a diocese, part or all of a church involving clergy and sometimes laiety.

Theodicy – the defence of a god who allows suffering and evil to exist.

Transfiguration – Christ's radiant and glorious appearance change in front of three Apostles.

Transubstantiation – miraculous change of bread and wine into Christ's body and blood at consecration.

Triptych – three panels with painting or writing on the inside, hinged to stand up or to close.

Milton Keynes UK
Ingram Content Group UK Ltd.
UKHW050434230324
439902UK00014B/366